Handbook of Research on E-Transformation and Human Resources Management Technologies:
Organizational Outcomes and Challenges

Tanya Bondarouk
University of Twente, The Netherlands

Huub Ruël
University of Twente, The Netherlands & American University of Beirut, Lebanon

Karine Guiderdoni-Jourdain
The Institute of Labour Economics and Industrial Sociology (LEST), Université de la Méditerranee, France

Ewan Oiry
The Institute of Labour Economics and Industrial Sociology (LEST), Université de la Méditerranee, France

INFORMATION SCIENCE REFERENCE

Hershey · New York

Director of Editorial Content:	Kristin Klinger
Senior Managing Editor:	Jamie Snavely
Managing Editor:	Jeff Ash
Assistant Managing Editor:	Carole Coulson
Typesetter:	Michael Brehm
Cover Design:	Lisa Tosheff
Printed at:	Yurchak Printing Inc.

Published in the United States of America by
Information Science Reference (an imprint of IGI Global)
701 E. Chocolate Avenue
Hershey PA 17033
Tel: 717-533-8845
Fax: 717-533-8661
E-mail: cust@igi-global.com
Web site: http://www.igi-global.com/reference

and in the United Kingdom by
Information Science Reference (an imprint of IGI Global)
3 Henrietta Street
Covent Garden
London WC2E 8LU
Tel: 44 20 7240 0856
Fax: 44 20 7379 0609
Web site: http://www.eurospanbookstore.com

Library of Congress Cataloging-in-Publication Data

Handbook of research on e-transformation and human resources management technologies : organizational outcomes and challenges / Tanya Bondarouk ... [et al.], editors.
       p. cm.

Includes bibliographical references and index.

Summary: "This book provides practical and unique knowledge on innovative e-HRM technologies that add competitive advantage to organizations"--Provided by publisher.

ISBN 978-1-60566-304-3 (hardcover) -- ISBN 978-1-60566-305-0 (ebook) 1. Personnel management--Technological innovations. 2. Management information systems. I. Bondarouk, Tanya, 1967-

HF5549.5.T33H36 2009
 658.300285'4678--dc22

                              2008052438

British Cataloguing in Publication Data
A Cataloguing in Publication record for this book is available from the British Library.

All work contributed to this book is new, previously-unpublished material. The views expressed in this book are those of the authors, but not necessarily of the publisher.

To our parents, partners, and children

—Tanya
—Huub
—Ewan
—Karine

Mohamed Omar Mahmud, *Kuwait Maastricht Business School, Kuwait*

Janet H. Marler, *University at Albany–State University of NY, USA*

Graeme Martin, *Glasgow University, Scotland*

Ariel Mendez, *University of Méditerrannée, LEST, France*

Valéry Michaux, *Reims Management School, France*

Frédéric Moatti, *Centre d'Etudes de l'Emploi, France*

Al-Ibraheem Nawaf, *Nawaf, KNET, Kuwait*

Miguel Olivas-Lujan, *Clarion University of Pennsylvania, USA*

Roxana Ologeanu, *University of Montpellier 2, France*

Leda Panayotopoulou, *Athens University of Economics and Business, Greece*

Emma Parry, *Cranfield University, UK*

Pramila Rao, *Marymount University, USA*

Martin Reddington, *Roffey Park Institute, UK*

Dino Ruta, *Catholic University of Milan, Italy*

Tyson Shaun, *Cranfield School of Management, UK*

Adam Smale, *University of Vaasa, Finland*

Stefan Strohmeier, *Saarland University, Germany*

Reima Suomi, *Turku School of Economics and Business Administration, Finland*

Carole *Tansley, Nottingham Trent University, UK*

Teresa Torres, *Universitat Rovira i Virgili, Spain*

Marc Van Veldhoven, *Tilburg University, The Netherlands*

Leon Wellicki, *Ono Software, Spain*

Hazel Williams, *Nottingham Trent University, UK*

Anabela Sarmento, *ISCAP, Portugal*

Gijs Houtzagers, *Kirkman Company, The Netherlands*

Marielba Zacarias, *Algarve University, Portugal*

List of Contributors

Table of Contents

Section I
e-HRM Transformation and Strategic HRM

Section II
User Involvement and User Participation

Section IV
E-Recruitment and National Culture

    Jonas F. Puck, Vienna University of Economics and Business Administration, Austria
    Dirk Holtbrügge, University of Erlangen-Nuremberg, Germany
    Alexander T. Mohr, Bradford University School of Management, UK

    Emma Parry, Cranfield School of Management, UK
    Shaun Tyson, Cranfield School of Management, UK

    Pramila Rao, Marymount University, USA

Section V
Modeling and Designing e-HRM Architectures

    Marielba Zacarias, Universidade do Algarve, Portugal
    Rodrigo Magalhães, Instituto Superior Técnico, Portugal
    José Tribolet, Instituto Superior Técnico, Portugal

    Elfi Furtmueller, University of Twente, The Netherlands
    Celeste Wilderom, University of Twente, The Netherlands
    Rolf van Dick, Goethe University Frankfurt, Germany

    Sven Laumer, University of Bamberg, Germany
    Andreas Eckhardt, University of Frankfurt a. Main, Germany

Detailed Table of Contents

Section I
e-HRM Transformation and Strategic HRM

Chapter I immediately confronts us with the complex issue of e-HRM transformation. Foster, an academician as well as an experienced consultant, observes that many organizations fail to take advantage of the transformational potential of e-HRM. He explains this idea with the concepts of sense-making and technological frames. These concepts are taken from the work of Orlikowski and Gash (1994), two scholars who have contributed heavily to the field of information technology research, and whose main work is inspired by the work of Anthony Giddens (Structuration Theory), a British sociologist. As Foster describes, the technological frames concept provides a useful analytical perspective for explaining and anticipating actions and meaning. Incongruence between frames held by different stakeholders is assumed to be a barrier to transformational change. Interestingly, Foster applies a grounded theory approach in order to reveal the different views HR managers and line managers hold towards e-HRM technology. More specifically, there is a significant frame incongruence regarding the relevance of e-HRM for achieving transformational outcomes.

Chapter II focuses on the role of e-HRM portals for intellectual capital development. Ruta starts with the observation that intellectual capital is of strategic importance to companies and that companies increasingly create HRM strategies to stimulate intellectual capital development. e-HRM portals function as intermediating tools between employees and the HR function, and offer opportunities to customize HRM practices to the individual employee's needs and preferences. The latter aspect in particular allows HR managers to align and leverage individual performances to the company strategy. This underlines the strategic and transformational role of the HR portal.

Chapter III

Barbara Imperatori, Catholic University, Milan, Italy
Marco De Marco, Catholic University, Milan, Italy

Chapter III presents a study on the impact of the introduction of e-work projects on labor transformation processes. The authors observe that values such as loyalty to a company and a job for life are giving way to concepts like employability, professionalization, and entrepreneurship. E-work solutions can facilitate or inhibit this process and the psychological contract between an employee and the organization. The case studies presented provide a number of critical issues and guidelines for the design and implementation of e-work solutions.

Section II
User Involvement and User Participation

Chapter IV

Gerwin Koopman, Syntess Software, The Netherlands
Ronald Batenburg, Utrecht University, The Netherlands

Chapter IV starts from the assumption that user involvement and participation are important factors for information systems success. They present five case studies of governmental organizations that deployed employee self-service applications and found that the deployment success of such systems was positively related to the extent of early user involvement and participation.

Chapter V

Karine Guiderdoni-Jourdain, The Institute of Labour Economics and Industrial Sociology
(LEST), Université de la Méditerranee, France
Ewan Oiry, The Institute of Labour Economics and Industrial Sociology (LEST),
Université de la Méditerranee, France

Chapter V analyzes HR intranet use by line managers in a large aeronautical firm. The results show that the managers hardly used the system since it conflicted with the dominant structures of their main activities, in which time constraints, a preference for face-to-face communication, and charisma as the basis for authority were considered important. A second version of the HR intranet was more successful when it met the expectations of the line managers. Especially the fact that the new version was coherent with the global corporate strategy increased the support of line managers for the HR intranet.

Chapter VI

Nawaf Al-Ibraheem, KNET, Kuwait
Huub Ruël, University of Twente, The Netherlands & American University of Beirut, Lebanon

The authors of Chapter VI assume that user involvement and participation in e-HRM systems developed in-house are higher than in off-the-shelf e-HRM projects. Therefore, they must also be more successful. Through a comparative case-study approach, an in-house e-HRM project and an off-the-shelf e-HRM project were compared. The results show that factors such as continuous user involvement, effective communication, and strong change management are considered more in the in-house e-HRM project, while business process reengineering, planning and vision, and project management are stressed more in the off-the-shelf e-HRM project. The in-house e-HRM project achieved increased efficiency, customer-oriented service excellence, and improved self-services.

Chapter VII

Pieternel Kuiper, Exxellence Group, The Netherlands
Betsy van Dijk, University of Twente, The Netherlands

Kuiper and Van Dijk describe how municipal electronic forms can be improved by adaptation. As municipalities offer more and more e-forms for citizens to place a request, adaptation of e-forms seems to be a step forward, they feel, to reduce the burden for citizens. Through an online questionnaire they surveyed the needs of citizens, municipal employees and local government organizations regarding the implementation of adaptation in municipal e-forms. All three respondent groups preferred the use of adaptation in e-forms and felt that municipal products and services could be improved by the use of adaptation.

Section III
e-HRM in Multinational Companies

Chapter VIII

Hazel Williams, Nottingham Trent University, UK
Carole Tansley, Nottingham Trent University, UK
Carley Foster, Nottingham Trent University, UK

The authors of Chapter VIII present a study of project teams working in a multinational organization implementing and maintaining the HR 'pillar' of a SAP global enterprise information system. The purpose of their study was to identify the human resource information system (HRIS) skills and knowledge in the key roles for the global project and to provide suggestions for the development of project team members. The authors provide a framework which can be used as a clarification tool by those responsible for managing people working in hybrid roles on global HRIS projects.

Chapter IX

Adam Smale, University of Vaasa, Finland
Jukka-Pekka Heikkilä, University of Vaasa, Finland

Smale and Heikkilä focus on the design and implementation of a globally integrated e-HRM system within a multinational corporation. This requires the parties involved to reach some form of agreement on which HR processes to standardize and which to adapt locally. By means of a longitudinal, in-depth case study approach, data was collected on micro-political behavior in an e-HRM system project in a Finnish subsidiary of a large, European-owned MNC over a period of nearly two years. The results showed that the key areas of conflict were system design, the standardized use of English, and grey areas of the HR policy. The three key parties involved used a range of negotiation resources such as business case logic, technical know-how, internal benchmarking, local constraints, and ignorance.

Chapter X

Huub Ruël, University of Twente, The Netherlands & American University of Beirut, Lebanon

Chapter X aims at demonstrating how adaptive structuration theory can be of use in studying human resource information systems. By applying key concepts of the theory to a global e-HRM case study, the author shows that those concepts help to increase our understanding of the social nature of e-HRM systems.

Section IV
E-Recruitment and National Culture

Chapter XI

Jonas F. Puck, Vienna University of Economics and Business Administration, Austria
Dirk Holtbrügge, University of Erlangen-Nuremberg, Germany
Alexander T. Mohr, Bradford University School of Management, UK

Chapter XI describes a study on the influence of the cultural context on the comprehensiveness with which companies in different countries make use of applicant information and selection strategies in corporate website recruiting. The results suggest that the use of the internet for management purposes is influenced by cultural factors.

Chapter XII
Emma Parry, Cranfield School of Management, UK
Shaun Tyson, Cranfield School of Management, UK

Parry and Tyson conducted a study on the potential of e-recruitment to transform the recruitment process and the role of the resourcing team. They observed that HR practitioners are often expected to be efficient administrators of the employment relationship and to act as a strategic partner. Based on the assumption that e-HRM may be a way of achieving these dual aims as technology can both improve the efficiency of HR processes and help the HR function to become more strategic, three case studies were conducted. They showed that the use of e-recruitment can potentially have an impact on both the strategic role and the efficiency of the resourcing team.

Chapter XIII
Pramila Rao, Marymount University, USA

Chapter XIII addresses the role of the national culture on e-recruitment practices in India and Mexico. According to the author, the role of culture on information technology is just emerging, and internet recruiting will definitely play a prominent role as the world becomes more digitized. Further, the author suggests that practitioners and researchers would benefit from making a 'what if' chart or spreadsheet based on cultural dimension scores and adaptability to internet usage.

Section V
Modeling and Designing e-HRM Architectures

Chapter XIV
Marielba Zacarias, Universidade do Algarve, Portugal
Rodrigo Magalhães, Instituto Superior Técnico, Portugal
José Tribolet, Instituto Superior Técnico, Portugal

Chapter XIV presents a bottom-up modeling framework. The framework can be used for the analysis and design of HR behaviors, starting from the assumption that the process of emergence lies at the root of the usage of technologies. The authors illustrate the way the framework should be applied and how it works out through a case study.

Chapter XV
Elfi Furtmueller, University of Twente, The Netherlands
Celeste Wilderom, University of Twente, The Netherlands
Rolf van Dick, Goethe University Frankfurt, Germany

Furtmueller, Wilderom, and Van Dijk propose applying the lead user method for e-service settings, a method stemming from the new product innovation literature. In their study registered applicants at an e-recruiting portal were compared with so-called lead users regarding new service idea proposals. The results showed that most users suggested social-network features they were already familiar with from other platforms, while lead users came up with more novel service solutions for different user segments.

Chapter XVI starts with an architecture for a next-generation holistic e-recruiting system. Based on this architecture, the authors propose to extend it by adding employer branding as a new component. They show how employer branding should be integrated in the existing architecture to develop and implement an effective employer branding strategy. As a result, Laumer and Eckhardt conclude that the newly proposed architecture is a first step towards a holistic e-HRM management system.

Guiderdoni-Jourdain focuses on the regulation between online HR designers and HR experts. She extends the concept of e-HRM by a systematic approach and uses it to study the interaction between the different actors involved in an e-HRM project.

Section VI
e-HRM Use and Performance Improvement

Chapter XVIII presents a study of the acceptance of HRIS in small and medium-sized organizations (SMEs). The authors looked at this topic by investigating perceptions about the use of these systems. Four case studies were conducted, and results showed that e-HRM tools in SMEs are perceived as useful, but not easy to use. The companies involved in the study considered the use of HRIS as helping them to make HRM more effective.

Chapter XIX focuses on the questions of how to improve the efficiency of HRM and enhance its status in organizations. The authors show that information technology can be of help in transforming the role of HRM departments in organizations. One of the challenges for managers nowadays is to determine the success factors for implementing HRIS.

Welicki, Piqueres Juan, Llorente Martin, and De Vega Hernandez their experience in building a Web-enabled workflow system for managing employee life-cycle processes. They describe how the system was able to successfully manage a large number of employee requests, brought reliability, traceability and auditability to employee life-cycle management processes. The web-enabled workflow system became a core system for supporting HRM operations.

Section VII

Extended e-HRM Topics

Chapter XXI describes a study on the impact of information technology on individual learning processes. The authors of this chapter started with the question of whether those technologies can possibly help increase an individual's competencies in order to improve learning. By using agent-based simulation, their results showed that communication through e-mail exchange appears to make individuals learn more slowly than on a Web forum.

Chapter XXII

Michaux presents a study aimed at identifying the main trends and international convergences when
analyzing the impact of IT on unions and trade unionism, and lists the challenges, opportunities, and
threats that IT poses to trade unions in industrialized countries. The author concludes that there is a
tension between the opportunities and threats, which can translate into four main types of challenges
posed by IT for trade unions.

Chapter XXIII deals with the question of coordination in virtual teams, more specifically how the coordination in such teams takes place. The author starts from the assumption that it is either trust or control
that is needed for the coordination in virtual teams. By means of a case study conducted in a high tech
firm, Parot presents findings showing that coordination in virtual teams is more formalized and more
control-oriented, and that the role of the project manager is essential in such teams.

Chapter XXIV is about information overload in the new world of work. A case study conducted at
Microsoft suggested that information overload is not perceived as a problem, but as a challenge and
a possible future problem. Interestingly, some of the interviewees in the case study suggested that the
next generation of workers, the NetGen, will be better able to handle information overload, as they may
have incorporated the search strategies for finding information in a large amount of data. The results of
this study also seem to contradict the popular belief that the phenomena of information overload is an
increasing problem.

Chapter XXV analyses the popular literature on HRM shared service centers. By using a grounded theory
approach, the authors analyzed 34 articles in the international HRM literature for practitioners. The
analysis shows that according to the popular HRM literature, brand development or service improvement
motivations for deploying HR shared service centers lead to more positive impacts and a higher success

rate. Solely economic motivations are not enough to achieve added value. Further, the anticipated risks are not a good predictor for eventual impacts, and finally, HR shared service centers have more positive impacts as they develop over time.

Preface

AIM OF THIS BOOK

Information technology (IT) continues to impact HRM. For a decade now, digital possibilities have been challenging the traditional ways of delivering HRM services within business. The huge investments in IT applications for HRM lead to new rounds of intra-organisational competition, challenging HRM and making it more complex to achieve organisational performance improvements.

The e-HRM field is fed (and complicated) by two academic backgrounds: studies oriented towards IT implementation and 'pure' HRM studies. The former usually investigate the usage of IT for HR purposes and mainly focus on the growing sophistication of the technology and the qualities necessary for its adoption. Such studies usually cover topics like IT acceptance, resistance, effectiveness, equality, information security and privacy in the context of e-HRM technology usage. However, they remain silent about changes in HR practices resulting from e-HRM. HR-based e-HRM studies, on the other hand, generally only examine single e-HR practices, focusing on the changes in HR processes and functions following automation. These studies tend to avoid issues related to implementation and the ongoing use of IT.

At the same time, we do not even know where e-HRM should be placed. Is it a new and substantial research area, or the 'crossroads' of two academic domains? Theoretical complexity has practical consequences for e-HRM projects and their management. It seems increasingly unclear exactly what the advantages of e-HRM are, and to what extent e-HRM helps to attain organisational HRM goals. The one-sided, scholarly e-HRM works fail to address this lack of clarity fully and, if anything, deepen the division between the two academic domains.

In order to reduce the aforementioned confusion, this volume has set a three-fold goal:

- To achieve a state-of-the-art overview of theoretical and empirical contributions on the impact of the integration of HRM and IT on the transformation of HRM.
- To address the integration of HR- and IT-based e-HRM research.
- To identify future cutting-edge research directions.

This book is a collection of interesting chapters on the intersection between HRM and information technology, predominantly referred to as electronic HRM or e-HRM since the mid-1990s. This is not the first book on e-HRM that collates chapters by a range of different scholars from around the world, but it is the first book that may count as a milestone because it aims to present the state of e-HRM research at this point in time! Research on e-HRM started in the mid-1990s and has resulted in books, journal articles, special issues and the like. Altogether, the number of scholarly journal articles on e-HRM is currently estimated at around 250. This is an impressive amount, based on the hard and persistent work of scholars and researchers from around the world. An analysis of the articles would result in a diverse picture in terms of the nature and focus of the works, from conceptual articles to mature empirical work.

As editors, we have been involved in e-HRM research from the beginning of this century. We have done research ourselves and published worked on e-HRM. In addition, from the very start, we aimed at bringing researchers on e-HRM together in order to foster the scholarly development of research on e-HRM. This has resulted in four international, scholarly, research-oriented events in four years' time. Researchers from the UK, USA, Mexico, Germany, France, the Netherlands, Italy, Spain, Finland, Portugal,and the Middle East were brought together to share insights, discuss each others' work, set agendas for further research, and establish collaboration.

This book is one of the results of these events, but it is a very special result. It contains 25 chapters on e-HRM, showing the very diverse nature of the e-HRM research area in terms of the topics, research approaches, theoretical perspectives, levels, and unit of analysis. This diversity is the strength and the uniqueness of this book, as it is a truly useful overview of what is going on in the field of e-HRM research. Once you have gone through all the chapters, you will hopefully have many new questions from whence to continue your own e-HRM journey.

CONTENT OF THIS BOOK

In this introduction we, the editors, would like to guide you through the chapters. First of all, it is interesting to identify a number of central themes that can be found throughout the book, and which are the key topics in e-HRM research so far: *user involvement, user participation, and user adoption of e-HRM applications; design and implementation of e-HRM; modeling; design of architectures of e-HRM systems and HR portals; e-HRM in multinational companies and global e-HRM; the role of culture; qualitative research methods as the dominant approach for empirical research; grounded theory for e-HRM-related theory development; strategic e-HRM and the transformation of the HR function; redefining the role of the HR function related to e-HRM implementation; e-recruitment; structuration theory as an approach to study e-HRM empirically; and human capital management and e-HRM.*

In combination with our own experience in the e-HRM research field, we derived seven e-HRM themes from the above-mentioned topics and ordered the 25 chapters in this book along them.

Section I, *e-HRM Transformation and Strategic HRM.* When it comes to expectations, it is assumed that e-HRM will spur a transformation of the HRM function in organizations, changing HRM into a truly strategic issue and the HRM function into a strategic business partner. **Chapter I,** written by Foster, immediately confronts us with this complex issue. Foster, an academician as well as an experienced consultant, observes that many organizations fail to take advantage of the transformational potential of e-HRM. He explains this idea with the concepts of sense-making and technological frames. These concepts are taken from the work of Orlikowski and Gash (1994), two scholars who have contributed heavily to the field of information technology research, and whose main work is inspired by the work of Anthony Giddens (Structuration Theory), a British sociologist. As Foster describes, the technological frames concept provides a useful analytical perspective for explaining and anticipating actions and meaning. Incongruence between frames held by different stakeholders is assumed to be a barrier to transformational change.

Interestingly, Foster applies a grounded theory approach in order to reveal the different views HR managers and line managers hold towards e-HRM technology. More specifically, there is a significant frame incongruence regarding the relevance of e-HRM for achieving transformational outcomes.

Chapter II, by Ruta, focuses on the role of e-HRM portals for intellectual capital development. Ruta starts with the observation that intellectual capital is of strategic importance to companies and that companies increasingly create HRM strategies to stimulate intellectual capital development. e-HRM portals function as intermediating tools between employees and the HR function, and offer opportunities to customize HRM practices to the individual employee's needs and preferences. The latter aspect in particular allows HR managers to align and leverage individual performances to the company strategy. This underlines the strategic and transformational role of the HR portal.

Imperatori and De Marco's contribution, **Chapter III**, presents a study on the impact of the introduction of e-work projects on labor transformation processes. The authors observe that values such as loyalty to a company and a job for life are giving way to concepts like employability, professionalization, and entrepreneurship. E-work solutions can facilitate or inhibit this process and the psychological contract between an employee and the organization. The case studies presented provide a number of critical issues and guidelines for the design and implementation of e-work solutions.

Section II in this book is *User Involvement and User Participation*. Information systems design and implementation aim at meeting the needs of an organization. The end-users are key players in determining whether or not these needs are met as they are the ones using the systems in their day-to-day work. The extent to which end-users should be involved in the design and implementation process and how they should be involved are ongoing major topics, also in the case of e-HRM systems.

Chapter IV, by Koopman and Batenburg, starts from the assumption that user involvement and participation are important factors for information systems success. They present five case studies of governmental organizations that deployed employee self-service applications and found that the deployment success of such systems was positively related to the extent of early user involvement and participation.

Chapter V, by Guiderdoni-Jourdain and Oiry, analyzes HR intranet use by line managers in a large aeronautical firm. The results show that the managers hardly used the system since it conflicted with the dominant structures of their main activities, in which time constraints, a preference for face-to-face communication, and charisma as the basis for authority were considered important. A second version of the HR intranet was more successful when it met the expectations of the line managers. Especially the fact that the new version was coherent with the global corporate strategy increased the support of line managers for the HR intranet.

Chapter VI, written by Al-Ibraheem and Ruël, assumes that user involvement and participation in e-HRM systems developed in-house are higher than in off-the-shelf e-HRM projects. Therefore, they must also be more successful. Through a comparative case-study approach, an in-house e-HRM project and an off-the-shelf e-HRM project were compared. The results show that factors such as continuous user involvement, effective communication, and strong change management are considered more in the in-house e-HRM project, while business process reengineering, planning and vision, and project management are stressed more in the off-the-shelf e-HRM project. The in-house e-HRM project achieved increased efficiency, customer-oriented service excellence, and improved self-services.

Kuiper and Van Dijk, the authors of **Chapter VII**, describe how municipal electronic forms can be improved by adaptation. As municipalities offer more and more e-forms for citizens to place a request, adaptation of e-forms seems to be a step forward, they feel, to reduce the burden for citizens. Through an online questionnaire they surveyed the needs of citizens, municipal employees and local government organizations regarding the implementation of adaptation in municipal e-forms. All three respondent groups preferred the use of adaptation in e-forms and felt that municipal products and services could be improved by the use of adaptation.

Section III covered in this book is *e-HRM in Multinational Companies*. As globalization is maturing, multinational companies (MNC) from the West go East and vice versa, issues such as requirements analysis, development, implementation and user adoption of e-HRM systems in a globalized world are attracting increasing attention.

Chapter VIII, by Williams, Tansley, and Foster, presents a study of project teams working in a multinational organization implementing and maintaining the HR 'pillar' of a SAP global enterprise information system. The purpose of their study was to identify the human resource information system (HRIS) skills and knowledge in the key roles for the global project and to provide suggestions for the development of project team members. The authors provide a framework which can be used as a clarification tool by those responsible for managing people working in hybrid roles on global HRIS projects.

Smale and Heikkilä, the authors of **Chapter IX**, focus on the design and implementation of a globally integrated e-HRM system within a multinational corporation. This requires the parties involved to reach some form of agreement on which HR processes to standardize and which to adapt locally. By means of a longitudinal, in-depth case study approach, data was collected on micro-political behavior in an e-HRM system project in a Finnish subsidiary of a large, European-owned MNC over a period of nearly two years. The results showed that the key areas of conflict were system design, the standardized use of English, and grey areas of the HR policy. The three key parties involved used a range of negotiation resources such as business case logic, technical know-how, internal benchmarking, local constraints, and ignorance.

Chapter X, by Ruël, aims at demonstrating how adaptive structuration theory can be of use in studying human resource information systems. By applying key concepts of the theory to a global e-HRM case study, the author shows that those concepts help to increase our understanding of the social nature of e-HRM systems.

Section IV, *E-Recruitmnet and National Culture*, is covered by three chapters. **Chapter XI**, by Puck, Holtbrügge, and Mohr, describes a study on the influence of the cultural context on the comprehensiveness with which companies in different countries make use of applicant information and selection strategies in corporate website recruiting. The results suggest that the use of the internet for management purposes is influenced by cultural factors.

Parry and Tyson, the authors of **Chapter XII**, conducted a study on the potential of e-recruitment to transform the recruitment process and the role of the resourcing team. They observed that HR practitioners are often expected to be efficient administrators of the employment relationship and to act as a strategic partner. Based on the assumption that e-HRM may be a way of achieving these dual aims as technology can both improve the efficiency of HR processes and help the HR function to become more strategic, three case studies were conducted. They showed that the use of e-recruitment can potentially have an impact on both the strategic role and the efficiency of the resourcing team.

Chapter XIII, written by Rao, addresses the role of the national culture on e-recruitment practices in India and Mexico. According to the author, the role of culture on information technology is just emerging, and internet recruiting will definitely play a prominent role as the world becomes more digitized. Further, the author suggests that practitioners and researchers would benefit from making a 'what if' chart or spreadsheet based on cultural dimension scores and adaptability to internet usage.

Section V in this book is *Modeling and Designing e-HRM Architectures*. e-HRM as a research field is an integration between IT-research and HRM-research. Both fields should mutually influence each other in order to find answers to the core research questions in the e-HRM research field. The IT-research side, in particular, can bring in a more engineering-based approach to counter-balance the social scientific-based HRM side. In this book we have four chapters that aim at providing design guidelines or architectures for e-HRM systems.

Chapter XIV, by Zacarias, Magalhães, and Tribolet, presents a bottom-up modeling framework. The framework can be used for the analysis and design of HR behaviors, starting from the assumption that the process of emergence lies at the root of the usage of technologies. The authors illustrate the way the framework should be applied and how it works out through a case study.

Furtmueller, Wilderom, and van Dijk, **Chapter XV**, propose applying the lead user method for e-service settings, a method stemming from the new product innovation literature. In their study registered applicants at an e-recruiting portal were compared with so-called lead users regarding new service idea proposals. The results showed that most users suggested social-network features they were already familiar with from other platforms, while lead users came up with more novel service solutions for different user segments.

Chapter XVI, by Laumer and Eckhardt, starts with an architecture for a next-generation holistic e-recruiting system. Based on this architecture, the authors propose to extend it by adding employer branding as a new component. They show how employer branding should be integrated in the existing architecture to develop and implement an effective employer branding strategy. As a result, Laumer and Eckhardt conclude that the newly proposed architecture is a first step towards a holistic e-HRM management system.

Guiderdoni-Jourdain, the author of **Chapter XVII**, focuses on the regulation between online HR designers and HR experts. She extends the concept of e-HRM by a systematic approach and uses it to study the interaction between the different actors involved in an e-HRM project.

Section VI in this book, covered by three chapters, is *e-HRM Use and Performance Improvement*. Fed by the numerous empirical observations of the problematic acceptance of e-HRM tools and how e-HRM tools can contribute to performance improvement, this issue demands continuous academic attention in order to increase our understanding of e-HRM user acceptance and performance improvement.

Chapter XVIII, by Bondarouk, ter Horst, and Engbers, presents a study of the acceptance of HRIS in small and medium-sized organizations (SMEs). The authors looked at this topic by investigating perceptions about the use of these systems. Four case studies were conducted, and results showed that e-HRM tools in SMEs are perceived as useful, but not easy to use. The companies involved in the study considered the use of HRIS as helping them to make HRM more effective.

Chapter XIX, written by Tahssain and Zgheib, focuses on the questions of how to improve the efficiency of HRM and enhance its status in organizations. The authors show that information technology can be of help in transforming the role of HRM departments in organizations. One of the challenges for managers nowadays is to determine the success factors for implementing HRIS.

Welicki, Piqueres Juan, Llorente Martin, and de Vega Hernandez, the authors of **Chapter XX**, present their experience in building a web-enabled workflow system for managing employee life-cycle processes. They describe how the system was able to successfully manage a large number of employee requests, brought reliability, traceability and auditability to employee life-cycle management processes. The web-enabled workflow system became a core system for supporting HRM operations.

Section VII, the final section covered in this book is what we call *Extended e-HRM Topics*. The previously described chapters cover topics that fit in a relatively narrow definition of e-HRM, namely the use of internet technology-based applications for human resource management strategy and practices implementation in organizations. However, within this definition, topics such as e-learning, trade unions and IT, virtual teams, information overload, and shared service centers do not fit very well. These are topics, though, that definitely interest researchers and practitioners within the e-HRM field. Therefore, we have given them a place in our book.

Chapter XXI describes a study on the impact of information technology on individual learning processes. The authors of this chapter, Guechtouli and Guechtouli, started with the question of whether those technologies can possibly help increase an individual's competencies in order to improve learning. By using agent-based simulation, their results showed that communication through e-mail exchange appears to make individuals learn more slowly than on a web forum.

Michaux, the author of **Chapter XXII**, presents a study aimed at identifying the main trends and international convergences when analyzing the impact of IT on unions and trade unionism, and lists the challenges, opportunities, and threats that IT poses to trade unions in industrialized countries. The author concludes that there is a tension between the opportunities and threats, which can translate into four main types of challenges posed by IT for trade unions.

Chapter XXIII, written by Parot, deals with the question of coordination in virtual teams, more specifically how the coordination in such teams takes place. The author starts from the assumption that it is either trust or control that is needed for the coordination in virtual teams. By means of a case study conducted in a high tech firm, Parot presents findings showing that coordination in virtual teams is more formalized and more control-oriented, and that the role of the project manager is essential in such teams.

Chapter XXIV is about information overload in the new world of work, written by ter Heerdt and Bondarouk. A case study conducted at Microsoft suggested that information overload is not perceived as a problem, but as a challenge and a possible future problem. Interestingly, some of the interviewees in the case study suggested that the next generation of workers, the NetGen, will be better able to handle information overload, as they may have incorporated the search strategies for finding information in a large amount of data. The results of this study also seem to contradict the popular belief that the phenomena of information overload is an increasing problem.

Finally, **Chapter XXV**, written by van Balen and Bondarouk, analyses the popular literature on HRM shared service centers. By using a grounded theory approach, the authors analyzed 34 articles in the international HRM literature for practitioners. The analysis shows that according to the popular HRM literature, brand development or service improvement motivations for deploying HR shared service centers lead to more positive impacts and a higher success rate. Solely economic motivations are not enough to achieve added value. Further, the anticipated risks are not a good predictor for eventual impacts, and finally, HR shared service centers have more positive impacts as they develop over time.

THE TARGET AUDIENCE

This book presents insights gained by leading professionals from research, consultancy, and the e-HRM projects practice. Therefore, we believe that the twenty-five chapters of this book provide useful information for academic researchers, consultancy firms, university graduates and e-HRM / HRIS practitioners.

We as editors wish you a very interesting journey through the state-of-the-art of e-HRM research.

Tanya Bondarouk, University of Twente, The Netherlands

Huub Ruël, University of Twente, The Netherlands & American University of Beirut, Lebanon

Karine Guiderdoni-Jourdain, The Institute of Labour Economics and Industrial Sociology (LEST), Université de la Méditerranee, France

Ewan Oiry, The Institute of Labour Economics and Industrial Sociology (LEST), Université de la Méditerranee, France

Acknowledgment

With gratitude, love, and respect we thank…

Our publisher, IGI Global who supported the book project, and especially Heather A. Probst, for her support, coaching and understanding during the intensive task of editing this book. The contents of this book were only possible because of the many contributors and the supportive work by the reviewers. Thanks to all the authors of the chapters in this volume, we are able to share the knowledge with a larger audience. And Yulia Bondarouk, our editorial assistant, for her dedication, her great competence, and for her great, warm, enthusiastic personality!

Tanya Bondarouk, University of Twente, The Netherlands

Huub Ruël, University of Twente, The Netherlands & American University of Beirut, Lebanon

Karine Guiderdoni-Jourdain, The Institute of Labour Economics and Industrial Sociology (LEST), Université de la Méditerranee, France

Ewan Oiry, The Institute of Labour Economics and Industrial Sociology (LEST), Université de la Méditerranee, France

November 12, 2008

Section I
e–HRM Transformation and Strategic HRM

Chapter I
Making Sense of e-HRM:
Transformation, Technology and Power Relations

Steve Foster
University of Hertfordshire, UK
NorthgateArinso, UK

ABSTRACT

Several organisations have adopted e-HRM technology as a platform for achieving transformational change, improving HR operational processes, allowing distributed access to employees / managers and providing better decision support. However, as a consultant working in this field, the author regularly encounters organisations that fail to take advantage of the transformational potential of e-HRM, particularly those in the United Kingdom public sector. This chapter argues that the concepts of sense-making and technological frames may explain the inertia experienced in some organisations. It contends that the analysis of technological frame domains provides a valuable lens for understanding and interpreting e-HRM, where high levels of frame incongruence may act as a barrier to transformational change. Research suggests that power relations between key groups of stakeholders, in particular HR Managers and line managers, may influence these frames and shape attitudes to technology. This approach may also provide the basis for strategies to manage e-HRM related change more effectively. Using a grounded theory approach, the research, currently work in progress in support of a professional doctorate (DBA), investigates how United Kingdom public sector organisations make sense of, plan for and implement HR technology.

THE TRANSFORMATIVE EFFECT OF e-HRM

A wide range of Human Resources (HR) processes and information can now be managed and devolved to line managers and employees through web-based technologies using **e-HRM** ('electronic Human Resource Management'), with potentially significant benefits in terms of cost reduction and improved service levels (Ashton, 2001; CedarCrestone, 2006). Organisations make a significant investment of time and resource in implementing e-HRM, with more than $1.5bn pa being spent in Western Europe on related software and implementation (Lykkegaard, 2007). At least 91% of midsize and large US organisations claim to be using web based HR technology in some way (Keebler & Rhodes, 2002).

As a consultant working in the e-HRM field, the author has observed that organisations typically choose one of three paths when implementing HR technology:

- **Replication:** Simply re-creating the content and functions of the existing system(s)—this is typically an IT 'refresh' activity, often because existing technology becomes non-viable or is simply out of date. There is generally no intention to restructure HR/Payroll services.
- **Enhancement:** New systems provide additional functionality (such as self-service, improved integration and reporting) but are intended to have only an *evolutionary* impact on the overall HR service delivery model.
- **Transformational:** Involving a *revolutionary* restructuring of HR service delivery, including the use of service centres, outsourcing and business partnering. E-HRM effectively becomes an enabler for these new approaches.

Reddington, Williamson & Withers (2005) claim that the greatest benefits of e-HRM arise when transformational outcomes are pursued and clearly, HR technology has a role to play in supporting the transformation effort. As Boroughs, Palmer and Hunter (2008) observe, *"The development of human resources is bound inextricably to the technology that serves it"* (p.3). While HR transformation appears to be the Holy Grail of e-HRM, the term 'transformation' itself is problematic, since it is often mis-used and abused, covering a range of activities from simple process redesign through to dramatic change. One definition that seems to capture the general spirit of current usage is *"the process of recreating or reinventing the HR function—such as re-engineering, restructuring, implementing new systems or a new HR service delivery model, outsourcing or co-sourcing—with the specific intent of enhancing HR's contribution to the business"* (Mercer, 2007).

Although a recent study by the UK's professional HR body, the Chartered Institute for Personnel and Development (CIPD, 2006), provided evidence that organisations are beginning to use technology to enable HR transformation, in practice, the main focus of many software implementation projects remains administrative efficiency and HR operational cost reduction rather than strategic, transformational outcomes (Ball, 2001). As Broderick & Boudreau (1992) note, *"most organisational investments in HR information technology support only a narrow range of administrative decisions"* (p.9) and the author's own experience suggests that the statement remains largely true. Projects often pursue a replication or enhancement strategy, implementing basic functionality during the first phase, then fail to capitalise on the full transformative potential of the investment in subsequent phases.

Research literature typically explains the impact of e-HRM technology on HR transformation under three, non-exclusive themes. The first of these sees technology as creating more **time** to be strategic—as HR processes become more efficient, HR functions are able to devote greater time to strategic matters. For example, Snell, Stuebner & Lepak (2002), suggest that e-HRM technology enables organisations to become not only cost-efficient, but also strategic and flexible, shifting the emphasis towards people management processes. The introduction of initiatives such as HR Business Partners, a concept championed by Ulrich (1997), is therefore enabled through the automation of transactional work. Several other writers, including Davenport (1993); Gourley & Connolly (1996); Hannon et al (1996); Liff (1997) and Tyson & Selbie (2004) also refer to this transitioning theme. Clearly, HR functions need to devote time to strategic activity—Lawler & Mohrman (2003) found that successful HR functions tend to invest more time in planning, organisational design and development, career planning and management development. However, we can be sure that the link is co-relational not causal—simply having more time will not make the function more strategic, even though most studies are light on explaining how the transition will take place.

Another common theme is that transformation is achieved through the greater use of strategic **information,** which refocuses the HR function. While technology has a strong capability for 'Automating', it also has the capacity for 'Informating' (a term first used by Zuboff in 1988), where informating refers to generating new forms of information to empower managers and provide data that HR specialists can strategically act upon. Othman (2003) for example, refers to the 'informated workplace'. Lawler & Mohrman (2003) found that the greater use of information technology may be associated with HR being more of a business partner, arguing that "*..it is much easier for HR to gather strategic data and analyze them in ways that can contribute to forming and implementing business strategy*" (p.21). At its boldest, technology provides opportunities for virtual and networked organisations, linking e-learning to knowledge management and the potential for new HR business models.

A third theme is the **symbolic** nature of technology. Kossek et al. (1994) have noted the role of technology in strategic positioning, that can "*practically and symbolically represent the transformation of Human Resources into a strategic business partner*" (p.137). Likewise, Tansley, Newell & Williams (2001) contend that technology plays a critical part in driving HR transformation, acting as a stimulus for a fresh approach to Human Resource practices and new employment relationships. Kovach et al (2002) conclude that the engagement of line managers in implementing HR technology exposes line managers to HR issues and gives them better appreciation of HR practices, with significant outcomes for HR transformation. The introduction of technology therefore makes a statement about transformational intent and becomes a powerful vehicle for driving change.

e-HRM AND THE UK PUBLIC SECTOR

The UK Public Sector generally has a poor reputation for Human Resource Management, being associated with low status, low influence roles and representing an 'enclave' in the personnel profession (Lupton & Shaw, 2001). While some research (Kelly & Gennard, 1996) found that some Personnel[1] Directors have developed a strategic role in managing the consequences of government changes, in others, the HR role has declined, as industrial relations issues have seemingly become less critical. Evidence seems to support the idea that the HR function in the public sector is relatively immature and less sophisticated than its private sector counterparts (Harris, 2002).

As a result of the Gershon Report (Gershon, 2004), there has been pressure on the UK Public Sector to become more efficient, by reducing overstaffing and inefficiency. Transformation of the HR function has therefore become a key priority in recent years, awakening an interest in technology. Although e-HRM has been widely used by the private sector over recent years, many public sector organisations are now embarking on a programme of investment in e-HRM as part of their transformation strategy, providing an excellent research platform for investigating perceptions of technology, its role and the approaches taken towards implementation.

THE e-HRM LANDSCAPE

One barrier to greater understanding of HR technology is that a multiplicity of terminology is used—HRIS, HRMS, web portals, e-HR and, of course, e-HRM, all of which serve to confuse potential users. However, for the purposes of this chapter, the term 'e-HRM' will refer to a fully integrated, organisation-wide electronic network of HR related data, information, services, databases, tools, applications and transactions, best summarised as:

The application of any technology enabling managers and employees to have direct access to HR and other workplace services for communication, performance reporting, team management, knowledge management and learning…in addition to administrative applications. (Watson-Wyatt, 2002)

Figure 1 highlights the wide range of functionality contained within contemporary e-HRM technology:

Functionality may be categorised into two areas, each of which has different but significant transformational potential. The first of these (Process Technology—lower half) provides support for basic transactions, now well-established and the foundation of all commercial HR technology. These functions include managing payroll, personal / organisational data and routine administration and are aimed at reducing costs and achieving HR operational efficiencies through automation.

The second group, shown in the upper half, are 'Human Capital' functions, aimed at supporting people management activities such as performance management, skills profiling and analytics. Because of the wider impact on business outcomes, these functions are more strategically oriented. It has been suggested elsewhere (Foster, 2006) that the term 'e-Human Capital Management', or 'e-HCM' should be used to describe these more sophisticated applications of HR technology.

This model, developed by the author, has proved to be highly useful as a strategic planning tool to demonstrate the 'art of the possible'. In reality, the impact of HR technology is likely to be some combination of process and human capital functions, analysis of which is beyond this chapter. However, the breadth of literature on these themes is rich enough to suggest that definitions of e-HRM which focus only on operational or administrative outcomes are likely to be inadequate.

While organisations are becoming more sophisticated and ambitious in their use of e-HRM, many HR professionals and line managers continue to

Figure 1. e-HRM landscape

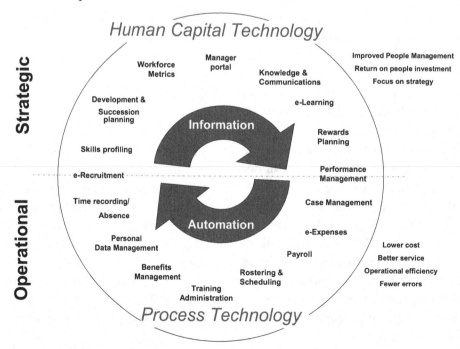

lack a clear knowledge of its transformative effect. For some, technology is seen as little more than an 'electronic filing cabinet', a basic repository of data, with little understanding of its potential for enabling change. As we have seen from the e-HRM landscape model (Figure 1), there is now a bewildering choice of functionality available, either as a module in a company-wide ERP solution, as standalone 'best-of-breed' software or as a series of modules in traditional HR software. Arguably, e-HRM technology is advancing faster than many organisations are able to comprehend and implement what is available, raising questions about how organisations make sense of what technology can offer. This has critical implications for the approach to e-HRM.

MAKING SENSE OF e-HRM

The concept of sense-making has its roots in the personal construct theories of Kelly (1955), which see our understanding of the world as a social process. Organisations are essentially a collection of people trying to make sense of what is happening around them through interpretations, translating events, developing models for understanding and assembling conceptual schemes—mapping out their world to create an intelligible whole (Daft & Weick, 1984). E-HRM takes place exclusively in an organizational setting, with technologies that are often new and unfamiliar. In order to interact with technology, people first have to make sense of it; in this sense-making process, users develop assumptions, expectations and knowledge of the technology, which then serve to shape subsequent actions toward it. These perceptions have a powerful influence on expectations—Ginzberg (1981) showed how users' expectations of technology influenced their perceptions of it and how cognitive and 'micro-level processes' became important to understanding these perceptions. The mental models formed when exploring technology are important sense-making devices during processes

of organizational change (Bartunek & Moch, 1987). As Weick (2005 p.411) states *"sense-making starts with chaos and involves labelling and categorising to stabilise the streaming of experience, connecting the abstract with the concrete"*. This idea of creating 'order out of chaos' will be familiar to anyone who has been involved in a technology project, where goals are discovered through social processes involving argument and debate (Daft, 1986).

If we accept that the use of e-HRM is fundamental to HR transformation, then being able to comprehend, plan for and ultimately implement e-HRM becomes a core organisational capability, not just for HR teams, but for all business leaders. Various explanations are available as to why organisations differ in their ability to make sense of e-HRM. One useful concept here is the idea of 'absorptive capacity'. Zahra and George (2002), adopting the earlier work of Cohen and Leventhal (1990), define absorptive capacity as the acquisition, assimilation, transformation and exploitation of knowledge to produce a new organisational capability. Those with higher absorptive capacity (i.e. those better able to make sense of its potential) will naturally be better able to exploit technology[2]. Likewise, group learning processes may also be seen as important mechanisms in understanding and developing technological knowledge. Bondarouk (2006) argues that acceptance of technology is related to group learning processes, which can only be achieved through complex interactions. Using Kolb's (1984) learning theory, Bondarouk describes a 5 step action-oriented group learning approach where individuals start to use technology in a haphazard way and gradually, through shared understanding, mutual adjustment occurs in which the use of technology is agreed.

TECHNOLOGICAL FRAMES

Orlikowski & Gash (1994) argue that the concept of 'technological frames' offers a useful analytic perspective for explaining and anticipating actions and meaning. Frames are related to sense-making and personal constructs, being cognitive structures or mental models that are held by individuals, typically operating in the background with both facilitating and constraining effects. These individual frames of reference have been described as "*a built-up repertoire of tacit knowledge that is used to impose structure upon, and impart meaning to, otherwise ambiguous social and situational information to facilitate understanding*" (Gioia, 1986 p.56). They have a powerful effect on people's assumptions, expectations and knowledge about the purpose, context, importance and role of technology. Frames can be both positive and negative—where they are positive, there is shared understanding and mutuality, whereas negative frames can become "psychic prisons" that inhibit learning because people "*cannot look at old problems in a new light and attack old challenges with different and more powerful tools—they cannot reframe*" (1991 p.4).

E-HRM implementation projects are often intensely political in nature, due to the challenges associated with the cost of investment and the changes to ways of working that are involved. Strong frame congruence may therefore be seen as a critical pre-requisite of project success and where frame incongruence exists, difficulties and conflict may arise. Orlikowski & Gash (1994), researching the introduction of Lotus Notes into a consultancy organisation, found that three 'domains' characterised interpretations of technology:

- **Technology in use:** People's understanding of how the technology will be used on a day-to-day basis.
- **Nature of technology:** People's images of the technology and their understanding of its capabilities and functionality.
- **Technology strategy:** Their understanding of why the organisation acquired and implemented the technology.

The current research is aimed at exploring how various organisational actors make sense of e-HRM by examining how the various frames of reference between stakeholders shape the planning and development of e-HRM, both before and during implementation. It suggests that this understanding is critical to an organisation's ability to plan for and ultimately deliver HR transformation. If stakeholders are unable to make sense of technology and agree common (congruent) technological frames, as a minimum there will be issues of resistance and potentially significant barriers to progressing beyond administration towards transformational HR.

RESEARCH METHODOLOGY

Approach

The underlying methodology of the research is based on the formative work on grounded theory by Glaser & Strauss (1967). Grounded theory is an inductive approach to theory development that attempts to account for observed behaviour through a series of theoretical propositions. In this case, the focus is on how organisations make sense of e-HRM, its use as a transformational tool, how it is perceived by HR and line managers and how those perceptions are manifested through to final implementation and use.

Research Sample & Approach

Several methods were used to collect data, the primary method being a series of semi-structured interviews. Research also included documentary analysis, workshops, participatory observation and the maintenance of a reflective diary. Interviews were aimed at obtaining an insight into the sense-making processes of human resource professionals and line managers with regard to the use of e-HRM technology. Participants were drawn from public sector organisations at different stages of their implementation of e-HRM technology, a mix of consultancy clients of the author or obtained via direct approaches through networking at conferences, events etc. Participants either used, or expected to use, a range of software products to meet their e-HRM needs. Some initial screening was performed against participants to understand the current stage of their project and whether reasonable access could be granted. The organisations participating were:

- 6 Local Councils (with extended access to one Council)
- 1 regional police constabulary
- 2 Government agencies
- 1 Health Authority

To date, 41 interviews have been conducted, including HR professionals, HR Directors and line managers on an individual basis, plus a series of group workshop discussions with line managers. Interviews lasted between 45 minutes and 2 hours and were recorded and transcribed for analysis. Interviewees were encouraged to engage in a broad-ranging discussion in order to provoke responses, rather than the interviewer being a 'speaking questionnaire'. Views were invited on the context of e-HRM, including an insight into what progress had been made with technology, concerns relating to its introduction and their perceptions of the impact of technology. They were also asked about the role of the HR function and the people management capability of the organisation. Line manager access has proved to be challenging—experience suggests that HR managers are protective of their 'customers' and initially act as gatekeepers. They are often reluctant to give permission to meet line managers until they have at least been through the research process themselves.

KEY THEMES

A prototype template analysis approach was used to analyse interviews. Although originally intended to provide context for the technology discussion, two key themes arose consistently throughout:

Theme 1: Risk-averse, bureaucratic and under-valued—An HR function under pressure.

It was no surprise to find that interviews supported the stereotypical idea of a public sector HR function, struggling to establish a credible reputation and highly concerned with demonstrating value. The HR functions studied were typically working under great pressure, with sub-optimal resources, often failing to deliver a good service. Line managers were especially critical of the quality of HR service delivered:

They don't give a s**t [Council, Line Manager]

And:

We get a c**p service [Council, Line Manager]

All too often, interviews portrayed organisations as highly rule-bound and bureaucratic. Line managers frequently expressed a concern that the HR function was defensive, risk averse and often uninterested in strategic people development issues:

We're probably a bit more slaves to the rules of the processes here. I think probably we made things a bit difficult for ourselves in areas—we do tend to tie ourselves up in knots and I do think it sets us back, a different way with more freedom would be good. [Council, Line Manager]

Even HR Managers confess a tendency to:

Play it safe, rather than make a decision which needs to be made. We're less bold in making decisions, we're good at administrative decisions but less bold on big decisions. [Council, HR Manager]

For many line managers, it seems that HR is 'only there for the bad things in life', rather than providing strategic support for organisation development activities:

HR is much more like a sort of emergency plumber service, there to give us help when things go wrong, such as where we have a long-term sickness issue or for sorting out the back-office processes like salaries and sickness. [Council, Line Manager]

The lack of strategic focus or direction was a source of frustration for managers:

I'm not sure we've all got a shared understanding of what the hell they're supposed to be doing. I think that's the problem. For me, it's a people business; we should have a very strategic view of what the role of our HR support is. [Council, Line Manager]

Of course, the meaning of 'strategic' in public sector HR terms invites wide interpretation, beyond the scope of this chapter. For one HR manager, strategic had a very operational meaning:

Strategic means assessing the policies, making sure the council operates in a consistent way and like any organisation employing people, that people abide by it. [Council, HR Manager]

One recurring theme was that line managers seemed to appreciate the contribution of individual HR people but were dismissive of the function as a whole. A complex relationship exists between line managers and functional HR staff that is beyond this chapter to explore.

Theme 2: Line Managers are perceived as lacking people management capability.

A second major theme was a series of strong concerns about the capability of line managers in their people management role. HR managers

expressed this in terms of a frustration with line management's need for constant 'hand-holding' whenever people management issues arose. A common view was that:

Some managers would like HR to come along and take away the people management function. [Council, HR Manager]

HR teams were typically cynical about the ability of line managers to cope with managing people and were critical of their ability to perform basic tasks such as attendance interviews, grievance discussions, or running performance management processes. As one HR manager stated:

I see it time and time again, one recent example is where a senior manager was in a terrible state, she had never thought that as part of being a manager, she would find herself in an employment tribunal, she didn't have the skills to manage the situation. [Council HR Manager]

Line managers themselves commented that their colleagues:

Won't face up to their responsibilities, disciplinary processes can take forever because the managers don't like disciplining, grasping the nettle and dealing with it. [Council Line Manager]

An often expressed sentiment was that line managers tend to see people management as a secondary activity to the 'real' management duties of managing a budget and providing an operational service, describing people management as *"a necessary evil"* [Council, Line Manager]. Some HR managers were even forgiving of poor people management:

There are some managers for whom it's impossible, they're managing huge numbers of people, there is legislation which requires them to work within boundaries, they don't have the luxury to be good people managers. [Council, HR manager]

However, one organisation, a Government Agency, saw the development of managerial capability as so important that they defined it as a key driver in their e-HRM strategy, seeking a need for a transformation in management culture and the HR approach:

That's part of the culture change, we've been trying to give managers more accountability and trust. It's been a hard year for the centre, because they feel they have to check everything—we said we're not going to be checking everything in future. Some of the managers think everything will get checked. [Government Agency, HR Manager]

Although not stated so explicitly, other HR managers expressed an aspiration that improved line management capability may be an additional outcome of the e-HRM investment, where technology acts as the 'symbolic' representation of a new way of working (see Tansley, Newell & Williams, 2001).

THEORY DEVELOPMENT

Following the structure proposed by Orlikowski & Gash (1994), research findings were analysed from the perspective of an interpretative technological frames model using the prototype template analysis structure. The three core technological domains form the basis for comparing differing views about the use, nature and strategy of technology, revealing varying degrees of frame congruence and some significant frame incongruence.

Technology in use: People's understanding of how the technology will be used on a day-to-day basis. This domain addresses the operational perception of e-HRM—that is, how technology is being (or will be) used to support HR delivery, particularly in administrative areas. Without exception, HR managers were enthusiastic about the automating impact of e-HRM:

What we're really hoping in terms of the new computer system we're introducing is that it will take away some of that pressure, particularly on some of the administrative things which will now be done automatically. We are relying very much on this new system doing that. [Council, HR Manager]

HR managers tended to assume that managers would intuitively understand the benefits of using the technology, making assumptions about how readily they would adapt to e-HRM in daily use:

Managers will see the benefits quickly ... they're not stupid, they will see it. There'll be a bit of work, but a lot of gain. So I'm hoping that there will be a balance and the fact that there is a vast amount of information available to them that they will actually appreciate that overall it is a good thing for them. [Council, HR Manager]

Line managers often had a different view on the benefits that had been achieved:

There was an attempt at trying to tell us what the benefits were but I don't think I've reaped those benefits yet. [Government Agency, Line Manager]

We were all trained some time ago, it may be that I haven't picked up on some of this. I think it's quite difficult. [Council, Line Manager]

Far from seeing the benefits, there was a sense that HR had simply transferred its work in another form:

I remember leaving the training session and thinking, well that's another load of extra work for me for no perceived benefits. I don't mind putting extra effort in if I'm going to get something tangible at the end of it, and I just thought well here we go, we've a great deal more to do. [Government Agency, Line Manager]

There was quite a bit of resentment initially about the system and I have to say my team were quite sympathetic, saying this is going to give you a lot more work and feeling sorry for me and they were kind. [Government Agency, Line Manager]

Even HR managers expressed cynicism at the benefits argument:

Let's be honest, however you dress self-service up, you're giving them an additional task to do that they didn't do before, that work doesn't actually go away and if you transfer it over you can fool yourself into thinking you've actually made some efficiency savings and you haven't. [Council, HR Manager]

Others had a desire to return to more traditional ways of working:

I always preferred the old system, where once a year you get a manual form and confirmed. This system doesn't pick up those people who have forgotten or can't be bothered to tell you they've moved home whereas it it's just relying on remembering to go in. It all sounds a bit dodgy. [Council, Line Manager]

I think it's good for processing between the managers and HR but I think between the staff and the managers it's cut the tie a little bit [Government Agency, Line Manager]

Some HR Managers expressed frustration at negative line management responses to e-HRM and recognised the need to embed the technology deeply into a new way of working:

I think they want the accountability but they don't want to fully own the responsibility that goes with it. I think managers do kind of want it both ways. The organisation is saying one thing and allowing another. We have to follow it through, let's say it much firmly, much more clearly. [Council HR Manager]

Although managers often placed a high value on improved management reporting, they were generally far less ambitious in their expectations than HR managers, often questioning whether e-HRM functionality would be relevant to them:

I'm not sure [managers] *would want too many fancy functions because they don't have very much freedom to act anyway... more sophisticated tools wouldn't be that much use to them.* [Council, Line Manager]

Although there is a broad level of agreement about the potential of e-HRM for administrative improvements, with high expectations about how it will be delivered, there appears to be a mismatch of views about e-HRM in practice, revealing shortcomings in the way that the new systems had been implemented.

Nature of Technology: people's images of the technology and their understanding of its capabilities and functionality.

This domain deals with the overall capabilities and potential of e-HRM and the perceived impact on the roles of HR and line managers. HR managers generally held a highly positive view of e-HRM capabilities, with several describing it in terms of a 'magic bullet', solving a variety of process problems. This is not uncommon in IT projects and can lead to highly unrealistic expectations (Markus & Benjamin, 1997). For example:

Self-service is going through meteoric development, isn't it, in terms of the potential of what it can do, there's nothing that we can't do through self-service. [Council, HR Manager]

Some HR managers saw e-HRM as a form of 'expert system', not just managing transactions but helping managers decide what to do next, in the form of online alerts to prompt actions. As one HR manager stated:

It would be the manager's friend—basically the manager would relate completely to that system and it would help him or her actually manage their staff. It gives them all the information they need, members might say we need to know the turnover in your area. In future, no matter what the personnel question is that comes up—I want the manager to feel confident they can interrogate the system easily and out it comes in a report. [Council, HR Manager]

Others were more realistic, yet saw the enabling potential:

It's partly about being an enabler, a large percentage of the personnel staff are out there professionally qualified, and I would like them to be using that as much as possible which means having fewer of them and fewer of them passing bits of paper, also it's much more motivating for them. [Council, HR Manager]

Others saw e-HRM as an opportunity to make a step change in the maturity of the HR function:

There were two drivers really, one was definitely efficiency to get the cost of the service down and the other driver was to get a more modern and professional service to meet the needs of the business. They were the two catalysts of change really, efficiency and modernising the service. [Government Agency, HR Manager]

HR teams often tended to see the implementation of e-HRM as having a positive impact on line manager roles, giving them a set of powerful tools to manage their staff. Indeed, a commonly held view was that once implemented, e-HRM had helped to raise the profile of the HR function as a result:

I think a year ago, some managers would have thought 'I don't know what HR does', but they are now trying to use HR technology to link into their

systems, their processes which in turn makes it better for everybody. [Council, HR Manager]

From an HR management perspective, e-HRM was often expected to have major impact on management accountability. Some organisations had integrated e-HRM into other management activity:

We do other things around reporting so that on the personnel intranet site you can set an alert which tells you for example when the latest turnover figures for your department are available so I'll do a report, put it on the intranet and you get an alert telling you about it. [Council, HR Manager]

Others saw e-HRM as a tool to monitor the activities of line managers, perhaps even 'weeding out' the weaker managers:

When I ask them what they've done about absence, with this new system, they can't say they don't know. [Government Agency, HR Manager]

With the system now, we can do compliance reports on who has done appraisals, who hasn't, who has recorded absence and who hasn't, and they are regular kind of reports... it goes to the Directors, it goes to members, they go to the chief executive. [Council HR Manager]

In fairness, many respondents were pragmatic about the 'policing' role of e-HRM:

I don't think that technology is seen as the tool for policing us. Managers can get a breakdown of absence and there are lots of reports available for monitoring so in that sense they are getting something out of the system. Staff may not have cottoned on to that yet but I personally think it's great that we've got the information there and we can do something about it. [Council, Line Manager]

It will take us out of the role of chasing managers, having to police them, instead the system should help them and only that small minority of managers that aren't capable will say the system is coercing them, that the technology isn't delivering. [Council, HR Manager]

However, interviews revealed major frame incongruence with regard to the capabilities and outcomes of e-HRM; whereas HR managers saw a step change in their capability, line managers often did not recognise or acknowledge the transformational outcomes or where e-HRM might change or enhance their line roles.

Technology Strategy: People's understanding of why the organisation acquired and implemented the technology.

This domain addresses the more strategic aspects of e-HRM and is particularly relevant to transformational objectives. Unless actors have a common point of reference and clear understanding of the transformational effect of e-HRM, a process-focused strategy is likely, so strong frame congruence about the strategic objectives of e-HRM would appear to be a pre-requisite. However, we find very different frames of reference among the two key stakeholder groups. Some HR Managers took the view that e-HRM would lead to a 'time-shift' transformation, where the automation or devolvement of administrative workload would allow the HR function to concentrate on strategic issues. Others saw a more active, direct transformational impact of e-HRM, where the technology itself would enable higher levels of managerial capability:

Eventually, we want to reduce HR administration, but also it's about strategic change, giving line managers the tools to be more effective, that's what it boils down to, putting things online, Personal Development Reviews, sickness etc. we're giving you all that technology, they will have to deal with it in future. [Police Authority/HR manager]

There is a chain—the technology can drive changes in the way that managers operate and the way we recruit—I also get really enthusiastic about this. [Council HR Manager]

Expectations of a transformational impact were high among many HR managers, many believing that technology would change their role at the strategic level by improving managerial capability. This view was also shared by some line managers:

It was always seen as a way of helping managers do their job better with better management information, understanding learning and development interventions, looking at their record of attendance, all of those things, so it was more a tool to do your job but not the end in itself. [Government Agency, HR Manager]

The other aspect to it is that you'd hope that not only will it allow us to take out posts across the organisation, but if set up properly it should allow mangers to manage their teams in a better way. [Council Line Manager]

There is also evidence in this domain that e-HRM has had a transformational impact. When asked about the relationship between HR and line managers, one HR Director responded that:

Yes, the good ones use the information or know the information is there and will ask us to get more involved in professional issues rather than processes. The less good ones will still complain about having to do personnel work. [Council, HR Manager]

The whole system coming has completely changed their perceptions they are now beginning to see the value of it, to take away the tedious systems and they'll see it pay back for all the work they've put in, I see self service as a starting point. [Government Agency, HR Manager]

While there were doubts about the true transformational potential of e-HRM, several line managers also saw see the strategic potential of technology, although they also questioned the capability of the HR function to deliver the strategic potential. Some HR interviewees were well aware of the limitations of technology:

The system won't make us strategic—because we have to believe we are already strategic. [Council, HR Manager]

However, one interviewee responded:

No, I think that's rubbish. I think because of the nature of HR you are driven operationally. I think the biggest barrier is professionals not having the capability to be strategic and really focusing. [Council HR Manager]

However, some managers were highly cynical about the likely impact of e-HRM:

My feeling is that time will just be swallowed up with day to day work. I've never yet seen—and one of the reasons why I've been a bit of a wet blanket in terms of supporting the system—I've never yet seen a successful personnel system and I've seen three. The reason is they all get watered down and Personnel say "we can't do this" and managers don't get engaged and the managers say that it does nothing for them. [Council, Line Manager]

Even where there are transformational aspirations, the ability of the function to realise those aspirations in the form of detailed plans is weak. As one HR professional said:

I don't think we've thought it through. We know we're going to save some costs, but beyond that we don't really know what to expect. [Council, HR Manager]

One finding of concern was that HR Business Partners (those staff directly supporting line managers in an internal consultancy role) tended to avoided involvement in e-HRM projects, seeing little or no relevance to technology beyond administration. It has been difficult to test this technological frame, since several planned interviews with Business Partners were cancelled at short notice. It may be that this subset of HR managers underestimates or misunderstands the potential transformational impact of technology, which would also restrict the scope of transformation programmes. Attempts will be made to explore this frame further as research progresses.

ANALYSIS OF FINDINGS

Interviews reveal that HR managers and line managers have very different views of technology in terms of its day-to-day use, capability and strategic value. Using the technological frames model developed by Orlikowski and Gash (ibid.), we can compare attitudes along the three core technological sense-making domains. Table 1 summarizes the key themes from interviews in tabular form against these domains:

There is an irony lurking here—while the HR function regards technology as an enabler of transformation and a tool to enhance its strategic impact, if the line managers it serves doubt the general strategic capability, why should they trust HR management to introduce a strategic HR system? A poor track record of strategic HR engagement is more likely to lead to a belief that technology will also be poorly implemented. If this is true, then an analysis of e-HRM limited to the three technological domains may provide an inadequate explanation of sense-making processes. We must also examine the context in which technology operates, in particular the power relations between groups of stakeholders, forming a three-way relationship to technology. This is consistent with Klein and Kleinman (2002), who argue that power relations play a key role in the social shaping of technology. As a result, the following proposition is made:

Table 1. Technological frames for HR managers and line managers

DOMAIN	STAKEHOLDERS	
	How HR Managers see e-HRM	How Line managers see e-HRM
Technology in use	Managers will understand and use the system and will intuitively grasp the system The manager's friend: alerts, warnings, guidance	Technology takes lot of time to get working and needs an investment from users to get benefits; it's just one more thing to learn HR is 'dumping its dirty work' Those with experience feel that that the system doesn't help them much
Nature of technology	Initially see technology as a way of reducing the cost of HR operations, reduced headcount Technology seen as a magic bullet, expert system, giving them greater control over non-compliant managers Believe that e-HRM will make managers better at their roles Believe e-HRM will produce better HR information	Technology should bring about process improvement "These things never work". Technology not likely to be 'sold' to managers properly. Assume that better management information will be delivered Cynicism that it will lead to meta-regulation from the centre
Technology strategy	Strategic aspiration often limited to administration and HR services Desire to make long-term shift in HR function (time shift) Doubt that technology will bring about a shift in strategic focus Technology is unlikely to impact on professional HR roles	Technology is an opportunity (but only one among many other strategies) HR needs to prove its operational capability before they can be trusted to implement technology

Context is critical: technological frames are moderated by the power relations between groups of actors, in this case, the mutual opinions of HR teams and line managers.

One particularly revealing interview with a Local Council Line Manager highlighted the need for transformational e-HRM decisions to be taken in the context of a clear HR strategy, by a credible HR function:

Without a clear vision of where the authority needs to be, we're struggling to fit with HR initiatives, it's still an authority with glib statements about what it wants to do. If it embeds properly, the information will be invaluable in helping to develop a strategic approach, but without the information, no, it will struggle to be any more than something that enhances processes. [Council, Line Manager]

Table 2 sets out these additional 'power relations' domains, examining how HR managers

Table 2. Power relations: Moderating frames

DOMAIN	HR Manager View	Line Manager View
HR function strategic capability	Under valued Lack good information or know how to use it Technology will improve strategic information	HR is bureaucratic and policy driven Value individual HR people but not the function as a whole No clear idea of the role and strategy of HR **Doubt that HR can deliver strategic e-HRM**
Management capability	Managers need a lot of 'hand holding to manage people Managers don't understand their people management responsibilities **Technology will improve managerial capability + weed out the weak managers**	People management sometimes seen as a 'necessary evil', secondary to operations Colleagues won't face up to their people management responsibilities **No coherent view on technology**

Figure 2. Relationship of core frames, moderating frames and technology strategy

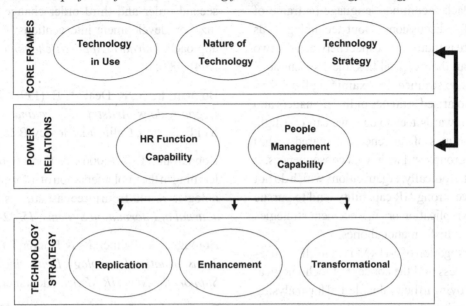

and line managers see one another. For example, whereas HR managers are likely to believe that e-HRM will improve strategic information, line managers often doubt that the HR function has the ability to deliver strategic e-HRM and deliver transformative change. Sadly, one key area of frame congruence is with regard to line manager capability—line managers believe their colleagues don't take it seriously and HR managers agree with this, seeing technology as a means of identifying poor managers. One conclusion from this is that transformational objectives with regard to technology are more likely to be supported and shared where good levels of credibility and capability are in place.

When viewed in conjunction with the three core technological domains, power relations domains offer a new insight into the context of e-HRM implementation. (see Figure 2)

DISCUSSION AND CONCLUSION

The technology to bring about transformational HR change has existed for some time. While some organisations have succeeded in e-enabling their HR organisation, others have created bold plans but have been unable to bring them to fruition. One reason for this is that software capability is often far ahead of organisational ability to take make sense of and take advantage of its potential. As a result, greater understanding is needed about the process through which organisations define and understand e-HRM, as well as how they plan for its use.

This chapter argues that this process is not simply about understanding technology in terms of the three core domains (use, nature and strategy), but that power relations between groups of stakeholders also moderate attitudes towards it. So, where the HR function doubts that line managers are capable of managing people effectively, or line managers doubt that HR knows how to get the best out of technology, there will be an impact on expectations of what technology can achieve. While there appears to be basic frame congruence about e-HRM as an administrative tool, there is likewise significant frame incongruence on the relevance of e-HRM for achieving transformational outcomes. These include a major gap between what HR feels it has achieved and the reality of those managers that are using it, who can tend to feel under-prepared and under-whelmed by their experience. It appears that HR managers and line managers lack a common language or frame of reference for discussions about technology—as long as there is mutual disrespect between the two groups about their capabilities, these discussions will always be strained. By examining the different, often polarised attitudes of line managers and HR teams towards technology, we can cast light on which frames of reference are shared within and across groups and with what consequences. It may be that, ironically, organisations which do not already have strong HR capability tend to pursue technology replication or enhancement strategies rather than transformational ones.

An investigation of e-HRM is in itself a sense-making process and the concept of technological frames is proving to be a valuable tool for analysing and categorising stakeholder attitudes. Research continues into this area and it would benefit from greater input by line managers, to understand better their relative technological frames and explore the impact of power relations. Of particular value would be to identify the conditions that lead to increased or decreased congruence, so that transformational objectives could be more precisely stated and realised. Frame analysis may also prove to be a useful tool in tracking changes in the meanings ascribed to technology over time. To address this, this research will continue into 2009 with further interviews planned with line managers. It is hoped that this work will make an important contribution to real-world usage of e-HRM and the development of tools to support change management initiatives.

REFERENCES

Ashton, C. (2001). *eHR Transforming the HR function*: Business Intelligence.

Ball, K. (2001). The use of human resource information systems: a survey. *Personnel Review, 30*(5/66), 677-693.

Bartunek, J. M., & Moch, M. (1987). First order, second order and third order change and organization development interventions: A cognitive approach. *Journal of Applied Behavioural Science, 23*(4), 483-500.

Bolman, L. G., & Deal, T. E. (1991). *Reframing Organizations: Artistry, Choice and Leadership*. San Francisco, California: Jossey-Bass.

Bondarouk, T. V. (2006). Action-oriented group learning in the implementation of information technologies: results from three case studies. *European Journal of Information Systems, 15*, 42-53.

Boroughs, A., Palmer, L., & Hunter, I. (2008). *HR Transformation Technology: Delivering Systems to Support the New HR Model*. Aldershot: Gower.

Broderick, R., & Boudreau, J. W. (1992). Human resource management, information technology and the competitive edge. *The Executive., Spring, 6*(2), 7-17.

CedarCrestone. (2006). *CedarCrestone 2006 Human Capital Survey*: Cedar Crestone.

CIPD. (2006). *Technology in HR: How to get the most out of technology in people management*. Wimbledon: CIPD.

Cohen, W., & Leventhal, D. A. (1990). Absorptive capacity: A new perspective on learning and innovation. *Administrative Science Quarterly, 35*, 128-152.

Daft, R. L. (1986). *Organization Theory and Design* (2nd ed.). St. Paul, MN: West.

Daft, R. L., & Weick, K. E. (1984). Toward a model of organizations as interpretation systems. *Academy of Management Review, 9*(2), 284-295.

Davenport, T. H. (1993). *Process Innovation*. Boston M.A: Harvard Business School Press.

Foster, S. (2006). A high tech future. *Payroll Manager's Review, November 2006,* (pp. 38-40).

Gershon, P. (2004). Releasing Resources to the Frontline: Independent Review of Public Sector Efficiency. In H. Treasury (Ed.).

Ginzberg, M. J. (1981). Early diagnosis of MIS implementation failure: Promising results and unanswered questions. *Management Science, 27*(4), 459–478.

Gioia, D. (1986). *The Thinking Organization.* San Francisco, California: Jossey-Bass.

Glaser, B. G., & Strauss, A. L. (1967). *The discovery of grounded theory: Strategies for qualitative research.* New Tork NY: Aldine.

Gourley, S., & Connolly, P. (1996). HRM and computerised information systems—have we missed a link? *Paper presented at conference—strategic direction of HRM.*

Hannon, J., Jelf, G., & Brandes, D. (1996). Human resource information systems: operational issues and strategic considerations in a global environment. *International Journal of Human Resource Management., 7*(1).

Harris, L. C. (2002). The future for the HRM function in local government: everything has changed- but has anything changed? *Strategic Change, 11,* 369-378.

Keebler, T. J., & Rhodes, D. W. (2002). E-HR becoming the 'path of least resistance'. *Employment Relations Today, 29*(2), 57-66.

Kelly, & Gennard, J. (1996). The role of Personnel Directors on the board of directors. *Personnel Review, 25*(1), 7-24.

Kelly, G. A. (1955). *The Psychology of Personal Constructs Vol 1 and 2.* New York: Norton.

Klein, H. K., & Kleinman, D. (2002). The Social Construction of Technology: Structural Considerations. *Science, Technology & Human Values, 27*(1), 28-52.

Kolb, D. A. (1984). *Experiential learning. Experience as the source of learning and development.* Englewood Cliffs, New Jersey: Prentice-Hall.

Kossek, E. E., Young, W., Gash, D. C., & Nichol, V. (1994). Waiting for innovation in the Human Resources Department: Godot implements a Human Resource Information System. *Human Resource Management, Spring, 33*(1), 135-139.

Kovach, K., Hughes, A., Fagan, P., & Maggitti, P. (2002). Administrative and strategic advantages of HRIS. *Employment Relations Today, 29*(2), 43-48.

Lawler, E. E., & Mohrman, S. (2003). HR as a strategic partner—what does it take to make it happen? *Human Resource Planning, 26*(3), 15-29.

Liff, S. (1997). Constructing HR information systems. *Human Resource Management Journal, 7*(2), 18-30.

Lupton, B., & Shaw, S. (2001). Are public sector personnel managers the profession's poor relations? *Human Resource Management Journal, 11*(3), 23-38.

Lykkegaard, B. (2007). *Western European Human Capital Management and Payroll Applications Forecast, 2007-2011:* IDC.

Markus, M. L., & Benjamin, R. I. (1997). The magic bullet theory in IT enabled transformation. *Sloan Management Review, Winter,* (pp. 55-58).

Mercer. (2007). *HR Transformation 2.0: It's all about the business.*

Orlikowski, W., & Gash, C. (1994). Technological frames: making sense of information technology in organisations. *ACM transactions on Information Systems, 12*(2), 174-207.

Othman, R. (2003). On developing the informated work place: HRM issues in Malaysia. *Human Resource Management Review, 13,* 393-406.

Reddington, M., Williamson, M., & Withers, M. (2005). *Transforming HR: Creating value through people.* Oxford: Elesevier:Butterworth-Heinemann.

Snell, S. A., Stuebner, D., & Lepak, D. P. (2002). Virtual HR departments: Getting out of the middle. In D. B. G. R. L. Henneman (Ed.), *Human Resource Management in virtual organisations* (pp. 81-101). Greenwich: Information Age Publishing.

Tansley, C., Newell, S., & Williams, H. (2001). Effecting HRM-style practices through an integrated human resource information system: An e-greenfield site? *Personnel Review, 30*(3), 351-370.

Tyson, S., & Selbie, D. (2004). People processing systems and human resource strategy. *International Journal of HR Development and Management, 4*(2), 117-127.

Ulrich, D. (1997). *Human Resource Champions: The Next Agenda for Adding Value and Delivering Results.* Boston MA: Harvard Business School Press.

Watson-Wyatt. (2002). *B2E/e-HR Survey Results.*

Weick, K., Sutcliffe, K. M., & Obstfeld, D. (2005). Organising and the process of sensemaking. *Organization Science, 16*(4), 409-421.

Zahra, S. A., & George, G. (2002). Absorptive capacity: A review, reconceptualisation and extension. *Academy of Management Review, 27*(2), 185-203.

Zuboff, S. (1988). *In the age of the smart machine.* New York: Basic Books.

KEY TERMS

e-Human Capital Management (e-HCM): Technologies that are specifically focused on supporting the people management aspects of an organisation, providing managers with the tools to support this activity

Enterprise Resource Planning (ERP): Systems such as SAP and Oracle, covering a wide range of business functions such as Finance, Manufacturing, Logistics and Procurement. These large systems typically have a Human Resources module.

HR Transformation: *"The process of recreating or reinventing the HR function—such as re-engineering, restructuring, implementing new systems or a new HR service delivery model, outsourcing or co-sourcing—with the specific intent of enhancing HR's contribution to the business"* (Mercer, 2007).

Human Capital Technology: Systems or parts of systems that support the management of people, such as providing decision support, planning and employee data

Process Technology: Systems or parts of systems that re aimed at supporting transactional HR processes such as payroll, personal data management, enrolment etc

Sense Making: People in organisations try to understand what is happening around them by making interpretations, translating events, developing models for understanding or bringing out meaning and assembling conceptual schemes. These sense-making processes are thought to be critical in influencing the decisions that are made about e-HRM

Technological Frames: Cognitive structures or mental models that are held by individuals that impose structure on and provide meaning for social and situational information to facilitate understanding. They influence our assumptions, expectations, and knowledge and can be positive and negative.

ENDNOTES

[1] Many UK Public Sector organisations still refer to the Human Resources function as 'Personnel'. The significance of this is beyond discussion in this chapter.

[2] I see the concept of absorptive capacity as analogous to a sponge, that becomes full of water and has no further capacity for ideas until more capacity becomes available

Chapter II
HR Portal:
A Tool for Contingent and Individualized HRM

Cataldo Dino Ruta
Bocconi University, Italy

ABSTRACT

Intellectual capital is today considered a key issue in analyzing the critical determinants of company performance. Companies design more and more human resource (HR) strategies when creating and developing intellectual capital. HR portals are applications that enable single personalized access points designed for specific user profiles and organizational positions. Our clarifications and recommendations highlight that HR portal implementation and use can be contingent if the HR function offers a specific set of HR applications to single employees based on differentiation strategies. HR portal implementation and use can also be individualized if the HR function offers a set of alternatives where the single employee can choose a personal HR configuration that is still aligned with the strategy and based on the differentiation of the workforce. Our contribution intends to underline the role of HR portals as a tool for the pursuit of a mature differentiation strategy of the workforce, where the technologies can increase the opportunities for negotiating and exchanging preferences and expectations between employees and the HR function.

INTRODUCTION

Recent studies have ascertained the positive relationship between HR strategy and organizational performances, such as individual performance and turnover (Arthur, 1994), market-based performance (Huselid, 1995), return on investment (ROI) (Delery & Doty, 1996), employee retention and firm productivity (Guthrie, 2001). Other authors have discussed how intellectual capital, which has been described as the sum of all knowledge firms utilize (Nahapiet & Goshal, 1998; Subramanian & Youndt, 2005) can be explained in terms of organizational performance, and more generally, competitive advantage. Furthermore, Youndt, Subramanian and Snell (2004) found that organizational performance can be enhanced by HR configurations, facilitating the development of intellectual capital. Despite the numerous studies on the theme, it is still not clear how the variables of HR configurations and intellectual capital interact. There is a gap in literature with regards to the current debate focusing on the development of some Information Technology (IT) tools that are intensely changing the HR function role (Lepak & Snell, 1998) and the contemporary organizations' way of doing business. Investigations and arguments are however intensifying, as the implementation of HR portals, state of the art IT applications which support HR practices, provide many relevant benefits to the creation and development of intellectual capital.

Objective of this study, aside from filling in some of those intermediate gaps, is to integrate HR strategy theories and configurations, intellectual capital, and information systems and explore the concept of HR portal alignment and personalized HR configuration as key variables for future HR strategies.

Proposition 1: *the HR portal configuration, if aligned with the HR strategy, will increase employee contributions to intellectual capital creation and development.*

Proposition 2: *the HR portal configuration, if offering a range of alternatives through which employees create a personalized HR configurations, will increase employees contribution to intellectual capital creation and development.*

The first section of this article discusses the theoretical background of the manuscript, linking strategic human resource management and information system theories. Thereafter, the interpretation of the contingent and personalized HRM strategies through the design of HR portals is presented. Implications for theory and practice are discussed in the final section.

INTELLECTUAL CAPITAL AND HR PORTALS

Intellectual Capital and Organizational Performance

Amongst the most widely accepted management constructs, intellectual capital has now been firmly established (Dean & Kretschmer, 2007) and defined as the gap between a firm's market value and its financial capital (Edvisson & Malone, 1997), collective brainpower (Stewart, 1997), knowledge and knowing capability of a social collective (Nahapiet & Ghoshal, 1998), and knowledge and competence for brand, reputation and customer relationships (Teece, 2000). The dimensions of knowledge employed and activated in the organization are emphasized by its holistic approach together with the impact of knowledge-based activities on the performance of the organization (Youndt, Subramanian & Snell, 2004). A considerable number of recent studies have examined the development, use, and performance effects of intellectual capital, contributing a more accurate classification of the intellectual capital dimensions (Bontis, 1998; Edvinsson & Malone, 1997; Stewart, 1997) and presenting intellectual capital as a multidimensional entity composed of three basic types of capital: human, social and intellectual (Subramaniam & Youndt, 2005). The entire knowledge base of the organization is grouped together by these three sub-domains according to its nature and knowledge-bearing entity—individual, network and organization.

Human capital is defined as the knowledge each employee has within the organization. Their knowledge, abilities and skills form part of the company's knowledge resources and constitute a unique source of innovation and strategic renewal (Shultz, 1961). Social capital instead, is the knowledge in groups and networks of people (Burt, 1992; Nahapiet & Ghoshal, 1998), consisting of knowledge resources embedded within, available through, and derived from, a network of relationships. Organizational capital includes a more comprehensive and formalized type of knowledge: codified experiences stored in databases, manuals, patents, routines, structures, and so forth (Tomer, 1987; Walsh & Ungson, 1991).

Treating human, social and organizational capital as discrete and independent constructs helps to understand more abstract concepts such as intellectual capital. Looking at an organization's overall profile of intellectual capital in the aggregate—as they can not be created, developed and leveraged in isolation—may be beneficial in order to comprehend how it develops and drives performance. A strict interconnection in fact exists between them and a single action on one of them is likely to have an impact on the intellectual capital in its entirety.

As can be seen from empirical evidence, the combination of human, social and organizational capital (Youndt, Sumbramanian & Snell, 2004) can form unique intellectual capital profiles for companies, whereas the tendency is to focus primarily on one type of capital and its development based on the perceived organizational performance and competitive advantage (Subramaniam & Youndt, 2005). For a better understanding of how HR portals can enhance knowledge flows in organizations, the classification of intellectual capital, its integrated character and unique profile based on strategy, must be considered.

The HR Portal Potential

Shilakes & Tylman (1998) defined the HR portal as an application that provides employees (users) with a single gateway to personalized information needed to make informed business decisions. Merril Lynch, an American financial institution, first used the word HR portal in 1998 to describe an integrated access point to their corporate information (Kakumanu & Mezzacca, 2005). A number of authors believe that HR portals are targeted at accomplishing different key functions according

to their basic characteristics (Bottazzo, 2005; Rose, 2003; Voth, 2002), and are able to design and structure a completely new way of working (Strohmeier, 2007), altering routines and based on national cultural characteristics (Ruta, 2005).

For the user, they represent first of all an information pool, combining data from different external or internal sources, and this *integration* process can be more dynamic and adaptive through portals: combining diverse documents, capturing changes in data and information and monitoring knowledge flows. Portals are therefore *interactive* tools enabling bi-directional exchange flows whilst the use that is made of the portal and views on corporate information can be personalized by tailoring ad hoc information and adapting the portal interface acccordingly. This *personalization* process is crucial as it enables people to set the portal in accordance with their own needs and requirements. Individual employees on the other hand, are responsible for uploading personal data (e.g. personal information, etc) and directly and autonomously consulting areas of personal interest (e.g. remuneration, benefits, working hours, holidays, communities of practice, databases, etc).

At the same time, HR portals allow HR staff to distinguish the various interventions, granting access to some areas of the portal according to needs and authorization and profiling the workforce whilst considering individual differences, preferences, capabilities, roles within the organization and future organizational and strategic needs and thereby gaining the highest value from the human capital.

HR portals are usually organized into macro areas and offer employees the following options in terms of access (Ruta, 2005):

- The HOME folder is mainly dedicated to general corporate information: different areas lead to different information, such as links to the most popular access functions, a search engine to surf the portal faster, a

People Finder to gain information on colleagues, a Frequent Questions and Answers area and a Feedback and Support area.

- The LIFE/WORK folder, with personal and password protected access for employees. This represents an area linked with the HR function: information is exchanged and transactions with the company take place here.
- The ORGANIZATION folder is a more content/country specific area sharing information on a specific division or country branch. A survey/poll area and a bulletin board is often included here.
- The MY portal folder represents the most personalized area of the whole HR portal. Each individual can customize this section according to their interests and needs and often includes a calendar of events and reminders akin to a personal diary.

The interpretation of the role of the HR portal needs further consideration within the intellectual capital framework. Youndt & Snell (2004) consider the information technology infrastructure as the basis for the development of high levels of organizational capital which leads to the assumption that an HR portal configuration that is focused on accessible, user-friendly, and integrated information systems can be considered part of a firm's organizational capital. Although acknowledging the HR portal as a crucial function of IT, its role can be amplified through boosting the development of the three dimensions of intellectual capital using a series of application that impact on skills, knowledge, networks, documents, etc.

The different HR applications that configure an HR portal need to be designed and implemented coherently with the HR strategy. Table 1 below synthesizes the most used HR applications with specific impact on the forms of capital supported (Ruta, forthcoming).

Table 1. A framework for the HR portal applications

Generic HR applications	Forms of Capital Supported		
	Human Capital	Social Capital	Organizational Capital
Personal folder (updating)	*	*	*
Training (e-learning, course selection)	***		*
Performance appraisal: management of the process and feedback reports	***		*
Competence Mapping: self assessment or third party evaluation	***		*
Career development	***		
e-Recruitment (external)	***		
Job posting (internal)	***	*	
People finder		***	
Expertise finder		***	
Community of practice (forum, chat, blogs)	*	***	
Community of practice (report, documents, best practices, etc)	*		***
Vision, Mission and Strategy			***
Organizational Structure (macrostructure and positions)			***
Processes and methods			***
Organizational values			***
Customers' profiles			***
Payroll data			***

Although the HR applications have generic titles in this model, it is quite common to find titles by IT products and brands. The objective is to gain an understanding of the general functionalities of these applications and their contribution in sustaining the three forms of capital.

A further benefit of the introduction of an HR portal is that it leads to a natural *reconfiguration of the HR function* and its tasks, allowing it to develop into a more strategic HR function. This only takes place if HR staff become relevant players in defining the organizational strategy, its implementation and management, which, in turn enhances HR's strategic role. HR staff become responsible for the critical task of aligning people into the firm's strategy and are accountable for monitoring resources and their development as well as for creating suitable opportunities to foster this development.

The use of a technological instrument such as an HR portal finally allows HR staff to differentiate between various interventions, profiling the workforce and taking into account individual differences, preferences, capabilities and roles within the organization and future organizational and strategic needs, extracting the highest value from the human capital. The HR function should also have the possibility to answer employees' and the organization's needs by adopting a new business and strategic point of view, trying to effectively measure the value of intellectual capital and the IT dimensions.

If HR managers strategically align the HR portal with the HR strategy, with the employees' preferences and adopting a new strategic point of view, then employees could be managed and monitored more easily. In the next section, the main issues of a strategic human resource management (SHRM) based on differentiation strategies are presented. The section on solutions and recommendations discusses the contingent and personalized approach for HR portal configurations, according to the propositions presented above.

CONTINGENT AND INDIVIDUALIZED HR

Managing a Differentiated Workforce

The development of intellectual capital is greatly affected by Strategic Human Resources Management (SHRM) . Training programs, for instance, help employees build relationships with their peers and transfer and share knowledge amongst themselves (increasing their social capital) but also increase employees' personal knowledge and human capital. Similarly, knowledge that potentially forms the foundation for organizational learning and knowledge accumulation (organizational capital) can be created as individuals learn and increase their human capital.

Although the correlation of HR investments with human capital has been evidenced (Guthrie, 2001; Huselid, 1995; Huselid, Becker & Beatty, 2005), very little research has examined the effects of HR configurations on social and organizational capital. This issue has successfully been addressed by Youndt & Snell (2004) with the development of three types of HR configurations: Acquisition and Developmental—in order to develop Human Capital (through intensive/extensive staffing, competitive pay, intensive/extensive training programs, promotions), Egalitarian and Collaborative—for the development of Social Capital (through broad banding, team structure, socialization, mentoring), Documentation HR and Information Systems—for the development of Organizational Capital (through soft management system to motivate employees to share and record their knowledge and experience and HR policies that reinforce knowledge capture and access). The implications are that HR activities do not directly boost the company's performance, but instead help the development of the three types of capital, which in turn, drive organizational performance. Every company can have a unique organizational capital profile and as a consequence a unique HR configuration when following a contingency perspective based on strategy.

When applying the contingency perspective within the organization, it is usually oriented to individualize positions that are most critical for executing the strategy (Huselid, Becker & Beatty, 2005; Lepak & Snell, 1999, 2002). Lepak & Snell (1999, 2002) argue that in order to appropriately manage employees it is not possible to rely on a single HR configuration (architecture) and thus developed a framework for differentiating employee groups on the basis of their strategic value and uniqueness. Huselid, Becker and Beatty (2005) suggested a strategy of differentiation among A, B and C positions, designing an appropriate HR configuration for each of these positions able to support the performances of players A, B, and C. A set of HR practices for each position must be coherent with the strategy (vertical fit) and coherent amongst themselves (horizontal fit).

On the basis of the theory presented, it can then be argued that there are core positions that directly impact on intellectual capital creation and development. In order to develop the unique intellectual capital profile each core position must have an HR configuration designed to chiefly support one of the three forms of capital: human, social and organizational. To introduce and integrate the HR portal potential of managing employees requires individualization of each HR configuration which then represents a single personalized access point designed for specific user profiles and organizational positions. A specific goal of the HR function, through an appropriate and strategic HR portal configuration, is to manage positions in order to create and develop intellectual capital which then increases its effectiveness.

Solutions and Recommendations: The Strategic Alignment of the HR Portal for Intellectual Capital Creation and Development

The importance of Information Technology (IT)-business alignment has been documented for some time now. Reich & Benbasat (2000) proposed a definition of alignment as the degree to which the information technology (mission, objectives, and plans) is designed and implemented according to the business mission, objectives, and plans. IT delivers systems and services that are crucial to the company's strategy, operations or user needs where such an alignment is present. Executives can consequently distinguish the contributions that IT makes and users are more likely to accept and utilize IT resources (Huang & Hu, 2007). This study adopts a contingency-based perspective according to which IT resources in themselves may add little value, and only when they are planned and used to support a firm's main strategic objectives, do they play a major role in improving a firm's performance (Oh & Pinsonneault, 2007). The lack of alignment between information systems (IS) and business strategies, according to Henderson and Venkatraman (1999), is the reason many businesses fail to realize value from investments in information technology. The correlation between IS alignment and performance or organizational effectiveness has instead been demonstrated by Chan, Huff and Copeland (1997). A key issue in information system management is the relationship between business strategy and IT alignment (Brancheau, Janz & Wetherbe, 1996), however, the alignment of information systems and business objectives has yet to be fully developed despite a profusion of research on this theme (Chan, 2002).

Henderson and Venkatraman (1999) developed a Strategic Alignment Model focusing on how IT based decisions enhance or threaten those made in the HR domain. The Strategic Alignment Model pertaining to this study requires that two types of alignment between business and the HR portal be specified: the *strategic integration*, contending with the HR portal capacity to both shape and support HR strategy, and the *operational integration*, referring to the link between organizational infrastructure and processes and IS infrastructure and processes. As the aim of this study is HR portal configuration, the focus is specifically on the strategic integration, examining the impact of the HR Strategy on the HR portal and vice versa.

The impact of the HR Strategy on the HR portal (HR portal substitution). This study assumes that HR managers are the HR strategy formulators who decide to leverage one or more dimensions of intellectual capital according to the overall business strategy objectives. The differing HR configurations are consequently designed according to positions within the organization, which in IT terms also means differentiating by profiling the access of those specific positions to the HR portal, thereby supporting the chosen HR strategy and configurations.

The "HR Portal Substitution" variable measures this concept. It measures the capacity of the HR portal to support all the HRM processes ensuring the correct balance between face-to-face and technology based activities. This measurement is calculated with the following ratio: the "Number of HRM Practices implemented in the HR portal that are not technology driven" by the "Number of HRM Practices defined in the HR configuration that are not technology driven". The specification "not technology driven" means that those practices can also be designed and considered without an IT infrastructure. In this case the IT infrastructure is a facilitator of the process itself (e.g.. performance appraisal, recruiting, etc)

The impact of the HR portal on the HR Strategy (HR portal leverage). Generating new HRM processes delivered through HR applications implemented in the portal is a further key role of the HR portal because it shapes the HR Strategy and contributes to its alignment. This effect is extremely crucial and relevant in the interpretation of the alignment in order to avoid a simple substitution effect. This study therefore assumes that "technology driven" HR practices (those that could not have been designed and considered without an IT infrastructure, i.e. e-learning, virtual communities, job posting, etc) can be implemented by the HR staff and planned,

supplemented and shaped directly by employees reinterpreting the technology for their own purposes (Ciborra, 1997).

The "HR Portal Leverage" variable measures this concept. It measures the capacity that the HR portal has to transform and shape a new HR configuration, to implement new applications and increase the number of HRM processes activated throughout the portal. The measurement is calculated by the "Number of HRM Practices implemented in the HR portal that are technology driven". The specification "technology driven" means that those practices could not have been designed and considered without an IT infrastructure (e.g.. e-learning, virtual communities, job posting, etc)

Considering the approach of a clear HR differentiation strategy where positions are valued and segmented based on their strategic contribution and uniqueness (Lepak & Snell, 1999), this study proposes a first measurement of HR portal alignment for each specific position in an organization. The formula shown in Figure 1 is the combination of the two variables presented above:

The HR Portal Alignment for one specific position is the result of the "HR Portal Substitution" multiplied by the "HR Portal Leverage". The alignment is zero when for that specific position (i.e. sales manager) none of the basic HR processes are implemented into the HR portal or when none of the technology driven HR practices are implemented in the HR portal. In both situations HR managers are not using the portal potential to better execute traditional processes or even to develop new ways to deliver HR processes.

In order to have a more reliable measure of alignment and to assess the HR portal Alignment for all the positions identified in a certain organization, this study proposes a second formula as shown in Figure 2.

Following the main model in Figure 1, the HR portal Alignment is linked to the creation of intellectual capital and can be explained based on the formula shown in Figure 3 that expresses the moderating effect:

Figure 1.

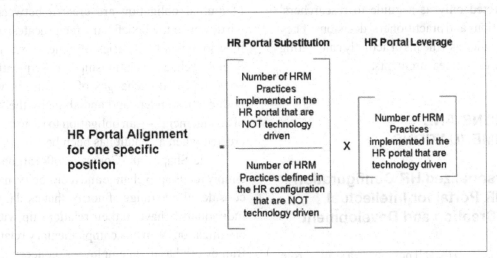

Figure 2.

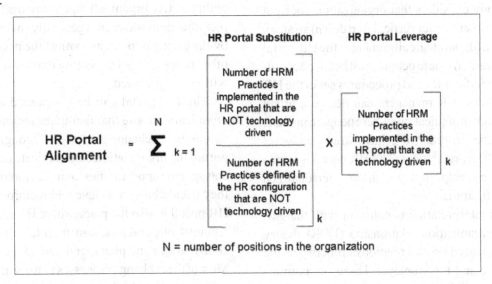

Figure 3.

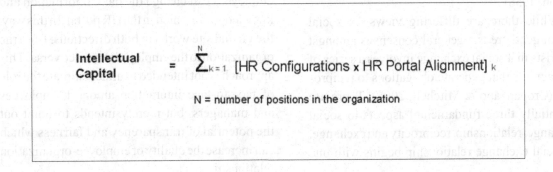

The formulae presented in this section should be interpreted only as a guide to researchers' interpretations and practitioners' decisions. They are not intended as a means of actually calculating indexes or exact measurements.

SOLUTIONS AND RECOMMENDATIONS

The Personalized HR Configuration of the HR Portal for Intellectual Capital Creation and Development

Can we be certain that all persons in a similar role are motivated, committed and treated fairly if the organization adopts the same HR configuration? This study considers that organization does not only consider a strict vertical (top down) strategy approach (the strategic alignment of the HR portal configuration) where people must behave according to specific rules and procedures set in the HR applications. HR managers can design a broad framework of applications where people can select alternatives in order to behave strategically yet follow their preferences. The HR portal is then a tool that can help employees attain a personalized HR configuration.

This interpretation is coherent with the employee-organization relationship (EOR) theory that is focused on the relationship between the employee and the employer, based on assumptions of social exchange (Blau, 1964) and the inducements–contributions model (March & Simon, 1958).

While there are differing views on social exchange, there is a general consensus amongst theorists that social exchange involves a series of interactions that generate obligations to reciprocate (Cropanzano & Mitchell, 2005). There are essentially three fundamental aspects to social exchange: relationship, reciprocity and exchange. A social exchange relationship begins with one party conferring a benefit on another. Feelings of mutual obligation are created between the parties once the beneficiary reciprocates, and is then followed by a series of benefit exchanges. Social exchange relationships consequently involve repeated exchanges of benefits in which both parties understand and abide by the "rules of engagement" — an obligation to reciprocate is created when a benefit has been bestowed.

Coyle-Shapiro and Conway (2004) argue that a simply focus on exchange and reciprocity may not consider all the range of norms that explain how individuals behave in their relationship with the organization. Whilst a complementary relational framework based on employees' concern for the welfare of the organization, termed communal exchange (Clark & Mills, 1979), may help explain positive organizational behaviors beyond a reciprocation motive, it is generally characterized by the giving of benefits to meet the needs of the other party without expecting that these benefits will be reciprocated.

The HR portal can be considered a virtual organizational site that facilitates reciprocal and communal exchange processes. Through the HR portal, the organization communicates and presents specific opportunities to single employees and they decide how to behave and reciprocate. The HR portal is also the place where HR managers, amongst other actors, can monitor employees' contributions and plan if and how to reciprocate. Most of the exchange processes that occurs among different actors in the organization can now be supported and tracked by the HR portal whilst employees can change the data, information and knowledge presented in the HR portal. In this way, the virtual site works in both directions: from the organization to the employees and vice versa. This approach is not intended to underestimate the role of face-to-face interaction amongst employees and managers, but merely intends to point out the potential of transparency and fairness which can increase the quality of employee-organization relationships.

As a consequence, one of the main issue of the EOR theory, aside from the relationship and the exchange process, is the specification of agents representing the organization (Coyle-Shapiro & Shore, 2007). According to Levinson, Price, Munden, Mandl and Solley (1962), employees view actions by agents of the organization as actions taken by the organization itself. The assumption in EOR research is therefore that employees view all possible agents and contract makers (even administrative contract makers such as human resource policies and mission statements) as grouped into one "humanlike" bundle. The humanization of the organization can be harnessed in the contract maker so that the employee has a relationship with one single entity (i.e., the organization).

An employee's immediate manager is likely to play an important role in shaping an individual's psychological contract according to Shore and Tetrick (1994) which is supported by Liden, Bauer, and Erdogan (2004) who claim that the "immediate supervisor plays a critical role as a key agent of the organization through which members form their perceptions of the organization" (pp. 228).

The role of the immediate manager may be one of facilitating the fulfillment of, or breaking the terms of, the more distal exchange which is however not likely to come to the forefront until triggered by an event such as the layoff, restructuring, removal or addition of benefits, or policy changes. Based on agency theory, they argued that a relatively narrow exchange with the employee is expected, and that the role assigned to the immediate manager is to put into practice formalized contracts that lay out clear expectations for the behavior and performance of the employee. Yet the opposite is expected from a dynamic capability perspective where, based on a rapidly changing environment (Coyle-Shapiro & Shore, 2007), EORs need to be highly individualized and regularly revised by the manager to address the changing needs of the organization. Theorizing therefore on the specification and role of the agent could begin from the context in which exchanges are embedded— the organizational strategy.

The HR portal changes the scenario of agents and relationships in EOR theory. The HR portal allows employees to interact directly with multiple and selected agents, and can be considered a channel where expectations and preferences are collected. Following a contingency perspective, the HR function doesn't offer the same set of practices to all employees. It differentiates the workforce and defines sets of practices for different positions, based on SHRM and the differentiation strategy. EOR theory suggests a balanced approach in the relationship, where employees can negotiate and exchange resources. For this reason, one possible option would be to design a range of alternatives (of the same practice) for each position (employee). In this way, the HR portal becomes a place where exchanges of resources occur (opportunities and preferences). Each position has a certain range of alternatives and employees build their own personalized HR configuration.

The HR portal can be interpreted as an "HR market place" that activates negotiation processes between employees and the organization (HR function, managers, etc). For instance, an employee has to develop a specific competence and can choose from among: training courses, e-learning, one-to-one or virtual learning; or an employee can decide the parameters of the incentive systems from among group, organizational or individuals goals or a combination of them; or an employee can contribute to the organization by formalizing methodologies or leading a community of practice. In these scenarios technology cannot be the only tool for negotiation, but it is certainly a strong facilitator. HR portals increase transparency and fairness, decreasing the risk of agent's opportunism.

A top down strategy must coexist with a bottom up approach of behaviors. The aim of the organization is to design organizational mechanisms, improving individual and organizational performance, where both these approaches work together. In the HR portal context, the HR function has to design HR portal configurations based on strategy, setting a range of alternatives in order to meet employees' preferences.

Researchers have theorized this approach known as the *individualized organization* (Lawler III & Finegold, 2000), however, only with the full potential of the HR portal is the HR function able to effectively design and manage employee-organization relationships.

FUTURE TRENDS

In the near future the concepts of e-transformation and human resource management technologies will simply become human resource management processes as technologies become familiar and available in all contexts. In this new scenario, the HR portal is not only a tool implemented to simplify the employees' access to data, information and knowledge, but will become a new way to set the employee-organization relationship. The HR function has to differentiate the workforce but at the same time has to make the portal a place where employees can create their own HR configurations, meeting their preferences.

Some significant future directions for research are indicated with this setting Firstly, relationships need to be tested through quantitative analysis with better and more reliable measurements of the contribution of the HR portal for the development of intellectual capital. Secondly, the design focus should be complemented with an in-depth analysis of the implementation process of HR portals. Not all well-designed and aligned HR portals are actually used by employees. Nonetheless, as employees consider the portal a good way of improving individual performance, alignment could be one variable to clarify usage. Thirdly, the effect of misaligned HR portals on individual performance and internal communication would be interesting to study. This is an important area of research that could explain the success of the HR portal as a crucial tool for HR effectiveness. Fourthly, how to design the set of alternatives

and how the employees make their choices is an important research area that can improve the efficacy of such technologies in the workplace.

CONCLUSION

This work is intended to offer an integrative model for HR portal and intellectual capital development. A firm's workforce should always be concentrated on increasing intellectual capital consistent with the company strategy. An organization's specific strategic position significantly influences the impact of HR practices on performance: the relationship between the use of specific HR practices and organizational performance is contingent on an organization strategy. Empirical evidence suggests that a tighter fit between human resource competencies and strategy leads to superior performance. Considering the theoretical background and the particular features and characteristics of the HR portal, some explicit advantages can be derived from the alignment and the design of the HR portal. It is HR managers who are accountable for HR Portal design; they are responsible for selecting the content and the proper configuration through the adoption of different applications and the design of specific practices. The different components and configurations they select will intrinsically guide and support employees' activities coherently with the company strategy. The expansion of human, social or organizational capital is impacted by different practices whilst different applications can be rejected according to their contribution to the development of the different components of intellectual capital.

Through the configuration of the HR portal, HR managers can align and leverage the workforce contribution to the company strategy. However, different alternatives of practices must be designed at the same time in order to meet employees' preferences. These findings, together with the existing literature on HR portals, confirm the propositions of this study and underline the strategic role of the

HR portal and the necessity of its management in order to achieve superior performance, both in a contingent and individualized approach.

REFERENCES

Arthur, J. B. (1994). Effects of human resource systems on manufacturing performance and turnover. *Academy of Management Journal, 37,* 670–687.

Blau, P. M. (1964). *Exchange and power in social life*. New York: John Wiley & Sons.

Bontis, N. (1998). Intellectual Capital: an exploratory study that develops measures and models. *Management Decision, 36(2),* 63-76.

Bottazzo, V. (2005). Intranet: A Medium of internal Communication and Training. *Information Services and Use, 25,* 77-85.

Brancheau, J. C., Janz, B. D., & Wetherbe, J. C. (1996). Key issues in information systems management. 1994-95 SIM Delphi results. *MIS Quarterly, 20*(2), 225-242.

Burt, R. S. (1992). *Structural holes: The social structure of competition*. Cambridge, MA: Harvard University Press.

Chan, Y. E. (2002). Why Haven't We Mastered Alignment? The Importance of the Informal Organization Structure. *MIS Quarterly Executive, 1*(2), 97-112.

Chan, Y. E., Huff, S. L., & Copeland, D. G. (1997). Assessing Realized Information Systems Strategy. *The Journal of Strategic Information Systems, 6*(4), 273-298.

Ciborra, C. U. (1997). De Profundis ? Deconstructing the Concept of Strategic Alignment. *Scandinavian Journal of Information Systems, 9*(1), 67-82.

Clark, M. S., & Mills, J. (1979). Interpersonal attraction in exchange and communal relationships. *Journal of Personality and Social Psychology, 37,* 12–24.

Coyle-Shapiro, J. A-M., & Conway, N. (2004). The employment relationship through the lens of social exchange. In J. Coyle-Shapiro, L. Shore, S. Taylor, & L. Tetrick (Eds.), *The employment relationship: Examining psychological and contextual perspectives*. Oxford: Oxford University Press.

Coyle-Shapiro, J. A-M., & Shore, L.M. (2007). The employee–organization relationship: Where do we go from here? *Human Resource Management Review, 17*(2), 166-179.

Cropanzano, R., & Mitchell, M. S. (2005). Social exchange theory: An interdisciplinary review. *Journal of Management, 31,* 874–900.

Dean, A., & Kretschmer, M. (2007). Can Ideas Be Capital? Factors of production in the post-industrial economy: a review and critique. *Academy of Management Review, 32*(2), 573-594.

Delery, J. E., & Doty, D. H. (1996). Modes of theorizing in strategic human resource management: Tests of universalistic, contingency, and configurational performance predictions. *Academy of Management Journal, 39,* 802–835.

Edvinsson, L., & Malone, M. S. (1997). *Intellectual Capital: Realizing Your Company's True Value by Finding its Hidden Brainpower*. New York: Harper Business.

Guthrie, J. P. (2001). High-involvement work practices, turnovers, and productivity: Evidence from New Zealand. *Academy of Management Journal, 44,* 180–190.

Henderson, J. C., & Venkatraman, N. (1999). Strategic alignment: leveraging information technology for transforming organizations. *IBM Systems Journal, 38.*

Huang, C. D., & Hu, Q. (2007). Achieving IT-Business strategic alignment via enterprise-wide implementation of balanced scorecards. *Information Systems Management, 24,* 73-84

Huselid, M. A. (1995). The impact of human resource management practices on turnover, productivity, and corporate financial performance. *Academy of Management Journal, 38,* 635–672.

Huselid, M. A., Becker, B. E., & Beatty, R. W. (2005). *The Workforce Scorecard: Managing Human Capital to Execute Strategy.* Boston: Harvard Business School Press

Kakumanu, P., & Mezzacca, M. (2005). Importance of portal Standardization and Ensuring Adoption in Organizational Environments. *The Journal of American Academy of Business*, Cambridge, *7*(2), 128-132.

Lawler III, E., & Finegold, D. (2000). Individualizing the Organization: past, present and future. *Organizational Dynamics*, *29*(1), 1–15.

Lepak, D. P., & Snell, S. A. (1999). The human resource architecture: toward a theory of human capital allocation and development. *Academy of Management Review, 24,* 31-48.

Lepak, D. P., & Snell, S. A. (2002). Examining the human resource architecture: the relationships among human capital, employment, and human resource configurations. *Journal of Management, 28*(4), 517-543.

Lepak, D. P., & Snell, S. A. (1998). Virtual HR: Strategic Human Resource Management in the 21st Century. *Human Resource Management Review, 8*(3), 215-234.

Levinson, H., Price, C. R, Munden, K. J., Mandl, H. J., & Solley, C. M. (1962). *Men, management and mental health.* Boston: Harvard University Press.

Liden, R. C., Bauer, T. N., & Erdogan, B. (2004). The role of leader–member exchange in the dynamic relationship between employer and employee: Implications for employee socialization, leaders and organizations. In J. A. -M. Coyle-Shapiro, L. M. Shore, Susan M. Taylor, & L. E. Tetrick (Eds.), *The employment relationship, examining psychological and contextual perspectives.* Oxford: Oxford University Press.

March, J. G., & Simon, H. A. (1958). *Organizations.* New York: Wiley.

Nahapiet, J., & Ghoshal, S. (1998). Social capital, intellectual capital, and the organizational advantage. *Academy of Management Review, 23,* 242–66.

Oh, W., & Pinsonneault, A. (2007). On the assessment of the strategic value of information technologies: conceptual and analytical approaches. *MIS Quarterly, 31*(2), 239-265.

Reich, B. H., & Benbasat, I. (2000). Factors that Influence the Social Dimension of Linkage Between Business and Information Technology Objectives. *Management Information Systems Quarterly, March,* 81-113.

Rose, J. G. (2003). The Joys of Enterprise portals. *The Information Management Journal, Sept/Oct,* (pp. 64-70).

Ruta, C. D. (in press). HR Portal Alignment for the Creation and Development of Intellectual Capital. *International Journal of Human Resource Management.*

Ruta, C. D. (2005). The application of change management theory to the HR portal implementation in subsidiaries of multinational corporations. *Human Resource Management, 35,* 33-53.

Schultz, T. W. (1961). Investment in human capital. *American Economic Review, 51,* 1–17.

Shilakes, C. C., & Tylman, J. (1998). *Enterprise Information portals.* New York: Merrill Lynch, Inc.

Shore, L. M., & Tetrick, L. E. (1994). The psychological contract as an explanatory framework in the employment relationship. In C. Cooper &

D. Rousseau (Eds.), *Trends in organizational behavior, 1* (pp. 91–109). New York: Wiley.

Stewart, T. A. (1997). *Intellectual Capital.* New York: Doubleday-Currency

Strohmeier S. (2007). Research in e-HRM: Review and implications. *Human Resource Management Review, 17*(1), 19-37.

Subramanian, M., & Youndt, M.A. (2005). The influence of intellectual capital on the types of Innovative Capabilities. *Academy of Management Journal, 18*(3), 450-463.

Teece, D. J. (2000). *Managing Intellectual Capital.* Oxford University Press, Oxford.

Tomer, J. F. (1987). *Organizational Capital: The Path to Higher Productivity and Well-Being.* Praeger Publishers.

Voth, D. (2002). Why Enterprise portal are the Next Big Thing. *E-learning,* (pp. 25-29).

Walsh, J. P., & Ungson, G. R. (1991). Organizational memory. *Academy of Management Review, 16,* 57–91.

Youndt, M. A., & Snell, S. A. (2004). Human Resource Configurations, Intellectual Capital and Organizational Performance. *Journal of Managerial Issues, 16*(3), 337-360.

Youndt, M. A., Subramanian, M., & Snell, S. A. (2004). Intellectual Capital Profiles: An Examination of Investments and Returns. *Journal of Management Studies, 41*(2), 335-361.

KEY TERMS

HR Portal: An application that enables companies to unlock internally and externally stored information, and provides users with a single gateway to personalized information needed to make informed business decisions.

HR Portal Alignment: The degree to which the HR portal is designed based on the business mission, objectives, and plans. When alignment exists, the HR portal delivers systems and services that are crucial to the company's strategy, operations or user needs.

Human Capital: There are four individual factors which, when combined, define human capital: the genetic inheritance, education, experience, and attitudes about life and business.

Intellectual Capital: The sum of the knowledge an organization is able to leverage in the process of conducting business to gain competitive advantage.

Personalized HR: The possibility that employees can create a personalized HR configuration, based on a range of alternatives that the HR function offer to employees.

Organizational Capital: All the knowledge within the company that has been institutionalized or codified through several instruments, such as databases, routines, manuals, patents, etc.

Social Capital: The connections at organizational level, within different individuals and parts of the organization, and at inter- organizational level and their ability to create and share knowledge.

Chapter III
E–Work and Labor Processes Transformation

Barbara Imperatori
Catholic University, Milan, Italy

Marco De Marco
Catholic University, Milan, Italy

ABSTRACT

The evolution of the managerial discourse is the result of fashion lifecycles that sometimes have no rational or technical foundations and find no real application within the firms. Taking our cue from the new-institutional perspective, the chapter explores the real labor transformation processes related to the introduction of e-work projects, considering their outputs, outcomes and impacts. The study is based on a multiple-case analysis and underscores the relevance and impact of information and communication technology (ICT) on both "rational" firm's productivity and "normative" employees' psychological contract, also considering different institutional environments. Some critical issues and guidelines inherent the design and implementation of technology-based work systems are discussed, such as the dual perspective approach (the organizational and the employer viewpoint) during the needs-analysis and goal-setting phases; the relevance of coherent organizational culture and human resource practices; the removal of organizational structural constraints; the management of cognitive resistance; and the importance of the evaluation and monitoring phases.

INTRODUCTION

Many economic business analyses confirm the strategic relevance of both internal resources and organizational flexibility: in the global scenario, modern firms can remain competitive if these are able to continually develop distinctive competencies (Grant, 1991, Lepak, Takeuchi & Snell, 2003, Prahalad & Hamel, 1990), maintaining their agility and efficiency (Sambamurthy, Bharadwaj & Grover, 2003). According to this double imperative, firms invest in their human capital to attract new talents and to generate new knowledge and skills (Taylor & LaBarre, 2006) and yet are also on a continual search for organizational solutions capable of responding to changes that are unpredictable. These dynamics have a substantial impact on the organizational structures and operating systems that influence the working practice and relationships within the firms (Rousseau & McLean Parks, 1993).

The new technological opportunities seem to bridge the two diverse outlooks of flexibility and knowledge development, yet have a huge impact on the labor processes (Empirica, 2003; Valenduc & Vendramin, 2001).

Is 'e-work' just a managerial fashion or a real practice? Do firms invest in technology to support new ways of working to create real business opportunities or to enhance their social legitimization among the institutional environment?

BACKGROUND AND MAIN FOCUS

In recent years, the academic and managerial literature (the "discourse") on e-work has developed by also taking into account the impact of the technology on work flexibility (Robinson, Kraatz & Rousseau, 1994).

Some scholars suggest that the evolution of the managerial discourse—what is said and written about managerial issues - is the result of fashion lifecycles that sometimes have no rational economic foundations (Abrahamson, 1996) and which do not always find valid application within the firms (Abrahamson & Fairchild, 1999).

According to the new-institutional theory, institutional pressures lead to convergence in an organization's structural features through a process of isomorphism. Indeed, the isomorphism of organizations that share a common context helps to legitimize the actual organizational methods, thereby increasing the likelihood of survival (Hinnings & Greenwood, 1988; Powell & DiMaggio 1991).

These institutional pressures include the legal aspects that characterize the socio-economic context, but also, and more generally, ideas, values, and beliefs that are exogenous to the organization. Isomorphic processes are social processes that could be the result of the dissemination of fashion "waves", which induce organizations to adopt (sometimes only formally) specific practices to enhance their legitimization among customers and stakeholders.

Management fashion-setters propagate fashions, by which we mean transitory collective beliefs that certain management techniques are at the forefront of management progress. These fashion-setters—consulting firms, management gurus, mass-media business publications—do not simply leverage fashions onto gullible managers. Indeed, to sustain their images as fashion-setters, they must lead the race to anticipate the emergent collective preferences of managers for new management techniques; develop rhetoric that describe these techniques as the vanguard of management progress; and disseminate these rhetoric back to managers and organizational stakeholders ahead of other fashion-setters (Abrahamson, 1997, Barley & Kunda, 1992; Guillen, 1994).

In recent years, the development of managerial literature on the technology mediated employee-organization relationship has mainly focused on the technology impact on work flexibility (Brodt & Venburg, 2007). ICT working solutions are undoubtedly a managerial fashion.

Several management scholars have recognized two contradictory types of employee-management rhetoric (McGregor, 1960), adopting the terms "rational" and "normative" to distinguish between the two.

The key assumption underlying the rational rhetoric is that work processes can be formalized and rationalized to optimize productivity. Therefore, management's role is to engineer or reengineer organizational machines and systems to maximize production processes and to reward employees for adhering to such processes.

The key assumption underlying the normative rhetoric is that employers can boost employee productivity by shaping their thoughts and capitalizing on their emotions. The role of managers is to meet the needs of employees and to channel their unleashed motivational energy through a clear vision and a strong culture. Therefore, the normative rhetoric prescribes methods of hiring and promoting those employees who possess the most suitable cognitive and psychological profiles, as well as techniques that satisfy the psychological needs of employees through benefits, enriched tasks and empowered management styles. These offer ways to survey and shape employee thoughts and loyalties with visionary leadership and organizational cultures in order to channel the motivational energy and creativity that these techniques release (Imperatori & De Marco, 2008).

We adopted the new-institutional perspective to analyze the new technological solutions for e-work as managerial fashion. Indeed, this "fashion perspective" focuses on two important aspects of the technology and work flexibility issue, which we want to test through our research project: first, does management adopt technical solutions in a rational way to enhance their productivity or in a normative way (i.e. socio-affective adoption) merely to legitimate themselves with their stakeholders? Second, could managerial fashion techniques have a lower impact in practice than in managerial discourse?

E-Work Solutions as a "Rational" Way of Organizing Labor

The advent of ICT is changing the traditional ways of working as well as affecting the individual's spatial relations within the company (McKinlay, 2002; Stover, 1999). ICT is a critical resource in creating organizational value (Kohli & Devaraj, 2004).

Mobile technology, which can support computing-on-the-move through the use of portable devices and wireless networks (Malladi & Agrawal, 2002, Varhney & Vetter, 2000), has emerged as the next wave of the IT revolution. Mobile technology includes technological connectivity infrastructure, such as Wireless Application Protocol (WAP), Bluetooth, 3G, and General Packet Radio Service (GPRS), as well as mobile information appliances, such as mobile phones, PDA, and laptop computers. By extending computing and the internet into the wireless medium, mobile technology allows users to have "anytime-anywhere" access to information and applications, which provides greater flexibility in communication, collaboration and information sharing (Shung et al., 2006).

The changes underway in the ICT sphere enable the progressive abandonment of the old work logics because sharing space is no longer a constraint to which to subject many types of employees. Indeed, not only does the organization transfer certain types of knowledge through the electronic channels to the workforce, but also the people working inside and outside the company exchange information and knowledge electronically (Anderson et al, 2003; Gavensky, 2002; Kakihara & Sørensen, 2004). Potentially, these factors translate into a gradual leaving behind of the traditional concept of work space to create the basis of the "e-worker" rhetoric, according to which technology is a mediator of the relation between the employee and the company and enables the work to be moved from inside to outside the organization. This can foster different positive outcomes for the organization, such as the possibility to relocate production and business units, trim labor costs, enhance organizational and workforce flexibility, coordinate geographically remote operations, and improve the use of organizational space and working time.

Nevertheless, several companies that have chosen or offered this method of distance work have retraced their steps and "e-working", cited in the managerial discourse as a flexible and innovative solution, is finding it hard to get off the ground.

E-Work as a "Normative" Way to Organize Labor

Rousseau and McLean Parks (1993) describe the employee-organization exchanges as promissory contracts, where commitment of future behavior is offered in exchange for payment. According to this definition, employees develop some expectations about the organization's context and adapt their behaviors according to their perception of the reciprocal obligation (Gouldner, 1960).

Research on labor contracts suggest that they are idiosyncratically perceived and understood by individuals (Rousseau, 1989; Schein, 1980). Subjectivity can lead to disagreements between the parties on terms and their meanings, especially in transforming organizations, where the reciprocal obligation can vary in time. The subjective interpretation of the labor contract has been called the "psychological contract". Originally employed by Argyris (1960) to underscore the subjective nature of the employment relationship, the present use of the term centers on the individual's belief in and interpretation of a promissory contract. Research has confirmed that employees look for reciprocity in a labor relationship and that their motivation to work is heavily influenced by their perceptions: the more the relationship is perceived as balanced, the more the employees are disposed to contribute and perform, even beyond the duties called for by their role (Organ, 1997; Van Dyne, Cummings et al.,1995).

ICT enables work solutions that move the work from inside to outside the organization and can have different positive outcomes on the employees' perception of the organization's determination to meet their needs. In a word, ICT solutions could have a positive impact in shaping psychological contracts as a form of signaling.

E-WORK: ADOPTION AND RESULT METRICS

To measure the two main adoption perspectives of our research project (rational vs. normative), we propose a framework that is generally used to evaluate the implementation of public policies, especially when the results: (a) may be both tangible and intangible; (b) have to be evaluated according to the different stakeholders, sometimes with objectives that do not coincide; (c) can be evaluated from both a "rational" and a "normative" viewpoint; and, ultimately, (d) when the "what", how" and "when" questions are of key relevance to the evaluation process because the decisions about these issues tend to determine the final results (Hirschheim & Smithson, 1999).

The evaluation model proposed assesses public policies according to three different effects: outputs (i.e. products-services generated), outcomes (i.e. results when products reach their target market), and impacts (i.e. underlying problems addressed or developed by the program in the longer term) (Pressman & Wildavsky, 1973).

The preliminary conditions are definitely applicable to the evaluation process of the aims and results of the projects analyzed. Therefore, we decided to use the same framework to measure the results of the four projects object of our case studies to identify and understand any differences and homogeneity between the projects and to classify and code their relative managerial process as "rational" or "normative", according to our research objectives.

Specifically, in line with the two formats adopted, we will operationalize our variables according to the following indicators. Normative adoption: dominant focus: impacts; secondary focus: outputs (as a mean); residual: outcomes. Rational adoption: dominant focus: outcomes and outputs (as investment); residual (but evident and persistent): impacts.

RESEARCH DESIGN

In accordance with the descriptive and explanatory nature of the research project, multiple-case studies were designed in order to analyze the organizational variables, including their development from when they were established to the present day, as well as identify the various determinant factors. Our research is based on a longitudinal study of four emblematic cases: the European Mobility Project at IBM; the Italian Tele-working Systems at I.Net, the Italian (international) Agile Mobile Worker Project at Unisys and the British BT Workstyle Project at British Telecom in the UK. All the projects analyzed had the goal of enhancing workforce mobility through technology.

The relevance and the significance of these projects to our research is confirmed by the fact that each of them: (a) centers on advanced technology solutions; (b) uses metrics to measure project success; (c) adopts the longitudinal perspective (from needs analysis to the implementation and evaluation phase); (d) produces different outcomes/results; and (e) are representative of different project phases.

While British Telecom, IBM, I.Net and Unisys are four separate companies, they each share several key features that make them good comparable for the purposes of our research. Indeed, each one focuses on internal technological innovation (i.e. employs technology-oriented people highly familiar with new solutions) and external technological innovation (i.e. supplies clients with technology solutions).

The heterogeneity of demographic variables was offset by the strict homogeneity of the sampling parameters directly connected to the research question (Miles & Huberman, 1984). E-work is an umbrella term for the working processes related to the new spatial dimension of organization enabled by the new ICT solutions.

The adoption of a longitudinal approach means we can move beyond the comparative analysis of static solutions and track the evolution of the project analyses themselves.

Data Collection

Data was gathered through document analysis, semi-structured interviews with the HR and, in some cases, the line managers, and project leaders of the four organizations.

Each case study followed a standard protocol (Yin, 1993). The first interview with the main contact person—usually the project leader or the HR manager—aimed to: (i) enrich our background information; (ii) identify the start-up and consolidation phases of the project; and (iii) identify the main project objectives and results. We asked our respondents to give a detailed description of the following variables: project objectives and overall aim, project sponsors, project organization, target population, project phases, main constraints and facilitators, technological supports and infrastructures and, finally, the project results (see Table 1).

All the interviews adopted a common structure, consisting of an open-ended format that enabled us to collect both factual data and personal impressions. Our respondents were first asked to reconstruct their personal experience of the project to distinguish the facts from individual observations. All the interviews were taped and transcribed. Information collected at a later stage requiring further probing or clarification of minor discrepancies meant that some respondents were interviewed more than once. Multiple interviews helped us to reconstruct a "story" for each process. Although, our reconstruction was based on our respondents' recall, combining multiple perspectives helped us move beyond individual perceptual biases and alleviated potential recall problems.

Data Analysis

The multiple data sources enabled us to compare the perceived, declared, and subjective organizational viewpoints of the actors involved, as well as gain an objective organizational perspective that described the organizational practices actually implemented by each company in their mobile projects.

Data analysis used common methods for grounded theory building (Glaser & Strauss, 1967; Miles & Huberman, 1984) and combined within-case analysis with cross-case comparison. Within-case analysis, based on rich information led to insights that were further developed and tested in the cross-case analysis. We began our analysis with a detailed chronological reconstruction of the project process. Each researcher independently highlighted "critical events", i.e. events or decisions that involved a change in the organization. Our later comparison of these independent analyses showed substantial agreement. Our goal at this stage was to identify the main features of each project and the "nature" of the adoption (i.e. rational versus normative). At the end of this process, independently, we gave a number to each variable of the evaluation model (i.e. focus on output, outcome and impact) to cluster the four projects studied. Furthermore, we asked five students to read the scripts of the cases and to grade the same variables. Finally, we computed the average of the ten values assigned to each of the variables, encoded according to the following Likert scales (see Table 2):

Focus on outputs: (scale: 1 = low to 10 = high) 1= no investments (low attention); 5= as mean to reach results (medium attention); 10= as an investment (high attention)

Focus on outcomes (scale: 1 = low to 10 = high): 1= not defined ex ante, not tangible; not monitored (low attention); 5= defined in a de-structured way (medium attention); 10= measurable, tangible, defined early; monitored (high attention).

Focus on impact: (scale: 1 = low to 10 = high); 1= no attention (low); 5= as by-product, to prevent constraints (medium attention); 10= as the main objective (high attention).

Finally, we analyzed the application of the e-work solutions taking into account the relative managerial processes. While our main research focus was on the organizational viewpoint, we also identified some organizational constraints and facilitators, as well as getting an idea of the employees' viewpoints, also thanks to internal climate surveys or similar methods.

Research Sample and Preliminary Results

Case 1: The IBM Mobility Project

In November 1999, IBM launched its Europe-wide Employee Mobility Project, an international and inter-functional project to develop and increase the work mobility initiatives offered by IBM, pinpointing and implementing technical and organizational solutions for mobile work. The project is still underway and has already produced numerous effects. The project was sponsored internally by two IBM vice-presidents and involved the identification and assignation of specific responsibilities, as well as the definition of organizational roles (Mobility Leader) and co-coordinating bodies (Regional Mobility Steering Committee and Mobility Project Team).

Project Design and Implementation
The project coded each IBM employee in a specific category that defines them in relation to their prevailing place of work. This enabled the identification of the home workers—who carry out almost all their work at home (otherwise known as e-workers); the mobile workers—meaning those who carry out almost 50% of their work off-site and who share a desk; the customer workers—those whose work is mainly carried out at the customer's offices and who are not allocated a desk, but if necessary can use a shared desk; and the transition worker—those who carry out part of their job off-site (30%

on average), but who are allocated a fixed desk for their exclusive use.

These combined workers are on the rise compared with earlier years and currently account for 41% of the total workforce. In addition, all those employees who do not occupy a fixed desk account for around 35% of the total. These data attest, on the one side, to the size of the mobility phenomenon in IBM EMEA and, on the other, to the fact that 35% of IBM EMEA's total workforce does not work regularly at the company's premises and does not have a fixed workstation. Currently, 85% of IBM employees have been given personal laptop computers to provide an incentive for e-working.

Further, the company carried out a survey in Italy that enabled it to segment the total IBM Italia employee population according to the time and uses of the remote connection method. This segmentation met the need to associate the different user segments with the most appropriate technical tools and supports in terms of efficacy and efficiency.

The survey produced three user segments: (a) the Anywhere & Always segment, which classifies those employees who normally use the remote connection to communicate with the company, who do not have a fixed desk and who use the remote connection for e-mails and to access the internet and the company's intranet, who spend an average of 18.5 hours per month online; (b) the Touchdown segment, which groups those workers who normally connect remotely from home for an average of 8.5 hours per month, and who use this access to hook up to the internet and the corporate intranet and, prevalently, to send/receive fairly hefty documents via e-mail; and (c) the Occasional segment, which comprises all those workers equipped with a laptop computer for remote access and who use it for a maximum of 11.5 hours per month, but not in a systematic way. These employees account for 22%, 43% and 35%, respectively, of the total number of users.

After identifying these three segments, the company studied specific support tools that would

respond to the diverse needs in an efficacious and efficient way. In particular, the Anywhere and Always workers get a laptop PC and a GPRS cell phone for connecting to the network. In addition, a small number of the Touchdown segment was wired with a dedicated ADSL line at home and, naturally, a laptop PC, while the Occasional group was equipped with a laptop computer.

Ultimately, to support the possibility of remote access, a dedicated corporate intranet website was designed specifically for IBM Italia. The website was launched in September 2001 and streams a quantity of useful information for distance working, promoting these methods also by presenting the direct testimonials of the mobile workers.

Organizational Project Setting

The IBM EMEA Employee Mobility project is part of the Business Operation function, a unit that encompasses all the activities supporting the group's core business, which, on the other hand, is related to sales and research and development.

IBM also created an international project group dedicated to the project on an ongoing basis. The project group is not only international, but also inter-functional, enabling the convergence of the different project members who head up the HR, Technology Development, Real Estate Management and Internal Communication corporate functions.

Measuring the Results

The Employee Mobility project also envisages the opportunity to heighten IBM's competitiveness through a number of expected benefits for the different categories of recipients, defined at the beginning of the project. The company. The project has enabled the company to improve its economic health, thanks to the development of a corporate image in line with the e-business era, the improved management of the infrastructure, and increased work productivity. This latter thanks to IBM's greater appeal in the job market and its improved capacity to retain the high-potential employees, reduce absenteeism, and increase the time that the employees dedicate to customers, but, above all, thanks to the quantifiable and easily monetized cost-savings in real estate management. In particular, much prominence is given internally to the enhancing of the real-estate management results, which are directly attributable to the project and have freed up financial resources.

The number of people sharing a desk at IBM EMEA has increased and the average number of employees per shared desk is currently 2.6. In addition, the density of the workforce has increased from 180sq.m. to 170sq.m per person.

Another result in Italy following the increase in mobile workers is the imminent quitting of two office buildings in the Milan and Rome areas in the current year, which will enable the company to more flexibly manage its work spaces.

The employees. The percentage of employees who use this work method has increased, despite the reduction in the overall number of staff employed by the EMEA group. Project-related results cited include an improvement and strengthening in the satisfaction of people generally; a more balanced management of family and working life; and greater flexibility and autonomy in the time management of clients (on a par with the hours worked). The employee's decision to join the project is usually voluntary and is discussed with their manager. More and more people in IBM interpret this new method of working as an opportunity.

The clients. The IBM client has experienced concrete benefits in the form of higher satisfaction, which derives from the greater amount of time dedicated to them by the IBM staff; a speeding up of the transmission times of critical information; and the more optimal response of the organization generally.

Nevertheless, some critical issues related to the social and interpersonal dimension of the work do exist, including the possible diminishing of the sense of belonging to the work group; the possible loss of identification with the IBM group; the loss of social relations with colleagues; and the

resistance related to the loss of status tied to the symbols of space.

Some difficulties also exist in terms of the inadequacy of the tools and/or human resource management politics, with people remaining anchored to the "traditional" places of work. Situations have arisen where the employee has complained of a feeling of being poorly valued by their boss, who, for their part, have reported a fear of losing control over their own staff.

Lastly, practical hurdles have been reported related to the need to have an "alternative work space", one that adequately meets needs, which is not always available at the employee's home, and to have access to the use of efficacious technological supports.

Case 2: The I.Net Tele-Working System

I.NET group is a market leader in business security and business continuity services and solutions. It offers businesses a stable and secure technological environment through its Internet Protocol and Business Factory networks where IP network-based applications are provided. I.NET's offering is therefore focused on designing, producing and managing solutions that respond flexibly, modularly and comprehensively to the ICT requirements of its client companies, drawing on a portfolio rich in services, solutions and know-how. At end-2007, I.Net had about 250 employees.

October 2000 saw I.Net launch its Tele-working System, an inter-functional pilot project to help some internal employees accommodate specific individual work and life balance needs. The project was coordinated by the Human Resource Dept. and involved different line managers. However, the project has now been closed and none of I.Net's employees are currently involved in the scheme.

Project Design and Implementation
The project involved ten Pre-sales Engineers. I.Net decided to focus on this organizational role only for the pilot version, due to both the nature of the

pre-sales work and the initial motivation of the sample group.

In addition, the company decided that the teleworking solutions were suitable only for those organizational roles/employees with the following features (based on the job level and the individual level of evaluation): (a) possibility to control productivity, even at a distance; (b) low level of paper document management; (c) high level of time-management and self-organization skills.

The project started with six workers on a voluntary basis. The employees were enabled to work from home two days a week. Of course, also at I.Net (like IBM) technological advancement is clearly the vehicle that makes it possible to activate and diffuse mobile work. The possibility of always being "connected" to the company's offices using technical tools, such as a personal laptop computer and cell phone, makes it practical to work from "a distance".

Each teleworker was supplied with a home ADSL connection, a company mobile phone, and an I.Net laptop computer.

Organizational Project Setting

The I.Net Tele-working project was designed and managed by the Human Resource function, which had to address a number of normative, structural and behavioral problems.

From the normative perspective, Italian legislation was a project constraint due to its rigidity, internal articulation, and ambiguity (especially in terms of the teleworking contract details). I.Net addressed these problems by deciding to stipulate a private agreement with each teleworker.

From the structural perspective, the company encountered some problems related to the control systems (of work content and times). To solve these problems, it decided to use an application system that enabled it to code the working processes. In addition, as mentioned earlier, it supplied the employees with the necessary technical equipment (i.e. laptop computer; mobile phone, and ADSL connection).

Finally, from the behavioral perspective, the company decided to limit flexible off-site working to only two days per week in order to prevent feelings of isolation, a low level of corporate identification, and ensure social interaction among all the employees.

Measuring the Results

After the first six months, the project was re-evaluated internally in a structured way based on internal interviews conducted by the HR department. The evaluation aimed to measure the employee satisfaction of all the teleworkers involved in the project, but also their bosses and some other employees to better understand the internal climate around the project.

The preliminary results of the project were favorable from all internal perspectives, leading to the involvement of additional employees and raising the total number of teleworkers to ten (from the initial six).

From the company's perspective, a key criticism was the lack of the employees' physical presence in the event of unforeseeable emergencies.

Case 3: The Unisys Mobile Working Program

In 2002, Unisys launched its Mobile Program in Italy. The program was incepted by the Italian HR department and channeled through the company intranet.

The e-working project was the idea of the Director of Human Resources, who personally promoted it to increase the Unisys employees' possibility of reconciling their working life with their private life.

Project Design and Implementation

The program was announced and a pilot program launched involving 20 employees, mainly volunteers, covering diverse corporate functions, including administrative and office staff.

The volunteers were given specific training and an ad hoc workstation at home from which they could also connect and work via the company's intranet. On average, these employees work two days per week from home and the other three days in the office

The program was open to all the company's employees (i.e. administrative staff, system developers) on a voluntary basis, although each volunteer had to have specific prerequisites, such as a good level of working autonomy, good past performance, and to have been on the payroll for at least one year.

Unisys supplied each mobile worker with a laptop, a home ADSL connection, a mobile phone, and a printer, while some were also given an ergonomic office chair.

Questionnaires were handed out six months after project launch to both the employees and their bosses to gauge their satisfaction with the e-working system.

The average results of that survey revealed a high level of employee satisfaction and a medium level of management satisfaction.

Since then the program has been hit by inertia (meantime the HR Director also changed) and the number of staff involved in the project was still 20 at end-2006 (although some have since left and others have come on board).

At the start of 2007, however, the project was given a new lease of life because of the project implemented by the parent company; called "Agile", this project has broad international scope and sets common goals for all the Unisys subsidiaries: the containing of real estate costs to 2.5% of sales. This new momentum has spawned a number of new initiatives for the re-launch of the Mobile project and as incentives for the employees to get involved.

First, the company decided to shape its own internal model for structuring and organizing its space to meet the new needs, setting up a Business Centre, where anyone could book a predefined time slot—through the corporate intranet from wherever they may be—to use a desk and a phone at the office. The goal is to ultimately organize all the offices in this way with the aim of reshaping and rationalizing the use of space.

Measuring the Results

To date, the results of the project launched in 2002 are modest, even though we clearly need to separate the period in question into two phases: the first between 2002 and 2006, the second from the beginning of 2007 to the present day.

Indeed, the nature of the project has changed considerably in this latter phase, when the company launched initiatives, also structural, to reorganize its work methods. The second part of the project is still in the launch phase, but has already produced the first visible results in terms of the growth in the number of employees enrolled in the program in the year to date and, above all, in terms of a new drive and orientation towards achieving the financial performance targets set.

The company has decided not to involve the labor unions for now, keeping the project in trial form with the aim of proceeding in an incremental logic so as not to trigger any internal resistance. In its present state of evolution, it is not possible to check results further, but the HR department says it has received favorable signs in terms of both the increase in the number of employees involved and the absence of internal resistance, along with the adaptation of the infrastructures deemed necessary.

Among the main problems and constraints, the most cited (from different perspectives) are: lack of a feeling of corporate identity (from the individual perspective) and inadequate country-urban technical infrastructures (i.e. in terms of connection speed and reliability). Finally, in this case study, surprisingly, the working culture was not perceived as a constraint but a facilitator, thanks to the advanced level of the Unisys technical culture and working practices. Indeed, at the worldwide level, Unisys had already adopted in 1996 an effective HR ERP system (i.e. PeopleSoft) that well supports and enhances the Agile Program output. Further, the company intranet also is highly developed and largely used as a managerial tool in the organization-employee relationship.

Case 4: The British Telecom (BT) Workstyle Project

BT is one of the world's leading providers of communication solutions and serves customers in 170 countries in Europe, the Americas and Asia Pacific. Its core business is mainly that of networked IT services, local, national and international telecommunication services, and higher-value broadband products and services. In the UK, BT serves over 18 million business and residential customers with more than 28 million exchange lines, as well as providing network services to other licensed operators. The group mainly operates four customer-facing business lines: BT Retail, BT Wholesale, and Open Reach, which operate almost entirely within the UK and serve the consumer, business and wholesale markets with a broad spectrum of communication products and services; and BT Global Services, which provides networked IT services to meet the needs of multi-site organizations. BT Group plc is listed on the London and New York stock exchanges.

The BT Workstyle project is one of Europe's most successful and largest flexible working program. Launched 20+ years ago, the BT Workstyle project counted 70,000 BT employees in 2006, of whom 11,600 are contractually employed by BT to work from home. Currently, around 50 employees sign up for home working every week in the UK alone.

Project Design and Implementation
BT pioneered its flexible working policies over 20 years ago to meet a clear business need. The starting point of the project was the awareness of the fact that the true competitive advantage of the digital networked economy is the ability to anticipate and respond quickly to change. BT perceived that

the traditional 9-5 working day could not satisfy the demands of either the business or the people working in the new economic and social environment. The group realized that its true competitive advantage would be created by its ability to attract talent on a global scale and the ability of that talent to anticipate change, the speed at which it could respond to new opportunities, and the 24/7 availability of products and services. BT's first official home workers were established in 1986. Between 1986 and 1998, the group launched a series of pilot and trial programs, introducing other forms of flexible working such as annualized hours, time banking, compressed hours, and the occasional home-based working. At end-1998, BT set a target of 2000 home workers for the year 2000, which it achieved in the first quarter of that year. By the end of the year, that number had increased to 5000 home workers.

Examples of flexible and home working can be found in every area of BT's business, from Systems and Solutions to Technical Design, HR, Finance, Directories, Customer Service and many others. Flexible working now extends to nearly 80,000 people across BT. A typical home worker is anyone from a Senior Executive to a Personal Assistant anywhere in its business.

Becoming a home worker is a very simple process. Each BT employee has the option to work from home and requires solely the approval of their line manager. BT's Workstyle website enables the manager to place an order for a new contract and authorize the purchase of equipment and/or furniture, while the individual is responsible for ordering their business e-mail address, stationery, and whatever else they may need.

Organizational Project Setting
The BT Workstyle project incorporates the following key elements: cultural change; creation of flexible estate; accommodation rationalization; a flexible technology platform.

The project was introduced from top to bottom. Senior executives were strongly encouraged to be early adopters in order to demonstrate management commitment. In addition, the HR, Estate Management and IT departments forged a close working relationship.

Clear polices and practices were established and publicized. Metrics such as quality of service, productivity, staff retention, and sick leave were employed. The focus shifted from rewarding people's attendance to rewarding people's contributions.

A key focus of the internal campaign was to celebrate those individuals who were working successfully in a new flexible environment.

In terms of accommodation and flexible estate, the company established several ad-hoc buildings around the world (about 170) and also remodeled the company flagship HQ as a workstyle building.

In terms of the technology platform, BT's workstyle technology architecture provides platforms for the ordinary flexible worker as well as for more

Table 1. Study sample: Initial comparison

	Project operative origin	Project sponsor	Project actual phase	No. of employees enrolled/tot (current)	Pre-requisites for program enrolment	Technical support	Organizational support	Main constraints	Main facilitators	Project results/ metrics (levels)
IBM MOBILE PROJECT	Strategic aim and costs reduction.	Business Operations Dept.	Maturity	3000/13000 (IBM EMEA Southern Region). Segmented.	Everyone is admitted on a voluntary basis.	Various, depends on the needs of the users: generally, an ADSL line, PC and mobile phone, intranet access.	Intranet campaign. Appropriate reward and performance evaluation systems. Skills assessment	"Presence = productivity" culture. HR systems. Social interaction	Sponsorship. IT culture. Intranet and HR ERP	At market level (legitimacy); at employee level (satisfaction); at company level (real estate cost-savings)
I.NET TELEWORKING SYSTEMS	Employee satisfaction Internal climate.	HR Dept.	Maturity /ended	Currently 0. Was 10/250 (total).	1. Possibility to control productivity; 2. Low paper document flow; 3. Good time-management skills. 4.Voluntary basis but only for some org. Roles	ADSL line, PC and mobile phone, Intranet.		Rigidity of legislation. Isolation. Controlling productivity. IT emergency. Infrastructure costs.	IT culture. Personal drivers (geographical dispersion).	At employee level (satisfaction); at company level (employer branding).
UNISYS MOBILE PROJECT (PHASE 1)	Employee satisfaction. Internal climate.	HR Dept. and Top Management	Maturity	Max 20/400 (total)	Voluntary basis. Good level of working autonomy; good performance; at least one year with the company	ADSL line, PC and mobile phone Intranet	HR support	Infrastructure reliability (connection speed). Lack of personal space at home (to use as an office).	Personal driver. Internal IT system and culture.	At employee level (satisfaction); at company level (legitimacy with clients).
UNISYS AGILE PROGRAM (PHASE 2)	Cost-savings	Top Management	Start-up	Currently 20/250, (number is increasing) expansion underway; segmented.	Voluntary basis idem as phase 1.	ADSL line, PC and mobile phone Intranet.	HR support plus office equipment and structure.	Infrastructure reliability (connection speed) Lack of personal space at home (to use as an office) Labor unions'.	Sponsorship IT culture Intranet, HR ERP Business Center.	Prospectively as for IBM.
BT WORKSTYLE PROJECT	Strategic aim and cost-savings	Top Management	Maturity	70,000/431.800 (number increasing).	Voluntary basis. Line manager approval (based on an internal agreement between the employee and his/her boss).	ADSL, ISDN, GPRS, 3G and Wi-Fi. Intranet. PC and mobile phone, Blackberry. Desk platform with ActivCard. Fixed/mobile telephony, working tools.	Training. Online help team. Public and transparent practices.	Cultural constraints (at the beginning). Necessary equipment and work space.	Sponsorship. Strategic driver. Clear policies. Metrics.	At market level (legitimacy); at employee level (satisfaction, productivity, retention..); at company level (real estate and HR cost-savings); at social level (lower pollution impact, whole CSR; diversity politics).

specialized staff who need to access corporate applications from home or other locations. Another crucial factor in the cultural change was fast access to the BT corporate intranet.

Measuring the Results

The move to flexible working has helped BT Group save more than 725 million of euro per annum in property management costs alone. BT has built a number of brand new buildings for BT employees around the world, installing hot desks and touchdown areas to move thousands of staff from fixed to flexible working. Part of the project also involved redesigning the BT Centre in Central London and BT currently has 1,500 workstations used by up to 4000 BT staff every day.

Introducing home-based working gave BT the opportunity to draw on a bigger pool of talent, retain workers in whom it had invested significantly in training and development, and make hefty savings in recruitment and training costs, while also reducing overheads—every fulltime home worker saves BT approximately £6000 per year and research has shown that these home workers are between 15 and 31 per cent more productive.

BT home workers are taking 63 per cent less sick leave than their office-based counterparts. The retention rate following maternity leave stands at 99 per cent compared with the UK average of 47 per cent.

Further, BT estimates that it has eliminated the annual need for more than 300 face-to-face meetings and the ensuing travel needs to get to those meetings.

On the customer side, the BT Workstyle Project means that BT people are more project-based and a virtual team across many disciplines can be put together quickly to address and solve problems.

E-WORK: ORGANIZATIONAL OUTCOMES AND CHALLENGES

The experiences of British Telecom, IBM and, partly, Unisys in its second phase attest to the feasi-

bility and usefulness of the new work methods and solutions in optimizing work space flexibility.

The projects have enabled the companies to improve their economic health, also thanks to the development of a corporate image in line with the e-business era, improve infrastructure management, and increase work productivity, above all, thanks to the quantifiable and easily monetized cost-savings in real-estate management. In particular, much prominence is given internally to the optimization of the use and management of the corporate real estate footprint, a factor directly attributable to the project and which has freed up financial resources. The BT Workstyle project has enabled the company and its people to become more agile and efficient in a 24/7 market. The number of people sharing a desk at IBM has increased and the current average number of employees per shared desk is 2.6. Unisys is also paring property management costs and has already sublet part of the office space released thanks to Project Agile.

All four companies have spurred the percentage of employees who use this work method, despite the reduction in the overall workforce. The project-related results outlined include an overall improvement and strengthening in staff satisfaction; a more balanced management by employees of their family and working life; and greater flexibility and autonomy in the time-management of clients (on a par with the hours worked). The employee's decision to join the project is usually voluntary and is discussed with their manager. As outlined in Table 2, we coded our results according to the evaluation model of outputs, outcomes and impacts. The IBM results are measurable as program outputs, outcomes and impacts, although less attention is paid to the program impacts at the beginning. The Unisys results are measurable as program outputs, given that these relate to the preliminary phase of the program, although recently, in line with project advancement, we can also factor in the program outcomes and impacts. The BT Workstyle project results are measurable as program outputs, outcomes and impacts.

On the other hand, the I.Net project had a very different organizational impact. Although it has since been wound up, it was a successful initiative that raised no internal resistance, either from the employees or the line managers, and the project was closed purely due to the changing needs of the employees themselves. This project can be easily compared with the first phase of the Unisys program.

The stated goal of both the organizations was to signal their employee focus, which they did successfully. However, no other more productive goals were perceived by the company. Currently, no employees are enrolled in the I.Net program and only a few are countable for the first stage of Unisys program. The projects, thanks to I.Net's and Unisys' internal climates and employer branding status in the job market, enabled the companies to improve their capacity to meet the work and life needs of their employees and reduce absenteeism. But even more importantly from the companies' standpoint, the projects have sent the employees an emotional signal that makes them feel more embedded organizationally.

The I.Net and Unisys (first phase) program results are measurable as the program impacts, while the emphasis on program outputs and outcomes are not as relevant.

Table 2 outlines the rational and normative framework of adoption and enables us to code the I.Net and Unisys (first phase) project adoptions as

normative and the adoption framework of the other three projects as rational.

In addition, each of these cases highlights the existence of common critical issues related to the social and interpersonal dimension of the employees' work, including potentially negative factors, such as a diminished sense of belonging to the work group; a loss of corporate identity; a loss of social relations with colleagues; and resistance related to loss of status and perceived career difficulties. Some difficulties also emerged in terms of the inadequacy of the tools and/or human resource management policies, with people remaining anchored to the "traditional" places of work. Situations have arisen where the employee has complained of a feeling of being poorly valued by their boss, while these latter have reported a fear of losing control over their staff.

Ultimately, practical hurdles have been reported related to the need to have an "alternative work space", one that adequately meets needs, which is not always available at the employee's home, and to have access to the use of efficacious technological supports.

These preliminary results lead us to draw the following conclusions:

First, the case studies confirm a substantial coherence between the managerial discourse and the effective situation analyzed, even though the scenario investigated seems privileged from this viewpoint and that even the actors describe it as unusual, especially those in Italy when compared

Table 2. Rational vs. normative framework adoption: operationalization

	IBM Mobile Project	I.Net Teleworking Systems	Unisys Mobile Project (Phase 1)	Unisys Agile Program (Phase 2)	BT Workstyle Project
Focus on outputs	10	5	8	9	10
Focus on outcomes	10	2	2	10	10
Focus on impacts	2 in advance 10 as results.	9 in advance; 0 as results.	8 in advance; 1 as results.	5 in advance (non yet measurable) as results.	6 in advance; 10 as results.

(scale: from 1 = low; to 10 = high)

with other successful European experiences (such as BT Workstyle). This corroborates the theory of Abrahamson and Fairchild (1999) on the temporal divergence, in some cases, between managerial discourse and practice, but, on the other hand, also helps us to better understand the dynamics that can help or hinder the convergence of practices with managerial discourse.

Second, IBM, BT and Unisys adopted the ICT solutions in a rational way, with measurable outputs on firm productivity. On the other hand, the adoption and implementation of ICT solutions by I.Net (and by Unisys in its first program phase) was more normative, achieving the primary goal of having a relevant impact on the psychological perceptions of the employees of the reciprocity of the contractual obligations.

These factors enable us to confirm the possible dual role of ICT-working solutions and their positive impact on the employees' psychological contract, even when the adoption is solely nominal. In fact, the employees tend to describe e-work as an opportunity that meets a number of specific working expectations, such as its positive effects on skill and performance levels, a better work and life balance, the saving of travel time (and costs).

Further, the case studies lead us to suggest that only a rational adoption can be successful and durable in the longer term. In fact, the adoption of non-rational solutions can translate into project hurdles when it comes to future development (i.e., not during initial implementation, but more in the longer term for large-scale programs).

Generally, however, this work method is not at all widespread, so it is certainly appropriate to speak of a managerial fashion that still seems to lack a consolidated following. Nevertheless, the implementation of these managerial practices in the four cases in question can help us identify several critical points related to the managerial discourse diffusion processes and also some useful guidelines.

E-WORK: PRELIMINARY EVIDENCE ON THE MANAGERIAL DISCOURSE

The cases analyzed and enable us to form a few preliminary considerations on the actual transformation of labor processes in e-work practices.

First, the adoption of specific technical-management models seems to differ sharply depending on the company's competitive scenario. Companies that operate in more dynamic environments subject to greater competitive pressure report a higher acceptance of the new management models, as the project survey has shown. Size also seems to be a key variable. That size is important is attested to by the fact that the larger companies are contaminated more quickly by or are more sensitive to managerial discourse. The poor diffusion of some logic could therefore be explained by the smaller average size of the Italian companies.

Second, given the distinctive characteristics of Italian companies, the differentiated use of particular flexible work methods could be explained by their corporate structures—closely held and controlled—where it is difficult to find a clear-cut separation between owners and management and where, in any case, the adoption stimuli are lacking.

Third, the theory on managerial fashions suggests that the diffusion of the managerial discourse goes through a "theorization" process, the goal of which is to make the adoption of specific techniques appealing to entire organizational categories, also those which group dissimilar forms between them but which share exposure to the same environmental stimuli. The non-homogeneous diffusion of the techniques in question can be explained by the weakness of that theorization process or, alternatively and more likely, by the difficulty Italian companies have in seeing themselves as similar, independently of size. Further, still referring to the weakness of the theorization process, we underscore the failure to identify the tools and univocal management systems required to manage the updated working models (partial theorization process). The literature supports the flexible work forms without, however, suggesting or prescribing new human resource management techniques and tools to align with the new work models (e.g., new methods of controlling and assessing performance).

Fourth, the theory on managerial fashions suggests that, in periods of expansion, the companies show a greater contamination of "rational" discourses, or those that promote job productivity through techniques that emphasize efficiency, while in periods of recession it is easier to find the implementation of techniques that emphasize the regulatory aspects of management and that implicate investments in the relationship between individual and company (Barley & Kunda, 1992).

Fifth, Guillen (1993) shows how the contamination is also influenced by the degree to which the companies are trade unionized. A higher level of unionization translates into a higher probability that the companies will adopt the diffused techniques of the managerial discourse. In recent years, Italy has seen the power of the trade unions diminish and, therefore, this variable could explain the irregular diffusion of the techniques in question.

Sixth, the institutional context can favor or inhibit the theorization process and in Italy neither the legal-judicial context nor the cultural context yet seem ready to embrace flexible solutions.

E-WORK: HOW TO IMPLEMENT LABOR PROCESS TRANSFORMATION

In terms of the cultural context, this paragraph aims to indicate several practical guidelines, based on the results of our case studies, to help address the different critical issues encountered in the process of designing and implementing flexible solutions to facilitate the "rational and aware" diffusion of the managerial discourse on the subject of technology and flexible work.

Our analysis, in a longitudinal and dynamic perspective, indicates clearly the importance of a logical development that envisages a first phase of (a) analysis and design; a second phase aimed at (b) the effective introduction of the flexible forms mediated by technology; and a third and final phase aimed at (c) the monitoring and measuring of the results achieved by the project. It is important that all these steps are designed and planned at the beginning of the project.

Bilateral Needs Analysis and Definition of the Goals

The redesign of the work times and spaces assumes the upstream production of a feasibility study that not only analyses the needs of both the organization and the employees, but also defines concrete and realistic objectives. These bases will enable the organization to introduce new forms of flexible work capable of marrying and reconciling the diverse needs of the company with those of the individuals without running the risk of designing projects that lack coherence and which are de-contextualized from the real needs of the interested parties. Several projects fail because the organizational presumptions about people needs.

Moreover, employees have different expectations, request and wishes, that are related with their individual motivational structures, life-cycles, life-styles and so on. It is necessary to understand what people really want and to categorize them also considering their different needs.

Those premises pave the way for another essential step, that calling for the clear definition of the objectives to be achieved by the organization and their levels and measurements: the lack of defined specific and measurable goals makes it hard, if not impossible, to embark on the project process.

As seen in our case studies, the successful projects are those that promote voluntary membership and take into account the real needs of the employees and their trends in the society. Moreover clear projects objectives are defined and monitored across the time.

Introduction of Flexible Work Forms Mediated by Technology

The managerial techniques used for dealing with the flexibility of the work space require the evaluation and overcoming of constraints (within and without the company) and the development of some organizational preconditions capable of maximizing adoption and acceptance.

In many cases, technology is a facilitator, a tool that enables new forms of flexible distance work, but there are other kinds of hurdles to leap, which are (1) structural, (2) regulatory, (3) cultural, and even (4) psychological in nature.

Structural Constraints

Some workers need to be in direct contact with the company's machinery and plants, which thus ties them to the place and time of machine loading, operation, and control: this constraint is typical of an industrial organization but affects a decreasing number of workers. Other jobs involve direct contact with the client - where this latter physically comes to the company at set times - or with other employees or even with colleagues who are members of the work group. Other restrictive factors might include information and documentation centers that cannot be decentralized. So, in theory, flexible solutions are not always a good fit for everyone: the corporate population needs to be segmented in line with the feasibility and the practicability of the various and possibly graded solutions.

That means it is necessary to design flexible and mobile solutions according to the specificity of the working processes.

This also applies to the cases presented here: even though the context is certainly more technology and service-oriented, the presence of different types of employees required the implementation of different solutions.

In addition, the office layout needed to be adapted to the needs of the mobile population as did the information technology structures (intranet, videoconferences, distance-working tools, virtual domains).

Regulatory Constraints

On the regulatory front, our case studies underscore how Italian labor legislation has long impeded the introduction of flexibility to the space-time aspect of the work performance, given that it has not yet been updated to cover the new working possibilities offered by technology. For example, the restrictions and clauses that still today obstruct the use of part-time or distance work methods, while provided for in the collective contracts and many company agreements, are not currently regulated by an organic law. Legislation on security and safety is also still lacking in this sense. However, the cases researched attest to the feasibility of flexible solutions despite such constraints.

Cultural Constraints

A particularly critical aspect in the adoption of flexible work forms is the popular view of the significance of "traditional" work forms and the values that it rewards or, to the contrary, penalizes. In Italy, the idea of "always being present" is still widespread, by which "presence = productivity". This logic is clearly antithetic to that of "working outside the company". Therefore, it is necessary to communicate the same level of value and to give status to the new forms of work, to debunk the idea that these are residual and sub-optimal.

That aspect is especially clear when we compare the Italian projects with the British. It is also clear that cultural change not only requires time, but involves other aspects of managing the cultural change processes, such as starting from the top, allocating training resources, and spreading information to support the managerial decision-making processes through the transition.

Psychological Resistances

Another factor that can impede a company's adoption of flexible work forms - at least in the initial phases - is the possible psychological resistance of the employees themselves. In the cases analyzed, diverse measures were taken to address the natural resistance to change deriving from the fact that any change in working methods necessarily and inevitably has an impact on the daily routines of the individuals, triggering fear and anxiety. Companies need to focus carefully on these aspects and start by preparing a communication plan that provides all the information and guidelines on the new solution to be introduced into the organization and guarantees a response to any requests for clarification by the employees. Our case studies also suggest that companies should not present such solutions as compulsory, but propose them as a choice to be made voluntarily by the employee.

Closely connected to the subject of the constraints to overcome are the organizational preconditions needed to ensure the successful outcome of the project, which therefore need to be planned in parallel with the other project design aspects. These comprise the corporate culture and the human resource management systems (Lengick-Hall & Lengick-Hall, 2006).

If the corporate culture tends to penalize (perhaps in terms of career) the flexible management of the work time, it will be difficult to get the employee to accept it. Therefore, flexibility needs to be given similar value and this value needs to be diffused throughout the company, rewarding it wherever it is represented.

The designing of transparent human resource management systems - thanks to which the value of flexibility is tangibly supported - is also closely related to this theme. Management systems are an indispensable organizational precondition for the adoption of flexible work forms. The existence of an organizational system of work processes to meet goals, which must be accompanied by an employee performance appraisal system to measure the results achieved, is an essential part of the effective project. It is necessary to switch from a logic centered on the physical presence of the employee, their activities and their duties in the company, to a logic oriented to achieving results in line with programmed yet flexible processes. This translates into new tools, but also new management logics that need to be transmitted across all levels of the organization (Martin et al., 2008).

Monitoring and Measuring Results

The last step in the introduction of flexible work forms calls for both the continuous monitoring and the final measuring of the results achieved by the company and the employees. Continuous monitoring is a key factor in enabling the correction of any errors and identifying any required changes; while the accurate measuring of the results achieved (better if concrete, tangible, quantitative) is of significant importance because it enables the objective assessment of the effects of the project implemented and, above all, supports future projects of a similar nature, as well as the decision-making process. This aspect is especially significant because it marries qualitative measures and indicators with other more quantitative parameters, which also have an immediately recognizable economic-financial impact and provide a people-climate index, such as the real estate implications (as in the cases of IBM, BT and Unisys) and the perceived satisfaction. Therefore, it is only possible to evaluate the results when the objectives have been accurately defined.

CONCLUSION

The projects discussed attest to the business opportunities sparked by the new technological solutions in supporting work flexibility, but, more generally, in supporting the emotional relationship (i.e. the psychological contract) between the employee and the organization. E-work solutions are particularly relevant when they come to the actual nature of the working relationship.

The employment market currently is the object of a far-reaching cultural revolution that is affecting the work relationship. Values and principles, such as loyalty to the company and a job for life are gradually giving way to concepts such as employability, professionalization, and entrepreneurship. Our case studies underscore how the cultural and institutional environment is a crucial factor in the success of the labor transformation processes.

The companies explain (and justify) this trend as instrumental to the flexibility and cost-reductions demanded by an increasingly competitive and global scenario. However, one might assume that all this would lead also to a change in the context and in the forms of social interaction between the individuals working for the company and between the company and the employee. Indeed, in this sense, companies are moving towards organizational forms that force them increasingly to make a trade-off between greater flexibility and the diminishing of the organizational commitment of the people who work for them.

The studied cases appear to confirm the alignment of the managerial discourse with organizational practices, although our results are also consistent with the "time-lag" theorized by Abrahamson & Fairchild (1999).

Ultimately, the cases enable us to pinpoint a number of critical issues and guidelines for the design and implementation of technology-based work systems—to sustain the contamination of practices - such as: the dual approach (the organizational and the employer viewpoint) during the needs-analysis and goal-setting phases; the relevance of a coherent organizational culture and human resource system (i.e., especially appraisal and reward systems); the removal of organizational structural constraints; the management of cognitive resistances; and the importance of the evaluation and monitoring phases during the project processes.

REFERENCES

Abrahamson, E. (1996). Management Fashion. *Academy of Management Review, 16,* 254-285.

Abrahamson, E. (1997). The Emergence and Prevalence of Employee-Management Rhetoric: The Effect of Long Waves, Labour Unions and Turnover. *Academy of Management Journal, 40,* 491-533.

Abrahamson, E., & Fairchild, G. (1999). Management Fashion. Lifecycles, Triggers, and Collective Learning Processes. *Administrative Science Quarterly, 44,* 708-740.

Anderson, M. C., Banker, R. D., & Ravindran, S. (2003). The new productivity paradox. *Communications of the ACM, 46*(3), 91-94.

Argiris, C. P. (1960). *Understanding Organisational Behaviour.* Homewood, IL: Dorsey Press.

Barley, S., & Kunda, G. (1992). Design and Devotion: Surges of Rational and Normative Ideologies of Control in Managerial Discourse. *Administrative Science Quarterly, 37,* 363-399.

Brodt, T. L., & Venburg, M. R. (2007). Managing Mobile Work—Insights from European Practice. *New Technology, Work and Employment, 22*(1), 52-65.

Empirica (2003). *SIBIS Pocket Book 2002/3.* Bonn, Germany: Empirica GmbH.

Gayeski, D. M. (2002). *Learning Unplugged; Using mobile Technologies for Organizational Training and Performance Improvement.* American Management Association, New York, :AMACOM.

Glaser, B., & Strauss, A. (1967). *The discovery of grounded theory.* Chicago: Aldine

Gouldner, A.W. (1960). The Norm of Reciprocity: A Preliminary Statement. *American Sociology Review, 25*(2), 161-178.

Grant, R. M. (1991). The Resource-based Theory of Competitive Advantage. Implication for Strategy Formulation. *California Management Review*, *33*(3), 114-135.

Guillèn, M. F. (1994). *Models of Management: Work, Authority, and Organization in a Comparative Perspective*. Chicago: University of Chicago Press.

Hinnings, C. R., & Greenwood, R. (1988). The normative prescription of organizations. In G. Zucker (Ed.), *Institutional Patterns and Organizations: Culture and Environment* (pp. 53-70). Cambridge, MA: Ballinger

Hirschheim, R., & Smithson, S. (1988). A Critical Analysis of Information Systems Evaluation. In N. Bjørn-Andersen & G. B. Davis (Eds.), *Information Systems Assessment: Issues and Challenges* (pp. 17-37). Amsterdam: North Holland.

Imperatori, B., & De Marco, M. (in press). ICT and Changing Working Relationships: Rational or Normative Fashion?" In A. D'Atri, M. De Marco, & N. Casalino (Eds.). *Interdisciplinary Aspects of Information Systems Studies*. London: Springer.

Kakihara, M., & Sorensen, C. (2004). Practicing Mobile Professional Work: Tales of Locational, Operational and Interactional Mobility. *INFO: The journal of Policy, Regulation and Strategy for Telecommunications, Information and Media*, *6*(3), 180-197.

Kohli, R., & Devaraj, S. (2004). Realizing the business value of information technology investment: an organizational process. *MIS Quarterly Executive*, *3*(1), 53-68

Lengick-Hall, C. A., & Lengick-Hall, M. L. (2006). HR, ERP and knowledge for competitive advantage. *Human Resource Management*, *45*, 179-194.

Lepak, D. P., Takeuchi, R., & Snell, S. A. (2003). Employment flexibility and firm performance: examining the interaction effect of employment

model, environmental dynamism and technological intensity. *Journal of Management*, *29*(5), 681-703.

Malladi, R., & Agrawal, D. P. (2002). Current and Future Applications of Mobile and Wireless Networks. *Communications of the ACM*, *45*(10), 144–146.

Martin, G., Reddington, M., & Alexander, H. (2008). *Technology, Outsourcing and Transforming HR*. Oxford: Butterworth Heinemann.

McGregor, D. (1960). *The Human Side of Enterprise*. New York: McGraw-Hill.

McKinlay, A. (2002). The Limits of Knowledge Management. *New Technology, Work & Employment*, *17*(2), 76-88.

McLean Parks, J., & Kidder, D. L. (1994). «Till Death Us Do Part...» Changing Work Relationships in the 1990s. In C. L. Cooper, & D. M. Rousseau (Eds.), *Trends in Organisational Behaviour*, 1 (pp. 111-136). Chichester, England: John Wiley & Sons.

Miles, M. B., & Huberman, A. M. (1984). *Qualitative Data Analysis*, *16*. Newbury Park, CA: Sage.

Organ, D. W. (1997). Organisational Citizenship Behaviour: Its Construct Clean-Up Time. *Human Performance*, *10*, 85-97.

Powell, W., & DiMaggio, P. J. (Eds.). (1991). *The New Institutionalism in Organizational Analysis*. Chicago-London: University of Chicago Press.

Prahalad, C. K., & Hamel, G. (1990). The Core Competence of the Corporation. *Harvard Business Review*, *68*, 79-91.

Pressman, J. L. & Wildavsky, A. B. (1973). *Implementation. How Great Expectations in Washington are dashed in Oakland.* Berkeley, L.A.: University of California Press.

Robinson, S. L., Kraatz, M. S., & Rousseau, D. M. (1994). Changing Obligations and the Psychological Contract: A Longitudinal Study. *Academy of Management Journal, 37*(1), 137-152.

Rousseau, D. M., & Mclean Parks, J. (1993). The Contract of Individuals and Organisations. In B. M. Staw & L. L. Cummings (Eds.), *Research in Organisational Behaviour, 15*, 1-43. Greenwich, CT: JAI Press.

Rousseau, D. M. (1989). Psychological and Implied Contracts in Organisations. *Employee Responsibilities and Rights Journal, 2*, 121-139.

Sambamurthy, V., Bharadwaj, A., & Grover, A. (2003). Shaping Agility though Digital Option. *MIS Quarterly, 27*(2), 237-263.

Schein, E., (1980). *Organisational Psychology.* Englewood Cliffs, NJ: Prentice-Hall.

Scott ,W. R., & Meyer, J. W. (1994). *Institutional Environments and Organizations: Structural Complexity and Individualism.* London: Sage.

Sheng, H., Siau, K., & Nah, F. (2005) Strategic Implications of Mobile Technology: A Case Study Using Value-Focused Thinking. *Journal of Strategic Information Systems, 14*(3), 23-55.

Starng, D., & Meyer, J. W. (1994). Institutional Conditions for Diffusions. In R. Scott & J. W. Meyer (Eds), *Institutional Environments and Organizations: Structural Complexity and Individualism* (pp. 100-112). Newbury Park, CA: Sage.

Stover, M. (1999). *Leading the Wired Organization.* New York: Neal Schuman Publishers

Taylor, W. C., & LaBarre, P. (2006). *Mavericks at work: why the most original minds in business win.* New York: William Morrow.

Valenduc, G., & Vendramin, P. (2001). Telework : from distance working to new forms of flexible work organization. *Transfer - European Review of Labour and Research, 7*(2), 244-257.

Van Dyne, L., Cummings, L. L., & Mclean Parks, J. (1995). Extra-Role Behaviours: In Pursuit of Construct and Definitional Clarity. In B. M. Staw & L. L. Cummings (Eds.), *Research in Organisational Behaviour, 17*, 215-285. Greenwich, CT: JAI Press.

Varshney, U., & Vetter, R. (2000). Emerging mobile and wireless networks. *Communications of the ACM, 43*(6), 73-81.

Vendramin P., & Valenduc, G. (2000). *L'avenir du travail dans la société de l'information, enjeux individuels et collectifs.* Paris: L'Harmattan.

Yin, R. K. (1993). *Case study Research: Design and Method.* London: Sage.

KEY TERMS

E-Work Solutions: Managerial rhetoric that means that employee-organization relationship is mediated by ICT. E-work could enable both spatial and time working flexible solutions.

Managerial Discourse: What is said and written about managerial issues.

Managerial Rhetoric: It is part of the managerial discourse and it describes managerial fashionable techniques as the vanguard of management progress.

Outputs, Outcomes and Impacts: They are three effects along with is possible to evaluate of public policies according respectively products-services generated, results when products reach their target market, and finally underlying problems addressed or developed by the program in the longer term.

Psychological Contract: It is the employee's expectations about his/her labor relationships (i.e. mutual obligations, values, expectations and aspirations) that operate over and above the formal contract of employment.

Section II
User Involvement and User Participation

Chapter IV
Early User Involvement and Participation in Employee Self–Service Application Deployment:
Theory and Evidence from Four Dutch Governmental Cases

Gerwin Koopman
Syntess Software, The Netherlands

Ronald Batenburg
Utrecht University, The Netherlands

ABSTRACT

This chapter theoretically and empirically addresses the notion that user participation and involvement is one of the important factors for IS success. Different models and studies are reviewed to define and classify types of early end-user involvement and participation. Next, five case studies are presented of Dutch governmental organizations (Ministries) that have recently deployed an employee self-service application. Based on interviews with developers, project managers and users it can be showed that the deployment success of such systems is positively related to the extent of early user involvement and participation. In addition, it was found that expectancy management is important to keep users informed about certain deployment decisions. In this way, employees can truly use the self-service applications without much support from the HR-departments.

INTRODUCTION

In 2007, the Dutch House of Representatives asked the Dutch Government questions about their ICT-expenditures. Concerns were raised about how much money was wasted by governmental ICT projects that resulted in failures. The Dutch Court of Audit was instructed to come up with a report on governmental ICT projects and the possible reasons for failures. When the report (Dutch Court Audit, 2007) was finished, it named several difficulties that can be faced when executing ICT projects for governmental organisations. Among this list is the impact of the changes caused by the implementation of the IT-system. Users current way of working may be completely changed by changing work processes when the system is introduced. Users therefore need to be informed an trained to completely benefit from the system. Another cause for problems is the need for clear goals and demands. If the software developer does not receive clear demands and wishes, the actual end-product might not be what the government thought it would receive.

In both of the mentioned problems users play an important role in making the system a success. There is already a lot of agreement on the fact that users should be involved to produce usable software programs. It is recommended in ISO standard 13407 to get better insights in the requirements for a software application. Most attention to user involvement is still on the usability testing of systems, which happens on a later stage in the development process. However, the sooner the end-user is involved, the more efficient it is (Noyes et al, 1996; Chatzoglou & Macaulay, 1996; Blackburn et al, 2000).

One of the challenges in involving users in IT developments is the time factor that plays a very important role in governmental IT projects. Most of the decisions to implement or develop new Information Technology have a political background. This means the project will have to be delivered at the end of the current cabinet's

term. This introduces a certain pressure for the project to be delivered as soon as possible. This conflicts with the idea that user involvement will take a serious amount of extra time needed in the development of a new system (Grudin, 1991). The systems that have the specific attention of this research on first sight also seem to conflict with this additional time needed in IT projects when involving users. Main reasons for implementing E-HRM systems and Shared Service Centres (SSC) are increasing efficiency and productivity (Verheijen, 2007; Janssen & Joha, 2006). For the current Dutch cabinet this is very important because it wants to decrease the number of civil servants with a number of 12,800 to achieve a cost cutback of 630 million Euros in four years (Ministerie van Binnenlandse Zaken en Koninkrijksrelaties, 2007).

Another difficulty in the involvement of users is the selection of the right groups of employees to have participating in the project (Grudin, 1991). This is especially true for most governmental organisations, because they employ a large amount of civil servants. As the applications that are the subject of the research are mainly aimed at self-service these are all potential end-users. This is a very diverse group and it can be considered a challenge to make the right selection of users from this total population.

In this paper we address the question which methods are currently used within the Dutch governmental institutions to involve end-users when deploying employee self-service applications. We also investigate the relationship between end-user participation and involvement and the success of such e-HRM applications. Four Dutch governmental organizations (Ministries) are investigated that have implementing employee self-service applications (i.e. e-HRM), which offers the possibility to compare the different development approaches that are followed. Semi-structured and topic interviews were held with stakeholders within the Ministries to explore which methods are already used to involve users in the process of deployment. Their experiences are described and reflected upon at the closing section of the paper.

THEORY

A Review on the Role of User Participation

DeLone & McLean (2003) evaluated empirical testing and validation of their original D&M IS Success Model (DeLone & McLean, 1992) by other researchers and developed an updated IS Success Model. An adaptation of this model is depicted in Figure 1. It is based on the three different levels of communication that were already defined by Shannon & Weaver (1949). The *technical* level is concerned with the physical information output of a system, and evaluated on accuracy and efficiency. The *semantic* level deals with the meaning of the output of a system, and specifically with how well the output conveys the intended meaning. The *effectiveness* level or *influence* level (Mason, 1978) concerns the effect of the information on the receiver.

The top layer of the model contains three different quality dimensions. The two dimensions at the left hand side of this layer are similar as in the original D&M model (DeLone & McLean,

Figure 1. Adapted from D&M (Updated) IS success model (DeLone & McLean, 2003)

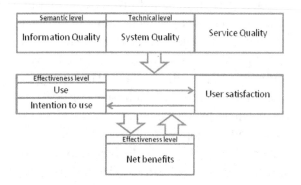

1992).Terms to measure *information quality* were accuracy, timeliness, completeness, relevance and consistency. This concept and the terms thus measure success on the semantic level. For *system quality* these terms were ease-of-use, functionality, reliability, flexibility, data quality, portability, integration and performance. These measures are related tot the technical success level. The concept of service quality was added, because of the changing role or IS organisations, they more and more deliver services instead of only products.

The *use* concept in the model measures success on the effectiveness level. It is considered an important indicator for system success, especially when it is "informed and effective" (DeLone & McLean, 2003). There are however some difficulties in the interpretation of the concept *use*. It has a lot of different aspects, for instance voluntariness and effectiveness. It therefore received critique in research of the original model. One example is that use is not a success variable in the case of mandatory systems. DeLone & McLean (2003) argue however, that no use is "totally mandatory" and that mandatory systems will be discontinued if they do not deliver the expected results. The differences are thus on the different levels: mandatory to use for employees, but voluntarily to terminate for management. Nevertheless, to overcome some of the difficulties, in the updated model a distinction is made between *intention to use* (attitude) and *use* (behaviour).

User satisfaction is considered a useful measure in evaluating the success of information systems (Ives, Olson, & Baroudi, 1983). In most cases this subjective judgment by users is considered to be more user practical, because of the difficulties in measuring the success of IS objectively (Saarinen, 1996; Lin & Shao, 2000). The *net benefits* concept is regarded as a set of IS impact measures, for instance work group impacts and organisational impacts. More specific measures are for instance quality of work, job performance and quality of work environment.

To reduce the complexity of the model these are all grouped together, and which impact will be chosen will depend on the information system that is evaluated. These two concepts (user satisfaction and net benefits) measure success on the effectiveness level.

Lin & Shao (2000) investigated the relationship between user participation and system success. They found a significant relationship between both concepts, but warn that the context should be taken into account. Both user participation and system success can be directly and indirectly influenced by other factors. Based on the outcomes of their data analysis they also suggest that "getting users involved in the development process may improve their attitudes toward the system and enhance the importance and relevance users perceive about the system". Other findings were the positive influence of user attitudes on user involvement and the fact that users are asked more to participate when the complexity of systems increases.

In a survey of 200 production managers Baroudi et al, (1986) found positive correlations between user involvement and user information satisfaction and system usage. User involvement in this case was conceptualised as activities during the development that enabled the users to influence the development. Although, this is more towards user participation, it does not completely distinct the behaviour and psychological concepts. Interviewing users and developers from 151 projects, McKeen & Guimaraes (1997) found a positive and significant relationship between user participation and user satisfaction. They also noted that projects concerning systems or tasks with a high complexity called for more user participation.

To positively influence the success of new software applications, developers often turn to user involvement. According to Kujala (2003) user involvement can be seen as a general term and refers to Damodaran (1996) who suggests a continuum from informative to consultative to participative. However, some researchers suggest a difference between user involvement and user participation. User participation will then be the "assignments, activities, and behaviors that users or their representatives perform during the systems development process" (Barki & Hartwick, 1989). User involvement can be regarded as "a subjective psychological state reflecting the importance and personal relevance that a user attaches to a given system" (Barki & Hartwick, 1989). McKeen et al, (1994) in their research on contingency factors also describe the development of the division of these two concepts. The refined model is even further extended, in that user the relationship between user participation and system success is influenced by other moderating variables like the *degree of influence, attitude, communication* and *type of involvement.* In this study therefore the distinction between the two concepts *user participation* and *user involvement* will also be used.

Several researchers do not only recognize the link between user participation and system success, but even stress the importance of involving end-users in the development of software. Kensing & Blomberg (1998) state the participation of end-users is "seen as one of the preconditions for good design" (see also Shapiro, 2005). The workers have the information about the working environment and organisation, which designers logically do not always possess. Combining the domain knowledge of the workers and the technical knowledge of the designers is considered a foundation for the development of a useful application (Kensing & Blomberg, 1998).

Reviewing several studies on user involvement Damodaran (1996) identified a number of benefits of participating end-users:

- **More accurate user requirements:** Numerous problems or defects in software applications can be traced back to poorly capturing requirements at the beginning of the development process (Borland, 2006). Pekkola et al. (2006) also argue one of the reasons for information system development projects to fail are incomplete requirements.

In their studies they found user participation useful in gathering "credible, trustworthy and realistic descriptions of requirements". In turn these accurate user requirements result in an improved system quality (Kujala, 2003).

- **Avoidance of unnecessary or unusable costly system features:** Two of the usability guidelines given by Nielsen (1993) are "Designers are not users" and "Less is more". Designers might think of certain features to incorporate in the application without consulting end-users. Functionalities that are completely logical for developers, might be completely incomprehensible for users. This might result in users having to spent too much time on learning how to use these functionalities or even not using them. Designers might also have the tendency of incorporating too many options to satisfy 'every' end-user. Besides the fact that users might never know of these options and use them, they can also work contra productive by overwhelming to users. A lot of time and effort for developing these features can be saved by participating end-users.
- **Improved levels of system acceptance:** The levels of system acceptance can be in positively influenced by user involvement in several ways. Among the list Ives & Olsen (1984) have found in other literature are for instance the development of development of realistic expectations about the information system (Gibson, 1977). Also decreasing user resistance against the new system and actually creating commitment for it are other results of user participation (Lucas, 1974). Cherry & Macredie (1999) state participatory design as a means to overcome the acceptability problems systems might encounter without the participation of users.
- **Better understanding of the system by the user:** Logically during the participation users will learn about the system by experiencing

the development (Lucas, 1974). This familiarisation also leads to the increase in chances users will come up with suggestions during the development, because they will feel more confident (Robey & Farrow, 1982). In the end this greater understanding should lead to a more effective use of the application.

- **Increased participation in decision-making within the organisation:** Clement & Van den Besselaar (1993) point to the fact that participation is not only restricted to the design of an IT-system. The application will probably change the way tasks are executed, thus affecting the entire organisation and by participating employees have the possibility to influence this (Robey & Farrow, 1982). It might thus not be restricted to the design of the application, but also to other decision-making processes within the organisation.

Although involving users is considered to be useful, it also introduces a number of difficulties. Firstly, a large amount of a user's knowledge about the process or task the software application will have to support has become tacit (Wood, 1997). It might therefore be hard to get information from these users about the way they work. An example of this was also visible at the Ministry of the Interior. Developers built a certain functionality based on the description of how a task was executed by employees without an application. After implementation however, it became clear in the former way of working an extra file was created by users to keep track of the status of the tasks at hand. Since this was not formally part of the process, they forgot to mention this to the developers. It was thus not incorporated in the new application, while this would have been relatively easy to realise. To overcome this kind of problems it is possible to perform field studies, which have the advantage that users do not have to articulate their needs (Kujala, 2003). Other researchers also suggest the use of (paper) prototypes to counter the difficulties users might have in articulating their needs (Pekkol aet al, 2006; Nielsen, 1993).

Users can also be reluctant to have developers observing them while they work (Butler, 1996). They might express concerns about justifying the time they would have to spent with the design team or disturbing their co-workers. Solutions to this problem are getting commitment from management (Grudin, 1991) and having sessions in separate rooms so no colleagues would have to feel bothered. Besides these problems Butler (1996) mentions the fact that these sessions are considered to consume a lot of time, as well in planning them, as in executing them. Several researchers also point out the fact that involving users most of the time delivers a large amount of raw data that is difficult to analyse and to use in decision making (Brown, 1996; Rowley, 1996). This will make projects where users participate more time-consuming and thus something development teams want to cut back on. Grudin (1991) also noted the judgement of developers that user involvement would take too much time. However, as already stated, allocating more time upfront will result in a faster cycle time for software developers (Blackburn et al, 2000).

Some members of the design team might simply not have the abilities needed to communicate efficiently with users (Grudin, 1991). They might find it difficult to understand the work situations of users or miss the empathy needed when communicating with users that do not possess the computer skills they have themselves. As a solution to the problematic communication between users and developers, mediators could be brought into action (Pekkola, Niina, & Pasi, 2006). They can act as a bridge between both groups, translating the different concepts from one group to the other. Mock-ups and prototypes from the design team are for instance discussed with users, while user input and feedback is given to the design team. Developers can then focus on

the design and implementation of the application instead of having to spent time and effort on user participation methods.

A challenge that occurs even before all of these mentioned is the selection of user representatives and obtaining access to them (Grudin, 1991). Even when a application is developed specifically for one organisation, developers might fear the risk of missing a certain user(group) in their selection. A possible solution is to define a few personas based on intended users. A persona is defined as "an archetype of a user that is given a name and a face, and it is carefully described in terms of needs, goals and tasks" (Blomquist & Arvola, 2002). This can be useful in organisations that have large groups of users, which makes it tricky to randomly take a small selection out of the total group. Subsequently getting hold of the 'selected' end-users might also pose some difficulties. There might be several barriers like information managers acting as user representatives, but who do not resemble the actual end-user. Also the physical distance between developers and users might create problems. One of the solutions is to; if possible, have the development team working on location of the customer. This way easy access to users is possible (planned or ad hoc).

Early Involvement and Participation of Users

The reasons of having user participation are clearly visible, but when should end-users engaged in the development process? Several researchers suggests that users should be involved early in the process. For instance, if users are used as sources in the requirements capturing process, the number of iterations are less than if they are not (Chatzoglou & Macaulay, 1996). Also capturing usability problems early in the process is very rewarding. Mantei & Teorey (1988) estimate that correcting problems early in the development process cost three times less than correcting them later on.

Nielsen (1993) also supports the involvement of users just after the start of the design phase. Regular meetings between users and designers could for instance prevent a mismatch the users' actual task and the developers' model of the task.

In comparing software development firms Blackburn et al. (2000) found that the ones that were considered to have a faster cycle time, were the ones that spent more time on for instance getting customer requirements at the early stages of the project. In their follow-up interviews of their quantitative data analysis, managers mentioned that much time in projects is consumed by rework. To reduce this time it is important to capture the needs of the users early in the development, so before the actual programming has started. In the end this will actually improve the speed and productivity of the software developer.

Damodaran (1996) underlines the justification of early user involvement by pointing to one of the principles of a number of social design approaches. That is, organisations will just postpone the detection of problems if there is no effective user involvement. Again, problems that have to be solved later on in the development, or even after implementation, will result in higher costs.

User participation can take on a number of forms in the development of a software product. Kujala (2003) suggests four main approaches are detectible, which are *user-centred design, participatory design, ethnography* and *contextual design*. Since involving end-users from the beginning of the project is considered very beneficiary, the focus will be on those approaches and methods that take place early in the development process.

Gould & Lewis (1985) in their research on *user-centred design* recommend the early focus on users and direct contact between development team and end-users. This implies doing interviews and discussions with end-users, even before any design has been made. Also people should be observed when performing tasks, as well in the present situation as with prototypes that are developed during the project. Also the design should

be iterative, this could for instance be realised by using prototypes that can be reviewed by users.

Participatory design is considered to be a design philosophy instead of a methodology (Cherry & Macredie, 1999). It is not prescriptive and therefore the set of techniques that could be used should be considered open-ended. The approach does have some identifiable principles however, firstly it aims at the production of information systems that improve the work environment. Secondly, users should be actively involved at each stage of the development and finally the development should be under constant review (iterative design). Cherry & Macredie (1999) also mention four important techniques, cooperative prototyping being the main technique. The other techniques are brainstorming, workshops and organisational gaming.

Ethnography consists of observing and describing the activities of a group, in an attempt to understand these activities (Littlejohn, 2002). In the design of information systems it is defined as developing "a thorough understanding of current work practices as a basis for the design of computer support" (Simonsen & Kensing, 1997). The reason for this is the occurrence of differences in what users say they do, and what they actually do (Nielsen, 1993). The approach is descriptive of nature, is from a member's point-of-view, takes place in natural settings and behaviours should be explained from their context (Blomberg et al, 1993). A typical method of ethnography is observing end-users while they perform their daily work. This can be done following them in their work, so designers being present at the office, or recording the tasks on video and then analysing this footage later on.

Similar to ethnography is *contextual design*. It goal is to help a cross-functional team to agree on what users need and design a system for them (Beyer & Holtzblatt, 1999). The approach focuses on the improvement of the current way of working within an organisation. It thus is not only limited to the design of a system, but also incorporates

Table 1. POTENTIAL early participation methods

Method	Approach (Kujala, 2003)
Observation	User-centred Design / Ethnography
Interviews	User-centred Design
Discussion	User-centred Design
Prototyping	User-centred Design / Participatory Design / Contextual Design
Brainstorming	Participatory Design
Workshops	Participatory Design
Organisational gaming	Participatory Design
Video analysis	Ethnography
Contextual Inquiry	Contextual Design

redesigning the work processes. Users are the main source for data to support decisions on what developments should take place. Specific methods to obtain information from users are (paper) prototyping and contextual inquiry. The latter method is a combination of observing users and interviewing them at the same moment (Beyer & Holtzblatt, 1999).

Co-development, ethnographic methods and contextual inquiry are participatory methods that are located early in the development cycle (Muller, 2001). Most of the approaches actually span the entire development. Table 1 summarises this section and lists the techniques that could be used in the early stages of the development.

THE CASE: EMPLOYEE SELF-SERVICE APPLICATIONS

As stated in the previous section the type of system and the contextual environment are important factors to keep in mind when measuring IS success. In this paper we focus on Employee Self-Service (ESS) systems that represent one of the fast developing trends in the domain of e-HRM (Strohmeier, 2007; Ruël et al, 2004). This type of systems is specifically relevant for this study as it directly relates to the issue of user participation, as it aims to empower employees within organizations.

ESS is defined by Konradt et al. (2006) as "corporate web portal that enables managers and employees to view, create and maintain relevant personnel information". Konradt et al. also identify four different basis channel functions the ESS can support:

- informing employees about rules and regulations
- providing interaction the access to personal information
- supporting transactions, like applications for leave
- delivering for instance payslips or training videos

All of the above tasks are normally done by the organisations' HR departments. Fister Gale (2003), in her study on three successful ESS implementations, describes reducing the workload of these personnel departments is a major reason for implementation. For instance, changing personal information of employees in often several databases normally had to be done by HR employees. This can now be done by employees themselves by filling in web based forms, resulting in (real-time) updates of the databases of the HR systems. The web based nature of the ESS also offer the possibility to significantly decrease the paperwork that needs to be handled. However, the benefits are not only on the organisations' side, employees also profit from the implementation of ESS. They have instant access to information and the effort needed for certain transactions, like expense claims, is reduced. Managers also benefit from the up-to-date information and easy access to for instance reports, resulting in a better overview over their resources.

ESS and User Satisfaction

Konradt et al. (2006) used the well-known Technology Acceptance Model (TAM; Davis, 1989) to describe the influences of a systems' usefulness and ease of use on user satisfaction and system use. The research model they used in their investigation is depicted in Figure 2. Ease of use related positively to user satisfaction, as well as to usefulness. Usefulness in turn positively influenced both system use and user satisfaction.

A final relationship was described between user satisfaction and system use.

A number of implications were drawn from these findings to ensure the success of an ESS implementation. The suggestion that system acceptance is mainly determined by the usefulness of the system and its ease of use, implies that enough attention should be paid to these factors. Informing and involving employees during the development is advised to influence the ease of use and usefulness of the application. It should be clear to employees why it is beneficiary to them to use the ESS, to ensure system acceptance. If users do not accept the system, the workload reduction for HR department will not be realised. Instead of the normal workload, HR employees will be flooded with help requests by users who do not understand the system or even are reluctant to work with it.

Data and Methods

To determine in what ways users are involved or enabled to participate in the development of

Figure 2. User participation and application success

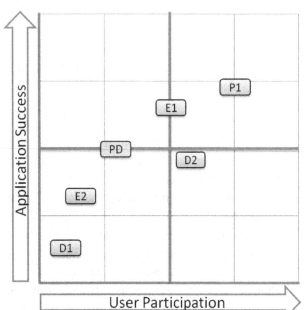

Legend	
E1	Emplaza (earlier versions)
E2	Emplaza 4.3
D1	PeopleSoft (Ministry of Defense, earlier versions)
D2	Peoplesoft (Ministry of Defense)
PD	HR-Portal (P-Direkt)
P1	P-Loket (Ministry of Health, Welfare and Sports)

software applications, interviews were held at four Dutch ministries. The cases are described below.

Emplaza at the Ministry of the Interior and Kingdom Relationships

The person interviewed representing the Ministry of the Interior and Kingdom Relationships is the project leader Self-Service / Emplaza. The application is called Emplaza, a combination of the words *Employability* and *Plaza*.

This self-service human resources application is used by approximately 5,500 civil servants within the Ministry of the Interior and Kingdom Relationships. The application is also used by the Ministry of Agriculture, Nature and Food Quality and the Ministry of Economic Affairs, resulting in a total number of about 17,000 users. The software supports up to twenty HR-processes, for instance applying for leave or filing an appraisal conversation. The application is actually a sort of web application and functions as layer over the actual administrative IT-system. It is built and managed by an external party.

At the time of the interview a new release of the application (version 4.3) was under development. This will be the base for this case description. Since the application is not entirely new some of the reactions of the users can be expected based on experiences from the previous releases. These experiences also influenced the way in which new releases or features are developed. This time however, the release has taken more than a year to develop because of some important differences with previous situations. First of all the builders were new to the project and therefore the advantage of having worked together (as with previous releases) was lost. Second, release 4.3 can be considered larger and more extended in words of number of functionalities. As a result testing the application a considerable amount of extra time was needed to test this version. Finally, the change in organizational structure with the introduction of

P-Direkt (see next section) also took some time to get used to. P-Direkt for instance now takes care of communication between the external builder and the user group of the Ministry.

For the development of the new releases key-users or super-users were selected to participate. These civil servants have a lot of knowledge about the process the application is supposed to support. By interviewing them they current way the process is executed is determined. A next step was to establish which forms should be available to support task within the process. After that the next task was to find out how the forms and workflow should look like in Emplaza. When agreement was found on these issues the Functional Designs were created by the software developer. Before the actual programming started, a number of applications that supported similar HR-processes were investigated. Findings from this analysis formed the starting point of how this should be realized in the Emplaza application.

The key-users are thus very involved in the business rules that need to be implemented in the system. Other aspects they are asked to judge, are the look-and-feel of the user interface and the performance of the application. To do this they have to use test-scripts that will force them through every step and part of the new functionality so they will be able to comment on all the new developments. Members of the HR self-service project team also test the application by looking at it from the viewpoint of a 'new' user. They specifically pay attention to the help texts that are created for the end-users to guide them through certain tasks.

A number of criteria were used in selecting employees to participate in the development of the new release. Participants had to have a lot of knowledge and experience in the field concerning the process at hand. Furthermore, they had to be available to cooperate, i.e. they had to be freed from their normal tasks. Finally, they also had to be able to think constructively about the new functionality. Most of the time it had become clear in earlier sessions whether or not people met this latter criterion. For testing the application managers are asked to cooperate, they are selected on their position within the organization and thus all have a different role in the HR-process that is going to be implemented in the system. It is tried to have two 'camps': those who are sceptical of ICT and those who feel positive about ICT.

End-users are actually involved just when the new release has gone 'live' i.e. has gone into production. Complaints and issues that come up during the use of the application are gathered and reviewed. These form the foundation for the change proposals that are discussed on a interdepartmental level. During these discussions decisions are taken on which changes really need to be implemented. If end-users are involved earlier after all, most of them come from the central apparatus of the Ministry. The reason for this is that they are located close to the test location. They are chosen as randomly as possible, so no real criteria are used to select participants. This way the development group hopes to get 'fresh' insights about the application.

P-Direkt to be Used Throughout Several Dutch Ministries

In July 2003 the Dutch cabinet chose to start the establishment of a Shared Service Centre (SSC) called P-Direkt. This should be a Human Resource Management SSC for Personnel registration and Salary administration. Although the project had some major problems, it is now still in progress with the same main goal. It should lead to a more efficient HR-column of the government (Ministry of Internal Affairs, 2006). Two identified conditions to reach this goal are joining administrative HR-tasks and the implementation of digital self-service. The latter of these recognised conditions makes P-Direkt an interesting subject to examine and see how user involvement or participation are applied in this project.

The respondent for this interview is the Test manager at P-Direkt and is responsible for the Functional Acceptation Tests and User Acceptation Tests of the HR-Portal that is currently developed. This self-service HR-portal should eventually be used throughout the entire government. In contrast to the Emplaza 4.3 release this is an entirely new application. It is built using mostly standard functionalities of SAP but, if necessary, customization is also applied.

In the process of developing the self-service application users are involved in different ways and at different stages. Right from the start several workgroups are formed. These consist of civil servants from several ministries that in the end will use the application. The members of these groups could be considered end-users, as they will eventually use the application in their normal work. However, they have a lot of knowledge about the HR-processes the application should support. These workgroups are full-time dedicated in the development of the application for a longer period of time. One workgroup for instance has been involved from the start in simplifying and standardizing the HR-processes within the Dutch Government. After twenty-four processes had been defined they formed the basis to build the technical system that should support them. The workgroups were then involved in incorporating the right business rules within this system. An example of such a rule is calculating the maximum compensation that should be granted in different situations.

At the final part of building the application a number of end-users are asked to test the application. This group of end-users do have knowledge about the processes that should be supported, however they were not earlier involved in the development of the application. The involved departments are asked to send one or two employees to take part in the User Acceptation Tests. Per session seven to ten participants are asked to complete the scenarios that are designed to guide them through a certain task. These tasks, for instance filing an expense claim, are subdivided in different steps. This way users cannot only comment on the application in general but also notate findings about specific steps in the process. In this way the scenarios also contribute to being able to easily group comments about certain steps in the process or specific parts from all the different test users. These grouped and summarized comments and findings are then discussed by P-Direkt and the builder of the application. During these discussions it is decided which findings need fixes and those are then built within two to three days. After that a new test session is held to examine whether or not the problems were sufficiently solved.

P-Loket at the Ministry of Health, Welfare and Sport

The Ministry of Health, Welfare and Sport uses an application which is very similar to Emplaza. It is called *P-Loket* and was also developed for the Ministry of Social Affairs & Employment and the General Intelligence & Security Service, because they use the same payroll application. *P-Loket* is a web application, and functions as a layer on top of this payroll application (PersonnelView, or P-View). This situation is thus very comparable to the one at the Ministry of the Interior.

P-Loket is a totally new developed application, which can be used by employees to support them in (personnel) tasks like for instance the filing of a request for leave. In June 2007 around 12 different forms are supported by the application, which can be used by approximately 2,250 civil servants. These numbers should grow to about 18 forms and 5,000 employees by January 2008. The forms and processes that should be supported were chosen based on the outcomes of the standardisation workgroup of the P-Direkt project. The P-Direkt project is also the reason that after the 18 forms are finished no further developments will be done. The P-Direkt application will eventually substitute *P-Loket*.

From the start of the development of the application (in 2006) it was already clear P-Direkt would be the governmental HR self-service application. However, for reasons of more rapidly realisable efficiency benefits and to get used to self-service applications, it was decided to still start the development of *P-Loket*. The first quarter of 2006 was used as preparation and to come up with a plan of how to approach the project. The second quarter of the year was used to prepare for the building, make a process design and setting up authorisations. By the end of June the actual creation of the application could start.

Building the application was done by an external software company that also created the P-View application. *P-Loket* was also a totally new developed application for them. However, P-View and P-Loket are quite similar web applications, which had some advantages. The links for instance that had to be available, were already more or less present and thus had not to be created completely from scratch. They had one developer working full-time on the project.

Employees of the Ministry were involved in several ways during the development. The project group that was formed at the start consisted of hr-employees, members of the audit service and two employees of the Information & Communication department. The latter two were experts on web (applications) and usability. Both these experts had the task to look at the application from a user perspective. The usability expert for instance discussed a number of prototypes (on screen) with the builder. By asking questions like "what will happen if a user clicks this button?" issues could already be addressed before anything was programmed. Apart from the experts the project group members did not attend to the User Interface of the application. Their focal point was on the business rules that should be implemented.

Next to the fact that users were represented in the project group, other civil servants were asked to cooperate in an usability test. This test was carried out by a third party and the main reason was to resolve usability issues the software builder and the usability expert from the project could not agree on. The test was carried out with one test person and a guide in one room, observers were in another room to take notes and film the session with a camera. In selecting employees to take part in this test, the project group tried to have a balance in computer skills, male/female ratio and office/field staff ratio. To find eight participants, contact persons were asked if they knew employees that fitted the necessary characteristics.

Another way to involve end-users was to have sessions with managers to discuss the functionality that supports performance review conversations with them. Per session the application was demonstrated to three to twelve managers. It took roughly five weeks to complete the sessions with two hundred and fifty managers. Managers could immediately deliver feedback in the form of questions or remarks during the demonstration. Although this way of involving end-users took considerable time and effort, it was considered to be very useful and contributing to the acceptance of the application. One of the strengths of having different sessions was that certain issues came up in numerous occasions. This made it easier to establish the importance of a problem or request. The issues from the different sessions were combined and for each issue the urgency was determined. Subsequently the impact of solutions for these issues was discussed with software developer.

Also the fact that the project group was located in the same offices as end-users that were not in the project group offered the possibility to ask these colleagues for their opinions in an informal ad hoc way. The project group gratefully made use of this opportunity during the development of P-Loket.

PeopleSoft/HR at the Ministry Of Defence

The Ministry of Defence started implementing self-service on HR-processes in 2004, but with-

out involving end-users. As a result the users started having wrong interpretations about the application. Therefore the Ministry started with improving the self-service parts of the application in 2006. The application is based on the PeopleSoft HR-system and the first processes to be supported were looking into personal data, filing requests for leave and filing requests for foreign official tours. Approximately 80,000 users make use of the software, of which about 65,000 are permanent staff of the Ministry. Besides this large group of users another point of consideration is the sometimes disrupted relationship with the formal superior. This is due to frequent shifts within the organisation, for instance staff being posted abroad for military operations. As a result the application should offer the possibility to delegate certain tasks to other superiors, planners and/or secretaries.

It took about one and a half years from the beginning of the project until the improved application went live. As a start it was determined which people and processes should be supported. Subsequently the possibilities of the (then) current application were investigated. There were three important points of departure:

- Outcomes of using should be visible to the user
- Employees use the application in good faith ("the user does nothing wrong")
- No training should be necessary to use the application.

The main idea behind this is that the development should not only be seen as supporting a processes by an application, but also supporting users in their actions when using the application. Usability research was done by someone from outside the Ministry who had no knowledge of HR-processes or PeopleSoft. This person asked the civil servants how the current application was used. Some consultancy was done by external parties, but it felt most of the work was done by the internal organisation to come up with the advises and reports.

Besides the usability research, users were also involved in other ways. Employees with reasonable knowledge and skills about IT were asked to name functional gaps in how the support of certain processes. Next to that case studies were done by randomly asking people in the organisation to perform tasks with the application. They only got a short introduction of the task and the reassurance they could do nothing wrong. So nothing about how the application worked was explained. After this users were observed completing the tasks, while they were invited to think-aloud. The moments when users hesitated or were in doubt, were explained as moments in the process the application should offer help. The outcomes of this test were thus:

- Information on how the application was used
- Whether or not concepts and descriptions were interpreted as intended
- Functional problems

Insights in perceptions on what has happened by performing this task ("what will be the next steps in the organisation?")

These outcomes findings were incorporated in the improved version of the software. It would be valuable to perform such a test again now the build is complete, however at the moment there is no time available to do this.

Demands for support and help options are not the same for every user, for instance because of the mentioned differences in IT-skills. One of the tools for help within the PeopleSoft application is the "See, Try, Know, Do" principle. Users can first look at a demonstration (see) before trying it themselves in a simulation mode (try). A next step is then to take a test to check if they understand everything (know), before finally actually performing the task with the application (do).

Users can use one or more of these functions to support them in the use of the software.

In choosing people for the tests information managers were asked if they could point out employees that met certain criteria. One criterion for instance was whether or not they were very skilled in using IT. Although there were some criteria, no standard profiles were used to categorise users in groups. To confront these users with the improved application, during the development, prototypes were used.

Cross-Case Comparison Analysis

The four case studies presented in the preceding sections have several things in common. First of all, they are of course all developments for a governmental organisation. Secondly, they clearly all support self-service on Human Resource processes. Thirdly, they all serve a large number of users, the HR self-service applications have a range from 5,000 to 80,000. The fourth parallel is that in all cases external organisations were

Table 2. Used methods to involve end-users

	Prototypes	Testing	Use-research
Emplaza at the Ministry of the Interior And Kingdom Relation-ships		✗	
P-Direkt to be used throughout several Dutch Min-istries		✗	
P-Loket at the Ministry Of Health, Welfare and Sport	✗	✗	
PeopleSoft/ HR at the Ministry Of Defence	✗	✗	✗

hired to assist in the development, although in the case of the Ministry of Defence this was mostly limited to advisory reports.

The previous sections also show that users are involved or are able to participate in the development of IT-systems in the Dutch government. Table 2 depicts the different ways users participated in the different cases that were discussed.

It is clearly visible that users get most attention during the test phase of the development. In all of the discussed applications end-users have participated in one or more tests during the development. Logically, this testing found place in later phases, however in three cases prototypes were used to be able to show users (parts of) the application earlier in the process of development. Non-expert end-users that participated from the start of the projects were visible in two cases (P-Loket at the Ministry Of Health Welfare and Sport and PeopleSoft/HR at the Ministry Of Defence). Most of the users that were engaged from the start had expert knowledge on the processes that were computerised by the implementation of the application.

Of particular interest is how the participation of end-users might have influenced the success of the applications in question. Figure 3 has the different applications from the interviews depicted in a diagram that scores them on success (y-axis) and user participation (x-axis). Their position on both axes is based on the interviews, but is of course subjectively determined. It is not meant to imply that any of the applications is 'better' than the others. The concept of 'application success' is seen from the viewpoint of each organisation and is based on:

- Time and effort needed for development (relative to the amount of features)
- Number of problems encountered during tests and implementation
- Satisfaction with the end-product
- Contribution to increase in efficiency of the supported tasks

As a final step to complete the four case studies among the Dutch Ministries, additional information about the (perceived) success of the ESS-applications was collected. This was conducted through one short personal e-mail sent to the interviewees, containing six system quality criteria for which an answer on a 5point scale was requested:

- The number of problems reported by users in the user (acceptation) tests (ranging from 1 being "very few" to 5 being "seriously many")
- The amount of rework needed after testing (ranging from 1 being "very little" to 5 being "very much")
- Current satisfaction with the application by end-users (ranging from 1 being "very dissatisfied" to 5 being "very satisfied")
- The amount of questions that reached the helpdesk shortly after implementation (ranging from 1 being "very few" to 5 being "seriously many")
- Contribution of the application to the increase in satisfaction (ranging from 1 being "very little" to 5 being "very much")
- The overall success of the application (ranging from 1 being "very low" to 5 being "very high")

Table 3 shows the answers of the respondents that were queried for four different Ministries/cases.

Based on these additional data, the actual relation between early user involvement, satisfaction and application success can be estimated for the four cases under investigation. Before we do so, some remarks beforehand.

First, it should e noted that for Emplaza both the latest version (4.3) and earlier versions were investigated (E1). During the interviews it became clear that in earlier versions a lot more user participation was applied. The short communication lines resulting from the programming

Table 3. Scores by respondents to extra questions

	Emplaza at the Ministry of the Interior and Kingdom Relationships	PeopleSoft/HR at the Ministry Of Defence	P-Loket at the Ministry Of Health, Welfare and Sport	P-Direkt to be used throughout several Dutch Ministries
1 Reported problems after test	5	3	2	2
2 Amount of rework needed	5	4	4	1
3 Current satisfaction level	4	4	4	n/a
4 Questions at helpdesk	2	3	4	n/a
5 Contribution to efficiency	4	2	4	n/a
6 Overall success	3	2	4	n/a

team working on the same location as users, made sure users could be frequently consulted. At the deployment of Emplaza 4.3 end-users were involved, but not at all before a working product was developed. A number of problems arose in the development and testing of the 4.3 version. Some functionalities could for instance not be implemented on time, because tests by key users revealed to many hick-ups. User satisfaction with the functionalities that could be implemented on time however, was considered to be reasonable high. Also, it would not be fair to let the low score on participation of end-users to be the only reason for the low score on application success. There were numerous other problems mentioned that contributed to the difficult development of Emplaza 4.3, as described in section 3.2.1. Before these problems are solved however, earlier versions can be considered relatively more successful than the latest one.

Secondly, it needs to be considered that the PeopleSoft/HR application also has earlier versions as ESS within the Ministry of Defence. In the use of the initial version users encountered too many problems. So, the second version was developed to be an improvement of the first version. A lot more attention for usability went hand in hand with the increasing possibilities for users to participate in the development. A lot of problems were therefore found, resulting in

quite a lot of rework. Although not all difficulties for users could be solved the second version was considered to be superior to its predecessor. This thus shows in participation, so the second version is placed more to the right of the graph. However, the success positioning is not as high as might be expected with regard to the amount of user participation. This mainly has to do with the low scores on contribution to efficiency and the overall success rating of the application by the respondent.

Thirdly, it appeared that the P-Direkt application to be used by several Ministries, is hard to compare with regard to its success as Table 3 indicates. For questions 1 and 2, the scores by the respondent were given 2 and 1 respectively. The current application is still only partly implemented and used by two departments, while the goal is to use it at all government departments. Therefore questions 3 to 6 are not applicable in this case.

Fourth and final, we need to clarify how we quantified user participation in order to score the four cases on this dimension and plot it against their application successes. We judged that the Ministry of Health, Welfare and Sports demonstrated relatively the most time and effort spent on user participation. For instance all managers were approached by demo sessions and invited to comment on the application. Although the different approaches used are less than with the

Ministry of Defence, the relative amount of time spent is considered to be more, so the P-Loket application is considered to score higher on user participation than the second ESS-version at the Ministry of Defence. Besides the delay in the start of the project, not a lot of problems arose during the development of the application. Also most of the problems users experienced with the application were caught in the different tests during the development. The amount of rework to be done, was therefore considered 'much', but it could be done early in the development. Since the application introduced self-service, it contributed a lot to the efficiency of the organisation. From the interviews it became clear that users participated less in the cases of Emplaza 4.3 and the first version of the Ministry of Defence, therefore the are ordered at the lower end of this dimension.

Given these remarks, the user participation and application scores for the different cases are plotted in Figure 3, recognizing that for two cases actually two measurements in time are included.

Without claiming to have precise measurements and quantifications, Figure 3 clearly confirms that user participation is positively related to (perceived) application success. This is supported by both cross-sectional comparing the four cases, as well as comparing the two Emplaza and PeopleSoft/HR cases over time. The implications of this hypothesized and convincing result are discussed in next closing section.

CONCLUSION AND DISCUSSION

This paper departed from an analysis of current literature on information system success, user satisfaction and user involvement. A number of researches were found that described what factors influenced the success of information systems. From the DeLone & McLean IS Success Model the concepts of system quality, (intention to) use and user satisfaction were found to be important influential factors. Other findings mentioned the influence of perceived usefulness and perceived ease of use on user satisfaction and intention to use. Subsequently these concepts could be influenced by the involvement of users in the development

Figure 3. User participation and application success

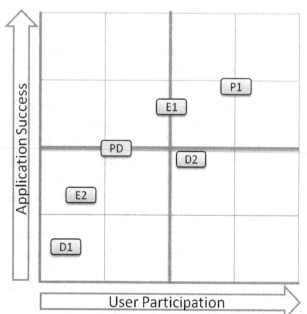

Legend	
E1	Emplaza (earlier versions)
E2	Emplaza 4.3
D1	PeopleSoft (Ministry of Defense, earlier versions)
D2	Peoplesoft (Ministry of Defense)
PD	HR-Portal (P-Direkt)
P1	P-Loket (Ministry of Health, Welfare and Sports)

process of new software applications. Next to this a distinction between the concepts of involvement and participation was suggested. Several findings of positive relationships between user participation, involvement and system success were presented. In the end the literature study was combined into a conceptual model. This model visualised the mentioned links between a number of concepts of the DeLone & McLean's IS Success Model, the Technology Acceptance Model and User Involvement & Participation.

The case studies portrayed are based on interviews with civil servants employed at different governmental organisations. One of the outcomes was a list of currently used user participation methods. In line with the findings from the literature study respondents also argued that users should be involved early, however, not too early because it would delay the development process too much. The challenges faced with involving users also did not deviate from the literature section.

Investigating the cases points also to the positive effect of user participation on the success of an application. Projects that have users participating in the development seem to be more successful than the ones that show less user participation. The only clearly visible exception is the case of the Ministry of Defence. It might be hard to compare the success of the different applications, however the differences between versions of applications are obvious (Emplaza and the Ministry of Defence).

Besides this confirmation of the positive results of user participation, also a number of lessons can be learned when studying these cases. A number of hints and points of attention were even explicitly mentioned by the respondents with regard to user participation. A number of important hints are listed below:

- **User participation requires time and a good schedule:** It is important to think about the consequences of participating end-users. Input from users will need gathered and put

in order, this takes time. Subsequently the results need to be analysed to for instance decide which requirements should be incorporated in the design or which findings should be solved. Using MOSCOW-lists, it is possible to rank requirements and suggestions in "must have", "should have", "could have" and "would have" items. To ensure the project stays on schedule, it is necessary to set deadlines when decisions need to be made, otherwise endless discussions might arise and requirements will keep changing. Also concerning scheduling is to make sure end-user are brought after some basic ideas are already thought of by the development team.

- **Try to find motivated end-users and have something to show them:** In choosing users to have participating in the project, try to find the ones that will be motivated to constructively think about the application. It might not be an easy task to do this in such large organisations, but the network of the project group or managers could be asked to produce a list of possible participators. To enable this set of end-users to come up with useful suggestions, it is wise to visualise parts of the application already. People will find it difficult to supply ideas without something they can see, even a simple mock-up will be fine to start a discussion.

- **Keep in mind the overall process that needs to be supported or automated:** The development of the self-service application itself is not the main goal of the project. There is a process or task that needs to be automated or supported. When designing, developing and testing always keep in mind this process or task. For instance observe users when executing a task to find out what other processes might be linked to this task. Or, when testing, ask the test person about his or her perceptions on what has happened and what the next step in the process will be.

- **Development team on location:** Having the development team close to end-users, for instance on location, shortens the communication lines. This enables more frequent consultation between end-users and programmers concerning for instance uncertainties about requirements or just asking user's opinions on what has been developed thus far. Being able to follow the progress more easily will also positively influence the involvement of end-users.

- **Expectancy management:** Make sure to tell participating users what will be done with their input and why. Not all of their suggestions and problems might be implemented or solved. In ensuring they maintain willing to cooperate it is important to communicate why certain decisions have been made and why some of their input is not visible in the developed application.

A number of additional lessons were mentioned by the respondents. It was mentioned to keep in mind employees should be able to use the self-service applications without too much support from the HR-departments. Otherwise it would only be a shift of the workload for the HR-department from HR-tasks to supporting users with the use of the application. In that case the organisations would not show the targeted improvements in efficiency. A third important aspect to take into account is the distinct decision process organisations like the Ministry have. This was a confirmation of one of the points in the report of The Netherlands Court of Audit. The decision process includes fairly a lot of people, takes considerable time and can be politically oriented.

REFERENCES

Barki, H., & Hartwick, J. (1989). Rethinking the Concept of User Involvement. *Rethinking the Concept of User Involvement, 13*(1), 53-63.

Baroudi, J. J., Olson, M. H., & Ives, B. (1986). An Empirical Study of the. *Communications of the ACM, 29*(3), 232-238.

Beyer, H., & Holtzblatt, K. (1999). Contextual design. *Interactions, 6*(1), 32-42.

Blackburn, J., Scudder, G., & Van Wassenhove, L. N. (2000). Concurrent Software Development. *Communications of the ACM, 43*(11), 200-214.

Blomberg, J., Giacomi, J., Mosher, A., & Swenton-Hall, P. (1993). Ethnographic field methods and their relation to design. In D. Schuler, & A. Namioka (Eds.), *Participatory Design: Principles and Practices* (pp. 123-155). Hillsdale: Lawrence Erlbaum.

Blomquist, Å., & Arvola, M. (2002). Personas in action: ethnography in an interaction design team. *Proceedings of the second Nordic conference on Human-computer interaction* (pp. 197 - 200). ACM.

Borland. (2006). Retrieved April 25, 2007, from http://www.borland.com/resources/en/pdf/solutions/rdm_whitepaper.pdf

Brown, D. (1996). The challenges of user-based design in a medical equipment market. In D. Wixon, & J. Ramey (Ed.), *Field Methods Casebook for Software Design* (pp. 157-176). New York: Wiley.

Butler, M. B. (1996). Getting to know your users: usability roundtables at Lotus Development. *Interaction, 3*(1), 23-30.

Chatzoglou, P. D., & Macaulay, L. A. (1996). Requirements Capture and Analysis : A Survey of Current Practice. *Requirements Engineering* (1), 75-87.

Chatzoglou, P. D., & Macaulay, L. A. (1996). Requirements Capture and Analysis: A Survey of Current Practice. *Requirements Engineering, 1*(2), 75-87.

Cherry, C., & Macredie, R. D. (1999). The importance of Context in Information System Design: An Assesment of Participatory Design. *Requirements Engineering, 4*(2), 103-114.

Clement, A., & Van den Besselaar, P. (1993). A retrospective look at PD projects. *Communications of the ACM, 36*(4), 29-37.

Damodaran, L. (1996). User involvement in the systems design process-a practical guide for users. *Behaviour & Information Technology, 15*(6), 363 - 377.

Davis, F. D. (1989). Perceived Usefulness, Perceived Ease of Use, and User Acceptance of Information Technology. *MIS Quarterly, 13*(3), 319-340.

DeLone, W. H., & McLean, E. R. (1992). Information system success: The quest for the independent variable. *Information Systems Research, 3*(1), 60-95.

DeLone, W. H., & McLean, E. R. (2003). The DeLone and McLean Model of Information Success: A Ten-Year Update. *Journal of Management Information Systems, 19*(4), 9-30.

Dutch Court of Audit. (2007). Lessons from IT-projects at the government [*Lessen uit ICT-projecten bij de overheid*] Retrieved from http://www.rekenkamer.nl/9282000/d/p425_rapport1.pdf .

Fister Gale, S. (2003). Three Stories of Self-Service Success. *Workforce, 82*(1), 60-63.

Gibson, H. (1977). Determining User Involvement. *Journal of System Management*, 20-22.

Gould, J. D., & Lewis, C. (1985). Designing for Usability: Key Principles and What Designers Think. *Communications of the ACM, 28*(3), 300-311.

Grudin, J. (1991). Systematic sources of suboptimal interface design in large product development organization. *Human Computer Interaction, 6*(2), 147-196.

Ives, B., & Olson, M. H. (1984). User Involvement and MIS Success: A Review of Research. *Management Science, 30*(5), 586-603.

Ives, B., Olson, M. H., & Baroudi, J. J. (1983). The measurement of user information satisfaction. *Communications of the ACM, 26*(10), 785-793.

Janssen, M., & Joha, A. (2006). Motives for establishing shared service centers in public administrations. *International Journal of Information Management, 26*(2), 102-115.

Kensing, F., & Blomberg, J. (1998). Participatory Design: Issues and Concerns. *Computer Supported Cooperative Work, 7*(3-4), 167-185.

Konradt, U., Christophersen, T., & Schaeffer-Kuelz, U. (2006). Predicting user satisfaction, strain and system usage of employee self-services. *International Journal Human Computer studies, 64*(11), 1141-1153.

Kujala, S. (2003). User involvement: a review of the benefits and challenges. *Behaviour & Information Technology, 22*(1), 1-16.

Lin, W. T., & Shao, B. B. (2000). The relationship between user participation and system success: a simultaneous contingency approach. *Information & Management, 37*(6), 283-295.

Littlejohn, S. W. (2002). *Theories of Human Communication.* Belmont: Wadsworth/Thomson Learning.

Lucas, H. J. (1974). Systems Quality, User Reactions, and the Use of Information Systems. *Management Informatics, 3*(4), 207-212.

Mantei, M. M., & Teorey, T. J. (1988). Cost/Benefit Analysis for Incorporating Human Factors in the Software Lifecycle. *Communications of the ACM, 31*(4), 428-439.

Mason, R. O. (1978). Measuring information output: A communication systems approach. *Information & Management, 1*(4), 219-234.

McKeen, J. D., & Guimaraes, T. (1997). Successful strategies for user participation in systems development. *Journal of Management Information Systems, 14*(2), 133-150.

McKeen, J. D., Guimaraes, T., & Wetherbe, J. C. (1994). The Relationship between User Participation and User Satisfaction: An Investigation of Four Contingency Factors. *MIS Quarterly, 18*(4), 427-451.

Ministry of Internal Affairs (2006). Press statement Retrieved July 21, 2007, from P-Direkt: http://www.p-direkt.nl/index.cfm?action=dsp_actueelitem&itemid=QKNGJL8E.

Ministerie van Binnenlandse Zaken en Koninkrijksrelaties. (2007). *Nota Vernieuwing Rijksdienst*. Retrieved Februari 08, 2008, from http://www.minbzk.nl/aspx/download.aspx?file=/contents/pages/89897/notavernieuwingrijksdienst.pdf

Muller, M. (2001). A participatory poster of participatory methods. *Conference on Human Factors in Computing Systems, CHI '01 extended abstracts on Human factors in computing systems*, (pp. 99 - 100).

Nielsen, J. (1993). *Usability Engineering*. San Diego: Academic Press.

Noyes, P. M., Starr, A. F., & Frankish, C. R. (1996). User involvement in the early stages of an aircraft warning system. *Behaviour & Information Technology, 15*(2), 67-75.

Pekkola, S., Niina, K., & Pasi, P. (2006). Towards Formalised End-User Participation in Information Systems Development Process: Bridging the Gap between Participatory Design and ISD Methodologies. *Proceedings of the ninth Participatory Design Conference 2006*, 21-30.

Robey, D., & Farrow, D. (1982). User Involvement in Information System Development: A Conflict Model and Empirical Test. *Management Science,, 28*(1), 73-85.

Rowley, D. E. (1996). Organizational considerations in field-oriented product development: Experiences of a cross-functional team. In D. Wixon, & J. Ramey (Eds.), *Methods Casebook for Software Design* (pp. 125 - 144). New York: Wiley.

Ruël, H., Bondarouk, T., & Looise, J. K. (2004). E-HRM: Innovation or Irritation. An Explorative Empirical Study in Five Large Companies on Web-based HRM. *Management Revue, 15*(3), 364-380.

Saarinen, T. (1996). SOS An expanded instrument for evaluating information system success. *Information & Management, 31*(2), 103-118.

Shannon, C. E., & Weaver, W. (1949). *The mathematical theory of communication* . Urbana: University of Illinois Press.

Shapiro, D. (2005). Participatory design: the will to succeed. *Proceedings of the 4th decennial conference on Critical computing: between sense and sensibility*, (pp. 29-38). Aarhus, Denmark.

Simonsen, J., & Kensing, F. (1997). Using ethnography in contextural design. *Communications of the ACM, 40*(7), 82-88.

Strohmeier, S. (2007). Research in e-HRM: Review and implications. *Human Resource Management Review, 17*(1), 19-37.

Verheijen, T. (2007). Gestrikt: E-HRM komt er uiteindelijk toch. *Personeelsbeleid, 43*(11), 20-23.

Wood, L. E. (1997). Semi-structured interviewing for user-centered design. *Interactions, 4*(2), 48-61.

KEY TERMS

Application Deployment: The adoption, implementation and usage of an information system or IT application within the context of a organization

Employee Self-Service: Corporate web portal that enables managers and employees to view, create and maintain relevant personnel information

Shared Service Centres (SSC): Newly created organization units, mostly implemented in large organizations to centralize supportive activities as administration, facilities, HR and IT-services

Semi-Structured (topic) Interviews: Case study method to collect qualitative and/or intangible data by questioning pre-selected respondents in a non-conditional, informal setting.

User Participation: Assignments, activities, and behaviors that users or their representatives perform during the systems development process

User Involvement: A subjective psychological state reflecting the importance and personal relevance that a user attaches to a given system

User Satisfaction: Subjective judgment of the information system by the user. Used as a measure for the success of an information system

78

Chapter V
Does User Centered Design, Coherent with Global Corporate Strategy, Encourage Development of Human Resource Intranet Use?

Karine Guiderdoni-Jourdain
The Institute of Labour Economics and Industrial Sociology (LEST),
Université de la Méditerranee, France

Ewan Oiry
The Institute of Labour Economics and Industrial Sociology (LEST),
Université de la Méditerranee, France

ABSTRACT

In organizations, researchers as well as professionals have generally observed insufficient use of computer technologies when compared to their expected outcomes before their implementation (Bowers, 1995). Reiterating in detail Orlikowski's theoretical propositions, the authors try to impart a clear theoretical status and to identify how transformation of the « artifact » can eventually transform uses. Using a longitudinal case study describing uses of a HR Intranet in an aeronautical firm, the authors want to show that: computer technology conception integrating user's needs, which scientific literature usually calls « user centered » conception, allows use development. However, data gathered in the interviews allows stating that this kind of conception achieved to develop uses only because it was in a strong interaction with corporate policy.

INTRODUCTION

In organizations, researchers as well as professionals have generally observed insufficient use of computer technologies when compared to their expected outcomes before their implementation (Bowers, 1995). This phenomenon can be explained through the characteristics of the individuals using them: some have a negative perception of technology, others fear the consequences on their own activity or on their influence within the organization (Markus, 1983; Marakas, & Hornik, 1996). Even if these criteria must not be minimized, the scope of this phenomenon constrains researchers to identify complimentary explanations.

In this reflection, the conceptual framework proposed by Wanda Orlikowski (2000) emerges as being clearly fundamental. This author offers a coherent and structured conceptual framework that allows analysis of the reasons that conduct an actor to develop a particular use « style » for a specific technology. She especially insists on creative user capacities by showing that uses of a given technology can be very different.

Reiterating in detail her theoretical propositions, our article develops her work on two points. First, even though her theory allows for it, Orlikowski does not develop concrete examples showing how use evolves. We propose an example. Then, by highlighting user's creativity, she seems to minimize the influence of the graphic interface (what is seen on the screen) in the uses. By naming it « artifact »—a term, which comes from Orlikowski (Orlikowski, 2000)—our article tries to impart a clear theoretical status and to identify how transformation of the « artifact » can eventually transform uses.

Using a longitudinal case study describing uses of a HR Intranet in an aeronautical firm, this exploratory research allows us to see that computer technology conception integrating user's needs, which scientific literature usually calls « user

centered » conception, (Beyer& Holzblatt, 1998), allows use development. But data gathered in the interviews allows stating that this kind of conception achieved to develop uses only because it was in a strong interaction with corporate policy. After a literature review centered on Orlikowski paper (2000), we will present our research design then detail main results of our exploratory research.

COMPUTER TECHNOLOGY USE LITERATURE REVIEW

In the computer technology research field the question of use occupies a paradoxical position. This question seems to have always been at the heart of conceptors preoccupations and still, literature offers few theories allowing to understand and to anticipate development of use in concrete company situations. On this level, Orlikowski's contribution (2000) is particularly motivating. After presenting it in detail we will continue by developing two areas that she explored less: technology use evolution and the role of the graphic interface (artifact) within this evolution.

Concrete Use are Relatively Absent in Research Analysis

In the area of computer technology research, the question of use occupies a paradoxical status. On one hand, the question has been the object of diversified and in-depth investigations. For example, the « Human Computer Interaction » (HCI) approach has focused on use since its goal is to improve the « usability» of technologies (Ruta, 2005). That is to say ergonomical technologies that demand minimal user learning in order to be used. In a more cooperative development logic, the Computer Supported Cooperative Work (CSCW) approach has also focused on use of IT solutions (Greif, 1988).

But, even if those literatures have placed the uses at the very centre of their reflection, they talk finally very little of «real» uses for their technologies. Indeed, the uses analyzed are more often those of the designers themselves—who test their tools in an attempt to improve them—or those of specific users, often placed outside their classical work conditions, put in the specific position of «testers» of a technology. Indeed, if scientific works and prototypes proliferate in those communities, the successful implantations of software remain rarer (Grudin, 1988; Markus & Connolly, 1990; Olson & Teasley, 1996). This fact makes the analysis of uses more delicate since it is known that the users positioned in a role of «co-designers» do not have the same behaviour as the «real» users and these test situations (even reconstructed or within the context of an experiment) are rather different to real use situations (Bardini & Horvath, 1995; Woolgar, 1991).

A New IT Structuration Perspective: Beyond Appropriation Towards Enactment

According to these considerations, we would like to focus on the major contribution of Orlikowski (2000). This author is one of the first to question and to place companies' employees' practices in the center of her reflexion as well as offering a theoretical framework to analyze them.

By revisiting the theory of structuration proposed by Giddens (1984) Orlikowski aims at branching out distinctively from the "social constructivism" approach (Mac Kenzie & Wajcman, 1985; Bijker & Alii, 1987; Woolgar, 1991; Bijker & Law, 1992).

According to her, in this approach researchers focus too much on technology conception methods. That led them to overestimate the role of conceptors. In particular, those works lay on a hypothesis which she felt unfounded: inventors could integrate a framework so structured into technology that users had only two choices, either adopt or reject it..

Orlikowski criticizes this hypothesis. She shows that a same technology can be used in extremely different ways. This furnishes the proof that technology does not embody structure.

In her IT structuration perspective, Orlikowski affirms that the concept of appropriation is too limited because its position is *related to the structure* that was embodied into the technology by the conceptors. So, for this author, in relation to a specific technology, users demonstrate a much greater creativity than "social constructivists" admit. That shows two things :

- Firstly, it is impossible to say that a technology is « stabilized », it can, however, be said that a technology is « stabilized-for-now » (Schryer, 1993) ;
- Secondly, the user's creativity is not in relation to the structure but in relation to numerous factors, which must be identified.

To accentuate these two elements, Orlikowski suggests replacing the term appropriation by « enactment », which she takes from Weick (1969), in order to designate the real use that actors make of a specific technology.

This conceptual shift allows Orlikowski to take distance with the « social constructivism » approach. However, she needs to propose a corresponding theory. The main question is to identify the factors, that explain why the enactment happens the way it does is needed. Orlikowski considers that when technology is used in recurrent social interactions, it corresponds to a « technology-in-practice » : an intangible shape, which intervenes in ongoing practices, through facilities, norms and interpretive schemes. Each type of « technology-in-practice » therefore shapes specific facilities, norms, and interpretive schemes which in turn transform the "technology-in-practice" that individuals enact.

Orlikowski (2000), considers "technology-in-practice" as structure she can then mobilize the theoretical framework of structuration to analyze it.

Figure 1. Enactment of technology-in-practice Orlikowski (Orlikowski, 2000, p.410)

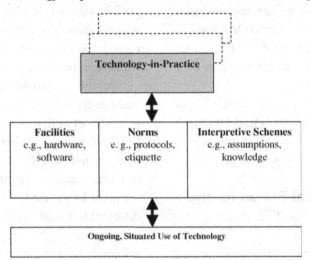

The structure « technology-in-practice » is in itself influenced by the other structures in the organization (hierarchy relations, remuneration/ incentive system, etc.)

All these structures and the interactions between structures are instantiated in recurrent social practice that employees maintain with the other members of the organization,

And the structures contribute in formalizing the facilities, norms, and interpretive schemes that shape their social interactions…

Therefore a detailed analysis of the different structures can explain a specific « technology-in-practice » that exists in the social environment of a individual and can be analyzed concretely through the facilities, norms and interpretive schemes by which the structures are instantiated in practice.

This IT structuration perspective developed by Orlikowski lead us to ask two questions: the first one concerns enactment transformation and the second one focuses on the role of the artifact in this transformation.

What Kind of Evolution for This Enactment?

In her article, Orlikowski (2000) clearly suggests continuing "the development of concepts that address the role of emergence and improvisation in technology" (p.411). Her propositions allow a better analysis of how improvisation can emerge. She also takes into consideration the fact that uses not only emerge: "users always have the potential to change their habits of use" (p.411). She even lists factors explaining the transformations: a change in the technology such as "deliberately modifying the properties of technology and thus how users interact with it" (p.411), a change due to experience ("users become more knowledgeable about using their technology" (p.412), or a change in their activity "they have changed jobs and now need to use technology differently"(p.412).

These changes can be deliberate as well as be produced by inadvertence. Because « technology-in-practice » is a structure, Orlikowski (2000) even adds that a change in structure will « change the facilities, norms and interpretive schemes used in their use of the technology » (p.412).

The case studies presented in this article are limited, however, they show how use emerges. It seems interesting to us to extend Orlikowski's reflexion by presenting a case study that describes how uses are transformed and not only how they emerge.

Over and above this first result, analysis will allow us to go more into depth in understanding certain use transformation mechanisms, which are merely evoked in Orlikowski's paper.

What Exact Theorical Status for the "Technology as Artifact"?

It seems that the very strong innovative side of Orlikowski's article (2000) has widened the gap between pre-existing literature and her own position. Particularly, it seems that her desire to show that users enact use that were not embodied into technology by their conceptors has led her to under estimate their role in technology construction.

More exactly, her article is ambiguous on this point. Firstly, she clearly states that conceptors do not embody structure into the technology they produce (Orlikowski, 2000, p.406) but later, she nevertheless, gives them certain recognition when she writes, « when people use a technology, they draw on the properties comprising the technological artifact—those provided by its constituent materiality, those inscribed by the designers, and those added on by users through previous interactions… » (p.410). She even conceptualizes this dimension when she states that technology has two aspects: « technology-in-practice » and « technology as artifact » (p.408). It still seems that she uses this difference to show that technology uses cannot be limited to analysis of its technological characteristics alone (p.409) and they must, necessarily, be linked to the actor's « technologies-in-practice ». This distinction allows for a true analytical breakthrough but there seems to be a crucial question still unanswered. Uses cannot be deduct from « technology as artifact » but it remains to be decided: Does « tech-

nology as artifact » play a role in enactment or not? Particularly, within the scope of our article, we will show how artifact transformation can be considered as a factor allowing for an enactment transformation.

On this question, Orlikowski's arguments leave us thinking that she accords a very limited role, almost null, to « technology as artifact » in use development. In her case studies she never actually makes a direct link between evolving enactment and « technology as artifact ». On the other hand, she links them systematically, to different forms of « technology-in practice ». As we have highlighted above, she has somewhat acknowledged the role of conceptor embodied technology characteristics. Citing some of her earlier work (Orlikowski and Gash, 1994), she also mentions that training and communication related to technology's functions could help develop uses. Finally, even if she does not mobilize them directly in her reflexion, her case studies start with a presentation of *Lotus notes* technical functions (Orlikowski, 2000, table 1, p.414). In her article, technology as artifact seems necessary in understanding enactment but it is not directly implicated in the analysis. An aim of our article is to offer several precisions on the status technology artifact could have in enactment analysis as drawn up by Orlikowski.

RESEARCH DESIGN

After describing how our research offers to extend Orlikowski's reflexion, we will present our methodology and detail our main results.

Technology as Artifact, User Centered Conception and Corporate Strategy

We have observed above that certain ambiguities in Orlikowski's presentation could be explained by the fact that she must position herself in relation to a dominant approach, that of "social constructivism". It seems to us that the ambiguities may also come from the way Orlikowski distributes the roles between conceptors and technology end-users. In fact, even if the text is not perfectly clear on this point, the reader could get the feeling that on one side there are technology conceptors and on the other people who use it. So, theoretical references exist which allow us to affirm that conception and use do not make-up two distinct phases in the technology life cycle and it is therefore, unjustified to oppose them (Akrich, 1998).

Based on this observation, more and more research conclude that a new type of « user centered » conception is necessary. Conceptors must take into consideration use when they create a new version to increase « user friendliness », responsiveness and therefore, user satisfaction. « User centered » conception first emerged in the Human Computer Interaction (HCI) community where conceptors goal is to create a more coherent link between a « new » tool and pre-existing user habits (Norman, 1988). Participative conception is a supplementary step in the intention to integrate users in the conception process from the very start (Darses, 2004). In fact, with this method, designers actually integrate users into conceptors teams (Cardon, 1997), instead of « representing » their needs through questionnaire statistics, situational work cases, films of user activities or use scenarios, etc. (Pascal, 2007). In this case, the users goal is to diagnose the problems encountered during use and to analyze videos of themselves using the prototype, etc. with the help of the researcher. Designers then, try to conceive a new prototype version that incorporates these remarks and reduces challenges encountered (Brun-Cottan & Wall, 1995).

Keeping in line with Orlikowski's approach, this type of conception could first avoid the main designer's errors. But, then, it could help us to give a more active role to artifact in use development. To analyze this situation completely it seems important to us, to stay in a strict « structurationist » framework, that is to clearly state that this « user centered » conception can favorize certain uses but that it can not lead users from a limited to a strategic use by itself, for example. To understand the role that this type of conception could eventually play in use transformation it seems essential to resituate it in relation to corporate structure and in relation to the dominant management style.

In fact, a reproach that can be made to this type of conception is to be too focused on the user. To develop technology use, conception must be based on more than just what the users want. For it, artifact modifications must answer user wishes as well as organizational strategic orientations. A use that represents a strong user demand but would be strictly opposite a firm's strategic aim seems generally unlikely to emerge. (Detchessahart & Journé, 2007). Some authors have already highlighted the importance of Top management's implication on uses (Deltour, 2004). Bhattacherjee (1998) underlines « organizational sponsoring » as being a major facilitator in corporate IT introduction. He explains it as management's effort to promote resource allocation and technology as added value within the organization.

Using the case study below, we will attempt to test the hypothesis, that a user-centered conception allows technology enactment transformation, when it is embedded into global corporate strategy.

Research Methodology

The research presented here is exploratory. Phenomena we will study are poorly known. Their boundaries and logics are uncertain. Therefore, the single case study seems to be the most adequate research method (Yin, 1994). Among data we collected in different firms[1], uses of an HR intranet in an aeronautical firm (called Aero) seem the most appropriate to develop insight. After presenting the firm and its intranet (2.2.1), we will describe the population we have selected for analysis (2.2.2).

Aero and its HR Intranet

Aero belongs to an international group in the Aeronautical and Space sector. In Europe, Aero has more than 12,000 employees. It is leader in High Tech apparatus construction. The group's activities occupy the complete supplier to customer process and range from R&D right through to specific hands-on training sessions for end users, including manufacturing (from raw materials), assembly lines, sales, delivery, after sales service, etc.

In 2000, a HR decision is taken to improve the management - employee communication policy. One of the actions was to develop a HR intranet offering access to all the employees from the firm's web site. Guiderdoni studied the use and social dynamics of this intranet from within the firm's communication department for four years from 2001 to 2005.

Two distinct phases can be identified in the intranet implementation. From 2000 to 2003, HR communication and information strategy is developed. Aero's HR director decides to grant the means and the tools necessary to manage and to control the diffusion and the quality of HR information. He creates an internal communication department under HR direction and implements simultaneous person-to-person actions as well as creating the "Corporate Intranet" (Kalika, Guillou & Laval, 2002) a HR intranet accessible to all the employees and offering, due to large diffusion, general HR information. From 2003, a new HR director reinforces the HR communication and information strategy. This translates into reinforcing the HR intranet team in quantity and in technical competencies. The "Corporate Intranet" then migrates towards a "Specialized HR Intranet" (Kalika, Guilloux & Laval, 2002) offering much more targeted HR information.

The aim of this article is to understand how and why the intranet was transformed this way and if that transformation affects the way certain employees use the tool.

Sample Population Description

To analyze use transformation, longitudinal research was necessary (King, Keohane & Verba, 1994). Data collection took place between 2001 and 2005. During this whole period, we used data triangulation and saturation (Miles & Huberman, 1994) by mobilizing different research methods: documentary analysis (in particular corporate archives), semi-directive interviews and participating HR intranet project observation.

We also administered two opinion surveys on the use of this intranet. The first phase of interviews took place in 2001. Three employee groups were identified: department managers or equivalent, level 1 (a department has about 200 people), sub-department managers or equivalent, level 2 (management of about 50 people) and team leaders, level 3 (management of about 10 people). 53 semi-structured interviews were conducted. The second phase of interviews took place in 2005 and there were 13 interviews. Only actors who were identified during the first phase as having specific uses (positive or negative) were targeted, the objective was to verify if the uses had been transformed.

With regard to this study, we have benefited by the use of coding techniques and derived 9 code labels from the interview tapes and have spread the data between these different themes. Throughout the coding analysis stage, the author made a number of changes to the list of codes; the coding stage was a interactive process through which patterns from the interviews emerged (Miles & Huberman, 1994). Initially, first-level coding was carried out as a data reduction technique summarising large segments of data, and finally pattern coding was employed as a way of identifying core themes across the interviews (Miles & Huberman, 1994).

The above sample shows that data on use was gathered all the way up the hierarchy. Nevertheless, in this article, we cannot present all our results. We have chosen to focus on one actor, the one for whom the eventual transformation of use best allows to complete Orlikowski's (2000) thought: the Assembly Line Manager.

In 2001, we identified this actor's dominant intranet use as a « limited use ». We identified the « facilities », the « norms » and the « interpretive schemes » he used to enact this "technology-in-practice" in his daily activity. We interviewed 4 Assembly Line Managers again in 2005 and analyzed the case of those with whom the HR intranet use was transformed. We were then able to identify their new « facilities », « norms » and « interpretive schemes » but we especially asked them to explain the reasons for this transformation. Their account shows that the 2001 opinion survey allowed user demands to emerge. On this basis, conceptors of Intranet developed a second version better adapted to user expectations (« user centered » conception phenomenon).

But that data highlight the fact that this conception mode is not solely responsible for strongly increasing intranet use. In fact, users underlined several times that this new HR intranet conception is pertinent because it allows a major corporate strategic axe to be implemented. Top management demands department chiefs to become real « *managers* » (this goes beyond intranet, itself). It seems, therefore, that it is the efficient combination of « user centered » conception and general corporate strategy, which allowed use transformation for certain Assembly Line Managers.

RESULTS

After positioning the Assembly Line Managers in the organization, we'll use Orlikowski's concepts (2000) to describe the way they used the HR intranet in 2001. After replace use within the overall corporate policy, we will describe how certain uses were recuperated by conceptors and integrated into the new 2003 Intranet version. Finally we will detail Assembly Line Manager's uses of the new 2005 HR Intranet.

Assembly Line Managers, « Very Managers », Less « Corporate » HR Intranet Users

The Assembly Line Manager's survey conducts us to enter a different world: the world of production, precisely industrial workshops and manufacturing lines (airplanes, helicopters, etc.). In « his » world, « his » workshop, the line manager is « master ». Corporate management has little hold on this world. The line manager is generally a charismatic leader, a man of action with a strong personality, respected for his integrity, an excellent technician with a human dimension capable of making « *fair* » decisions.

Nevertheless, he is under the pressure of high production rates. Respecting final assembly dates push him to be very demanding (overtime, Sundays, etc.) of the different teams he manages. The work rhythm is so intense that the border between private and professional life is often over stepped. This leader must be extremely close to his « *guys* » in order to achieve objectives.

« *We are also top management's representatives in the shop, so it's our job to maintain a positive social atmosphere, that means we have to be on the field constantly, so the guys are happy to come to work every day. It's also a sensitive position, because you must be attentive: if a worker is not right or upset, you have to go and see him quickly. Talking with him, you understand that his child is sick or his wife left him ... so, that's when you have to take the time and support him. You have to maintain direct contact* ». (William)

He is considered as the guarantor of team spirit that can be found in the sectors used to working with permanent urgencies[2]. This leader manages an average of more than 200 workers. Generally he works his way up through the ranks. Because of that, he usually holds the technicity of the product close to his heart.

How does this type of person consider the HR intranet? He spontaneously states: « I feel more at home in the workshop than behind a computer » (William). In 2001, the survey results are therefore not very surprising: use of the HR intranet is rare or inexistent. The tool is seen as « a waste of time » because « we can get the information elsewhere » (Jean). Orlikowski's concepts of (facilities, norms et interpretive schemes) allow to better describe this « limited use ».

By limiting facilities analysis to the sole HR intranet artifact, we can observe it is of a « corporate » type: the same space is accessible to all the employees, whatever their hierarchy level. The HR information is very general. It cannot satisfy specific demands of line managers (bonus management, salary increases, etc.). Concerning behavioral « norms », production rate pressure makes them favorize face to face or telephone communication systematically (William, Jean, Jesus). This behavior is also possible in the HR field because there is a decentralized HR manager in each workshop. The line manager has quick contact (which corresponds to his work rhythm) with that person on a targeted subject (corresponds to his needs). The HR intranet is, therefore, rarely

Figure 2. Assembly line bosses use HR intranet in 2001

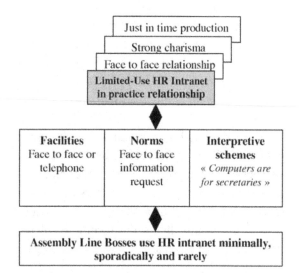

used because it is contrary to these exchange modes. Finally, in terms of interpretive schemes, a computer is associated to secretarial tasks by these actors. We can see here a supplementary reason for limited use of the intranet by this population.

Using Orlikowski's (2000) conceptual schema shown in Figure 2, we can describe the line manager's « limited uses ».

A « User Centered » HR Intranet Re-Conception Coherent with Global Corporate Strategy

The team in charge of the HR intranet requested that 53 interviews to be administered to collect users opinions. Criticisms listed below are potential improvements for second version conception of the system. In fact, it can be deducted that if managers found information on the intranet corresponding to their real needs and that if they found strategic information that they could not find « elsewhere » their use could increase. During these interviews, they also added an element that we had not yet evocated : they would like to find more tools to manage team member's competencies, careers, etc.

These wishes expressed by the users were globally taken into account by the conceptors of the second version. In the latest version there is no longer a global platform for all the employees. There are now three distinct and independent portals: one for employees, one for managers and one dedicated to Human resources. The first platform is still open to all employees and continues to contain general HR information.

On the other hand, the second platform, reserved for managers, answers the questions expressed by line managers directly. This space contains the HR tools they requested, specific and adapted HR information and strategic information they should not be able to obtain through other channels (telephone, informal discussions, etc.), informations about corporate projects, strategic evolution, etc. Reporting of regular round table discussions between the CEO and a few managers can also be found here. This information offers a strategic dimension that the first version did absolutely not have. As we mentioned above, it's possible to consider that in 2003 the firm evolved from a « corporate » HR intranet to a « specialized HR intranet » in order to satisfy user expectations.

The intranet artifact reforming seems to have been positive because several line managers we interviewed in 2005 stated they used intranet more at that time than they had before. They did, however, systematically link their increased use of the system to a global transformation of general corporate policy. In fact, in 2003 a whole new team of general managers (CEO, HRD, etc.) moved into the firm. The line managers, along with all the others, received at that time, an order to change their management styles. Communication around management was « *omni-present in the firm, they lay it on us in every meeting that we have* » (Gilles). Even if certain managers can criticize the new management's latest trend, most of them are not chocked by the obvious will for change. In fact, the firm's management had not waited for 2003 to start evolving and finally, the arrival of a new team is often perceived as intensifying existing and relatively legitimate policies.

The precisions on this context are important because they allow to gain perspective about, on one hand, uses developed by certain people, use that stays unchanged for the majority and hence, the interest but the limits of « user centered » conception. Indeed, the line managers, who use intranet more in the second version, do so undoubtedly, because the « user centered » conception bred an artifact more in line with their expectations but especially because the new approach led to a specific intranet that helped them to play their new role in a privileged fashion such as in information transmission. This role is now expected of them from their direct hierarchy as

well as top management. They do not consider intranet, in and of itself, but as a tool allowing them to embody the role they want and the role that management wants them to take on.

Everyone does not, however, follow this logic because some of the line managers met in 2005 did not accept to take on the above-mentioned role. Despite reaffirmed corporate policy and « user centered » conception as a means, we observe that a significant number of managers have maintained their traditional role as leaders preferring face-to-face relations rather than computerized tools even if they are specific and strategic.

Certain Uses Have Been Deeply Transformed With the New HR Intranet

To specify the new use characteristics of some of the line managers, we suggest using Orlikowski's (2000) analysis grid again. In 2001, most uses were limited. In 2005, some of them have a more intensive use that can be qualified as « utilitarian ». Concerning « facilities », these line managers say they now read and use top management's information tools on strategic communication. They also use certain HR team management tools that were put on line such as absence management workflow charts.

In terms of behavioral norms, the face-to-face relationships are still privileged as one manager declared "*I participated in* [a round table discussion with the CEO]. *I found it good because it allowed me to ask direct questions. Direct communication is the best kind of communication.*" (Jean) However, some leaders evolve in relation to this point and, in fact, find themselves more in phase with supports offered on the intranet, as another manager states: « *what's new is the way top management initiated change ... We aren't passive anymore but active... Concerning intranet, the novelty is that it's a reference for us... We have never used the manager's platform as much. It's a credible system, more user friendly.* » (Jesus)

Figure 3. Assembly line bosses use HR intranet in 2005

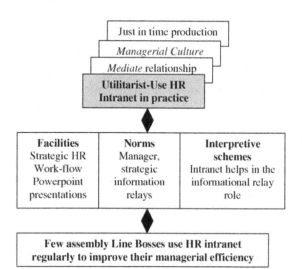

In coherence with these new norms, interpretive schemes have also evolved. Even if some managers continue to say, "*in production, a good manager is in his workshop most of the time*", a manager who uses the intranet states, "*Communication has really evolved... I'm in corporate training, the intranet is really interesting, we can find references to management books, I received a Powerpoint presentation about global corporate strategic orientations and major priorities. The document was reproduced down to the lowest level. For me, I'm in perfect coherence with my company's, [as well as, the group it belongs to] strategic objectives*" (Jean). We are far from the idea that "*computers are for secretaries...*" (William).

Orlikowski's (2000) concepts allow a synthesis of HR intranet uses by « utilitarian » line mangers using the schema shown in Figure 3.

CONCLUSION

The literature review showed that we have few elements on use of IT developed in firms. Orlikowski's (2000) work seems to be the first

to offer a real theoretical frame to analyze and understand it.

Based on this author's concepts, we have analyzed HR intranet use by line managers in an important aeronautical firm. The voluntary managers barely used the system because it was in profound contradiction with dominant structures of their activity: very strong time constraints, preference for face-to-face communication and charismatic based authority. Even though use was extremely low, the survey, which aimed at identifying the reasons for the low engagement, allowed the intranet management team to develop a second version that partially satisfied expectations, that is to say, it offered HR tools and "hot" HR informations on major projects and corporate strategy.

During the second phase interviews, certain actors clearly certified that the « user-centered » HR intranet conception allowed them to develop their own uses but they added that because the IT system was coherent with global corporate strategy (all the tools, and not only the HR intranet, were used to promote the new managerial vision) it played such an important role in use development.

This exploratory research seems to develop a concrete example of how use can be transformed (and not only emerge as Orlikowski's case studies demonstrate) but also the role that technology artifact can play in the development of use.

REFERENCES

Akrich, M. (1998). Users and Players of Innovation. *Education permanente, 134*, 79-89.

Bardini, T., & Horvath, A.T. (1995). The social construction of personal computer use. *Journal of communication, 45*(3), summer, 40-65.

Beyer, H., & Holzblatt K. (1998). *Contextual Design: Defining Customer-Centred Systems.* New York: Morgan Kaufmann.

Bhattacherjee, A. (1998). Management of emerging technologies experiences and lessons learned at US West. *Information and Management, 33*(5), 263-272.

Bijker, W. B., & Law, J. (Ed.). (1992). *Shaping Technology/Building Society: studies in socio-technical change.* Cambridge/MA, London: MIT Press.

Bijker, W. E. (1987). The social construction of Bakelite: Toward a Theory of Invention. In W. E. Bijker, T. Hughes, & T. Pinch (Eds.), *The Social Construction of Technological Systems: New Directions in the Sociolo.gy and History of Technology.* Cambridge MA/London: MIT Press.

Bowers, J. (1995). Making it work. A field study of a CSCW Network. *The Information Society, 11*, 189-207.

Brun-Cottan F., & Wall P. (1995). Using Video to Re-Present the User. *Communication of the ACM, 38*(5), 61-71.

Cardon, D. (1997). Social sciences and machines for cooperation. *Réseaux,* (85), 11-52.

Darses, F. (2004). *Psychological Processes of Collective Problem Resolution Conception: Contribution to Ergonomic Psychology.* Unpublished HDR in Ergonomic Psychology, University of Paris V, France.

Deltour, F. (2004). *Satisfaction, acceptation, impacts: A Multi dimensional and Contextualized Analysis of Individual Intranet Assessment.* Unpublished doctoral dissertation, University of Paris IX, France.

DeSanctis, G., & Poole, S. (1994). Capturing the complexity in advanced technology use: Adaptive structuration theory. *Organization Science, 5*(2), 121-147.

Detchessahar M., & Journé B. (2007). Une approche narrative des outils de gestion. *Revue française de gestion, 174*, 77-92.

Giddens, A. (1984). *The Constitution of Society.* Berkeley, California: University of Canada Press.

Greif, I. (Ed.). (1988). *Computer Supported Cooperative Work.* New-York: Morgan Kaufman.

Grudin, J. (1988). Why CSCW applications fail. Problems in the design and evaluation of organizational interfaces. *Proceedings of the CSCW'88* (pp. 85-93). New-York: ACM/Sigchi and Sigois.

Guiderdoni, K. (2006). Assessment of an HR intranet through middle managers' positions and uses: how to manage the plurality of this group in the beginning of an e-HR conception. *Proceeding of the 1st European Academic Workshop on E-HRM,* University of Twente, The Netherlands.

King, G., Keohane, R. O., & Verba, S. (1994). *Designing Social Inquiry.* Princeton, Princeton University Press.

Laval, F., Guilloux, V., & Kalika, M. (2002), HR Intranets: Firms' Practices and Problematics In F. Laval, V. Guilloux, M. Kalika, & M. Matmati (Eds.), *E-GRH: Revolution or Evolution? Manage the Challenge of IT Integration in the HR Function* (pp. 63-90). Paris : Editions Liaisons.

MacKenzie, D., & Wajcman, J. (Eds.). (1985). *The Social Shaping of Technology: How the Refrigerator Got Its Hum.* Milton Keynes: Open University Press.

Marakas, G. M., & Hornik, S. (1996). Passive resistance misuse: Overt support and covert recalcitrance in IS implementation. *European Journal of Information Systems, 5*(3), 208-219.

Markus, M. L. (1983). Power, Politics and MIS Implementation. *Communications of the ACM, 26*(6), 430-444.

Markus, M. L., & Connoly, T. (1990). Why CSCW applications fail. Problems in the adoption of interdependent work tools. *Proceedings of the CSCW'90* (pp. 7-10). Los Angeles.

Miles, M. B., & Huberman, A. M. (1994). *Analysis for qualitative data: collection of new methods.* Bruxelles : De Boeck University.

Norman, D. (1988). *The Psychology of Everyday Things.* New-York: Basic Books.

Olson, T. K., & Teasley, S. (1996). Groupware in the wild. Lessons learned from a year of virtual collocation. *Proceedings of the CSCW'96* (pp. 362-369). Boston: ACM Press.

Orlikowski, W., & Gash D.C. (1994). Technological frames: Making sense of information technology in organizations. *ACM Transactions on information systems, 2*(2), 143-169.

Orlikowski, W., & Robey D. (1991). Information Technology and the Structuring of organisations. *Information Systems Research, 2,* 143-169.

Orlikowski, W. (2000). Using technology and constituting structures: a practice lens for studying technology in organizations. *Organization Science, 11*(4), 404-428.

Pascal, A. (2006). *Conception of an IT Solution to Favorize Innovative Project Emergence: Approach by Use. The KMP Experience.* Unpublished doctoral dissertation, University of Nice-Sophia Antipolis, France.

Pascal, A., & Thomas, C. (2007). Role of boundary objects in the coevolution of design and use: the KMP experimentation. *Proceedings of 23rd EGOS Colloquium.* Vienna July 5—7.

Ruta, C. D. (2005). The application of change management theory to the HR portal implementation in subsidiaries of multinational corporations. *Human Resource Management, 44*(1), 35–53.

Schryer, C. F. (1993). Records as Genre. *Written Communication, 10,* 200-234.

Strohmeier, S. (2006). Coping with contradictory consequences of e-HRM, *Proceedings of the 1ˢᵗ academic workshop on e-HRM research,* University of Twente, The Netherlands .

Weick K. E. (1969). *The social Psychology of Organizing.* Reading, MA: Addison Wesly.

Whisler, T. L. (1970). *The impact of computers on organisations.* New York: Praeger.

Woolgar, S. (1991). Configuring the user The case of usability trials. In J. Law, (Ed.), *A sociology of monsters. Essays on power, technology and domination* (pp. 58-99). London: Routledge.

Yin R. K. (1994). *Case Study Research : Design and Methods.* London: Sage.

KEY TERMS

HR Intranet: Intranet is a network based on TCP/IP protocol, which can be linked to Internet. HR intranet is the part of this tool dedicated to on-line services offered by the Human Resources department.

Middle Management: The category of population characterizes by its specific position between the Board of Management and the staff. This population is one of the most important HR clients to satisfy, because they are considered as a key factor in the company's transformation through managerial style and discourse.

Strategy: Global mid-term orientation of an organization supposed to give it a strong advantage compared to other firms in the market.

Structurational Perspective on Technology: Wanda Orlikowski (2000) proposes to mobilize the structurational theory (Giddens, 1984) to explain why users develop different uses of a common technology. She distinguishes two aspects in a technology :
- **Technology as a technical artifact:** "which has been constructed with particular materials and inscribed with developers' assumptions and knowledge about the world at a point in time" (Thomas, Pascal, 2007),

- **Technology as a technology-in-practice:** "which refers to the specific structure routinely enacted by individuals as they use the artifact in recurrent ways in their everyday situated activities" (Thomas, Pascal, 2007).

Those recurrent interactions and those "situated activities" are different by themselves but, more than that, they are "situated in the structural properties of social systems. Thus, in interacting with a technology, users mobilize many structurals, those borne by the technology itself, and those deriving from different contexts (group, community, organization, company, etc.) in which their uses are developed." (Thomas, Pascal, 2007). In this perspective, those different interactions and those different structurals explain the diversity of uses of a common technology.

User-Centered Design (UCD): User-centered design is a project approach that puts the needs, wants and limitations of intended users of a technology at the centre of each stage of its design and development. It does this by talking directly to the user at key points in the project to make sure the technology will deliver upon their requirements. In this project approach, such testings are necessary because it is considered as impossible for the designers to anticipate how real users interact with the technology they propose.

Chapter VI
In–House vs. Off–the–Shelf e–HRM Applications

Nawaf Al-Ibraheem
KNET, Kuwait

Huub Ruël
University of Twente, The Netherlands & American University of Beirut, Lebanon

ABSTRACT

Companies new to the e-HRM technologies are overwhelmed by the dilemma of choosing either the ready-made, off-the-shelf e-HRM systems, or develop their own e-HRM systems in house in order to implement the e-HR transformation. Therefore, this research was done to shed some light on the differences and similarities between off-the-shelf e-HRM systems and in-house developed ones, with regards to some elements developed in a preliminary framework, such as the implementation and development approaches, e-HRM activities they facilitated, application types and characteristics, and e-HRM outcome and benefits. This comparison provided insightful information that could help companies make the most effective choice between the two systems. It was found through this research that factors such as continuous user involvement, effective communication, and strong change management are most considered by companies that develop e-HRM in house, while advocates of off-the-shelf e-HRM systems are most affected by success factors such as business process reengineering, planning and vision, and project management. Another finding was that increasing efficiency, providing customer-oriented service excellence, and improving self services were top goals accomplished by companies developing their e-HRM system in house. These findings, beside many other ones discovered in this research, would help companies decide which system best fits their needs and accomplish high levels of effectiveness gained from the transformation of their HR function to e-HR.

INTRODUCTION

Human Resources Management has always been the first business process to use the emerging technologies of the new era. As a matter of fact, Payroll Administration is known to be one of the earliest business processes to be automated (Lengnick-Hall and Mortiz 2003, p.365). Through the use of technology and information systems, human resources departments of companies around the world are able to use computers to log employees' data and interact electronically with them. These functions and more are offered to Human Resources personnel and other employees through what is called the *Electronic Human Resources Management*, or e-HRM.

Since the 1960s many firms (large and small) all over the globe have been implementing IT-based Human Resources Management applications in order to reduce the amount of associated costs. Ball (2001) pointed out that by 1998, 60 percent of the Fortune 500 companies used a Human Resources Information System (HRIS) to support daily HRM operations. The main benefits of HRISs are focused on improved accuracy, the provision of timely and quick access to information, and the savings of costs (Ngai & Wat, 2006 based on Lederer, 1984; Tetz, 1973; Wille & Hammond, 1981). For the human resources activities, e-HR has the potential to enhance efficiency by reducing cycle times for processing paperwork, increasing data accuracy, and reducing human resources workforce (Lengnick-Hall and Mortiz, 2003). Effectiveness can also be influenced by empowering both employees and managers to make better, accurate, and timely decisions (Lengnick-Hall and Mortiz, 2003).

HRIS started to be more internet-technology based since the second half of 1990's, where its aim was not only to support the HR department itself, but to target managers and employees' effectiveness. The term electronic Human Resources Management (e-HRM) was coined and has become a dominating label for HRM services delivered through internet-technology based applications. Ruël et al (2004) define e-HRM as a way of consciously implementing HRM practices, policies and strategies supported by or fully delivered through internet-technology based applications. Terms like Management Self-Service (MSS) and Employee Self Service (ESS) started to be used as well. The purposes of implementing e-HRM systems broadened in comparison to those connected to HRISs.

During the e-commerce era in the 1990s, the term e-HRM emerged to basically refer to conducting Human Resources Management functions using the Internet (Lengnick-Hall and Mortiz 2003, p. 365). Nowadays, many organizations are implementing e-HRM within the strategic design of their core businesses. Some Organizations require the use of standardized HR management tools such as payroll, employee benefits, recruitment, training, etc. These organizations mainly refer to off-the-shelf e-HRM solutions offered by third party such as Oracle, PeopleSoft, SAP, or IBM, where they perceive efficiency and fulfilment in these ready-made systems. Others require customized Human Resources Information Systems (HRIS) tailored to best fit their business's needs. One of the key advantages of in-house developed HRISs is that they save HR staff time in dealing with the elements of the application as they already know and understand the parameters of their own software (Thaler-Carter 1998, p.22).

One objective therefore becomes the main purpose of this research and that is to compare and contrast the in-house developed and off-the-shelf e-HRM systems with regards to their implementation, associated costs, usage, and effectiveness.

LITERATURE BACKGROUND

An essential step in e-HRM systems implementation is the decision whether to buy an off-the-shelf e-HRM software package (in many cases part of an Enterprise Resource Planning (ERP) package like Oracle/Peoplesoft or SAP) or to develop e-HRM systems in-house. As Kovach et al. (2002) describe, a small company might prefer to depend on consultants and outsource all aspects of design, implementation, and operation, while a large company could prefer to opt for in-house development of e-HRM systems by their own IT department. Widely believed benefits of off-the-shelf systems in general are time-saving, proven system quality, and availability of expertise through the provider. On the contrary, disadvantages of off-the-shelf systems are the lack of customization/flexibility and dependency on vendor-expertise. In order to avoid these down-sides companies might opt for in-house development of an HRIS system. Exact figures regarding the differences/similarities between off-the-shelf e-HRM and in-house developed e-HRM, do not really exist.

To take further the point issued by Kovach et al (2002), in case of e-HRM, the acceptance and usage of applications by employees and managers is critical to successful implementation and the generation of results. That makes the decision whether to 'buy or make' even more important, and seems to favor in-house development over off-the-shelf implementation. However funded knowledge on this issue is lacking so far.

The annual CedarCrestone survey (2006) shows that many organizations lay out more expenses for outsourced solutions (mainly off-the-shelf) than they do for in-house development. Three main reasons are explained: organizations with in-house software development mostly have fragmented system operations which cause them to overlook embedded costs within distributed operations; outsourcing assures better view and control of costs; and outsourcing is a solution for organizations that struggle to control costs due to the complexity of their operations (*HR Technology Trends to Watch in 2007* 2007, p. 1). On the other hand, the CedarCrestone survey (2006) notes that some respondents sense that in-house HR solutions positively affect employees' productivity and can be easily and swiftly integrated into the current

system, while off-the-shelf software would cause difficulties during the integration phase.

In this study, the authors will concentrate on the issue of the differences and similarities between off-the-shelf and in-house developed e-HRM implementations. We define implementation broadly, from the first initiation to the evaluation of results of e-HRM, and semi-technical (i.e. type of applications/functionality/design) and organizational issues (i.e. change management, HR restructuring, etc).

Technology plays the role of enabler that helps HR to deliver the workforce support and management based on business needs (Gueutal & Stone 2005, p. 2). New web technologies have enabled HR to perform certain paperless tasks that used to consume time and human resources in the old ages of HR. Furthermore, technology-enabled HR functions have evolved into human capital management (HCM), as Gueutal and Stone (2005, p. 2) agree with Ruël et al. in stating that HCM and e-HR are the responsibilities of everyone in an organization, from employees to executives. Nevertheless, Hendrickson (2003, p. 383) stresses the fact that this change in information technology has created significant challenges for HR professionals to get updated with the latest information technology while simultaneously transforming HR processes to e-processes.

From these definitions arises a general understanding of what e-HRM is. In this research, e-HRM is the management of an HR network that connects employees, managers, and HR staff through web-technology-enabled channels that provide them with an electronic access to human resources transactions, strategies, policies, and practices.

Benefits, Goals, and Objectives of e-HRM

The fast changing world of business stipulates organizational flexibility, capability, and rapid response in order to succeed (Lepak & Snell

1998, p. 215). Therefore, e-HRM must attain objectives such as strategy-oriented focus, flexibility, cost containment, and service-providing excellence (Lepak & Snell 1998, p. 215). Strategic orientation can be achieved by concentrating on the transformational HR activities mentioned in section 2.2, while flexibility can be reached by updating HR processes, policies, and practices to counter the rapidly changing business world. Efficiency, on the other hand, can be achieved by many ways such as staff reduction, elimination of manual processes, and timeliness. However, cost reduction can only be considered beneficial if there is no loss of effectiveness or deterioration of customer service excellence (Schramm 2006, p. 3). Hendrickson (2003) agrees that efficiency is one of the goals of implementing e-HRM that can be rendered by increasing number of HR transactions and timeliness without affecting needed resources.

Another benefit of using e-HRM is the increased effectiveness of human resources management through the use of technology which simplifies HR processes and enhances performance (Hendrickson 2003, p. 385). Beer et al. (1984) distinguish four different benefits or outcomes from e-HRM: commitment, competence, congruence, and cost effectiveness. Commitment is achieved by motivating employees to interact with managers cohesively during changes to achieve organizational goals (Ruël et al. 2004, p. 369). High competence is when employees learn new tasks and gain competitive skills to enhance their contribution, effectiveness, and creativity. Congruence is also another benefit of implementing e-HRM that involves structuring the business from the inside out in the best interest of stakeholders (Ruël et al. 2004, p. 369). Cost effectiveness aims at increasing the level of economical value based on the tangible and intangible benefits produced by the amount of resources spent (i.e. money, time, human resources, etc). A cost effective e-HRM system, however, is one that provides adequate e-HRM services for the reasonable HR-related costs it incurs during and after the implementation stage such as employee turnover, resistance, and confusion.

A typical agreement by most authors proves that efficiency is a top goal considered by many organizations that use e-HRM. Cost reduction is also agreed upon to be the main benefit of e-HRM. Other benefits might not be as noticeable or tangible as efficiency. Lengnick-Hall and Moritz (2003) divide the outcome of e-HRM into tangible and intangible benefits. Tangible benefits include process and administrative cost reduction, staff reduction, transaction processing speed-up, elimination of information errors, and improvement in tracking and controlling HR activities (Lengnick-Hall & Moritz 2003, p. 369). Intangible benefits are mostly associated with the indirect effect of e-HRM on the HR function. Such benefits are improvement in employee productivity and morale, decision making, and information sharing. Innovation enhancement and time-to-market acceleration might also be considered as intangible benefits of e-HRM (Lengnick-Hall & Moritz 2003, p. 369).

To summarize this section, the author will consider the following main goals of implementing e-HRM within organizations:

- Increase efficiency by reducing cost and eliminating unnecessary functions.
- Provide management and employee self-service mechanisms.
- Improve HR's strategic focus.
- Achieve client service excellence.

On the other hand, different outcomes can be gained from implementing e-HRM within an organization. For this research, the following outcomes will be considered:

- Commitment.
- Competence.
- Cost Effectiveness.
- Congruence.

e-HRM Applications

e-HRM applications (as depicted in Figure 1) represent the outmost layer of the human resources management model suggested in this research. This model suggests that the outer layers comprise all of the elements of the inner ones. Therefore, the application layer includes all the basic requirements and functions of HRM and e-HRM including its types, goals, and benefits. E-HRM applications are wide in range and they provide a variety of automated HR activities that enchant the HR function with flexibility and ease of use. In an exclusive survey by IOMA (2002) professionals reported that e-HRM applications which are most preferred by users are those that possess high levels of integration and processing capabilities, user friendliness, robustness, and reporting. Furthermore, e-HRM studies with emphasis on the Technology Acceptance Model (Davis et al. 1989) has exhausted the use and outcome of e-HRM applications and determined that they are mainly dependant on the *usefulness* and *ease of use* of such applications (Ruta 2005). On one hand, usefulness is defined by Davis et al. (1989, p. 985) as "the prospective user's subjective

probability that using a specific application system will increase his or her job performance within an organizational context". This means in order for the e-HRM system to be perceived by users as useful, positive impact on the organizational performance of an employee must be observed during or after the use of the e-HRM applications. Davis et al. (1989, p. 985), on the other hand, define the perceived ease of use as "the degree to which the prospective user expects the target system to be free of effort." E-HRM applications could be perceived by employees as "easy to use" if it doesn't require effort to be operated.

The combination of e-HRM definition produced in section 2.1 with the general understanding of e-HRM applications mentioned here yields a predominant meaning for e-HRM applications:

E-HRM applications are the software programs that offer a useful and easy-to-use electronic medium, through which the e-HRM goals are accomplished by performing different types of human resources activities electronically to yield the desired outcome and benefits.

This definition explains the layered approach shown in Figure 1 but, nevertheless, it doesn't explain the types of these software applications. The following section suggests a few types of e-HRM applications that have been discussed in previous literature.

Types of e-HRM Applications

e-HRM applications can be specified under different categories according to the HR activities they facilitate electronically. Seven types have been identified by Florkowski and Olivas-Luján (2006) and divided into two predominant groups: software applications that target HR staff as end users, and those that target internal staff (managers and employees) as end users. The types that target HR staff are *HR functional applications*

Figure 1. e-HRM layers

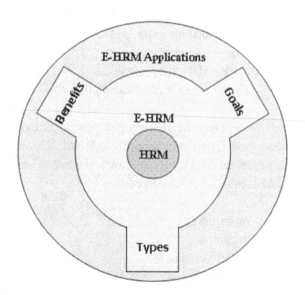

and *integrated HR suite applications*. Those that focus on managers and employees as end users are *Interactive Voice Response (IVR) systems, HR intranet applications, self-service applications, HR extranet applications, HR portal applications* (Florkowski & Olivas-Luján 2006, p. 687).

The CedarCrestone annual report (2007), on the other hand, divides over 30 e-HRM applications into the following groups:

Administrative applications, including core HR functions such as payroll, benefits, and HR management system. This category handles most of the operational type of HR activities—mentioned under section 2.2—that are administered by the HR staff. The report identifies three major activities that belong to this group as payroll, HR management system, and benefits administration (CedarCrestone annual report 2007).

Employee and manager productivity applications which provide self service transactions that aim at improving service delivery, reducing cost, and enabling employees and managers to concentrate more on core processes (CedarCrestone annual report 2007). These applications also provide access to operational HR activities performed only by managers and employees such as benefit-related self service (BSS), simple management reporting (SMR), pay-related self services (PSS), employee self services (ESS), time management self service (TMSS), total benefits statements (TBS), HR-oriented help desk, and manager self service (MSS).

Strategic HCM applications, such as talent management, training enrollment, competency management, e-learning, compensation, performance, succession planning, and career planning. These applications transform relational HR activities into their electronic version.

Business intelligence applications comprise HR data warehousing, operational reporting, HR scorecard, and analytics that help develop the strategic focus of an organization. These applications are the protagonists of e-HRM. They facilitate the transformational activities that help develop the strategic orientation of the HR function.

Looking at the adoption level of e-HRM applications, Financial Services seem to top other businesses in leading the e-commerce market of human resources management by automating most of its HR activities with the help of the application sets mentioned above (CedarCrestone annual report 2007). On the contrary, CedarCrestone reports that the least business categories to adopt e-HRM technologies are Retail and Public Administration. The top players in e-HRM application software market are Oracle/PeopleSoft, ADP, SAP, and Kronos, as most of the applications mentioned above are supported by these giants and favored by a plethora of HR departments around the world.

e-HRM Applications Implementation and Development Approaches

The implementation and development of the e-HRM application doesn't require a set of critical success factors or approaches different than those constituted by Enterprise Resource Planning (ERP) projects or large enterprise portal projects, as e-HRM is considered a part of ERP implementation itself. These large projects differ from traditional information system projects in scale, scope, complexity, organizational changes, costs, and need for business process reengineering (Remus 2007, p. 538). As a result, technical and business difficulties during the implementation and development of these systems (including e-HRM systems) are imminent. Literature has it that these difficulties are widely spread, but only fragmented research was done regarding the critical success factors and approaches to ERP implementation (Nah et al. 2001, p. 286). These approaches were narrowed down to the ones shown in Table 2, which have been previously identified by academic articles as shown in the table.

Table 1. e-HRM approaches

	Lee & Lee (2001)	Nah et al. (2001)	Al-Sehali (2000)	Remus (2007)
User involvement	✗		✗	✗
Business process reengineering	✗	✗		✗
Planning & strategy	✗	✗	✗	✗
Training & education	✗		✗	✗
Change management		✗	✗	✗
Top management support		✗	✗	✗
Effective communication		✗		✗
Project management		✗		✗

User Involvement

User involvement in the early stages of the implementation and development phases of the e-HRM system allows users to make adjustments to the system to satisfy their needs. Consequently, organizational resistance to the new changes implied by the use of the e-HRM applications is minimized and customer satisfaction is increased (Lee & Lee 2001, p. 208). Change management processes in this case are minimized and easily controlled.

Business Process Reengineering

Achieving benefits through the implementation of an enterprise system is impossible without the inevitable alignment of processes and activities with the new system requirements (Remus 2007; Bingi et al. 1999). This means that when a company implements a new e-HRM system, some of the HR processes must be reengineered in order for the e-HRM system to be more effective. Such reengineering mechanism is applied when transforming HR manual processes to paperless forms. Reengineering should begin before choosing the software system to make sure changes are accepted by the stakeholders and the processes can actually be aligned with the new system (Nah et al. 2001, p. 294).

Planning and Vision

A solid business plan needs to be defined in order for the ERP project to be directed toward the proposed strategic and tangible benefits, resources, costs, risks, and timeline (Buckhout et al. 1999). This means for e-HRM implementation to be successful, a plan must be agreed upon by the project manager or the responsible parties to follow during the project life cycle. This plan will guarantee the alignment of the e-HRM goals and strategy with the HR and corporate strategies to ensure maximum effectiveness, integration, and alignment. Lee and Lee (2001) insist that good planning consumes a considerable amount of time prior to implementation. This ensures that the e-HRM system is thoroughly exploited and efficiently implemented to coincide with the corporate strategies.

Training and Education

Since the e-HRM system offers new methods of processing transformed or new HR activities, proper training must be given to all users of the system. This becomes crucial since the new interface provides functionality that has never been used before and needs to be related to the newly reengineered business processes (Remus 2007, p. 544). Education is the catalyst that brings the knowledge of the users up to the point where they can familiarize themselves with the new e-HRM system quickly and sufficiently.

Change Management

Managing change within the organization could be a full time job by itself, as it requires the management of people and their expectations, resistance to change, confusion, redundancies, and errors (Remus 2007, p. 541). For the e-HRM to be successfully implemented, the organization should realize the impact of this new change on employees, managers, and HR staff and understand its dimensions in order to manage the effects with a corporate strategy that is open to change. Furthermore, emphasis on quality, computing ability, and willingness to accept the new technology would positively assist the implementation effort (Nah et al. 2001, p. 293). Training and education is a critical step in managing change itself, as employees must be educated about the new system to understand how it changes business processes (Nah et al. 2001, p. 293).

Top Management Support

One of the most critical success factors for implementing an ERP system is the support and involvement of top managers in the project during its life cycle (Al-Sehali 2000, p. 79). In order for e-HRM implementation to be successful, top managers have to approve and continuously support the responsible parties during the implementation stage to make sure no obstacles prevent or delay the progress of the project. Also, an executive sponsor should be appointed to coordinate, communicate, and integrate all aspects of the project between the development team and top management (Remus 2007, p. 544). The executive sponsor should communicate, integrate, and approve the shared vision of the organization and the responsibilities and structures of the new e-HRM system (Nah et al. 2001, p. 291).

Effective Communication

Interdepartmental communication as well as communication with customers and business partners is a key element in the success of implementing an ERP system (Remus 2007, p.544). Communication helps employees and involved parties better understand the new e-HRM system to keep up with the development and implementation stages of the project. Employees should also be informed in advance the scope, objectives, activities, and updates implemented by the new system in order to meet their expectations (Nah et al. 2001, p. 291)

Project Management

Managing the implementation and development of e-HRM system is a crucial step toward successful results. The scope of the project must be clearly defined, including aspects such as the amount of systems implemented, involvement of business units, and the amount of business process reengineering needed (Nah et al. 2001, p. 292). A company must assign a project manager to lead the project of developing and implementing an e-HRM system professionally according to profound business rules. The project itself must have clearly defined business and technical objectives and goals corresponding to the project deliverables (Remus 2007, p. 543). Such E-HRM goals (mentioned in section 2.3) are embedded within the different e-HRM activities (mentioned in section 2.2) as part of the project management scheme.

Recent Studies on e-HRM Application Implementation

An essential step in e-HRM implementation and development is the decision whether to buy an off-the-shelf e-HRM systems (in many cases part of an Enterprise Resource Planning (ERP) package such as Oracle/Peoplesoft or SAP), or to develop such systems in-house. As Kovach et al. (2002) describe, a small company might prefer to depend on consultants and outsource all aspects of design, implementation, and operation, while a large company could prefer to opt for in-house development of e-HRM applications by their own IT department. Widely believed benefits of commercial off-the-shelf (COTS) systems in general are time-saving, proven system quality, and availability of expertise through the provider. Furthermore, COTS systems help reduce the amount of time and resources used during the design and implementation phases of the software project, as the software is already professionally designed and implemented to fit most of customer's needs (Amons & Howard 2004, p. 50). Silverman (2006) offers a few reasons why most organizations opt for COTS solutions. First, avoiding lengthy and complex software design and development cycles (by using COTS solutions) saves time, money, and human resources. Second, risk is minimized by the fact that COTS systems are professionally provided and supported by experienced entities. Third, COTS vendors take responsibilities of supporting and maintaining the software, which leads to reducing the cost of supporting the software itself. Fourth, COTS systems are virtually up to date as vendors keep investing in developing the software itself (Silverman 2006, p 10). It is also known as a fact that most IT managers first evaluate COTS software when money and time-to-market are at the top of the priority list (Traylor 2006, p 20). This evidence makes it clear that off-the-shelf software saves on time and money resources. On the contrary, disadvantages of off-the-shelf systems are illustrated by the lack of customization/flexibility and the dependency on vendor-expertise. Amons and Howard (2004) insist that buying an already-made software packages will increase time and other resources spent on the integration and deployment phases of the IT project. Indeed, COTS systems need to be perfectly aligned and integrated within the practices of the organization, and deployed in a matter that best fits the company's vision. One particular disadvantage of COTS is of an intangible nature; when most companies adjust their practices to conform to the COTS software standard offerings they lose their competitive advantage, as their technology-based processes become replicas of each other (Carr 2003, p. 6). For e-HRM, this means that companies cannot strategically position their HR activities or improve its strategic orientation by the use of electronic means.

Although it is believed that off-the-shelf software usually contains industry's best practices, but Yeow and Sia (2007) posit that the notion that "best practices" are context-free and can be conveniently acquired, stored, used, and transferred across organizations is questionable. For example, implementing off-the-shelf ERP systems such as Oracle, PeopleSoft, and SAP, in the context of non-US/European and non-private organizations (i.e. governmental institutes in Kuwait) can be quite challenging and might not even fit the environment's needs. Any discrepancies between the organization's needs and the off-the-shelf software's features will most likely affect the overall project success (Lucas et al., 1988; cited by Yeow and Sia 2007, p. 2)

In order to avoid these down-sides, companies might opt for in-house development of an HRIS system. Building e-HRM applications in house requires a special team of developers that is fully skilled and dedicated to do the job of designing and implementing the software. One of the reasons companies choose to develop their HRIS in-house is that they can design the software precisely to fit the organizational goals, as they know their own processes better than anyone else (Zizakovic 2004, p. 4). This way companies gain the competitive advantage and have full control of their proprietary software.

Pearce (2005) provides three key elements for software implementation and development. First, organizations must consider the function of the IT application (i.e. e-HRM application) to determine the level of standardization required by the operations of the application and whether COTS software can provide these standard operations (Pearce 2005, p. 93). For example, e-HRM activities such as payroll and benefits can be suitably offered by COTS systems. Second, organizations must consider the life cycle of the application and how it will be modified, updated, maintained, and supported over the years to come (Pearce 2005, p. 94). This consideration helps organizations to set forth a long-term strategic plan for its e-HRM practices in order to continue sharpening its competitive edge. The third key element in deciding on the best software implementation strategy is to consider the return on investment, or ROI. Pearce (2005) insists that companies must practice the strategy of weighing the associated costs of implementing and developing different software methods against the potential outcome of the IT project itself.

To take further the point issued by Kovach et al (2002), in case of e-HRM the acceptance and usage of applications by employees and managers is critical to successful implementation and the generation of results. That makes the decision whether to 'buy or build' even more important, and seems to favor in-house development over off-the-shelf implementation. However funded knowledge on this issue is lacking so far. The annual CedarCrestone survey (2006) shows that many organizations lay out more expenses for outsourced solutions than they do for in-house development. Three main reasons are explained: organizations with in-house software development mostly have fragmented system operations which cause them to overlook embedded costs within

distributed operations; outsourcing assures better view and control of costs; and outsourcing is a solution for organizations that struggle to control costs due to the complexity of their operations (*HR Technology Trends to Watch in 2007* 2007, p. 1). On the other hand, the CedarCrestone survey (2006) notes that some respondents sense that in-house HR solutions positively affect employees' productivity and can be easily and swiftly integrated into the current system, while off-the-shelf software would cause difficulties during the integration phase.

Theoretical Framework

The suggested framework for this research is depicted in figure 2. This framework combines the main elements discussed in the literature review. Since studies on the different e-HRM applications are scarce, this framework is used primarily to study different elements of implementing software applications and to focus predominantly on implementing e-HRM software applications and the effect they might bring onto the HR function.

This framework suggests three dependant stages of e-HRM systems' implementation and deployment. First stage is the e-HRM software implementation and development approaches, which is affected by the type of system used by the organization—whether it is a commercial off-the-shelf e-HRM system or one that is developed in house. Another factor affecting this stage is the predetermined e-HRM goals as suggested in the literature review. E-HRM goals constitute the implementation and development approaches and set a course of action to be followed during all three stages. The second stage consists of the main elements of e-HRM application deployment such as e-HRM activities handled by the system, application types, and application characteristics. These application criteria help an HR department to provide the necessary e-HR functions to accomplish the goals mentioned in the first stage and meet the needs of the stakeholders. Note that

Table 2. Research constructs

Constructs/Variables	Description
Overview	This strategy is used to start a case study research by collecting general information about the organization to be researched and the e-HRM system it uses.
Implementations and Development Approaches	The factors affecting the implementation and development of e-HRM system and how the company deals with them
E-HRM Goals	The main goals of implementing the e-HRM system and how they coincide with corporate strategy
E-HRM Activities	The HR-related activities offered by the new e-HRM system and how employees work with them
E-HRM Application Characteristics	The characteristics of the e-HRM software application as defined by ISO 9126 standards
E-HRM Outcomes	The four C's of HR: commitment, competence, congruence, and cost effectiveness and how they are impacted after the implementation of the e-HRM system
HRIS Benefits	Usefulness and ease of use of the new e-HRM system

each of the e-HRM activity types fit under at least one of the e-HRM application types. Furthermore, e-HRM application and activity types, and the application characteristics are interdependent (represented by the up-down arrow). For example, relational e-HRM activities such as training, recruitment, and performance management depend mainly on the level of reliability and usability of the e-HRM system, while functionality and efficiency of the e-HRM system might change with the type of e-HRM activity types. The last stage is not in any means of less value than the other stages. It represents the outputs and benefits an HR department aims for during the e-HRM transformation. These outputs consist of the "four C's of HR"—namely commitment, competence, cost effectiveness, and congruence—and user benefits suggested by the Technology Acceptance Model—such as usefulness and ease of use.

METHODOLOGY

Deciding which research strategy to adopt depends solely on the nature of the research question and how the author plans to answer it. The strategy consists of a plan with clear objectives derived from the research question and specifies the sources from which to collect data (Saunders et al. 2003, p. 90). Since the aim of this research is to compare the two types of e-HRM system implementation methods, the author assumes a comparative, descriptive case study strategy. A Comparative study scrutinizes the differences and similarities between the two e-HRM implementation methods, whilst a descriptive study attempts to construct a precise profile of the different e-HRM system implementation methods (Robson 2002; cited in Saunders et al. 2003, p. 97). Furthermore, the descriptive study is a perfect strategy that helps with the proliferation of the inductive research approach. This strategy helps to reach a theoretical conclusion about the outcome and level of effectiveness induced by both implementation methods. A case study research strategy implies the use of detailed and empirical investigation within the real context of a particular phenomenon (Cassell & Symon 2004, p. 323). While the case study strategy provides a good challenge and a source of new hypotheses of an existing theory, it can also help with the creation of a new theory using different means of data collection methods such as questionnaires, interviews, observation, and documentary analysis (Saunders et al. 2003, p.

93). This, indeed, makes a perfect strategy that fits the research philosophy and approaches suggested in the previous sections, as Cassell and Symon (2004) agree that the case study strategy begins with a primitive framework which then will be reproduced or developed under a new theoretical framework that makes sense of the collected data and can be systematically examined for plausibility. This strategy also facilitates the collection of data through multiple research instruments such as participant observation, direct observation, interviews, focus groups, and documentary analysis (Cassell & Symon 2004, p. 325). Consequently, this means that a variety of research instruments can be utilized to understand how the different e-HRM implementation methods affect the HR function.

All in all, case study strategy can be considered a prudent choice for this research as it offers a flexible environment for the researcher to work with and attempts to collect as much information as necessary to conclude how the two E-HRM systems can be compared and contrasted.

For the purpose of this research, two descriptive case studies were conducted on local organizations that have been chosen according to the e-HRM system they used:

- **Case Study 1:** This case study was conducted on a well known company that uses a commercial off-the-shelf e-HRM system by Oracle, called "Oracle ERP". The reason this company was chosen because of the amount of experience it had with the e-HRM system and the strong reputation it possessed in the Kuwaiti marketplace.
- **Case Study 2:** The second case study was conducted on a governmental institute that had gained its competitive advantage mainly through leveraging its IT capabilities to provide the latest technological trends to its customers. The reason this organization was chosen is that it was one of the few local

companies that had developed their e-HRM system in house.

The main constructs used in this research are shown in the table below. These variables can then be used to create a set of questions that help the researcher with gathering appropriate research data for analysis. This process is called the "operationalization of construct" and is explained in the next section.

Operationalization of Constructs

Boiling down the constructs into research questions helps the researcher with the design of the appropriate research instruments to be used to collect and test enough data about the commercial off-the-shelf and in-house developed e-HRM systems. By doing so, the constructs are "operationalized" so that they can be measured accordingly. Table 3 shows the operationalization of constructs mentioned in the previous section.

Research Instruments

Case study is a strategy that includes multiple methods (or instruments) suited to research questions that require detailed understanding of a particular phenomenon due to the large amount of data collected in the context (Cassell & Symon 2004, p. 323). For this research, the following data collection instruments were used:

- **Semi-structured interviews:** These types of non-standardized interviews use list of questions that vary between interviews according to the context (Saunders et al. 2003, p. 246). These interview questions are the outcome of the operationalization of constructs process mentioned in the previous section. Table 4 shows the position of the interviewees and the related questions used during the interviews.

Table 3. Operationalization of constructs

Constructs/ Variables	Definition/Dimension	Operationalization of Constructs
Overview		
Background	General information about the company	- Business establishment - Number of employees - Type of Business
Current HR practices	Where the HR practices currently stand	- Main function/mission of HR department - Level of employee/manager involvement
E-HRM Application	The e-HRM application currently in use	- e-HRM system brand/name - Reason to chose this system - criteria used to make the decision
E-HRM Activities	HR activities utilized/offered by the new e-HRM system	- HR activities handled by the system - New HR activities introduced by the system - level of employee/manager involvement in e-HRM activities
Implementation & Development Approaches		
User Involvement	Involving employees and managers in the e-HRM implementation and development process	- Type of users involved - Stage(s) at which users were involved - Level of involvement
Business Process Reengineering	Reengineering/redesigning of HR business processes	- HR processes reengineered - HR processes eliminated by BPR - New HR processes introduced
Planning & Vision	The planning process and strategy used to implement the e-HRM system	- Type and quality of business plan - Plan outline - Project strategy alignment with corporate strategy and vision
Training & Education	Plan taken to train and educate users of the new e-HRM system	- Level of training/education - Training material - Training delivery
Change Management	How the change/conflict implied by the new e-HRM system is managed	- Resistance, conflict, or confusion by staff/users - Handling of conflict - Corporate strategy toward change
Top Management Support	The support of the e-HRM system implementation by top managers	- Level of top management involvement
Effective Communication	Inward/outward communication needed during the implementation phase	- Level and type of communication between different parties involved - communicating project scope, objective, activities, updates
Project Management	Managing and administering the e-HRM implementation project	- Implementation management - Responsible PM team - Project milestones
e-HRM Goals		
Increase Efficiency	Make HRM more efficient by reducing time, costs, human resources, etc	- Achieving cost reduction - Cost, time, staff, other resources reduction - Processes eliminated to achieve efficiency
Provide Self Service	Provide a mechanism for employees and managers to perform HR functions	- Employee Self Services (ESS) - Manager Self Services (MSS)
Achieve Service Excellence	Provide HR high quality services to employees and managers	- Customer orientation of HR department - How customers perceive the quality of services
Improve Strategic Focus	The strategic orientation and focus of the organization should be improved through the use of the e-HRM system	- The effect of the e-HRM implementation on HR strategy - Changes made to improve HR strategy

continued on following page

Table 3. continued

Constructs/ Variables	Definition/Dimension	Operationalization of Constructs
e-HRM Activities		
Operational Activities	Routine HR tasks such as payroll, attendance, vacation, etc	- Transformed operational activities - New operational activities introduced by e-HRM - Effect of e-HR operational activities on HR function
Relational Activities	Internal and external relational activities such as recruitment and selection, training, performance management, etc.	- Transformed relational activities - New relational activities introduced by e-HRM - Effect of e-HR relational activities on HR function
Transformational Activities	HR activities aimed at improving the strategic orientation of the HR department such as knowledge management, competence management, strategic redirection, downsizing, upsizing, rightsizing, etc	- Transformed transformational activities - New transformational activities introduced by e-HRM - Effect of e-HR transformational activities on HR function
e-HRM Application Characteristics		
Functionality	How the e-HRM system functions with regards to suitability, accuracy, interoperability, and security	- Fulfilment of stated needs - Appropriate set of HR functions - Expected results - Information and data security
Reliability	How reliable the e-HRM system in delivering HR needs	- System maturity - Fault tolerance - Recoverability
Usability	How easy is it to understand, learn, and operate the e-HRM system	- Understandability - Learnability - Operability - Attractiveness
Efficiency	Performance of the e-HRM system with regards to time and other resources utilization	- Time utilization - Resources utilization
Maintainability	The stability of the e-HRM system when analyzed, changed, and tested	- Analyzability - Changeability - Stability - Testability
Portability	How the e-HRM system can adapt new requirements, be installed in different environment, coexist with other software programs, and can be replaced	- Adaptability - Installability - Co-existence - Replaceability
e-HRM Outcomes		
Commitment	Employees commitment to organization due to the implementation of the new e-HRM system	- Change in level of employee commitment to organization
Competence	Development of employees competencies due to the implementation of e-HRM	- Influence of e-HRM on employee competencies
Cost Effectiveness	Benefits of implementing e-HRM such as providing adequate e-HRM services should outweigh costs such as employee resistance and turnover	- Cost of delivering e-HRM practices and services such as staff turnover and resistance - Benefits versus costs
Congruence	The effect of e-HRM on the level of congruence between employees' own goals and those of the organization	- Relationship between managers and employees - Relationship between employees
HRIS Benefits		
Usefulness	How useful the e-HRM system is in enhancing employee performance	- Enhancement of employee performance
Ease of Use	Easiness of performing e-HRM activities	- Effort needed to perform e-HRM tasks

Table 4. Interviewees & related questions

Interviewee position	Related questions (Appendices)
HR manager / administrator	A1, A2, B2-B5, C1-C5, D1-D4, G1-G2, G4-G5
End users (employees & managers)	B1, B7, C2-C3, F3-F4, G1-G2, G4, H1-H2
Project Manager of e-HRM project	A3-A4, B2-B9, C1, C4-C5, D1-D4, G1, G3-G5
IT personnel	A3-A4, B1-B2, B8, C2-C3, D1-D4, E1-E5, F1-F5

- **Documentary analysis:** Company documentation of the e-HRM system implementation is analyzed to understand how the system works. This data, if available, provides a secondary source of information that could potentially assist the researcher to reach a final conclusion about the research question.
- **Participant's observation:** This method allows the researcher to observe first-hand the day-to-day e-HRM experiences, activities, feelings, and interpretations of the users in order to collect information related to some of the constructs mentioned in the previous section (Cassell & Symon 2004, p. 154).
- **Group interviews:** The purpose of group interviews is to collect data from feedbacks and interpretations of multiple interviewees (with similar experiences) during one gathering. An advantage of the group interviews is to hear different opinions of the phenomenon at the same time (Cassell & Symon 2004, p. 143). This gives the researcher an opportunity to observe a sufficient amount of different feelings and experiences about the e-HRM system at the same time.

Sampling Methods

The criteria for selecting case study samples were mainly based on the type of e-HRM system used by an organization—whether it is off-the-shelf or in-house developed e-HRM system. The author also wanted to conduct intensive, comparative, and descriptive investigations of both e-HRM systems

and, therefore, selected only two case studies to concentrate on. Secondly, the requirement to collect large amount of data to analyze the systems put a constraint on the author to select samples with vast experience in the context of electronic HR. This, indeed, narrowed down the search for perfect samples to those organizations with a minimum of 2 years of e-HRM experience. Thirdly, the two sample organizations operate in different markets and have different cultures, as to generate more interesting and variable results. For example, the first sample organization was a mid-size, privately-owned company with a market culture that is profit oriented, while the second sample organization was a government-owned entity with a culture that is more oriented toward bureaucracy. Fourthly, the size of the sample organizations was not a major criterion; however, it gave the organization more of an initiative to implement an e-HRM system. For example, middle to large size organizations feel more pressure to implement an HR system that would keep human resources management under control. Lastly, technologically advanced organizations were preferred by the author as they are more likely to adopt e-HRM technologies at early stages of their life cycle.

Data Analysis Methods

Intensive interviews were first conducted at both sites and recorded on a digital recorder, and then transcribed into separate sets of data for each case. The data was then categorized into multiple sections according to the operationalization Table 3.

FINDINGS

The data analysis starts with transcribing the recorded interviews to capture as much necessary data as possible. The transcripts are then studied and paragraphs rephrased and rearranged under the corresponding instruments depicted in the framework.

The following sections contain those analyzed transcripts from both case studies, where case 1 represents the company that uses off-the-shelf Oracle ERP, and case 2 represents the governmental institute that has developed its own e-HRM system in house. Data collected from each case is displayed side by side according to the theoretical instruments to show a clear comparison between the two different systems.

e-HRM Overview

The aim of this section is to explain some of the general issues associated with the implementation of the e-HRM systems of both cases. The overview allows the researcher to get a feel of the researched systems before getting into the detailed interviews that would confirm or refute the propositions suggested in the theoretical framework.

Case 1: The implementation of Oracle ERP system started in 2004. Before that, in 2001, an initiative from the Board to perform a total restructuring and business process reengineering took place. The aim of this BPR was to transform all business processes into the IT era, including the transformation of the HR practices into e-HR technologies. The main steps of reengineering were diagnostics, analysis, and implementation. HR reengineering (i.e. transformation to e-HR using Oracle ERP) was 30% of the whole BPR process of the organization. It took about 3 years to progress through the diagnostics, analysis, and implementation stages, and about one year to complete the transformation of the HR function. In order to implement such a big change

within a large organization, the bureaucratic and centralized culture needed to be changed as well. This culture was changed to reflect the open environment that accepted change and forward movement.

As for why this organization opted for Oracle ERP, it was recommended by the Chairman to choose this system as the best offer because of its flexibility, changeability, adaptability, and reputation between other vendors such as SAP and Anderson. The second reason was that the IT department at this company didn't have the qualified resources to implement such a fully integrated enterprise system that could support the new structure and culture. As a matter of fact, the IT department was mostly outsourced to a third party that was able to arrange and manage the e-commerce transformation. Oracle ERP needed lots of customizations to remove unwanted processes such as taxation and add or modify the HR processes to fit the company's HR needs.

About 80% of manual work was eliminated by the new system. The BPR, along with the ERP implementation, has caused the reduction of manpower from 900 to approximately 200, as most processes were eliminated, reduced, or outsourced. The other 20% of manual and paperwork cannot be changed due to the nature of the work that requires to be done in professional and manual way such as memorandums and official letter.

Case 2: The e-HRM system was developed by the Systems Development team in this organization's IT department. The reason behind developing this e-HRM system in house was that there was no system out in the market that could fulfill the complex HR requirements implied by the country's laws and by this governmental institute. The IT department manager indicated that if they had chosen an off-the-shelf e-HRM system, customization would have cost them incredible amount of time and money. Second, this system was developed and implemented in order to fit it to the user's needs and not to adjust the user to the system's offerings.

The system development started in 2002 and took about 2 years to complete. It is totally web based using Oracle database, Microsoft .NET framework, and object oriented programming methods. Long before that, in 1976, there was an initiative by top management to automate most of the HR processes in order to minimize time and associated costs. Paperwork was costing the organization lots of time and money to store the voluminous data in multiple cabinets. Also, data integrity and security was a top priority and major concern that would justify the need to transform all HR processes into the e-commerce era. At that time, a mainframe system called "Tandem" was used to build the infrastructure that would support the renovated business. The current system was therefore developed and implemented in accordance to the vision of top management which encouraged the IT department to integrate the latest and most flexible and reliable electronic technologies. This upgrade required the replacement of the old mainframe system with the more flexible and compact Microsoft system.

The e-HRM system provides user with many facilities such as attendance, which is totally secured and tied up to a biometric system that scans users fingerprints for authentication. Also, the main HR functions provided by COTS systems have been extracted and implemented within this in-house developed system, with a touch of flexibility to fit those functions to the organizational needs.

Presentation of Results

While the data collected might specifically describe the contextual situation of e-HRM systems used by these two cases, some general remarks about the differences and similarities between off-the-shelf and in-house developed E-HRM systems can be drawn. Referring back to the main question of this research—which compares off-the-shelf

with in-house developed e-HRM with regards to the implementation and development approaches, e-HRM goals, e-HRM activities they facilitate, application types and characteristics, and e-HRM outcomes—one can provide conclusive evidence about the differences and similarities at hand.

In general, organizations transform their HR function to e-HR in the hope to reduce the amount of time spent on processing HR activities. The automation of HR processes, therefore, is a necessary requirement and a major step in the transformation process, as mentioned by Lengnick-Hall and Moritz (2003, p. 367). A minimum of 90% of HR's paperwork at both cases has been eliminated and/ or replaced by automated functions. It is also true that companies evaluate the capabilities of their IT department and accordingly decide whether they can develop and support enterprise-quality software in house. Furthermore, the point of Pearce (2005) about the organizations' concern of whether off-the-shelf software can provide standard e-HRM functions is touched upon by both cases. On one hand, the first case saw that Oracle ERP would provide just about the right e-HRM functions with minimal customization needed. On the other hand, the second case believed that no single COTS system could provide standard e-HRM functions that best fit their business needs. Also, to confirm the point of Amons and Howard (2004), off-the-shelf e-HRM systems dramatically reduce the amount of time spent on design and implementation stages, as the system has already been professionally designed and only needs to be integrated and deployed. However, the integration and deployment stages are overwhelmingly critical due to the fact that off-the-shelf systems need to be customized to properly bolt onto the company's environment. It took case 1 a whole year to completely integrate and deploy Oracle ERP. On the other hand, as Amons and Howard (2004) suggest, design and development stages are lengthy using in-house developed software, especially with the second case in this research where the development team's experience was limited.

Looking at the development and implementation approaches, a general theme can be depicted. When implementing either e-HRM system (i.e. COTS or in-house developed), the organizations look for satisfying the HR's department needs as the main user, and the needs of all other users such as employees and managers. However, some approaches might be emphasized more than others according to the type of e-HRM system. For example, when implementing in-house developed e-HRM systems, the users are continuously involved, trained, and educated throughout the product life cycle to ensure that the software works for the best interest of its users, and to build a high level of trust in the IT department. This new experience for the IT department meant a new challenge and a new chance to prove its competence. Also, change management and communication management had to be perfected to provide the proper support for the development team and to make sure no conflict or confusion would cause the deterioration of trust between key players. As for project management, the second case believes that organizations who develop their e-HRM software in house must appoint a project manager from within the development team for two reasons. First, it is best to manage this first experience in house to avoid conflict of interest and to impose more control on decision making. Second, no one knows how to orchestrate the development team and leverage their capabilities better than a person who works closely with them.

Factors that affect off-the-shelf e-HRM implementation the most are business process reengineering, planning, and project management. The reason being is that HR process reengineering and project management are two essential elements handled professionally by the vendor within a well organized plan to implement off-the-shelf e-HRM software. In other words, vendors do not just deliver the software, but they rather manage the whole project through planning, reengineering, training, and implementation. From a realist point

of view, one can also conclude that implementing off-the-shelf e-HRM system is a professional experience that must be handled by those who are most skilled and knowledgeable about the product itself, where this knowledge needs to be transferred to the acquiring party in an organized and well planned manner.

A new predominant factor has been extracted during this research, which affected the implementation of e-HRM systems at both cases. Teamwork plays an essential role in implementing e-HRM systems as it triggers a synergistic effect between the teams involved in the transformation project. Cross-functional teams work cohesively in both cases to achieve planned targets and meet project gates.

Flexibility, timeliness, and elimination of manual processes are advocates of efficiency when implementing both e-HRM systems. Increasing efficiency, therefore, is the most critical goal of transforming the HR function to e-HR. Efficiency can also be measured by the amount of HR staff reduced after the implementation. In both cases, less staff members could handle more tasks using the e-HRM systems. Providing employee and manager self services also came on the top of most effective e-HRM goals list. ESS and MSS are implemented within both e-HRM systems to provide easy access for employees to perform multiple e-HRM services swiftly and without interaction with the HR office. Third, achieving service excellence is considered crucial for organizations that develop e-HRM software in house. It is concluded through this research that when an e-HRM system is developed in house, users' expectations of results are at peak, due to the fact that this software is developed under the same organizational culture, by staff that commemorate this same culture. Last and perhaps least considered by both cases is the goal of improving the strategic focus. It is evident that due to the lack of market competition in Kuwait, companies spend less effort to improve their strategic orientation.

Operational, relational, and transformational e-HRM activities are common between the two systems. However, these types of e-HRM activities become the most competitive advantage of in-house developed e-HRM systems. It is concluded through this research that when developing an e-HRM system that best fits the users' needs, many of those needs become reality in an attempt to achieve maximum customer satisfaction and meet those high expectations. The outcome of this phenomenon is a system that harbors the best practices of off-the-shelf e-HRM systems with a competitive twist tailored to the last details of users' needs.

As for the e-HRM application characteristics, supporters of off-the-shelf systems (i.e. case 1) believe that corporations such as Oracle and SAP implement the markets best practices into their software solutions to gain a competitive advantage and increase market share. This leads to the creation of state-of-art enterprise solutions such as Oracle ERP. Also, case 1 agrees with Silverman (2006) that risk of implementing off-the-shelf e-HRM systems is minimized by the fact that those systems are professionally provided and supported by experienced entities. On the other hand, software quality characteristics as depicted by ISO 9126 might not have been seriously considered by the amateur development team of the second case. This might have been caused by the fact that software development is not in conjunction with this organization's profession. However, features like accuracy, suitability, security, reliability, usability, and maintainability become adhesive during the design and development phases.

Comparing the e-HRM outcomes of the two cases, an apparent theme emerges. Because of the amount of trust, confidence, and support shown to the in-house development team during the design, development, and implementation stages, employees' commitment may substantially increase. As the HR senior staff at case 2 phrases it: "supporting the hometown team eventually pays off." Another reason for such a phenomenon is due to

the amount of customer satisfaction implemented into the system, as most of the users' needs are catered for to create a system that best fits those needs. Cost effectiveness, on the other hand, is most favored by those organizations that use off-the-shelf system. Traylor (2006) agrees that although the amount of money spent on acquiring, integrating, and supporting the enterprise off-the-shelf system is incredibly high, more cost effectiveness is achieved for both implementation and ongoing maintenance. Case 1 felt that using the renowned Oracle ERP system and the support package offered by the vendor avoided software obsolescence in the long run, as professional software providers keep on implementing the latest technologies into their provided services. Another outcome observed by the first case was changing the attitude of employees, which remains questionable. The change in attitude might have been partially affected by the open environment created during the e-HRM transformation, but it is believed that the organizational-level business process reengineering had the bigger effect on people's attitude.

Finally, usefulness and ease of use become natural effects of implementing both e-HRM systems. However, both benefits are most noticed by the users of in-house developed e-HRM systems because those systems are made to specifically fit the user's needs.

The following table provides a summary of those findings and a clear comparison between the two systems with regards to the variables in the suggested framework.

FUTURE RESEARCH

Further research can be done to determine the best practices for implementing e-HRM systems in the Kuwaiti context. Yeow and Sia (2007) found out, from a social constructivist point of view, that "best practices" are socially enacted knowledge that requires organizational power

Table 5. Off-the-shelf vs. in-house developed e-HRM systems

Variables	Off-the-shelf	In-house
Implementation & Development Approaches		
User Involvement	- Moderate	- High - Users continuously involved throughout all stages
Business Process Reengineering	- Considered a major factor since HR processes need to be reengineered to conform to off-the-shelf standards	- Some processes reengineered to eliminate time-consuming manual work
Planning & Vision	- More planned - Strategy and vision are professionally outlaid	- Informal plan and strategy
Training & Education	- Standardized - Delivered by vendor	- More emphasized to gain proper organizational support
Change Management	- Handled professionally with the help of the vendor - More rejection of the foreign system	- Handled by project manager to increase effective-ness - Less rejection and more support of the friendly system
Top Management Support	- Moderate support - High trust in professional services	- High level of support for the home-made product
Effective Communication	- Formal communication through awareness sessions	- Different informal communication channels for maximum effectiveness
Project Management	- Outsourced to experienced entity for more effective-ness	- In-house for more effectiveness
Teamwork	- Highly emphasized	- Highly emphasized
e-HRM Goals		
Increase Efficiency	- Time and cost reduction are guaranteed by vendor and their professional e-HRM	- Efficiency accomplished by utilizing resources, minimizing time and errors, and eliminating manual work
Provide Self Service	- ESS and MSS as provided by vendor	- ESS and MSS shaped to better fit users' needs
Achieve Service Excellence	- Customer-oriented culture imposed by the system and not necessarily by organization	- Crucial due to the high level of users' expectations
Improve Strategic Focus	- Strategic solutions offered professionally by the system	- Not critical
e-HRM Activities		
Operational Activities	- Standardized	- Tailored to the last details of users' needs
Relational Activities	- Standardized	- Tailored to the last details of users' needs
Transformational Activities	- Standardized	- Tailored to the last details of users' needs
e-HRM Application Characteristics		
Functionality	- Very secure, accurate, and interoperable - Moderately suitable with a number of customizations	- High suitability - Very secure and accurate - Limited interoperability
Reliability	- High maturity, fault tolerance, and recoverability	- Immature but recoverable - Limited errors
Usability	- Easy to understand, learn, and operate - Normal attractiveness due to the standard graphical interface	- High usability levels due to the implementation of most users' needs - Very attractive GUI
Efficiency	- High levels of timeliness and resource utilization	- High efficiency
Maintainability	- Professionally maintained by vendor through service and support agreements	- Easy to analyze, install, and test - Limited changeability

continued on following page

Table 5. continued

Variables	Off-the-shelf	In-house
Portability	- Easily adopted in multiple environments	- Limited to Windows-based environments
e-HRM Outcomes		
Commitment	- Mildly imposed by the software's culture	- Substantially high due to the amount of users' needs implemented in the system
Competence	- Moderate increase	- Moderate increase
Cost Effectiveness	- Substantially high due to the professionalism of the system	- Normal
Congruence	- High	- High
HRIS Benefits		
Usefulness	- Normal	- Meets or exceeds expectations
Ease of Use	- Normal	- Meets or exceeds expectations

through politics, and discourse to influence different technological assumptions, expectations, and knowledge until this difference is resolved into what is logically called "best practices". This means that politics and discourse in the context of Kuwaiti organizations can be studied to determine what the best practices are for implementing e-HRM systems.

Another augmented approach to future research could be done after the fact that e-HR transformation in Kuwait has reached its maturity and the market is saturated with diverse organizations that use different e-HRM systems. Infusing e-HRM technologies in Kuwait's organizations is inevitable, however it could be long before any such technologies are enforced by cultural values and/or organizational needs due to the fact that legislations for electronic technologies have yet to be considered by Kuwaiti laws.

CONCLUSION

The comparison between off-the-shelf and in-house developed e-HRM applications has been exploited in this research to find out the differences and similarities between development and implementation approaches, e-HRM goals, e-HRM activities, application types and characteristics, and the outcome of implementing both systems. Realism philosophy was used to extract facts about the suggested theoretical framework introduced in chapter three. Further, two cases were used as the best candidates for this research because of the different corporate cultures and markets they operated in, which lead to more interesting remarks.

Looking back at the theoretical framework developed in chapter three, one can suggest a few minor adjustments. One of the elements that became irrelevant to this comparative study was the e-HRM application types. E-HRM systems are divided into four main types as described in the literature, namely administrative, employee/manager productivity, strategic HCM, and business intelligence applications. Each of these sets handles a number of e-HRM activities (i.e. operational, relational, and transformational activities). However, these application types do not provide relevant information and, therefore, cannot be used as a credible variable of the theoretical assumptions that are made about the differences and similarities between off-the-shelf and in-house developed e-HRM systems. Another adjustment would be to add "teamwork" as one of the major factors affecting the implementation and development of the e-HRM systems, as it was observed greatly by both cases.

Generally, the decision of choosing between off-the-shelf and in-house developed e-HRM is dependent on factors such as the IT department capabilities, amount of time and resources spent on development and implementation phases, and the purpose of e-HR transformation. We saw that when companies plan a total business process re-engineering, for example, the best practice would be to seek the assistance of professional services that can provide enterprise-level qualities.

One of the most interesting findings in this research is that when e-HRM systems are developed in house, users' expectations are high. Also, trust and confidence levels in the development team must be increased in order for the development to meet those high expectations. On the other hand, organizations who implement a certain off-the-shelf e-HRM system automatically develop a high level of trust in the professional expertise of the provider. This is due to the fact that software providers implement industry's best practices and software quality (i.e. ISO 9126) into their solutions to gain a competitive advantage and increase market share.

Teamwork and cross-functional team cooperation are on the top list of factors affecting the development and implementation of both systems, as they create a synergistic environment that leads to more efficiency and effectiveness. User involvement, effective communication, and change management are the most critical success factors for implementing in-house developed E-HRM software. On the other hand, planning and vision, project management, and business process reengineering are factors that affect the implementation of off-the-shelf e-HRM systems the most due to the fact that these systems are handled professionally by the vendors.

Increasing HR efficiency is a critical objective behind implementing both e-HRM systems. This goal can be mainly achieved through increasing the flexibility and timeliness of HR processes and eliminating a big portion of the manual processes. Reducing HR manpower is a consequent effect of the e-HR transformation that can also be counted as an efficiency measure.

The fact that an e-HRM system is developed and supported internally by the IT department increases the level of pride and support by users toward the system and the team who develops it. This high level of support instantiates high congruence between employees and line managers, and improves the alignment between departmental and organizational goals. Furthermore, employees' commitment increases as the level of confidence and support of the "home-made" e-HRM system increases. On the contrary, companies who implement off-the-shelf e-HRM systems increase cost effectiveness during the life cycle of the product due to the fact that those systems are "built to last".

REFERENCES

Al-Sehali, Saud, H. (2000). *The Factors that Affect the Implementation of Enterprise Resource Planning (ERP) in the International Arab Gulf States and United States Companies with Special Emphasis on SAP Software*. D.I.T. dissertation, University of Northern Iowa, Iowa.

Amons, P., & Howard, D. (2004). Buy it, Build it, or Have it Built? *Catalog Age, 21*(3), 50.

Ball, K. S. (2001). The Use of Human Resource Information Systems: a Survey. *Personnel Review, 30*(6), 677-693.

Beer, M., Spector, B., Lawrance, P., Mills, Q., & Walton, R. (1984). *Managing Human Assets*. New York: The Free Press.

Bingi, P., Sharma, M. K., & Godla, J. (1999). Critical Issues Affecting an ERP Implementation. *Information Systems Management, 16*(3), 7-14.

Buckhout, S., Frey, E., & Nemec, J. Jr (1999). Making ERP Succeed: Turning Fear into Promise. *IEEE Engineering Management* Review, (pp. 116-23).

Carr, N. G. (2003). IT doesn't matter. Harvard Business Review, *81*(5), 41-49.

Cassell, C., & Symon, G. (2004). *Essential Guide to Qualitative Methods in Organizational Research*. London: SAGE Publications.

CedarCrestone 2006 HCM Survey: Workforce Technologies and Service Delivery Approaches – 9th Annual Edition.

CedarCrestone 2007-2008 HR Systems Survey: HR Technologies, Service Delivery Approaches, and Metrics – 10th Annual Edition.

Davis, F. D., Bagozzi, R. P., & Warshaw, P. R. (1989). User Acceptance of Computer Technology: a Comparison of Two Theoretical Models, *Management Science, 35*(8), 982-1004.

Exclusive IOMA Survey: What do Users Like (and Dislike) About Their HRIS? (2002, December). IOMA's Payroll Manager's Report, *02*(12), 1.

Florkowski, G. W., & Olivas-Luján, M. R. (2006). The Diffusion of Human Resource Information Technology Innovations in US and non-US Firms. *Personnel Review, 35*(6), 684-710.

Gueutal, H. G., & Stone, D. L. (2005). *The Brave New World of eHR: Human Resources Management in the Digital Age*. San Francisco: Jossey-Bass.

Hendrickson, A. R. (2003). Human Resource Information Systems: Backbone Technology of Contemporary Human Resources. Journal of Labor Research, *24*(3), 381-394.

HR Technology Trends to Watch in 2007 (2007). *HR Focus, 84*(1), 1.

International Organization for Standardization. (ISO) (2001). ISO/IEC: 9126 Software Engineer-

ing – Product Quality – Part 1: Quality Model – 2001. Retrieved November 21, 2007 from http://www.iso.org.

Kovach, K. A., Hughe, A. A., Fagan, P., & Magitti, P. G. (2002). Administrative and Strategic Advantages of HRIS. *Employment Relations Today, 29*(2), 43-48.

Lee, C., & Lee, H. 2001. Factors Affecting Enterprise Resource Planning Systems Implementation in a Higher Education Institution. *Issues in Information Systems, 2*(1), 207-212. Retrieved November 24, 2007 from http://www.iacis.org.

Lengnick-Hall, M. L., & Mortiz, S. (2003). The Impact of e-HR on the Human Resource Management Function. *Journal of Labor Research, 24*(3), 365-379.

Lepak, D. P., & Snell, S. A. (1998). Virtual HR: Strategic Human Resource Management in the 21st Century. *Human Resource Management Review, 8(3),* 215-234.

Madill, A., Jordan, & A., Shirley, C. (2000). Objectivity and Reliability in Qualitative Analysis: Realist, Contextualist and Radical Constructionist Epistemologies. *British Journal of Psychology, 91*(1), 1-20.

Nah, F. F., Lau, J. L., & Kuang, J. (2001). Critical Factors for Successful Implementation of Enterprise Systems. *Business Process Management Journal, 7*(3), 285-296.

Ngai, E.W.T., & Wat, F.K.T. (2006). Human Resource information systems: a review and empirical analysis. *Personnel Review, 35*(3), 297-314.

Pearce, J. (2005). In-House or Out-Source? Three Key Elements for IT Development. *Franchising World, 37*(4), 93-95.

Remus, U. (2007). Critical Success Factors for Implementing Enterprise Portals: A Comparison with ERP Implementations. *Business Process Management Journal, 13*(4), 538-552.

Ruël, H., Bandarouk, T., & Looise, J. K. (2004). E-HRM: Innovation or Irritation. An Explorative Empirical Study in Five Large Companies on Web-Based HRM. *Management Revue, 15*(3), 364-380

Ruta, C. D. (2005). The Application of Change Management Theory to the HR Portal Implementation in Subsidiaries of Multinational Corporations. *Human Resource Management, 44*(1), 35-53.

Saunders, M., Lewis, P., & Thornhill, A. (2003). *Research Methods for Business Students*, 3rd edition. Essex: Pearson Education Ltd.

Schramm, J. (2006). HR technology Competencies: New Roles for HR Professionals. *HR Magazine, 51*(4), special section, 1-10.

Silverman, R. (2006). Buying Better to Buy Better. Contract Management, *46*(11), 8-12.

Thaler-Carter, R. E. (1998). Do-It-Yourself Software. *HR Magazine, May 1998*, 22.

Traylor, P. (2006). To Buy or To Build? That is the Question. *Info World, 28*(7), 18-23.

Valverde, M., Ryan, G., & Soler, C. (2006). Distributing HRM responsibilities: a classification of organisations. Personnel Review, *35*(6), 618-636.

Wright, P. M., & Dyer, L. (2000). People in the E-business: New Challenges, New Solutions. Working paper 00-11. Center for Advanced Human Resource Studies, Cornell University.

Yeow, A., & Sia, S.K. (2007). Negotiating "Best Practices" in Package Software Implementation. *Information and Organization*. Retrieved from doi:10.1016/ j.infoandorg.2007.07.001.

Yumiko, I. (2005). Selecting a Software Package: From Procurement System to E-Marketplace. The Business Review, Cambridge, *3*(2), 341-347.

Zizakovic, L. (2004). *Buy or Build: Corporate Software Dilemma*. Retrieved November 11, 2007, from http://www.insidus.com.

KEY TERMS

BPR: Business Process Reengineering

BSS: Benefit-related Self Service

COTS: Commercial Off-The-Shelf

E-HRM: Electronic Human Resources Management

ERP: Enterprise Resource Planning

ESS: Employee Self Services

HCM: Human Capital Management

HRIS: Human Resources Information Systems

HRM: Human Resources Management

ISO: International Organization for Standardization

IVR: Integrated Voice Response

MSS: Manager Self Services

PSS: Pay-related Self Service

ROI: Return on Investment

SMR: Simple Management Reporting

TBS: Total Benefits Statement

TMSS: Time Management Self Service

Chapter VII
Adaptive Municipal Electronic Forms

Pieternel Kuiper
Exxellence Group, The Netherlands

Betsy van Dijk
University of Twente, The Netherlands

ABSTRACT

Adaptation of electronic forms (e-forms) seems to be a step forward to reduce the burden for people who fill in forms. Municipalities more and more offer e-forms online that can be used by citizens to request a municipal product or service or by municipal employees to place a request on behalf of a citizen. The impression exists that not all users of municipal e-forms are entirely satisfied about the current e-forms. To improve the customer satisfaction a shift must be made from a supply-led to a demand-led approach, including possibilities for tailored information and services. A municipal e-form can automatically adjust to the background, knowledge, interest, goals and restrictions of the user. The user can also adjust the form to his/her needs. Adaptive municipal e-forms can be used for different purposes, that is to make an appointment, to announce a change of address, or to request a passport or building permit. This chapter describes how municipal e-forms can be improved by the use of adaptation.

INTRODUCTION

To adapt or to be adapted: that is the question. This chapter describes how municipal electronic forms (e-forms) can be improved by the use of adaptation. The impression exists that not all users of municipal e-forms are entirely satisfied about the current e-forms. To improve the cus-tomer satisfaction a shift must be made from a supply-led to a demand-led approach, including possibilities for tailored information and services. (Advies Overheid.nl, 2006)

Adaptation of e-forms seems to be a step forward to reduce the burden for people who fill in forms. (Dijk, 2005). Municipalities more and more offer e-forms Online (through a website or portal) that can be used by citizens to request a municipal product or service or by municipal employees to place a request on behalf of a citizen. The form can automatically adjust to the background, knowledge, interest, goals and restrictions of the user. The user can also adjust the form to his/her own needs. Adaptive municipal e-forms can be used for different purposes, e.g. to make an appointment, to announce a change of address, or to request a passport or building permit.

The Dutch program *Overheid heeft Antwoord*, assigned by the Dutch Department of Internal Affairs and Kingdom relations (*Binnenlandse Zaken en Koninkrijksrelaties - BZK*), describes that municipalities must offer at least 65% of their services through the Internet in 2007. For the total government this required percentage is 67%. *Overheid heeft Antwoord* gives out a yearly report called the *Overheid.nl Monitor*. The *Overheid.nl Monitor* 2007 describes the most important progressions and bottlenecks in the design of the electronic government and it stimulates governments to perform better. The *Overheid.nl Monitor* is based on a elaborate checklist and consists of both a yearly and continue monitor. The results of the *Overheid.nl Monitor* 2007 are inspiring and confirm that we are heading in the right direction. 67% of the public services are offered electronically in 2007. This means that the goal of 65% in 2007 is widely accomplished. The results also indicate that personalized services to citizens and companies, have increased rapidly in 2007 from 19% to 36%. This has been made possible by doubling the implementation of DigiD (see (DigiD, 2008) for more information), personalized front offices and the Internet pay desks. The priority in 2008 will be on projects regarding personal services. The *Overheid.nl Monitor* will also focus on the accessibility and the quality of the government services. The goal is that government services are rewarded with a 7 (out of 10) by citizens. A better and more efficient service will safe the citizens but also the government time and money. (Garnier, Flos & Romeijn, 2007).

One of the most prominent cases in the area of e-government is the implementation of a digital front office, e.g. a digital service counter. Due to this, services can optimally be adapted to users/citizens, the interaction between citizens and the government can be improved, and various internal front offices can be supported. A digital request of a municipal product and/or service can for example lead to a higher efficiency because of a higher quality of the request and the possibility for semi-automatized testing. A disadvantage is that if the municipality can not digitally process the request in their back office systems there is a big change that the digital request will only lead to a shift of the administrative burdens and to an increase of the costs. (Hoogwout & Vries, 2005) In this case the request will be send through email to an municipal employee. The employee has to process the request in the back office system manually. With, e.g., the implementation of a Mid Office, the municipalities can process the requests digitally in the back office systems. In this case intervention of an municipal employee is not necessary anymore. For more information about a Mid Office, see (Expertisegroep Usability, 2006).

When implementing e-government one of the main points of interest is that everyone gets access to public services to avoid the risk of digital diversion. One way to handle this risk is to adjust the municipal e-forms (adaptation). This can be done by adjusting the form to the user (personalization) or the user can adjust the form him/herself (customization). There are numerous potential advantages. Time can be saved when the content matches with the choices of the user. The field of attention can be increased by pointing out which choices similar users made. The forms can also adapt to the expectations of the user by showing adapted content after the system has recognized the user. But are users actually interested in adaptation implemented in municipal e-forms? A user might get the feeling that he/she has no control since the system decides which offer the user gets. Moreover, a user might get the feeling that his/her privacy is violated since the system monitors the (Online) behaviour of the user. (Kroon, 1998)

This chapter answers the question if and in which way citizens, municipal employees, and municipalities appreciate the implementation of adaptation in simple and complex municipal e-forms and if adaptation can improve the quality of municipal e-forms. To get an answer to this question a research has been performed by the University of Twente in cooperation with the Exxellence Group (Kuiper, 2006). This research consisted of two parts. In the first part a theoretical research was performed regarding the implementation of adaptation in general and in municipal e-forms in particular. As a result of this theoretical research, three questionnaires were created to discover the need of adaptive municipal e-forms under citizens, municipal employees and municipalities. The second part of the research consisted of the design and evaluation of prototypes to demonstrate how adaptivity can be implemented in municipal e-forms.

The next sections give an overview of the different types of adaptation and adaptation techniques, the difference between paper forms and e-forms, and the way adaptation can be applied in e-forms in general and in municipal e-forms in particular. In the following sections the questionnaires performed under citizens, municipal employees and municipalities, including their results, are discussed. The last sections of this chapter describes the prototypes that are designed based on the theoretical research and the results of the questionnaires. They also describe the evaluation of these prototypes including their results. The prototypes are evaluated under citizens and municipal employees in an end-user evaluation and under municipalities in a focus group evaluation.

OVERVIEW OF ADAPTATION

Adaptation deals with the ability of an application to collect user information, to analyze this information, and to adapt the application to the needs of the user based on the analysis (Kobsa, Koeneman & Pohl, 2001). Figure 1 shows an overview of adaptation.

Types of Adaptation

There are two types of adaptation; personalization and customization, which can occur simultane-

Figure 1. Overview of adaptation

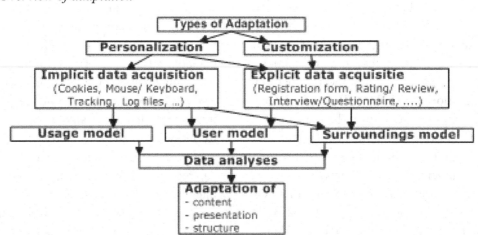

ously. Customization is based on explicit data, i.e. a user can adapt the applications' data or layout. Personalization is handled by the system and is based on implicit data, e.g. user behavior, and/or explicit data, e.g. information entered in a form. Hereby an application can adapt to an individual or a group. For personalization three types of models are used: user models, surroundings models, and usage models. For customization two of these models are used: user models and surroundings models. User models describe personal information or presumptions about the user. Surroundings models describe the users' software, hardware and location. Usage models describe the users' behavior by looking at user actions. User models and surrounding models contain explicit and implicit data. Usage models only contain implicit data. To create a more elaborated model, the data in these models must be analyzed using various data analysis methods, e.g. content-based filtering, collaborative filtering, rule-based filtering and usage mining. Content-based filtering is a method that is based on individual user interest and preferences. Information comparable to these interests and preferences is offered. Collaborative filtering compares the current user with comparable users to predict unknown attributes of the current user. With rule-based filtering decision rules, that are based on static or dynamic profiles and that can be used for content adaptation, can be specified in advance. In this way association rules can determine that a user who has seen two pages will also be interested in the third related page. Usage mining applies statistic and data mining methods to log data which results in user patterns that describe the user behavior of the user. (Kobsa, Koeneman & Pohl, 2001), (Germanakos, 2005), (Bearman & Trant, 2004), (Eirinaki & Vazirgiannis, 2003).

Adaptation based on usage, user and surroundings models can be presented in three ways: adaptation of content (methods to adjust the content to users), adaptation of presentation (methods to adjust the presentation, media formats, and interaction elements to the user), and adaptation of navigation (methods to adjust the navigation to the user), which can appear in combination. (Kobsa, Koeneman & Pohl, 2001), (Serengul Guven Smith, 2000).

Adaptation of Content

Adaptation of content can be described according to different personalization functions and techniques. The following personalization functions can be distinguished (Kobsa, Koeneman & Pohl, 2001):

- **Optional explanation of detailed information.** Explanations can help users to better understand items when they miss certain background information. However, such explanations can also be unnecessary or even distractive for users who do have the necessary knowledge. Optional explanations of detailed information of items can improve the relevancy of a page for users who are interested in the item. It can also help to keep a page interesting for users who are already familiar with the item.
- **Personalized recommendations.** They inform the user about available options in which they might be interested by presenting or highlighting the items or emphasizing the parts the user is possibly interested in.
- **Optional opportunistic hints,** which are based on possible user interest and current circumstances.

The following personalization techniques can be distinguished (Kobsa, Koeneman & Pohl, 2001), (Serengul Guven Smith, 2000):

- **Conditional text:** Conditional text means that text has been divided in different parts, each part associated with a condition regarding the user knowledge of a user model (e.g. an expert or novice user). Only these parts are presented in which case the condition is true.

- **Page variants:** A page can exist of two or more variants, in which each variant presents information on a different level or in a different way. Adaptation simply means selecting a page variant. This technique can easily be implemented by selecting a page variant. A disadvantage of this method is that for each variant a new page must be created. It could also be inflexible since all relevant pages should be adapted when something changes and it can easily become inconsistent since items should be adapted on multiple places.
- **Fragment variants:** This is a more refined implementation of the page variant technique. Each page is subdivided in a number of fragments. Two or more variants of one fragment can exits in which each variant is created for a certain user group. Fragment variants can be used in combination with page variants. A suitable page variant can be selected according to the background of the users, after which other adaptation techniques can be used by selecting a suitable fragment variant according to the knowledge of the user.
- **Fragment coloring:** Fragment coloring can only be applied in areas where content is presented in the same formulation to all users and where the variability of adaptation across all users is relatively low. Using colors, for individual users some elements can be marked as being important, irrelevant or demanding. The advantage of fragment coloring is that users can see all available information. In this case mistakes that are self-assessed have less critical effects than with page/fragment variants.
- **Adaptive strechtext:** Adaptive strechtext is text that gives explanations about a term or word and which can be "unfolded" by the users, which can automatically be folded and

unfolded by the system, or which a pop-up screen can show when a user clicks on it or moves over it with the mouse. The advantage is that the user can adapt the content manually when the automatic adjustment is not suitable or wanted.

- **Adaptive natural-language generation:** Adaptive natural-language generation can be used to formulate alternative descriptions for different users. It can also be used as an addition on strechtext.

Adaptation of Presentation

With adaptation of presentation the information content of the object ideally stays the same while the format and the layout of the object change, e.g. images are replaced by text and/or text is replaced by audio, and/or video is replaced by still images. This can be relevant for users with a physical disability, e.g. blind people. Adaptation of presentation can be used in combination with adaptation of content and adaptation of navigation (Kobsa, Koeneman & Pohl, 2001).

Adaptation of Navigation

The goal of adaptation of navigation is to support users in decision making by manipulating navigation recourses, e.g. links, labels or hot words. It should also prevent problems like disorientation and information overload. Adaptation of navigation can be described according to a number of personalization techniques and functions. The following personalization techniques can be distinguished (Kobsa, Koeneman & Pohl, 2001), (Serengul Guven Smith, 2000):

- **Collateral structure adaptation:** Content adaptation can create implicit adaptation of links ("wanted" side-effects) when fragment variants contain links that are not shown to the user in one of the variants.

- **Adaptive link sorting:** This can be used for non-contextual links. Links can be arranged according to user interests, goals, and availablitliy (e.g. presenting recommended items) or based on frequent use (e.g. creating personalized views).
- **Adaptive link annotation:** This can be used for contextual and non-contextual links. Adaptive link annotation annotates links in a personalized way using different colors, font types, sizes or pictograms. In a lot of systems annotations are adjustable.
- **Adaptive link hiding or disabling:** Hiding links removes the visual indicator of a link (the link looks like a normal text or icon). Disabling links removes the functionality of a link but not the visual representation. The goal of adaptive link hiding is to simplify the link in a visual way to support the navigation behavior of the user and to guide him/her to those parts of which the system thinks that they are relevant or understandable based on the supposed knowledge level of the user.
- **Adaptive link removal/addition:** This adds or removes the link of non-contextual links as a whole. The idea behind this is also to simplify the link in a visual way by removing links that point to non-relevant information. By adding links a complete new link, such as a link that points to a page that contains information that corresponds to information on the current page of the user.

The following personalization functions can be distinguished (Kobsa, Koeneman & Pohl, 2001), (Serengul Guven Smith, 2000):

- **Adaptive recommendations.**
- **Recommendations regarding products and information:** Lists with links to products/services and information are filtered or arranged according to usage and user data and presented to the user.

- **Navigation recommendations:** Links are filtered or arranged according to usage, user and surroundings data. Filtering can also mean that inferior links are removed and therefore recommendations are enforced.
- **Adaptive guidance and orientation.**
- **Personalized maps:** Maps help users to understand the content and structure of an application. Hiding/disabling, annotation and direct guidance techniques can also be used to improve a map.
- **Personalize direct guidance:** This points the user to the most suitable route. Users only have to click on the 'next' button to get to the next page, which the system determines according to the user/usage model. Normally the user does not get the freedom to ignore the suggestions of the system. The destination of the 'next' button is not directly connected to the current node but can be determined dynamically.
- **Personal views and spaces:** The possibility to create ordered bookmarks gives users personalized access to websites (views). Personalization techniques can support users creating personal views and more elaborate information spaces. Personal spaces can namely be used for looking up browser history, creating shortcuts, and saving documents.

Possible Disadvantages of Adaptation

Next to the mentioned advantages, adaptive systems can also lead to usability problems. The usability principles 'predictability', 'transparency', 'controllability' and 'unobtrusiveness' are principles that can easily be violated by adaptive systems, as well as the principles 'privacy' and 'breadth of experience'. People may become concerned about the possibility that their data will be used inappropriately. When the user completely delegates a task to the system or the system relies excessively on an incomplete user model the consequence might be that the adaptive system does not work as it should. To reduce these problems the user should have the possibility to choose between complete control over a task and complete delegation of it. (Anthony, 2003), (Kroon, 1998)

Conclusion

Adaptation can be divided in personalisation and customization, uses explicit and implicit data, and is based on user, usage an surroundings models. Adaptation can be presented in three ways: adaptation of content, adaptation of presentation and adaptation of navigation. These adaptation methods can be used in combination. The use of adaptation has a lot of advantages, but also some disadvantages e.g. the problem that users can have the feeling that they have no control and problems regarding privacy issues.

PAPER FORMS VS. E-FORMS

A lot of governments replace their paper forms with Online e-forms. The main reason for this replacement is to enhance the efficiency. Next to this, the assumption was made that filling in e-forms is easier than paper forms and that the amount of forms filled-in incompletely would decrease. There are a number of standard problems that can occur when filling in paper forms and that can be solved by the use of e-forms (Dijk, 2005):

- **Routing problems:** Routing problems can be eliminated by the use of a branching program that only asks relevant questions depending on the answer of the previous questions.
- **Verification of calculations:** Verification of calculations will be less important since the computer performs all the calculations. Next to this, computers can contain built-in checks

that detect implausible or contradicted answers to question. Such features can inform the user about possible mistakes.

- **Terminology problems:** Terminology problems can be solved with the use of pop-up definitions and explanations.
- **Explanations:** Explanations can be offered through Online help. Some explanations can even be replaced by wizards that do not explain how the answer to a question can be found but that guide the user to the correct answer.

It has been said that there is no significant difference in accuracy, mental load, or motivation when filling in paper or e-forms. However, the use of adaptation in e-forms seems to be a step forward in reducing the administrative burden for persons who fill in forms. With adaptation answers can be prefilled in the forms and questions can be skipped if the answer is already known or irrelevant. (Dijk, 2005).

ADAPTATION IN E-FORMS

This section describes the different adaptation techniques that can be used in e-forms according to the theory described so far (overview of adaptation) and theory about dynamic forms (Frank & Szekely, 1998), (Girgensohn, 1995), (Serengul Guven Smith, 2000). It also describes the different possible advantages and disadvantages of the implementation of adaptation in e-forms.

Adaptation Techniques

As a result of the theory about adaptation in general, as described in the previous sections, and the theory about dynamic forms the following adaptation techniques can be used with e-forms to enhance the usability and flexibility of the form: dynamic visibility of fields, active fields, nested forms, adaptive link hiding and disabling, sorting, built-in checklists, personalized direct guidance, personalized maps, page variants, fragment variants, and frame-based techniques. The adaptation techniques that are already discussed in the previous sections are only mentioned shortly. The new adaptation techniques are described in a more elaborate way:

- **Dynamic visibility of fields:** Dynamic visibility of fields adds and/or removes fields or links (see also adaptive link removal/addition, as discussed in the section Adaptation of navigation). When fields are added or removed they are repositioned automatically in the form to prevent empty spaces. This technique can be used to prevent the user from being exposed to unnecessary items and helps the user to focus on relevant information.

- **Active fields:** Active fields corresponds to formulas linked to a cell used in spreadsheet programs. If the content of one field changes this can lead to other automatic changes in the form. This can especially be useful for the calculation of certain data in a form.

- **Nested forms:** Nested forms is a form of adaptive strechtext (see the section Adaptation of content). The content of a window is organized in sections and subsections that the user or system can open and close.

- **Adaptive link hiding/disabling:** Adaptive link hiding or disabling is discussed in the section Adaptation of navigation. It hides the visual indicator of a link or disables the functionality of a link.

- **Sorting:** Sorting corresponds to adaptive link sorting, as discussed in the section Adaptation of navigation, but also aims at text, fields, and sections.

- **Built-in checklists:** Built-in checklists is a form of adaptive link annotation, as discussed in the section Adaptation of content, and of fragment coloring, as discussed in Adaptation of navigation. It uses colors to make sure no obligatory fields are forgotten and guides users to perform tasks. Checklists can adapt themselves according to previous choices and it can determine if a step is unnecessary, finished or still has to be performed.

- **Personalized direct guidance:** Personalized direct guidance, as discussed in the section Adaptation of navigation, dynamically determined destination of 'next'-button.

- **Personalized maps:** Personalized maps, as discussed in the section Adaptation of navigation, helps users to understand the content and structure of the form.

- **Page variants:** With page variants, as discussed in the section Adaptation of content, one page consist of two or more variants representing information on a different level or style.

- **Fragment variants:** Fragment variants, as discussed in the section Adaptation of content, is the refinement of page variants. One page is divided in different fragments consisting of two or more variants representing different user groups.

- **Frame-based technique:** The frame-based technique uses adaptive natural-language generation (see the section Adaptation of content) to create alternative descriptions for different users, e.g. offering different explanations or different details of information, e.g. depending on the knowledge of the user.

(Dijk, 2005), (Frank & Szekely, 1998), (Girgensohn, 1995), (Kobsa, Koeneman & Pohl, 2001), (Serengul Guven Smith, 2000).

Advantages and Disadvantages

Implementing adaptation in e-forms has a number of possible advantages and disadvantages in comparison with e-forms without adaptation. The following advantages can be distinguished:

- The run time of filling in the form can be reduced since unnecessary fields and remarks/explanations are omitted and adapted help functions and interface can be offered. The user will not be distracted by irrelevant items.
- The user can fill in the form uninterrupted without consulting a separate guidebook; the user does not have to switch between the form and the Online guidebook. In this way the form can be filled in faster and obscurities can be solved faster.
- The help function will be ignored less by the user, it will take less effort to find relevant information and there is more chance that the help function will be used. For example, when a user consults a help function more than 50% of the time the following help functions will automatically be showed by the system.
- An adaptive application, like adaptive municipal e-forms, will reduce the costs of extra support on problem solving. For example, when a user has problems filling in a non-adaptive municipal e-form to request a service he/she might decide to call or visit the municipality to do the request or to ask for help. Implementing adaptation in municipal e-forms can reduce these costs.

Next to these advantages the following disadvantages can be distinguished []:

- Designing e-forms and replacing the current forms will result in extra "costs"
- When adaptation is not applied correctly by the system this could lead to irritation of the user when he/she must restore the "mistake".

Conclusion

As a result of the theory about adaptation in general and theory about dynamic forms different adapta-

tion techniques can be distinguished that can be implemented in e-forms. If all of these adaptation techniques are also suitable for municipal e-forms is discussed in the next sections. Implementing adaptation in e-forms has a number of possible advantages: the run time of filling in forms can be reduced, the user can fill in the form uninterrupted without consulting a separate guidebook, the help function will be ignored less by the user, and an adaptive application, like adaptive municipal e-forms, will reduce the costs of extra support on problem solving. The possible disadvantages is that it will result in extra costs and that when adaptation is not implemented correctly it could lead to irritations by the user.

ADAPTATION IN MUNICIPAL E-FORMS

Adaptation has mostly advantages for public (but also private) organizations that use a lot of administrative and on forms based communication, like municipalities and the *Belastingdienst*. Improving the efficiency of (electronic) forms is not only an advantage of adaptation for the organization but also for the users: the administrative load of filling in forms by the user (citizen or municipal employee) shifts to controlling, adding and updating information, that is offered by the application. Additionally, adaptive e-forms can help organizations to reduce operational costs by elimination time-consuming, error-sensitive (paper) document processing, and to improve the user satisfaction by offering certain services in a faster and easier way. At municipalities adaptive e-forms can be used for different issues/tasks, e.g. making an appointment, request for an official document or a permit, asking a question. (Dijk, 2005).

User Groups

According to the Dutch government, government websites and municipal websites have to conform to a number of standard requirements. One of these requirements is that a municipal website should be accessible. Here accessibility means that a website should be usable for all Internet users, e.g. citizens (regardless their physical or technical disabilities) or companies. A real accessible website does not exclude any visitors. (Advies Overheid.nl, 2005)

When researching the implementation of adaptation in municipal e-forms it is sensible to make a distinction between users and to take into account different backgrounds, knowledge, interest, wishes, goals and restrictions of the user. Looking at the accessibility and the different users the following standard user groups can be distinguished that are relevant for municipal e-forms:

- citizens
- companies
- municipal employees
- municipalities

For these four user groups possible physical and technological restrictions should be taken into account. They can also be subdivided in subgroups, e.g. novice and expert users, depending on the experience level of the user.

Experience Level of Municipal E-Forms

As mentioned in the introduction the Dutch program *Overheid heeft Antwoord* presents a yearly report called the *Overheid.nl Monitor*. The *Overheid.nl Monitor 2007*, that describes that municipalities must offer at least 65% of their services through the Internet in 2007, is based on an elaborate checklist and consists of both a yearly and continue monitor. The checklist is renewed every year, since the government organisations improve their services/website throughout the year. (Garnier, Flos & Romeijn, 2007).

To measure to which extent/percentage the services offered by the different government organizations are offered through the Internet different experience levels are used (Winkel, 2005):

(0) **no information:** The municipality has no website or does not offer any or insufficient information on the website about a certain service.

(1) **information:** Essential information about services is present on the website, e.g. a description of a service and information about procedures or rules.

(2) **download application form:** The website offers an application form for certain services that can be downloaded from the website. The user can print, fill in and send this form to the municipality.

(3) **upload application form:** The website offers an application form on the website for certain services which the user can fill in Online.

(4) **electronic transaction:** When a user or company has submitted an electronic request, the municipality offers the possibility to receive the product or service electronically or sends an digital message that the request is being processed.

For example, the service *Announcement of a change of address* can be offered on level 4 (electronic transaction). In the checklist of the *Overheid.nl Monitor 2007* the actual level, e.g. level 3, offered by a municipality is compared with the maximum level (in this case level 4). In this way the percentage is been determined. To read more about the (yearly and continue) monitor the website of *Overheid.nl Monitor* can be consulted, see (Overheid heeft Antwoord, 2008), (Garnier, Flos & Romeijn, 2007).

Conclusion

Adaptation has the biggest advantages for public organizations that use a lot of administrative and on form based communication, like municipalities. However, it is important to take privacy and security rules into account. Three user groups can be distinguished that are relevant for municipal applications: citizens, companies, and municipal employees. According to the *Overheid.nl Monitor* of the Dutch government 65% of the public services should be offered through Internet in 2007. The results of the *Overheid.nl Monitor* 2007 is that 67% of the public services in 2007 are offered digitally, which means that That year's goal of the monitor is accomplished.

ONLINE QUESTIONNAIRE

There are four main choices that are important when governments/municipalities deal with adaptation: the choice between personalization, customization, or a combination, the choice between adaptation to an individual or a group, the choice between implicit acquisition, explicit acquisition, or a combination, and the choice between adaptation of content, adaptation of presentation, adaptation of navigation, or a combination. Next to these choices it also important to make sure the different options correspond to the needs of the user groups of municipal e-forms: citizens, companies, municipal employees and municipalities. To discover the needs of these user groups three Online questionnaires were created as part of a research on Adaptive municipal e-forms conducted by the University of Twente in collaboration with the Exxellence Group (Kuiper, 2006). In this research the group companies has not been taken into account.

Method

The questionnaire for citizens, municipal employees and municipalities was created to discover the wishes and needs of these user groups regarding adaptation with municipal e-forms. The citizens questionnaire aimed at all citizens in the Netherlands who have access to Internet. Citizens were approached by a posting (Computable forum) and by email (78 persons) including the request to send it on to others. The municipal employees questionnaire aimed at municipal employees who fill in municipal e-forms on a regular base. About 800 municipal employees were approached in a newsletter of the Exxellence Group. Next to this, an email was send to all 483 municipalities in the Netherlands. Both with the question to send it on to municipal employees who fill in forms. The municipality questionnaire aimed at all municipalities in the Netherlands. Municipalities (mostly clients of the Exxellence Group) were personally approached by email. In total 53 municipality employees were emailed.

Before the questionnaires were designed it was necessary to find out which options (adaptation methods/models) should be used in adaptive municipal e-forms and which products/services could be improved with adaptation. The questionnaires were designed to be understandable for everyone, since they aimed at different people, e.g. men/women, young/old people, people with different educational levels. The main problem was how to ask things of which the user has no knowledge. To do this the questionnaires used examples of announcing a change of address, where the use of adaptation was described by approaching different users in a different way when filling in the form. The questionnaires also used pictures based on this example to explain items, e.g. adaptation of content. The user was explicitly asked to indicate his/her preference, e.g. personalization, customization, or a combination.

Questionnaire Results

54 out of 78 citizens have filled in the citizen questionnaire. The effect of request to send the questionnaire to others and the response on the posting is not known. The response rate of the municipal employees who were approached in a newsletter of the Exxellence Group was less than 1%. The response rate of the municipal

employees that were approached indirectly (who got the request from another person) was also less than 1%. The response rate of the municipal employees who were approached by sending an email to all 483 municipalities in the Netherlands was 11%. In total 51 municipality employees have filled in the questionnaire. The response rate of the municipalities was 26% (14 persons (13 municipalities) out of 53).

Citizens and municipal employees indicated that they had different problems when filling in municipal e-forms. Striking differences between the two user groups are be mentioned when relevant.

- **Explanation problems (69%):** it was not clear that an explanation could be consulted; the correct information was difficult to find in the explanations.
- **Knowledge problems (65%):** not all terms and fields that had to be filled in were clear to the user.
- **Selection problems (64%):** it was not clear enough which questions had to be answered.
- **Orientation problems (58%):** the overview was not clear enough when filling in the form.
- **Control problems (53%):** the user was not interested in or had no time to control the filled in form on mistakes.
- **Shift problems (52%):** because other documents needed to be consulted when filling in the form, the user had to shift between the form, the explanation an other Online documents.
- **Calculation problems (27%):** the user had difficulties with the calculation of problems. Notable is that 36% of the municipal employees had calculation problems comparing with only 17% of the citizens.

The problems mentioned above can be prevented with adaptation. Citizens and municipal employees also indicated that the following adaptation items could be improved in (municipal) e-forms:

- **Relevant fields (72%):** the program should only show the questions or fields that are relevant for the user.
- **Unlikely fields (69%):** the program has to give signals when a very unlikely data or illogical combinations of data are filled in.
- **Combination forms (67%):** the program offers combination forms if this is relevant for the user.
- **Sums (65%):** the program should calculate sums automatically for the user. The user should only fill in the numbers.
- **Suggestions (62%):** the program should make suggestions for other forms that could be relevant for the user.
- **Instructions (58%):** the program should give instruction about "difficult" terms and fields when relevant to the user.
- **Relevant explanations (58%):** the program should only show relevant and understandable explanations and detailed details to the user.
- **Link problems (56%):** the program should prevent link problems by showing information in the same screen, e.g. in the form of an explanation. Notable is that 70% of the municipal employees indicated that link problems should be improved comparing with only 41% of the citizens.
- **Modal data (45%):** data that has to be filled in on a frequent base, as personal data, should be filled in automatically by the program.

Assuming that the approached end-users were representative for the whole end-user group it can be concluded that they all prefer the use of adaptation with municipal e-forms (citizens: 82%, municipal employees: 67%, and municipalities: 62%). Striking is that especially the highly educated persons were more positive than people with a lower education. The users also had the opinion that most of the municipal products and services could be improved by the use of adaptation. The following products and services could be improved the most: 'Announcement of a change of address' (according to citizens), 'Permit to fell trees' (according to municipal employees), and 'Building permit' (according to municipalities). Citizens, municipal employees and municipalities generally have the preference for:

• Adaptation to an individual AND adaptation to a group
• Combination of personalisation and customisation (e.g. for people with poor eyesight)
• Combination of explicit (e.g. DigiD) and implicit acquisition
• Adaptation of content
• Adaptation of presentation (especially for people with poor eyesight)
• Adaptation of navigation. Notable is that 63% of municipal employees preferred the use of adaptation of navigation comparing with 84% of the citizens and 77% of the municipalities.

Since people with poor eyesight are seen as an important subgroup by the end-users, this should also be taken into account in the design phase (of the prototypes).

Conclusion

An Online questionnaire was conducted to discover the needs of citizens, municipal employees and municipalities regarding the implementation of adaptation in municipal e-forms. Before the questionnaires were designed it was necessary to find out which options (adaptation methods/models) should be used in adaptive municipal e-forms and which products/services could be improved with adaptation. All three user groups preferred the use of adaptation with municipal e-forms and they had the opinion that most of the municipal

products and services could be improved by the use of adaptation. As a result of the results of the Online questionnaire and the theory studied two prototypes were created and evaluated in an end user evaluation.

END USER EVALUATION

The end user evaluation uses a so-called usability test that measures the usability by examining how easy and effective a certain user can use an application and which problems occur. It can also collect information about problems, difficulties and weak point and areas that need improvement. (Lee, 1999) In this case the usability test is used as a comparison test, where the usability of an adaptive municipal e-form has been compared with a municipal e-form without adaptation. In this way the effects of adaptation could be measured.

Method

As a result of the results of the Online questionnaire and theory studied two municipal prototypes were designed and evaluated that would benefit the most from the use of adaptation or that could be improved the most according to the user groups; one relative simple form 'Announcement of a change of address' and one relative complex form 'Building permit'. Both prototypes contained the preferred methods indicated by the end-users. During the evaluation the focus was on fill in mistakes, explanations, mental efforts (quantitative results), and the use of the help function, the function page style, the appreciation, and the choice between adaptive and non adaptive (qualitative results).

The prototypes are evaluated in a face-to-face evaluation where the users (citizens and municipal employees) could give feedback while interacting with the prototype. The end user evaluation has been performed to examine if the implemented design choices correspond to the demand of these end-users. The evaluation used different test methods (Expertisegroep Usability, 2006):

- **Scenario-based testing:** gives better insight in the product and shows the items the user actually has problems with.
- **Prototype testing:** gives early insight in design mistakes and gives users an accurate view of the level in which the system corresponds to the wishes and expectations of the user.
- **Work out loud method:** is applied in an easy way, it gives direct feedback over how the application will be welcomed by the user since they get an active roll in the designs process, and it gives a clear overview of bottlenecks.
- **Interview techniques:** makes it possible to get clarifications to prevent misunderstandings.
- **Questionnaire techniques:** makes it possible to get feedback in a fast and effective way from the perspective of the user.

Users interacted with the prototype according to a scenario where he/she had to say out loud what he/she was thinking and doing. After the prototype test the user had to fill in a short questionnaire and an interview was conducted to compare the adaptive and non-adaptive version.

End User Evaluation Results

The end users (citizens and municipal employees) preferred the adaptive forms over the non adaptive forms. This was the case for both the relatively complex form 'Building permit' and the more simple form 'Announcement of a change of address'. Certain features of adaptation were more appreciated in complex forms than in the relative simple variant. The context specific help function in the form 'Building permit' was more appreciated than in the form 'Announcement of a change of address'. On the other hand, the use of DigiD was more appreciated in the form 'Announcement of a change of address', since the number of fields that had to be filled in was drastically reduced by it. In the simple form the option built-in checklists was most appreciated by the citizens and the page style option the least. With the municipal employees the option dynamic visibility of fields was most appreciated and the personalized recommendations the least. In the complex form the option dynamic visibility of fields was appreciated the most and the page style option the least. With municipal employees the option built-in checklists was appreciated the most and the page style option was also appreciated the least. However, it was also indicated by the municipal employees that the choice of the page style should depend on the interaction behaviour of the user and not of his/her personal data, e.g. age of the user.

Conclusion

As a result of the results of the Online questionnaire and theory studied, two municipal prototypes that would benefit the most from the use of adaptation or that could be improved the most according to the user groups were designed and evaluated in an end user evaluation. In the end user evaluation the citizens and municipal employees could give feedback on the adaptive and non adaptive variants of the e-forms while interacting with the prototypes. Both citizens and municipal employees preferred the adaptive forms over the non adaptive forms. The option dynamic visibility of fields and built-in checklists were most appreciated by the users and the page style option the least. Next to the evaluation under citizens and municipal employees an evaluation under municipalities has been performed: focus group evaluation.

FOCUS GROUP EVALUATION

After the end user evaluation under citizens and municipality employees a focus group evaluation was performed under municipalities to investigate if municipalities are interested in offering adaptive municipal e-forms to citizens and/or municipal employees and in which way these forms should be offered.

Method

The goal of the focus group evaluation was to get reactions on the prototypes, to get insights by group interactions, and to get the opinions, attitudes, and preferences of the group. Both adaptive municipal e-forms 'Announcement of a change of address' and 'Building permit' were presented and discussed during the group evaluation to see if these types of e-forms are appreciated by the municipalities. The focus group evaluation is a qualitative evaluation where the focus was on the use of the help function, the function page style, built-in checklists, DigiD, adaptive 'next button', dynamic visibility of fields, and personalised recommendations. Discussed were appreciation of these functionalities and the preference of an adaptive or a non adaptive version.

The target group of the evaluation consisted of a representative focus group of municipalities that offer municipal e-forms to citizens. Five (of the thirteen) approached municipalities participated in the focus group evaluation. The group consisted of ICT advisers, ICT managers etc. of expert (40%) and middle (60%) municipalities. The novice group was also approached but they indicated that they were not far enough with their digital services to evaluate the use of adaptation with municipal e-forms.

Focus Group Evaluation Results

The municipalities preferred adaptive forms and indicated that the use of adaptation contributed to municipal e-forms since it enhanced the usability of the form. This was the case for the relative complex form 'Building permit' and the more simple form 'Announcement of a change of address'. According to the municipalities the use of adaptation should be standard in the implementation of all types of forms. Some adaptive functionalities were more appreciated than others, however according to the municipalities all functionalities contributed to the forms and should be used in standard implementations.

Conclusion

A focus group evaluation was performed under municipalities to investigate if they are interested in offering adaptive municipal e-forms to citizens and/or municipal employees and in which way these forms should be offered. The municipalities preferred adaptive e-forms and indicated that the use of adaptation contributed to adaptive municipal e-forms since it enhanced the usability of the form. They also mentioned that it should be used as the standard implementation in all types of (municipal) e-forms.

CONCLUSION

The question was if and how municipal electronic forms (e-forms), used to request municipal products and services, can be improved by the use of adaptation. The impression exists that users are not totally content with the current municipal e-forms. To discover if the use of adaptation contributes to municipal e-forms different researches were performed where the focus was on the user and the client.

First a theoretical research was performed regarding the implementation of adaptation in general and in municipal e-forms in particular. As a result of this theoretical research a more detailed research has been performed by means of an Online questionnaire and user evaluations to examine how citizens, municipality employees and municipalities, think about the use of adaptation with municipal e-forms. First a questionnaire was conducted under citizens, municipal employees and municipalities. The questionnaire results were used to develop two prototypes which were tested in an end-user evaluation with citizens and municipal employees and during a focus group evaluation with municipalities. The results of the Online questionnaire indicated that citizens (82%), municipality employees (67%) and municipalities (62%) had a preference for the use of adaptation. They indicated that the major part of the discussed products and services could be improved with the use of adaptation. For citizens this was especially the service 'Announcement of a change of address', for municipality employees it was the product 'Request for a felling permit' and for the municipalities it was the product 'Request for a building permit'. Four prototypes have been created. Two variants of the relatively simple service 'Announcement of a change of address' and two variants of the more complex product 'Request for a building permit'; an adaptive and a non adaptive variant. Citizens, municipality employees and municipalities preferred the adaptive version of the form 'Announcement of a change of address' as well as of the form 'Request for a building permit'. However, they mentioned that improvements should be made with respect to the content of the form 'Request for a building permit'. Remarkable was that at first municipalities were least positive about the implementation of adaptation in municipal e-forms (62%) and that they were most positive after the evaluation of the prototypes (100%). They also mentioned it should be the norm to implement adaptation in municipal e-forms, both simple as complex ones.

It is recommended to municipalities to standard implement adaptation with municipal e-forms, to monitor user behaviour and use known (personal) data and data about corresponding users as an input for adaptation. Municipalities should also examine the municipal e-forms internally and improve them internally prior to the implementation of adaptation. It is recommended to use DigiD and built-in checklist in municipal e-forms and to offer personalised guidance and links; dynamic and active fields, page variants and context dependent help functions on different levels.

When implementing adaptation in municipal e-forms different items should be taken into account. The implementation of adaptation costs money; a part can be 'earned back' because less counter and call centre employees will be necessary if citizens are able to request municipal products and services Online without the aid of a municipality employee. By monitoring the user behaviour the user can have the feeling that he/she is being watched. The user can also fear the possibility that his/her personal data will be abused; the municipalities should show a disclaimer which clearly mentions why and how the user data will be used. If adaptation is not being correctly applied by the system this could lead to irritations for the end-user, who has to recover the 'mistake' him/herself.

Because of the positive feedback of all three user groups (citizens, municipal employees and municipalities) added value of the use of adaptation in municipal e-forms is evident and municipalities should seriously consider to use it in standard practice.

REFERENCES

Anthony, J. (2003). Adaptive Interfaces and Agents. In J. Jacko & A. Sears (Eds.), *Human-computer Interaction Handbook* (pp. 305-330). Mahwah, NJ: Erlbaum.

Advies Overheid.nl (2005). Webrichtlijnen Overheid.nl 2005, Richtlijnen voor de toegankelijkheid en duurzaamheid van overheidswebsites. Retrieved from http://webrichtlijnen.overheid.nl/webrichtlijnen-1.1.pdf

Advies Overheid.nl (2006). Overheid.nl Monitor, Prestaties van de e-overheid gemeten. Retrieved from http://www.minbzk.nl/contents/pages/54678/overheid.nl_monitor_2005.pdf

Bearman, D., & Trant, J. (2004). *Museums and the Web 2004, Proceedings.* Toronto: Archives & Museum Informatics. Retrieved from http://www.archimuse.com/mw2004/papers/bowen/bowen.html

DigiD (2008). *Over DigiD.* Retrieved August 2008 from http://www.digid.nl/burger/.

Dijk, van J. A. G. M. et al. (2005). *Alter Ego: State of the art on user profiling. An overview of the most relevant organisational and behavioural aspects regarding User Profiling,* Telematica Instituut. Retrieved from https://doc.telin.nl/dscgi/ds.py/Get/File-47289/UT_D1.10a.pdf

Eirinaki, A., & Vazirgiannis, M. (2003). *Web Mining for Web Personalization.* Retrieved from http://www.db-net.aueb.gr/magda/papers/TOIT-webmining_survey.pdf. Athens University of Economics and Business.

Expertisegroep Usability 2006 Regio Randstad-Noord (2006). *Usability Testing, Kenmerken van Methoden, Sogeti Nederland B.V.* Retrieved from http://www.tmap.net/Images/Usability%20Testing%20versie%201.01_tcm8-31182.pdf#search=%22voordelen%20%22usability%20testing%22%22.

Exxellence Group (2008). *Partner van de elektronische overheid.* Retrieved from http://www.exxellence.nl.

Frank, M. R., & Szekely, P. (1998). Adaptive forms: an interaction technique for entering structured data. *Knowledge-Based Systems, 11,* 37-45.

Garnier, M., Flos, B., & Romeijn, H. (2007). Overheid.nl Monitor 2007, Overheid heeft Antwoord©. Retrieved from www.advies.overheid.nl/attachment.db?7698.

Germanakos, P., et al. (2005). Personalization Systems and Processes Review based on a Predetermined User Interface Categorization, III CONGRÉS INTERNACIONAL COMUNICACIÓ I REALITAT. Retrieved from http://cicr.blanquerna.url.es/2005/Abstracts/PDFsComunicacions/vol1/05/GERMANAKOS_MOURLAS_PANAYIOTOU_SAMARAS.pdf.

Girgensohn, A. et al. (1995). Dynamic forms: An enhanced interaction abstraction based on forms. In *Proceedings of Interact'95, Fifth IFIP Conference on Human-Computer Interaction,* (pp. 362-367). London: Chapman & Hall.

Hoogwout, M., Vries, de M., et al. (2005). Onderzoek: Digitale indiening omgevingvergunning Mijlpaal op weg naar de Andere Overheid, Zenc. Retrieved from http://www.vrom.nl/pagina.html?id=18487.

Kobsa, A., Koeneman, J. J., & Pohl, W. (2001). Personalized hypermedia presentation techniques for improving online customer relationships. *The knowledge Engineering Review, 16*(2), 111-115.

Kroon, J. P. (1998). *Hoofdstuk 10: Het belang van klantinformatie voor E-commerce. Ecommerce Handboek.* Retrieved from http://www.netmarketing.nl/downloads/files/Voorbeeldhoofdstuk%20E-commerce%20Handboek.pdf.

Kuiper, P. M. (2006). *Adaptieve Gemeentelijke eFormulieren,* Formulieren die met u meedenken, Universiteit Twente, Exxellence Group, Nederland.

Lee, S. H. (1999). *Usability Testing for Developing Effective Interactive Multimedia Software: Concepts, Dimensions, and Procedures,* Hanyang University, Department of Educational Technology, Seoul, Korea. Retrieved from http://ifets.ieee.org/periodical/vol_2_99/sung_heum_lee.html.

Overheid heeft Antwoord (2008). *Actueel.* Retrieved August 2008 from http://www.advies.overheid.nl.

Serengul Guven Smith, A. (2000). *Application of Machine Learning Algorithms in Adaptive Web-based Information Systems*, School of Computing Science Technical Report Series. Retrieved from http://www.cs.mdx.ac.uk/staffpages/serengul/Pdf/chapter%204.PDF.

Winkel, N. (2005). *Publieke dienstverlening 65% elektronisch, Viermeting van de elektronische dienstverlening van de overheid in 2005*, Advies Overheid.nl en Ministerie van Binnenlandse Zaken en Koninkrijksrelaties. Retrieved from http://advies.overheid.nl/3137/.

KEY TERMS

Back Office: The back office forms the hart of the organisation were, invisible for the outer world, the primary (data distributing) processes are performed.

Back Office System: A back office system/application offers data distributing functionality and is used in this way by a mid office .

Customisation: Customisation is the adaptation of a website to his/her personal preference s of a user.

E-Form: An e-forms is a given procedure designed to register, read, edit, transport, reproduces, save and search data in an uniform, systematic and complete way (fill in and fill up).

E-Government: E-government is the use of ICT in government services in combination with organizational changes and new abilities of the employees.

Electronic (digital) Service Counter: An electronic service counter is a (government) service counter where the government and the citizens/companies communicate through electronic channels with the goal to optimally adjust their services to the demand of the citizens/companies.

Front Office: The front office forms the presentation layer of the organisation to the outer world; all interaction with the outer world is being performed by the front office.

Mid Office: The mid office is a collection of functionalities that connects the processes and corresponding applications and data in the front office and the back office.

Personalisation: Content is offered in a personalized way by a website to individuals or groups of persons, based on profiles, demographic data and/or previous transactions.

Portal: A portal offers functionality to offer relevant information and applications to (groups of) end users in a personalized way.

Section III
e–HRM in Multinational Companies

Chapter VIII
HRIS Project Teams Skills and Knowledge:
A Human Capital Analysis

Hazel Williams
Nottingham Trent University, UK

Carole Tansley
Nottingham Trent University, UK

Carley Foster
Nottingham Trent University, UK

ABSTRACT

Global, enterprise-wide, information systems (GEIS) projects are often delayed with budget over-runs often due to a lack of understanding of the key roles required on the project. The "hybrid" knowledge and skills requirement of functional GEIS teams, typically composed of both IT personnel and representatives from the departments where the system is going to be used, are generally not acknowledged and understood. This chapter presents the findings of a study conducted with project teams working in a multi-national organisation implementing and maintaining the HR "pillar" of an SAP GEIS located in four countries. The main purpose of that study was the identification of HRIS skills and knowledge in the key roles on the global project and make suggestions for development of project team members. Using a human capital frame of reference, we provide a guiding framework which can be used as a sensemaking tool by those responsible for managing people working in hybrid roles on such projects.

INTRODUCTION

The development of human resource information systems (HRIS) over the last twenty years has been driven by imperatives to improve the service of the HR function, further compounded by the growth of global enterprise-wide information systems (GEIS). A GEIS is a software system that allows an organisation to share common data across functional areas of enterprises operating transnationally and which produce and access information in a real-time environment (see Davenport, 1998; Klaus et al., 2000). During the 1990s, enterprise resource planning (ERP) systems became the *de facto* standard for replacement of legacy systems in large and, in particular, multinational companies (Holland et al 1996; Holland et al 1999).

Adoption of GEIS can be long, complicated and problematic, involving major technical and organisational challenges of business process reorganisation, often involving delays and budget over-runs and ending in failure (Cozijnsen et al 2000; Matta and Ashkenas 2003; Robey et al 2002; Shanks and Seddon 2000). In addition, a number of writers note the role of human factors in the failure or the success of these technological changes (Guérin et al 2001; Martinsons and Chong 1999; Paré and Elam 1995). There can be many reasons for this, but often overlooked is whether the skills and knowledge requirements of those on international project teams are available at the right time and place. Each functional GEIS is typically composed of both IT personnel and representatives from the departments where the system is going to be used in the representative country. Such teams are populated by individuals with a blend of knowledge, skills and talents and who necessarily traverse different disciplines as 'hybrids'. However, there is often a lack of understanding of the key roles required on the project and the need for 'new' roles for specialist areas (because of the multi-disciplinary nature of the knowledge and skills required).

Historically human resourcing specialists have focused their skills and knowledge on HR management processes, such as resourcing, training and development, rewards, performance management and employee relations. However in recent years, and mirroring other functional specialisms, another role has been added to the HR specialist's remit: responsibility for the implementation and management of human resource management information systems (HRIS) projects. The introduction of this technological resource suggests the introduction of new skills and competencies for the HR specialist, in particular project management and information systems. The requirement for these new skills and knowledge sets has been a challenging learning journey for many within the HR profession.

Although there has been a growing body of academic interest in HRIS, the majority of interest is around how HRIS supports and integrates with corporate strategy to enable competitive advantage (Broderick and Boudreau 1992; Hannon et al 1996; Minneman 1996; Tansley et al 2001; Williams 2000), and the presence and 'fit' in different organisations (Ball 2001; CIPD 2007). There is limited and dated research around the information systems skills and knowledge of the HR specialist (Beaumont et al 1992; Kinnie and Arthurs 1996).

We present here the findings of a study conducted with project teams working in a transnational organisation implementing and maintaining the HR 'pillar' of an SAP GEIS on their UK, Germany, Canada and the USA sites. The main purpose of that study was the identification of HRIS skills and knowledge in the key roles on the global project and the clarification of talent management issues relating to project team members. Using a human capital frame of reference, in this paper we identify key issues of resourcing project teams and offer a framework for identifying the appropriate mix of skills and knowledge requirements.

THE ROLE OF HUMAN CAPITAL MANAGEMENT IN HRIS PROJECT TEAM RESOURCING

Examining the skills and knowledge of a global HRIS project team can be a complex undertaking because no diagnostic tools are available for this hybrid occupational group. Using a human capital 'lens' is useful as it provides a valuable and rigorous way of framing the diverse attributes of project team members. This approach has not yet been promoted in the literature to date and thus offers an innovative opportunity for scholars and practitioners to examine an HRIS project team. The ultimate aim is to provide a descriptive framework for future action.

The notion of human capital is a relatively new concept which focuses on the valuation of human effort, knowledge, competence and contribution to economic performance. It is an organisational strength which is becoming increasingly recognised as an important strategic contributor to organisational success (Becker et al 1997; Snell et al 1996; Wright et al 1994) and a competitive differentiator (Fitz-Enz 1997, 2000; Gebauer 2003; Rastogi 2003; Ulrich and Lake 1991). As Rastogi (2000: 196) argues: "well-developed human resources serve to provide the foundation on which an edifice of human capital may be built". A number of writers have shown that individuals with high levels of human capital are able to implement new technologies more effectively (Bartel and Lichtenberg 1987, 1990; Link and Siegel 2007; Siegel 1999; Siegel et al 1997). This suggests that organisations need to continually invest in their human capital to build and develop individuals' knowledge, skills and competencies, to continue to ensure organisational success (Youndt et al 2004).

Becker's (1975; 1993) work is considered seminal in this area, where in the broadest sense, human capital is defined as knowledge, skills, health, or values and is produced by investment in *formal* education and training (rather than

informal which is considered more difficult to measure). Another clear implication is that within this definition, human capital is embedded within the employee and cannot be separated from that person. Although Becker considered human capital from a macro-national perspective, his observations are valid at the micro level in that one can study the training, formal and informal education of the individuals who, in the case presented, constitute a project team.

There are three distinct positions taken in the human capital literature that we will consider in the context of HRIS project teams. The first position advocates human capital being the *aggregate* or sum of the workforce capabilities (physical strength, intelligence and demographics) of a particular population. The second position focuses on the *constituent parts* that make up individual human capital, such as the proprietary knowledge, skills, experience and competencies of individuals (Scarbourgh and Elias 2002). The third position, (mainly found in the economics and the finance literature) takes the view that human capital is a result of a variety of investments made to enhance an individual's organisational offering and potential (Schultz 1961).

This short historical overview of human capital literature is intended as background for the focus of this paper. Additionally it provides context for a more in-depth human capital analysis of the research study.

RESEARCH DESIGN

Background Information on the Case Study

The organisation being studied, known here as CHC Plc, is a leading power-systems company operating in a variety of engineering markets. The company manufactures in 20 countries, employs approximately 38,000 people worldwide and serves customers in 150 countries. Market operations are becomingly increasingly challenging with rising costs (particularly raw materials), fierce competition from established players in a mature market and the search for innovation around new investments. However, the organisation's strong product portfolio means that they are involved in many of the major future projects in the markets they serve.

The focus of this study was on the team implementing and developing the SAP human resourcing (HR) system used by the company, which is part of a global enterprise-wide system used by their HR function to deliver excellence to its stakeholders. The HR system had a number of different elements: personnel administration; organisation management; reward; time management; payroll; resourcing; travel and expenses; training and events management; global mobility; occupational health and reporting and personal development. It was first rolled out in the UK five years ago. Prior to this 1600 legacy HR systems had existed. Future project work on SAP includes the development of the ES HR information system (HRIS) with countries other than the UK, Germany, the USA and Canada.

There are many different stakeholders involved in the project, including: project managers, IS designers, HRIS developers and maintainers, HR clients as system users, and a number from outside the organisation, such as external consultants. It also needs to be noted that at the time of the study the company had totally outsourced its IT function to EDS, a world leading IT service provider. This was a complex project to manage as all stakeholders are involved at different points of time as future system-owners (Hammer and Champy 1995) but not on a continuous basis as Luftman (2000) suggests, but, rather, with different degrees of intensity.

The CHC PLC HRIS development team responding to client needs has grown organically over the last 10 years, rather than being designed and developed strategically. This growth has been driven both by embracing and expanding

SAP HR technology and functionality in the UK and the addition of different parts of the business operating in different countries (USA, Canada and Germany). It has meant that there are eight members on the UK central HRIS team and six in the other geographies.

By April 2007 a growing number of problems had been reported, by both team members and clients from the company's HR shared-service centre in the UK. For example, as the UK team has grown there has been the problem of indistinct and ambiguous reporting lines and ambiguity of role responsibilities impacting on service quality. This came about because individuals did not have clearly defined roles or role boundaries. Work tended to be allocated on a basis of who was free at a particular time with the specialisms and interests of team members allied to allocation of work tasks wherever possible. Part of the reason for this was lack of a suitable level of personnel on the team. However, this did cause confusion for HRIS colleagues based in other countries, the internal HR client and for representatives of the outsourcing firm. For example, for the HR client there is often confusion as to where responsibilities lie: with the internal HRIS team or the outsourcing firm. Some of this confusion is due to budgetary arrangements, called 'head count politics' by one interviewee; i.e. how a project is defined will depend on how it is then resourced.

To help address these issues, the head of the HRIS team realised that the team would need to be adequately resourced, communication processes across the globe needed to be improved and individual members developed. A talent pool from which the team could draw upon was therefore of strategic importance. The team leader had been in charge of the team since its inception 10 years ago, which meant unusual stability for a project team, although he is due to retire within the next year. Although not a primary driver for this research, succession planning for his critical role is a key future task for this project. Overall, then, it was identified that the key element which was missing and which was the foundation of solving the current issues was the identification of all roles in the global team, the mapping of key knowledge and skills of individuals on the team, a development plan for their future work needs and a gap analysis to fill knowledge and skills needs for current and future projects. At this point the researchers were briefed on these requirements and this study began.

Research Methodology and Methods

The research methodology of this study was interpretive in approach and the methods comprised of observation, focus groups, meetings and individual interviews. A total of 25 semi-structured interviews were conducted over a two-month period. Respondents included HRIS team members in the UK, USA, Germany and Canada senior HR managers and key internal and external clients and stakeholders with whom the team has had significant contact with. Three interview protocols were developed to take account of the different roles of the respondents and all interviews were recorded and transcribed. Interview questions were aimed at examining how the skills, knowledge and experiences of the HRIS team impacted on the team's objectives for servicing clients' needs for satisfying wider organisational goals. Interviewees were not asked to prioritise or weight answers at this stage, therefore we do not draw inferences in terms of the relative importance of responses.

The approach adopted when conducting the interviews was a narrative one in order to gather stories about the respondent's day-to-day work, exploring how individuals employed their current and previous experiences, knowledge and skills in various settings to "generate data which give an authentic insight into people's experiences" (Silverman 2001: 87). Outcomes of this approach were accounts of participants' work, their feelings about their work, of internal and external organisational colleagues' work, of the politics and the

interpersonal dynamics within and external to the organisation. These accounts were therefore saturated with the respondents' physical, emotional and intellectual experience (Abna 2003; Gold et al 2000; Taylor et al 2004) and were "not simply representations of the world; they are part of the world they describe" (Hammersley and Atkinson 1983: 107). Observational material collected was from two workshops where the skills and knowledge of HRIS specialists were explored. These workshops were facilitated by the authors and attended by members of the UK HRIS team (both in company and consultant representatives). Documentary evidence, such as organisational charts and meeting notes supplied by respondents in the UK, US, Canada and Germany were also drawn upon.

Our analysis involved loading of research materials such as interview transcripts into the qualitative data analysis package NVivo, then sharing initial findings with all or some of the company team, such as the project manager and team members. Their observations were recorded and transcribed. Following this, each researcher individually reviewed the qualitative data they had personally collected then they met as a team to articulate the themes emerging from each research episode. These reflections were added to NVivo as additional themes for theorising and in order to compare the cases and consider the principles of dialogical reasoning and suspicion in order to further improve our interpretive accounts (Klein and Myers, 1999). In analyzing the data we looked for pattern codes which can provide explanatory or inferential meta-codes that allowed us to identify an emergent theme, configuration, explanation or 'repeatable regularities' (Miles and Hubermann 1994, p69). An iterative process of cross-study discussion and fine-tuning of themes aided our identification of the over-arching theme related to elements of human capital frameworks. The analytical themes were then organised around these mechanisms which allowed us to develop a coherent sense of the impacts across the case study.

CASE STUDY ANALYSIS & DISCUSSION

At this point we move to examine the case study and its analysis. Instead of discussing our research findings and analysis separately, we propose to amalgamate these elements. Initially, we presents our understanding of aggregated and consistent human capital (Figure 1), refining and extending Becker's (1975; 1993) thinking by considering human capital in a commercial and economic context. We will apply this understanding to material drawn from our study, noting the challenges inherent in each of these positions with regard to our study.

Types of Human Capital

The types of human capital noted in Figure 1 are drawn from literature analysed elsewhere (Williams 2008) and used here as a framework for discussion.

Aggregate View of Project Team Human Capital

Aggregated data are not new descriptors; they have been used for many years in the human resource planning lexicon and tend to express a top-level view, of whole or part of an organisation's human capital. So in organisational practice they can be used as collective data on individuals to describe the aggregate organisational population (Tansley et al 2001). The main difficulty with this type of data is that there is an underlying assumption that organisations are characteristically homogenous, whereas in reality they are heterogeneous. This said, this type of data does have value when considering a global HRIS project team. Here we consider three aspects of aggregated data: physical location; education levels; and tenure.

The physical location of a project team is likely to influence the geographic context of an individual's knowledge, orientation to that body of knowledge and potentially their exposure to particular work practices.

Figure 1. Types of human capital

Aggregate human capital

The aggregate view of human capital provides for a collection of employee details comprising, for example, age, gender, marital status, previous work experience, competencies and physical location. This can be taken as a whole or part of an organisation.

Constituent elements of individual human capital

The constituent view of human capital comprises an individual-level perspective. This has a number of features:

1. **Personal attributes:** Individual human capital is characterized by the repertoire of personal attributes (particularly values and beliefs, education, knowledge, skills, experience, commitment and motivation) owned, developed and created by an individual that are productive (or have the potential to be productive) in an economic context and taken with the individual when they leave the firm. (Williams, 2008)
2. **Specialist attributes:** Individual human capital can also be characterized by specialist attributes (Lepak & Snell, 1999) that are observed in those who are considered "experts" in their field and who are vital to the continued competitive success of organisation and an essential part of its core competence. These "experts" have explicit and tacit knowledge and skills (Polanyi, 1958, 1967, 1998) that can only be found within particular professions and roles. Where specialist attributes of human capital exist they need to be attached to appropriate roles in an organisation with "different occupations... [requiring] investments in different kinds of capital" (Polachek & Siebert, 1993, p. 175); this is echoed in the work of Heijke et al. (2003).
3. **Firm-specific attributes:** Individual human capital finally can be characterized by firm-specific attributes, notable an individual's specific skills, experiences and learning that can only be gained and employed within a particular organisation and are not transferable outside of that sector or organisation. (Bingley & Westergaard-Nielsen, 2003) This type of attribute is developed through long-term tenure within a particular organisation.

Table 1. Summary of CHC PLC HRIS team member functional backgrounds

Functional specialism	UK			Germany			USA			Canada		
	No. in team	Education	Tenure (years)	No. in team	Education	Tenure (years)	No. in team	Education	Tenure (years)	No. in team	Education	Tenure (years)
HR	4 FT	1 C 1 H+M	29 17 8	0	n/a	n/a	0	n/a	n/a	1 FT	1D+M	7
IS	2 FT	1U	37	2 PT	2D	5 5	2 FT	1B	4 1	0	n/a	n/a
Finance & Payroll	2 FT	1G	29 17	0	n/a	n/a	0	n/a	n/a	1 FT	1U	7

Legend:

Academic qualifications:		Professional qualifications:
C = Craft	D = Degree	H = Human resourcing
G = School leaver at 16	M = Masters	B = Business

Other:

U = unknown	FT = Team member whose time is fully allocated the a HRIS role
n/a = not applicable	PT = Team member who time is partially allocated to a HRIS role

Table 1 summarises the geographical location of interviewees and their functional specialisms.

The HRIS team members are a collection of individuals that, in general, have been with CHC PLC for a significant number of years and all are full-time members of the team (see Table 1). All team members are over 30 years of age, with three nearing retirement age. The eight members of the UK team in particular have long experience within the organisation, ranging from eight to 37 years and totalling 137 years, with a mean average of 23 years. Four of the UK team have an extensive human resourcing background, supported by other key individuals who have significant payroll and financial experience. At least two have completed a craft level engineering apprenticeship. The other four members of the UK team primarily come from a financial background with some infor-

mation system skills. When asked, interviewees found it difficult to place their initial functional background as most have moved both horizontally and vertically in the organisation over many years and through different functional specialisms. The general picture was one of deep understanding of the historical development of the organisation, the inter-weaving of different functional and policy areas and an awareness of the wide-ranging internal political dimensions.

This differs from the two part-time HRIS team members based in Germany who have an information systems background. Although they have each been with the CHC PLC for five years, they have significant experience with the company with which they were originally employed, so they have a deep understanding of the local organisational context. There are two full-time HRIS team members located in the United States of America: one is an employee of four years standing; the other is a consultant on an open-ended service contract for the last year. Like the Germany team, both have a significant information systems background. The consultant has worked on SAP consultancy projects, particularly payroll projects, on a self-employed basis. The Canadian team also has significant employment with CHC PLC. These two full-time employees have each been with the company for seven years. Although one employee has a HR-related masters, both have a preference for work associated with information systems knowledge sets. The average length of service for the other geographies is five years with CHC PLC, but this does not take into consideration service with the previous employing organisations that were acquired by CHC PLC.

This aggregated analysis is a useful practice especially for transnational organisations where teams are based in various geographical locations. The ability to summarise disparate data highlights human capital gaps, for example in terms of basic education levels. However this 'snapshot' approach is problematic if undertaken infrequently as project teams are often, by their very nature, transient and temporary arrangements (Dainty et al 2004; O'Donohue et al 2007) and radical change can take place within short periods of time. The extended tenure and wide-spread location of this particular project team suggests potential concerns for the distribution of skills and knowledge. An examination of the constituent attributes of individual human capital will add a depth of understanding not gained through consideration of the aggregated approach.

Constituent View of Human Capital

As noted earlier, individual human capital can be taken to comprise three constituent attributes: personal; specialist; and firm-specific.

Table 2. The attributes of an HRIS specialist

HR IS attributes:	IS attributes:
Calm in a crisis	Attention to detail
Inquisitive mindset	Enquiring mindset
'Lark' or 'Owl'	Analytical mindset
Practical	Problem-solver
Integrity	Tenacious
Open-minded	

Personal Attributes of Individual Human Capital

Various attempts have been made to articulate the personal attributes of individual human capital in recent years (Cressy 1996; Laing and Weir 1999; Marsden 1993). An outcome of this study was a discussion around the attributes of the HRIS specialist. Interviewees were asked to describe the skills resident and admired within the team they considered characterised an effective HRIS specialist. All found this very difficult to do, but Table 2 below summarises the words they used to describe personal attributes they admired in their colleagues or valued in themselves.

As the HRIS project team comprises individuals with a variety of different backgrounds it is not appropriate to consider personal attitudes drawn from either a HR or information systems studies for comparison. Nonetheless, for HR specialists, an analytical, problem-solving mindset has not been a distinctive feature in the past. HR specialists have traditionally been associated with attributes that demonstrate emotional intelligence and a people-orientation rather than hard analytical characteristics. The hybrid HRIS specialist studied here clearly values analytical attributes, illustrated by a Canadian-based member of the team, who notes, "one of my strongest points or aspects would be I'm a very logical person and I'm a very thorough person... I need to make sure that all options are considered and I have answer for all of them". This opinion was echoed in a number of interviews.

Specialist Attributes of Individual Human Capital

From the data analysis (see Table 1) we found that the eight members of the HRIS team based at the UK corporate headquarters have excellent skills and knowledge in the development of the systems specific to operational HR client requirements. Half of the team emanate from functional HR where they had experience in HR line operational roles. Their move to HRIS provides an excellent example of a potential resourcing strategy for this role. CHC PLC legacy systems were replaced during 1997-2000 with an enterprise-wise system, SAP. Four of the UK HRIS team members were all part of this process, with two taking on functional super-user roles. This provides a strength of understanding of particular pillars of SAP HR. Their deep knowledge and skills in these areas, coupled with their high length of service within the HR function and the organisation, are the basis for their initial move and continued development in the HRIS role. Two of the UK team members have moved from an information systems background into the HRIS role. Two of the team have a strong processing background in finance and payroll, supported by substantive experience implementing the payroll pillar in the UK and other the geographies. The payroll application is considered a critical system: should this pillar fall the impact on the whole organisation would be dramatic. A critical concern for the team leader and indeed the whole team is that the knowledge and skills that reside only in these two individuals for the whole of the UK. There is a lack of knowledge within the UK team of strategic understanding and none described themselves as HRIS business analysts to take any visioning forward for the HR function as a whole. There are limited formal qualifications in the UK team: two have craft engineering qualification

gained some 20 years ago; one has the UK HR qualification awarded by the Chartered Institute of Personnel and Development, this individual is also in the process of studying for a Masters in Project Management.

By contrast the knowledge of the German, US and Canadian team members has been gained by exposure to a number of large organisations. Experience has also been gained via professional consultancy in Canada and the USA. This is particularly relevant for the US-based consultant who is Dutch by birth, but has dual nationality with the US. He has experience in both Europe and the US in SAP related work. His deep knowledge has been gained via exposure to similar projects and he has proactively developed a scarce expertise. Although one of the Canadian team does have a HR qualification and a *Masters in Labor Relations*, the others all have degrees in information systems related disciplines: these formal qualifications underpin the practical knowledge of these individuals.

Project management knowledge and skills are generally associated with the information systems professionals: an area considered important by all interviewees. Individuals with formal IS qualifications are assumed to have these knowledge and skills; this is the case for HRIS team members in Germany, the USA and Canada, but not the case for members of the UK-based team. The two team members based in the UK who consider they have a significant background in IS draw on knowledge and skills acquired informally through exposure to a number of years 'doing the job'. Other members of the UK-based team consider that they are still learning, via informal mechanisms. One team member, with HR qualifications has recognised the need to acquire a formal qualification and is studying for a *Masters in Project Management*.

Some of the key elements of knowledge and skills identified by the respondents as necessary for an effective HRIS specialist were generated from 'free lists' (Weller and Romney 1988) are listed in Table 3.

Table 3. Typology of knowledge and skills required by the HRIS specialist

Process knowledge:		
Human resourcing:	Resourcing Development	Professional qualification
Financial:	Payroll	Professional qualification
Information systems:	Data migration Data testing Design Implementation	Infrastructure Maintenance Programming Technical lead
Project management:	Budgeting Development Governance	Management of Project planning Professional qualification
Global:	Languages	Cultural awareness
Interpersonal skills:	Negotiation Team player	Trustworthy Emotional intelligence

Table 3 illustrates some of the knowledge and skills sets interviewees' considered essential for the effective HRIS specialist. This typology is presented with three core areas: process knowledge; global knowledge; and interpersonal skills. The process knowledge is sub-divided further into four core areas: human resourcing; financial areas; information systems; and project management. Table 3 is not presented as a complete list of the knowledge required by and HRIS specialist. It is directly drawn from participant interviews. We suggest that further investigation is required to identify the full range of consistent elements. Nevertheless we can make a number of observations at this stage.

Interviewees distinguished between four types of process knowledge. HR knowledge is derived from individuals who have undertaken practitioner roles at some point in the past. For example, of the team members in the UK, four individuals have had roles as HR specialists, although only one, younger member of the team has a CIPD qualification. The Canadian team member a psychology degree and labour relations masters. The interviewees' 'talk' illustrated how their previous experiences as a practising HR specialist informed their current work as a HRIS specialist. All members of the global HRIS

project team considered that the contribution of individuals with an HR practitioner background differentiated the HRIS project team from the ERP IS team. This distinctiveness is noted elsewhere: for example "ideal project team members, especially the project team leader, are to some extent multidisciplinary" (Fischer 1995 : 2), although there is limited literature at this time. Indeed CHC team members welcome each other's contribution even though there are still some challenges in working such a cross-functional team, where critical success factors (such as task design, group composition, organisational context, internal processes and boundary, management, and group psychosocial traits) (after Holland et al 2000) are constantly renegotiated.

We follow Becker's (1975; 1993) position and focus on the formal education undertaken by our interviewees. Fundamentally the education levels of the HRIS team are split geographically: the UK and the other geographies. Interestingly although there is a great deal of knowledge in the UK-based team, this has been gained through tenure, rather than formal study with one significant exception. On the other hand those based in the Germany, the US and Canada bring more formal academic knowledge sets to bear. Interviewees found it very difficult to discuss their tacit and explicit knowledge and skill-base. They did not really think in terms of how they employed their knowledge and skills in their day-to-day work

What is clear from the lists in Table 3 is the range and depth of knowledge and skills needed in the HRIS team member role. It might be argued that these can all be learned, however it is unlikely that external qualifications and training exist currently that encompass these areas. This suggests that organisations may have to choose to resource individuals who have some of these competences and provide development for others: here, a strategically balanced approach is proposed.

Professional development tends to be balkanised in that individuals will chose to specialise in their early 20's. The syllabuses for the human resourcing qualification in the UK and the USA have limited financial studies, information systems studies or project management studies. These appear in only one module and are not considered by the majority of students to be primary skills. Most students study HR in order to acquire the range of process knowledge associated with the HR function. It is only in the last three years that this has begun to change. Likewise the information systems qualifications do not make a detailed study of other functional process areas such as HR. In the UK the Skills Framework for the Information Age (SFIA) "provides a common reference model for the identification of the skills needed to develop effective information systems making use of information communications technologies" (SFIA 2008 [online]). A recommendation from this study is that CHC PLC review their information systems skills development and competences in line with SFIA. However significant attention is given to project management processes. This suggests that an individual will need to initially specialise in one area and then acquire the knowledge necessary for the other discipline.

The question is which discipline should be studied first. This is further complicated by the fact that the attributes generally associated with one discipline are not associated with the other: information systems and project management vis-à-vis human resourcing. Analysis of the HRIS team studied shows that half of the team are drawn from one discipline area and half from the other. Although this was not a deliberate strategy at the time, particularly given the emergent nature of the team over considerable time, it would appear that this is an appropriate balance. Nevertheless the team is unbalanced geographically and this is its greatest weakness. This has implications for resourcing and development strategies for this talent pool.

The definition we use here (Figure 1) recognises that individual human capital is owned by the individual, and suggests that potential talent may not yet be exploited fully within their current position. It is clear from the interview data that individuals are proud of the work they do and the contribution they make to the organisation. What is not clear at this stage is how their talents can be further developed within the current structure, given the limited number of team members. The development of individual members of the HRIS team to date has been very ad hoc. There is no clear career and succession planning so any development that has taken place has been instigated by individuals. A significant example is that of a UK-based project leader from an HR background who has gained sponsorship for an MSc in Project Management.

If formal development processes are not available to such specialists, it is very likely that those, particularly with less tenure, will look to other organisations for positions that will support development of the knowledge and skills not yet acquired in Table 3. Given the breadth and depth of human capital owned by these individuals, it is likely that they will not have difficulty in finding suitable, highly remunerated positions. It is also important to note that being employee-owned this form of human capital is highly mobile and will leave when the individual leaves and organisation, representing a measurable loss. The greater the horizontal development and breadth of knowledge and skills, the greater the potential loss of human capital to the organisation. Thus career planning for this specialist talent pool within a talent strategy is vital and should be considered a priority as the loss of even one individual in such a small and unique team will have a significant impact.

It seems from the evidence so far that this is a large, global organisation with well established information systems and human resourcing operational teams and dedicated HRIS team that operates both locally and globally. However, the HRIS team examined is a collection of highly specialist individuals who emanate from disparate backgrounds. They constitute a *community of practice* and have an "evolving form of membership" (Lave and Wenger 1991: 53), but the HRIS team studied does not currently have a sense of identity. Here we explore how the organisation can "sponsor the creation of certain loose organisational structures around which it is hoped that communities of practice may then interact" (Thompson 2005: 151) and suggest the skills, knowledge and behaviours (that is, the individual human capital) that makes up such a global community of HRIS practice.

The team studied represents a unique collection of knowledge and skills and, in their day-to-day work, they act on this tacit knowledge and expertise (Becker 1964; Perrow 1967); it is this that draws them together into a community of practice. Lepak and Snell (1999: 35) note that "these skills often involve idiosyncratic learning process [therefore] it is not likely to find these skills in the open labor market". This suggests both an organisational strength and a weakness. Because it is not easy to develop the skills and knowledge needed in the role of the HRIS Specialist, it is not easy for competitors to replicate SAP HR developments at a global level (echoing Barney's (1991) work at a corporate level) since it is necessary for team members to draw on different kinds of human capital at the same time: the innate attributes embedded in generic human

capital; the formal and informal education and learning embedded in individual human capital; and the organisational knowledge embedded in firm-specific human capital. Thus these three elements necessarily precede the development of HRIS specialist human capital. For the individual the advantage of acquiring specialist has clear ramifications in terms of tenure.

Firm-Specific Attributes of Individual Human Capital

Developing the firm-specific attribute of the constituent view, we can see from Table 1 that particularly within the UK HRIS team there is long term tenure, averaging 23 years, which has breadth and depth across different operational, support function arena as well in the specialist HRIS team. Even within teams based in the US, Canada and Germany there is still significant tenure at a local level, with the six team members averaging five years tenure.

Individuals with high levels of firm-specific attributes are a repository of organisational knowledge and skills that are difficult or impossible to replace or replicate in the short- and medium-term. Their tacit understanding of the 'way it works here' is often underestimated and may not be fully exploited, particularly during mergers and acquisitions, or when an outsourcing or insourcing decision is considered.

It is the combination of these constituent attributes that offer individual uniqueness for particular project team members. It is important for a HRIS project team leader to understand and appreciate the combination of these attributes to ensure that these experts are retained within the project team and organisation. Such understanding can provide stability for the team and projects undertaken.

Realistically this tacit knowledge and experience cannot be acquired except over time. This has implications for *aggregate* human capital, particularly in terms of the demographic character of those concerned. However although tenure can we quantified and aggregated, it is more challenging to quantify tacit knowledge. For transnational organisations competing in an international arena, it is vital to acquire and retain firm-specific attributes (Schuler and Rogovsky 1998) for future use, particularly when such tacit knowledge is resident in so few members of an organisation. The challenge is to find an appropriate metric that allows tacit knowledge to be assessed.

Individuals with high firm-specific human capital are a repository of knowledge and skills that are difficult or impossible to replace or replicate in the short- and medium-term. Their deep understanding of the 'way it works here' is often underestimated and may not be fully exploited, particularly during mergers and acquisitions, or when an outsourcing or insourcing decision is considered. It has been suggested for a number of years that there is a positive relationship between tenure and performance, enhanced by group cohesiveness (Keller 1986). Realistically this deep knowledge and experience can not be acquired except over time. This has implications for the generic human capital, particularly in terms of the demographic character of those concerned, particularly as three member of the UK are likely to retire within the next five years. For transnational organisations competing in an international arena, it is vital to acquire and retain firm-specific human capital (Schuler and Rogovsky 1998) for future use, particularly when such deep knowledge is resident in so few members of the team.

IN CONCLUSION: THE 'RIGHT KIND' OF HUMAN CAPITAL

In this paper we present the findings of a study conducted with project teams working in a multinational organisation implementing and maintaining the HR 'pillar' of an SAP GEIS on their UK, Germany, Canada and the USA sites. The main purpose of that study was the identification of HRIS skills and knowledge in the key roles on the global project and suggestions for development of project team members. Using a human capital frame of reference, we provide a guiding framework which can be used as a sensemaking tool by those responsible for managing people working in hybrid roles on such projects. Our purpose is to explore how this sensemaking framework can be usefully employed by practitioners to resource, develop and retain HRIS project teams.

The guiding framework, noted in Figure 1, explores two views of human capital drawn from the literature. The aggregate view of human capital provides for a collection of employee details comprising, for example, age, gender, marital status, previous work experience, competences and physical location. This can be taken as a whole or part of an organisation. Whereas the constituent view of human capital comprises an individual-level perspective, comprise three distinct sets of attributes. Personal attributes are owned, developed and created by an individual that are productive (or have the potential to be productive) in an economic context and taken with that individual when they leave the firm. Secondly, specialist attributes consist of explicit and tacit knowledge and skills (Polanyi 1958, 1998, 1967) that can only be found within particular professions and roles are vital to sustaining competitive advantage. Thirdly, firm-specific attributes are those specific skills, experiences and learning that can only be gained and employed through long-term tenure within a particular organisation and are not transferable outside of that sector or organisation.

It is clear that an aggregated analysis can provide a useful overview of human capital for transnational organisations with specialists located in different geographical locations. Where individuals have high mobility, this 'snapshot' approach offers a picture of the current situation. However the constituent perspective of individual human capital offers a deeper analysis of a project team's skills and knowledge and is likely to be a more appropriate tool for management.

Although here we have considered each of the three constituent attributes separately, in practice project leaders and HR specialists review human capital as a whole as it resides in an individual team member. Given the wide range personal, specialist and firm-specific attributes identified in this study, it is not surprising that current incumbents tend toward a particular professional area.

A fundamental conundrum for many organisations is the decision to 'make or buy' its human capital. Developing the work of Williamson (1975; 1981; 1994) essentially an organisation can 'buy' this human capital by recruiting individuals, and it can 'make' human capital via providing a variety of training and development, work experience and exposure to particular situations and contexts: it may chose to do both. Care needs to be taken to design supportive HR polices concerning resourcing, retention and remuneration solutions. Although overly simplistic, this duality does provide a practical starting point for organisations in terms of the strategic investment decision for human capital. Lepak and Snell (1999) provide an overview of the essential arguments for this decision and develop the discussion further. This decision of 'make or buy' is influenced by the talent strategy for this group and here we explore some of the dilemmas and considerations for future research and exploration.

In the first instance the conundrum is that this type of project team consists of a scarce, niche talent pool of highly knowledgeable individuals globally dispersed, but locally utilised, with a deep knowledge of the local context, and an appreciation of the wider applications. There are clear resourcing implications for such a team of specialists that need three forms of individual human capital discussed in this paper, with particular issues around the HR, IS and project management knowledge, skills and personal attributes of HRIS specialists. Of particular concern is the discipline background of team members and care should be taken to acquire a balance of individuals with IS and HR qualifications and experiences across the geographies.

A second consideration is one of career development for the HRIS specialist. Horizontal application software development to provide a wider and deeper understanding of a dynamic and ever changing sector is a necessary knowledge set for the HRIS specialist. HRIS projects require intense concentration and individuals with broad project responsibilities are likely to feel overburdened which may lead to stress related absence. Many HRIS specialists will also be looking for vertical career development. This is difficult even in a large, global organisation as HRIS specialists are likely to belong to a small team that may not have an internal or external sense of identity; how does such a specialist move their career forward in such circumstances? This is particularly important for ambitious individuals. It is possible that overtime they may feel siloed and not able to progress within an organisation. If vertical progression is not possible, individuals may look for a change of scene, even if this means taking on the same role in a different organising. The outcome of this type of voluntary termination is the possibility of a demand market bidding war.

Strategically, a GEIS HRIS team of specialists suggests global, service-orientated organising structures led by a globally-focused team leader at a senior level of the organisation in order to gain local commitment from purchasing HR clients. This has implications for the team leader's span of control, management and personal style. In addition there are clear resourcing issues particularly with regard to team financing.

According to Huselid and Barnes (2002: 10) "little academic work has been completed regarding human capital management systems. Practitioners are relatively light years ahead of the academic work in progress or already completed". So it is worthwhile to examine practice within organisations to offer a contribution to the limited empirical literature to date. We believe that descriptions of human capital to date tend to stem from academic deliberations and do not do justice its complexity in practice. With this as our starting point, our purpose here was to examine definitions of human capital within a guiding framework of a specific HRIS project team to attempt to provide a basis for further exploration and research, thus contributing to both a scholastic and practitioner understanding of human capital. We believe that organisations need to take account of the constituent elements of human capital owned by the individual and jointly developed within an organisational context for continued project success. We suggest that organisations should extend this analysis further to include all aspects of the organisation, including human resourcing.

This discussion explored the evidence presented within one research project with particular reference to a particular HRIS project team. We do not consider that we have answered the questions relating to the composition of individual human capital for HRIS project teams. Rather we have raise questions that require further research and study. The complexity and diversity of knowledge and skills needed accompanied by attributes necessary to carry out the role, imply further attention to the constituent view of human capital.

REFERENCES

Abna, T. (2003). Learning by Telling: Storytelling Workshops in an Organizational Learning Intervention. *Management Learning, 34*(2), 221-240.

Ball, K. S. (2001). The Use of Human Resource Systems: A Survey. *Personnel Review, 30*(6), 677-693.

Barney, J. (1991). Firm resources and sustainable competitive advantage. *Journal of Management, 17*(1), 99-120.

Bartel, A. P., & Lichtenberg, F. R. (1987). The Comparative Advantage of Educated Workers in Implementing New Technology. *Review of Economics and Statistics, 69*, 1-11.

Bartel, A. P., & Lichtenberg, F. R. (1990). The Impact of Age of Technology on Employee Wages. *Economics of Innovation and New Technology, 1,* 1-17.

Beaumont, J. R., Kinnie, N. J., Arthurs, A. J., & Weatherall, C. B. (1992). *Information technology and personnel management: issues and educational implications.* Unpublished paper, School of Management, University of Bath:

Becker, B. E., Huselid, M. A., Pinkus, P. S., & Spratt, M. F. (1997). HR as a Source of Shareholder Value: Research and Recommendations. *Human Resource Management, 36(1)*, 39-47.

Becker, G. (1964) *Human Capital: a Theoretical and Empirical Analysis, with Special Reference to Education.* New York: Columbia University Press (for NBER).

Becker, G. (1975) *Human Capital.* Chicago, IL: University of Chicago Press.

Becker, G. (1993) *Human Capital.* Chicago, IL: University of Chicago Press.

Bingley, P., & Westergaard-Nielsen, N. (2003). Returns to tenure, firm-specific human capital and worker heterogeneity International. *Journal of Manpower, 24*(7), 774-788.

Broderick R. and Boudreau, J. W. (1992). Human Resource Management, Information Technology, and the Competitive Edge. *Academy of Management Executive, 6*(2), 7-17.

CIPD (2007). *HR and Technology: Impact and Advantages, Research into Practice.* Chartered Institute of Personnel and Development: London

Cozijnsen, A. J., Vrakking, W. J., & van IJzerloo, M. (2000). Success and failure of 50 innovation projects in Dutch companies. *European Journal of Innovation Management, 3* (3), 150-159.

Cressy, R. (1996). Are Business Start-ups Debt Rationed. *The Economic Journal, 106*(438), 1253-1270.

Dainty, A. R., Raiden, A. B., & Neale, R. H. (2004). Psychological contract expectations of construction project managers. *Engineering, Construction and Architectural Management, 11*(1), 33–44.

Fischer, R. L. (1995). HRIS quality depends on teamwork. *Personnel Journal, 74*(11), 1-3.

Fitz-Enz, J. (1997). Are Your Human Assets Outperforming the Market? *Management Review, 86*(2), 62-66.

Fitz-enz, J. (2000). *The ROI of Human Capital.* New York: Amacon.

Gebauer, M. (2003). Information Systems on Human Capital in Service Sector Organizations. *New Library World, 104*(1184/1185), 33-41.

Gold, J., Watson, S., & Rix, M. (2000). Learning for Change by Telling Stories. In J. McGoldrick, J. Stewart, & S. Watson (Eds.), *Understanding Human Resource Development: A Resource-based Approach.* London: Routledge

Guérin, G., Ouadahi, J., Saba, T., & Wils, T. (2001). La mobilisation des employés lors de l'implantation d'un système d'information: ébauche d'un cadre théorique. *Actes de la 19e université d'été de l'Institut d'audit social*, (pp. 145-159).

Hammer, M., & Champy, J. (1995). *Re-engineering the Corporation: A Manifesto for Business Revolution.* London: Nicholas Brealey.

Hammersley, M., & Atkinson, P. (1983). *Ethnography principles in practice.* London: Routledge.

Hannon, J., Jelf, G., & Brandes, D. (1996). Human Resource information systems: operational issues and strategic considerations in a global environment. *The International Journal of Human Resource Management, 7*(1), 245-269.

Heijke, H., Meng, C., & Ramaekers, G. (2003). An investigation into the role of human capital competences and their pay-off. *International Journal of Manpower, 24 (7)*, 750-773.

Holland, C. P., Light, B., & Kavalek, P. (1996). *A critical success factors model for enterprise resource planning implementation.* Proceedings of the Seventh European Conference on Information Systems, Copenhagen: Copenhagen Business School

Holland, C. P., Light, B., & Kawalek, P. (1999). *Beyond enterprise resource planning projects: innovative strategies for competitive advantage.* Proceedings of the Seventh European Conference on Information Systems, Copenhagen: Copenhagen Business School

Holland, S., Gaston, K., & Gomes, J. (2000). Critical success factors for cross-functional teamwork in new product development. *International Journal of Management Reviews, 2*(3), 231-259.

Huselid, M., & Barnes, J. (2002) *Human capital management systems as a source of competitive advantage.* Unpublished manuscript, Rutgers University, New Jersey.

Keller, R. T. (1986). Predictors of the performance of project groups in R&D organizations. *Academy of Management Journal, 29*(4), 715-726.

Kinnie, N. J., & Arthurs, A. J. (1996). Personnel specialists' advanced use of information technology: evidence and explanations. *Personnel Review, 25*(3), 3-19.

Laing, D., & Weir, C. (1999). Corporate performance and the influence of human capital characteristics on executive compensation in the UK. *Personnel Review, 28*(1/2), 28-40.

Lave, J., & Wenger, E. (1991) *Situated Learning: Legitimate Peripheral Participation.* Cambridge, UK: Cambridge University Press.

Lepak, D. P., & Snell, S. A. (1999). The human resource architecture: toward a theory of human capital allocation and development. *Academy of Management Review, 24*(1), 31-48.

Link, A. N.,& Siegel, D. S. (2007) *Innovation, Entrepreneurship and Technological Change.* Oxford: Oxford University Press.

Luftman, J. (2000). Assessing Business-IT Alignment Maturity. *Communications of the Association for Information Systems, 14*, 1-51.

Marsden, R. (1993). The politics of organizational analysis. *Organization Studies, 14*(1), 93-124.

Martinsons, M. G., & Chong, P. K. C. (1999). The influence of human factors and specialist involvement on information systems success. *Human Relations, 52*(1), 123-152.

Matta, N. F., & Ashkenas, R. N. (2003). Why Good Projects Fail Anyway. *Harvard Business Review, 81(9)*, 109-114

Miles, M. B., & Hubermann, A. M. (1994) *Qualitative Data Analysis: An Expanded Sourcebook.* London: Sage.

Minneman, W. A. (1996). Strategic justification for an HRIS that adds value. (Human resource information systems). *HR Magazine, 41*(12), 35-38.

O'Donohue, W., Sheehan, C., Hecker, R., & Holland, P. (2007). The psychological contract of knowledge workers. *Journal of Knowledge Management, 11*(2), 73-82.

Paré, G., & Elam, J. J. (1995). Discretionary Use of Personal Computers by Knowledge Workers: Testing of a Social Psychology Theoretical Model. *Behavior and Information Technology, 14 (4)*, 215-228.

Perrow, C. (1967). A Framework for the Comparative Analysis of Organizations. *American Sociological Review, 32*(2), 194-208.

Polachek, S., & Siebert, W. (1993) *The economics of earnings.* Cambridge, England: Cambridge University Press.

Polanyi, M. (1958, 1998) *Personal Knowledge. Towards a Post Critical Philosophy.* London: Routledge.

Polanyi, M. (1967) *The Tacit Dimension.* New York: Doubleday & Co.

Rastogi, P. N. (2000). Sustaining enterprise competitiveness - is human capital the answer? *Human Systems Management, 19*(3), 193-203.

Rastogi, P. N. (2003). The Nature and Role of IC - Rethinking the Process of Value Creation and Sustained Enterprise Growth. *Journal of Intellectual Capital, 4(2)*, 227-248.

Robey D., Ross, J. W., & Boudreau, M.-C. (2002). Learning to Implement Enterprise Systems: An Exploratory Study of the Dialectics of Change. *Journal of Management Information Systems, 19*(1), 17-46.

Scarbourgh, H., & Elias, J. (2002) *Evaluating Human Capital Chartered Institute of Personnel and Development.* London

Schuler, R. S., & Rogovsky, N. (1998). Understanding Compensation Practice Variations across Firms: The Impact of National Culture. *Journal of International Business Studie, 29*(1), 159-168.

Schultz, T. W. (1961). Investment in human capital. *American Economic Review, 51(1)*, 1-17.

SFIA (2008) *The Skills Framework for the Information Age (SFIA)* Retrieved 23 May 2008, 2008 from http://www.sfia.org.uk/

Shanks, G., & Seddon, P. (2000). Editorial Enterprise resource planning (ERP) systems. *Journal of Information Technology, 15*(4), 243-244.

Siegel, D. S. (1999). *Skill-biased Technological Change: Evidence from a firm-level Survey.* Kalamazoo, MI: W E Upjohn Institute Press.

Siegel, D. S., Waldman, D. A., & Youngdahl, W. E. (1997). The Adoption of Advanced Manufacturing Technologies: Human Resource Management

Implications. *IEEE Transactions on Engineering Management, 44*, 288-298.

Silverman, D. (2001). *Interpreting Qualitative Data: Methods for Analysing Talk, Text and Interaction.* London: Sage.

Snell S. A., Youndt, M., & Wright, P. (1996). Establishing a Framework for Research in Strategic Human Resource Management: Merging Resource Theory and Organizational Learning. In G. Ferris (Ed.), *Research in Personnel and Human Resource Management.* Greenwich, CT: JAI Press, *114,* 61-90.

Tansley, C., Newell, S., & Williams, H. (2001). Effecting HRM-style practices through an integrated Human Resource information system: An e-greenfield site? *Personnel Review (Special Issue: Managing the Employment Relationship in Greenfield sites), 30(3),* 351-370.

Taylor, S., Fisher, D., & Dufresne, R. (2004). The Aesthetics of Management Storytelling: A Key to Organizational Learning'. In C. Grey & E. Antonacopoulou (Eds.), *Essential Readings in Management Learning.* London: SAGE

Thompson, M. (2005). Structural and epistemic parameters in communities of practice. *Organization Science, 16*(2), 151-164.

Ulrich, D., & Lake, D. (1991). Organizational capability: Creating competitive advantage. *Academy of Management Executive, 5*(1), 77-92.

Weller, S. C., & Romney, A. K. (1988). *Systematic Data Collection.* London: Sage Publications Ltd.

Williams, H. (2000). *How Can Human Resource Information Systems Inform and Enable Strategy Making?* Human Resource Management Nottingham Business School, Nottingham Trent University: Nottingham

Williams H. (2008). *How do organisations make sense of their talent as valued assets?* The Literature Human Resource Management Nottingham Business School, Nottingham Trent University: Nottingham

Wright, P., McMahn, G., & McWilliams, A. (1994). Human Resources and Sustained Competitive Advantage: A Resource-based Perspective. *International Journal of Human Resources Management, 5*, 301-326.

Youndt, M. A., Subramaniam, M., & Snell, S. A. (2004). Intellectual Capital Profiles: An Examination of Investments and Returns. *Journal of Management Studies, 41*(2), 335-361.

KEY TERMS

HCM: Human capital management

HRIS: Human resource information systems

Project Teams

Project Management

Chapter IX
IT–Based Integration of HRM in a Foreign MNC Subsidiary:
A Micro–Political Perspective

Adam Smale
University of Vaasa, Finland

Jukka-Pekka Heikkilä
University of Vaasa, Finland

ABSTRACT

The design and implementation of a globally integrated e-HRM system within a multinational corporation (MNC) requires different parties to reach some form of agreement on which HR processes must be standardised and which must be locally adapted. In this respect, the IT-based integration of HRM presents an intriguing setting in which to study micro-political behaviour during HRM integration, that is, how parties promote their own interests and the strategies they use during negotiations. Accordingly, the study's aims were to identify those issues which generated the greatest degree of conflict during the IT-based integration of HRM, the key actors involved and the resources that were deployed during negotiations. A longitudinal, in-depth case study approach was used, and followed the integration of a global e-HRM system in the Finnish subsidiary of a large European-owned MNC over a period of nearly two years. Qualitative data was collected via semi-structured interviews with key subsidiary HR personnel and was complemented with company documentation. The findings indicate that the key areas of conflict were system design, the standardised use of English, and grey areas of HR policy. Three key parties were identified as being involved in subsequent negotiations. These parties utilised a range of negotiation resources including business case logic, technical know-how, internal benchmarking, local constraints and ignorance.

INTRODUCTION

One weakness that has been highlighted in the extant literature on HRM in multinational corporations (MNCs) is the over-emphasis on structural explanations of HRM practices in foreign subsidiaries and insufficient consideration of the role of organisational politics (Edwards & Kuruvilla, 2005). Case-study research suggests that our knowledge about how and why HRM integration takes place will remain incomplete if the contested nature of parent-subsidiary relations is not taken into account (Ferner, 2000; Ferner *et al*, 2005). These arguments essentially refer to the significance of subsidiary attitudes and the strategic responses that are open to subsidiary managers in the face of pressures to integrate parent HRM practices. Oliver (1991) cites this lack of attention to organisational self-interests as one weakness of institutional theory explanations of subsidiary behaviour and suggests that it should be complemented with a resource dependence perspective, which better acknowledges the strategies and tactics subsidiaries might use to resist institutional pressures.

In particular, these case studies highlight the seemingly important role that power relations and micro-political processes play in determining the use and effectiveness of different HRM integration mechanisms (Martin & Beaumont, 1999; Ferner, 2000). Empirical work by Ferner *et al.* (2004, 2005) elaborate further by presenting a dynamic view of HRM integration whereby mechanisms of HRM integration, centralisation in particular, are subject to continual negotiation between parent and subsidiary and are thus better viewed as contested processes of 'oscillation' between global integration and local responsiveness. The role played by subsidiary managers as interpreters of the local HRM environment is seen as a key determinant in patterns of HRM integration in this respect.

As will be argued throughout this paper, the implementation of an e-HRM system presents an excellent opportunity to observe how the global integration of HRM is negotiated and contested in MNCs. In essence, this is because e-HRM implementation is often accompanied with a fundamental re-think in how HRM is delivered, which requires the parties involved to reach some form of agreement, in a relatively short period of time, on what must be globally standardised versus what must be locally adapted, and why.

Thus, adopting a micro-political perspective, the study's main objective is to explore the ways in which the IT-based integration of HRM is negotiated and contested within a foreign MNC subsidiary setting. More specifically, the study aims to identify those issues which generate the greatest degree of conflict during the IT-based integration process, they key actors involved and the resources that are deployed by those actors during negotiation. The setting of the study is a Finnish subsidiary of a well-known European MNC, INTRACOM [1].

The paper starts by reviewing the literature on the mechanisms used by MNCs to achieve greater integration of HRM practices within foreign subsidiaries. The focus is then turned to the field of e-HRM as an IT-based mechanism of integration, and the micro-political perspective. Following a description of the methods used, the paper presents the results on the key areas of conflict and the resources used in negotiation. The paper concludes with a discussion of the findings and some suggestions for future research.

LITERATURE REVIEW

HRM Integration in MNCs

Evidence suggests that MNCs are shifting their attention more and more towards the integration and cohesion side of the integration-responsiveness tension (Ghoshal & Gratton, 2002). This trend would also seem to be having widespread implications for how the HR function and its contingent HRM practices are coordinated (Taylor, 2006). Indeed, from an evolutionary perspective, it is argued that the required organisational levels of coordination now necessary to execute global strategies has provoked the emergence of a strategic global HRM agenda (Kiessling & Harvey, 2005).

The case for global HRM notwithstanding, the majority of research on HRM in MNCs has focused on the characteristics of HRM practices in foreign subsidiaries and those factors that lead to either greater parent or local firm resemblance. A feature of this literature is that unlike most other business functions, HR is generally regarded to be the most culture- and institution-specific and thus the most difficult to integrate, typically requiring higher levels of local responsiveness (Tayeb, 1998). Accordingly, contributions to this literature have drawn on a range of theoretical approaches in trying to provide explanations for patterns of HRM integration and/or local responsiveness, including resource dependency theory (e.g. Hannon *et al*, 1995), cultural theory (e.g. Gill & Wong 1998), institutional theory (e.g. Björkman & Lu 2001), and the national business systems approach (e.g. Ferner & Quintanilla 1998).

Whilst the above contributions provide a detailed list of structural factors (e.g. MNC characteristics, parent-subsidiary relations) and contextual factors (e.g. country-of-origin, isomorphic pressures) that are likely to affect patterns of HRM integration and local responsiveness, the research is comparatively silent on those factors associated with the process (the 'how') of integration (Smale, 2007). In this regard, a wide variety of organisational mechanisms have been documented in the literature, including expatriation (e.g. Björkman & Lu, 2001), internal benchmarking (Martin & Beaumont, 1998), global expertise networks and HR centres of excellence

(Sparrow *et al*, 2004), and IT-based integration (e.g. Hannon *et al*, 1996; Tansley *et al*, 2001; Ruta, 2005), to which we now turn.

IT-Based Integration of HRM

For the purpose of clarity, this paper distinguishes between the use of IT in human resource information systems (HRIS) and e-HRM. In line with the definitions provided by Ruël *et al* (2004) and Reddington and Martin (2007), whilst HRIS refers to the automation of systems for the sole benefit of the HR function, e-HRM is concerned with the application of internet and web-based systems, and more recently mobile communications technologies, to change the nature of interactions among HR personnel, line managers and employees from a face-to-face relationship to one that is increasingly mediated by technology. Based on a study of human resource articles published in the top HRM journals from 1994 to 2001, only one percent of the articles focused on the influence of IT in HR (Hoobler & Johnson, 2004). Although the field of e-HRM has started to mature, historically academics have paid insufficient attention to the impact of IT on HR (Lepak & Snell, 1998).

The case for the adoption of integrated e-HRM systems have been argued from a number of different perspectives. From a business case perspective, three drivers of integrated e-HRM systems have been cited (Stone & Guetal, 2005, Reddington & Martin, 2007). Firstly, e-HRM systems can reduce HR transaction costs and headcount. Secondly, e-HRM can substitute physical capability by leveraging digital assets, i.e. HR information can be used flexibly on an infinite number of occasions at little or no marginal cost. And thirdly, the effective use of integrated e-HRM systems can transform the HR "business model" by e-enabling the HR function to provide strategic value to the business that it previously could not do.

From a control perspective, e-HRM has been identified as facilitating the greater integration of HRM practices in foreign subsidiaries in three main ways (Smale, 2008). Firstly, e-HRM can serve as a form of bureaucratic control by establishing procedural standards about how the system is used (Clemmons & Simon, 2001) and thus how HRM processes are carried out. Secondly, e-HRM presents an opportunity for output control in its role of communicating goals and monitoring them through an array of management reporting functions. Thirdly, e-HRM can accommodate varying degrees of control via centralisation by restricting access rights and introducing layers of transaction authorisation.

The arguments for adopting integrated e-HRM systems notwithstanding, case study evidence indicates that firms have been active in their implementation (e.g. Tansley *et al*, 2001; Shrivastava & Shaw, 2003; Ruta, 2005). Collectively, however, this body of research appears to have more to say about the problems encountered in implementation, especially in terms of end user acceptance (e.g. Fisher & Howell, 2004), than any far-reaching transformation of the HR function. Indeed, there is a danger that the adoption of e-HRM may even have negative consequences for HR professionals and their internal clients if change management and technology acceptance issues are handled ineffectively (Reddington *et al*, 2005).

Given the potential that e-HRM has for the transformation of HR, it is reasonable to expect that the sizeable changes required, both in organisation and mindset, are likely to provoke resistance from various end users. At the very least, since e-HRM models of HR delivery encourage a fundamental re-think about how HRM is carried out, their exists a big incentive for various end users to ensure that their own interests are considered in subsequent decisions regarding e-HRM design and implementation. This is not least true for foreign MNC subsidiaries which must communicate convincingly their interests to the parent—a task that is likely to involve conflict and negotiation.

A Micro-Political Perspective on the IT-Based Integration of HRM

Compared to the dominant economic and deterministic approaches to studies on MNCs, the socio-political dimension of managing MNCs has been largely neglected in the international business literature (Ferner, 2000; Geppert & Williams, 2006). Conceptualisations of MNCs as hierarchical structures based on formal authority relations between headquarters and subsidiaries are becoming increasingly inappropriate given the complex interdependencies that characterise the modern MNC (e.g. Doz & Prahalad, 1993). Indeed, MNCs have come to be described as 'loosely coupled political systems' where power games and political influence over decision-making are useful in explaining the nature of internal processes (Forsgren, 1990).

Organisational micro-politics has been defined in general terms as "*an attempt to exert a formative influence on social structures and human relations*" (Dörrenbächer & Geppert, 2006: 256), but is suggested more specifically to focus on "*bringing back the actors and examining the conflicts that emerge when powerful actors with different goals, interests and identities interact with each other locally and across national and functional borders*" (2006: 255). In this sense, studies on micro-politics are argued to provide a deeper understanding about internal processes within MNCs and managing the complexities associated with transnational reorganisation by concentrating on the strategies of local/subsidiary actors (Mense-Petermann, 2006). One common theme within the micro-politics literature, which is also the focus of the present study, is where concepts, systems and/or practices developed elsewhere require subsidiaries to engage in local adaptation and translation—processes that often involve conflicts.

With regards to studies in the field of HRM in MNCs one major critique concerns the assumptions made about how HRM practices become established in foreign subsidiaries and the roles played by different actors in the integration process. In this regard, Edwards *et al.* (2007) suggest such studies should adopt a political economy approach. This conceptual approach, they argue, integrates a focus on markets, distinct national institutional frameworks, and the micro-political activity of multinationals. The *market-based* approach focuses on the competitive pressures firms face to transfer 'best practices' and is rooted in resource-based explanations of HRM in foreign subsidiaries (see e.g. Taylor *et al*, 1996; Bae *et al*, 1998). The *cross-national comparative* approach focuses on the influence of distinct political and socio-economic structures in shaping an MNC's international HRM activities (see e.g. Rosenzweig & Nohria, 1994; Gooderham *et al*, 1999). Lastly, the *micro-political* (or power-based) approach focuses on "*how actors seek to protect or advance their own interests, the resources they use, and the resolution of conflicts*" (Edwards *et al*, 2007: 203).

Rather than adopting all three conceptual approaches, this paper predominantly focuses on the micro-political approach in its study of the IT-based integration of HRM. The reasons for this are firstly, that this paper shares the view of Geppert and Mayer (2006) when they state that,

Only rarely, if ever, does the literature engage in more than a passing way with the agency of actors in shaping the lived 'reality' of corporate coordination and control mechanisms and in defining the adoption—and adaptation—of organizational and managerial practices as they move throughout the organization, particularly across national boundaries (2006: 2).

In this sense, the paper seeks to contribute to this under-researched approach on HRM integration in MNCs and extend it to the specific field of e-HRM. The second reason for adopting the micro-political approach concerns the IT-based integration of HRM specifically. It is argued here

that the IT-based integration of HRM presents a somewhat unique setting in which to observe how the global-local dilemma plays out in foreign MNC subsidiaries. This is because the design and implementation of an integrated e-HRM system explicitly requires the parties involved to reach some form of agreement in a relatively short period of time on what must be standardised versus what must be locally adapted, and why. Accordingly, the IT-based integration of HRM will typically involve the relevant parties to enter into systematic negotiations regarding the system's appearance, content and processes—potentially on the full range of HRM practices. This would appear to be particularly fertile ground on which to conduct an investigation into how parties promote their own interests during the IT-based integration of HRM and the resources that each party uses during the ensuing negotiations.

METHOD

Research Design

This paper adopts a single, in-depth case-study design. The unit of analysis is the IT-based integration of HRM in a Finnish subsidiary owned by a well-known, European MNC. The study can be classified as holistic (Yin, 2003) since it concerns the integration of HRM into the focal subsidiary and no further sub-units of analysis. In connection with the 'how'-type question of the study, which itself justifies a case-study approach (Ghauri & Grønhaug, 2002), the study's analytical focus is on issues of process—in this case the process of negotiation during the IT-based integration of HRM and the involvement of key actors. Ferner *et al* (2005) argue that an emphasis on processual issues favours an in-depth case-study approach, especially when the aim is to unravel the dynamics of bargaining processes between HQ and subsidiary. Moreover, the single case-study method is instructive when the issue of contextuality, crucial to studies on subsidiary-headquarters relations, is of key importance in interpreting the data (Yin, 2003). Lastly, the use of exploratory research methods has especially been advocated in fields within HRM such as technology due to its relative infancy (Hoobler & Johnson, 2004).

According to Yin (2003), single case-study designs are appropriate if they fit one of five circumstances or rationale. In order of importance, the study firstly falls under the rationale of the *longitudinal* case where interest lies in how the phenomenon develops over time and how certain conditions may change, thus allowing for a deeper understanding (Ghauri, 2004). Secondly, the study contains elements of a *representative* or typical case in its acknowledgement that the IT-based integration of HRM has become increasingly commonplace yet has remained under-researched.

Data Collection and Analysis

The study was conducted over a period of almost two years (2006-2007), approximately one year after the decision was made to include INTRA-COM Finland in the global, IT-based integration process (see below for details). Since the study's emphasis was on uncovering how local actors shape the lived 'reality' of corporate control and coordination mechanisms (Geppert & Meyer, 2006), the key informants were the HR personnel of the Finnish subsidiary. This foreign subsidiary 'view from below' (see e.g. Ferner *et al.*, 2004) allows for the more accurate identification of conflict areas and the resources used in negotiation, which are central to the micro-political approach.

Data were collected using in-depth face-to-face interviews with the HR personnel of the Finnish unit and via a detailed review of company documentation on the integration process. In total, five in-depth, face-to-face interviews were conducted with the Finnish Country HR Manager, the HR Account Manager and the HR Advisor at even intervals over the two years. In addition,

the Nordic HR Manager and one of the e-HRM third-party consultants were also interviewed. The interviewees were invited to comment on their own experiences of the HRM integration process. In particular, interviewees were asked to state which issues produced the greatest conflict and how they sought to resolve these issues with the parties involved. Interviews were conducted in English, lasted an average of sixty minutes and were all recorded and *verbatim* transcribed. The company documentation included presentations from INTRACOM headquarters, Nordic presentations on the integration process, minutes of the project meetings, as well as communication on the main problem areas and subsequent actions taken.

The data was content-analysed, coded and categorised into groups relating to the conflicts identified. Further analysis within these groups enabled a detailed identification of the conflicts, the parties involved and the resources used in negotiation. Collecting data from multiple sources within the Finnish subsidiary allowed for the comparison of personal experiences and the identification of where responses converged and diverged thus enhancing the validity of the research via informant triangulation (Denzin, 1978). Direct citations of the raw data are used to illustrate and support the analysis presented in the results.

Introduction to INTRACOM

INTRACOM[1] is a well-known European MNC, operating in over 100 countries and employing more than 100,000 people. Having grown via acquisitions into a large and diversified MNC with operations dispersed on a global scale, IN-TRACOM found that it had become a collection of semi-autonomous subsidiaries with insufficient integration between businesses. The complexity and weaknesses of this multidomestic structure and strategy came to a head in the late 1990's and prompted a significant organisational restructuring effort whereby INTRACOM launched its new 'Global Organisation' approach. Features of this 'Global Organisation' included, amongst other things, the streamlining of its core businesses, a matrix structure organisational design, and far-reaching efforts at process standardisation. In short, INTRACOM's focus was on reducing complexity, speeding up decision-making, creating economies of scale and changing the culture.

In recent years the above 'global' strategic realignment has led to an equally sizeable transformation in INTRACOM's Group HR strategy. The three major goals of the new group HR strategy have been HR's greater functionality in how it serves INTRACOM's newly defined lines of business, the greater standardisation of HR processes and the creation of a single global HR system.

Integral to the achievement of these three goals has been the global, IT-based integration of HRM. More specifically, IT-based integration in the case of INTRACOM has meant the design and implementation of a globally integrated e-HRM system (SAP HR), referred to hereafter as their 'global e-HRM system'. In addition to the three goals of the Group's new global HR strategy, the rationale behind adopting the global HR system included; (i) HR process simplification, alignment and standardisation as a necessary step prior to setting-up HR shared service centres (a Nordic service centre is already in operation with plans to migrate to a single European service centre within three years); (ii) to increase employee and manager self-service roles, and thus accountability, allowing for a focus on more value-adding HR activities by HR representatives; (iii) to improve HR strategic decision-making via more sophisticated management reporting tools (e.g. identifying talent pools throughout the Group); and (iv) to reduce compliance costs by assuming greater control over HR processes and monitoring them.

Group-wide implementation of the global HR system commenced in 2001 and, after a failed attempt to roll it out globally at the same time in

all locations, has been introduced in the different foreign operations in order of their strategic importance to the Group. INTRACOM Finland was established nearly 100 years ago and currently employs around 350 people across more than 200 service outlets. The HR department consists of three full-time personnel (all included in this study). Being a relatively small foreign unit, involved in fewer strategic lines of business, INTRACOM Finland began implementing the global e-HRM system in the summer of 2005. This study reports the experiences of the HR personnel in INTRACOM Finland throughout the integration process and their dealings with other key parties involved.

RESULTS

In line with the study's aims, the results are structured in such a way so as to indicate the key areas of conflict, the key parties involved, and the resources used in negotiation. Content analysis revealed that the key sources of conflict revolved around three main issues; (i) system design components, (ii) the standardised use of English, and (iii) institutionally 'grey areas' of HR policy. The parties involved in negotiations and the tools they used are summarised in Table 1.

Omitted from the above list is the initial decision to integrate the system in the Finnish subsidiary in the first place. Although this presented an opportunity for the subsidiary to resist and negotiate, the reason for its omission is because the Finnish HR personnel accepted the decision as ultimately a positive thing. As described by the Country HR Manager:

My Line Manager told me last August "I have good news. You are going live with the (system) in six months time." Of course my first reaction was that I started to scream "no, we're not going to do it!" Then I said, "Oh, good. Good to be part of the family." He said afterwards that

Table 1. Areas of conflict, key parties and resources used in negotiation

Area of conflict	Key parties	Resources used in negotiation
System design components	• Group HR; • Finland HR; • System consultants	• Business case (cost), internal benchmarking, authority, use of third-party consultants • Business case (operational), local constraints • Systems know-how, Group mandate, ignorance
Standardised use of English	• Group HR; • Finland HR • System consultants	• Strategic mandate, business case (cost), no resource allocation for translation services • Business case (operational), linguistic ability, employee discontent, contradictions in Group policy • Group mandate, ignorance
Grey areas of HR policy?	• Group/Nordic HR; • Finland HR	• Steering committee, verifying local 'interpretations,' internal benchmarking • Local norms, local legislation

he had been very surprised about my reaction, and that he had prepared lots of arguments that he could have used had I started to argue that we can't do it.

Another reason for the decision of integrating the system not provoking a round of negotiation was the explicit use of authority- (or hierarchy-) based resources from the outset by INTRACOM Group HR. As the Country HR Manager vividly recalls:

The number one HR person in the INTRACOM Group said that "one hour used up talking about whether to have (the system) or not is an hour wasted." So, I think it was quite clearly put! We knew what was expected from us. It was repeated so many times that we finally understood it.

Indeed, the Finnish subsidiary response to the decision quickly turned to acceptance as the integration process appeared to be inevitable. Interestingly, this response was described to differ noticeably from that of the Swedish subsidiary, which was reported as sitting in meetings discussing all the possible reasons for not adopting the new system. Certain HR colleagues in other INTRACOM units interpreted this as Finland's high power distance and subservience to hierarchy, or that they just didn't understand the implications.

From the Finnish perspective, however, their lack of resistance reflected their belief that the decision had already been made. The only issues that were offered up for negotiation at this stage were the amount of extra resources needed to facilitate the system implementation and the reasons why they might not be able to complete it in the given time schedule. These issues are explored next in connection with the three substantive areas of conflict.

System Design and Components

The first substantive area of conflict was the design of the new e-HRM system. More specifically, there was disagreement over which HR modules should be included in the system and which ones should be left out. This was most evident in the case of the payroll function. Most other components of the system, with some exceptions such as the learning module (i.e. booking training events), were stipulated as compulsory. However, payroll was less clear cut and invited the parties involved to discuss the relative merits of including payroll processes under the new system.

The parties involved in this particular negotiation were Group HR representatives and the Country HR Manager. The primary resource used by Group HR in the ensuing negotiation was the business case, which followed that the costs of integrating the payroll module into the system would be too costly in relation to the size of the Finnish unit. Internal benchmarking was also used as a tool in negotiation whereby Group HR reinforced its business case argument through the use of comparisons with other similar sized units. In response, the Finnish Country HR Manager argued the case for including payroll also based on the business case, but from an operational perspective:

It was more or less a given fact that the figures show it is cheaper to run (payroll) by building an interface. [...] They (Group HR) were more or less giving the figures and there was not much resistance from our side. We tried, because we saw the complexity of having two systems with only a one-way interface. But the discussion was more or less stopped.

Nearly two years later it is interesting to note that the costs of running the interface have been higher than anticipated and the inclusion of payroll is back on the agenda. Nevertheless, whilst IN-TRACOM Finland did not succeed in negotiating the inclusion of payroll, they were successful in negotiating more autonomy in certain other HR processes. In this regard, the third-party system consultants employed by the INTRACOM Group played a key role in conflict generation and nego-tiations. Indeed, the e-HRM system consultants could be considered as being, on the one hand, a resource used by Group HR in negotiating the tighter integration of the system, and on the other hand, as being influential actors themselves with their own interests and negotiation resources.

Regarding the latter, the consultants were sometimes perceived as having their own agenda and, in reference to their systems know-how, were seen to shape the system's design in ways that were in conflict with what Finland HR wanted. For example,

I felt that we had agreed that "OK, this is the scope" and suddenly we started getting business process procedures, describing processes that we had already said that we don't want to have in the system. So there were some consultants who thought, if I want to look at it positively, that we wanted to have something we didn't know we wanted to have. We had to fight back and say "sorry, we said that we don't need this bit. It doesn't work here." (Country HR Manager)

In these cases the negotiations were between INTRACOM Finland HR personnel and the third-party consultants. The negotiation resources used by the consultants typically rested on systems know-how and repeating what they had been in-structed by their client, the INTRACOM Group (Group mandate). When those resources failed to resolve the conflict, consultants were perceived to resort to ignorance in the sense that they lacked sufficient knowledge of the local environment and made little efforts to learn or adapt,

One example was our (production) plant, where there are fifty blue-collar workers, who don't have their own individual PC's. [...] The recommenda-tion from the consultants was that, at the beginning of every month, they would fill out themselves the shifts they have worked during the previous month. We just imagined those fifty guys queuing for this one PC [...]. The solution from the consultants was "well, go and buy more PC's," but we knew it wouldn't work in that environment so we said "we won't be taking that part of the system." (Country HR Manager)

When we had meetings, they (consultants) would say "yeah, you should really take this." They didn't consider what's suitable for Finland. I think it was a problem in many cases that they didn't really know how payroll in Finland works, or annual leave issues, or any HR issues in Finland. (HR Advisor)

As reflected above, the reasons used by Finland HR in negotiations again centred on the operational case and the local constraints connected to certain HR processes. In essence, the consultants' lack of local HR knowledge was a source of conflict with Finnish HR personnel, but at the same time it provided the HR personnel with an opportunity to resist certain components in the system's design.

Standardized Use of English

The second key area of conflict centred around the strict, standardised use of English in the new e-HRM system. Indeed, the use of English was so standardised that the system did not recognise certain characters within the Finnish alphabet. As a result, Finland HR repeatedly used the business (operational) case in negotiating with the consultants for some local, linguistically-related modifications. The reasons varied from people not being able to enter their own names and employees' salary slips being lost in the post because the system didn't allow for the correct spelling of addresses. Eventually, the consultants conceded and added a separate field for addresses, but all other language-related change requests were rejected. Again, Finland HR felt that the resources consultants used in negotiations were more or less borne out of ignorance. For example:

It was very difficult to explain to the consultants that in Finnish we have Scandinavian characters and the system doesn't recognize them. And they said, "Well, if there's a name with dots, just write it without dots." They didn't understand that the word could have a totally different meaning. [...] So that's something we will now have to enter in two places. (Country HR Manager)

The seemingly straightforward decision to use English throughout the system had the accumulative effect of handing all necessary translation

tasks to local HR personnel. Although one of the key objectives behind the globally integrated e-HRM system and shared-service model was to free HR personnel from administrative duties, local HR personnel claimed that these duties were more than being replaced with their new role as translators. This role included translating global HR policies, providing detailed notes to payroll staff regarding what different fields in the e-HRM system meant and taking telephone calls from employees who could not understand, for example, their own pay policy.

For example, the pay policy document is sixty pages and in addition to that we have a local policy for blue-collar workers. We don't apply the global pay policy for blue-collar workers, because they are so attached to the collective bargaining agreement. So, that's really a challenge, how to balance the global and local policies and what to translate into English and what then to translate into Finnish. (HR Advisor)

Interestingly, the standardised use of English transformed the role of local HR personnel into that of a communication filter. Since many subsidiary employees struggled to understand English, local HR personnel were forced to make quick judgements about what HR information, policies and processes needed to be translated and what did not. Consequently, the source of this communication and the designers of the e-HRM system had to rely on the personal judgement and linguistic skills of local HR if the messages were to get across. This was sometimes described to be extremely challenging given technical nature of the terms and legal jargon.

From the perspective of local HR staff, the stance of Group HR towards language was self-evident in their decision to provide no extra provisions or resources to the translation work. In a sense, this was a resource used in negotiation—you cannot do what you don't have the resources to do. One consequence of this decision was for Finland HR to include English language skills into all recruitment and selection criteria for new employees. The second key resource used by Group HR was the re-emphasising of the strategic mandate behind the introduction of the e-HRM system, in this case the pursuit of process standardisation and data integrity. By adopting a common language these two goals could be more easily achieved. To follow up this argument in negotiations, access rights to the system in many areas were reduced to viewing only.

However, in reference to certain strategic goals like freeing HR personnel from more administrative tasks not actually being achieved, the standardised use of English was contested by Finland HR on the grounds that it contradicted other INTRACOM goals. This was also evident in Finland HR's concern that the standardised use of English sat in direct contrast to the Group's recent large-scale promotion of workforce diversity and inclusiveness. In their view, using a language many employees found difficult to understand was having precisely the opposite effect.

This language issue comes up every time we have a staff council meeting. […] There are lots of people that feel excluded, because they can't understand what is being talked about and there are thousands of e-mails and intranet messages arriving in English. And we really don't have the resources in HR, or in any other departments, to do the translating.

In terms of negotiation outcomes, the arguments for local system adaptations for linguistic reasons have largely been unsuccessful regardless of the resources used in negotiations. Evidently, the costs of adaptation and the threat to process standardisation and data integrity have outweighed local, operational concerns and apparent contradictions in Group policy.

Grey Areas of HR Policy?

INTRACOM's Group HR strategy clearly spelt out the need for greater HR process standardisation and the movement towards a single, global HRM system. Taken together, the strategic mandate from the Group's perspective did not leave much room for manoeuvre in terms of local adaptation. However, they did acknowledge the need to adhere to local regulations. The Finland Country HR Manager interpreted the Group approach as follows:

We're moving towards having more global processes in HR, and then some local processes. The local [processes] *are the ones we refer to as being defined in collective bargaining agreements or local law. But there should actually be nothing in between.* (Country HR Manager)

Indeed, subsidiary HR came to understand that this approach really meant that everything will be standardised up until the point where it is deemed illegal. Over time, Finland HR personnel thus found it increasingly difficult to negotiate for greater flexibility due to this approach of global, local and nothing in between. Their scope for negotiation was effectively limited due to the Group's stance that there should not be any grey areas.

In reality, of course, this approach was not so easy to follow and a number of resources were used by the different parties either to convince the other that something was or wasn't illegal, or that it really is or isn't a grey area of HR policy. One of the tools used in such negotiations was HR steering committees, which were used as a forum to present arguments for local adaptation and process standardisation and return a decision on how to proceed. The steering committee consisted of HR representatives from the different European regions and Group HR. The logic was that serious local requests for deviating from the standard process would be discussed by the committee. Over time, Finland HR came to learn which arguments never succeeded in this process (e.g. language) and which ones stood a chance. Based on experience, the Nordic HR representative would also sometimes refuse to put certain subsidiary requests on the committee table knowing that they were not convincing enough. In addition, the bureaucratic nature of the decision-making process itself seemed to act as a disincentive to formulate a case for adaptation. Collectively, the INTRACOM Group appeared to have used their resources in negotiation in such a way so as to persuade Finland HR to not enter into negotiations in the first place.

Another important feature of the steering committee was its use as an internal benchmarking tool. Via a process of coercive comparison (Ferner & Edwards, 1995), the committee would compare the experiences and arguments of similar units and use them as a resource in negotiating for greater standardisation. In other words, if one unit could standardise the process or adopt English as the common language without any problems then the others could too. Sometimes as a result, supposedly grey areas looked a lot more clear-cut.

The definition of what contravened local law and what didn't was strictly verified by Group HR. By explicitly requiring Finland HR personnel to provide independent legal proof that a certain part of Group HR policy was illegal, including which paragraph of the law, INTRACOM was effectively reducing Finland HR's ability to 'interpret' the local context in their favour—a potentially powerful resource for subsidiaries in such negotiations:

You can only deviate from [Global HR policy] *if you have a legal reason. And we actually need to confirm it through our Head of Legal Affairs, that this is a legal requirement in Finland. It isn't enough that the answer comes from us.* (HR Advisor)

In some cases the Group's tough stance in negotiations has forced Finland HR to shift their emphasis from operational arguments or arguments based on local norms to legal arguments. One example of this was the letters sent out to new employees. The new e-HRM system, to be used shortly by the shared service centre, was designed so that standardised 'new joiner' letter templates were sent out in English. Rather than argue that certain employees would not understand the letter or "that wouldn't be the way things are done here", which would most likely have been insufficient reasons, instead Finland HR have had to find the appropriate piece of local legislation that stipulates that firms are obliged to provide such letters in Finnish and/or Swedish.

DISCUSSION AND CONCLUSION

By adopting a micro-political perspective, the main objective of the present study was to explore the ways in which the IT-based integration of HRM is negotiated and contested within a foreign MNC subsidiary setting. The specific aims of the research were to identify those issues which generate the greatest degree of conflict during the IT-based integration process, they key parties involved and the resources used by those parties during negotiation. In doing so, the study acknowledges the potentially significant role of micro politics in the MNC's use of control mechanisms in general (e.g. Geppert & Meyer, 2006) and HRM integration in particular (e.g. Martin & Beaumont, 1999; Ferner *et al*, 2004; Edwards *et al*, 2007).

The study's findings provide broad support for the argument made here that the implementation of a globally integrated e-HRM system not only provides fertile ground for revisiting the HRM global-local debate, but furthermore, that it generates a somewhat transparent forum in which to observe key actors forced to come together in a relatively short period of time to make their case for either the standardisation or local adaptation of a range of HRM practices. Accordingly, researchers are presented with a fairly unique opportunity to investigate where the most conflict arises, what arguments each party is using, and the resources each party deploys to advance their own interests.

Three issues were identified as generating the most conflict. Firstly, the e-HRM *system design* generated conflict perhaps because it represented the first genuine opportunity for parties to shape local HRM practices and processes. Accordingly, system design negotiations involving three main parties—Group HR, Finland HR and the IT system consultants—were characterised by all parties deploying multiple negotiation resources. In terms of the parties involved, the role of the third-party consultants was particularly significant. On the one hand, the consultants commanded a powerful negotiating position by being able to switch from Group orders (or mandate) to technical know-how to plain ignorance in resisting requests for local modifications from subsidiary HR personnel. On the other hand, the consultants' lack of local contextual knowledge also handed subsidiary HR with additional bargaining power. Indeed, scholars have identified the potentially unconstructive and powerful role played by consultants who may be trying to sell inappropriate e-HRM packages as part of a broader ERP solution (Walker, 2001; Lengnick-Hall & Lengnick-Hall, 2006). Supported by the findings of the present study, critical investigation into the roles of consultants in e-HRM system design and integration would be a constructive area for further research.

The second area of conflict was the *standardised use of English*, which caused widespread discontent throughout the Finnish subsidiary. Despite the number of negotiation resources deployed by Finland HR personnel, the strategic mandate (process standardisation, data integrity etc.) and the business case of cost seemed to out-

weigh most obvious language-related concerns. In terms of designing an effective globally integrated e-HRM system, which in turn facilitates moves towards a shared service model of HR delivery, the standardised use of English is a logical decision. However, the far-reaching implications of a strictly standardised language policy such as end users failing to understand what they are expected to do and lack of clarity and resources concerning translation responsibilities points to the pervasive role of language in multinational management and how it is often overlooked (e.g. Marschan *et al*, 1997). This is not to mention the feelings of exclusion that result.

Globally integrated e-HRM systems are not well suited to addressing potentially *grey areas of HR policy*. Instead, the huge costs associated with adaptation together with the system's key strengths in streamlining HR processes, are more likely to encourage a black and white approach to HRM standardisation and local adaptation. This was clearly evident in this study whereby the black and white approach was reinforced by questions of legality. Indeed, in terms of negotiation resources, the message being communicated by Group HR was that only verified legal constraints will suffice in negotiating deviations from Group-wide HR policies and processes. An interesting question warranting further research in this respect is whether the MNC parent uses certain arguments (or negotiation resources) more when seeking to achieve global integration via e-HRM systems compared to other situations. In this study the issue of cost, as a business case, played a significant role. Thus, there appeared to be connections to the cost-minimisation approach to the HRM global-local decision presented by Schmitt and Sadowski (2003), who argue that MNC decisions on this issue can be explained by applying rational economic thinking about the relative costs of achieving HRM centralisation and decentralisation.

On a more general note, the present study reported an MNC's attempts at greater HR process standardisation, facilitated by the global integration of an e-HRM system. In reference to the international HRM literature, this is an intriguing development given HRM's reportedly high cultural sensitivity (e.g. Tayeb, 1998). However, it is also worth noting here precisely what is being standardised and what is not. As Schuler (1992) argues, there are various levels of HRM ranging from HRM philosophies to HRM policies and practices. Research has since shown that the extent of HRM integration and responsiveness is likely to differ between these levels (e.g. Tayeb, 1998; Sippola & Smale, 2007). From this perspective, e-HRM systems may be able to standardise certain levels of HRM such as the philosophy behind its delivery and a range of transactional HRM processes, but it may be less successful in achieving the global integration of certain institutionally sensitive HRM practices.

In the IT literature we have come to understand that the key strengths of large-scale IT systems, such as ERP-based solutions, risk being undermined by excessive concessions and local modifications. This study has demonstrated at least that there can be few sufficiently compelling reasons for local adaptation. In this sense, will globally integrated e-HRM systems of this kind become somewhat of an oxymoron and lead to a disappointing uptake by end users, or will local HR personnel have to assume additional responsibilities in ensuring that end users do not become disenfranchised. Either way, it would appear that although HR professionals might benefit from such systems by allowing them to hand over more routine administrative HR transactions (e.g. Reddington & Martin, 2007), these tasks could just as easily be replaced not by more strategic roles, but by other administrative tasks aimed at limiting the negative impact of the system itself. If this is the case, the transformational effect of e-HRM systems on the HR function will be limited.

LIMITATIONS AND FUTURE RESEARCH

Any interpretations or conclusions based on the present study must of course be made in light of its limitations. Nevertheless, the limitations outlined below can also serve as potentially fruitful avenues for future research. Firstly, in order to establish a picture of the lived 'reality' of corporate control and coordination mechanisms (Geppert & Meyer, 2006), the study only drew upon the experiences and perceptions of subsidiary HR personnel. To alleviate potential respondent bias, interviews with representatives from headquarters and third-party consultants would have provided a more balanced account and served as an effective means through which to gain insights about each party's responses to the other's tactics and political stratagems (Oliver, 1991). Future studies in this area might therefore benefit from viewing HRM system integration outcomes as the result of complex negotiations between these different parties.

Secondly, and related to the first limitation, some of the findings of the study could be explained by the relatively small size of the Finnish subsidiary and its institutional setting. However, the aim of the study was not to explain negotiation outcomes, but rather to identify the main areas of conflict, which parties were involved and which negotiation resources were used. In this sense, it would be interesting to investigate whether these issues of conflict and use of negotiation resources differ across subsidiaries of different size and background. Furthermore, future studies could go on to evaluate the effectiveness of various negotiation resources in terms of their ability to promote interests and successfully achieve more room for manoeuvre.

Lastly, the findings are based on data from one MNC. As is typical to any single, in-depth case study, the generalisability of the findings is limited. However, when positioned methodically as a longitudinal and representative case

(Yin, 2003), this paper has contributed to our understanding about how HRM integration is negotiated between different key actors and the role that micro politics plays in this process. More specifically, it is demonstrated here that the introduction of a globally integrated e-HRM system offers academics in the field of HRM a rare opportunity to observe how HRM practices are established and controlled in MNC subsidiaries as well as the rationale used.

REFERENCES

Bae, J., Chen, S., & Lawler, J. (1998). Variations in human resource management in Asian countries: MNC home-country and host-country effects. *International Journal of Human Resource Management, 9*(4), 653–670.

Björkman, I., & Lu, Y. (2001). Institutionalization and bargaining power explanations of HRM practices in international joint ventures—the case of Chinese-Western joint ventures. *Organization Studies, 22*(3), 491–512.

Brewster, C., Sparrow, P., & Harris, H. (2005). Towards a new model of globalizing HRM. *International Journal of Human Resource Management, 16*(6), 949–970.

Clemmons, S., & Simon, S. J. (2001). Control and coordination in global ERP configuration, *Business Process Management, 7*(3), 205–215.

Denzin, N. K. (1978). *The Research Act: Theoretical Introduction to Sociological Methods*. New York: McGraw-Hill.

Doz, Y., & Prahalad, C. K. (1993). Managing DMNCs: A search for a new paradigm. In S. Ghoshal & D. E. Westney (Eds.), *Organization Theory and the Multinational Corporation* (pp. 24–50). MacMillan: Basingstoke.

Dörrenbächer, C., & Geppert, M. (2006). Micropolitics and conflicts in multinational corpora-

tions: Current debates, re-framing, and contributions of this special issue. *Journal of International Management, 12*(3), 251–265.

Edwards, T., & Kuruvilla, S. (2005). International HRM: national business systems, organizational politics and the international division of labour in MNCs. *International Journal of Human Resource Management, 16*(1), 1–21.

Edwards, T., Colling, T., & Ferner, A. (2007). Conceptual approaches to the transfer of employment practices in multinational companies: an integrated approach. *Human Resource Management Journal, 17*(3), 201–217.

Ferner, A. (2000). The underpinnings of 'bureaucratic' control systems: HRM in European multinationals. *Journal of Management Studies, 37*(4), 521–539.

Ferner, A., & Edwards, P. K. (1995). Power and the diffusion of organizational change within multinationals. *European Journal of Industrial Relations, 1*(2), 229–257.

Ferner, A., & Quintanilla, J. (1998). Multinationals, national business systems and HRM: the enduring influence of national identity or a process of 'Anglo-Saxonization'. *International Journal of Human Resource Management, 9*(4), 710–731.

Ferner, A., Almond, P., Clark, I., Colling, T., Edwards, T., Holden, L., & Muller-Camen, M. (2004). The dynamics of central control and subsidiary autonomy in the management of human resources: case-study evidence from US MNCs in the UK. *Organization Studies, 25*(3), 363–391.

Ferner, A., Almond, P., & Colling, T. (2005). Institutional theory and the cross-national transfer of employment policy: the case of 'workforce diversity' in US multinationals. *Journal of International Business Studies, 36*(3), 304–321.

Fisher, S., & Howell, A. (2004). Beyond user acceptance: an examination of employee reactions to information technology systems. *Human Resource Management, 43*(2-3), 243–258.

Forsgren, M. (1990). Managing the international multi-centre firm: Case studies from Sweden. *European Management Journal, 8*(2), 261–267.

Geppert, M., & Mayer, M. (2006). Introduction. In M. Geppert & M. Mayer (Eds.), *Global, National and Local Practices in Multinational Companies* (pp. 1–14). Basingstoke: Palgrave Macmillan.

Geppert, M., & Williams, K. (2006). Global, national and local practices in multinational corporations: Towards a sociopolitical framework. *International Journal of Human Resource Management, 17*(1), 49–69.

Ghauri, P. (2004). Designing and conducting case studies in international business research. In R. Marschan-Piekkari & C. Welch (Eds.), *Handbook of Qualitative Research Methods for International Business* (pp. 109–124). Cheltenham: Edward Elgar.

Ghauri, P., & Grønhaug, K. (2002). *Research Methods in Business Studies: A Practical Guide.* Harlow, UK: Financial Times and Prentice Hall.

Ghoshal, S., & Gratton, L. (2002). Integrating the enterprise. *Sloan Management Review, 44*(1), 31–38.

Gill, R., & Wong, A. (1998). The cross-cultural transfer of management practices: the case of Japanese human resource management practices in Singapore. *International Journal of Human Resource Management, 9*(1), 116–135.

Gooderham, P. N., Nordhaug, O., & Ringdal, K. (1999). Institutional and rational determinants of organizational practices: human resource management in European firms. *Administrative Science Quarterly, 44*(3), 507–531.

Hannon, J., Huang, I-C., & Jaw, B-S. (1995). International human resource strategy and its determinants: the case of subsidiaries in Taiwan. *Journal of International Business Studies, 26*(3), 531–554.

Hannon, J., Jelf, G., & Brandes, D. (1996). Human resource information systems: operational issues and strategic considerations in a global environment. *International Journal of Human Resource Management, 7*(1), 245–269.

Hoobler, J. M., & Johnson, N. B. (2004). An analysis of current human resource management publications. *Personnel Review, 33*(6), 665–676.

Kiessling, T., & Harvey, M. (2005). Strategic global human resource management research in the twenty-first century: an endorsement of the mixed-method research methodology. *International Journal of Human Resource Management, 16*(1), 22–45.

Lengnick-Hall, C., & Lengnick-Hall, A. (2006). HR, ERP and knowledge for competitive advantage. *Human Resource Management, 45*(1), 79–94.

Lepak, D. P., & Snell, S.A. (1998). Virtual HR: Strategic human resource management in the 21st century. *Human Resource Management Review, 8*(3), 215–234.

Marschan, R., Welch, D., & Welch, L. (1997). Language: The forgotten factor in multinational management. *European Management Journal, 15*(5), 591–598.

Martin, G., & Beaumont, P. (1998). Diffusing 'best practice' in multinational firms: prospects, practice and contestation. *International Journal of Human Resource Management, 9*(4), 671–695.

Martin, G., & Beaumont, P. (1999). Co-ordination and control of human resource management in multinational firms: the case of CASHCO. *International Journal of Human Resource Management, 10*(1), 21–42.

Mense-Petermann, U. (2006). Micro-political or inter-cultural conflicts?—An integrating approach. *Journal of International Management, 12*(3), 302–317.

Oliver, C. (1991). Strategic responses to institutional processes. *Academy of Management Review*, *16*(1), 145–179.

Reddington, M, & Martin, G. (2007). Theorizing the links between e-HR and strategic HRM: A framework, case illustration and some reflections. *Proceedings of the First European Academic Workshop on Electronic Human Resource Management*.

Reddington, M., Williamson, M., & Withers, M. (2005). *Transforming HR: Creating Value Through People*. Oxford: Butterworth Heinemann.

Rosenzweig, P., & Nohria, N. (1994). Influences on human resource management practices in multinational corporations. *Journal of International Business Studies*, *25*(2), 229–251.

Ruël, H. R., Bondarouk, T. & Looise, J. K. (2004). E-HRM: Innovation or Irritation. An Explorative Empirical Study in Five Large Companies on Web-based HRM. *Management Revue*, *15*(3), 364–380.

Ruta, C. D. (2005). The application of change management theory to HR portal implementation in subsidiaries of multinational corporations, *Human Resource Management*, *44*(1), 35–53.

Schmitt, M., & Sadowski, D. (2003). A cost-minimization approach to the international transfer of HRM/IR practices: Anglo-Saxon multinationals in the Federal Republic of Germany. *International Journal of Human Resource Management*, *14*(3), 409–430.

Schuler, R. S. (1992). Strategic human resources management: linking the people with the strategic needs of the business. *Organizational Dynamics*, *21*(1), 18–32.

Shrivastava, S., & Shaw, J. B. (2003). Liberating HR through technology. *Human Resource Management*, *42*(3), 201–222.

Sippola, A., & Smale, A. (2007). The global integration of diversity management: A longitudinal case study. *International Journal of Human Resource Management*, *18*(11), 1895–1916.

Smale, A. (2007). *Mechanisms of Global HRM Integration in Multinational Corporations*. Unpublished dissertation, No.181, University of Vaasa, Finland.

Smale, A. (2008). Foreign subsidiary perspectives on the mechanisms of global HRM integration. *Human Resource Management Journal*, *18*(2), 135–153.

Sparrow, P. (2006). Global knowledge management and HRM. In G. K. Stahl & I. Björkman (Eds.), *Handbook of Research in International Human Resource Management* (pp. 113–138). Edward Elgar, Cheltenham.

Sparrow, P., Brewster, C., & Harris, H. (2004). *Globalizing Human Resource Management*. London: Routledge.

Stone, D., & Gueutal, H. (2005). *The brave new world of e-HR: human resources management in the digital age*. San Francisco: Jossey-Bass.

Tansley, C., Newell, S., & Williams, H. (2001). Effecting HRM-style practices through an integrated human resource information system. *Personnel Review*, *30*(3), 351–370.

Tayeb, M. H. (1998). Transfer of HRM practices across cultures: An American company in Scotland. *International Journal of Human Resource Management*, *9*(2), 332–58.

Taylor, S. (2006). Emerging motivations for global HRM integration. In A. Ferner, J. Quintanilla & C. Sánchez-Runde (Eds.), *Multinationals, Institutions and the Construction of Transnational Practices* (pp. 109–130). Basingstoke: Palgrave Macmillan.

Taylor, S., Beechler, S., & Napier, N. (1996). Toward an integrative model of strategic international human resource management. *Academy of Management Review*, *21*(4), 959–985.

Walker, A. (2001). *The Technologies and Trends that are Transforming HR: Web-Based Human Resources*. NewYork: McGraw Hill/Towers Perrin.

Yin, R. K. (2003). *Case Study Research: Design and Methods*. 3rd edition, Thousand Oaks, CA: Sage.

KEY TERMS

Micro-Political Perspective: Turns the spotlight on the conflicts that emerge when powerful actors with divergent goals, interests and identities negotiate with each other locally and across national and functional borders.

Standardization: Establishing a standard procedure or practice for optimising the economic use of resources.

Localization: Adapting a system to take into account different languages, customs, symbols and legislation.

ENDNOTE

[1] For confidentiality reasons a pseudonym is used and certain details concerning the organisation's titles have been kept vague.

Chapter X
Studying Human Resource Information Systems Implementation using Adaptive Structuration Theory:
The Case of an HRIS Implementation at Dow Chemical Company

Huub Ruël
University of Twente, The Netherlands & American University of Beirut, Lebanon

ABSTRACT

Research on Human Resource Information Systems (HRIS) implementation lacks theoretical depth and richness. For that reason this paper applies a theory to HRIS implementation developed by Gerardine DeSanctis and Marshal Scott Poole originally for studying information systems implementation, namely Adaptive Structuration Theory (AST). AST is based on Structuration Theory, a theory from sociology, and assumes that information systems and organizations are fundamentally interrelated. They influence each other mutually. In this paper concepts from AST are applied to a HRIS implementation at Dow Chemicals. The case shows how a HRIS' philosophy through appropriation by end-users is being realized in HRIS outcomes.

INTRODUCTION

Human Resource Information Systems (HRIS) research lacks theoretical depth and richness. For that reason this chapter applies a theory to HRIS implementation developed by DeSanctis & Poole (1994), originally for studying information systems implementation, namely Adaptive Structuration Theory (AST). AST assumes that information systems and organizations are interrelated. In this paper concepts from AST are applied to study the HRIS implementation at Dow Chemicals. In this way the case of Dow shows how an HRIS' philosophy, in AST terms called spirit, is brought to life through appropriation by end-users and is shown in expected and unexpected HRIS outcomes.

In this first section, HRIS research up to date is summarized. Subsequently, Adaptive Structuration Theory will be described and some interesting results provided with the help of this theory presented. In section three the research methods applied are described, and after that in section four the HRIS implementation at Dow Chemicals will be presented.

Human Resource Information Systems Research Up to Date

In this paper we define HRISs as all IT-based information systems and applications, either stand-alone or networked, for human resource management purposes, be it for facilitating HR practices, policies or strategies. In earlier studies HRISs have been excluded from the e-HRM area since some authors were of the opinion that there was a fundamental difference between HRIS and e-HR in that. Basically, HRISs were directed towards the HR department itself. Users of these systems were mainly HR staff as these types of systems aimed to improve the processes within the HR department itself (RuëL, Bondarouk & Looise, 2004).

In this paper however, we consider the term HRIS to encapsulate the whole area of IT, internet technology and HRM. The commonly used terms nowadays like e-HRM, web-based HRM, and IT based HRM are considered as developments within the area of HRISs. Although we agree that HRISs in the early days concerned mainly IT-based information systems for the HR department, we do not agree that a line can be drawn between IT-based information systems for HR and internet-based HR applications, they are basically similar: IT technologies for HR activities, whether performed within the HR department or outside the HR department, for example by line managers and employees.

HRISs in their current appearance emerged from a number of developments in society and business. Following Lengnick-Hall & Moritz (2003) the first building block for HRIS' was the worldwide distribution of PC's that facilitated managers and employees with the hardware to perform HR tasks electronically. However, with the availability of PCs computer literacy had to increase in order to enable managers and employees to use the technology. The Internet opened the way to connect PC's and to communicate in real-time. In this way many physical hurdles that before formed obstacles for efficient interaction and smooth business processes were bypassed. On top of that enterprise resource planning (ERP) systems created the opportunity to link all business processes. Databases that before were isolated could be integrated and "into a seamless whole for real-time transaction processing and decision making" [3; p. 367]. The final stage arrived when HR professionals and information technology specialists joined forces and developed electronic information systems "that moved HR information and decision making from file drawers to computers" [3; p. 367]. HR processes were reengineered to eliminate steps and to speed up cycle times.

Broadly speaking, HRISs appear in three types: operational HRIS's, relational HRISs, and transformational HRISs. This division is based upon RuëL, Bondarouk and Looise (2004). The first type, operational HRISs, concern systems that are used for basic HR activities in the administrative area, such as payroll and personnel data administration (employee's personal data, job description, CV, holiday leave etc.). The second type, relational HRISs concerns more advanced HRM activities, those that involve interaction between a professional source, a HRIS application and employees and/or management. Examples of relational HRISs are recruitment and selection systems, training and development systems and performance management systems. The system contains the professional instruments, such as a professional questionnaire assessing an employee's development level, and employees and management have the online access to use them wherever, whenever. Transformational HRISs, the third type, are the ones for HR activities with a strategic character like organisational change processes, strategic re-orientation, strategic competence management. Examples of HRIS applications of this type are corporate online discussion platforms, weblogs or applications that guide employees through the objectives, stages and methods of an organisational change process, or applications for assessment of professional skills and offering online advice for skill development aligned with strategic HR objectives.

So far, large companies have tried to implement HRISs of all the three types whereas smaller and mid-size companies implemented mostly the operational and relational HRISs.

HRIS Research Up to Date

Research on HRISs started to take off in the second half of the 1980's, but it developed slowly and it for sure did not mature. Research articles from those 'early days' are from DeSanctis (1986); Kavanagh, Gueutal & Tannenbaum (1990); Cascio & Awad (1981); Haines & Petit (1997), Limburg, Looise & Ruël (1998). The research topic received renewed attention with the growing importance of Internet technology. Since the second half of the 1990's organizations started to apply this technology for Human Resource Management purposes. 'Early birds' on the role of Internet-based applications for HRM in particular were Lepak & Snell (1998) and Wright & Dyer (2000). However, these papers mainly aimed at outlining the importance of the issue, and limitedly empirical. Overall, Strohmeier (2006) found 18 appropriate studies that can be labelled as empirical HRIS (he prefers to use the

term e-HRM) studies, nine from the pre-Internet era, nine from the Internet-era. Only a few new empirical articles have appeared since Strohmeier's last study mentioned (RuëL, Bondarouk and Looise, 2004) was published. Bell, Sae-Won Lee & Yeung(2006) studied the impact of e-HR on professional competence in HRM and found through interviews with HR professionals from 19 firms that "[HRIS] is a driving force in the transformation of the HR function" (p. 306). Their data suggest that this transformation is reshaping the competencies that define HR professionals' success (p. 306). Guiderdoni (2006) concludes that different types of middle managers, she distinguishes four, respond differently to HRISs. Bondarouk & Ruël (2006) and Ruël, Bondarouk & van der Velde (2007) conclude that especially the content and the structure of a web-based HRIS application has a positive influence on perceived HRM effectiveness.

Overall, we are of the opinion that HRIS research is in its infancy, though trying to mature if we look at conference initiatives and upcoming special journal issues and books on HRIS/e-HR. Existing research foci still need to be broadened and to be deepened in order to let HRIS research mature. This conclusion becomes even more evident if we look at the theoretical development of the HRIS research area.

Martin, Wood & Collings (2006) note, together with Shrivastave & Shaw (2004) RuëL, Bondarouk and Looise (2004) were the first to provide a theoretical framework for HRIS adoption. Strohmeier (2006) ignores even Shrivastava & Shaw's framework and only recognizes two studies that employ frameworks in order to systematise examined consequences: Gardner, Lepak & Bartol (2003), and RuëL, Bondarouk and Looise (2004). A very recent attempt to theorize and model HRIS drivers, intervening factors, and consequences comes from Stone, Stone-Romero & Lukaszewski (2006). However, yet next to a limited empirical basis we observe that the HRIS field is also under-theorized, an opinion shared by

Reddington & Martin (2006) and Martin, Wood & Collings (2006). For that reason, in this paper we apply a powerful theory developed by DeSanctis & Poole, Adaptive Structuration Theory.

ADAPTIVE STRUCTURATION THEORY (AST): A BRIEF INTRODUCTION

DeSanctis & Poole (1994) and Poole & DeSanctis (1990) ; Poole & DeSanctis (1989), were inspired by the basic ideas of Structuration theory and developed an extended theory, initially to study groups using group decision support systems (GDSSs). In more recent publications the focus has been broadened towards advanced information technologies in general (DeSanctis & Poole,1994) .

With AST, DeSanctis and Poole tried to develop a theory that holds the 'middle ground', inspired by the work of Anthony Giddens they want to position themselves between technological determinism (or objectivism) and voluntarism (or subjectivism). Initially, AST was developed for studying groups which were using an electronic group decision support system. "It looks into the process of human usage of computer systems and at the nature of group-computer interaction", was the argument advanced by [22, p. 150]. Poole & DeSanctis (1989) were of the opinion that the concept of information technology should be reconsidered, and that structuration theory would assist them to achieve this and to formulate their adaptive structuration theory. Poole & DeSanctis (1989) state: "Building on the theories of structuration advanced by several European social theorists, the theory of adaptive structuration attempts to explain how technology affects group and organizational processes and resultant outcomes" [22 ; p.149]. Their AST holds that it is the active use of technology by people that determines the observable outcomes, rather than the view that technology is a direct, causal, influence on human

behavior. This is the approach we adopt in this study. Therefore, we begin with a closer look at the basics of AST.

The Basics of Adaptive Structuration Theory

As has already been noted, AST initially in particular focused on group processes for the purpose of studying the *use* of group decision support systems. The reason for labeling it as 'adaptive' is that adaptation to the situation is seen as the primary goal of group action. This approach can accept differences in outcomes that occur even when the same conditions exist, since AST accepts that groups are not merely information processing entities but that they have a social existence that has to be considered when using group technologies (Chin, Gopal & Salisbury, 1997). DeSanctis & Poole (1994) developed a model that presents AST in its full context, as presented in Figure 2.1. The eight arrows in the model reflect seven hypotheses:

1.   Advanced information technologies (AIT) provide structures (in terms of structuration theory) which can be described in terms of their spirit and features. Different sets of spirits and features lead to different forms of interaction with the technology.

2.   Use of AIT structures can vary depending on other contingencies that offer alternative sources of structures.

3 & 4. New sources of structure emerge as the technology and other sources of structure are applied during the course of interaction.

5.   New structures emerge in group interactions as the spirit and features of an AIT are appropriated in a given context and then reproduced in group interactions over time.

Figure 1. The original adaptive structuration theory model (adapted from DeSanctis & Poole, 1994)

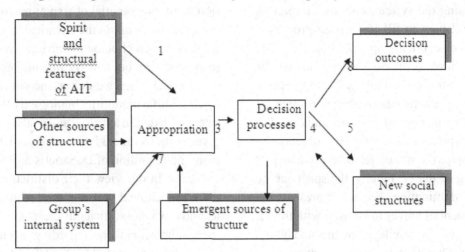

6. Group decision processes will vary depending on the nature of AIT appropriation.

7. The nature of AIT appropriation will vary depending on the group internal system.

8. Given AIT and other sources of structure (n1, n2, n3, etc.) ideal appropriation processes, and decision processes that fit the task at hand, then the desired outcomes of AIT use will result.

Figure 1, and the seven hypotheses represent the original AST model. They are based upon two main ideas: firstly that advanced information technologies are social in nature. This is expressed by the concept of *spirit*. Secondly that advanced information technologies are being 'realized' by its use. This is expressed by the concept of *appropriation*.

Since AST was initially developed to study group decision support systems in use, the model and the hypotheses contain 'decision processes', 'decision outcomes', and 'group's internal system'. Good examples of applying AST in studying electronic group system use do exist and include Poole & DeSanctis (1992), Wheeler, Mennecke & Scudder (1993), Chin, Gopal & Salisbury (1997),

Kahai, Sosik & Avolio (1997), and Majchrzak, Rice, Malhotra, King & Ba (2000).

However, DeSanctis & Poole (1994) stress that AST is also useful for studying other advanced information technologies. We are especially interested in applying it to HRIS implementations. Furthermore, AST can be considered as a general framework from which more specific hypotheses can be drawn. In this paper it is especially the concepts of spirit and appropriation, that we believe are promising and these have not been used before in studies on HRISs.

Applying AST to office technology gives our study an interesting challenge. In the following sub sections we elaborate on the spirit and the appropriation of office technology.

Spirit of Technology

One of the central elements of AST is the belief that advanced information technology is social in nature. Hence, the introduction of the concept of spirit. DeSanctis & Poole (1994) define spirit as follows: "Spirit is the general intent with regard to values and goals underlying a given set of structural features" (p. 126). The concept of spirit concerns the 'official line' which the technology presents to people regarding how to act when using the system, how to interpret its features, and how to fill in gaps in procedure which are not explicitly specified (p.126). The spirit of a technology provides what Giddens calls 'legitimation' to the technology by supplying a normative frame with regard to behaviors that are appropriate in the context of the technology" [1 ; p.126). The spirit can also give 'signification' to users, as it helps them to understand and interpret the meaning of the IT. Finally, the spirit can be a means of 'domination', because it presents the type of influential moves to be used with the IT. Some users may be privileged by this and others constrained. Therefore, in terms of structuration theory, the concept of spirit concerns the total set of possible structures promoted that may be called upon by means of the structural features (later on in this section we will discuss how to define the structural features). The concept of spirit suits very well what Orlikowski & Robey (1991) calls the 'interpretive flexibility' of information technology. The implication of this assumption is that the realization of any object may differ between situations, and that the object itself can change as people change their mode of using it.

In terms of AST, structural features are the specific rules and resources, or capabilities, offered by the system. This suggests that an office technology must contain 'visible' structures but we do not agree with this point of view. In AST, the concepts of spirit and structural features are not clearly separated. Structural features only refer to the technical capabilities of a system. Structures never have a physical form, structures can only become 'visible' *in* human action. Information technology, in our perception, may consist of dozens of technical capabilities, but it is the technology's spirit that enables users to make sense out of these capabilities. Therefore we prefer to speak of *technical features*, rather than structural features.

In the context of information technology, it can be said that, when users work with a specific

information technology means, they make a selection from the potential of structures 'offered' by the spirit, by means of the technical features. This implies that a technology's spirit can enable users to appropriate, but it also can constrain them.

In conclusion, we define the concept of the spirit of information technology as the general intent with regard to values and goals underlying a given set of technical features. This differs a little from the definition of DeSanctis & Poole (1994) , because in our view their distinction between the non-technical part and the technical part of technology is not sufficiently clear. A technology's spirit is the 'official line' regarding how to act when using a technology. HRISs (and thus its spirit) can only be realized in actual use, which is referred to as appropriation. If, in a certain context, users do not appropriate an HRIS in accordance with its spirit, this may lead to unanticipated outcomes. In this way, it can be theoretically understood why similar office technologies, even in similar contexts, can lead to different outcomes. Related ways of referring to a technology's spirit in this paper will be through the use of terms such as 'underlying philosophy' or 'intention' of an information technology.

After having explained the concept of spirit, the following section elaborates further on the concept of appropriation.

Office Technology Appropriation

AST considers information technology use as a matter of appropriation. In the relatively short history of AST, its developers have gone through some changes in the way they conceptualize appropriation. Initially, AST distinguished three dimensions of appropriation: *faithfulness of appropriation, attitudes towards appropriation,* and *the level of consensus on the appropriation.* However, after rethinking the theory of adaptive structuration, DeSanctis & Poole (1994) distinguish four dimensions of appropriation: *appropriation moves, faithfulness of appropriation, attitudes towards appropriation,* and *instrumental uses.* So, they added *appropriation moves* and *instrumental uses,* and removed *consensus on appropriation.* We believe that a combination of DeSanctis & Poole (1994) and Poole & DeSanctis (1992) provides the most useful concept of appropriation. We therefore include all the dimensions in our concept of appropriation.

So far, in our elaboration, we have adopted from AST the two central concepts; the spirit of an HRIS and appropriation. These concepts will be our main 'sources' in developing a research model that suits our study on HRISs.

HRIS Outcomes

It is assumed that an HRIS is not implemented in organizations without reason. We suppose, if an HRIS is appropriated in accordance with its spirit, that the expected effects will arise. In general, the main reason for the implementation of an HRIS is to increase business performance (productivity, efficiency, quality of services).

We assume, based upon Beer et al.'s ideas about the expected results or outcomes of HRM, that HRISs also aim to achieve a certain set of outcomes. As stated earlier, implementing an HRIS in our view, is a way of carrying out HRM, it is a way of thinking about and implementing HRM strategies, policies, and practices. By following a specific HRIS direction, an organization expects to achieve certain goals: an improvement in the HR's strategic orientation, an improvement in client focus and satisfaction, and a decrease in costs or increased efficiency.

Besides these goals that can lead to anticipated outcomes, a number of so-called 'overall' organizational goals can be distinguished regarding an organization's 'social capital'. All HRM activities, and therefore also all e-HRM activities, will implicitly or explicitly be directed towards these 'overall' goals. Beer, Spector, Lawrence, Mills & Walton (1984) distinguish four possibilities: high

commitment, high competence, cost effectiveness, and higher congruence. By high commitment they mean that the workforce is motivated and understanding, and that they are willing to interact with the management about changes in the organizational environment and the impact that this can have on the internal organization. For HR itself, this means that it should be able to play the role of change agent, to use (Ulrich, 1997) terminology. High commitment implies a high level of trust between management and workforce. High competence points towards the capacities of employees to learn new tasks and roles if the circumstances require it. For HR itself it means, in Ulrich's framework, playing the employee champion role. Cost effectiveness refers to the competitiveness of pay levels and employee turnover rate, and to the acceptability of costs resulting from employee resistance such as strikes. As Ulrich (1997) states, HR itself has to be able to play the administrative expert role in order to contribute to an organization's cost effectiveness. Finally, higher congruence refers to the internal organization, the reward system, and the 'input, throughput, and output' of personnel, which need to be structured in the interests of all stakeholders.

Towards a Research Model

In this section we will combine the above-described 'ingredients' in a research model, which will then guide our study on HRIS implementation:

RESEARCH METHOD

In this paper we apply a case study approach. Within the case study approach, specific techniques have to be selected for collecting the data. One of the components of the method is that the data collected must be suitable for answering the

Figure 2. The research model

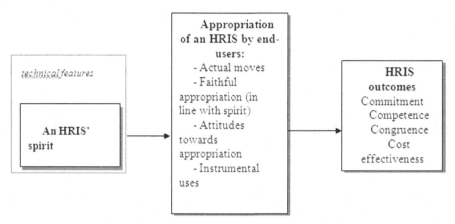

research questions and for testing the hypotheses. As noted earlier, our research is basically of a soft-line deterministic nature, as our research model, is based on AST.

We have several techniques at our disposal, such as conversational interviews, non-conversational interviews or written questionnaires, participant observation, and document analysis. For our study we have chosen conversational and non-conversational interviews (written questionnaires) as the dominant techniques. The conversational interviews particularly are used to describe the variables in the research model, the non-conversational interviews are used for testing the hypotheses which represent the relationships between the variables in the research model.

Conversational interviews are adequate for the following reasons. Firstly, we studied an HRIS implementation retrospectively. Because of time constraints it was not possible to participate in a HRIS projects from start to end. Secondly, through the use of conversational interviews with representatives of all groups of participants, it was possible to reconstruct an HRIS implementation from start to end. In this sense, the conversational interviews are used as an instrument for *ethnographical* purposes. 'Traditional' ethnographical methods concern participant observation within

a specific context, often for a considerable a period of time; the researcher is in fact the research instrument. Because of the practical constraints it was not possible to participate in a number of office technology projects over a period of time. Therefore we had to choose an alternative; we used project participants who had been able to observe the project as 'researchers' and let them tell their story. As this includes representatives of all the project parties, we have a so-called multi-view of the project, and are able to describe the variables as discerned in our research model. The non-conversational interviews, which we will refer to as questionnaires from now on, were used to test our hypotheses.

Besides the two types of interviews as the dominant techniques, and the analysis of documents as additional techniques, we also used immediate participant observations as a source of data. As explained, it was not possible to be constantly present in the projects, but in all of them we observed a number of users of the newly implemented HRIS over a short period of time. The data collected in this way is in addition to the data obtained from the dominant techniques. How we developed the instruments for use in the case studies is described below.

Table 1. Concepts, definitions and indicators

Concept	Definition	Indicators
Spirit of HRIS	The extent to which the general intent regarding the values and goals underlying an HRISs set of technical features is clear to users.	the technology's goals the 'thought behind' an HRIS knowing where effective use of an HRIS leads to knowing what developers aimed for knowing how an HRIS is used optimally
Technical features	The visible, technical capabilities users are offered being a part of an HRIS.	Level of restrictiveness Level of sophistication Degree of comprehensiveness
Appropriation	The physical and mental activities that users of HRIS carry out while making a selection from the potential set of structures of an HRIS, represented by the spirit and the technical features, for the day-to-day practices.	Actual use (moves) Use in line with the spirit (faithful appropriation) Usefulness of an HRIS Ease of use of an HRIS Instrumental use of an HRIS Consensus about use
HRIS outcomes	The extent to which the day-to-day activities of the group of users of an HRIS have to be carried out to meet the standards required.	Commitment Congruence Cost effectiveness Competence

RESULTS: AN HRIS IMPLEMENTATION AT DOW CHEMICALS

The Dow Chemical Company is one of the largest chemical companies in the world. This US-based company (Midland, Michigan) is now active in 33 countries around the globe. Dow was until recently a country-oriented company, with fairly autonomous sites around the world only loosely coupled with Dow sites in other countries. During the mid-1990s this changed, and Dow aimed to become a global company in which the globally dispersed sites would be turned more into business-oriented units. Dow's current organizational structure is flat (a maximum of six layers) and based upon worldwide-organized businesses. This provides employees with a high level of independence and accountability, and employees work in self-managing teams, process operators as well as managers.

The Research Site: Dow Benelux B.V.

Dow Benelux is part of the global Dow Company, and has ten production locations and three office locations. Dow's largest production site outside of the United States is located in Terneuzen (the Netherlands). This site consists of 41 units, of which 26 are factories. Dow's European accounting unit and its Research and Development unit are also located in Terneuzen. The total number of employees at Dow Benelux is about 2800, with about 600 in Belgium and 2200 in the Netherlands (with 2100 in Terneuzen). The average period that the employees have been working at Dow Benelux is 16 years, and their average age is 42.

Dow Benelux produces more than 800 different products, most of which are semi-manufactured goods for application in all kinds of products used in aspects of our daily lives. Examples of markets where Dow is a major 'player' are: furniture and furnishings (carpets, furniture materials), maintenance of buildings (paint, coatings, cleaning materials, isolation), personal care (soap, creams, lotions, packing materials), and health and medicine (gloves for surgeons, diapers, sport articles).

Starting with e-HRM at Dow: The Spirit of the People Success System

In 1997, Dow started to introduce the People Success System (PSS): "a system of Human Resource reference materials and tools that help provide the underpinnings of Dow's new culture". Before the introduction of PSS (which is technically based upon Peoplesoft), Dow already had a number of electronic HR systems in use. PSS's difference was that it was based upon the idea of having one database, and more importantly, with PSS, a completely new HR philosophy was introduced.

With the PSS, Dow's management aimed to provide an integrated Human Resources system that supported Dow's strategy and enabled the culture that is necessary for individual and business success to flourish. Further, Dow's management aimed to support a global business organization, empower employees, support a de-layered organization and self-directed teams, and create a change-ready workforce.

The Spirit of the PSS

The People Success System is a result of Dow's strategic, global, competence-based HR policy. It is a system of 'Human Resource reference materials and tools that help provide the underpinnings of Dow's new culture'. The electronic tool is seen as a necessary enabler. The PSS consists of four components, visualized as four pieces of a puzzle: one in the center, and the other three around it. The middle piece, the heart of the 'People Success puzzle', is *Performance Expectations* and seen as the central component of the entire system. It describes the required contributions from both the employees and the company for success. The other pieces are compensation, development, and opportunities.

Dow plans and decides on how many, and what kinds of, talents are needed for the future through its Corporate Staffing strategy, Strategic HR Planning, and Workforce of the Future. It is

claimed that Dow attracts new employees through providing them with challenging and interesting work, extensive resources for personnel development, empowerment, competitive pay and global scope.

Appropriation of the HRIS at Dow Chemicals Company

This part describes the way people at Dow appropriate the People Success System, that is how people incorporate the PSS' spirit through using the web-based tools and resources available into their day-to-day work.

The first reaction to the People Success System from people working in the plants was one of hesitance (*appropriation moves*), and the supporting staff were also hesitant but in a more open way. The difference can be attributed to three aspects. Firstly, the differences in PC experience: the people working in the plants were generally less used to working with a PC, especially the elderly workers. Secondly, there was a lack of available PCs in the plants. Thirdly, the dominant language in the People Success System was English, and the plant workers were, on average, less skilled in English.

Overall, people at Dow appreciated the fact that, with the PSS, information became available that was not previously accessible (*consensus about use*). The global compensation system especially received a lot of hits at the beginning, because it provided information about salaries at all job levels at all Dow sites around the world (*appropriation moves/faithful use/usefulness*). People could compare between countries and between job levels. This contributed to the open culture that had been announced as part of the HR changes at Dow.

Interestingly, due to the introduction of a whole new HR philosophy, there was so much information available that it discouraged people from exploring the system (*appropriation moves/ usefulness*). It could create a feeling of getting lost, not knowing how to find the way.

Initially, employees had a lot of questions about the system (*ease of use*), but after some time these tailed off. Coaches organized meetings to explain the system to employees, especially for those in the plants. Employees were stimulated to use the system, and to investigate the system. The impression is given that the problems people experienced with the implementation of the system were not exceptional in comparison to other changes. The large resistance to using the PSS (*appropriation moves*) was similar to resistance experienced during other change processes.

As the system became more sophisticated, the enthusiasm for using the system itself increased (*appropriation moves/usefulness*). Quite soon after the implementation, in 1997, Dow's Job Announcement System (JAS) became available. Until then, the people at Dow had been reluctant to believe that this system would really create the transparent and flexible internal labor market promised. At Dow, the traditional way of filling vacancies was to contact friendly colleagues or line managers within the company. Some people expected to be blocked by their managers if they wanted to apply for a job elsewhere in the company. However, the JAS has been the greatest success story with the PSS, initially and still today (*appropriation moves/faithfulness of appropriation/ usefulness*). Line managers have to publish job vacancies on the JAS, and employees, right from the very start, have used the opportunities offered to apply internally for jobs. Some line managers were not pleased by the fact that their employees 'walked out', and complained to HR "Help, my people are walking out". HR's reply in such cases was "Then you have a problem" meaning that the line managers had to work on the way they managed their people.

Six Months Later

It can be said that various groups appropriated the People Success System differently (*faithfulness of appropriation*). Supporting staff were 'getting along' with the PSS more easily than plant employees (*easiness of use*). The impression exists that many people still do not go deeply into the system (*faithfulness of appropriation/usefulness/ easiness of use*). A lack of time is one of the explanations that people give. Others think that this is just an excuse for not accepting responsibility for one's own development (*faithfulness of appropriation*). The People Success System stresses learning and development, which is a difference to Dow's 'old' situation. One half a day every two months can be an appropriate amount of time for using the system.

In 2001 most of the material on the PSS was translated into Dutch, so language should no longer be a motive for not using the tools and resources. However, the view exists that this did not lead to a change in attitude towards using the PSS (*appropriation moves*).

Generally, departments seem to have two or three employees who are interested in searching using the internet. In particular, young people were the more enthusiastic users (*appropriation moves/ usefulness*). Elderly workers in the beginning did not want to work with the system because of their lack of PC skills and because most of the information was in English. However, much information has now been translated, as remarked upon earlier. Tools such as feedback and learning tools are used by some employees, but others find these tools to vague and difficult (especially operators). A significant group of employees did not use the 360 degrees feedback tool (*appropriation moves*) because they were afraid that a negative outcome would be used by their managers as evidence of a negative performance. This is despite Dow's management having announced that the result of the 360 degrees feedback tool is confidential: the employee decides what, if anything, to do with the result (*consensus about use*).

Although everybody has received all the information about the system, it could be that there are too many screens and steps to go through. It could be that operators, in particular, need more precise interfaces (*easiness of use*).

One interesting aspect is that the opinion exists that the PSS stresses very much the social issues (training, conflict management, language, and social skills) rather than the professional technical skills. As one person close to this topic said: *"We simply rely on their (new employees) education; presuming that they have their technical and professional skills. In my view, many mistakes were made in the recruiting of new employees because of the issues in the system: too much attention is given to the social aspects and not to the normal professional skills".*

In conclusion, it can be said that the organization's members, in the first stage of appropriation, worked with the PSS mainly as an operational e-HR tool. They used it a source of information (*faithfulness of appropriation*). When more tools and resources were added in 1997 and 1998, especially when the JAS was added, appropriation switched, to some extent, towards relational e-HR, albeit with caution (*faithfulness of appropriation*). Since then, we have concluded that the PSS appropriation has slightly moved towards transformational e-HR, given that young new employees use the competency assessment tool for new employees right from their start at Dow (*faithfulness of appropriation*). They use the development tool to compile their development plan for the near future, are happy to be immediately exposed to the JAS, and are used to learn@dow. In this way the workforce has become more change ready (*faithfulness of appropriation*).

HRIS OUTCOMES

Commitment

The new system has not in itself changed the commitment of employees at Dow. If commitment has improved, and this is difficult to prove, then it is not because of the system.

At the same time we have found an indirect connection: the transparency of the company has increased and its policies have become more open—the same information is available to the management and to the employees. The most impressive example is the openness of the compensation part of the PSS. Salaries of all positions are visible to everybody, anyone can see how much the leaders earn, and in all countries.

There is no direct and linear relationship between the commitment and trust—whether the relationship was strengthened due to the PSS is uncertain. However, our respondents were certain that the system had not destroyed it.

Competence

Overall, it can be said that the competencies of people at Dow have increased: 60-70% of the employees have developed their competencies by using the PSS. There are amusing anecdotes in the company about some employees who had to start to learn how to operate a PC because of the PSS implementation. Some older employees now proudly tell their grandchildren that they have learned to work with a PC...

With the new Strategic Blueprint and the new HR philosophy (competence-based) there can be more people than before on a senior level within a group of workers. There can now be more than one 'first operator' working on a shift, and an increase in the number of team members who can do specific tasks, and this makes job rotation possible.

Since the implementation of the PSS, employees can see how to change and develop, and this is very new to them. According to some views, the idea of career self-management is not yet fully working: employees need more time and this has to be granted by their team leader. Within Dow, a more revealing opinion can be heard about the opportunities the PSS gives. There is a commonly held view that there are many examples of individuals who have wanted to develop themselves at Dow, and who have been successful due to the PSS. With about 2000 operators, it cannot be expected that all of them will develop careers at Dow. Further, time and the availability of the privacy needed to work on a PC are always limited. However, those who are motivated will find a solution, and the system has given people the opportunity to develop their basic educational level (the level they entered Dow with). This is desirable because the plant has become more complex, and more highly educated people are necessary. However, there are still people who do not accept this responsibility.

The Job Announcement System (JAS) has contributed greatly to personal development. Being a user-friendly and well-designed tool, it provides the opportunity to plan a career within Dow. Some of the respondents found the JAS the best part of the PSS.

People learnt the English terminology used in the PSS very quickly, and did not need to wait until the information was translated. Also people's PC skills improved. Furthermore, the extent of communication with non-Dutch managers, 'outsiders', has increased.

The learning component was also experienced as very new. Now, if you want to learn, you can. An impression gained is that the general opinion is that the e-learning tool is used in a different manner than it was intended. This could be due to the American style of the courses that sometimes seem to teach obvious things. The e-learning tool in itself is a good idea, but the content is not always relevant to a person's position and needs.

Congruence

Communication is now very fast and it is very simple to communicate with anybody. In the plant, however, there are still employees who never check their e-mail. However, one hears that direct contacts have been dramatically reduced.

Overall, in the plants there are still voices that say that there is too much information that employees have to go through, there are too less PCs, there is little time to work with the PSS, and

some employees have difficulties with English (although at least the materials have now been translated).

The philosophy of the PSS, however, is sound and important: it empowers the company, but it is valid to ask whether you need an intranet/ electronic tool to achieve this. Most of the information was already available before the PSS was introduced, and to find that the new system contains already familiar information can be disappointing.

HR specialists say that people are now more aware of what the company wants from them. People are trying to do something about their knowledge and skills. All the information needed about how to develop is on-line, so there is no need to physically go to the HR department.

Now that the performance evaluation criteria and processes are clear, and information about this can be found on the web, leaders cannot do whatever they want because the employees are better informed.

Cost Effectiveness

In terms of cost effectiveness, it is difficult to determine whether the PSS has helped in reducing costs. However, one interesting detail is that, ten years ago, Dow employees used less paper than they do now. So, probably the PSS did not help to reduce paper usage.

The e-learning component Learn@dow has saved money. It reduced costs in terms of space, time and human resources. The number of courses that can be offered through the HR intranet is also far more than the number that could be offered class room-based.

Further, there remain people at Dow who believe that 30-50% of employees will never access the People Success System. They would not know what it is, where to find information, and why they should access it. Potentially it is still difficult for half the employees to use the system in accordance with its initial idea, for example, to search out and manage their own personal development.

REFERENCES

Beer, M., Spector, B., Lawrence, P., Mills, Q., & Walton, R. (1984). *Managing Human Assets.* New York: The Free Press.

Bell,B. S., Sae-Won Lee, & Yeung, S. K. (2006). The impact of e-HR on professional competence in HRM: implications for the development of HR professionals. *Human Resource Management,* (Fall), 295-308.

Bondarouk, T. V., & Ruël, H. J. M. (2006). E-HRM effectiveness at a Dutch Ministry: Results from discursive analysis. In: *Proceedings of the 1st European Academic Workshop on E-HRM,* Enschede (Netherlands).

Cascio, W. F., & Awad, E. M. (1981). *Human resources management: an information systems approach.* Reston (Virg.): Restion publishing company (a Prentice-Hall Company).

Chin, W., Gopal, A., & Salisbury, W. (1997). Advancing the theory of adaptive structuration: the development of a scale to measure faithfulness of appropriation. *Information Systems Research, 8,* 343-367

DeSanctis, G., & Poole, M. S. (1994). Capturing the complexity in advanced technology use: Adaptive Structuration Theory. *Organization Science, 5,* 121-145.

DeSanctis, G. (1986). Human resource information systems: a current assessment. *MIS Quarterly, 10,* 217-234.

Gardner, S. D., Lepak, D. P., & Bartol, K. M. (2003). Virtual HR: The impact of information technology on the human resource professional. *Journal of Vocational Behavior, 63*(2), 159-179.

Guiderdoni, K. (2006). Assessment of an HR Intranet through middle managers' position and users. How to manage the plurality of this group in the beginning of an e-HR conception. In: *Proceedings of the 1st European Academic Workshop on E-HRM,* Enschede (Netherlands).

Haines, V.Y., & Petit, A. (1997). Conditions for successful human resource information systems, *Human Resource Management, 36*(2), 261-275.

Kahai, S. S., Sosik, J. J., & Avolio, B. J. (1997). Effects of leadership style and problem structure on work group process and outcomes in an electronic meeting system environment. *Personnel psychology, 50,* 121-146.

Kavanagh, M. J., Gueutal, H. G., & Tannenbaum, S.I. (1990) *Human resource information systems: development and application.* Boston, Mass: PWS-Kent publishing company.

Lengnick-Hall, M., & Moritz, S. (2003).The impact of e-HR on the Human Resource Management Function. *Journal of Labor Research, 24*(3), 365-379.

Lepak, D. P., & Snell, S. A. (1998). Virtual HR: strategic human resource management in the 21st century. *Human Resource Management Review, 8*(3), 215-234.

Limburg, D., Looise, J. C., & Ruël, H. (1998). HRM and ICT in the Knowledge Company. An explorative study to the integration of strategic HRM, production organization and ICT. In *Conference Proceedings of the Sixth conference on International HRM.* Paderborn (BRD).

Majchrzak, A., Rice, R. E., Malhotra, A., King, N., & Ba, S. (2000). Technology adaptation: the case of a computer-supported inter-organizational virtual team. *MIS Quarterly, 24,* 569-600.

Martin, G., Wood, G., & Collings, D. (2006). Institutions, HR strategies and the Adoption and exploitation of e-HR. In: *Proceedings of the*

1st European Workshop on e-HRM. Enschede , Netherlands.

Orlikowski, W. & Robey, D. (1991). Information technology and the structuring of organizations. Working paper No. 220, CISR. Sloan School of Management, Massachusetts Institute of technology.

Poole, M. S., & DeSanctis, G. (1989).Use of group decision support systems as an appropriation process. In: *Proceedings of the 22nd Annual Hawaii International Conference on System Sciences* (pp. 149-157). New York: ACM

Poole, M. S., & DeSanctis, G. (1990). Understanding the use of group decision support systems: the theory of Adaptive Structuration. In J. Fulk, & C. Steinfield (Eds.), *Organizations and communication technology* (pp. 173-193). Newbury Park/London/New Delhi: Sage Publications

Poole, M. S., & DeSanctis, G. (1992). Micro-level structuration in computer-supported group decision-making. *Human communication research, 19,* 5-49.

Reddington, M., & Martin, G. (2006). Theorizing the links between e-HR and strategic HRM: a framework, case illustration and some reflections. In: *Proceedings of the 1st European Workshop on e-HRM,* Enschede (Netherlands).

Ruël, H. J. M., Bondarouk, T. V., Velde, & M. van der (2007). Does e-HRM influence HRM effectiveness? *Employee Relations, 24,* 16-25.

RuëL, H. J. M., Bondarouk, T.V., & Looise, J.C. (2004). *E-HRM:Innovation or Irritation?* Utrecht: Lemma/Purdue University Press.

Shrivastave, S., & Shaw, J.B. (2004). Liberating HR through technology. *Human Resource Management, 42,* 201-222.

Stone, D., Stone-Romero, E., & Lukaszewski, K. (2006). Factors affecting the acceptance and effectiveness of electronic human resource systems. *Human Resource Management Review, 16,* 229-244.

Strohmeier, S. (2006). Coping with contradictory consequences of e-HRM. In: *Proceedings of the 1st European Workshop on e-HRM,* Enschede (Netherlands).

Ulrich, D. (1997).*Human Resource Champions.* Boston, MA: Harvard Business School Press.

Wheeler, B., Mennecke, B. E., & Scudder, J. N. (1993). Restrictive group support systems as a source of process structure for high and low procedural order groups. *Small group research, 24,* 504-522.

Wright, P., & Dyer, L. (2000). People in the e-business: new challenges, new solutions. Working paper 00-11, Center for Advanced Human Resource Studies, Cornell University.

KEY TERMS

Appropriation: The process of incorporating the functionalities of an application into daily work life.

AST: Adaptive Structuration Theory

HRIS: Human Resource Information System.

People Success System: A IT-based system that offered Human Resource Services to employees.

Structuration Theory: Theory developed by Anothy Giddens, a British sociologist, on how to analyze the social world.

Spirit of Technology: The goals and intents of an application.

Section IV
E–Recruitment and National Culture

Chapter XI
Applicant Information and Selection Strategies in Corporate Web Site Recruiting:
The Role of National Culture

Jonas F. Puck
Vienna University of Economics and Business Administration, Austria

Dirk Holtbrügge
University of Erlangen-Nuremberg, Germany

Alexander T. Mohr
Bradford University School of Management, UK

ABSTRACT

This chapter empirically analyses the influence of the cultural context on the comprehensiveness to which companies in different countries make use of applicant information and selection strategies in corporate web site recruiting. The elements of informing and selection are discussed as critical elements of corporate Web site recruiting in the literature. Based on Hofstede's 4-Dimensions model of culture, seven hypotheses are developed and tested against data from 420 companies in 14 countries. The results indicate that cultural effects are relevant even though a management technique is provided on the World Wide Web. From a practitioner's perspective, the results of this study have implications on at least three different levels. At first, companies have to train both their HR- and IT-personnel with regard to the influences of culture. Secondly, job applicants have to be aware of the different intensities of corporate Web site recruiting across countries. Thirdly, companies developing corporate Web site recruiting software should consider the development of culture-specific applications to allow for a culture-consistent implementation.

INTRODUCTION

The use of technology in human resource management (HRM) has increased tremendously within the last few years. In particular, the World Wide Web (www) has gained importance for personnel recruiting (see, for example, Bussler and Davis 2001; Piturro 2000). Different ways of electronic recruiting have been developed, i.e. job boards, career networks, newsgroups or corporate web site recruiting (Pearce and Tuten 2001; Puck 2002). The latter is regarded as the most important method, since it allows the presentation of a company within its corporate identity, as well as an easy integration of (incoming) applicant data with the companies' IT network (Brice and Waung 2002; Finn 2000). For those reasons, the use of a firm's web site is viewed as more authentic than other ways of electronic recruiting (Gale 2001). Web site recruiting can also be expected to be relatively cheaper, as companies with high levels of traffic on their homepage can reap scale effects.

It is often argued that the strong growth of the internet may lead to a world-wide convergence of organizational practices, although the question as to how services provided over the internet (like corporate web site recruiting) are affected by contextual variables is controversially discussed. Agre (1998), for example, sees an influence of the culture on the extent to which firms use knowledge management software on the internet, while Graham (2001) and Soderberg and Holden (2002) suggest that the internet is helping to overcome cultural barriers between countries and see a convergence effect of the internet. Surprisingly, extant literature is short of studies examining this topic, especially with regard to corporate web site recruiting, even though it has become a widely used human resource management practice: 91% of all companies in the "Fortune Global 500" use corporate web site recruiting (iLogos Research 2002). Therefore, the aim of this study is to test the influence of national culture on the comprehensiveness with which firms from different countries

use corporate web site recruiting. Particularly, we will analyze whether the comprehensiveness of the use of this HRM instrument may be explained by cultural differences.

The remaining part of this paper will be organized as follows. The study starts with a short introduction into corporate web site recruiting. Afterwards, Hofstede's model of national culture is used to develop hypotheses about possible cultural influences on this HRM instrument. Then the measures, the empirical basis and the methodology of the study are explained. The corporate recruiting web sites of 420 companies from 14 countries were analyzed in order to test the hypotheses. Finally, the results of the study are discussed and implications for both management practice and further research are indicated.

CORPORATE WEB SITE RECRUITING: FOUNDATIONS OF A NEW HRM INSTRUMENT

Personnel recruiting is understood as the combination of personnel pooling and personnel selection, with the objective of obtaining (personnel pooling) and selecting (personnel selection) an adequate number of applicants with the necessary qualifications (Holtbrügge 2005, pp. 93). It is open to discussion whether the definition of recruiting should include induction and other successive activities (like mentoring), or exclude the process of selection. For the purpose of this article, all induction and introductory activities have been excluded. This, however, does not imply that these post-selection activities are less important or cannot be assisted electronically.

Four aims of ***personnel pooling*** can be distinguished: *information, acquisition, selection* and *action*. According to Puck et al. (2006), the objective of a*cquisition,* the creation of interest, is not as important in the case of corporate web site recruiting because of the selective use of the internet: a user visiting a company's homepage already has a general interest in the company and its services and/or job opportunities. The *action* function, i.e. getting qualified people to apply, is mostly seen as a structural and not a content function. Action can only be reached if the personnel homepage is easy to use (see, for example, Yu and Roh 2002 for the importance of menu design), e.g. by a direct link from the company's homepage to the webpage where job offers are located.

The aims of applicant information and (pre)-selection are discussed as the critical content related elements of CWSR. The objective of *information* is to fulfill the applicants' information needs. As compared to newspaper advertising, homepages enable companies to provide far more information to potential applicants, due to the interactive and multimedia capabilities of the internet (Murphy 1999; Terri et al. 2004). In particular, the ability to connect job advertisements with multimedia company presentations allows for meeting the individual applicant's information needs more efficiently (Capelli 2001; Nielsen 2000). At the same time, however, many users complain about problems in finding the specific information they are looking for (see, for example Charles 2000; Feldmann and Klaas 2002; Martinez 2000; Rosen et al. 2004; Zall 2000). In the case of corporate web site recruiting, a more important role is played by the *selection* function, since electronic recruiting makes it easier for an applicant to apply for a job. Numerous applications can be sent within a very short period of time. Since a large volume of (potentially unsuitable) job applicants may exceed the information-processing capabilities, companies attempt to improve and assist the self-selection of applicants (Hays 1999). Some companies try to achieve this by offering "culture-fit" tests on their homepage, which candidates can use to test whether they fit into the corporate culture. The process of selection in personnel pooling can easily be distinguished from true personnel selection, since in the process of pooling no data about the applicant is transmitted to the company.

As to the process of *personnel selection*, the conventional wisdom is that corporate web site recruiting will not take over the complete selection process, because neither the company nor the job applicant can generate sufficient valid information (Mooney 2002). Nevertheless, web-enabled pre-screening is going to play an important role in the future, and so called "online games" are already used by various companies. In these games the player, i.e. the job applicant, has to carry out a number of different tasks on-line; the company then evaluates the suitability of the candidate for a given position. Similarly, chats are used in the pre-screening process, but their use is not very common. Other pre-screening methods are either not used on the internet or their use is very uncommon, even though online assessment-centers are seen as a possible development in the future (Kotlyar and Ades 2002).

THEORY AND HYPOTHESES: THE INFLUENCE OF CULTURE ON THE INFORMATION & ACTION ELEMENTS OF CORPORATE WEB SITE RECRUITING

In order to examine the effects of cultural differences on corporate web site recruiting, the framework developed by Hofstede (1998; 2001a; 2001b) was used. He identified four dimensions along which different cultures vary: power distance, individualism-collectivism, masculinity-femininity and uncertainty avoidance[1]. The claim that differences in national culture can be represented in terms of these four dimensions has been subject to criticism, not least because Hofstede's data was confined to one company, his questions focused exclusively on work values and his research framework has been considered to be biased by Western standards (see, for example, Erez and Early 1993 for a summary). It is not the intention of this study to enter into the debate about the validity of Hofstede's model. His study continues to be the largest empirical study connecting cultural orientation with observable institutional differences between countries within a single framework. In addition, the framework has successfully been used in similar studies before (see, for example, Snape et al. 1998; Ryan et al. 1999; Newman and Nollen 1996). Thus, Hofstede's model will be applied in this study. In the following, each of the four dimensions is examined for its influence on the information and action elements of corporate web site recruiting used by HR departments.

Power distance describes the extent to which inequalities in the distribution of power are expected and accepted by the members of a culture (Hofstede 1991). Power distance influences the degree of centralization, participation, leadership style and use of status symbols. Most important for this study is the impact of power distance on the organizational decision process. Hofstede (2001a) proposes that managers in companies from countries with low power distance have a more participative and independent attitude towards work. In countries with high power distance managers are more likely to show and use their power. Since the information function of electronic recruiting allows a company to better present itself, its employees and its way of business within its corporate identity than in the print media, companies from cultures with a high degree of power distance can be expected to use this function of corporate web site recruiting more comprehensively than companies from cultures with a lower degree of power distance. On the other hand, the application of web-based selection and pre-selection methods delegates some power of decision to the computer and reduces the responsibilities of the managers. Thus, it seems plausible that selection and pre-selection methods are more intensely applied in companies from cultures with a lower degree of power distance. Thus, the following hypotheses are proposed:

Hypothesis 1a: *The higher the index of power distance in a culture, the less comprehensive is the use of pre-selection and selection methods in that culture. (cp.)*

Hypothesis 1b: *The higher the index of power distance in a culture, the more comprehensive is the use of the information function of corporate web site recruiting in that culture. (cp.)*

Individualism-collectivism describes the degree to which individuals identify with groups and are integrated into the community. In individualistic societies ties between individuals are loose. In collective societies, people are born into and remain, with great loyalty, in strong and cohesive groups throughout their lives (Hofstede 1991; Early 1994). In companies, individualism is manifested in high levels of autonomy of employees, an employee-employer-relationship that is predominantly based on the employment-contract, and in work conditions that provide employees with sufficient personal time. Collectivism (or low individualism), on the other hand, is manifested in work unit solidarity, group responsibility for results, moralistic/family-like relationships with employers, and the priority of relationships over tasks. Furthermore, collective societies are characterized by putting the group interest above the interest of the individual (Hofstede 2001a). The internet, not only when used for recruiting purposes, is often described as anonymous (see, for example, Allen 1999). It might be argued that companies from collectivist societies are reluctant to pre-select and select job-applicants from the internet. The fact that individuals find their way into the group through the anonymous internet contradicts the central ideas of a group, and might even be viewed as a threat to it. On the other hand, more collectivist cultures rate the group higher than the individual and may thus be more interested in presenting a clear view of the organization to possible applicants since this may lead to an increased number of applicants that feel familiar with the company's culture.

Thus, the following hypotheses are formulated:

Hypothesis 2a: *The higher the degree of individualism in a culture, the more comprehensive is the use of selection and pre-selection methods in corporate web site recruiting by companies in that culture. (cp.)*

Hypothesis 2b: *The higher the degree of individualism in a culture, the less comprehensive is the use of the information function in corporate web site recruiting by companies in that culture. (cp.)*

Masculinity and femininity describe the extent to which a society emphasizes assertive and competitive, as opposed to nurturing, values. In feminine societies managers strive for consensus; equality, solidarity and quality of life are emphasized, and conflicts are solved by negotiation and compromise. In masculine societies managers are expected to be assertive and decisive, emphasis is laid on performance and competition among colleagues (Hofstede 1991; 2001a). Since only hard facts count within the selection process of corporate web site recruiting it seems to be linked with the attribute of decisiveness that Hofstede (1998) used to describe masculine societies, since selection criteria are definite and identical for all applicants. Thus, the following hypothesis is proposed:

Hypothesis 3: *The higher the degree of masculinity in a culture, the more comprehensive is the use of pre-selection and selection methods in corporate web site recruiting by companies in that culture. (cp.)*

Uncertainty avoidance is defined as the extent to which the members of a culture feel threatened by uncertain or unknown and ambiguous situations. This feeling of threat results in a greater need of individuals for predictability and for (written or unwritten) rules. In companies, uncertainty avoidance manifests itself in an increased clarity of reporting relationships, procedures and systems in order to reduce employees' feelings of anxiety stemming from unknown situations. Emphasis is placed on punctuality and precision. Individuals from societies with a low degree of uncertainty avoidance are more tolerant towards other cultures and opinions, and try to keep the number of rules to a minimum: "People in such societies will tend to accept every day as it comes. They will take risks rather easily. They will not work hard. They will be relatively tolerant of behavior and opinions different from their own because they do not feel threatened by them" (Hofstede 1983, p. 81). The efficiency of corporate web site recruiting as a new form of personnel pooling and selection has rarely been empirically tested. Therefore, its use is combined with a high insecurity about the risks and benefits of this method. As a consequence, companies from cultures with high uncertainty avoidance will not be pioneers in the application of corporate web site recruiting. Thus, analogous to the results of Ryan et al. (1999), the following impact of uncertainty avoidance on the use of corporate web site recruiting is expected:

Hypothesis 4a: *The lower the degree of uncertainty avoidance in a culture, the more comprehensive is the use of pre-selection and selection methods of corporate web site recruiting by companies in that culture. (cp.)*

Hypothesis 4b: *The lower the degree of uncertainty avoidance in a culture, the more comprehensive is the use of information methods of corporate web site recruiting by companies in that culture. (cp.)*

CONTROL VARIABLES

A series of control variables were included as they were expected to be crucial factors when analyzing variances in the use of corporate web site recruiting across countries: internet access, unemployment rate and market capitalization.

Internet access. The extent to which people of a country have access to the internet obviously puts a ceiling on the comprehensiveness of use of the internet by companies for recruiting purposes in the respective country. Companies take into account the number of potential users when setting it up. If the number of potential users is expected to be low, companies will be reluctant to set up comprehensive web sites. For example, there is a higher user rate of the internet in the United States than in Europe, and corporate web site recruiting is therefore more comprehensively adopted in the US (iLogos Research 2002).

The ***unemployment rate*** was included as a second control variable. The more people are unemployed, the bigger the pool from which applicants can be selected. This reduces the necessity to put a high effort on the pooling function, both in print media and on the internet. Therefore, it can be expected that the unemployment rate of a country is negatively related to use of web recruiting by firms in that country.

Finally, it can be assumed that the comprehensiveness of corporate web site recruiting is also influenced by the size of a firm. Larger firms have greater financial and personnel resources and might therefore be more likely to use web recruiting activities. For the purpose of this study, we decided to use the ***market capitalization*** as a measure of firm size as this data was easily available and accessible.

Beyond these three control variables others (such as HRM strategy or employee image) may be expected to influence the use of corporate web site recruiting. For these variables, however, no secondary data are available. Since this study is based on an online research design (see below) we restricted the set of control variables to those explained above where data are easily accessible.

METHODOLOGY

This section of the paper describes the methodology of the empirical study. It starts with an overview of the sample followed by the methodology, the development of the measures and the control variables included in the survey. An overview of the methodology and the predicted influences can be found in Figure 1.

Figure 1. Cultural and control variables and proposed influences

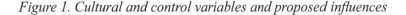

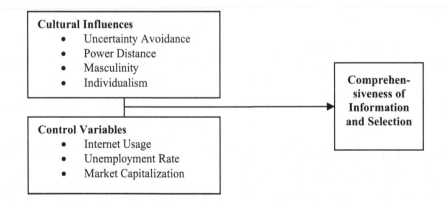

Sample

The sample consists of the 30 largest publicly listed companies—measured by their market capitalization—in each of the following 14 countries: Canada, Czech Republic, Finland, Germany, Hong Kong, Hungary, Italy, Norway, Peoples Republic of China, Poland, Sweden, Taiwan, United Kingdom and the United States of America. Thus, in total the sample comprises 420 companies from 14 different countries and three continents. These countries were selected because they show significant differences along Hofstede's cultural dimensions, and therefore allow for a detailed study of cultural influences (contrast approach). The second criteria for the selection of these countries were the language skills of the authors. Since detailed analyses of corporate web sites were necessary, only those countries could be included where the corporate languages of companies are understood by the authors. Data were collected in autumn 2002.

Research Design and Measures

First of all, the market capitalization (MARK-CAP) and the home country of each company were noted. Then the company's home-country homepage was visited. If a link to a personnel homepage was found, we followed this link. In the case that more than one personnel homepage existed, the page of the company's head office was chosen.

We applied the scales presented by Puck et al. (2006) to measure the functions of corporate web site recruiting: By visiting the personnel homepage the *quality and quantity of information* in personnel pooling was measured with five dichotomous items. Are there any specific job offers (INFORM01)? Is there a newsletter about jobs available (INFORM02)? Are the multimedia possibilities of the internet used (INFORM03)? Is information about career opportunities available (INFORM04)? Has a Chat been installed

giving the visitor the possibility to "talk" with HRM managers of the company (INFORM05)? All items were then aggregated into one variable (INFORMCOMP). The internal reliability, as tested with the Kuder-Richardson Formula 20 (KR20 = .871), presented strong support for our scaling.

The *selection function* was measured with two items: PRESELECT, with "0" indicating "No Self Selection Tests", "1" indicating "One Self Selection Test Available", "2" indicating "Two Self Selection Tests Available", and so on. The same approach was applied to measure the amount of selection methods available SELECT. After that, both items were combined into one variable, representing the combined comprehensiveness of personnel selection and pre-selection (SELECTCOMP).

RESULTS

Descriptive Statistics

As mentioned above, the data of 420 companies from 14 countries was collected and evaluated. The data gathered was analyzed using the SPSS 11.5 and STATA 8 statistical packages. The following Table 1 reveals the values of the four dimensions as suggested by Hofstede's model, as well as the internet user rate and the standardized unemployment rate for those countries. Furthermore, the table shows the means and standard deviations for the dependent variables (INFCOMP; SELECTCOMP) for each country included in our survey.

The descriptive statistics regarding the comprehensiveness of web site recruiting in Table 1 show that the use of corporate web site recruiting varies markedly between the countries included in this study. Additionally, it can be seen that only a very limited number of companies used selection and/or pre-selection methods. This may be explainable by the fact that online selection tools

Table 1. Data overview (Sources: Hofstede, 2001; OECD, 2002; CIA, 2002)

	PD	IND	MAS	UA	UNEMRATE	NETUSE	INFCOMP	SELCOMP
							Mean (SD)	Mean (SD)
Canada	39	80	52	48	7.2%	9.1%	1.30 (1.06)	.00 (.00)
Czech Rep.	35	60	45	60	8.2%	8.76%	.50 (.75)	.00 (.00)
Finland	33	63	26	59	9.1%	43.86%	1.04 (.74)	.00 (.00)
Germany	35	67	66	65	7.7%	21.68%	2.03 (.96)	.07 (.25)
Hong Kong	68	25	57	29	7.3%	40.53%	1.63 (1.52)	.00 (.00)
Hungary	45	55	79	83	5.8%	6.43%	.21 (.69)	.00 (.00)
Italy	50	76	70	75	9.4%	20.11%	.60 (.86)	.00 (.00)
Norway	31	69	8	50	3.6%	52.40%	.61 (.79)	.00 (.00)
Poland	55	60	65	78	18.2%	7.25%	.21 (.42)	.00 (.00)
PR China	80	20	66	30	4.0%	5.27%	1.43 (.87)	.00 (.00)
Sweden	31	71	5	29	5.1%	50.70%	1.04 (.99)	.00 (.00)
Taiwan	58	17	45	69	5.2%	38.50%	1.89 (.696	.00 (.00)
UK	35	89	66	35	5.0%	32.63%	1.10 (.89)	.10 (.31)
USA	40	91	62	46	4.8%	53.23%	2.13 (.86)	.00 (.00)
Mean(SD)[1]	47.40	62.55	52.95	55.78	7.18%	30.67%	1.19 (1.09)	.01 (.11)

were still in the development phase by the time of data collection.

Regression Analysis

Since the hypothesized relations in our model are highly interrelated a high level of heteroskedasticity and contemporaneous correlation of the variables can be expected. Therefore, a simple linear regression is not suitable to further analyze the proposed dependencies. Instead of this we applied a parametric seemingly unrelated regression (SUREG) using multivariate regressions for each of the two dependent variables. The SUREG method estimates the parameters of a model, accounting for heteroskedasticity and contemporaneous correlation in the errors across equations (Zellner, 1962; Timm, 2002) and is frequently applied in social sciences to estimate regressions in models with two or more dependent variables (e.g., Globerman and Shapiro, 1999; Agarwal et al., 2004). To check for multicol-

linearity, Table 2 provides the means, standard deviations and bivariate Pearson correlations for the variables used. Although there are significant inter-variable correlations among the independent variables, none of the coefficients exceeds .40. Due to these low levels of inter-variable correlation multicollinearity does not appear to be a serious problem.

We computed three distinct models for each dependent variable to allow for an interpretation of differences in explanatory power of cultural and control variables: the first model included only the control variables, the second only the cultural variables, and a third model combined the cultural factors and control variables to explain variances in the dependent variables.

Testing of Hypotheses

First, we computed two equations using only the control variables as independents. While equation 4 (DV: comprehensiveness of information) was

Table 2. Means, standard deviation and correlations

	Mean	SD	1	2	3	4	5	6	7	8
1. SELCOMP	.01	.11	1							
2. INFCOMP	1.19	1.09	.04	1						
3. PD	47.40	14.96	-.094	.120*	1					
4. IND	62.55	23.52	.085	-.347**	-.342**	1				
5. MAS	52.95	22.51	.066	-.015	.312**	.072	1			
6. UA	55.78	20.42	-.049	.133**	.133	.076	.375**	1		
7. NETUSE	29.83	17.54	-.010	.263**	-.284**	.195*	.233*	.248*	1	
8. UNEMRATE	7.17	3.54	-.035	-.255**	.225*	.213*	-.213**	-.243*	-.209**	1
9. MARKCAP	26.45	51.82	.143*	-.180**	-.147	.175**	.236*	-.234*	-.218**	.204**

* Level of significance ≤ .05; ** Level of Significance ≤ .01 in two tailed Tests (Pearson's correlations), n=440

significant and delivered significant statistics for the unemployment rate and the internet userrate (R-square: .0555), equation 1 (DV: comprehensiveness of selection and preselection) was not significant and contained no significant variables except for the constant. Looking at the following equations with comprehensiveness of selection and preselection as dependent variable, the results are the same: neither the equation nor the variables are significant on a satisfying level. Thus, Hypotheses 1a, 2a, 3a and 4a cannot be supported by our data.

In a **second model** we included only the cultural variables, which led to an increased R^2 of 9.05%.

Finally, we combined both cultural and control variables in equations 3, which caused an increase of R^2 to 24.42% (Table 3). In general, the differences in explanatory power between the models suggest that cultural factors – when compared to the control variables in our study – have a higher influence on the comprehensiveness to which firms make use of their web site for recruiting purposes. Overall, the results suggest that cultural factors significantly influence the use of corporate web site recruiting across national boarders.

Precisely, it was predicted in **hypothesis 1b** that the level of power distance (PD) will positively influence the comprehensiveness of information in corporate web site recruiting. As proposes, correlation analysis delivers a positive correlation coefficient of r=.120* on a good level of significance (p≤.05). This positive correlation between PD and WRCOMP is also supported by the results of the equations 5 and 6 (see Table 3). As a consequence, hypothesis 1b is supported by our data.

Hypothesis 2b suggested a negative influence of the degree of individualism (IND) on the comprehensiveness of information in corporate web site recruiting. The correlation results in Table 2 lend support for hypothesis 2 (r= -.347; p ≤.01). The regression analyses (euqations 5 and 6) show a similar result: the coefficient for individualism is negatively and significantly associated with the comprehensiveness of information in web recruiting, again supporting hypothesis 2b.

Hypothesis 4b proposed that the comprehensiveness of information in corporate web site recruiting is negatively associated with the degree of uncertainty avoidance (UA) in a society. This hypothesis is supported. With r=-.251 (p ≤.01) in the correlation analysis and similar results in the regression models our study shows that the level of uncertainty avoidance has a negative influence on the comprehensiveness of corporate web site recruiting.

Table 3. SUREG results

Related Hypothesis	Variable	Estimated Coefficient	Standard Error	t-statistic
Equation 1; Dependent variable (DV):Comprehensiveness of Selection and Preselection; R^2 =.0015; χ^2 = .38				
CONTROL	Unemployment Rate	-.001	.0004	-.37
CONTROL	Internet Userrate	-.001	.0001	-.48
CONTROL	Company Size	-.000	.0000	.27
	Constant	.0154	.0073	2.11*
Equation 2; DV: Comprehensiveness of Selection and Preselection; R^2 = .0034; χ^2 = 1.03				
H1a	Power Distance	-.0001	.0002	-.54
H2a	Individualism	-.0001	.0001	-.58
H3	Masculinity	.0001	.0001	1.01
H4a	Uncertainty Avoidance	-.0001	.0001	-.44
	Constant	.0184	.0159	1.15
Equation 3; DV: Comprehensiveness of Selection and Preselection; R^2 = .0068; χ^2 = 1.99				
H1a	Power Distance	-.0001	.0002	-.96
H2a	Individualism	-.0001	.0001	-.74
H3	Masculinity	.0001	.0001	.66
H4a	Uncertainty Avoidance	-.0001	.0001	-.83
CONTROL	Unemployment Rate	.0001	.0004	.35
CONTROL	Internet Userrate	-.0001	.0001	-.95
CONTROL	Company Size	.0000	.0000	.58
	Constant	.0298	.0179	1.66†
Equation 4; DV: Comprehensiveness of Information; R^2 = .0555; χ^2 = 14.10**				
CONTROL	Unemployment Rate	.-.0292	.0108	-2.27**
CONTROL	Internet Userrate	.0062	.0025	2.51**
CONTROL	Company Size	.0001	.0001	.129
	Constant	3.9420	.1244	10.76***
Equation 5; DV: Comprehensiveness of Information; R^2 = .0905; χ^2 = 24.34***				
H1b	Power Distance	.0107	.0037	2.88**
H2b	Individualism	-.0076	.0021	-3.59***
H4b	Uncertainty Avoidance	-.0059	.0018	-3.20**
	Constant	2.6048	.3177	8.20***
Equation 6; DV: Comprehensiveness of Information; R^2 = .2442; χ^2 = 105.23***				
H1b	Power Distance	.0159	.0049	3.21**
H2b	Individualism	-.0173	.0027	-6.46***
H4b	Uncertainty Avoidance	-.0051	.0021	-2.14*
CONTROL	Unemployment Rate	-.0119	.0094	-2.16*
CONTROL	Internet Userrate	.0127	.0116	4.25***
CONTROL	Company Size	.0001	.0000	1.05
	Constant	2.4714	.4231	5.84***

*Breusch-Pagan Test of Independence: $\chi^2(15) = 1974.231$****

N = 420; †<.1 *p<.05 **p<.01 ***p<.001;

The control variables were significantly related to the comprehensiveness of information of corporate web site recruiting in both correlation analysis and regression. We suggested a positive influence of the *spread of the internet in a country* on the comprehensiveness of information. The regressor for this control variable is positive on a .001-level, thus confirming the crucial role of internet access outlined above. As a second control variable, we expected the *unemployment rate* to have a negative influence on the comprehensiveness of information provided by firms in that country. As expected, the coefficient is significantly negative, supporting our arguments. The regressor for the *market capitalization* of the sample firms was expected to be positive, as larger firms were argued to be more likely to have the financial and personal resources necessary for the use of web recruiting. As shown in Table 3, in line with our argumentation the coefficient is positive but surprisingly does not enter in the regression significantly.

DISCUSSION

As a first result, all hypotheses regarding the (pre-)selection function cannot be supported by our data. As can be seen from the descriptive statistics, this surprising result probably results from the very small number of companies that actually applied recruiting techniques in their corporate web site recruiting approach by the time we collected the data. Thus, future studies may repeat this approach.

On the other side, the findings support our argumentation that variations in the comprehensiveness of information in corporate web site recruiting can partly be explained by cultural differences. In particular, the influence of *power distance* was in line with our expectations, i.e. this variable is significantly negatively related to the comprehensiveness of information in corporate web site recruiting. Furthermore, the results show

that the level of *individualism* significantly negatively affects the comprehensiveness of information in corporate web site recruiting. Firms from cultures with a high level of collectivism tend to provide more information than firms from more individualist societies. Furthermore, as proposed, companies from cultures with a high level of *uncertainty avoidance* make a less intensive use of corporate web site recruiting. This is in line with the findings of Ryan et al. (1999) on traditional recruitment who revealed that companies from cultures with high uncertainty avoidance might not be the pioneers in the application of new recruiting methods. They quoted that if the effectiveness of a new method is not securely proven "it might be that uncertainty about the usefulness of methods themselves is what is the cause for concern" (Ryan et al. 1999, p. 383).

In conclusion, the results of this study show that the use of the internet for management purposes, i.e. the comprehensiveness of information in corporate web site recruiting, is affected by cultural factors. This is especially interesting, since many software products for web related management techniques such as knowledge management or corporate website recruiting are highly standardized. Moreover it is often argued that the growth in worldwide communication leads to a convergence of management practices around the world (Levitt 1983). Thus, contrary to the convergence hypothesis that "the common requirements of management – or a common logic of industrialism – disregards the importance of cultural factors" (McGaughey and De Cieri 1999, p. 236) the results of our study lend support to the divergence hypothesis that firms maintain their culturally based dissimilarities irrespectively of emerging major trends.

IMPLICATIONS AND LIMITATIONS

This study significantly contributes to our state of knowledge concerning the relationship between national culture and the use of web-related management techniques such as corporate web site recruiting. In particular, it shows that the four dimensions of culture proposed by Hofstede are to some extent able to predict the comprehensiveness to which electronic recruiting is used in different countries of the world. Among these four dimensions, individualism has the strongest influence which is in accordance with other studies in the field of intercultural management (e.g., Triandis 1995; Bhagat et al. 2002). Obviously, companies from collectivist countries are reluctant to implement web-based management-techniques since the anonymity of the internet contradicts their basic values of solidarity, group responsibility and personal relationships.

From a practitioner's perspective, the results of this study have implications on at least three different levels. At first, companies have to train both their HR- and IT-personnel with regard to the influences of culture. Since the findings of this study support the existence of cultural barriers to the implementation of corporate web site recruiting, both HR- and IT-personnel have to be aware of these barriers and have to develop strategies to deal with them. One way to achieve this cultural awareness might be the employment of intercultural training (see, for example, Landis et al. 2004).

Secondly, job applicants have to be aware of the different intensities of corporate web site recruiting across countries. Since, for example, companies from collectivist countries make less use of this management technique, applicants have to align their application strategies to this cultural context. This finding is particularly relevant for individuals who apply for jobs in more than one country or even worldwide (e.g., academics, flight attendants, musicians).

Thirdly, companies developing corporate web site recruiting software should consider the development of culture-specific applications to allow for a culture-consistent implementation. This argument is in line with other studies (e.g.,

Schuler et al. 1993) which argue that the adaptation of human resource practices to the cultural context may lead to achieving strategic advantage. If this is also true for corporate web site recruiting it has to be tested in future studies which include measures of its efficiency.

Considering the results of this study, some limitations should be taken into account. Firstly, the study is based on a relatively small sample (n=420) and limited to the 30 largest firms in each country. Secondly, the caveats associated with Hofstede's model (as mentioned above) have to be borne in mind, and future research might use different conceptualizations of (national) culture (e.g., House et al. 2004). Finally, the canon of control variables (internet user rate, rate of unemployment and market capitalization) could be extended to better explain variances in the comprehensiveness of corporate web site recruiting across nations. For example, future studies might include the influence of industry, employee image, HRM strategy or corporate culture. Since no secondary data on these variables are available, questionnaires or other methods of primary data collection have to be used. That would, however, reduce the response rate significantly.

According to Hofstede (2001a), cultures are inert and not susceptible to short-term changes. The internet, on the other hand, develops and changes very rapidly. Therefore, it would be interesting to replicate our study in some years when corporate web site recruiting will be a far more elaborate management technique and to find out whether the findings will differ significantly or not.

REFERENCE

Agarwal, R., Echambadi, R., Franco, A. M., & Sarkar, M. B. (2004). Knowledge Transfer through Inheritage: Spinout Generation, Development, and Survival. *Academy of Management Journal*, *47*, 501-522.

Agre, P. (1998). Building an Internet Culture. *Telematics and Informatics*, *15*, 231-234.

Allen, C. (1999). Internet Anonymity in Contexts. *Information Society*, *15*, 145-147.

Bhagat, R. S., Kedia, B. L., Harveston, P. D., & Triandis, H. C. (2002). Cultural Variations in the Cross-Border Transfer of Organizational Knowledge: An Integrative Framework. *Academy of Management Review*, *27*, 204-221.

Brice, T. S., & Waung, M. (2002). Web Site Recruitment Characteristics: America's Best Versus America's Biggest. *Advanced Management Journal*, *67*, 4-8.

Bussler, L., & Davis, E. (2001). Information Systems: The Quiet Revolution. *Human Resource Management Journal of Computer Information Systems*, *42*, 17-20.

Capelli, P. (2001). Making the Most of On-Line Recruiting. *Harvard Business Review*, *79*, 139-146.

Charles, J. (2000). Finding a Job on the Web. *Black Enterprise*, *30*, 90-95.

CIA (2002). *The World Factbook 2001*. Retrieved from http://www.odci.gov/cia/publications/factbook, on 15.07.2002.

Early, C. P. (1994). Self or Group? Cultural Effects of Training on Self-Efficacy and Performance. *Administrative Science Quarterly*, *39*, 89-117.

Erez, M., & Early, C. P. (1993). *Culture, Self-Identity and Work*. Oxford University Press, New York et al.

Feldmann, D. C., & Klaas, B. (2002). Internet Job Hunting: A Field Study of Applicant Experiences with On-Line Recruiting. *Human Resource Management*, *41*, 175-192.

Finn, W. (2000). Screen Test. *People Management*, *6*, 38-43.

Gale, S. F. (2001). Internet Recruiting: Better, Cheaper, Faster. *Workforce*, *80*, 74-77.

Globerman, S., & Shapiro, D. M. (1999). The Impact of Government Policies on Foreign Direct Investment: The Canadian Experience. *Journal of International Business Studies*, *30*, 513-532.

Graham, J. L. (2001). Culture and Human Resource Management. In A. M. Rugman, & T. L. Brewer (Eds.), *The Oxford Handbook of International Business*. Oxford University Press, New York et al., 503-537.

Hays, S. (1999). Hiring on the Web. *Workforce*, *77*, 76-84.

Hetrick, S. (2002). Transferring HR Ideas and Practices: Globalization and Convergence in Poland. *Human Resource Development International*, *5*, 333-351.

Hofstede, G. (1983). The Cultural Relativity of Organizational Practices and Theories. *Journal of International Business Studies*, *14*, 75-89.

Hofstede, G. (1991). *Cultures and Organizations: Software of the Mind*. McGraw-Hill, London.

Hofstede, G. (1998). Think Locally, Act Globally: Cultural Constraints in Personnel Management. *Management International Review*, *38*(2), 7-26.

Hofstede, G. (2001a). *Culture's Consequences. International Differences in Work Related Values*, second ed. Sage, London/Beverly Hills.

Hofstede, G. (2001b). Culture's Recent Consequences: Using Dimension Scores in Theory and Research. *International Journal of Cross Cultural Management*, *1*, 11-30.

Holtbrügge, D. (2005). *Personalmanagement*, (2nd Ed.). Springer, Berlin et al.

House, R. J., Hanges, P. J., Javidan, M., Dorfman, P. W., & Gupta, V. (Eds.) (2004). *Culture, Leadership, and Organizations. The GLOBE Study of 62 Societies*. Sage, Thousand Oaks et al.

iLogos Research (2002). *Global 500 Web Site Recruiting: 2002*. Survey, San Francisco.

Kotlyar, I., & Ades, K. (2002). Don't Overlook Recruiting Tools. *HR Magazine, 47*, 97-102.

Landis, D., Bennett, J. M., & Bennett, M. J. (Eds.) (2004). *Handbook of Intercultural Training*, (3rd Ed.). Thousand Oaks, CA: Sage.

Levitt, T. (1983). The Globalization of Markets. *Harvard Business Review, 61*(3), 92-102.

Martinez, M. N. (2000). Get Job Seekers to Come to You. *HR Magazine, 45*, 44-52.

McGaughey, S., & De Cieri, H. (1999). Reassessment of Convergence and Divergence Dynamics: Implications for International HRM. *International Journal of Human Resource Management, 10*, 235-250.

Mooney, J. (2002). Pre-Employment Testing on the Internet: Put Candidates a Click Away and Hire at Modem Speed. *Public Personnel Management, 31*, 41-52.

Murphy, H. L. (1999). Top Job Sites. *Marketing News, 33*, 13-17.

Newman, K. L., & Nollen, S. D. (1996). Culture and Congruence: The Fit between Management Practices and National Culture. *Journal of International Business Studies, 27*, 753-778.

Nielsen, J. (2000). *Designing Web Usability*. New Riders Publishing, Indianapolis.

OECD (2002). *Standardised Unemployment Rates*. Retrieved from http://www.oecd.org/pdf/M00030000/M00030784.pdf, on 15.07.2002.

Pearce, C. G. & Tuten, T. L. (2001). Internet Recruiting in the Banking Industry. *Business Communication Quarterly, 64*, 9-18.

Piturro, M. (2000). The Power of E-Cruiting. *Management Review, 89,* 33-37.

Puck, J. F. (2002). *Personalrekrutierung über die Personalhomepage*. Ibidem, Stuttgart.

Puck, J. F., Mohr, A. T., & Holtbrügge, D. (2006). Cultural Convergence through Web-Based Management Techniques? The Case of Corporate Web Site Recruiting. *Journal of International Management, 12*, 181-195.

Rosen, D. E., Purinton, E., & Lloyd, S. J. (2004). Web Site Design: Building a Cognitive Framework. *Journal of Electronic Commerce in Organizations, 2*, 15-29.

Ryan, A.M., McFarland, L., Baron, H., & Page, R. (1999). An International Look at Selection Practices: Nation and Culture as Explanations for Variability in Practice. *Personnel Psychology, 52*, 359-391.

Schuler, R. S., Dowling, P. J., & Cieri, H. D. (1993). An Integrative Framework of Strategic International Human Resource Management. *Journal of Management, 19,* 419-459.

Snape, E., Thompson, D., Yan, F. K., & Redman, T. (1998). Performace Appraisal and Culture: Practice and Attitudes in Hong Kong and Great Britain. *International Journal of Human Resource Management, 9*, 841-861.

Soderberg, A.-M. & Holden, N. (2002). Rethinking Cross Cultural Management in a Globalizing Business World. *International Journal of Cross Cultural Management, 2*, 103-121.

Terri, A. C., Goes, P. B. & Gupta, A. (2004). GIST: A Model for Design and Management of Content and Interactivity of Customer-Centric Web Sites. *MIS Quarterly, 28*, 161-182.

Timm, N.H. (2002). *Applied Multivariate Analysis*. New York et al., Springer.

Triandis, H.C. (1995). *Individualism and Collectivism*. Boulder, Westview.

Yu, B.-M., & Roh, S.-Z. (2002). The Effects of Menu Design on Information-Seeking Performance and User's Attitude on the World Wide Web. *Journal of the American Society for Information Science, 53*, 923-933.

Zall, M. (2000). Using the Internet to find your next job. *Strategic Finance, 81*, 74-78.

Zellner, A. (1962). An Efficient Method of Estimating Seemingly Unrelated Regressions and Tests of Aggregation Bias. *Journal of the American Statistic Association, 57*, 348-368

KEY TERMS

Applicant Selection Strategies: Applicant selection strategies combine strategies with regard to the selection and pre-selection of applicants.

Applicant Information Strategies: Applicant information strategies combine strategies with regard to pre-selection information of applicants.

Corporate Web Site: The Corporate Web Site is the Web-Site of a Firm on the World Wide Web.

Electronic Recruiting: Electronic Recruiting can be defined as personnel recruitment using the World Wide Web.

Hofstede's Framework of Culture: Hofstede identified four dimensions along which different national cultures vary: power distance, individualism-collectivism, masculinity-femininity and uncertainty avoidance.

National Culture: National Culture is the combination of symbols, beliefs and artefacts typical for members of one nation.

Seemingly Unrelated Regression Analysis: The Seemingly Unrelated Regression Analysis (SUREG) method estimates the parameters of a model, accounting for heteroskedasticity and contemporaneous correlation in the errors across equations and is frequently applied in social sciences to estimate regressions in models with two or more dependent variables.

ENDNOTE

[1] Hofstede presented a fifth dimension after collecting additional data in Asia: Long term orientation. Anyhow, since scores for this dimension weren't evaluated for all cultures within our sample, this dimension was not used in our study.

Chapter XII
What is the Potential of E–Recruitment to Transform the Recruitment Process and the Role of the Resourcing Team?

Emma Parry
Cranfield School of Management, UK

Shaun Tyson
Cranfield School of Management, UK

ABSTRACT

HR practitioners are often expected to be both efficient administrators of the employment relationship and to act as a strategic partner to the business. Some authors have suggested that the use of e-HRM may be one way of achieving these dual aims as technology can both improve the efficiency of HR processes and help the HR function to become more strategic by freeing up time from the burden of administration and by providing reliable information on which to make strategic decisions. The authors investigated the potential of technology to transform the HR function into one that is both efficient and strategic by focusing on a single process area, recruitment. Through the use of three detailed case studies we showed that the use of e-recruitment can potentially have an impact on both the strategic role and efficiency of the resourcing team.

INTRODUCTION

HR practitioners have long been under pressure to transform the HR function into one that is both efficient and can contribute to an organisa- tion strategically. More recently, there has been the suggestion that e-HRM could be a means to achieve these dual objectives. A number of authors, particularly in the US, have examined the proposition that e-HRM can facilitate the move to an HR function that is both efficient and strategic through broad examinations of the impact of technology on HRM. However this is more difficult to do in the UK where the use of e-HRM across the whole spectrum of HRM is still relatively new and its full impact may not have been realised. This chapter will address this issue by taking a more detailed look at the use of e-HRM in a process area which is more mature in the UK, that of recruitment. We will examine how our three case study organisations have used technology to transform the recruitment process and to help the resourcing teams achieve the dual aims of being efficient and operating at a strategic level.

The transformation of the HR function to one that is more strategic has long been a subject of the academic literature with authors such as Legge (1978) noting that the HR function should be more involved in senior management decision-making. Paauwe (2004) summarised this literature by saying HR needed to become "more business oriented, more strategic and more oriented towards organisational change" (p183). Academics such as Guest and Peccei (1994) and Boxall and Purcell (2003) have set out the theoretical and empirical background to the claims that HR roles have strategic impact. HR practitioners have therefore become more concerned to add strategic value within an organisation and to become a 'business partner' to line managers (Ulrich, 1997).

Whilst this shift in focus to one of a "strategic business partner" has received much attention in the literature, there remains a need for HR to be efficient, and indeed, the desire to be more strategic may be accompanied with moves to reduce overhead costs. Ulrich, in his popular 1997 framework, suggested that HR professionals must learn to master both strategic (long term) and operational (short term) processes and be good business partners through the deliverables that include both strategy execution and administrative efficiency. According to this view, HR practitioners must therefore find ways in which

they can both promote efficiency and facilitate a shift to a more strategic HR role.

There is an extensive literature on the strategic aspects of HRM, and on the challenges HR managers face in achieving such a role (Tyson, 1995; Purcell, 1999; Paauwe, 2004). These include the difficulties that HR managers experience in changing the expectations of line managers who have become content with the HR function as a largely administrative and transactional activity. HR staff may have little business experience and have often not been exposed to risk bearing action.

There are also questions about what HR strategy is, and whether there should be an HR strategy separate from an organisational strategy. Many of these issues are centred around the extent to which HR management can demonstrate its contribution to business performance. Studies, for example by Huselid (1995), and by researchers examining the impact of particular initiatives such as high performance work systems (Osterman, 1994; Youndt *et al*, 1996), learning organisations (Senge, 1990), the employee-customer value chain (Rucci *et al*, 1998; Murphy and Zandvakili, 2000), encouraged HR specialists in the view that there are strategic directions to be initiated and sustained which demonstrate the value of the alignment of an HR strategy with business goals. This has been further reinforced by the resource-based view, which has shifted the perspective of HRM towards playing a major role in the management and development of human capital to achieve competitive advantage. In order to become more strategic therefore HR managers need to take a different perspective in order to free themselves from administrative and often fire fighting roles so that they become more data driven and can show the business results from their interventions.

It has been suggested that the use of technology within HRM may both improve efficiency and facilitate the shift to a more strategic role for the HR function. Ruël, Bondarouk and Looise (2004) defined e-HRM as "a way of implementing HR strategies, policies and practices in organisations through a conscious and directed support of and/or with the full use of web-technology-based channels" (p.365). Snell, Stueber and Lepak (2002) observed that HR could meet the challenge of becoming more strategic as well as more customer focused and cost efficient by using information technology. Bussler and Davis (2002) concluded that "with the use of technological solutions, HR is no longer transactional and reactionary but strategic and proactive" (p17).

In discussing the impact of e-HRM on efficiency, Enshur, Nielson and Grant-Vallone, (2002) concluded that the shift from traditional HR to e-HR can lead to "substantial reductions in cost and time for many HR activities" (p. 238). Snell, Stuber and Lepak (2002) also noted that IT may potentially enable HR to lower administrative costs, increase productivity and reduce response times. Likewise, Lengnick-Hall and Moritz (2003) suggested that e-HR not only reduces process and administrative costs but can speed up transaction processing, reduce information errors and improve the tracking and control of human resource actions. Lengnick–Hall and Moritz go on to note that many of these effects are likely to be realised early in the implementation of an e-HR system so can provide compelling evidence of the benefits of such a system to stakeholders.

The literature has also discussed the use of e-HRM to facilitate a change in the role of the HR function. This literature discusses two main impacts of e-HRM that may support HR practitioners in making this change. Firstly, the use of e-HRM means that much administration can be accomplished using automated or self-service systems, so that the amount of time that HR practitioners need to spend on administration tasks is greatly reduced. This allows the HR function time to manage human resources strategically and to become a full partner in the business (Groe, Pyle and Jamrog, 1996; Lawler and Mohrman, 2003). Indeed, research by Watson-Wyatt (2002) demonstrated that the most commonly recognised

business benefit of e-HR was "allowing HR to re-focus on becoming a business partner" (p.11). Shrivastiva and Shaw (2004) suggested that technology could have a transformational impact by redefining the scope of the HR function by enabling it to focus on more strategic activities.

Secondly, the shift to a more strategic role for the HR function has led to an increase in the demand for accurate and detailed information about a company's human resources (Ball, 2001). The use of e-HRM means that such information can be produced at the touch of a button. Kovach and Cathcart (1999) noted that this information can be used both for efficiency purposes, to reduce costs and time, and also for more analytical decision support, while Wilcox (1997) proposed that the HR function can better use data to drive strategic organisational decisions. The use of an HRIS may therefore allow the HR function to develop data-driven HR strategies and to play a greater part in strategic business decision-making.

Ulrich and Brockbank (2005) acknowledged the efficiency benefits from IT applied to HR, and the possibilities for removing transactional work and thus freeing up time for a more strategic role, but their discussion of the potential contribution to the 'bottom line' stated: "Nevertheless, technology accounts for just 5 percent of HR's total influence on business performance, making this the only HR competency domain that is not significantly related to financial performance" (p.239). Clearly then, the potential of using e-HRM to transform the HR function into one that is both efficient and a strategic business partner needs further investigation.

Ruël, Bondarouk and Looise (2004) summarised the past literature on e-HRM and suggested three types of goals for the introduction of e-HRM in organisations, based on the four "pressures" of virtual HRM suggested by Lepak and Snell (1998). Firstly, improving the strategic orientation of HRM, secondly, cost reduction or efficiency gains and thirdly, improving their service to clients and facilitating management and employees. As a result of their empirical work, Ruël *et al* added to these the goal of achieving global orientation. Ruël *et al* also distinguished between these four goals of e-HRM and other outcomes that emerge as a result of the use of technology such as cost reduction and a reduction of the administrative burden on the HR function. We will use Ruël *et al*'s proposition as a framework for our research.

Most of the academic literature in this area has discussed e-HRM broadly across the entire domain of human resource management, without detailed attention to particular process areas. This may be problematic as the impact of e-HRM could vary according to the process area in which it is implemented. In addition, the use of e-HRM may be more mature or developed for particular areas and could therefore have more impact. For instance, in the UK, a survey by the CIPD (2005) has shown that e-HRM is more commonly used in absence management, training and development and recruitment and selection, than in HR planning, knowledge management and expenses administration. Much of the empirical research in this area has been conducted in the United States where the use of e-HRM may be more common and more mature generally. In addition, the broad studies on HRM in general may not allow the detailed examination that is necessary to fully understand the potential of e-HRM for the transformation of the HR function. It is for the reasons above that we will focus on a single HR process that is reasonably developed within the UK, that of recruitment.

For the purpose of this research, we will define e-recruitment as the use of any technology to attract, select or manage the recruitment process. We will limit this to technology that is within the organisation itself, such as a corporate recruitment website or applicant tracking system, as this is the technology over which the HR or resourcing team have control. The use of online jobs boards and external agency software will therefore not be included in our examination. Technology is now commonly used for recruitment within the UK, to attract, select and manage candidates. For instance, the CIPD found that 75% of UK organisations used their corporate website to attract applicants and 30% used online testing for selection (2007). Similar CIPD research in 2006 showed that 72 % used online job applications.

Despite the widespread use of technology in recruitment, research regarding e-recruitment is sparse, particularly from an employer's perspective. Bartram (2000) noted that 'The topic of study is relatively new...A search of PsychLit for papers concerned with the Internet and selection or recruitment found nothing.' Our own search suggests that the situation has changed very little since Bartram's paper, with the majority of interest in online recruitment remaining from the candidate's perspective. Indeed, Lievens, Van Dam and Anderson (2002) also noted that research into online recruitment is "very scarce" and that "all the studies we retrieved focused on applicant reactions". For instance, Dineen and others have examined the use of online information to promote person-organisation fit (Dineen, Ash and Noe, 2002; Dineen, Ash and Del Vecchio, 2007), and Cober, Brown, Keeping and Levy (2004) addressed the impact of website characteristics on applicant attraction. A number of authors have researched the use of technology for personnel selection (for example, Buckley, Minnette, Jay and Michaels, 2004; Sinar, Reynolds and Paquet, 2003; Jattuso and Sinar, 2003), but to date, authors have paid very little attention to the impact of technology on the recruitment process as a whole. One exception to this is O'Leary, Lindholm, Whitford and Freeman's (2002) case study of e-recruitment in the US Government. O'Leary *et al* concluded that information technology had radically changed recruitment within the UK Government and cited outcomes such as reduced costs, a shorter time to hire and increased efficiency.

The lack of research into the impact of technology on recruitment is perhaps particularly surprising if we consider the importance of recruitment to organisations. Recruitment 'performs the essential function of drawing an important resource - human capital- into the organisation' (Barber, 1998, p. 841). The strategic significance of recruitment is often reported in the literature (Boxall and Purcell, 2003), the emphasis being upon the need to attract and retain high quality people in order to gain a competitive advantage, as is consistent with the resource-based view of companies (Barney 1991; Barney and Wright, 1998; Wright and McMahon, 1992). In addition to providing insights about the use of technology to transform HRM therefore, we will also use this research to add to knowledge about the impact of e-recruitment on the end-to-end recruitment process from an employer's perspective.

The research on e-HRM discussed above would indicate that the use of technology should have an impact on both the efficiency of the recruitment process and also on the role of the recruitment or resourcing team. Our research is therefore designed to explore these ideas within the framework of Ruël *et* al's four goals of e-HRM, through three case studies with users of e-recruitment. The primary question that we will seek to answer is therefore *"What impact does the use of technology have on the recruitment process and the role of the resourcing team?"*

METHODOLOGY

In order to explore the impact of the use of technology on the recruitment process in some detail, case studies in three organisations were conducted. While it was not possible to be fully representative of the population through three case studies, a range of organisations were chosen to examine the use of e-recruitment in a number of different contexts. The organisations were selected from a range of different industry sectors, which used a range of technological solutions within recruitment. As we were interested in the impact of technology on e-recruitment, organisations

were selected that had used their e-recruitment system for at least one year. These organisations were medical charity Cancer Research UK, retail chain Marks and Spencer, and manufacturing firm BOC Gases. The case studies were conducted between 2006 and 2007.

The case studies consisted of interviews with HR Directors and Managers, HR and Resourcing Administrators, Resourcing Specialists and Line Managers, as appropriate to the case. In some of the case studies, focus groups were held with managers or employees where this was the most convenient method to gather data. Ruël, Bondarouk and Looise (2004) proposed that conversational interviews such as those used in our study are adequate for use in case studies in order to "reconstruct" (p.369) the progress of an e-HRM project from its start to the time of the interview. In our research these interviews were used in order to construct a picture of the use of e-recruitment and the impact that the introduction of technology had had on the recruitment process.

The information collected as a result of the case studies was analyzed using the content analysis software NVivo, in order to draw out themes that emerged in the data.

The three case studies are described in full below.

Cancer Research UK

Cancer Research UK is the world's leading independent organisation dedicated to cancer research. The organisation is almost entirely funded by donations from the public and therefore conducts a large amount of fundraising through over 30,000 volunteers. Cancer Research UK has approximately 3500 paid employees and funds the work of over 3000 doctors, nurses and scientists that are based (bar one) in the UK. The organisation has expanded considerably since its formation in 2002, and recruits to over 1000 vacancies per year. Recruitment is managed by a single team, based in London.

The resourcing team introduced an online recruitment system in 2005 in response to a number of business needs. This business case included the following items:

- Reduction of costs, through a reduced head count and less paper-based work.
- Faster and more efficient recruitment.
- Increased accuracy of data entry.
- Increased reach to overseas job seekers.
- Efficient management of speculative applications.
- Maintenance of their 'cutting edge' image.
- The bulk of the organisation's target population in terms of employees is online.

The use of online recruitment is also in accord with the organisation's resourcing strategy to attract the best talent from all over the world. An off the shelf recruitment system (AMRIS) was chosen based on the developed specification and on price. The system is used to manage the recruitment process from end to end.

Vacancies are advertised on the corporate website via the system and applicants are encouraged to apply online either by completing an online application form or by submitting a CV, depending on the vacancy. People are also driven to the website via external advertising. Each new application for a particular vacancy is sent to the relevant manager directly via email. The system allows the resourcing team to manage both the vacancy and candidates through to the end of the recruitment and selection process. It is also used to respond to candidates, to provide information regarding vacancies (by downloading role profiles), provides email alerts to candidates and stores candidate details. The system also has the capacity to search the database of candidates for particular characteristics and to provide online selection tools and can also send text alerts/invites to candidates, but this functionality has not yet been adopted by the organisation. The system is managed by the resourcing team so line

managers have to contact this team to advertise a position. They currently still use paper-based recruitment in addition to online recruitment in order to maintain accessibility for all candidates. However, they are encouraging as many applicants as possible to apply online in order to reduce workload. The department does not want to remove human contact totally from the recruitment process so they still accept telephone calls and emails. They do not currently use online selection processes but may do in the future. The system is not currently linked to the main HRIS as this is still in development. Eventually data regarding candidates who take up positions within the organisation will be automatically transferred into a personnel file, therefore saving the time required to enter this data.

Prior to the implementation of the online recruitment system, the organisation's recruitment processes were paper based. A copy of each CV that had been received for a particular vacancy would be sent to the appropriate line manager, for consideration, while another copy would be filed and stored by the resourcing team. This process was described by members of the resourcing team as "slow" due to the reliance on the postal service and also "cumbersome" due to the need to process and store large quantities of paper. In addition, candidate details were entered into a computer database manually. This led to a number of mistakes in data entry due to human error. These processes are now conducted entirely online and communications are via email. Candidate data is entered by the candidate via the online application process. This has had a number of effects on recruitment processes. Firstly, the process is considerably faster. The system has "revolutionised" the way that jobs are loaded onto the website. Previously this had been a slow, time-consuming manual process, which often resulted in errors, but now happens "at the press of a button". Closing dates for applications can be maintained due to the speed of communicating via the online system (they no longer have to "wait for the post"), applications are sent immediately to line managers and the data is readily accessibly via the recruitment portal. Secondly, as the candidate data is now entered directly by the candidate, there are fewer errors in the information, therefore making the process significantly more accurate. In addition, if a mistake with regard to an online vacancy is found, or details need to be changed, this can be done instantly whereas previously it would have taken several days and would have required the help of another team.

Applicant feedback, via online questionnaires, has been mostly positive in that applicants find the online system more efficient, effective, faster and easier to use compared to the paper-based system. Anecdotal feedback from managers was also positive in terms of the speed and efficiency of the process. The system can produce metrics with regard to the numbers of people applying online. However, these had not been analyzed in order to identify changes in the volume or type of applications. The volume of applications was perceived to have significantly increased.

The system is managed on a candidate by candidate basis. This means that each candidate file on the system has to be updated individually once a post is filled. There was some feeling among the resourcing team that this was a time consuming process and could be improved. This difficulty means that for some positions with a large number of applicants (e.g. the graduate recruitment scheme) there is time lag in keeping the system up to date however it is still faster than the previous paper based system. Generally, the resourcing team felt that the system was a positive development for the organisation.

The Resourcing Manager explained that cost savings had already been achieved in two areas. Firstly, because candidate data no longer needed to be entered into a database manually, the headcount within the resourcing team has been reduced by one. As the price of maintaining the online recruitment system is lower than this individual's salary and costs per annum, this represents a significant cost saving. In addition, the move from a system that used a large amount of paper to an online system has saved administration costs, although he was unable to supply a figure for either of these cost savings.

An output of the online recruitment system is the production of accurate and accessible information. Information regarding vacancies and the recruitment process is now "at their fingertips" and is always available. This means that the team can "work smarter" by targeting their recruitment advertising for instance. At a higher level, the Head of Resourcing has access to faster, "real time" information and can monitor who is applying for jobs etc. and use this information in order to make better decisions. It is also possible to track the workload of each individual on the resourcing team in order to examine operational efficiency.

The automation of systems in recruitment has meant that the Resourcing team has more time to focus on other "better value" issues so that they can "add more value" to the organisation. The fact that they have more time has encouraged the resourcing team to be more proactive with their work and to take more responsibility for vacancies. Their role has shifted to one that is more customer-focused as they spend more time interacting with managers. The shift in the role of the resourcing team has led to a change in the skills requirements of HR staff. The HR team has needed to develop their communication and consultancy skills so that they can work with their customers effectively. They needed to develop skills in analysing and interpreting data so that they can make effective use of the information that is now available. The team has also had to develop skills in using the technology.

Marks and Spencer

Marks and Spencer is a large retail chain selling clothing, home furnishings, beauty products, food and financial services. The organisation has over 450 stores located throughout the UK and another 200 stores worldwide, operating in 30 countries. The company has approximately 68,000 employees worldwide. The HR structure within Marks and Spencer is based loosely upon the Ulrich model, with centres of excellence and a shared services centre. The business is split into two areas - Head Office and Retail. Recruitment is carried out by store managers and recruitment advisors on the retail side, with support from the shared services centre. In Head Office, recruitment is carried out by line managers with support from the HR shared services centre. Marks and Spencer needs to recruit an extremely high volume of workers annually, especially at a store level.

An e-recruitment system was introduced in 2006 in order to manage the volume of vacancies and applicants more efficiency. The business case for the introduction of this system centred on:

- Reduction of recruitment costs
- Increased efficiency
- Improved experience for candidates
- Release of store managers time to focus on customer-centred activity, rather than recruitment

The candidate portal for store employees is accessed via the careers and recruitment part of the Marks and Spencer website. Potential applicants can search for opportunities by role, region, store, contract type and number of hours. The available roles are then displayed and the candidates can choose to apply for one or more of these. Initially, each applicant is pre-screened online according to their eligibility and suitability for the role. This pre-screen is based upon a number of questions such as "can you provide proof that you are legally allowed to work in the UK?" and "Can you confirm that you are no longer of compulsory school age?" Unsuitable candidates are then automatically rejected and are provided with a specific explanation for this rejection online. If they pass the eligibility screening, applicants are taken to a help and instructions page explaining

how they should proceed with the next stage of their application. They are then asked to complete a few basic details such as their name and equal opportunities information, before being asked to complete an online talent screening. This test assesses their skills and experience against what is required for the role for which they are applying. Those candidates that are successful following the talent screen can then book an interview with the appropriate store manager online.

Store managers or recruitment advisors enter the details of a vacancy into the system and then are not involved in the recruitment process until the interview stage. The system provides a schedule for interviews to each store manager/recruitment advisor.

Managers are recruited via a multi-stage process. Applicants search for opportunities via the candidate portal in the same way as applicants for customer assistant positions. If there are no live vacancies in their area, they can register their interest via the system and are automatically notified when a vacancy arises. Management candidates are screened on 'killer' questions and, if they pass this stage, they complete an online application form. At this stage applicants are either invited for interview or are asked to complete a test online at which point they are either automatically rejected or invited for interview.

Recruiters can edit, approve, archive and look at statistics on vacancies at any time via the system. The use of the online system means that the comparatively high workload in raising, approving and posting vacancies is minimized. Potentially high volumes of inappropriate applications are screened out and potential 'stars' are identified through the use of online testing and killer questions. The use of the online system has made the process more user-friendly and eased sourcing and associated expenses through the creation of a talent database.

Graduates are also recruited via a multi-stage process. They access vacancies via the candidate portal on the Marks and Spencer website and are then pre-screened by function and some applicants are rejected automatically at this stage based on minimum criteria. Those that have passed this stage complete an online application form, at which point they may be rejected based on the need for a work permit, mobility or shift patterns. If they pass this stage they are automatically invited to complete a verbal test online. Those that pass the verbal tests are invited to complete a numerical test online. Those that pass this test are invited to complete the OPQ personality test, also online. On completion of the OPQ they are either rejected or invited to an assessment centre. Candidates can book their assessment centre place online.

The use of online recruitment for store employees has improved efficiency by reducing administration by 60% through automation. It has also created consistency in recruitment practices across 400 stores as everyone now has to go through the same process. The system is more reliable and minimizes administration and the time to hire for over 45,000 recruits per year. In addition, customer service has been improved as store managers now have more time to devote to customers rather than to recruitment.

The use of an online system for graduate recruitment has led to improvements in both the efficiency and rigour of the recruitment process. Manual screening has been reduced to zero, consistent and robust screening methodologies are used and candidates can check their progress and have the facility to book assessment centre's online. The graduate system manages over 6000 applicants per campaign.

The graduate system is also used to produce a variety of statistics about graduate recruitment which are used to review each recruitment campaign and to plan the next. These statistics are available in real time so current data can be accessed at any time. The induction process for successful candidates is started online via a portal that is personalised for each candidate. This system provides information to new starters and allows new employees to communicate with each other via message boards in order to encourage them to build relationships and ask questions.

The recruitment team at Marks and Spencer feel that the use of the online system has strengthened their position relative to other graduate recruiters by providing a high level of candidate service and cutting the amount of time to from application to offer. In addition, the system allows recruiters to focus on "value-adding" candidate-facing tasks by automating administration and selection.

Internal research has shown that the use of online recruitment has led to improved candidate service and employer brand. 97% of candidates rated the recruitment process as good to excellent. The system has allowed the company to save 60% of costs in some areas. The system also provides detailed management information to drive improvement and to plan future campaigns and supports induction.

BOC Gases

BOC Gases is a large manufacturer of industrial gases that is divided into three lines of business—Process Gas Solutions, Industrial and Special Products and BOC Edwards, in addition to a specialist logistics business, Gist. They employed over 30,000 people and work in 50 countries. At the time of the case study the company had just been taken over by Linde so were undergoing a merger process. BOC Gases has had a shared services HR structure in place since 1999. Business Unit HR partners report to the MD for each unit. These work in conjunction with specialists in the shared services centre.

The company uses a system called Provitrack for recruitment. The business case behind introducing an automated recruitment system was:

- High visibility spend
- Quick access to candidate information

- To reduce headcount by reducing administration
- Real time recruitment
- Quicker advertising

The company needed to introduce a system that suited all of the different recruitment systems internationally in a 'one size fits all' approach. Provitrack was chosen as it was cheapest for the functionality provided.

Provitrack consists of a central recruitment database which is linked to a number of different career centres that each has a unique URL. They may also have their own application form. Each location within the company generally has an internal and external career centre and may also have career centres linked to different levels of recruitment such as for graduates. The system has different access levels for managers, vendors, administrators and HR recruiters.

Managers can create their own vacancies but in the UK this is generally done by the resourcing team. This goes through an approval process and an advertisement is then posted to the corporate website, intranet and jobs boards. This can be posted in multiple languages. Applicants complete the form online—they only have to complete this once and then it is saved for future applications. This also creates a database that the company can proactively search. The system sends out automated acknowledgements and can be instructed to issue letters in batches. Managers can log in to look at active vacancies, and, as the process happens in real time, they can log in and view CVs and screen them themselves. They can also view a summary of candidates, their status, interview scheduled and source. There is also the facility to add multiple choice questions to the application form and screen candidates on these. The system also has a reporting function and can produce standard reports by, for example, equal opportunities information or agency information, or can produce ad hoc reports.

The move to using Provitrack and online recruitment has saved the company half a million pounds in recruitment fees over the first three years since its implementation. Cost savings are more than the cost of the system through headcount and agency fees. The company wanted to be perceived as leading edge in terms of the recruitment market and their interface with candidates and to be able to handle volume.

It was expected that the introduction of Provitrack would lead to the resourcing team spending more time liaising with managers but actually they have spent more time working with the front end of the system as managers like to shortlist candidates themselves. This means that the team have more time and freedom to do "added-value" work. For instance, they can make sure that they really understand the job brief and concentrate on sourcing strategies and selection.

FINDINGS

We have examined the use of e-recruitment and the impact of this technology on the efficiency of the recruitment process and the role of the resourcing team. The literature has proposed that the use of technology in HRM can lead to both improved HR efficiency and facilitate a shift to a more strategic HR role, by providing both the time and information required for the HR function to act more strategically within an organisation (Lawler and Mohrman, 2003; Shrivastiva and Shaw, 2003, Snell, Stueber and Lepak, 2002).

An examination of the evidence that emerged from the three case studies above, allowed us some insight into the potential impact of technology on the efficiency of the recruitment process and the role of the resourcing team. We have examined this evidence within the framework of the four goals suggested by Ruël, Bondarouk and Looise (2004). In order to do this we will examine the outcomes of the introduction of e-recruitment and discuss whether these have led to the achievement of the goals specified by Ruël *et al* - improving the strategic orientation of HRM; cost reduction or efficiency gains; improving their service to clients and improving the global orientation of the firm.

Cost Reduction and Efficiency Gains

Our three cases studies provided a significant amount of evidence that the use of e-recruitment can lead to cost reduction and efficiency gains. Indeed, the drivers for introducing e-recruitment in each company included both cost reduction and a number of items around efficiency, including speed and accuracy of the recruitment process. Each of our three organisations had also experienced a series of positive outcomes from using e-recruitment that had helped them to achieve a more efficient recruitment process. For instance, in Cancer Research UK, the previous, paper-based process was described as "slow", "cumbersome" and "inaccurate" compared to the online process. The organisation has seen great savings in time and accuracy as a result of introducing e-recruitment. Similarly, Marks and Spencer has experienced massive increases in efficiency with the reduction of administration by 60 percent as a result of the move to e-recruitment. BOC have achieved significant cost savings through a reduction in headcount and in agency fees. There would seem to be no doubt therefore from our case studies that the goals of cost reduction and efficiency gains have been realized. This supports O'Leary *et al*'s (2002) experience of the impact of e-recruitment in the US Government and also other research on efficiency gains from e-HRM in general (Enshur *et al*, 2002; Snell *et al*, 2002; Lengnick-Hall and Moritz, 2003).

Improved Service to Clients

We also found some evidence that the use of e-recruitment could lead to an improved service for clients. Recruitment is perhaps a more difficult HR

process to evaluate in this regard than some others, as the clients include external candidates as well as line managers. However, both line managers and applicants praised the speed and efficiency of the e-recruitment system in Cancer Research UK, suggesting that the efficiency savings alone were resulting in service improvements. In addition, the resourcing team now has the time to interact more with managers and to take more responsibility for vacancies. Internal research at Marks and Spencer showed that the use of e-recruitment had led to improved candidate service and that 97% of candidates rated the recruitment process as good to excellent. In BOC, recruiters have been able to spend more time understanding the job brief thus enabling them to provide a better service to the line managers they work with. It was clear from the interviews with line managers carried out in two of our case study organisations that line managers will only appreciate the service improvements that e-recruitment may lead to if they have been fully educated in its use and the rationale behind its introduction. If steps have not been taken to engage managers in this way, they may resent the changes, rather than perceiving the benefits.

Improving the Strategic Orientation of HR

Our case studies provided some evidence that the use of e-recruitment could facilitate a change in the role of the resourcing team, to one that is more strategic. Firstly, we found that the reduction in administrative work needed had allowed recruiters more time to spend on "value-added" tasks. In Cancer Research UK, the resourcing team's role had shifted to more of a consultancy role. In BOC, recruiters now had time to focus on developing appropriate sourcing and selection strategies, rather than concentrating on transactional tasks. This idea that the use of e-HRM allows HR practitioners more time to focus on more strategic roles is in support of the literature in this area (Groe *et al*, 1996; Lawler and Mohrman, 2003; Shrivastiva and Shaw, 2004). Our results also supported the suggestion that e-HRM can facilitate data-driven, strategic decisions through the provision of accurate and detailed information (Kovach and Cathcart, 1999; Wilcox, 1997). Within Cancer Research UK, the Head of Resourcing used the information now available about vacancies and the recruitment process to make better decisions and to improve operational efficiency. Marks and Spencer also used the statistics from the e-recruitment system to review and plan each recruitment campaign.

Improving Global Orientation

The fourth of ë *et al*'s goals, 'to improve a company's global orientation' was not found to be a commonly cited factor within our case study organisations. This may be because four out of the five companies studied by Ruël *et al* operated internationally, whereas two out of our three case studies focused primarily on UK markets. The only strongly international company, BOC, conducted its UK recruitment separately from that of other countries. However, within the context of recruitment, this goal could be interpreted as a widening of the candidate base to one which is global. Indeed, to "reach overseas candidates" was a driver for the introduction of e-recruitment in Cancer Research UK, but whether this had been achieved had not been assessed.

Our analysis of the case studies suggests that, for recruitment at least, we may add a fifth goal to Ruël et al's framework, that of *employer branding* or promoting the image of the company. One of Cancer Research UK's reasons for introducing e-recruitment was to maintain their "cutting edge image" to job seekers. This was also the case within BOC gases where the company wanted to be seen as "leading edge" in terms of the recruitment market. This idea of image is particularly important in recruitment as an outward facing activity so may be specific to this process rather than being relevant across the whole spectrum of human resource management. However, the suggestion of 'image' or 'employer branding' as a fifth goal needs further investigation.

The use of e-recruitment may therefore facilitate a transformation of the recruitment process to one that is more efficient and also a shift in the role of the resourcing team to one that is more strategic. Our results are in support of those from Ruël *et al*'s (2004) study, in that the outcomes experienced by our case study organisations—increases in speed and accuracy, reduced costs, a reduction in necessary administration and the provision of data—have led to the achievement of at least three of Ruël *et al*'s four goals of e-HRM. Our case study organisations represented three very different industrial contexts and yet similar conclusions can be drawn for each of them.

It is important to note that, in Cancer Research UK, the use of e-recruitment and the resulting change in the HR role had led to some different demands on the resourcing team's skills. Aside from the skills needed to use the technology itself, the team needed to develop consultancy and analytical skills. This raises an interesting implication for companies introducing e-recruitment or e-HRM in order to improve the strategic orientation of the HR function. These organisations must be careful that their HR team has the skills and experience to make this transformation effectively, if they are not to be left behind.

Our research is not without limitations. The experience of three UK organisations can not be described as generalisable to other organisations in different industries and different countries. We have adopted this approach to allow us to look at the detail of what is occurring in these organisations, but there is now a need to validate these findings on a wider level. In addition, similar detailed examinations must be performed for other HR process areas. Nevertheless, we have shown the way in which e-HRM may help to facilitate the transformation to an HR function that is both efficient and strategic.

CONCLUSION AND FUTURE TRENDS

This chapter has used detailed case studies in a single process area, recruitment, in order to provide further insight into the transformational impact of e-HRM on the HR function. This enabled us to overcome the difficulties inherent in using a more general approach to examining e-HRM in a country where companies are at different stages of e-HRM development. On one level, our findings support the more general findings of Ruël, Bondarouk and Looise (2004) that e-HRM can be used to achieve the goals of cost reduction and efficiency gains, client service improvement and improving strategic orientation. We can therefore also lend some support to the general literature on the use of e-HRM to facilitate a more efficient and strategic HR function.

We must add a word of caution to these assertions. There could be two main reasons why technology might enhance the strategic role of HR managers, according to the literature we have summarized earlier. The reduction in the administrative resources required to operate a manual system could provide more time or budget for more strategic level work. However, recruitment activity as a process is usually managed at a fairly junior level. Therefore, the release of more junior HR managers' time is unlikely to produce more time for strategic activity; rather it will offer opportunities for efficiency savings, with reduced HR headcount. Nor is the budget saving necessarily reinvested in more senior HR specialists, but might, for example, be used to absorb the cost of new e-recruitment, or e-HRM, systems.

The second reason advanced for new technology in HR enhancing the strategic role is through the production of more accurate data, routinely collected. For this to occur requires there to be an organisational need, well understood at the time of the system design which incorporates the collection and analysis of strategically valuable data, and also for HR staff to possess skills in statistical analysis so they can go beyond descriptive statistics into studies of causes, forecasting and of variation. Thus, the functionality of the system as a data generating activity is limited by prior knowledge of what data is required, and the skills and knowledge of how to analyze the data meaningfully.

There is a third possible reason which is more indirect and contingent upon sector, occupational groups and the labour market. This concerns the strategic importance of a well managed recruitment process, for example in building an employer brand, and in accessing talent ahead of the competition.

There is some evidence in the data gathered here that all three reasons for the positive impact of technology may have a strategic value. The most striking of our findings are around the impact of e-recruitment on the efficiency of the recruitment process. All three of our case study organisations had experienced significant efficiency savings as a result of using technology. However, while the outcomes of releasing HR practitioners' time and providing HR data were certainly realised, and HR practitioners were using this time and information in order to act more strategically, it cannot be said that this impact was of great magnitude. This supports Ulrich and Brockbank's (2005) assertion that, while promoting efficiency, technology accounts for only a small proportion of the HR function's impact on business performance. This may be because the practitioners concerned lacked the necessary skills to make this transformation effectively. It may also be because the changes were emerging organically as a result of the outcomes of using e-recruitment, rather than being strategically driven by the organisation. If an organisation wishes to take full advantage of the possibilities that e-HRM allows, then it must develop a strategy by which to do this. Organisations must look at how their resourcing team (or wider HR team) can be restructured and the roles and work re-designed to facilitate this transformation to a more strategic role. In addition, future research should analyze how e-HRM can be used in conjunction with these processes in order to achieve the transformation of the HR function.

REFERENCES

Ball, K. (2001). The use of human resource information systems. *Personnel Review, 30*(5/6), 677-693.

Barber, A. E. (1998). *Recruiting Employees.* Thousand Oaks, CA: Sage Publications.

Barney, J. B. (1991). Firm Resources and substantial competitive advantage. *Journal of Management, 17*(1), 99-120.

Barney, J. B., & Wright, P. M. (1998). On becoming a strategic partner: The role of human resources in gaining competitive advantage. *Human Resource Management, 37*(1), 31-46.

Bartram, D. (2000). Internet recruitment and selection: Kissing frogs to find princes. *International Journal of Selection and Assessment, 8*(4), 261-274.

Boxall, P., & Purcell, J. (2003). *Strategy and Human Resource Management.* London: Palgrave Macmillan.

Bussler, L., & Davis, E. (2002). Information systems: the quiet revolution in human resource management. *Journal of Computer Information Systems, 42*(2), 17—20.

Chartered Institute of Personnel Development (2007). *Recruitment and Retention 2005*; CIPD, June 2007

Chartered Institute of Personnel Development (2006). *Recruitment and Retention 2005*; CIPD, June 2006

Chartered Institute of Personnel Development (2005). People management and technology: progress and potential. London, CIPD.

Cober, R. T., Brown, D. J., & Levy, P. E. (2004). Form, content and function: an evaluative methodology for corporate employment websites. *Human Resource Management (USA), 43*(2/3), 201- 218.

Dineen B., Ash, S., & Noe, R. (2002). A web of applicant attraction: person organisation fit in the context of web-based recruitment. *Journal of Applied Psychology, 87*(4), 723.

Dineen, B., Ling, J., Ash, S., & Del Vecchio, D. (2007). Aesthetic properties and message customisation: navigating the dark side of web recruitment. *Journal of Applied Psychology, 92(2),* 356.

Enshur, E., Nielson, T., & Grant-Vallone, E. (2002). Tales from the hiring line: effects of the Internet technology on HR processes. *Organisational Dynamics, 31*(3), 224-244.

Groe, G., Pyle, W., & Jamrog, J. (1996). Information technology and HR. *Human Resource Planning, 19*(1), 56-61.

Guest, D., & Peccei, R. (1994). The nature and causes of effective human resource management. *British Journal of Industrial Relations, 32*(2), 219-240.

Huselid, M. A. (1995). The impact of human resource management practices on turnover, productivity and corporate financial performance. *Academy of Management Journal, 38,* 635-672.

Kovach, K., & Cathcart, C. (1999). Human resource information systems (HRIS). Providing business with rapid data access, information exchange and strategic advantage. *Public Personnel Management, 28*(2), 275-282.

Lawler, E., & Mohrman, S. (2003). HR as a strategic partner: what does it take to make it happen? *Human Resource Planning, 26*(3), 15-29.

Legge, K. (1978). *Power, Innovation and Problem Solving in Personnel Management.* London: McGraw-Hill.

Lengnick-Hall, M., & Moritz, S. (2003). The impact of e-HR on the human resource management function. *Journal of Labor Research, 24*(3), 365-379.

Lepak, D., & Snell, D. (1998). Virtual HR: strategic human resource management in the 21st century. *Human Resource Management Review, 8*(3), 215-234.

Lievens, F., van Dam, K., & Anderson, N. (2002). Recent trends and challenges in personnel selection. *Personnel Review, 31*(5), 580-601.

Murphy, T. E., & Zandvakili, S. (2000). Data and metrics driven approach to human resource practices using customer, employees and financial metrics. *Human Resource Management, 39*(1), 93-105.

O'Leary, B., Lindholm, M., Whitford, R., & Freeman, S. (2002). Selecting the best and brightest: leveraging human capital. *Human Resource Management, 41*(2), 325-340.

Osterman, P. (1994). How common is workplace transformation and who adopts it? *Industrial and Labor Relations Review, 47*(2), 173-188.

Paauwe, J. (2004). *HRM and Performance: Achieving long-term viability.* Oxford University Press.

Purcell, J. (1999). Best practice and best fit: Chimera or cul-de-sac? *Human Resource Management Journal, 9*(3), 26-34.

Rucci, A., Kirn, S., & Quinn, R. (1998). The employee-customer-profit chain at Sears. *Harvard Business Review, 70*(1), 82-87.

Ruël, H., Bondarouk, T., & Looise, J. (2004). E-HRM: Innovation or irritation. An explorative empirical study in five large companies on web-based HRM. *Management Revue, 15*(3), 364—381.

Senge, P. M. (1990). *The fifth discipline.* Century Business.

Shrivastava, S., & Shaw, J. (2003). Liberating HR through technology. *Human Resource Management, 42*(3), 201-222.

Snell, S., Stueber, D., & Lepak, D. (1992). Virtual HR departments: Getting out of the middle. In R. L. Heneman & D. B. Greenberger (Eds.), *Human resource management in virtual organizations* (pp. 81-101). Greenwich, CT: Information Age Publishing

Tyson, S. (1995). *Human resource strategy.* Pitman.

Ulrich, D. (1997). *Human Resources Champions.* Boston: Harvard Business School Press.

Ulrich, D., & Brockbank, W. (2005). *The HR Value Proposition.* Harvard Business School Press.

Watson Wyatt (2002). B2E/EHR: Survey results 2002. Retrieved from *www.watsonwyatt.com.*

Wilcox, J. (1997). The evolution of human resources technology. *Management Accounting, June 1997,* 3-5.

Wright, P., & McMahan, G. C. (1992). Theoretical perspectives for strategic human resource management. *Journal of Management, 18,* 295-320.

Youndt, M. A., Snell, S. A., Dean, J.W., & Lepak, D. P. (1996). Human resource management, manufacturing strategy and firm performance. *Academy of Management Journal, 39*(4), 836-866.

KEY TERMS

Business Partner: An HR professional that works with a specific client usually at the senior management level and contributes to the design of the business strategy from a people perspective and helps advise or find advice on key strategic issues.

E-Recruitment: The use of any technology to attract, select or manage the recruitment process.

e-HRM: A way of implementing HR strategies policies and practices in organizations through a conscious and directed support of and/or with the full use of web-based technology channels.

Human Resource Information System (HRIS): Any system that helps an organisation to acquire, store, manipulate, analyse, retrieve and distribute information about an organisation's human resources.

Killer Questions: Questions that are used to sift candidates. Those candidates that answer questions incorrectly are rejected at this stage.

Online Application Form: An application form that is completed and submitted via the Internet.

Chapter XIII
The Role of National Culture on E–Recruitment in India and Mexico

Pramila Rao
Marymount University, USA

ABSTRACT

This chapter will address the role of national culture on e-recruitment practices in India and Mexico. The GLOBE (Global Leadership and Organizational Behavior Effectiveness) cultural study on 61 countries will be used to discuss the role of cultural dimensions on e-recruitment practices in these two countries. The chapter will also discuss the beginnings of e-recruitment trends in India and Mexico, challenges of e-recruitment for United States multinationals, national culture profile, and implications for multinational managers. This conceptual chapter will provide hypotheses for the cultural dimensions discussed. Specifically, this study will address the role of power-distance, in-group collectivism, gender egalitarianism and uncertainty-avoidance on e-recruitment practices.

INTRODUCTION

E-HRM (electronic human resource management) is the process of using online technology for human resource management activities, such as recruitment, training, performance appraisal and benefits. E-recruitment is maintaining the entire recruitment process online-right from placing the job advertisements to receiving the resumes and communicating back to potential applicants (Othman & Musa, 2007; Rudich, 2000).

E-recruitment can either be in the form of corporate or third-party recruiters. Corporate recruiters allow potential job applicants to post their resumes directly on their job sites without using any other intermediaries. Statistics reveal that 80% of the world's US 500 companies use corporate websites for recruiting (Epstein & Singh, 2003). Third-party recruiters, such as Monster.com, are synonymous to job advertisement pages of the newspapers identifying thousands of employment vacancies (Epstein & Singh, 2003). They usually charge employers a cost for posting their advertisements for certain duration of time (Tong, & Sivanand, 2005). Usually third party recruiters and corporate recruiters collaborate together to provide best recruitment and career solutions to potential applicants (Pollit, 2005; Mollsion, 2001). The goal of this paper is to discuss the role of national culture on e-recruitment practices in emerging economies like India and Mexico as multinationals seek to establish a strong presence in these countries (Friedman, 2005).

Multinationals are proactively seeking the best talent worldwide. The method of online recruiting allows organizations to transcend geographical boundaries from Monterrey to Mumbai seeking the best in human capital (Birchfield, 2002). E-recruitment has several other advantages; such as its low cost (Rudich, 2000; Galanaki, 2002), quick response time (Hays, 1999), broad range of applicants (Sessa and Taylor, 2000), more educated applicants (Othman & Musa, 2007), and of course worldwide accessibility (Galanaki, 2002; Vinutha 2005). Specifically, it has demonstrated a shorter recruitment cycle and lower cost-per-hire (Sridhar, 2005; Jasrotia, 200; Pollitt, 2005). For instance, Nike has demonstrated with the use of e-recruitment the average time to fill job positions reduced from 62 to 42 days and the recruitment costs reduced by 54% (Pollitt, 2005). From the employees' perspective, it has made the recruitment process a very proactive one – now passive applicants post their resumes online in anticipation of an interview (Mollison, 2001).

Further, online recruitment allows applicants the luxury of accessing jobs online at their own convenience 24 hours 7 days a week. It provides the comfort of scrutinizing jobs without physically going through the stress of an interview. Finally, it allows applicants to get a thorough understanding of the organization and its culture before joining the organization (Vinutha, 2005).

On the other side, the disadvantages of e-recruitment are that it could create disparate impact as economically disadvantaged groups might not have access to online facilities. This becomes even more distinct in emerging economies where there is a stark difference between the rich and the poor due to social and economic classes, creating what scholars have termed a "digital-divide" (Olivas-Lujan, Ramirez & Zapatu-Cantu, 2007; Curry and Kenney, 2006; Lancaster, 2003).

Further, employees from the older age groups might perceive themselves to be less tech-savvy than the current "digital-generation" of employees, and therefore feel a sense of alienation (Othman & Musa, 2007). Also, several cultures, such as India and Mexico, do not like to use e-recruitment for upper-level executives who have to lead, direct, and manage organizations. These cultures feel that they have to trust and know such cadre of executives before recruiting them (Chokkar, 2007; Davila & Elvira, 2005). Finally, e-recruitment is known for its deluge of unqualified applicants (Othman & Musa, 2007).

The primary objective of this chapter is to provide readers an overview on e-recruitment challenges in two emerging economies, India and Mexico. Both these countries are increasing their trade relations with other countries in the world and aggressively promoting foreign investment (Friedman, 2006). Therefore as multinationals scramble to these nations to establish their foothold, it is important to understand cultural impediments on staffing practices, such as e-recruitment, in these two growing economies.

The next section discusses perspectives and problems of e-recruitment in these economies (India and Mexico) and is organized as follows 1) beginnings of e-recruitment 2) challenges of e-recruitment 3) national culture, with specific reference to power-distance, in-group collectivism, gender egalitarianism and uncertainty-avoidance and their impact on e-recruitment practices.

BEGINNINGS OF E-RECRUITMENT: INDIA AND MEXICO

The United States pioneered the global trend of e-recruitment when Jeff Taylor launched Monster.com in 1994 (Taylor, 2003; Murray, 2001) with 20 clients and 200 job openings (Anonymous, 2007). Monster.com launched the concept of posting and storing resumes online (Taylor, 2003; Mollison, 2001). The beginning of e-recruitment coincided with a business culture that was becoming increasingly global with the trade reforms such as the NAFTA and the breaking down of political and trade barriers (Friedman, 2005).

The Indian government's proactive liberalization policy in 1991 opened the doors to numerous multinationals. Today 125 Fortune 500 companies have their R &D centers in India (Zakaria, 2006). Microsoft, IBM. & Hewlett-Packard are eagerly increasing their operations in India (Solomon, 2005; Ramamurthi, 2001) requiring increased staff. Dell is planning to double it work staff in India over the next three years to almost hire 20,000 technical workers. Microsoft is going to add another 3000 jobs in India over the next three-four years (Frauenheim, 2006).

Mexico opened its doors to foreign policy when it changed it trade policy from an import-substitution to an export strategy. With the NAFTA opening the doors to increased trade, Mexico has become the 15th largest exporter economy of the world. In the IT sector, the Mexican government is heavily investing in the Information Technology (IT) industry as it realizes that it lags behind several Asian economies in the IT field. The government has announced an incentive program called Prosoft to achieve $5 billion worth of Mexican software by 2013 and also make Mexico a software leader in the Latin American region (Emmond, 2005; Navarrete & Pick, 2002).

In March 1997, an Indian company, Naukri.com, began its first internet portal operation with basic HTML (Hypertext Markup Language)

operation. At that time, India had only 14,000 internet connections with most of them being text-only connections. However, today Naukri.com is India's largest e-recruitment portal with 3.5 million users and 15,000 corporate clients (Srinivasan, Babu & Sahad, 2005). The main players of the e-recruitment industry in India today are Naukri.com, Timesjob, Careerindia.com, and Jobstreet.com (Sridhar, 2005). Job.street provides a certification that ensures absolute privacy about applicant's employment details (Suryanarayanan, 2001), which is very important in the Indian organizational culture that values qualities such as loyalty and trust (Chokkar, Brodbeck & House, 2007).

The pioneers of online recruitment in Mexico are Bumeran.com and Laborum.com, both non-Mexican firms, established around 1999. The corporate offices of Bumeran are in Argentina and that of Laborum are in Chile (Fitzgerald & Liburt, Peterson, 2000; Anonymous, 2001). Scholars suggest barriers, such as high business costs, complicated ownership laws for new firms, and a lack of capitalist culture prompts non-Mexicans to dominate the e-commerce business in Mexico (Curry, Contreras, Kenney, 2001).

The online revolution pioneered by Monster.com in the US in 1994 (Murray, 2001) set the stage for emerging economies like India and Mexico to experience the flattening of the world (Friedman, 2005).

CHALLENGES OF E-RECRUITMENT: INDIA AND MEXICO

US multinationals frequently use online recruitment as a predominant method to leverage talent across the globe. On an average, about 804 of the Fortune 1000 companies use Monster.com as one of their recruitment portals (Mollison, 2001). The US culture promotes sharing work experiences more openly than many other cultures- hence posting resumes on web sites is not a difficult choice for applicants (Mollison, 2001). US multinationals seeking off shoring and outsourcing resources to countries such as Mexico and India are challenged by local economic and cultural practices (Friedman, 2006).

In India, the sheer magnitude and size of online recruiting is staggering by Western standards. On an average, large Indian companies recruit about 10,000 entry-level positions annually (Sachitanand & Sheth, 2007). The process of screening resumes for authenticity and relevance is a staffing nightmare for online recruiters as the population of India staggers over a million (Vinuta, 2005; Sridhar, 2005).

Second, a strange paradox called "digital-divide" exists, although India is acknowledged as the information technology (IT) leader of the world (Friedman, 2005). Therefore, the rich have the benefits of the technological revolution while the poor are left behind. Apart from economic costs, poor telecommunications infrastructure and undependable power shortages are the norm for most rural villages in India. India's population of one billion has only 3.7% internet penetration with approximately about forty-two million internet users (Lath, 2006). While the big metropolitan cities of Mumbai, Bangalore, Chennai, Delhi and Hyderabad are very well-connected, internet connection in inner cities are not of global standards. The low internet penetration can be a challenge for US multinationals where a laptop at every desk is so ubiquitous (Lath, 2006).

Similarly in Mexico, there is a "digital inequality (Olivas-Lujan, Ramirez & Zapatu-Cantu, 2007; Curry and Kenney, 2006) - where there is a stark distinction between those who can afford access to the internet and those who cannot. Such digital disparity is widely prevalent because of poor telecommunications infrastructure, distinct economic classes of the rich and poor, and also high costs associated with Internet usage. On an average, about 37% of the households in Mexico have internet access (Anonymous, 2005). In the corporate world only 28.6% firms have internet

Table 1. Internet users and Internet penetration: India and Mexico for 2007 (Adapted from http://www.internetworldstats.com)

Country	Users	Population	Penetration
India	42,000,000	1,129,667,528	3.7 %
Mexico	22,700,000	106,457,446	21.3 %

connection, while 71.4 % of the corporate do not have internet access (Olivas-Lujan, Ramirez & Zapatu-Cantu, 2007).

Table 1 provides details of internet users and penetration for these two countries.

Third, cultural preferences dictate a very personal and controlling approach outlook to staffing in both India and Mexico because of their high power-distance and collectivist ties (Chokkar, Brodbeck & House, 2007; Davila & Elvira, 2005). High power distance cultures prefer to be personally involved in staffing as it provides authority. Collectivist cultures are characterized by a very tight social framework and therefore prefer to hire employees known to them through social connections, regardless whether employees are qualified for the job (Awasty & Gupta, 2004). This is more relevant to upper-level positions which require a lot of trust and loyalty and can be developed only through personal relationships (Chokkar, Brodbeck & House, 2007; Davila & Elvira, 2005).

Finally, cultural dimensions such as uncertainty avoidance create a sense of anxiety about the unknown. Mexican employees fear loss of confidentiality in submitting their resumes to the Internet (Mejias, 2000). Loyalty is a very important cultural trait (Davila & Elvira, 2005) and applicants fear their employers (bosses) might see their resumes online (Mejias, 2000). Several online fraud activities, such as credit card transactions, have made Mexican cautious of the credibility of internet communications (Peterson, 2000). In India, some online recruiters have certification to ensure absolute privacy about applicant's employment details (Suryanarayanan, 2001), as employees do not want their superiors to know that they are looking for jobs elsewhere (Chokkar, Brodbeck & House, 2007).

Several studies Chokkar, Brodbeck & House, 2007; Davila & Elvira, 2005) have explored the effect of culture on human resource management practices but very few studies have addressed the role of national culture on e-recruitment practices (Gong, Li & Stump, 2007). This article will address the paucity of research in this domain. The next section will provide the national culture profile of India and Mexico and its influence on e-recruitment practices.

NATIONAL CULTURE: INDIA AND MEXICO

This study uses the GLOBE (Global Leadership and Organizational Behavior Effectiveness) cultural dimensions as it one of the most recent studies (Chokkar, Brodbeck & House, 2007) on organizational values and cultures. It has synthesized cultural findings from 61 countries on nine core cultural dimensions. The predominant cultural dimensions are assertiveness, future-orientation, gender egalitarianism, humane orientation, institutional collectivism, in-group collectivism,

performance orientation, power distance and uncertainty-avoidance. The definitions of these cultural dimensions are provided in Table 2.

Six of these dimensions have their origins from Hofstede's cultural studies (1980). The collectivism construct has been divided into two specific dimensions, institutional and in-group collectivism, to reflect differences between culture in the society at large and culture in organizations. The masculinity dimension has been developed into assertiveness and gender egalitarianism to reflect both individual differences and gender equity. Future and humane orientation have their origins from studies of Kluckholm and Strodbeck and the performance orientation was derived from McClelland's work on achievement (Chokkar, Brodbeck & House, 2007).

India ranked high on three dimensions namely; in-group collectivism, (Rank 4), power distance (Rank 16), and humane-orientation (Rank 9), while for other cultural dimensions it had the following ranks among the 61 countries surveyed; uncertainty-avoidance (Rank 29), institutional collectivism (Rank 25), future-orientation (Rank 15), performance-orientation (Rank 23) gender egalitarianism (Rank 16) and assertiveness (Rank 53).

Mexico ranked high on three dimensions namely; in-group collectivism (12th rank), assertiveness

Table 2. Definition of cultural dimensions (Adapted from Chhokar, Brodbeck, & House, 2007)

#	Cultural Dimension	Definition
1	Assertiveness	The degree to which individuals in organizations or societies are assertive in social relationships
2	Future-Orientation	The degree to which individuals in organizations or societies plan for the future
3	Gender Egalitarianism	The degree to which organizations or society promotes gender equality
4	Humane Orientation	The degree to which individuals in organizations or societies reward individuals for positive behavior
5	Institutional Collectivism	The degree to which organizational and institutional practices encourage collective action
6	In-group Collectivism	The degree to which individuals in societies reflect collectivist behavior
7	Performance Orientation	The degree to which upper management in organizations and leaders in societies reward group members for performance excellence
8	Power Distance	The degree to which organizations and societies accept power
9	Uncertainty-Avoidance	The degree to which organizations and societies avoid uncertainty by relying on practices and procedures

Table 3. National cultural dimension scores for India and Mexico

#	Cultural Dimension	India (Rank)	Mexico (Rank)
1	Assertiveness	3.73 (53)	4.45 (16)
2	Future Orientation	4.19 (15)	3.87 (26)
3	Gender Egalitarianism*	2.90 (55)	3.64 (16)
4	Humane Orientation	4.57 (9)	3.98 (34)
5	Institutional Collectivism	4.38 (25)	4.06 (38)
6	In-Group Collectivism	5.92 (4)	5.71 (12)
7	Performance Orientation	4.25 (23)	4.10 (32)
8	Power Distance	5.47 (16)	5.22 (30)
9	Uncertainty-Avoidance	4.15 (29)	4.18 (26)

(16th rank) and gender-egalitarianism (16th rank). Mexico had the following ranks for the other cultural dimensions. Uncertainty-avoidance (Rank 26), institutional collectivism (Rank 38), future-orientation (Rank 26), performance-orientation (Rank 32) gender egalitarianism (Rank 16) and assertiveness (Rank 16) (Chhokar, Brodbeck, & House, 2007). Table 2 provides scores and ranks for India and Mexico on these various cultural dimensions.

The next section will discuss the role of the GLOBE national cultural scores on e-recruitment practices in these India and Mexico. Specifically, this study will address the role of power-distance, in-group collectivism, gender egalitarianism and uncertainty-avoidance on e-recruitment practices.

POWER DISTANCE

Both the Indian and Mexican corporate world is characterized by clear hierarchies and formal structure. Employees are very reluctant to disagree with their boss or even call them by their first names (Gordon, 2002; Davila & Elvira, 2005). Formal titles such as Mr., Mrs., Dr, Sir or Madam are widely used in Indian corporate (Chokkar, 2007) and job titles such as "*licenciado*" or "*jefe*" are used in the Mexican corporate. Subordinates rarely circumvent their bosses', as such behavior is considered defiance to authority (Awasthy & Guptha, 2004; Davila & Elvira, 2005).

Scholars (Bagchi, Hart & Peterson, 2004) examined the influence of national culture on adoption of information technology (IT) products (such as internet, cell, and pagers) on 31 countries. They concluded that high power distance countries do no adopt IT products very easily into their work lives. The internet, cell phones and pagers promote a participatory method of interaction between subordinates and superiors, which the low power distance cultures enjoy and support. On the other hand, high power distance cultures prefer to keep a distance and maintain an autocratic decision style, and therefore rely less on information technology products that will increase such horizontal participation between superiors and subordinates.

Therefore, high power-distance cultures will not incorporate e-recruitment easily in their work lives as employers from such cultures would like to maintain an autocratic decision style, with a single person or persons making the staffing decisions. India and Mexico have high scores and ranks in power distance (India: 5.47, Rank 16; Mexico: 5.22; Rank 30), with India having higher scores than Mexico. The higher the power distance, the greater will be the resistance to absorb new technology, such as e-recruitment. Therefore organizations from these countries are less likely to incorporate e-recruitment into their staffing process than US multinationals which predominantly seek e-recruitment to get the best talent worldwide (Mollison, 2001). Therefore this leads to the first hypothesis:

H1: *Indian organizations are less likely to adopt e-recruitment practices than Mexican organizations.*

H2: *Indian and Mexican organizations are less likely to adopt e-recruitment practices than US multinationals operating in their countries.*

IN-GROUP COLLECTIVISM

Collectivist cultures are characterized by a very tight social framework where members distinguish themselves from their in-groups and out-groups. In-group members could be employees from the same caste, religion or family. In-group members always favor members from the same group. In India, it is very easy to distinguish a person's caste (social class) and religion by her or his last name, making it possible to make biased staffing decisions (Budhwar & Baruch, 2003). In Mexico, family and close friends are of paramount importance, such that recruiting practices are based on strong personal bonds that usually supersede organizational hiring criteria (Davila & Elvira, 2005).

Bagchi, Hart & Peterson, (2004) in a study on adoption of information technology (IT) products concluded that individualistic cultures adopt internet easily into their work lives. This is because individualistic cultures like the autonomy and impersonal interaction that IT products offer. Therefore, employees in such cultures feel connected with their employers albeit maintaining a good physical distance. On the contrary, collectivist cultures feel a strong sense of personal interaction between employers and employees rather than being connected by the wireless technology. In another study by Lim, Leung, Sia & Lee (2002) on individualism and internet shopping concluded that high individualistic cultures used the internet widely and had higher internet shopping rates. On the contrary, collectivist cultures rely on personal recommendations from a trusted source, such as friend, family or co-worker who has bought the product rather than shopping from an unknown (Internet) source.

Therefore, collectivist cultures will use less of the internet resources, such as e-recruitment, because they prefer to recruit and hire employees from the same in-group members. Therefore, they would not prefer to recruit applicants from the internet who are unknown and consequently cannot be trusted. India and Mexico have high scores and ranks in in-group collectivism (India: 5.92, Rank 4; Mexico: 5.71; Rank 12), with India having higher scores than Mexico. The higher the in-group collectivism, the greater will be the resistance to absorb new technology, such as e-recruitment. Therefore organizations from these countries are less likely to incorporate e-recruitment into their staffing process than US multinationals which predominantly seek e-recruitment to get the best talent worldwide. Therefore this leads to the second hypothesis:

H1: *Indian organizations are less likely to adopt e-recruitment practices than Mexican organizations.*

H2: *Indian and Mexican organizations are less likely to adopt e-recruitment practices than US multinationals operating in their countries.*

GENDER EGALITARIANISM

In Mexico, the strong *macho* culture focuses on promoting men to upper-level positions, while women are considered as glamorous support staff. Physical appearances are very important in Mexico, and women have to be physically attractive to climb up the corporate ladder, putting undue pressure on women. The masculine Mexican culture openly state in their job advertisements for physical characteristics such as slim and fair-skinned from their female applicants. The strong masculine orientation is demonstrated in exaggerated titles and open display of power and wealth (Messenger, 2004).

Similarly in India, there is a societal preference towards male dominance both in the corporate and social settings, although India had a female Prime-minister ruling the nation. In staffing, there is a strong preference for recruiting men in upper-level management positions (Chokkar, 2007). Multinationals, such as Motorola and Coca-Cola, are trying to reverse the skewed representation of women in upper-management positions by proactively hiring women and also making women a part of the recruiting panel for upper-level management positions (Agrwal, 2006).

Researchers (Bagchi, Hart & Peterson, 2004) in a study on information technology concluded that cultures with high femininity adopt new information technology, such as the internet and its resources, very easily into their daily work lives. Highly feminine cultures prefer to have a work-life balance which is supported by increased reliance on information technology products, such as internet. Gong, Li & Rodney (2007) examined the role of national culture and the usage of internet in 58 countries and concluded that masculinity hinders internet usage. Masculine cultures rely less on the internet usage as such advances in technology creates a sense of cyber equality at the work place – which might not be congruent with the assertive, dominating masculine cultures.

Therefore, high masculine cultures will not incorporate e-recruitment easily into their work lives as employers from such cultures would like to maintain a sense of personal domination by being involved in the hiring process at the work place. India and Mexico have different scores and ranks in masculinity (India: 2.90, Rank 55; Mexico: 3.64; Rank 16), with India having much lower scores than Mexico. The higher the masculinity, the greater will be the resistance to absorb new technology, such as e-recruitment. Therefore organizations from these countries are less likely to incorporate e-recruitment into their staffing process than US multinationals which proactively seek new applicants through the worldwide web

(Mollison, 2001). Therefore this leads to the third hypothesis:

H1: *Mexican organizations are less likely to adopt e-recruitment practices than Indian organizations.*

H2: *Indian and Mexican organizations are less likely to adopt e-recruitment practices than US multinationals operating in their countries.*

UNCERTAINTY-AVOIDANCE

Many Indian social customs suggest a culture that is very ritualistic and avoids the uncertain or unknown. Most business arrangements, such as beginning a new plant, have a very strong reliance on astrological predictions to identify if the time is favorable and therefore avoid any possible mishaps (Chokkar, 2007). In staffing, such uncertainty about the future makes organizations seek elaborate information through employment testing and employers conduct several interviews to seek elaborate information about applicants (Som, 2006). Similarly in Mexico, to reduce anxiety or the unknown, employers seek elaborate information of applicants, such as current age, family background, work background, marital status, photos, and number of children through interviews and biodata (O'Connell, Hattrup, Doverspike and Cober, 2002).

Lim, Leung, Sia & Lee (2002) examined the role of uncertainty avoidance on internet shopping in thirty-three countries. Their study concluded that cultures with low uncertainty avoidance had higher internet shopping rates. Cultures high in uncertainty-avoidance viewed internet shopping as risky and a complete change in shopping style, which is anxiety producing.

Therefore, cultures high in uncertainty avoidance will not incorporate e-recruitment easily into their work lives as employers from such cultures feel a sense of anxiety of the unknown (e-recruitment) rather than their traditional methods of hiring. India and Mexico have almost similar scores and ranks in uncertainty avoidance (India: 4.15, Rank 29; Mexico: 4;18; Rank 26), with India having slightly lower scores than Mexico. The higher the uncertainty-avoidance, the greater will be the resistance to absorb new technology, such as e-recruitment. Therefore organizations from these countries are less likely to incorporate e-recruitment into their staffing process than US multinationals which proactively seek the best global talent through the internet (Agrwal, 2006). Therefore this leads to the fourth hypothesis:

H1: Mexican organizations are more likely to adopt e-recruitment practices than Indian organizations.

H2: Indian and Mexican organizations are less likely to adopt e-recruitment practices than US multinationals operating in their countries.

IMPLICATIONS FOR MULTINATIONALS

Western Multinationals have to be wary as they compete for worldwide talent that transferring Western staffing practices, such as e-recruitment, might not work well in other cultures. Several cultures consider e-recruitment an impersonal approach to staffing. In a case study of four Mexican companies, the HR departments reported a sense of alienation with the applicants with the use of e-recruitment (Olivas-Lujan, Ramirez & Zapatu-Cantu, 2007).

Multinationals would benefit from making a cultural chart to understand the role of national cultural dimensions on e-recruitment practices in different countries. This chart would help them understand why certain cultures are slow to absorb this method of staffing. High power distance cultures have a strong need to dominate. Therefore in staffing, personal interviews and tests

gives them undeniable power. High masculine cultures thrive on assertiveness and open display of power, which personal methods of staffing provide. Collectivist cultures have a strong need to know and trust the applicant before hiring, which is not possible through e-recruitment. Cultures with high uncertainty do not trust any information that does not come from a reliable authentic source and therefore are unsure of the applicants' veracity (Bagchi, Hart & Peterson, 2004; Lim, Leung, Sia & Lee, 2002).

Most emerging economies are experiencing a "digital-divide", where distinct regions in their country have internet access and other regions do not (Lancaster, 2003; Curry and Kenney, 2006). This might come as a big surprise to US multinationals where computers are ubiquitous at almost every office. The national average for internet penetration in the US is 59%, with the Pacific states of Washington and Oregon boasting of a high average of 68% (Anonymous, 2003). Therefore US multinationals would benefit from making a chart that identifies internet penetration based on the different states or regions of the countries they are planning to establish overseas operations. The emphasis here is that identifying exact areas/states of internet usage in various countries to give a better perspective for multinationals to adopt their staffing practices overseas (Curry and Kenney, 2006; Lancaster, 2003).

FUTURE TRENDS

The role of culture on information technology is just emerging (Leidner & Kaysworth, 2006) and this paper advances to this promising research by identifying the role of culture and IT (information technology) adoption in two entirely different national contexts. Leidner & Kaysworth (2006) in their recent interesting theory on IT-culture conflict propose three main conflicts that result with the interaction of IT and national culture; systems, contribution, and vision.

A "system conflict" can occur when an IT application (such as e-recruitment) brings cultural nuances to the fore. E-recruitment brings out the cultural importance of a very personalized and collective approach that some national cultures have towards staffing. The "contribution conflict" occurs when group member core values contradicts with IT application (such as e-recruitment). Studies in Mexico have shown that managers felt a sense of isolation and of being disconnected with potential applicants in the process of e-recruitment. The core Mexican management values are being in close contact with the potential applicants (Olivas-Lujan, Ramirez & Zapatu-Cantu, 2007). A "vision conflict" occurs when the group's values about technology conflicts with the actual values of the IT application (such as e-recruitment). While e-recruitment is considered more efficient and time-saving (actual values), the groups values (such as those in Mexico or India) may consider it unreliable as they do not like to experiment with processes or systems that are unknown (Leidner & Kaysworth, 2006). Therefore researchers and practitioners have to be cognizant of these "conflicts" and their impact on e-recruitment.

Second, this research makes a strong connection between the concept of e-recruitment and national culture, which has not been previously examined. This is significant as multinationals are relying increasingly on this staffing method to leverage worldwide talent (Epstein & Singh, 2003). Multinationals should be cognizant that national cultures exert a strong influence on the outcomes of IT usage and adoption (Leidner & Kaysworth, 2006).

Third, this paper focuses on IT adoption in emerging economies, predicted to be the future business leaders. Most research articles focus on Western economies leaving emerging economies largely unexplored (Friedman, 2006). This article provides a good perspective on internet usage, internet penetration and role of culture in two leading emerging economies.

CONCLUSION

Internet recruiting will definitely continue to play a very prominent role as the world becomes more digitized. Multinationals are going to rely increasingly on this method of recruitment as it proven to bring high-caliber worldwide talent to your doorstep. Practitioners and researchers would benefit from making a "what if" chart or spreadsheet based on cultural dimensions scores and adaptability to internet usage. This would help identify as to why some countries still prefer a very different approach to staffing (Bagchi, Hart, Peterson, 2004).

REFERENCES

Anonymous (2001). Headhunters hit by slowdown. *Country Monitor, 9*, (22), 5.

Anonymous (2005). Internet penetration mainly a coastal thing. *Chain Store Age, 79*(10), 80.

Anonymous (2007). The coming crisis in employee turnover. *Growth Strategies, 1004*, 1-3.

Awasty, R., & Gupta, R. (2004). An Indo-Japanese MNC operating in India. *South Asian Journal of Management, 11*(3), 94-113.

Bagchi, K., Hart, P., & Peterson, M. (2004). National culture and information technology product adoption. *Journal of Global Information Technology Management, 7*(4), 29-46.

Budhwar, P., & Baruch, Y. (2003). Career Management practices in India: An empirical study. *International Journal of Manpower, 24*(6), 699-721.

Chokkar, J. (2007). India. Diversity and Complexity in Action. In J. Chhokar, F. Brodbeck, & R. House (Eds.), *Culture and Leadership across the World. The GLOBE book of In-depth studies of 25 societies*. Lawrence Erlbaum Associates. Mahwah, New Jersey.

Chhokar, J., Brodbeck, F., & House, R. (Eds.). (2007). *Culture and leadership across the world. The GLOBE book of in-depth studies of 25 societies.* Lawrence Erlbaum Associates. Mahwah, New Jersey.

Curry, J., & Kenney, M. (2006). Digital divide or digital development? The Internet in Mexico. *First Monday, 11*(3), 1-21.

Curry, J., Contreras, O., & Kenney, M. (2001). The Internet and E-Commerce Development in Mexico. Working Paper 144. *The Berkely Roundtable on the International Economy.*

Davila, A., & Elvira, M. (2005). Culture & Human Resources Management in Latin America in (Ed) *Managing Human Resources in Latin America.* New York: Routledge.

Emmond, K. (2005). Investing in IT. *Business Mexico, 15*(5), 22-28.

Epstein, R., & Singh, G. (2003). Internet Recruiting Effectiveness: Evidence from a biomedical device firm. *International Journal of Human Resources Development and Management, 3*(3), 216-225.

Fitzgerald, M., & Liburt, E. (1999). Spanish-language job site launches. *Editor & Publisher, 132*(48), 3.

Feldman, D., & Klas, B. (2002). Internet job hunting: A field study of applicant experiences with on-line recruiting. *Human Resource Management, 41*(2), 175.

Friedman, T. (2005). *The World is flat.* New York: Farrar, Straus and Giroux.

Friedman, T. (2006). The World is Flat. Updated and Expanded. New York: Farrar, Straus and Giroux.

Frauenheim, E. (2006). Indian Leaders in demand amid rapid expansion. *Workforce Management, 85*(7), 6-9.

Galanaki, E. (2002). The decision to recruit online. *Career Development International, 7*(4). 243-250.

Gong, W., Li, Z., & Stump, R. (2007). Global internet use and access: Cultural considerations. *Asia Pacific Journal of Marketing and Logistics, 19*(1), 57-73.

Gordon, J. (2002). India or Bust. *Fortune, 169*(8), 65-69.

Jasrotia, P. (2001). E-recruitment market registers major growth. *Express Computer.* Retrieved from http://www.itpeopleindia.com/20011008/cover1.htm

Lancaster, J. (2003). Village Kiosks Bridge India's Digital Divide. *Washington Post, Oct 12th*, A01.

Lath, S. (2006) The Battle of Two Portals; Yahoo and MSN; are getting ready to fight it out in the Indian market, which may still be small but promises a lot. *Business Today, 128.*

Leidner, D., & Kayworth, T. (2006). A Review of Culture in Information Systems Research: Toward a Theory of Information Technology Culture Conflict. *MIS Quarterly, 30*(2), 357-370.

Lim, K., Leung, K., Sia, C., & Lee, M. (2002). Is e-commerce boundaryless. Effects of individualism-collectivism and uncertainty avoidance on Internet shopping. *Journal of International Business Studies, 35*(1), 545-559.

Mejias, C. (2000). *Latin American Trends in Human Resources. Society for Human Resource Management.* V.A.: Alexandria

Messenger, R. (2004). Style Matters. *Business Mexico, 14*(7), 30-32.

Mitra, K. (2006). The New Dotcom Millionaire. *Business Today* (p. 124).

Mollison, C. (2001). The Internet World Interview. *Internet World Magazine.* Retrieved from http://

www.iw.com/magazine.php?inc=050101/05.01.0
1interview.html.

Murray, S. (2001). From tiny job boards into mighty career networks. A brief history of online recruitment. *Financial Times*, 04.

Navarrete, C., & Pick, J. (2002). Information technology expenditure and industry performance: The case of the Mexican Banking Industry. *Journal of Global Information Technology Management, 5*(2), 7-29.

O'Connell, M., Hattrup, K., Doverspike, D., & Cober, A. (2002). The Validity of "Mini" Simulations for Mexican Retail Salespeople. *Journal of Business and Psychology, 16*(4), 593-599.

Olivas-Lujan, M., Ramirez, J., & Zapata-Cantu, L (2007). E-HRM in Mexico: Adapting innovativeness for global competitiveness. *International Journal of Manpower, 28*(5), 418-434.

Othman, R., & Musa, N. (2007). E-reccruitment. Pros Vs Cons. *Public Sector ICT Management Review, 1*(1), 35-39.

Peterson, A. (2000). Opening a Portal: E-Commerce apostle target Latin America. *Wall Street Journal* (*Eastern Edition*), A1.

Pollitt, D. (2005). E-recruitment gets the Nike tick of approval. *Human Resource Management International Digest, 13*(2) 33-36.

Ramamurthi, R. (2001). Wipro's Chairman Azim Premji on building a world class Indian company. *Academy of Management Executive, 18*(12), 13-19.

Rudich, J. (2000). Job hunting on the web. *Link up, 17*(2), 21-25.

Sessa, V., & Taylor, J. (2000). *Executive Selection: Strategies for Success.* San Francisco: Jossey-Bass and The Center for Creative Leadership.

Solomon, J. (2005). India poaches U.S executives for tech jobs. *Wall Street Journal.* (Eastern Edition), B1.

Som, A. (2006). Bracing for MNC competition through innovative HRM practices: The way ahead for Indian firms. *Thunderbird International Review, 48(*2), 207-237.

Srinivasan, P., Babu, V., & Sahad, P. (2005). Durable Dotcoms. *Business Today*, 60.

Sridhar, B. (2005). E-Recruitment, the right way. *The Hindu.* Retrieved from http://www.hinduonnet.com/jobs/0503/2005030900350600.htm

Suryanarayanan, M. (2001). A Guide to Better Positions and Better Performance. *The Hindu.* Retrieved from http://www.hinduonnet.com/jobs/0105/05230014.htm.

Taylor, J. (2003). Decisions. Jeff Taylor founder and chairman, Monster. *Management Today*, 26.

Tong, D., & Sivanand, C, (2005). E-recruitment Service Providers Review. International and Malaysian. *Employee Relations, 27*(1/2), 103-118.

Vinuta, V. (2005). E-Recruitment is here to Stay. *Express online Computer.* Retrieved from http://www.expresscomputeronline.com/20050418/technologylife01.shtml

Zakaria, F. (2006). India Rising, *Newsweek, CXLVII* (10), 34-43.

KEY TERMS

Contribution Conflict: A conflict that occurs when group members' core work values contradicts with IT application (such as e-recruitment)

Digital Divide: A split between people who have access to the Internet and people who do not have access to the Internet due to economical and technological reasons.

E-Recruitment: The complete automation of the recruitment process whereby applications and resumes are screened online.

Internet Penetration: Indicates the percentage of internet users in any country.

Naukri.com: An employment website in India that means "job" in the Indian national language, Hindi.

System Conflict: A conflict occurs when an IT application (such as e-recruitment) brings cultural differences to the vanguard.

Vision Conflict: A conflict that occurs when the group's values about technology conflicts with the actual values of the IT application (such as e-recruitment).

Section V
Modeling and Designing e-HRM Architectures

Chapter XIV
Modeling Human Resources in the Emergent Organization

Marielba Zacarias
Universidade do Algarve, Portugal

Rodrigo Magalhães
Instituto Superior Técnico, Portugal

José Tribolet
Instituto Superior Técnico, Portugal

ABSTRACT

This chapter asserts that a proper integration of HRIS within organizations entails extending the scope of HRM technologies to encompass modeling frameworks enabling the analysis and (re)design of HR behaviors. Furthermore, it argues that the process of emergence, which constitutes the cornerstone of contemporary sociological thought on organization, lies at the root of the usage of technologies capable of addressing the emergent nature of HR behaviors. This chapter describes and illustrates a bottom-up modeling framework that takes into account the problem of emergence and allows (1) an enhanced traceability of HR, (2) a situated, context-aware HR modeling, and (3) HR modeling from action repositories. The present framework is illustrated with a case study, where it is used to capture, model, and analyze work practices.

INTRODUCTION

An agenda for Human Resources Information Systems (HRIS) research is put forward by Magalhaes and Ruel (2008), who propose an inte-grative perspective for HRIS research, and stress that research in organizational and information systems cannot be separated. They argue that the integration of HRIS within organizations can be seen as an intricate web of many causes and consequences and that HRIS cannot be studied separate from the organizational context where they are interwoven. This assertion has two main implications; (1) when researching HRIS from an integrated perspective, it is crucial that the researcher approaches the topic from an appropriate ontological point of view, and (2) the scope of Human Resource Management (HRM) should not only include applications to support traditional HRM functions, but also frameworks to capture, analyze, and eventually modify the behavior of human resources (HR). Such frameworks should be developed accordingly to the ontological position defined. Social emergence is the ontological point of view defended by those authors. Sawyer (2005: 213) explains that the emergence paradigm research "focuses on the micro-interactional mechanisms by which shared social phenomena emerge and on how those emergencies constrain those mechanisms".

In this paper we discuss an issue, which is relevant to HRIS, i.e. the problem of modeling individual-level behavior in the context of broader organizational action. Hence, it is important that the problem under review is placed within an ontological framework of the organizational phenomenon. Ontology and methodology are two sides of the same coin, meaning that the methodology used to research a particular phenomenon will depend entirely on the ontological perspective that one holds. It is submitted, firstly, that the emergence of the organizational phenomenon depends to a large degree upon the alignment between the individual and the organization. Secondly, that such alignment cannot be taken for granted; rather, it requires conscious, systematic and continuous efforts. Thirdly, that the alignment of the individual and the organization can be facilitated by (1) the development of a semi-formal models of agent behaviour at different organizational levels and (2) methods and tools to build, update and analyze the representations based on those models.

Whereas current modeling efforts are mostly directed at organizational perspectives, little attention has been paid to individual or inter-personal perspectives. Several approaches to modeling organization strategy, processes and resources have been developed. However, models for individual or inter-personal levels are scarce and have typically, different purposes. Research is needed to address the modeling of individual and interpersonal behaviors and the definition of proper ways of linking these behaviors with perspectives of higher organizational levels. More specifically, research is needed to raise awareness and to illustrate the benefits of aligning individuals and the organization. The aims of such modeling are as follows:

- Enabling the organization to capture and visualize different concerns of individual behavior.
- Enabling individuals to understand the relationship of their daily actions with organizational resources and activities.
- Facilitating the analysis, discussion and (re)design of individual and inter-personal work.

Organizational modelings are of interest to HRIS due to the closeness of this category of information system and all organizational phenomenon. If organizations are defined essentially as groups of people working for a common goal, then it is clear that any information system dealing with human resources will tightly interwoven with the organization itself. There are many schools of thought in organizational modeling but in this paper we are particularly interested in a school of thought guided by the following principles: (1) agents have acting, deliberation, and learning capabilities, (2) agent exhibit multiple behaviors that depend of specific contexts of execution, and (3) such behaviors should be captured from agent actions and interactions.

The school of thought in organizational modelling which is followed in this paper considers organizational phenomena as being emergent in nature. Hence, we begin the article by putting forward a model of emergent organization. The model is inspired on the evolutionary logic of autopoiesis which explains the construction of social groups starting from their biological origins and on Mingers' (2001) hierarchy of self-referential social systems. Each level exhibits to the same autopoietic characteristics of *operational closure* and *self-referentiality* and represents a level of sensemaking at which the organization can be analysed or diagnosed. The remainder of the paper is devoted to an exposition on the proposed modelling approach.

THE EMERGENT ORGANIZATION

Mingers (2001) argues that although autopoiesis cannot be transferred as a whole to social theory, there is one key principle of autopoiesis which can—the principle of organization closure. Such argument is based on the assumption that throughout the entire hierarchy of systems, as proposed by Boulding (1956), all the systems' levels exhibit characteristics of organizational closure. As we have seen above, for autopoiesis the main guideline for the characterization of living, autonomous systems is not a set of inputs and outputs, but the nature of their internal coherence, which arise out of their interconnectedness (Varela, 1984). In turn, organizational closure "requires some form of self-reference, whether material, linguistic or social, rather than the more specific process of self-production" (Mingers, 2001: 111). Thus, it is suggested that organizational closure and self-referentiality are criteria which unequivocabily define social systems.

There are many simple examples of organizational closure and self-referentiality in every-day life. Conversations are one case in point. In order to maintain its internal coherence, a conversation between two persons has to be self-referential, meaning that it must anchored on statements already made and for the conversation to remain meaningful it must build on past knowledge. Our own perception of events around us is also self-referential. An example comes from Gestalt theory in psychology and concerns the phenomenon of apparent movement. When the light in one place is turned off and the light in another place is immediately turned on, we experience the perception of light movement. This illusion is the basis of the apparent movement of neon advertising signs. The observer does not see two lights going on or off and she immediately infers that something is moving. The immediate perception, on the basis of past knowledge, is one of movement and it is only by careful analysis that the observer realizes that there was no physical movement (Hill, 1997).

In Table 1 it is explained how social systems evolve from the level of the individual to the level of society, consistently maintaining the attributes of organizational closure and self-referentiality. Starting from the non-social individual, enacted cognition theory (Varela et al, 1991) posits that knowledge of the world is formed through the establishment of enduring relationships between the movement of the body and the changes in the neuronal activity of the brain. In the words of Varela (1992: 260) "to know is to evaluate through our living, in a creative circularity".

The next stage is the stage where the first inter-personal bonds are created. In order for the non-social individual to become a social individual the first and crucial ingredient is communication, the most fundamental social category. As defined by Luhmann, communication is "the reciprocal interaction between two individuals" (in Mingers, 2001:116). Whereas actions may not be inherently social, communication is always social and for action to be classified as social there must be communication involved. Furthermore, communication generates understanding, meaning, emotions and behaviour, the bases for the formation of bonds between people. "Double contingency" is the basic mechanism behind the creation of such bonds.

"Double contingency" is an expression coined by Luhmann (in Mingers, 2001: 117) to explain the situation that everybody faces in interpersonal interactions of not knowing what the other person knows or thinks. Given that knowledge is personal and self-referential, when we speak or when we listen our interpretation of what we said or of what we heard is always subjective and we are permanently engaged in an ongoing effort to "guess" what the other person's expectations are. Thus, double contingency can be summed up in the following sentence: "I will do what (I think) you expect of me if you do what (you think) I expect of you". Still according to Luhmann, it is the resolution of this daily conundrum that leads to the establishment of an emergent order of regular patterns of behaviour known as social structure.

The explanation regarding the level of social networks and its evolution to the level above— society/organization—rely also on the social theory developed by Anthony Giddens. Giddens (1984) makes an important contribution to an understanding of how social systems are formed and how reality is socially constructed. For that author, the evolution of society is radically different from the evolution of living organisms in that society is a human production. Giddens' central proposition—structuration theory—provides a conceptual basis for explaining how social systems are formed through communication, with new meanings and new words being generated through a continuous process of narrative making by social actors.

Social boundaries, social norms, and the emerging social practices transcend the individual and remain even after the individuals have departed. Particular members may join or leave but the social organization carries on. This is true of small groups, such as families, micro-communities or sub-cultures in the workplace but it is also true of larger groups such as clubs, associations, firms, armies or nations. The transcendental or extra-subjective properties of social organization are the same at both the level of social networks and of society/organization.

THE INDIVIDUAL-ORGANIZATION ALIGNMENT

The problem of aligning individuals and organizations has been acknowledged in several works. Agency theory (Alchian, 1972) defines an agency

Table 1. Emergent levels of self-referential (social) systems (adapted from Mingers, 2001)

Level	Type of component	Structural relations	Mode of organizational closure or self-referentiality	Emergent properties
Society/ Organi-zation	Societal communication	Interaction generates society and society structures interaction	Closed communication domains	Closed networks of communication bound by structural rules re-produced through social interaction
Social networks	Recurrent interaction within groups	Structural coupling to a behavioural domain in terms of meaning, legiti-mation and power	Conversations	Enduring social or cultural practices
The social individual	Direct interaction between people	Expectation of other's behaviour in terms of meaning, emotion and behaviour	Double contingency	Creation of inter-person-al bonds
The embodied individual	Body, action and ner-vous system	Neuronal and bodily relations	Enactive or embodied cognition	Self-awareness. Learn-ing

relationship as a contract between two parties; the principal, integrated by one or more persons, who engage another party, enacted by another person (defined as the agent) to perform some service on their behalf (Jensen,1976). Assuming that both parties to the relationship are utility maximizers, there is good reason to believe that the agent will not always act in the best interests of the principal.

In Agency Theory, the alignment between individuals and organizations is regarded in terms of inducing an "agent" to behave as if he were maximizing the "principal's". In this sense, it is a 'one-sided' notion. The principal can limit divergences from his interest by establishing appropriate incentives for the agent and by incurring in monitoring costs designed to minimize undesirable activities of the agent. The agency structure is applicable in a variety of settings, ranging from macro-level issues to micro-level dyad phenomena (Eisenhardt, 1989). In summary, the domain of agency theory is relationships that mirror the basic agency structure of a principal and an agent engaged in cooperative behavior, but with different goals or attitudes toward risk.

In the "The Power of Alignment", Labovitz (1997) describes the benefits of aligning organization's strategy, processes and people. In this book, organizational alignment entails both integrating key systems and processes to environmental changes, and developing capabilities that enable managers to; (1) shape business strategy with real-time information from customers, (2) link teams and processes to the changing needs of customers, (3) connect employees' behavior to the mission of the company, and (4) developing a culture where all these elements work together seamlessly.

The authors of this book distinguish two types of alignment; vertical and horizontal. A vertical alignment is achieved when employees understand organization-wide goals and their roles in achieving them. A horizontal alignment

means aligning business processes with customer needs. More specifically, it means understanding what customers want, as well as creating and delivering what the customers want, when and how they want it.

The need of aligning individual and organizational concerns has also been acknowledged in the work of V. Dignum (Dignum,2004). According to Dignum, only when the organization and its individuals work together to organize the flow of processes and resources in a way that they simultaneously address individual requirements and the strategic objectives of the organization, innovation is enabled and, thus, a competitive and sustainable advantage of the organization. Consequently, enterprise models need to reflect this interaction between individual and organizational views.

When regarding the individual-organizational alignment problem from the ontological viewpoint of social emergence, departing from the individual level (non-social individual) of organizational emergence discussed in section 2, there are some key questions that individuals may legitimately ask about their organizations. These include questions made from an individual perspective such as: *who am I in this organization, that is, which roles do I play? how, when, where or why is work accomplished here?,* and questions from a collective i.e. organizational perspective, such as; *who are our members, what roles do they play? How, when, where or why do they accomplish their work?*

Answers to these questions will clearly help in the effort of understanding the evolution from the first to the second level of emergence, i.e. the non-social and social individual levels. Such evolution is done through a process known as *sensemaking* (Di Paolo, 2005). Sensemaking is defined as the mechanism that allows the process of socialization to evolve in human beings. Organizations exist largely in the minds of organization members in the form of cognitive maps, or images. These maps require a certain level of social agreement and cooperation derived from human propensity for social interaction. Furthermore, in mapping and talking about organizations and their environments, they are reified, that is, they are made real. Sensemaking shifts the focus of the individual-organizational problem to achieving shared understandings as an essential pre-requisite of reaching inter-agent agreements. Under this viewpoint, the alignment between individuals and organizations is always partial, and requires conscious and continuous efforts. Hence, it is regarded both as a process and a product.

Consequently, the individual-organization alignment refers firstly, to the capacity of answering the questions related to the individuals and organizations as a whole. Second, it refers to achieving an acceptable level of coherence between individual and organizational answers. For example, the roles a given individual play in the organization should be consistent with the roles the individual thinks he plays; or the particular ways that individuals have of accomplishing activities should be in line with organization's processes and goals. Lastly, achieving this coherence should require a reasonable amount of effort. On one side, the organizations should be tooled with methodologies and technologies to retrieve the proper information about individuals. On the other side, individuals should be able to relate their work to organizational processes and resources.

An individual-organizational alignment means that the organization and its individuals work together to organize the flow of processes and resources such that they both address individual requirements and the strategic objectives of the organization (Dignum, 2004). An adequate alignment level between individuals and organizations enables innovation and, consequently, a competitive and sustainable advantage of the organization. Organizational models need to reflect this interaction between individual and organizational views.

ENTERPRISE MODELING

Modelling is present in almost every discipline. One overlapping work area of both organization science and IS communities is Enterprise –or Organization- Modelling (EM). Organizations communicate, document and understand their activity through models (Caetano et al., 2004). In organization sciences, models are visual representations of given theories, described in terms of concepts and their relationships (Hatch and Cunliffe, 2006). Organization theorists use them to make abstractions more tangibles. In this field, the main goal of models is to provide ways of thinking about the organization and to produce management principles based on these ways of thinking. These models have a high level of abstraction and are described in natural language. Thus, they are limited to human use and may lead to different interpretations.

EM has also been addressed by two fields related to computer sciences: IS and Artificial Intelligence (AI). In these fields, it has been mainly used as communication tools to facilitate the design and implementation of business applications (Shekkerman, 2004). Despite their differences, the frameworks developed in these fields share some characteristics. First, they allow representing different concerns of enterprise in terms of several perspectives, dimensions or architectural viewpoints. Second, these perspectives are inter-related, that is, means of relating concepts from different perspectives are provided. Third, enterprise models are described with semi-formal or formal languages and most of them enable graphical representations.

The development of IS/AI EM languages have proved the communication power of these languages and particularly, of its graphical representations. The effect of using more formal syntax and semantics, is two-fold; first, they allow its processing by automated agents. Second, they reduce the possibilities of giving raise to different, inconsistent interpretations. The communicational advantage of graphic enterprise models seems promising for purposes beyond systems development. They can be valuable tools in analyzing and (re)designing not only the organization itself, but also its members. Nonetheless, achieving this purpose entails overcoming some limitations.

Current EM frameworks are restricted to concerns relevant to system stakeholders. Moreover, these models are not consistent with the contemporary paradigm of organizations, since they are based on static, mechanistic and deterministic views of the phenomenon. They are also based on an objective position of reality, that is, organizational representations offer an 'aerial' view, are assumed to be unique and shared by all members of the organization. Another limitation of current EM approaches stems from the model acquisition process. Several frameworks provide means to capture the data required to build the models. These means have varying levels of detail and support among the different approaches. In general terms, the building process is mostly manual, and supported by data collection techniques including interviews, surveys, text/document analysis, among others. This type of acquisition requires effort and is time-consuming, thus hinders updating representations to reflect organizational changes, as soon as they take place.

Regarding model construction, the development of information technologies (IT) has increased dramatically the number and frequency of computer mediated interactions among individuals. The value of emerging IT is not restricted to supporting daily operations. Footprints of these interactions can be found within the repositories of all these applications. Enterprise applications also provide analytical power, with tools allowing the discovery of hidden patterns in data. Several frameworks have been proposed to use these applications to enhance and accelerate sensing and reacting capabilities of organizations. The development of semantic technologies allows the extracting relevant patterns from non-structured computer-mediated interactions. Hence, these technologies can be used in further enhancing the analytical power of enterprises. The combined use of all these technologies looks promising in facilitating the acquisition and update of enterprise representations from actual actions and interactions among organizational members.

It is important to note however, that an essential pre-requisite for the successful use of all these technologies entails overcoming the former limitation. This means developing models addressing different concerns of organizations and its human resources. The definition of these models need necessarily to be supported by exploratory research works reflecting on the nature of organizations, its human resources, and the critical questions that need to be answered.

AN AGENT AND CONTEXT-CENTRIC FRAMEWORK TO MODEL HR

The ontological position of emergence focuses on how organizational behavior and hence, the behavior of its human resources, is constructed in a bottom-up fashion by increasingly complex agents and contexts. However, current EM approaches are essentially process-centered views where the complexity and adaptiveness of organizational agents is completely disregarded. The model briefly described in this section aims at overcoming current EM limitations in addressing agent-centric behaviors, and was developed as part of a doctoral research program (Zacarias, 2008).

This work makes the case for an enterprise perspective centered on agents and contexts. More specifically, this research (1) develops an agent-centric perspective that is complementary to activity, technology, information, and strategy/organization perspectives, and (2) proposes a way to link the agent perspective with these perspectives. The concept of context provides the key for this 'linkage'. The proposed view is part of a conceptual framework, integrated by a layered model of organizational agents, and a methodological approach to build representations based on this model. This framework aims at enriching enterprise modeling, providing an analytical tool for organizational analysis and (re)design ends.

An "Architected" Model of Organizational Agents

The model departs from five essential concepts (resource, activity, agent, role, and context), and integrates agent and enterprise architectures to acknowledge in a single framework multiple concerns of agent behavior.

Resources are the entities relevant for the operation of the organization. Resources may be concrete (tools, materials, people) and abstract (information, knowledge or skills). **Activities** describe what organizations do. Activities are always abstractions. Acknowledging the abstract nature of activities is essential in addressing the alignment between daily actions of individuals with organizational activities and resources because it highlights the fact that the relationship of a single

action with activities depends on how each activity is defined or regarded by a given agent.

Agents are individual and collective human resources. This model explicitly acknowledges that agents have acting, deliberation and learning capabilities. As a result, agent behavior is captured in terms of inter-dependent activity and resource-related roles, which are organized in three layers; (1) action, (2) deliberation, and (3) change/learn layer (fig. 1). The separation of behavioral concerns in different layers allows not only addressing more complex concerns such as deliberation and change, but also defining modes of representation consistent with the complexity level of each behavioral layer. Moreover, it provides a means of exploring and uncovering the influence between different concerns.

Another distinctive feature of this model is that it also acknowledges that agents play different roles in different interaction contexts, at different times. Action layer **roles** define agent observable behaviours, which is expressed in a particular set of actions. It is noteworthy that this particular set of actions may vary from agent to agent. Hence, this model acknowledges that agent behaviour is *partially* determined by roles.

Figure 1. Architecture of organizational agents

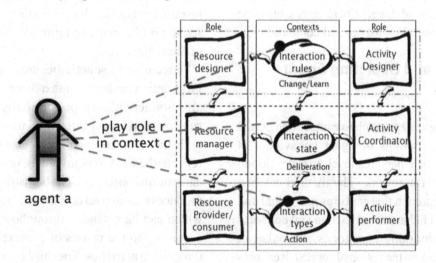

Actions are acts that change the state of particular resource items. Actions typically use and/or produce one or more resource items. Actions may be communicative or non-communicative. Communicative actions involve sender and receiver agents, and are mostly succeeded by a reply. In this model, **interactions** are defined as ordered pairs of communicative actions where the second is a reply to the first. Due to the abstract nature of activities and resources, the relationship of a single action or interaction and its associated resource items with activities and resources, is not necessarily straightforward. Understanding this relationship requires situating such actions within their corresponding context.

Contexts are defined as situations created and updated by streams of actions. These streams reveal observable context features such as typical action types, resource items, as well as the action history. Contexts have also some non-observable features such as the commitments that reflect the state of interactions and can be inferred from the types of actions and interactions observed. Other non-observable features such as rules governing agent actions and interactions, need to be elicited from the participating agents. The analysis of context features is essential in defining the meaning of actions. The specific feature to be analyzed will depend on the specific behavioral layer addressed. Hence, in this model, agent behaviors cannot be dissociated from their associated contexts.

Capturing and Depicting Agent Behaviors

A methodological approach to capture and depict model representations of agent behaviours at personal and inter-personal levels was developed as part of the framework. The method offers a bottom-up approach that captures individual and inter-personal behaviours of action and deliberation layers from action repositories, and makes an instrumental use of the notion of context. It encompasses six activities; (1) bootstrapping, (2) action capture, (3) context discovery, (4) context-based analysis and (5) context integration (fig 2).

In **bootstrapping**, the basic action types and resources to be registered are defined, and their meanings discussed. Ideally, action and resource definitions are registered. **Action capture** creates the action repositories. Actions are captured in natural language, using a structure <subject, verb, object>, where the subject represents the agent performing the action, the verb represents the type of action performed, and the object the resources involved. **Context discovery** entails identifying, characterizing, and labelling *personal* contexts. Personal contexts define the personal view that an individual has o a given context. In this activity, personal contexts become 'entities' characterized by a set of keywords. **Context visualization** displays context main characteristics to their owners, for validation purposes. In **context-based analysis,** personal contexts are used as units of analysis in representing individual and inter-personal strategies. Context-based representations offer situated 'pictures' of the observed subjects and the relationships between them, and allow discussing which behaviours should be standardized or (re)designed. **Context integration** takes places when strategies are considered good practices, and they are standardized as formal organizational behaviour and consequently, update current task/resource models. The case study described in section 6 illustrates and provides further details of these activities.

Executing these activities creates three cycles. First, action capture, context discovery and visualization activities are performed by the observed subjects, and are repeated until they are satisfied with the contexts identified. The second cycle reflects the iterations involving observed agents and external observers. The bootstrapping activity produces an initial set of action and resource types, which can be extended throughout the process, according to the results of context analysis and integration activities. The third cycle is due to the evolution of agent behaviors, requiring new iterations of the whole process from time to time.

Figure 2.Capturing and depicting agent-centric behaviors

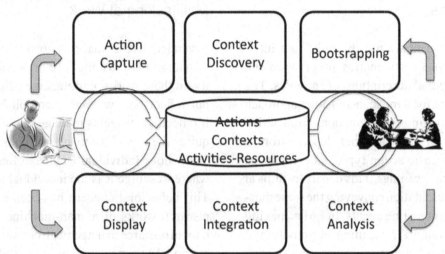

Regarding Emergence in HR Modeling

The ontological position of emergence poses several requirements on organizational and HR models. The model put forward proposes some solutions that aim at overcoming the shortcomings of organizational modelling in satisfying such requirements.

Enhanced Traceability of HR

Current EM modelling approaches address organization's complexity defining several, inter-related perspectives. Nonetheless, none of these approaches fully acknowledge that agents themselves are complex entities, which also needs to be handled with their own architecture. Consequently, EM frameworks provide limited support in addressing questions about organizational agents. A framework that integrates agent and organizational architectures and contributes

to an uncovering of agent-centric behaviours is needed.

Situated HR Modeling

Current EM approaches assume the existence of unique, external viewpoints, and produce 'aerial' representations i.e. representations seen from the outside of the organization. These representations, while meaningful for some organizational members, are meaningless or incorrect for others. Enterprise representations make sense for specific agents, and specific contexts. Departing from actual actions and interactions, and the inclusion of the notion of context enables situated enterprise representations. Modeling frameworks that take this fact into account and allow the modeling of behaviors situated within specific contexts are needed. Developing 'context-aware' representations provides the conceptual richness required to address more properly, the complexity of organizations and their HR. It also enables a proper understanding and comparison of such representations, as well as their evolution in time.

Capturing HR Behaviors from Action Repositories

Enterprise models are mostly built from interviews, surveys, questionnaires, observation and analysis of textual descriptions of activities. The requirement is for a model acquisition approach that allows creating representations from action repositories, an approach that departs from a discussion of basic action types, and resources, as well as their meanings. This departure aims at building representation conveying the same message to all participating agents. In EM achieving consensus around the meaning of activity and resource names requires is a time consuming processes. The usage of small semantic units such as actions and resource-related items as the basic building blocks of the approach eased the process of achieving consensus around their meaning.

Capturing and Modeling Work Practices

Current EM frameworks capture generic task, activity, and process model that define behaviour at a role level. Modelling work practices require the capability of answering the question; "How does Individual i perform Activity A? Which resource(s) use?". This compound question has been addressed by independent research in systems development and simulation, but not by EM frameworks.

Capturing and modeling work practices means building diagrams situated in particular contexts, reflecting the particular action types, action flows and resources employed by given individuals in performing given tasks. Since these resources can be human, diagrams reflecting inter-personal patterns must be built. This means the ability to answer questions such as (1) "Who (Individual i1) interact with who (Individual i2)?", and (2) "How does Individual i1 interact with Individual i2?" These questions must be addressed using a representation language and model acquisition approach better fitted for purposes of organization analysis.

Capturing and Modeling Human Multitasking at Work

Several researchers have acknowledged the impact of human multitasking in individual productivity. In these works, multitasking behaviour does not reflect how work is accomplished. Rather, it reflects how agents manage themselves. It requires the capability to answer question such as "How does Individual I manage Resource R?", where Resource R is the individual him/herself. This behavioral concern has been addressed in research works of human-machine interaction, human resource management, cognitive sciences, but no EM framework has addressed it.

Capturing and modeling multitasking requires using a deliberation layer which means using the notion of context to define work fragmentation, rather than tasks. Multitasking behavior is modeled in terms of context interleaving, and context activation rules. Different tasks may require similar resources. Likewise, the same task may require different resources, at different stages. Since switching costs are caused by the need to 'pull' different set of physical and cognitive resources, and contexts reflect resource groupings, this criteria is more appropriate to measure work fragmentation than tasks.

Aligning Design with Execution

The problem of linking individual behaviours with organizational activities and resources is disregarded by EM acquisition approaches, which depart from higher level of abstraction. The problem of aligning organization's design with actual execution using action logs, has been acknowledged and addressed by the process mining research. However, the focus of this field is restricted to the alignment of pre-defined application workflows, with workflows acquired from execution data collected from logs produced by WFMS, and enterprise applications. This work does not collect data from non-structured actions stored in message-based, groupware applications, where messages are not associated with tasks. It also disregards non-computer mediated actions and interactions, which require to be registered manually. Without unstructured, non-classified actions, it is not possible to get accurate definitions of actual organization workflows.

CASE STUDY: CAPTURING AND MODELING WORK PRACTICES

Work practice is a concept that originates in socio-technical systems, business anthropology, work systems design and management science (Sierhuis, 2000). Work systems involve people engaging in activities over time, interacting with each other, and with machines, tools, documents, and other artifacts. Work systems and work practice evolve slowly over time. The integration and use of technology, the distribution and allocation of people, organizational roles and procedures, and the facilities where the work occurs largely determine this evolution (Sierhuis, 2002).

Degani and Wiener (1997) distinguish between procedures and practices. Procedures are predefined specifications of tasks. Practices encompass what people do with procedures. People either conform to procedures or deviate from it, even if the procedure is mandatory. Whereas process, activity, and task models are appropriate to represent standard operating procedures, they are not able of representing actual work practices.

Modeling work practices offers a means of uncovering problems not detected in process or tasks models. Capturing work practices means understanding how specific individuals accomplish tasks in specific circumstances. The importance of modeling and simulating work practices in improving work systems design has been acknowledged and addressed in (Sierhuis 1997; 2000; 2002), and in (Brèzillon, 2001; Pomerol, 2002). According to Sierhuis, modeling and simulating work practice should emphasize:

- What people actually do, not just official job functions
- What people are doing every minute of the day, where they are, and what they are perceiving, not just working on one task at a time
- The collaboration between two or more agents, such as face-to-face conversations, telephone calls, etc.
- That people have personal identity, and are not interchangeable resources

These research works show that modeling work practices is not restricted to support IS/IT systems. Rather, it is valuable in (re) designing practices themselves, and consequently the people performing them. Thus, a better knowledge of work practices is useful not only for IS developers but also for organization analysts and managers. Even workers can benefit by having better understandings of how their daily work relates to business processes and resources of their organizations.

Organizational Setting

The organizational setting is a furniture retail company. This is a Portuguese organization, in the market for more than 30 years. Nowadays the companay employs more than 1000 workers in 20 stores and 5 warehouses distributed throughout Portugal. In 2001, the company adopted the ERP SAP R/3© to support its operations. The adoption of SAP streamlined the company business processes. In spite of this effort, the need of further optimizing some activities persists, particularly to face the stiff competition posed by Ikea, a transnational furniture retail, which has already opened two stores in Portugal. The case study is centred in the company commercial unit. This department is composed by three subunits:

- Product line managers, responsible for product management and suppliers' contracts,

- Central purchasing unit, in charge of buying products or services from suppliers, and managing the relation with suppliers after the product/service acquisition and
- Containers unit, responsible for buying and managing the orders provided by suppliers whose merchandise comes in containers.

The study developed encompasses the purchasing and imports units. However, since the framework was fully applied only on the former, this section summarizes the results related to the purchasing unit. The intervention main purpose was to facilitate (1) the discussion of current work practices of the team members, and (2) standardization of those considered the best practices. The purchasing unit manager defined this purpose at the outset in a briefing.

The individuals to be observed were defined in the same briefing. Six members of the purchasing unit were included in the study: (1) João Cardoso, (2) Maria Alvega, (3) Pedro Cabrita, (4) Sandra Pereira, (5) Susana Gomes, and (6) Susana Pauleta. These individuals interacted with the following external agents: Warehouse, Sales department, Distributors, Suppliers Category managers, Isabel, Stores, Reception, Marco Pinheiro, and Transporters.

The observation and action capture period was also discussed. An initial duration of a month was defined, which could be extended depending on the amount of information acquired after the initial period. In this case, a web-based application to support data capture, and analysis phases was developed.

Results

This section presents a sample of the results of the application of the proposed approach for each activity.

Bootstrapping

A preliminary observation period served to define basic action and resource types, as well as their meanings. The action types and resource items defined for this case are the following.

Action Types: alter, update, analyze, annotate, block, unblock, calculate, confirm, reconfirm, create, print, inform, request, ask, search.

Resource items: calculator, pencil. Ruler, e-mail, printed e-mail, Excel, exported Excel sheet, fax, printed fax, telephone, SAP component

The unit manager provided a set of context types as input. This set defined the most typical conversations and/or situations observed at the observed setting. The initial action and resource set was discussed and validated by the unit manager and the team. The initial set was further extended along the observation period. The following shows resulting set of contexts;

- provisioning
- product codes
- product catalog
- supplier contact information
- containers
- new orders
- order status
- damaged supplies
- incomplete supplies
- sales orders
- pending orders
- substitute products
- suppliers price
- advertising
- client claims

Action Capture

A set of 711 actions was collected through a three-week observation period Most of the actions registered in the log were actions performed by the individuals included in the study. A very small number (4), captured actions performed by external agents. Of the total actions registered, an external observer, who spent some time in the setting, registered 227. The remaining actions (482), were registered by the case study individuals.

Visualizing Personal Contexts

Personal context boundaries were defined by the set of context types identified at bootstrapping. Hence, the characterization and display of personal contexts was straightforward; personal contexts were identified grouping actions performed by a given individual, associated to the same type of context. Personal context characteristics were manually extracted from the action repositories captured by the web-based application and displayed in a tabular format. The owners of each personal context validated these characteristics.

Since the observed subjects have similar responsibilities, they all performed actions related to some or all the identified contexts during the observation period. However, personal contexts are not necessarily identical and revealed different resource usage preferences. Figures 3 and 4 show the provisioning contexts of João and Sandra. The context keyword 'Excel' is present in João's context. Moreover, it is present in most of the actions belonging to Joăp's provisioning context, revealing a frequent usage of this tool. In Sandra's context though, the 'Excel' keyword does not appear. There are also differences in the SAP modules used. Whereas in Sandra's context appears the usage of the ME21 module, in João's,

Figure 4. "Provisioning" context of Sandra

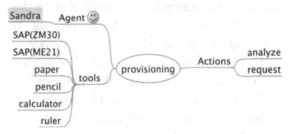

appear the ZM26. Module ZM30 appears in both contexts. Further differences appear in information items, human resources and action types. João's context is characterized by information items not present in Sandra's context. Suppliers also appear as (human) resource in his context while not in Sandra's. In terms of action types, the action type 'calculate' is present in most actions of João's context but not in Sandra's.

Context-Based Analysis

Several context-based depictions were elaborated in this phase, including actions and resource usage in each personal context. Due to space limitations we will only show one of the most relevant depictions. Figure 5 depicts the action distribution by subject. This figure shows that in average, the actions related to the "order status" subject doubled and sometimes, tripled the actions related to new orders. When this chart was presented to the com-

Figure 3. "Provisioning" context of João

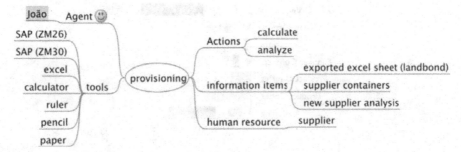

pany sales director, he declared: "this situation is anomalous, and points to the need of further streamlining the "*order fulfillment*" process'. To understand the reason why so many actions were registered with this subject, an analysis of the most common action types related the "order status" subject was done. Distinguishing the individual performers, directed the discussion towards the individuals with more registered actions related to this particular subject (Pedro Cabrita, Maria Alvega and Susana Pauleta).

The analysis of most common actions allowed noticing that "confirm", "inform" and "update" actions have a similar number of records (48,47 and 46, respectively), and are followed by the "ask" action type (34). These action types are by far, the most recurrent action types related to this particular subject. From these results it was concluded that the actions of the "order status" subject are mostly associated with: (1) confirming pending orders, (2) informing (or answering someone's questions) about the state of an order and (2) updating the state of an order.

Context Integration

This activity encompassed three steps (1) identification of the team activities and sub-activities, (2) identification of action patterns within and between personal contexts, and (3) discussion of these patterns to define practices allowing to improve the areas identified in the context-based analysis. The unit manager indicated the main activities related to the purchasing unit and provided a description of them. Four main activities were identified; (1) Manage Purchases, (2) Manage Claims, (3) Manage products and (4) Create Advertising. The Manage Purchases activity encompasses the Manage Containers and Manage Orders sub-activities.

The second step identifies the particular ways employed by each individual in performing those tasks. This phase involved several steps. First, the relationship between subjects and tasks was defined. This allowed relating personal contexts and tasks. Second, the actions within the personal contexts related to a given task, were analyzed. For

Figure 5. Number of actions in each personal context

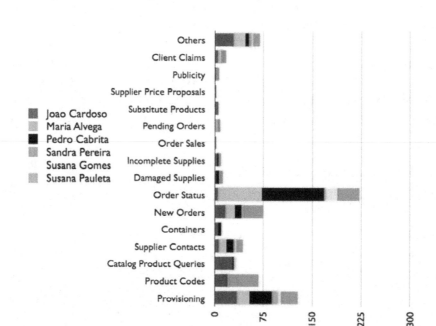

246

example, the *create orders* task is related to the provisioning, product codes, new orders, and supplier contacts contexts. Hence, to identify which individuals were performers of the create order task (and how they performed it), the actions of the corresponding personal contexts were selected and their action types and resources (human and non-human) analyzed.

Table 2 depicts a sample of the actions belonging to personal contexts related to the *create order* task. This sample shows the action types, as well as the technical and human resources employed by given individuals. The analysis of recurrent action types and resources used within each given context allows first, 'filling the boxes' of the company generic "create order" task model, with the specific tools used by different individuals. Second, it allows to identify the name of the specific individuals performing each part of the task. In some cases, variations in action types and sequences between strategies are also uncovered.

Summarizing, individual practices are represented with 'specialized' task models. Figures 6-7 depict the resulting diagrams representing the practices of two different individuals (Maria Alvega and Pedro Cabrita), used in performing the create order task. All diagrams were validated by their owners. The diagrams were displayed in the web application, along with a form where the individuals corrected actions, flows or completed missing actions (along with their associated flows) and resources, that did not appear in the original task model or the action repository. Solid line boxes represent explicitly present within the action repository or task model. Traced line boxes represent actions 'filled' by their owners in the validation phase.

The analysis of these diagrams shows first, that there are no differences in the action types and flows employed in performing the task. The differences appear in the resources used at each action. Pedro Cabrita estimates provision needs manually, using as input printed stock reports from the SAP (ZM26/30) modules. He also supports the task, with an excel sheet containing suppliers, orders and delivery information. In the case of Maria Alvega, she does not use excel in any of her tasks. She performs the whole task combinig SAP-provided support and manual means.

Table 2. Actions of the create order task

Agent	Context	Action	Technical Resources		Human Res.
Pedro Cabrita	Provisioning	Calculate	SAP (ZM30)	Calculator, Pencil, Ruler	
Pedro Cabrita	Provisioning	Calculate	SAP (ZM26)	Calculator, Pencil, Ruler	
Pedro Cabrita	Provisioning	Calculate	SAP (ZM30)	Calculator, Pencil, Ruler	
Pedro Cabrita	Provisioning	Calculate	SAP (ZM26)	Calculator, Pencil, Ruler	
Pedro Cabrita	Provisioning	Calculate	SAP (ZM30)	Calculator, Pencil, Ruler	
Pedro Cabrita	Provisioning	Calculate	SAP (ZM26)	Calculator, Pencil, Ruler	
Pedro Cabrita	Provisioning	Calculate	SAP (ZM26)	Calculator, Pencil, Ruler	
Pedro Cabrita	Product Catalog Queries	Ask	SAP		Sales Dept.
Pedro Cabrita	Supplier Contacts	Search	Excel	Telefone	
Pedro Cabrita	Supplier Contacts	Search	Excel		
Pedro Cabrita	Supplier Contacts	Search	Excel		
Pedro Cabrita	Supplier Contacts	Search	Excel		
Pedro Cabrita	New Orders	create	SAP (ME21)		
Pedro Cabrita	New Orders	create	SAP (ME21)		
Pedro Cabrita	New Orders	create	SAP (ME21)		
Joao Cardoso	Product Codes	(un)block	SAP		
Joao Cardoso	Product Codes	(un)block	SAP(ZM171)		
Joao Cardoso	Product Codes	(un)block	SAP		Store
Joao Cardoso	Product Codes	(un)block	SAP		
Susana Pauleta	Product Codes	(un)block	SAP (ZM171)		Sales Dept.
Susana Pauleta	Product Codes	(un)block	SAP (ZM171)		Warehouse
Susana Pauleta	Product Codes	(un)block	SAP (ZM171)		Sales Dept.
Susana Pauleta	Product Codes	(un)block	SAP (ZM171)		Sales Dept.

Figure 6. Create order practice of Maria Alvega

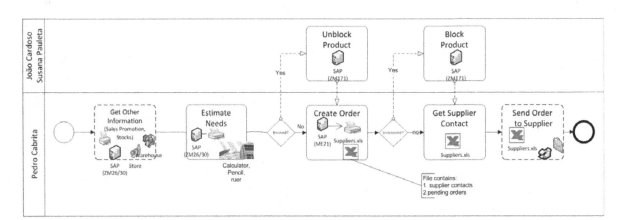

Figure 7. Create order practice of Pedro Cabrita

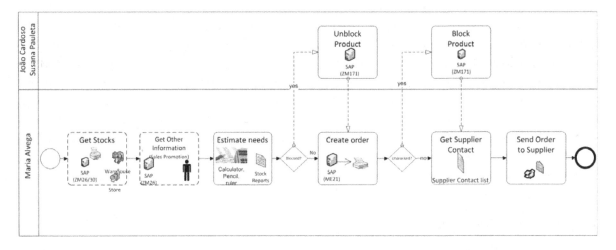

CONCLUSION

Over the years organizational research has identified forces within the organization, which are more enduring and hard to change as opposed to others with, are more ephemeral or amenable to adoption. The former are usually of an informal nature (e.g. cultural norms) and the later are of a more formal character (e.g. HRIS). From the point of the view of the researcher these kinds of forces are quite unrelated and often difficult to reconcile. However, the implementer of systems in the real world knows that these kinds of forces *are* related and that neglecting either of them

could mean failure of the project. Hence, when researching HRIS from an organizational and integrated perspective, as recommended by Ruel and Magalhaes (2008), it is crucial to combine concepts from the sociology of organizations with techniques from organizational and systems modeling. This is what we have tried to achieve in the present paper.

Social emergence is the ontological point of view which we defend in this paper. In line with the autopoietic view, Fuchs (2003) argues that society can only be explained consistently as self-reproducing if man is recognized as a social being and has a central role in the reproduction process. Through social actions, social structures are constituted and differentiated, meaning that social interaction makes new qualities and structures emerge which cannot be reduced to the individual level. This is a process of *bottom-up emergence*. If we concur that the study of HRIS has crucial organizational implications, then the study of HRIS should encompass the HR modeling considerations we have put forward in this paper.

We describe a conceptual framework to model HR whose main purpose is to facilitate the alignment between individuals and organizations. Nonetheless, organizations have several levels of complexity, which are typically structured around individual, inter-personal, group, organization-wide levels, as well as inter-organizational levels. Hence, aligning individuals and organizations need to be accomplished on a level-by-level basis. The proposed framework defines an approach to align individual and inter-personal views with group-level views. At these levels, alignment entails addressing several concerns of individual and inter-personal behaviors, and relating these behaviors with individual tasks, organizational activities and resources.

The key modeling propositions contained in this framework are as follows: (1) Enhanced traceability of HR, (2) Situated HR modeling, (3) HR modeling from action repositories, (4) Capturing and modeling work practices, (5) Capturing and modeling human multi-tasking at work, and (6) Aligning design and execution. We have illustrated the framework by means of a case study which aims at highlighting some crucial modeling criteria of emergent phenomena present in modeling HR. The case study illustrates a specific key modeling proposition; how the proposed framework can be used as a bottom-up approach in capturing and modeling work practices from action repositories.

REFERENCES

Alchian, A. A., & Demsetz, H. (1972). Production, Information Costs and Economic Organization. *American Economic Review, 62*(5),777-795.

Brèzillon, P., & Pomerol, J.-Ch. (2001). About Some Relationships between Knowledge and Context. In V. Akman, P. Bouquet, R.H. Thomason & R. A.Young (Eds.), *3rd International and Interdisciplinary Conference on Modeling and Using Context* (pp. 461-464). Springer LNCS(LNAI) 2116.

Caetano, A., Silva, A., & Tribolet, J. (2004). Separation of concerns in object-oriented business process modeling. *7th International Conference on Information Systems Implementation Modelling*, Rožnov pod Radhošťem, Czech Republic.

De Jaegher, H., & Di Paolo, E. (2007). Participatory Sensemaking: an enactive approach to social cognition. *Phenomenology and the Cognitive Sciences, 6*, 485-507.

Degani, A., & Wiener, E.L.(1997). Procedures in Complex Systems: The airline cockpit. *IEE Transactions on Systems, Man and Cybernetics-Part A: Systems and Humans, 27*(3), 302-312.

Dignum, V. (2004). *A model for organizational interaction: based on agents, founded in logic.* SIKS Dissertation Series No. 2004-1. Utrecht University, Netherlands.

Di Paolo, E. (2005). Autopoiesis, Adaptivity, Teleology, Agency. *Phenomenology and the Cognitive Sciences, 4*, 429-452.

Einserhardt, K. M. (1989). Agency Theory: An assessment and review. *Academic of Management Review, 14*(1), 57-74.

Fuchs, C. (2003). Structuration Theory and Self-Organization. *Systemic Practice and Action Research, 16*(2), 133-167.

Jensen, M. C., & Meckling, W. H. (1976). Theory of the firm: Managerial behavior, agency costs and ownership structure. *Journal of Financial Economics, 3*(4).

Giddens, A. (1984). *The Constitution of Society: outline of the theory of structuration.* Cambridge, UK: Polity Press.

Hatch, M. J., & Cunliffe, A. L. (2006). *Organization Theory.* Oxford: Oxford University Press.

Hill, W. F. (1997). *Learning: a survey of psychological interpretations.* New York: Longman.

Labovitz, G., & Rosansky, V. (1997). *The Power of Alignment.* New York: Jonh Wiley & Sons.

Liles, D. H., & Presley, A. (1996). *Enterprise modelling within an enterprise engineering framework.* Winter Simulation Conference, Association for Computing Machinery), San Diego, CA, USA.

Mingers, J. (2001). Information, Meaning and Communication: an autopoietic approach. In F. Geyer & J. van der Zouwen (Eds.), *Sociocybernetics: complexity, autopoiesis and observation of social systems.*Westport, CT: Greenwood Press.

Pomerol, J.-Ch., Brèzillon, P., & Pasquier, L. (2002). Operational Knowledge Representation for Practical Decision Making. *Journal of Management Information Systems, 18*(4), 101-116.

Ruel, H., & Magalhaes, R. (2008). *Human Resource Information Systems: an Integrated Research Agenda.* Forthcoming book chapter, Elsevier Science.

Sawyer, R. K. (2005). *Social Emergence: societies as complex systems.* Cambridge, UK: Cambridge University Press.

Sierhuis, M., & Clancey, W. J. (1997). Knowledge, Practice, Activities and People, AAAI Spring Symposium on Artificial Intelligence in Knowledge Management, 142-148. AAAI Press.

Sierhuis, M., Clancey, W. J., Hoof, R., & Hoog, R. (2000). *Modeling and simulating work practices from Apollo12 .* 6th International Workshop on Simulation for European Space Programmes, ESTEC.

Sierhuis, M., & Clancey, W.J., (2002). Modeling and Simulating Practices, a Work Method for Work Systems Design. *Intelligent Systems, 17*(5), 32-41.

Varela, F. J. (1984). Two Principles of Self-Organization. In H. Ulrich and G.J.B. Probst (Eds.), *Self Organization and Management of Social Systems.* New York: Springer Verlag.

Varela, F. J., Thompson, E., & Rosch, E. (1991). *The Embodied Mind.* Cambridge, MA: MIT Press.

Zacarias, M. S. (2008). *A Conceptual Framework for the Alignment of Individuals and Organizations.* PhD Dissertation. Lisbon, Portugal: Instituto Superior Tecnico.

KEY TERMS

Agent: Term given to individual and collective human resources of organizations

Agent Architecture: Organizing principles of agent models. The typical agent architecture commonly defines three layers; action, deliberation and change/learn layers. Each layer addresses a different behavioral concern of agents.

Alignment: Degree of shared understandings achieved among interacting agents.

Autopoiesis Theory: Theory that argues that living systems are organizationally closed, autonomous, and self-referent systems. These three aspects provide them auto-creation or auto-renovation capabilities.

Context: Situations created and continually modified by agent interactions.

Emergence: Phenomenon through which complex systems and patterns emerge from multiple simple and local interactions. Emergence is central to the theory of complex systems.

Enterprise Modeling: Term commonly used in defining efforts to model organizations in terms of different, but interrelated perspectives. Several enterprise modeling frameworks including concepts, methodologies and tools have been developed mostly within Information Systems and Artificial Intelligence disciplines. Within the information systems discipline such frameworks are commonly known as Enterprise Architectures, while in Artificial Intelligence they are better known as Enterprise Ontologies.

Methodology: Assumptions about the appropriate research approaches to generate valid evidence. Certain research methods have a natural affinity with certain ontological assumptions.

Ontology: Branch of philosophy concerned with theories of reality. Ontological assumptions or positions concern the essence of phenomena.

Work Practice: Particular ways that individuals or groups have of accomplishing their activities. Work practices are always defined by specific agents and contexts.

Chapter XV
Utilizing the Lead User Method for Promoting Innovation in E–Recruiting

Elfi Furtmueller
University of Twente, The Netherlands

Celeste Wilderom
University of Twente, The Netherlands

Rolf van Dick
Goethe University Frankfurt, Germany

ABSTRACT

In order to maintain their customer base, many e-recruiting firms are in need of developing innovations. The Lead User (LU) Method has been heralded in the new product innovation literature but not yet applied often in e-service settings. Based on an e-recruiting portal, the authors compare new service ideas emerging from interviews with 60 registered applicants to the ideas derived from 15 so-called lead users. Whereas most users offered us social-network features they already know from other platforms, lead users came up with more novel service solutions for different user segments. From both type of users we learned that applicants are more inclined to re-use the same e-recruiting portal if it includes community and social network features for specified user segments, sharing a similar social identity supplementing offline ties. Thus, carefully specifying and treating differentially various user groups at the outset of an e-service innovation project is likely to pay off. This and other practical findings have prompted us to sketch implications for innovating e-recruiting services.

INTRODUCTION

While most of today's innovations are incremental advances of existing products and services, the LU method has been found to help in generating breakthrough innovations (von Hippel, 2005; Franke et al., 2006). Innovative companies such as 3M, Johnson & Johnson, Philips or Hilti (Luethje & Herstatt, 2004) --and even governmental agencies-- are increasingly interested in applying lead user studies for commercial advantage or innovations. The Danish Government, for instance, just made user-driven innovation a national priority. The LU method is built around the assumption that the most innovative new product and service ideas are held by just a few highly innovative *"lead users."* If these lead users are drawn into a process of joint development with the management team of an organization, they have been shown to contribute more to idea generation and innovation than through internal organizational idea generation methods or external market research methods.

The innovations by lead users have been found to be crucial particularly for the long-term performance of firms because lead users face needs that are latent among a larger group of potential users; a lead user is able to identify and explain these needs months or years before the rest of the potential users (von Hippel, 1988, 2005). Typically, lead users benefit from their own innovations, therefore they are motivated to think in innovative, new ways along with their suppliers. Also, users who have real-world experience with an unsatisfied need have been found to provide the most accurate data in the form of need-specification and ideas to meet their needs. Despite the fact that breakthrough innovations through lead user studies have been regularly cited in the innovation literature for the past 10 years (Morrison et al., 2000; Olsen & Blakke, 2001; von Hippel, 2005; Schreier et al., 2007), only a small number of firms have integrated lead users into their product or service development processes. This is especially

salient in the context of service firms (offering, for instance, e-recruiting). Most LU studies have been conducted in manufacturing with the purpose of enhancing new product development.

In this chapter, we contribute to lead user theory by inductively studying how to innovate and develop radical innovations outside of manufacturing firms. Our focus is on innovating e-recruiting services. In our study we explore which services an online career platform would need to offer to trigger its re-use or loyalty. The overall question we address is: *which service innovations do e-recruitment platforms require in order to achieve long-term participation of its users?* We compared the service ideas emerging from 60 interviews with registered users (applicants) with the ideas derived from the LU method.

This chapter is organized as follows: First, we review the literature on user involvement in service innovations and summarize the relevant aspects of the e-recruiting literature. We specifically focus on the LU method as a primary driver of breakthrough innovations. Then, we describe the empirical portion of this paper, a case study of a nationwide e-recruiting service. Finally, we present the findings with the aim of sparking future research on innovating e-recruiting.

BACKGROUND

User Involvement in Service Development

The idea of involving users in product and service development stems from the belief that involving users provides multiple benefits. These include first users' stronger intention to actually (re)use services, and second, increased user accountability for the system's design, resulting in users' higher satisfaction, commitment and identification with the service (Buchanan, 2007; Wagner & Piccoli, 2007). In particular in the area of IT service innovation, higher levels of IT services' success have been associated with the active involvement of members of the user community (e.g., Doherty et al., 2003). Moreover, development times can be reduced if continuous acceptance tests are carried out during service development (e.g., Iansiti & MacCormack, 1997).

Also, the service management literature emphasizes that a deeper understanding of customers' needs is vital for achieving high service quality (e.g., Berry, 1995; Grönroos, 2000; Matthing et al., 2006; Zeithaml, 2000). However, the exact timing of when and how extensive user involvement needs to be organized into the (re-)design process of services is unknown (e.g., Rondeau, Ragu-Nathan & Vonderembse, 2006). While it has been found that involving users can lead to innovative service ideas, sometimes the users' ideas are too difficult to obtain or too costly to realize (Magnusson, 2003). A common definition of user involvement is still lacking as well. It has been seen as synonymous with *contacting with users* (Grudin, 1991), *participation of users* (Ives & Olson, 1992), *user-centred design* (Noyes et al., 1999), and *user engagement* (Wagner & Piccoli, 2007). There are many different approaches to the involvement of users in the generation of potentially innovative activities. For instance, in participatory design studies, users actively take part in design activities, whereas in other approaches users are involved as providers of information, as quasi consultants or users are involved as objects of observations in experiments. Hence, the level of user involvement may broadly be characterized as being on the continuum starting from informative, through consultative to participative (Kujala, 2003). One of the major problems in involving users and understanding their needs is that part of users' knowledge is tacit and to some extent not consciously available. Thus, the kind of user involvement needs to be carefully thought through when aiming to collect user data on how to innovate a particular type of service.

Research into different sources of user involvement and innovation has expanded to include one particularly promising concept, focusing on the concept of "lead users." Lead users share the following characteristics: They (1) anticipate the future needs of a specific market and do so significantly earlier than the majority of other users, and they (2) profit strongly from the suggested innovations, in the sense that these innovations help solve their problems or enable new opportunities (von Hippel, 1986). A classic example of a lead user is Berners-Lee, who did not set out to invent the internet as a contemporary cultural phenomenon, but rather just aimed to develop a tool for his work. He wanted to simply solve a problem that was hindering his efforts as a consulting engineer. By sensing service innovations and future opportunities well before ordinary customers, lead users have a strong desire for innovations that will solve their problems in ways that existing products and/or services cannot. Hence, lead users have been found to be an extremely valuable cluster of customers and/or potential customers (von Hippel, 1988; Franke et al., 2006; Olson & Bakke, 2001).

Perhaps the one firm that has most publicly adopted the LU method is 3M. Like many firms, 3M desired a method that would help their managers and engineers to create more and better breakthrough innovations. 3M conducted an internal study, comparing the outcome of traditional ways of doing new product development (with focus groups, customer interviewing, brainstorming, conjoint analysis etc.) with the lead user method. They found that the ideas generated by the lead user method were more novel and original (i.e., more breakthrough-like), had higher success rates, higher market share, as well as a better fit with the firm's strategic plans and functional capabilities. Further, research showed that successfully introducing breakthrough innovations creates large profits and sales growth (Lüthje & Herstatt, 2004; Thomke & von Hippel, 2002; von Hippel, 2007). Similarly, Lilien et al. (2002) proved empirically that lead-user innovations have a significantly higher sales potential and generation of new product lines compared to innovations generated by traditional market research techniques.

Lagrosen (2005) emphasizes that the mere act of involving customers in the development of new services is not enough. In the same vein, von Hippel (2005) coined the term "sticky information" in order to describe the transfer of the "right" information between lead user and producer. Von Hippel equated the stickiness of information with the cost associated with transferring such information; if information stickiness is low, the retrieving of important information for new service development is a minor issue. However, von Hippel's research shows that information stickiness is often high, especially in the field of information technology. The LU method addresses the issue of sticky information and seems to render the traditional means of customer involvement (such as the focus group or interview) less functional for breakthrough innovation. Thus the tacit nature of information, as a common reason for information stickiness, can be reduced by the LU method and easier than in traditional user involvement procedures.

These traditional methods are less suitable for overcoming the information asymmetry between producer and user. A new product or service developer might consider the sticky information needed for an innovation to be too expensive. He or she typically chooses, instead, to develop the new service based on more easily available information that might already exist in the organization. Similarly, Shane (2000) identifies the role of prior knowledge in opportunity recognition. Prior knowledge may consist of information about markets, technologies, as well as customer problems, needs and how to serve customers. Lead users acquire knowledge about problems, needs and skills when using a certain product or service. They then leverage this knowledge to develop solutions to the problems on their own. Von Hippel notes that a special setting in the form of a face-to-face lead-user workshop helps the individual lead-user participants to interact,

thereby enabling the transfer of tacit knowledge (Nonaka & von Krogh, 2006).

Furthermore, it is important to include lead users with different kinds of experiences, information, needs and knowledge. Ideally, lead user workshops include different external lead users with various needs and use(r)-related knowledge as well as various internal engineers and employees with solution-related, technical knowledge (von Hippel, 2005). Consequently, radical innovations developed during a lead user project face less internal resistance, are easier to integrate and more widely accepted by an organization's employees (Lilien et al., 2002). Conducting a lead user project also indicates a positive attitude toward radical innovation on an organization's side. Based on this literature review on (lead) user involvement in innovation projects, we found the lead user method promising for the identification of breakthrough ideas for innovating e-recruiting services.

E-Recruiting Service Research

The current e-recruiting literature points towards next generation e-recruiting portals with web 2.0 applications. In reality, most existing e-recruiting portals are simple job listing boards serving to replace traditional newspaper ads. In most if not all industrialized countries, company recruiters are increasingly using the internet to advertise job postings and search applicant pools in order to attract a wider set of prospective candidates than traditional recruiting processes would allow (Gueutal & Stone, 2005).

Although research on e-recruiting is still scant (Parry, 2008; Smith & Rupp, 2004), the increasing number of recent academic publications show that there is an increase in the attention paid to these services (e.g., Anderson, 2003; Bauer et al., 2004; Lievens & Harris, 2003; Stone et al., 2006). So far, most studies have focused on applicant reactions (e.g., Dineen et al., 2007; Feldman & Klaas, 2002; Zusman & Landis, 2002). Less research attention has been paid on company employers' or recruiters' views on the effectiveness of different e-recruiting services (Zhao, 2006). Although e-recruiting services (e.g., www.monster.com) and professional networks (e.g., www.linkedIn.com, www.xing.com) have improved access to talent, large numbers of these services suffer from little user participation, outdated profiles and lurking. Consequently, many fail (Feldman & Klaas, 2002; Lin & Stasinskaya, 2002). It is thus quite difficult to design technical features of e-recruiting services and seed their social practices in a way that generates ongoing contributions from a larger fraction of its perhaps initially instrumentally oriented users (Preece et al., 2004; Szmigin et al., 2005). E-recruiting service organizations face many challenges such as keeping registered applicants profiles up-to-date or delivering semantically accurate search results when offering applicant-pool search functions. Also, the many current e-recruiting services hardly differentiate themselves from each other. Hence, we set out to gather empirical data on innovating e-recruiting service offerings: in an effort to achieve more long-term commitment of the various customer groups.

The Case Company

The firm central to the empirical part of our study is an Austrian e-recruiting service actively involved in developing web 2.0 applications for niche recruiting platforms. Since its establishment in 2005, the company has developed many partnerships with public institutions and companies across Austria and has obtained research grants for developing next-generation technologies for e-recruiting services. On an ongoing basis, employees regularly participate in international conferences as well as in programming competitions. Also, a considerable amount of time is spent on collaboration with users (applicants) and other customers such as company recruiters or media personnel in an effort to capitalize and distribute knowledge for system design improvements (e.g.,

von Hippel, 2007). Another unique attribute of this young high-tech firm is its target-specific focus on different applicant segments, for instance, an engineering recruiting portal separate from the business recruiting portal. As a starting point, we studied its engineers' career portal.

RESEARCH STRATEGY

Next to our substantive interest in user-driven, new e-recruiting paths, in order to compare the extent to which the ideas collected in traditional user interviews were –according to von Hippel's theory—less innovative than the ideas derived through the LU method, we collected two sets of qualitative data. We will now describe how we conducted first the traditional interviews, and then how we proceeded during the LU project.

Traditional Interviews

For purposes of traditional interviewing, we randomly selected one registered user from each engineering college in Austria. There are a total of 60 so-called Higher Technical Colleges (HTLs) in Austria; we sampled and interviewed only those engineers/users from each college who had a minimum of 3 years of work experience. He or she was telephone interviewed. Companies is Austria are very keen on recruiting HTL engineers as they are younger than traditional university graduates, said to be easier to align with the organizations' missions, and have already gained practical experience while gaining 5 years of engineering education in various field such as mechanical engineering, electrical engineering or computer science etc. In Germany, the former HTLs were transformed more than 20 years ago into universities of applied science, but the Austrian government runs the 60 HTL engineering schools parallel to the 26 universities of applied sciences. The interviews with the applicants aimed to identify service ideas in order to increase the platform's long-term usage. We probed in detail for users' ideas of what functions an e-recruiting service should offer so that users would make use of it for the long run, rather than just for finding just a single job. All interviews were tape-recorded. While tracking, observing, and asking questions, we kept a record of field notes that enhanced the quality of later in-depth analyses. We also paid attention to Chatman's (1984) advice of establishing rapport with our informants so that they were more open and felt comfortable during our interactions. A second aim of these interviews was to identify a subset of users in the sample with both of the two lead user characteristics mentioned (i.e., being ahead on the trends identified and expecting high benefit from innovations).

Lead User Workshops

In line with the prior literature, we followed the four steps of the LU method, described in detail in von Hippel (1986) and Urban and von Hippel (1988). Figure 1 shows how each of the four steps were carried out in this particular study.

In the 1ˢᵗ step, the broad research goal, the scope (focus on the engineering recruiting portal), financials and other resource requirements of the LU project were planned. Lead User projects require the dedication of an interdisciplinary internal organization team, usually consisting of people from marketing, sales, R&D, and production. In this study, the Marketing & Operations Manager, the Chief Technical Engineer and one researcher with a background in HR planned this together. Research has shown that engineers from R&D often have difficulties imagining that users of a company's products and services can develop technically sophisticated and innovative solutions. Hence, in order to ensure the commitment to customer involvement in new services design, we included employees from different functional lead roles right from the beginning.

The 2ⁿᵈ step involved analyzing key trends and services discovered by studying more than 200 e-recruiting websites, screening the relevant academic literature on e-recruiting and following market trends about e-recruiting services in mainly German and American e-business, management and human resource magazines (such as Business 2.0; MIT Sloan Management Review; Personal Magazin; Personalwirtschaft; Personal Manager etc.). Identification of needs and trends was also supported by weekly viewings of various, mostly Silicon-Valley originating, podcast series on different e-services start-ups. Also, external experts with expertise in e-recruiting were identified and interviewed. Reports from visits to 12 career fairs and interviews with 73 recruiters, done with the aim of exploring service quality criteria, also included analysis of limitations in e-recruiting services and possible ways to enhance current services (see, e.g., Ettinger, Wilderom & Ruel, 2009). Participation in academic conferences helped to think through various academic lenses, i.e. to take into account perspectives of researchers from a variety of fields such as internet research, information systems, semantic technology, psychology and marketing. Once we had identified the major trends and needs, we prioritized them based on their potential service innovation. Although more trends came up such as innovating by means of semantic technologies, one striking need all e-recruiting services faced was finding a solution for keeping their registered applicant profiles up-to-date and for enhancing user return rates (applicants as well as paying recruiters or media personnel). Typically, as soon as registered applicants have found a new job, they hardly have any reason to re-visit a career site in the near future. Similarly, if recruiters have filled their open position, there is no guarantee that they will return to the same recruiting service. As the competition between the vast amounts of recruiting services is increasing, other players may win the battle for the chance for cooperation, and consequently, an organizations' recruiting budget the next year/period. Also, media personnel such as personnel marketers are continuously looking for new portals that have the best links to their target group(s). Accordingly, we had one central research question: *Which service innovations do e-recruitment platforms require in order to achieve the long-term participation of its users?*

In the 3rd step, we identified the lead users. Empirical evidence has shown that average users are restricted by familiarity to actual products and contexts. However, the situation is different if users are progressive and leading or setting trends. These users experience dissatisfaction with current services and are familiar with needs that will become popular in the future marketplace. We aimed to include different user groups into the lead user study. The typical users of e-recruiting services are registered applicants, recruiters, and media (mostly personnel marketing) personnel. We aimed to get users from all three categories to participate. However, due to time restraints of several participants and the time needed to identify and recruit lead users, we split the workshop in two parts. The proxy used for identifying lead users included evaluating to what extent the users appeared ahead of others on our identified trends. Following prior research (Herstatt & von Hippel, 1992; von Hippel, 2005), we operationalized "ahead on identified trends" into the following two criteria: (1) the degree to which the interviewees agreed that the trends that had been previously identified were in fact needed and important from their points of view and (2) the ways in which the interviewees articulated technically interesting innovations regarding these trends. The proxy used for "user innovation benefit expectations" was that users expressed a benefit for the suggested services. Thus, we were looking for critical users that were unsatisfied with their current or former use of e-recruiting services and were able to articulate these negative experiences. Following earlier research, we needed to include people with different skills and those who had informally identified unusual needs

and who expected benefits from service solutions to their needs.

Workshop 1: In the first workshop we brought together the Chief Technical Engineer, the Marketing & Operations Manager, the lead researcher of this study, and three recruiters and two personnel marketers. We ensured to include different types of recruiters including one company recruiter, one recruiter from a personnel agency and one so-called personnel headhunter. One personnel marketer works at a large corporation in need of marketing their organizations to engineers while the other works at a large educational institution in need of engineering students. The process for searching out these lead users was based on a networking approach that the portal-offering firm pursued from its outset. We will now briefly compare the two types of search processes commonly used in lead user studies.

The first is a rather quantitative, standardized screening approach which is applied when the number of customers in the market is manageable and an acceptable screening of all users is possible. This approach was impossible to realize in this case considering the large customer groups of e-recruiting services (customer size-indication is impossible as all larger organizations employ several recruiters). In addition, some organizations employ personnel marketing in case there is a specific need to advertise the organization to certain applicant groups and build relationships with them, in addition to the actual recruiting. The fact that recruiters and personnel marketers do not tend to be a loyal group of customers—they are open to any new cooperation agreement to meet their staffing and advertising needs—made the selection process difficult. We also thought through the issue of how innovations created in the workshop may become an issue of intellectual property in dealing with external parties. Therefore, we relied on the second approach for identifying valuable lead users which is the non-standardized networking approach where informal references help to identify lead users.

While the company was interacting with many recruiters and personnel marketers throughout the year (by means of email communications, phone, in-person at career fairs or in business meetings, or through recruiters and media personnel visiting the e-recruiting services office) only those users that appeared to have built some lasting impression on one of the management team were approached. The three initiators of the lead user study (Chief Technical Engineer, Marketing & Operations Manager and the researcher) engaged in this networking search procedure. A firm deadline of one month was set to get confirmations from potential lead users to participate in the workshop. We created a list of potential participants and the researcher contacted one after the other to check how they fared in terms of our identified trends. Other key selection criteria were that they (1) need to have noted some dissatisfaction with the current e-recruiting services on the market, (2) articulated some suggestions for improving e-recruiting services, and (3) expect some personal gain from innovative solutions. We received five confirmations accompanied by a strong interest to participate. For their participation, those five lead users were given 15 free job ad postings on the website, free online company presentation for one year, their company logo printed on 10,000 flyers distributed at 60 engineering schools in 2007 and four lines of text in the e-career letter to graduates.

Workshop 2: Although about a third of the sample of 60 registered applicants interviewed by telephone met our pre-defined selection criteria for becoming lead users; from that pool of 20 only the three most highly innovative applicants were recruited to participate in the lead user workshop. Those three users agreed that long-term usage of recruiting portals is a problem and that they have had negative experiences with e-recruiting services. Also, they were highly interested in the research project and finding a solution that benefits them as well. One user voluntarily offered a follow-up interview to discuss things more deeply,

another one suggested his desire to think more about these issues and that he would get back to the interviewers with more ideas via email. The third user verbally articulated different stories about how he experiences e-recruiting services—his likes and dislikes—without our probing. This made us invite those three users to participate in the lead user workshop. The case company labelled this LU workshop as their Vision Workshop which ran a full day from 11:00am – 9:00pm. Food during the day, travel expenses in the amount of a second-class train ticket (one came by car who received 0,38 €/km) and € 100 cash were given to the lead users for their participation. The applicants were happy to be invited and enjoyed participating and expressing their ideas in lively discussions. Other workshop participants included two system designers and two programmers of the platform, and the same company team who initiated the lead user workshop.

In the 4th and final step, we held the two lead user workshops. The first workshop with the recruiters, personnel marketers and the company team was held at the end of the summer of 2007 while the second workshop with the applicants and the company team was held in the early fall of 2007. Both workshops started with the overall goal of the group interaction, i.e., how to innovate e-recruiting services. All participants introduced themselves and the company presented its organizational structure; its current products and services; financial growth since its business start; market trends and expected future challenges. In both workshops, the key question was presented (*Which service innovations do e-recruitment platforms require in order to achieve long-term participation of its users?*) Following discussions and a first idea collection phase on flipcharts, the participants quickly identified the need for different service innovations, depending on the three key customer groups of e-recruiting services: (1) applicants, (2) recruiters and (3) personnel marketers. While there are other customer groups as well, these three groups represent the core customers of e-recruiting services. We found that meeting and exceeding their needs will contribute most to the financial firm figures and consequently, to long-term platform sustainability. More specifically, we were interested in improving the services for these customer groups with the goal of enhancing their long-term usage of the platform. Other customer groups are different public agencies (unions, associations, clubs, etc.) and other private self-employed persons or companies (e.g., self-employed consultants such as interview coaches interested in cooperation with the e-recruiting service, publishing companies, etc.). However, those were classified as partners with mostly mutual exchange of services without financial compensation and therefore were not targeted in this study.

Throughout the workshop, field notes were taken and then typed right after the workshop. Memos were only taken during group discussions of new service ideas and/or when summarizing discussion-themed results. Further, flipcharts were used for visualizing the research goal, the process of idea generation and for drafting the results.

Data Analyses

The traditional telephone interviews were analyzed as follows. The involved researcher first listened to all audio tapes. Then, she compiled narratives of the interviews and compared them with the content of the field notes made during the interviews. Themes in the data were identified and reduced into broad categories (Miles & Huberman, 1994; Yin, 2003). The preliminary categories were posted on the company intranet and employees were invited to make suggestions, improve the wording of the labels and cluster related service ideas. Importantly, the service innovation ideas for enhancing long-term usage were presented and discussed with a group of six registered applicants who worked on or had already finished (at the time of the service category validation) their Bachelor or Master theses which were sponsored by the e-recruiting firm. We found this group validation of the individual interview results important to see if any other service ideas would emerge and if the clustering was regarded as appropriate. Similarly, in the lead user workshop we compared the tape-

Table 1. The lead user method as applied in the four processes

STEP 1 **Plan Project Scope**	STEP 2 **Identify e-RecruitingTrends**	STEP 3 **Identify Lead Users**	STEP 4 **Lead User Workshop**

• Define broad research scope: Innovating e-recruiting services
• Build an interdisciplinary internal project team
• Plan finance and other resource requirements
	• Review academic and business literature
	• Listen to podcasts series on e-services start-ups
	• Competitors' trends analysis, review 200 e-recruiting sites
	• Internal reports from visits at 12 career fairs with interview data from 73 recruiters
	• Interviews on services for long-term usage with 60 registered applicants
	• Visit conferences
	• Prioritize major needs/ trends: Which service innovations do e-recruitment platforms require in order to achieve long-term participation of its users?
		• Aim for a total of 15 participants
		• 5 lead users (3 recruiters and 2 personnel marketers) through network search
		• 3 lead users (applicants) from telephone interviews
		• 7 members from the company team:
		  ○ 1 Chief Technical Engineer
		  ○ 1 Marketing & Operations Manager
		  ○ 1 Researcher
		  ○ 2 System Designers
		  ○ 2 Programmers
			• Workshop 1:
			  ○ 3 recruiters
			  ○ 2 personnel marketers
			  ○ 1 Chief Technical Engineer
			  ○ 1 Marketing & Operations Manager
			  ○ 1 Researcher
			• Workshop 2:
			  ○ 3 Applicants
			  ○ 2 System designers
			  ○ 2 Programmers
			  ○ 1 Chief Technical Engineer
			  ○ 1 Marketing & Operations Manager
			  ○ 1 Researcher
			• Triangulation, Comparison, Evaluation of Service Ideas

recorded memos, field notes, presentation slides and handwritings and we transformed this data into a few themes. Also, this set of service ideas was posted on the intranet: in an effort to further enrich the collected ideas.

Following, participants of the lead user workshop systematically compared the service ideas collected from both sets of data (Strauss & Corbin, 1988). We noted patterns and overlaps of the identified service ideas, but also significant differences of service ideas collected through the traditional interviews compared to ideas from the lead users. Not surprisingly, the innovation literature shows that innovativeness is multidimensional and difficult to operationalize. However, the recent literature treats the degree of innovativeness as comprising market, technological and organizational dimensions (e.g., Lettl et al., 2008; Dahlin & Behrens, 2005; Garcia & Calantone, 2002). We operationalized innovativeness according to these dimensions. After both workshops, the core ideas were compiled and emailed to the workshop participants.

They were asked to individually evaluate the service ideas in regard to the degree of innovativeness. For practical reasons, lead users only rated the market dimension, whereas the involved participants of the company team (i.e., the Chief Technical Engineer, Marketing & Operations Manager, Researcher, 2 System Designers, and 2 Programmers) rated all three dimensions. It was felt not meaningful to let company-external lead users rate the internal organizational fit of the derived service ideas. Also, we found the company engineers in the best position to rate the technological feasibility, but it was not opportune to ask lead users working in recruiting or marketing or applicants themselves to rate the innovativeness along the technological dimension.

Specifically, the dimensions were operationalized as follows: (1) *Market Dimension*: how original and novel is the service idea compared to existing services in terms of (a) new benefits for a user, (b) higher benefits for a user, (c) po-

tential for the firm's competitive advantage. (2) *Technological Dimension*: how quickly can the service idea be realized or technical feasibility,:(a) newness of the technology needed to realize the service idea, (b) complexity to realize the service idea, (c) uncertainty about development time and (3) *Organizational Dimension*: how well does the service innovation fit into existing firm structure: (a) required change in competencies, (b) required change in strategy. The users rated the service ideas either as 1 (high) or 0 (low). A similar procedure has been applied in a recent LU study by Franke et al. (2006) and we found that it matches the LU method's aim of spotting finding attractive innovations only.

FINDINGS

Table 2 contains a summary of the main ideas on innovative e-recruiting services. The lead user method offered a clear differentiation between service innovations for the three customer groups of e-recruiting services: applicants; recruiters and personnel marketers. Moreover, lead users came up with new product lines with services valuable for all three customer groups, i.e., including a *Blog Service* so that applicants, recruiters and personnel marketers can have their own blog and communicate with their intended target group. In innovative companies such as Apple, it is often standard that people in important functions (e.g., Steve Jobs) have their personal blog or company blogs to update the general public on news, things of general interest and things that matter to them. If recruiters and marketers could link from their company logo to their blog, they could inform potential applicants on more firm-specific data in a rather informal way without needing to meet each applicant face-to-face. Note that most recruiters or marketers publish their organization's logo or banners on e-recruiting sites and/or present their organization profile online.

This new type of blogging practice has implications also for employer branding initiatives as it can build up large-scale, weak-tie relationships with potential applicants. Many blogs nowadays have developed wide readerships of people regularly re-visiting blogs of specific individuals or companies. To subscribe to a company blog via RSS newsfeed has become a much used feature and may well work for recruiting services as well. Also, personnel marketers from educational institutes could use such blogs to keep a real-time overview of their services, announce guest speakers, events, upload pictures from graduation ceremonies etc. Further, by using blogs to communicate with the general public, the problem of space (line) limitations—which are usually much more restricted in newspaper ads—would be solved. Besides this, newspapers appear in cycles and depend on people reading them at a certain point of time. With a company's or educational institution's blogs, recruiters and marketers could chronologically order their blog entries, invite applicants to comment or join different discussions, and more selective application might become a reality which might reduce significant HRM-administrative costs.

Also through the LU method the idea came up to offer an applicant blog: where applicants could initiate the communication with registered recruiters of the companies they target and exchange information with other registered applicants on experiences gained in different work settings. Such applicant blogs may serve as sort of discussion boards, enabling authentic and social support from peers. Also, it could enable the entire application process to turn 360 degrees: i.e., if all applicants were to put their own blogs out and recruiters "apply" to their "ads." In the traditional interviews, applicants exclusively suggested service innovations for their personal use. Even when probing long-term sustainability of e-recruiting services in general, in the traditional interview applicants made only references to themselves; they did not identify service innovations for other

potential customer groups. For instance, in regard to communication tools, we note that applicants were only suggesting services for communication with other registered applicants via social networks as commonly known in other platforms. While applicants suggested including text-based information on employers with some sort of branch categorization, phone, address and email, they did not identify new communication services --such as *Blogs or Live Chat*-- to communicate online with recruiters or educational institutes. Lead users further suggested enhancing the communication by including an *Avatar* in the form of a Digital Application Coach instead of FAQ or customer service links. This was found to create more personal customer service than traditional text information. Both, the lead user and the users from traditional interviews came up with many ideas on how to integrate social network and community features into e-recruiting services. The regular users suggested career related and private use services so as to connect with each other, share music or videos, play games, and communicate online with other registered engineers. The users predominantly emphasized interest in communicating online with offline-known fellow acquaintances: from their prior schools or via extended networks (friends of friends). Interestingly, the interviewed engineers didn't seem to be keen on developing or maintaining a strong network with fully unknown engineers. Fifty-six of the sixty interviewed engineers confirmed that they would use an online career service for the long run if it was specifically targeted at engineers' needs. However, most of the interviewed users are not inclined to sign up at a general online job board that attracts many different job searchers. General jobs boards are seen as exchange-based career tools for finding a job when needed, but among them it is not desirable to connect online in such job boards with unknown users.

Social presence theory (Biocca et al. 2003) has noted that the presence of other members (which can be complemented by offline interactions) may foster stronger ties of participants to their online service. Consequently, applicants who know that people similar to them are involved as users are more likely to maintain an up-to-date profile in niche career platforms. Moreover, we assume that determinants of long-term sustainability of e-recruiting services need to range from understanding how users judge online features, such as the quality of a career community's service, its system, and the provided information (DeLone &Mclean, 2003) to understanding offline features, such as the offline activities of users (Wellman & Haythornthwaite, 2002). Studies on online communities found that people's offline activities do indeed increase the solidarity and cohesiveness of online interactions (Boyd & Ellison, 2007). Thus, offline activities strengthen the ties between members of an online portal which may cause applicants to stay connected to a specific online service.

While lead users recommended to include *Newsfeeds and Statistics* for transparent updates depending on the different customer groups, users in the traditional interviews came up with a *Newsletter* with the latest jobs matching their skills; new information on hiring companies; info on continuing education; and other career related topics. Most e-recruiting services offer such newsletters or job-alerts functions to keep applicants informed of new jobs and other career-related news. However, the new services that were identified by the lead users added additional value, including that a transparent newsfeed may enhance the trust of the customer groups to the platform, and consequently improve long-term use. For instance, recruiters and personnel markets should have the possibility for automatic updates on the number of unique visitors and page impressions in different time frames (such as per week/month etc). Also, newsfeeds on new applicants that registered and would fit an open position in a ranking order would be valuable. Further, services such as regular updates on which applicant clicked on a specific job ad or company logo may cause

recruiters interest. Such features would enable recruiters and marketers transparency into their advertising investment and also estimate latent demand. Another trust-related service would be to let recruiters, marketers and applicants who used different career services rate those services. There is certainly the danger here that competitors would be inclined to write negative comments on purpose. People who rate such services, therefore, may need to include some personal data, or careful monitoring of the posted comments would need to be undertaken.

For educational institutes, Newsfeed could include the number of requests for certain study programmes or the amount, demographic and geographic information of people registering for educational programs. Also, the strength of cooperation with other media channels and possibilities for recruiters and marketers to include their advertising on partner channels (such as newspapers) is interesting to estimate a portal's effectiveness in reaching specific target groups.

Further, for applicants, newsfeed services may cause them to keep their profile up-to-date and return to the site as they get a better overview of who is interested in their profile. This may enhance users' curiosity to re-visit the site and possibly also their self-esteem if many people viewed their profile or left messages. Also, some notification of jobs where only few applicants applied may save the applicants time so as to not apply to jobs where hundreds of other candidates already applied. Also, applicants should get an automatic individual newsfeed on jobs matching their skills instead of receiving traditional mass newsletter. Further, if applicants don't have the skills available yet to apply for a specific job, they should be offered educational links to institutes where they can best acquire the missing knowledge/degrees. Some other innovative services for applicants include ranking employers who pay most for graduates from different schools, and a search possibility to find friends or FoF (friends of friends) work at same organization or area.

One new service relates to visualizing applicant data by tag clouds. Such "identity clouds" can be used to indicate things in different pixel sizes, depending on how closely related and characteristic certain terms are associated with a specific person. Creating such a tag cloud for an applicant could include visualizing attended schools, skills, and work experiences. If an applicant is an expert user of a certain computer program, for instance, this would appear in larger font while computer programs he has only basic knowledge about would appear in small font. Also, organizations where an applicant has collected longer work-experience would appear larger than work settings where the applicant has done only an internship. The service for recruiters and marketers *Visualizing Applicants* may also include a map showing black spots (no suitable applicants) and green spots (suitable applicants), regional distribution in line with skills: For example, where do more chemical engineers live? Similarly, the services for applicants *Visualizing Jobs* may include a map showing black spots (no fit with my profile) and green spots (fit with my profile) or visual info in what region and company I have already friends working.

Another interesting LU suggestion (fostering potentially long-term participation and up-to-date profiles) relates to the *Integration of external eHRM systems in which job ads and* profiles are automatically updated. While the very large recruiting services such as Monster already have created data transfer interfaces (e.g. HR-XML) with large corporations, this feature is not applied much yet. In order to give each other the possibility to transfer sensitive employee data via shared interfaces, it requires technological savvy and trust from both cooperation partners. However if recruiting services can get more of such cooperation agreements for convenient data transfer, it is likely to enhance long-term cooperation. A major advantage of effectively working data transfers and reliable updates relates to time and cost savings. Further, applicants may re-use the services

of a specific e-recruiting site if they have the opportunity to create a neutral and free application webpage for use outside the e-recruiting service and general future use.

Recruiters and marketers are also likely to benefit from the LU generated *Fan Club* service idea. This holds that applicants who have an interest in a specific organization simply add companies of interest to their search status. However, for applicants this service should rather be labelled *Insider* or *VIP Club*. The careful consideration of wording (Insider instead of Fan) is suggested to enhance applicants' feelings of special as "insiders," getting more and better information about an organization since they directly communicate with recruiters of desired companies. Certainly, it is beneficial for companies to see which applicants have real and current interest in the organization. Direct interaction with a selected Fan Club audience should be enabled by different means of communications, starting with text messaging or discussion boards. Research has shown that recruiting from standard applicant pools can be highly frustrating for recruiters. This is because of the small and slow response rate of applicants. Besides this, applicants may have already found a job elsewhere and are still registered as job searching though in fact not available anymore. While recruiters are already looking forward to invite candidates from applicant pools for interviews, they often find themselves with no response from the registered candidates (Ettinger, Wilderom & Ruel, 2009). Therefore such Fan Club features may flag who among their applicants has a current interest in a specific organization, enabling relationship building with candidates and consequently employer branding.

Moreover, a *Career Letter* service might address a segmented target audience instead of general newsletter services, as proposed by the lead users. Companies should be able to decide who exactly should get certain information, e.g. only mechanical engineers in a specified region or who have graduated from a specific school.

From the traditional interviews, users suggested information on how find jobs, how to prepare application documents, info on trainee programs, links to companies and continuing education.

Other user-generated new ideas include a differentiation between applicants' personal and private page. This idea came from lead users as well as regular users. Importantly, recruiting services are challenged to create private (for friends) and public (for HR recruiters) spaces of the users' applicant profile so that trust is built, in order to ward off the fear that personalized resume data will be abused. As one applicant described: "How can you make sure that my boss will not find my profile in the database?" and "Sure, I want my profile for friends to look different than my applicant profile."

Further, implementing more selection criteria to enhance users' *Privacy, Security* and *Control* was strongly associated with long-term use of e-recruiting portals. Moreover, a service labelled *Career Cockpit* would help recruiters to put previously selected or interviewed candidates in a history folder, save comments on interactions with candidates etc. Having such an overview of all interactions with users of a specific recruiting portal enhances not only the transparency but also the administration of data. For marketers this could relate to saving the advertising history in such a Career Cockpit, i.e. subscriptions, successful placements etc.

We also noted that services aiming to enhance applicants' *Self esteem/ Competency* might well be received by users. One possible feature would be to include *Crowd-sourcing*: integrate users to expand skill ontologies; user experts can compare themselves to other users and get ranked depending on their performance. Applicants may even use such skill test scores for their online applicant profile. In addition, if applicants can match their resume profile with different job ads, this may cause users to search for jobs where they are the top candidate, consequently strengthening platform bonding.

With the prospective service, *Check your Market Value,* users should be able to compare how well they would fit a specific job description compared to other users, friends, people in a certain region, the whole network etc. This feature also relates to playfulness which has been found very important in re-using online services. Users from the telephone interviews suggested to add games and to rank winners. However typical online games may not fit the strategy of e-recruiting portals. The ideas suggested by the lead user in regard to "gaming" which allow applicants to assess their skills, compete against other users for expanding skill ontologies and to motivate users to check their market value are strategically related to career services.

Finally, when interpreting Table 3, one needs to be cautious. First of all, the degree of innovation along the market dimension has been evaluated by all workshop participants (n=15) while the technological and organizational dimension has been only evaluated by the involved company team (n=7). Evaluators either judged statements as 1 (high) or 0 (low). We did not include other variation in the evaluation in an effort to only select service ideas perceived as highly innovative or not innovative. We summed up the numbers per statement to get an overview of which service ideas score high on our operationalization of innovation. Clearly, service ideas from the lead users score higher than service ideas from the traditional interviews. There is one exception, *Social Network/Community features* which represents a summary term for all ideas suggested by traditional users in regard to such applications. As discussed in earlier sections of this chapter, social network and community features in general have been found as innovative. However, the ideas suggested in the traditional interviews largely revealed service ideas such as inviting, blogging, and tagging which are commonly known from other platforms. Nevertheless, most of the workshop participants already stated during the workshop that any advancement to include such

Table 2. Innovations from the LU method compared to new-service ideas obtained with traditional interviews

Lead User Method			Traditional Interviews
Innovations for Recruiters	**Innovations for Personnel Marketers**	**Innovations for Applicants**	**Innovations for Applicants**
Recruiters Blog • Directly communicate with target group	**Marketers Blog** • Directly communicate with target group	**Applicant Blog** • Directly communicate with recruiters • Discussion Board: social exchange of positive/negative job experiences	**Applicant Communication** • Internal communication with friends or FoF, exchange experiences **Social Network/Community features** • Inviting, blogging, tagging services • Keep in touch with friends for career purposes • Connecting based on branches, city groups, school groups, sports groups • Recommending friends
Newsfeed for Transparency/ Statistics • #Visitors, # page impressions • Detailed information which applicant has clicked on job ad or company logo • Ranking services: who is the best suitable applicant for an open job position, 1st, 2nd, 3rd etc. • Evaluation service of different recruiting sites: other recruiters rank services they used	**Newsfeed for Transparency/ Statistics** • #Visitors, # page impressions • Detailed information which applicant has clicked on ad or company logo • # Incoming information requests on marketers products and services • # People registering, applying or buying the marketers services • # and strength of cooperation with other media agencies to advertise more efficiently	**Newsfeed for Transparency/ Statistics** • # Recruiters and detailed info who has visited applicant profile • # and detailed information on new jobs matching applicant profile • Show educational links if skills are missing • Notification on jobs where only few applicants applied or only view applicants clicked the job ad • Matching which employer pays most for graduates from different schools • Friends or FoF work at same company, area?	**Newsletter** • Email new job offers • Events for graduates, alumni • Info on continuing education
Visualizing Applicants • Map showing black spots (no suitable applicants) and green spots (suitable applicants), regional distribution in line with skills: where are e.g. more chemical engineers living? • Tag cloud	**Visualizing Applicants** • Map showing black spots (no suitable applicants) and green spots (suitable applicants) • Tag cloud	**Visualizing Jobs** • Map showing black spots (no fit with my profile) and green spots (fit with my profile) where are the jobs I fit best • Tag cloud	**Career info pages** • How to find jobs • How to prepare application documents • Info on trainee programs • Company online presentation
Live Chat • Text or video	**Live Chat** • Text or video	**Avatar** • Digital Application Coach	**Employer communication** • Employer list with phone, address, email
Integration with e-HRM systems • HR-XML so as to automatically update profiles and job ads	**Integration with e-HRM systems** • HR-XML so as to automatically update customer database	**Flexible Application Homepage** • Free page with individual address for independent, outside platform, future use	**Data transfer** • Download section, share pics, videos, music, e-books etc.

continued on following page

Table 2. continued

	Lead User Method		Traditional Interviews
Innovations for Recruiters	**Innovations for Personnel Marketers**	**Innovations for Applicants**	**Innovations for Applicants**
Fan Club • Applicants join company groups, better overview of interested applicants, relationship building, employer branding	**Fan Club** • Applicants join company groups, better overview of interested applicants, relationship building, employer branding	**Insider/VIP Club** • Applicants join company groups, feel special to be "insides" and directly communicate with recruiters	
Career Letter • Target specific groups of users	**Career Letter** • Target specific groups of users	**Career Letter** • Target specific groups of users	**Newsletter** • Email new job offers
		Differentiation between personal and private page • Invitation by friends necessary to register, exclusivity, extended privacy settings	**Differentiation between personal and private page** • Contact info, hobbies, events, friends etc. • Private page with career info
Career Cockpit • Search status: who is actively/ passively searching a new job • Save selected candidates, successful placements etc.	**Career Cockpit** • Search status: who is actively/ passively searching a new job • Save advertising history, subscriptions, successful placements etc.	**Career Cockpit** • Search status: who is actively/ passively searching a new job • Save selected jobs	
		Self esteem/ competency features • Crowd-sourcing: integrate users to expand skill ontologies, user experts can compare themselves to others • Enable applicants to use score for resume • Check your market value: show users how they score compared to other users, friends	**Playfulness** • Online games with other users, rank winners
Open ID, APIs	**Open ID, APIs**	**Open ID, APIs**	
Control/Security	**Control/Security**	**Control/Security**	

features in e-recruiting portals is innovative. However, when reviewing the first part of the table on the lead user ideas, one sees that social network and community features have been split into different innovative services ideas, scoring high on the market dimension.

We need to emphasize that high scores on the technological innovation dimension is not necessarily beneficial for organizations wishing to advance their e-recruiting services. For instance, high scores on *Uncertainty about development time* make it difficult for the organization to plan advertising efforts until the products and services are readily available. A high score on *Complexity to realize the service idea* can be positive, as it is harder to imitate the new service, but also often requires competencies that may currently not be available in the organization. When looking at the organizational dimension, both a low score on *Required change in competencies* and *Required change in strategy* means the organization does not need to adjust their internal structure. In this case, a lower score seems beneficial as service innovations can be realized without requiring the

Table 3. Categorizations of the new- e-recruiting service ideas (LU method versus traditional interviews)

E-Recruiting Innovation	Market Dimension (n=15)			Technological Dimension (n=7)			Organizational Dimension (n=7)	
	New benefits for user	Higher benefits for user	Potential for the firm's competitive advantage	Newness of the technology needed to realize the service idea	Complexity to realize the service idea	Uncertainty about development time and	Required change in competencies	Required change in strategy
Lead User Method								
Blog	6	7	7	0	0	0	0	2
Newsfeed for Transparency/ Statistics	15	15	15	4	6	5	3	3
Visualizing Applicants/Jobs	12	11	9	3	3	1	3	3
Live Chat	8	8	7	2	2	0	0	2
Avatar	9	12	8	4	4	5	2	2
Data integration with eHRM systems	12	13	13	6	6	5	3	4
Flexible Application Homepage	9	8	5	0	0	0	0	0
Fan Club/Insider/VIP Club	11	12	10	0	0	0	0	0
Career Letter	9	8	8	0	0	0	0	0
Differentiation: Personal/Private page	7	8	7	0	2	0	0	0
Career Cockpit	12	13	9	3	2	2	0	0
Self esteem/Competency features	15	14	13	4	5	4	2	5
Open ID, APIs	9	10	8	0	0	0	0	2
Control/Security	6	11	7	3	4	2	0	2
Traditional Interviews								
Applicant Communication	7	6	7	2	1	0	0	0
Social Network/Community features	8	9	6	4	3	3	2	4
Employer communication	0	0	0	0	0	0	0	0
Data transfer/Download	6	7	3	1	1	1	0	0
Career info pages	2	2	0	0	0	0	0	0
Newsletter	0	3	0	0	0	0	0	0
Differentiation: Personal/Private page	7	8	7	0	2	0	0	0
Playfulness/Online games	6	4	2	2	1	0	0	2

organization to adjust much of its current strategy or recruit new employees. We have to admit that a more quantitative evaluation with recruiters, marketers and applicants may reveal quite different evaluations along the three innovation dimensions. However, organizations undertaking innovation projects frequently do it to get an overview for their own purposes. It is quite obvious that the management team of organizations—when having identified radical innovations—is not always open to share these innovations with the general public and may risk competitors imitating their innovative service ideas before the initiating company can bring it to the market. After identification of the innovative service ideas, the case company did not aim to ask outsiders to evaluate and further validate the service ideas identified in this study. In conclusion, many new ideas for innovating e-recruiting were collected. As presented in this chapter, most of these ideas relate in some form to social network and community features with different ways for communicating and bonding online. We hope that the overview of service ideas provided in this chapter provides fresh substantive insights for purposes of further developing online career services.

FUTURE TRENDS

A major and understudied challenge in today's (service) innovation management regards the combination of a deliberate customer orientation with the aim of creating breakthrough service innovations. Companies that cope well with this challenge add to the probability that their new services will perform successfully in the market. Although most writings on the Lead User Method herald its promise, empirical illustration and analysis is scarce. Therefore, we carried out an exploratory study on the practical application of this method in the field of innovating e-recruiting. As expected, we find that service ideas evolved in the lead user workshop appear more innovative

than those collected in the interviews. On this basis, we find ground to assume that e-recruiting platforms can only be sustainable if they evolve or transform into highly participative and continuously innovating e-community platforms, organized around niches of users sharing a similar social identity. Further, our findings point to the insight that sustainable virtual career communities require not only useful information on careers and continuing education, but also can encourage friendship, social activities as well as (virtual) experiences that may enhance users' self esteem. These results require more customer-centric and niche approaches to e-recruiting than most current providers of e-recruiting offer. General and exchange-based e-recruiting platforms might thus need to develop into comprehensive career networks or at least offer the possibility of such networking activities. However, as the needs of the interviewed lead users are not necessarily the same as the needs of the users who will make up the major share of tomorrow's e-recruiting market, more research is needed to examine the extent to which the service ideas identified by the lead users in our study will be valued by the more typical future users in their target markets.

CONCLUSION

In this chapter we present the rationale for and findings from employing the lead-user method in an effort to further innovate in an extant, Austrian e-recruiting platform. We collected data from 60 registered applicants, including 15 lead users. The resulting Table 1 contains the service ideas with which e-recruiting platforms may serve its key stakeholders better. In terms of our key substantive question, that of more sustainable use of an established niche portal, we found that users of this portal are more inclined to re-use the same portal if it includes community and social network features for specified user segments, sharing a similar social identity by enabling offline ties.

Concerning our application of the LU method, we find that the service ideas emerging from the lead user method appear more innovative than those collected in the traditional interviews. Whereas most of the registered applicants identified social network and community features they already knew from other platforms, lead users came up with innovative service solutions for different user groups: applicants, recruiters and personnel recruiters. Thus, carefully specifying potential customer groups at the outset of an innovation project can lead to more targeted service offerings. It is likely – as both sets of interview data show—that social networks and a sense of community (i.e., shared identity) matters for long-term sustainability of e-recruiting services, and thus that the general users will welcome "a sense of community" to be built into online career portals. In developing such portals along these lines, we may need to review the traditional community psychology as well as customer loyalty literatures where we might find mechanisms that can be effectively transposed into this virtual, e-recruiting type of commercial setting.

Some limitations to our study need to be noted. First, the theoretical foundation of the lead user identification process needs more work and appears to be different from case to case (Lüthje & Herstatt, 2004). While the assessment process used in this application study is not optimal, we found it worked well as a first step to tapping a high degree of practical innovativeness. The service ideas generated by the lead users in this study already built upon the ideas gathered through the 60 traditional user-interviews, a feature that must have increased the innovativeness of the workshops by itself. Certainly, in the future, more fundamental research work in this realm would need to assess more independently, objectively and precisely the degree of innovativeness of the user-driven ideas, based on various data-collection methods, engaging various e-recruiting platforms. Furthermore, social scientists may criticize the use of the LU method as suffering

from the self-fulfilling prophecy, namely that those (lead) users who are expected to be more innovative than the typical user might indeed turn out to be more innovative because they are treated differently by the portal organization. Hence in a pure, scientifically sound test of both user groups we might need to ensure that this and other biases are removed, but for application purposes the LU method worked extremely well, particularly when using the traditional interview method first for purposes of identifying the best external candidates for the lead-user workshops, as we did in this case.

Moreover, despite our promising application of the LU Method , we are intrigued by the question to what extent the group setting, in our case the lead-user workshops, when compared to individual interviews with lead users would have led to even more innovative ideas; it may well be that several users derive better ideas in isolation than in group settings (see, e.g., Thompson, 2003: "Brainwriting"; Heslin, 2008). As we noted difficulties to get all identified lead users together at one place and date, individual interviews with (some) lead users would have proven even more beneficial. Hence, (resource) planning needs to be carefully integrated into undertaking a similarly successful LU-innovation project.

REFERENCES

Anderson, N. (2003). Applicant and recruiter reactions to new technology in selection: a critical review and agenda for future research. *International Journal of Selection and Assessment, 11,* 121-136.

Bauer, T. N., Truxillo, D. M., Paronto, M. E., Weekley, J. A., & Campion, M. A. (2004). Applicant reactions to different selection technology: Face-to-face, interactive voice response, and computer-assisted telephone screening interviews. *International Journal of Selection and Assessment, 12,* 135-148.

Biocca, F., Harms, C., & Burgoon, J. K. (2003). Toward a More Robust Theory and Measure of Social Presence: Review and Suggested Criteria. *Presence, 12*(5), 456–480.

Boyd, D., & Ellison, N. B. (2007). Social network sites: Definition, history, and scholarship. *Journal of Computer-Mediated Communication, 13*(1), article 11.

Buchanan, R. (2007). Understanding your users: A practical guide to user requirements: Methods, tools, and techniques. *Design Issues, 23*(1), 92-92.

Chatman, E. A. (1984). Field research: Methodological themes. *Library and Information Science Research, 6*, 425-38.

Dahlin, K. B., & Behrens, D. M., (2005).When is an invention really radical? Defining and measuring technological radicalness, *Research Policy, 34*, 717–737.

DeLone, W.H., & McLean, E.R. (2003). The DeLone and McLean Model of Information

Systems Success: A Ten-Year Update. *Journal of Management Information Systems, 19*(4), 9-30.

Dineen, B., Ling, J., Ash, S., & Del Vecchio, D. (2007). Aesthetic properties and message customisation: Navigating the dark side of web recruitment. *Journal of Applied Psychology, 92*(2), 356-372.

Doherty, N. F., King, M., & Al-Mushayt, O. (2003). The Impact of Inadequacies in the Treatment of Organizational Issues on Information Systems Development Projects. *Information & Management, 14*, 49-62.

Ettinger, E., Wilderom, C.P.M., & Ruel, H. (Jan 2009). Web recruiters service quality criteria: a content analysis. *Proceedings of the 42nd Hawaii International Conference on System Science*, Hawaii.

Feldman, D., & Klaas, B. (2002). Internet job hunting: A field study of applicant experiences with online recruitment. *Human Resource Management, 41*(2), 175-201.

Franke, N., von Hippel, E., & Schreier, M. (2006). Finding commercially attractive user innovations: a test of lead-user theory. *Journal of Product Innovation Management, 23*, 301-315.

Garcia, R., & Calantone, R. (2002). A critical look at technological innovation typology and innovativeness terminology: A literature review. *Journal of Product Innovation Management, 19*, 110–132.

Gueutal, H. G., & Stone, D. L. (2005). *The Brave New World of eHR: Human resources management in the digital age.* San Francisco: Jossey-Bass.

Grönroos, C. (2000). *Service Management and Marketing: A Customer Relationship Management Approach.* New York, NY: Wiley.

Grudin, J. (1991). Interactive systems: Bridging the gaps between developers and users. *IEEE Computer, 24*(4), 59-69.

Herstatt C., & von Hippel E. (1992). From experience: developing new product concepts via the lead user method: a case study in a "Low Tech" Field. *Journal of Product Innovation Management, 9*, 213–221.

Iansiti, M., & MacCormack, A. (1997). Developing products on the Internet Time. *Harvard Business Review, 75*(5), 108-117.

Ives, B., & Olson, M. (1992). User Involvement and MIS Success: A Review of Research. *Management Science, 30*(5), 586-603.

Kujala, S. (2003). User involvement: a review of the benefits and challenges, *Behavior & Information Technology, 22*(1), 1-16.

Lin, B., & Stasinskaya V. S. (2002). Data warehousing management issues in online recruiting. *Human Systems Management, 21*(1), 1-8.

Magnusson, P. R., Matthing, J., & Kristensson, P. (2003). Managing user involvement in service innovation. *Journal of Service Research*, *6*(2), 111-124.

Matthing, J., Kristensson, P., Gustafsson, A., & Parasuraman, A. (2006). Developing Successful Technology-Based Services: The Issue of Identifying and Involving Innovative Users. *Journal of Service Marketing*, *20*(5), 288-297.

Noyes, J., & Baber, C. (1999). *User-Centered Design of Systems*. Heidelberg, Germany: Springer Verlag.

Lagrosen, S. (2005). Customer involvement in new product development: A relationship marketing perspective. *European Journal of Innovation Management*, *8*(4), 424-436.

Lettl, C., Hienerth, C. & Gemuenden, H. G. (2008). Exploring How Lead Users Develop Radical Innovation: Opportunity Recognition and Exploitation in the Field of Medical Equipment Technology. *IEEE Transaction of Engineering Management*, *55*(2), 219-233.

Lilien, G., Morrison, P. D., Searls, K., Sonnack, M., & von Hippel, E. (2002). Performance Assessment of the Lead User Generation Process for New Product Development. *Management Science, 48*, 1042-1059.

Lievens, F., & Harris, M. (2003). Research on Internet recruiting and testing: Current status and future directions. In C. Cooper & I. Robertson (Eds.), *International Review of Industrial and Organizational Psychology*, *18*, (pp. 131-165).

Lüthje, C., & Herstatt, C. (2004). The Lead User method: An outline of empirical findings and issues for future research. *R&D Management*, *34*(5), 553-568.

Miles, M. B., & Huberman, A. M. (1994). *Qualitative data analysis: An expanded sourcebook*. (2nd Ed.). Thousand Oaks, CA: Sage.

Morrison P. D, Roberts J. H., & von Hippel E. (2000). Determinants of user innovation and innovation sharing in a local market. Management Science, *46*(12), 1513–1527.

Nonaka, I., von Krogh, G., & Voelpel, S. (2006). Organizational knowledge creation theory: Evolutionary paths and future advances. *Organization Studies*, *27*(8), 1179–1208.

Olson, E. L., & Bakke, G. (2001). Implementing the Lead User Method in a High Technology Firm: A Longitudinal Study of Intentions versus Actions. *Journal of Product Innovation Management*, *18*, 388-395.

Parry, E. (2008), Drivers of the adoption of online recruitment: An analysis using diffusion of innovation theory. In. T.V. Bondarouk & H.J.M. Ruël (Eds), *E-HRM in theory and practice*. Amsterdam: Elsevier.

Preece, J., Nonnecke, B., & Andrews, D. (2004). The top five reasons for lurking: Improving community experiences for everyone. *Computers in Human Behavior*, *20*(2), 201-223.

Rondeau, P. J., Ragu-Nathan, T. S., & Vonderembse, M. A. (2006). How involvement, IS management effectiveness, and end user computing impact IS performance in manufacturing firms. *Information and Management*, *43*(1), 93-107.

Schreier, M., Oberhauser, S., & Pruegl, R. (2007). Lead users and the adoption and diffusion of new products: Insights from two extreme sports communities. *Marketing Letters, 18*(1–2), 15–30.

Smith, A. D., & Rupp, W. T. (2004). Managerial challenges of e-recruiting. *Online Information Review*, *28*(1), 61-74.

Stone, D. L., Stone-Romero, E. F., & Lukaszewski, K. (2006). Factors affecting the acceptance and effectiveness of electronic human resource systems. *Human Resource Management Review*, *16*(2), 229-244.

Strauss, A., & Corbin, J. (1998). *Basics of qualitative research: Techniques and procedures for developing grounded theory.* (2nd Ed.), Thousand Oaks, CA: Sage.

Szmigin, I., Canning, L., & Reppel, A. E. (2005). Online community: Enhancing the relationship marketing concept through customer bonding. *International Journal of Service Industry Management, 16*(5), 480-496.

Thomke, S., & von Hippel, E. (2002). Customers as innovators: A New Way to Create Value, *Harvard Business Review, 4*(80), 74-81.

Thompson, L. (2003). Improving the creativity of organizational work groups. *Academy of Management Executive, 17*(1), 96-109.

Heslin, P. A. (in press). Better than Brainstorming? Potential Contextual Boundary Conditions to Brainwriting for Idea Generation in Organizations, (June 21, 2008). *Journal of Occupational and Organizational Psychology.*

Urban, G., & von Hippel, E. (1988). Lead user analyses for the development of new industrial products, *Management Science, 34*(5), 569-582.

von Hippel, E. (1986). Lead users: A source of novel product concepts. *Management Science, 32*(7), 791-805.

von Hippel, E. (1988). *The Sources of Innovation.* New York: Oxford University Press.

von Hippel, E. (2005). *Democratizing Innovation.* Cambridge: MIT Press.

von Hippel, E. (2007). Horizontal innovation networks: By and for users. *Industrial and Corporate Change, 16*(2), 293-315.

Wagner, E. L., & Piccoli, G. (2007). Moving beyond user participation to achieve successful IS design. *Communications of the ACM, 50*(12), 51-55.

Wellman, B., Boase, J., & Chen, W. (2002). The networked nature of community on and off the Internet. *IT and Society, 1*(1), 151-165.

Yin, R. K. (2003). *Case Study Research: Design and Methods.* Third Edition, Thousand Oaks, CA: Sage.

Zeithaml, V. A. (2000). Service quality, profitability, and the economic worth of customers: What we know and what we need to learn. *Journal of the Academy of Marketing Science, 28*(1), 67-85.

Zhao, H. (2006). Expectations of recruiters and applicants in large cities of China. *Journal of Managerial Psychology, 21*(5), 459-475.

Zusman, R., & Landis, R. (2004). Applicant preferences for web-based versus traditional job posting. *Computers in Human Behaviour, 18,* 285-296.

KEY TERMS

E-Recruiting: Is any form of online recruitment service including job boards, specialized niche job sites, resume databases and career networks.

Innovation: Is the new development of a product, service, or idea that is perceived by individuals as new.

The Lead User Method: Is a qualitative workshop similar setting heralded in the new product innovation literature as enhancing radical breakthrough innovations.

Online Communities: Are places where users with similar interests meet for social online interaction.

Organizational Performance: Means the sustainability of an e-recruiting portal.

Service Innovation: We define service innovation as any new services developed during innovation processes which are valuable for customers.

Social Networks: Are the representation of connections among registered users of an IS system.

User Participation: Is the decision of users to use a service for the long run.

User Involvement: Is the engagement of users in the generation of potentially innovative activities.

Chapter XVI
What Makes the Difference?
Introducing an Integrated Information System Architecture for Employer Branding and Recruiting

Sven Laumer
University of Bamberg, Germany

Andreas Eckhardt
University of Frankfurt a. Main, Germany

ABSTRACT

In 2007 Erickson and Gratton asked "What it means to work here" and discussed the need for a structured approach to establishing an employer image among potential employees. In July 2007, Lee also proposed an architecture for a next-generation holistic e-recruiting system. Based on these ideas and a design science approach we propose an extension of this framework by adding employer branding as an important new component and structured sub-process. Based on an extensive review of IS and HR literature, we show how employer branding should be integrated into the existing architecture to develop and implement an effective employer branding strategy. The results are a first step towards an architecture for a holistic e-HR management system.

INTRODUCTION

"What it means to work here". In a 2007 discussion Erickson and Gratton asked the question, "What makes a firm attractive for employees?" Many applicants might prefer large companies with strong brand reputations. However, prod-

uct brand and employer brand are different, and there are substantially more firms looking for employees than most candidates realize. In fact, it is easy to conclude from the literature that a top-notch image is the exclusive province of a select few (e.g. Keller, 2002). Hence, firms need to develop a strategy to promote themselves as an attractive employer (Erickson and Gratton, 2007). In a competitive labor market, one way for a business to stand out is to develop an employer 'brand' that will attract good candidates. An employer brand is a set of tangible and intangible attributes and qualities that make an organisation distinctive, promise a particular kind of working experience, and appeal to those people who will thrive and perform their best in its culture (Lievens et al. 2007, Know & Freemann, 2006). However, as Erickson and Gratton (2007) point out, "companies—even very large ones—don't need to be all things to all people. In fact, they shouldn't try to be." While e-recruiting has matured substantially over the years, the recruiting sub-process of employer branding is considered to be particularly important but not sufficiently mastered by HR executives. As our review of marketing, recruiting and IS literature indicates, there is a need for a structured approach to managing the recruiting process and supporting it with information systems. The existing models of the recruiting process cover all important aspects other than employer branding.

The approach of our paper is therefore to extend the architecture of the holistic e-recruiting system introduced by Lee (2007) to structure both the process and the supporting information systems for the recruiting process and the employer branding approach.

Therefore we chose a design science approach (Hevner et al., 2004) to develop an IT-architecture which would align the holistic e-recruiting system with the Employer Branding process. Our research design is based on the approach with seven guidelines created by Hevner et al. (2004). However, we have not yet addressed the evaluation of our architecture design and suggest this for further research. To provide a rigorous research design we followed these guidelines (Hevner et al. 2004) and structured our paper as follows. The following section analyses the problem of whether or not there is a need for a structured recruiting process. A rigorous theoretical background to the concept

of employer branding as discussed in the marketing and recruiting literature and an overview of existing models of the recruiting process can be found in section 3. This section also analyzes the need for extending the existing architecture of an e-recruiting system as propounded by Lee (2007). In section 4 we discuss an extension by adding the process steps of developing and implementing an employer branding strategy. Section 4 explains the design as a search process and leads to the artifact of this research, and we extend e-recruiting architecture in section 5. A brief summary pointing out the research contribution of our results with a statement of their implications for further research finalizes the paper in sections 6 and 7.

PROBLEM RELEVANCE

This section discusses the relevance of our research topic and presents the findings of our literature review. Due to a global talent shortage, for example for groups of engineers and IT workers, we identified corporate staff recruitment as an interesting research area. As shown by a current call for papers by the European Journal of Information Systems (EJIS) (Riemenschneider et al. 2008) and surveys such as Luftman's issues for IT-executives (Luftman et al. 2006), the successful hiring of specific target groups as IT professionals is a major challenge in both theory and practice.

In 2002 Agarwal and Ferratt forecast that talent shortage on the IT labor market will cause an enduring problem. The imbalance between demand and labor supply can be traced back to the 1980s. At that time the Fortune 500 firms in the US often had more than 100 vacancies for IT-specific work profiles. In economically underdeveloped regions of the country in particular, it became extremely difficult for companies to recruit qualified IT-workers (Rifkin 1989). The importance of both information technology and its workforce increased over the following years due to competition in almost every branch of industry and the disappearance of traditional boundaries (Keen, 1991). This growing demand for IT services led to a serious shortage of sufficiently qualified IT professionals (King, 1997). Among the reasons for the specific shortage of IT talents were the greater demand for specific technical knowledge and process management skills required from IS staff compared to average employees (Gillian, 1994). Therefore King stated in 1997 that one of the biggest challenges for the IT- and IT-related industries would be attracting and retaining talent.

In anticipation of this upcoming problem a few researchers started to develop human resources strategies for more effective IT-professional recruitment. The first step was to design strategies to facilitate the definition of the IT skills required for the vacant work profiles and to identify the sources of potential hires. Results of a study by Smits et al. (1993) showed that the description of the vacant job profile within the job ads was a valuable opportunity for attracting highly skilled candidates for a specific company. Agarwal and Farrett (1998) chose a different approach and observed successful companies and their practices in staff recruitment in order to build up a taxonomy of IT recruiting practices. Their results showed that successful hires could sometimes be traced back to a company's network. The use of networks to disseminate an employer's attractiveness represented a completely new way of effecting staff recruitment. Closer relationships with universities or further academic institutions offered an effective channel for hiring top students directly from college (Agarwal & Farrett, 1998). Referrals represented not only an effective recruiting mechanism in relationships with academic institutions but also for hires through the networks of the company's employees. For example, one company within their survey managed to recruit 60% of all hires from internal referrals.

The first step towards a defined strategy for recruiting IT-professionals was a taxonomy which included the practice categories for IT-staff recruitment. This taxonomy is separated into four divisions: sourcing, skills sought, competitive differentiation elements and one-off inducements. Sourcing means a source from which a need for IT-professionals is met. A further part of the taxonomy was the mix of skills sought to identify prospective hires for the IT organization. Competitive differentiation elements are the basis upon which an IT corporation demonstrates itself to be an attractive place to work during the whole process of IT-staff recruitment. Finally, one-off inducements on a limited basis help to attract the relevant candidate to the organization. (Agarwal & Ferratt, 1998) This framework with four categories is the first step in showing what practices companies follow within their staff recruitment.

The general framework with four categories was extended in subsequent years. Ferratt et al. (1999) observed that the seriousness of the shortage problem determined the importance of the recruitment practices used for hiring IT professionals. The results showed that the importance ratings for particular recruiting mechanisms differed according to whether or not recruitment where there was a talent shortage was seen to be a significant problem. For example, the use of online instruments is regarded as very important by companies who assess IT-staff recruitment as a major problem. The reason for this lies in the opportunity it offers to reach and attract a larger number of applicants beyond the regular catchment area. Moreover, the companies should be able to process a larger number of applications compared to traditional methods. In the category of competitive differentiation, it is obvious that those companies who regard IT-talent shortage as a serious issue need to make extra effort. Another clear result reveals that companies negatively affected by an overall IT-talent shortage believe that they must demonstrate the company's unique strengths, overall reputation, visibility and vision with the objective of attracting IT professionals on a long term basis (Ferratt et al. 1999).

A further step towards defining a combined IT-HR strategy for the recruiting of IT-professionals is the application of five strategic levers. The first of these five levers is located in the point of recruitment, and focuses on the HR practices essential for influencing the application behavior of IT-professionals. Compensation packages also tend to be effective in attracting candidates to a particular company. Balancing the needs of both productivity and the individual could be further strategic levers, consisting of HR practices focused on the work of IT professionals, while maintaining their productivity, work arrangements, performance measurement and employability training and development. The fifth lever is career development and security for each candidate. This lever represents the direct linkage between the recruiting, attracting and developing of candidates (Agarwal & Ferratt, 2001).

A necessary condition for the successful implementation of strategies in IT-staff recruitment is also strongly related to the relationship between the IT and HR-departments (Schwarzkopf et al. 2004). A case study of 30 senior managers of 15 companies compared these internal relationships. This showed that the IT-departments regarded the related HR departments either as a nuisance, a service bureau or a valued partner. As a result of this observation, Schwarzkopf et al. (2004) specify four main IT-employment approaches. The first strategy dealt with the use of external contractors and consultants to control uncertainty of talent shortage. IT departments undoubtedly benefit from better relationships with HR; HR specialists could give valuable support in terms of legal risk, skills tracking, skills assessment, and other trends that can reduce IT staffing uncertainty. Better information systems provide better forecasting and a closer connection with their organizations' overall business planning process. Finally, lateral relationships help to delegate skill development decisions to departments or individuals.

IT-professionals are a group of candidates who display specific behavior in the application process. IT-professionals act in the recruiting process in more or less defined patterns. They use certain channels to seek information about potential employers and job descriptions. The companies need to adjust to these behavioral patterns and attract their candidates using the channels the IT-professionals prefer. The group of IT-professionals tends to look for vacancies published on corporate websites and on internet job boards. Speaking generally for companies, the most promising way to attract IT-professionals is the internet (Keim & Weitzel, 2006). The following subchapter describes the underlying theories for the development of long-term candidate attraction. This long-term candidate attraction is also known as employer branding.

RESEARCH RIGOR

As discussed in the previous section, the labor market for IT professionals can be characterised as an especially competitive one. The challenge for the organisations is to differentiate themselves in order to successfully attract and recruit talented staff. Therefore in this section we summarize prior research findings about the concept of employer branding as well as the recruiting process as a whole.

Research Rigor: Employer Branding

Our review of marketing, recruiting and IS literature indicates that one possibile way of meeting this challenge is to communicate an attractive image of the firm to potential employees. Stern et al. (2001) suggest that "image is generally conceived of as the outcome of a transaction whereby signals emitted by a marketing unit are received by a receptor and organized into a mental perception of the sending unit." They cite Ind (1990) to support their definition of an employer image: it "is simply the picture that an audience has of an organisation through the accumulation of all received messages". In addition de Chernatony and Dall'Olmo Riley (1998) conclude that 'brand' is "a multidimensional construct whereby managers augment products or services with values and [which] facilitates the process by which consumers confidently recognise and appreciate those values". For our research we define 'image' and 'brand' as presented here and specify the usage of the term consumer and brand as "the consumers are potential recruits and the 'brand' is the augmentation of recruitment services provided by recruiters as they espouse the firm's attributes and values during the recruitment process" (Knox & Freemann, 2006).

Marketing literature recognises the importance of combining a company's internal and external image to manage the correlation of all brand concepts that can be recognised by customers, employees and job seekers (Dukerich & Carter, 2000; Duncan & Moriarty, 1998). This not only impacts the perception of the image among employees, potential employees and customers, it also aligns employees with the brand (Keller, 2002). Ind (2001) points out that some companies such as Nike have de facto employer brand without an explicit human resource marketing strategy. However, most companies do not have the level of recognition by jobseekers that Nike has. For example, Eckhardt et al. (2007) present a case study of a German company and their need to evaluate an employer branding strategy to attract potential candidates. Indeed, there are a lot of different marketing methods that contribute towards the formation of the employer brand: recruitment marketing plans, outputs which may require advertising, press coverage, sponsorship, word-of-mouth endorsement and contacts with employees (Kennedy, 1977; Dowling, 1994; Dowling, 2001; Stuart, 1999).

In addition, the recruiting literature agrees that employer brand image is a significant predictor of early decisions made by new recruits about their employers (Gatewood et al. 1993). The perception of an employer influences on the one hand the perception of the recruiter's behaviour by an applicant and on the other hand the job itself and its perceived organisational attributes after the interview (Truban et al. 1998). Taylor and Bergmann (1987) explain that the influence of communication on an employer brand image is particularly important in the early stages of the recruitment process. With respect to the 'war for talent', Ewing et al. (2002) and Ambler and Barrow (1996) introduce the notion of branding the firm to potential and existing employees in order to develop this as a distinguishing feature. They use the terms 'employment brand' and 'employer brand' respectively to characterise the package of functional, economic and psychological benefits provided by employment and identified with the employing firm.

Erickson and Gratton (2007) discuss "what it means to work here". They emphasize that "companies that successfully create and communicate signature experiences understand that different types of people will excel at different companies and that not all workers want the same things". They propose three elements of engagement by which a company might foster deep commitment from their employees. First, a comprehensive understanding of potential employees' characteristics is needed. Second, it is also necessary to have a structured strategy of communicating an employer image that on the one hand conveys the attributes and values of the organization to potential hires while at the same time intensifying those of employees. Third, the communication must include a coherent employee experience. Erickson and Gratton (2007) conclude that companies need more than one employer branding strategy because of the different characteristics of the employers' target groups. Each group must be addressed by a different strategy. In addition, Mitchell (2002) points out that, to enhance productivity, a branding strategy has to be designed not only for external candidates but also for employees already working for the company.

Some research has been done which discusses the impact and design of employer branding. Backhaus (2004) analyses how companies use an online recruiting platform (monster.com) to communicate their employer branding and Lievens et al. (2007) evaluate the situation from both the applicant's and the employee's point of view, to consider what aspects are important for an internal and external employer image. Kirchgeorg and Lorbeer (2002) introduce a model to include the different aspects of employer branding. Figure 1 illustrates that socio-demographic factors, personal values, the course of study, the current career status and occupational group influence information and application channels used by job seekers, and the establishing of employer and job requirements. An employer branding strategy has to address all five factors that affect the formation of an individual's understanding of employer and jobs requirements.

As explained in section above, an integrated employer branding strategy is necessary. This section discusses the concepts of employer branding and image to communicate to employees the attractiveness of working for the company. The next section will present different approaches to structuring the different concepts of the recruiting challenges.

Research Rigor: Recruiting Process

Various research contributions contain valuable approaches to the definition of the structure and stages of classic staff recruitment in large-scale enterprises. These processes differ much more than recruitment in small and medium-sized enterprises. Recruitment in SME's is more related to the availability of a known individual than to the process itself. Atkinson and Meager (1994) found evidence of a correlation between business size and the adoption of formal recruiting procedures and confirmed this hypothesis. Several authors recommend a systematic four-stage procedure for starting a recruiting process; assessing if vacancies need to be filled, a definition and broad analysis of the job profile, the production of a job description and a person specification (Carroll et al. 1999). The overall process was sectioned in three phases: generating applicants, maintaining applicant status and influencing job-choice decisions (Barber, 1998). These phases require that certain activities be carried out. To generate applicants the companies have to advertise their vacancies in paper based or digital media. The maintaining of applicants' interest could be strengthened by professional treatment during a site visit. Finally certain recruitment actions (e.g. the timeliness of a job offer) may increase the likelihood of whether an applicant accepts a job offer or not (Barber 1998). Breaugh and Starke (2000) used this phase-model to portray the recruitment process as a combination of activities, variables and strategic measures to achieve a number of recruitment objectives whose outcomes are compared afterwards. Figure 2 now visual-

Figure 1. Analytical model explaining job seekers' behaviours (Kirchgeorg & Lorbeer 2002)

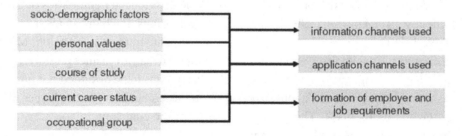

Figure 2. A model of the organizational recruitment process (Breaugh & Starke 2000)

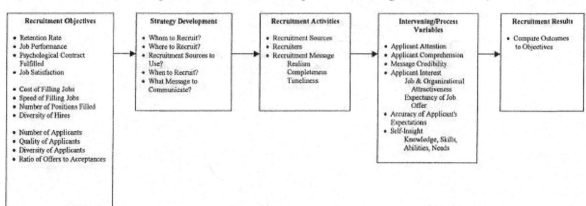

izes the model of the organizational recruitment process (Breaugh & Starke, 2000).

In a next step Faerber et al. (2003) integrated the different recruitment functions within the process. Their model showed which tasks are related to the recruitment of new employees starting from the first contact between candidate and company till the signing of the contract. Based on previous work (Albert, 1998; Schneider, 1995), the process design contained the recruiter's five main tasks: short- and long-term candidate attraction, applicant management, pre- and final selection of candidates. The focus in this approach is the management and tracking of applications in organizations as well as the integration of being attractive to applicants in the long term to build up the image of an attractive employer.

As can be seen, a lot of research has been done on the design of recruiting processes and its related tasks. Despite the increasing use of information technology, little is known about the design of recruiting processes and their supporting IT-functions. A valuable initial approach to designing an e-recruiting process was made by Lee (2005), who developed a business process diagram to visualize intra-organizational information flows and internal processing events (Figure 3). A simulation using this business process diagram showed that the e-recruiting process produces

better results for the time-to-hire (average process time) and costs per hire than the traditional recruiting process.

The opportunities offered by e-recruiting compared to the traditional process are clearly visible not only in terms of process time and cost but also for process quality and external circumstances such as a talent shortage on the IT labor market. It is our aim to extend an existing architecture of an e-recruiting process (Lee, 2007) to assure a constant high number of applicants in addition to providing an efficient measure for the recruitment of IT professionals.

DESIGN AS A SEARCH PROCESS

"Finding and retaining valued workers in information technology demands bold and innovative solutions" (Agarwal & Ferratt, 2002). So we tried to extend an existing technology to improve the e-recruiting process. For this we chose the architecture of the holistic e-recruiting system invented by Lee (2007).

We extend this architecture by adding a new component for the e-recruiting process. We based this component on existing literature (e.g. Erikson & Gratton, 2007, Kirchgeorg & Lorbeer, 2002) and tried to solve existing problems in staff re-

Figure 3. The business process diagram for the recruiting process (Lee 2005)

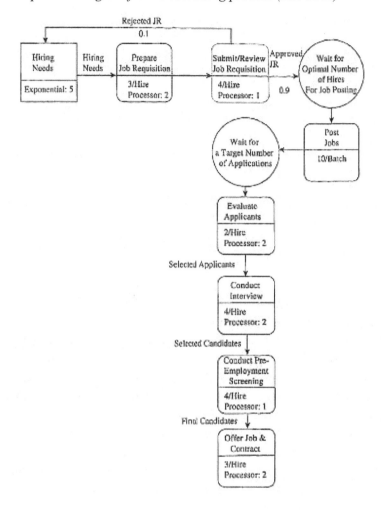

cruitment identified in theory and practice. These problems are:

- A talent shortage for several target groups, especially IT-professionals
- No chance to influence and convince candidates before or early in the recruiting process
- A cyclical recruiting of all companies on the labor market
- Appropriate alternatives to attract candidates

DESIGN AS AN ARTEFACT

We designed and developed one specific artifact in our research. The artifact produced is an extended IT-architecture for a holistic e-recruiting system including the sub process of Employer Branding. Figure 4 shows the holistic e-recruiting system described by Lee (2007) and our extensions to this approach (highlighted). Additionally to the new component of candidate attraction with employer branding campaigns, we also added the dataflow between this component and an image campaign requisition management subsystem as well as the

Figure 4. An extended architecture for a holistic e-recruiting system

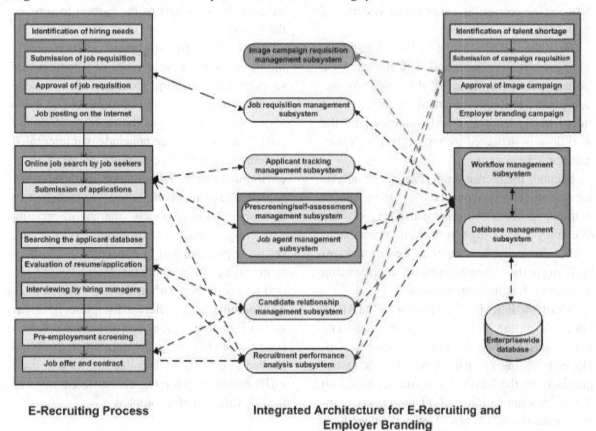

E-Recruiting Process   **Integrated Architecture for E-Recruiting and Employer Branding**

workflow management system. We also linked the component with a candidate relationship management system because the data of potential candidates gained in this phase are important for candidate relationship management. The dataflow to the recruitment analysis performance subsystem will help to analyse this attraction measure (Figure 4).

SYSTEMS

The development of employer branding campaigns and the approval of a specific action are the two major tasks related to the employer branding process. The process is managed by the "image campaign requisition management subsystem"

and its performance is analyzed by the "recruitment performance analysis subsystem". Thus, the focus of the system is to streamline the developing of employer branding campaigns and to establish an employer image of a company among actual and potential employees. Therefore the manager responsible for employer branding is the main user of the system, but recruiting managers and top-management may also use the systems.

INTERFACES

The "image campaign requisition management subsystem" (ICRM) is the central system for managing employer branding activities and its activities are strongly connected with recruiting ones. Thus, this section points out the interfaces between the recruiting management system and the ICRM.

First, the ICRM is connected to the workflow management subsystem and with the database management subsystem. All data and information related to employer branding activities are stored in the enterprise wide database and the workflow is managed by the central workflow management system.

Second, the recruiting performance analysis subsystem (RPAS) is connected with the employer branding process to measure the performance of employer branding activities. It is possible to analyze for example whether a specific employer branding activity is responsible for an increasing number of qualified applications.

Third, the ICRM is connected with the RPAS via the workflow management subsystem. The ICRM can identify the need for specific employer branding campaigns based on statistics provided by the RPAS. For example, based on the decreasing number of IT-professional applications, the ICRM can identify the need for a specific IT-employee campaign and for the ICRM advice employer branding managers to develop valuable activities.

Fourth, if existing employer branding campaigns are valuable in job ads, the job requisition management subsystem can scan the enterprise database for specific implementation activities to add them to their communication strategy.

RESEARCH COMMUNICATION

The limitation of our research is that our approach is based solely on a literature review. We have discussed concepts of marketing, recruiting and information systems. The concept we recommended must be validated by a case study or empirical research to highlight the benefits of a holistic e-recruiting system. Even so, as Lee (2007) suggested, the holistic e-recruiting system is expensive and complex and a lot of companies have to choose a part of the system to support their needs.

Nonetheless the suggested architecture is the basis for the development of a system that supports the recruiting process. This is indeed a major implication for practitioners. The motivation for our paper was the shortage of skilled staff. Therefore we can conclude that integrated system architecture is essential for a competitive environment on the labor market. To develop our approach to employer branding we conducted an extensive literature review,. thereby integrating marketing (brand), recruiting (employer brand, ecruiting process) and IS concepts (IS architecture) concepts into a holistic system.

Future research can benefit from this approach. The combination of different disciplines like marketing, human resources, recruiting, information systems, talent management, psychology etc. is needed to develop an architecture for a holistic e-HR system which integrates different tasks of the HR-function of a company.

RESEARCH CONTRIBUTIONS

Our paper suggests an extension of the architecture of the holistic e-recruiting system by Lee (2007). Based on a design science approach (Hevner et al. 2004) we extend the model by including the concept of employer branding and model the process with the steps 'Identification of talent shortage', 'submission of campaign requisition', 'approval of image campaign' and 'employer branding campaign'. Furthermore we added the 'image campaign requisition management subsystem' to support this process with IT. This subsystem is connected with the 'workflow and database management subsystem', 'candidate relationship management subsystem' and the 'recruiting performance analysis subsystem'. With this proposal, employer branding can be support by IS to develop and implement effective employer branding campaigns.

REFERENCES

Agarwal, R., & Ferratt, T. W. (1998). Recruiting, Retaining, and Developing IT Professionals: An Empirically Derived Taxonomy of Human Resource Practices. In R. Agarwal (Ed.), *Proceedings of the 1998 ACM SIGCPRLSIGMIS Conference* (pp. 292-302). New York, NY: Association for Computing Machinery.

Agarwal, R., & Ferratt, T. W. (2001). Crafting an HR strategy to meet the need for IT workers. *Communications of the ACM, 44(7)*, 58-64.

Agarwal, R., & Ferratt, T.W. (2002). Enduring Practices for Managing Information Technology Professionals. *Communications of the ACM, 5(9)*, 73-79.

Albert, G. (1998). *Betriebliche Personalwirtschaft*. Kiehl: Ludwigshafen.

Ambler, T., & Barrow, S. (1996). The Employer Brand. *The Journal of Brand Management, 4(3)*, 85-206.

Atkinson, J., & Meager, N. (1994). Running to stand still: the small firm in the labour market. In J. Atkinson & D. Storey (Eds.), *Employment, the Small Firm and the Labour Market*. London: Routledge.

Backhaus, K. B. (2004). An exploration of corporate recruitment descriptions on monster. com. *Journal of Business Communication, 41(2)*, 115-136.

Barber, A. E. (1998). *Recruiting employees*. Thousand Oaks, CA: Sage Publications.

Breaugh, J. A.,& Starke, M. (2000). Research on Employee Recruitment: So Many Studies, So Many Remaining Question. *Journal of Management, 26(3)*, 405-434.

Carroll, M., Marchington, M., Earnshaw, J., & Taylor, S. (1999). Recruitment in small firms: Processes, methods and problems. *Employee Relations, 21(3)*, 236-250.

Ferratt, T. W., Agarwal, R., Moore, J. E., & Brown, C. V. (1999). Observations from 'the front': IT Executives on practices to recruit and retain information technology professionals". In: *Proceedings of the SIGCPR '99*. New Orleans LA, USA.

De Chernatony, L., & Dall'Olmo Riley, F. (1998). Defining a 'Brand': Beyond the Literature with experts' Interpretations. *Journal of Marketing Management, 14*, 417-443.

Duncan, T., & Moriarty, S. E. (1998). A Communication Based Marketing Model for Managing Relationships. *Journal of Marketing, 62(2)*, 1-13.

Dukerich, J. M., &Carter, S. M. (2000). Distorted Images and Reputation Repair. In M. Schultz, M. J. Hatch & M. H. Larsen (Eds.), *The Expressive Organization: Linking Identity, Reputation, and the Corporate Brand* (pp. 97-112). Oxford: Oxford University Press.

Dowling, G. R. (1994). *Corporate Reputations: Strategies for Developing the Corporate Brand*. Melbourne: Longman Professional Publishing.

Dowling, G. R. (2001). *Creating Corporate Reputations: Identity, Image and Performance*. Oxford: Oxford University Press.

Eckhardt, A., Laumer, S., & Weitzel, T. (2008). Extending the Architecture for a Next-Generation Holistic E-Recruiting System. In: *Proceedings of the 2008 International Conference on Information Resources Management (Conf-IRM)*, Niagara Falls, Ontario, Canada.

Eckhardt, A., Weitzel, T., Koenig, W., & Buschbacher, J. (2007). How to Convince People who don't like IT to use IT—A Case Study on E-Recruiting. In: *Proceedings of the Thirteen Americas Conference on Information Systems 2007 (AMCIS)*, Keystone, Colorado, USA.

Ewing, M. J., Pitt, L. F., de Bussy, N. M., & Berthon, P. (2002). Employment Branding in the

Knowledge Economy. *International Journal of Advertising, 21*, 3-22.

Erickson, T. J., & Gratton, L. (2007). What it means to work here. *Harvard Business Review, 3,*104-112.

Faerber, F., Keim, T., & Weitzel, T. (2003). An Automated Recommendation Approach to Personnel Selection. In: *Proceedings of the 2003 Americas Conference on Information Systems*, Tampa.

Gatewood, R. D., Gowan, M. A., & Lautenschlager, G. J. (1993). Corporate Image, Recruitment Image and Initial Job Choice. *Academy of Management Journal, 36*, 414-424.

Gillian, P. (1994). Tame the Restless Computer Professional. *HR Magazine, 39*(11), 142-144.

Hevner, A. R., March, S.T., Park, J., & Ram, S. (2004). Design Science in Information Systems Research. *MIS Quarterly, 28*(1), 75-105.

Ind, N. (1990). *The Corporate Image*. London: Kogan Page.

Ind, N. (2001). *Living The Brand: How to Transform Every Member of Your Organization into a Brand Champion*. London: Kogan Page.

Keen, P. G. W. (1991). *Shaping the Future: Business Design Through Information Technology*. Cambridge, MA: Harvard Business Press.

Keller, K. L. (2002). *Strategic Brand Management*. Second Edition, New Jersey: Prentice Hall.

Keim, T., & Weitzel, T. (2006). Strategies for Hiring IT Professionals: An Empirical Analysis of Employer and Job Seeker Behavior on the IT Labor Market. In: *Proceedings of the Twelfth Americas Conference on Information Systems*. Acapulco, Mexico.

Kennedy, S. H. (1977). Nurturing Corporate Images. *European Management Journal, 11*(3), 120-164.

Kirchgeorg, M., & Lorbeer, A. (2002). Anforderungen von High Potentials an Unternehmen. *Arbeitspapier der Handelshochschule Leipzig (HHL), 49*.

King, J. (1997). IT Labor Emergency Promots Feds to Study, Fix Shortage. *Computerworld*, October 6.

Knox, S., & Freemann, C. (2006). Measuring and Managing Employer Brand Image in the Service Industry. *Journal of Marketing Management, 22*, 695-716.

Lee, I. (2005). An integrated economic decision and simulation methodology for e-recruiting process redesign. *International Journal of Simulation and Process Modelling, 1*(3/4), 179-188.

Lee, I. (2007). The Architecture for a Next-Generation Holistic E-Recruiting System. *Communications of the ACM,50*(7), 81-85.

Lievens, F., Hoye, G.V., & Ansell, F. (2007). Organizational Identity and Employer Image: Towards a Unifying Framework. *British Journal of Management, 18*, 45–59.

Luftman, J., Kempaiah, R., & Nash, E. (2006). Key Issues for IT Executives 2005. *MIS Quarterly Executive, 5*(2), 81-99.

Mitchell, C. (2002). Selling the Brand Inside. *Harvard Business Review, 1-2,* 73-80.

Riemenschneider, C., Moore, J. E., & Armstrong, D. (2008). Call for papers - Special Issue on Meeting the Renewed Demand for IT Workers. *European Journal of Information Systems (EJIS)*. Retrieved from http://www.palgrave-journals.com/ejis/CFP-EJIS-ITWorkers.pdf.

Rifkin, G. (1989). Recruiting in MIS: Facing Up to Hire Stakes. *Computerworld, 23*(6), February 13.

Schneider, B. (1995). *Personalbeschaffung*. Frankfurt: Peter Lang Europaeischer Verlag der Wissenschaften.

Schwarzkopf, A. B., Mejias, R. , Jasperson, J., Saunders, C., & Gruenwald, H. (2001). *Effective practices for IT skills staffing", Communications of the ACM, 47*(1), 83-88.

Stern, B., Zinkhan, G. M., & Jaju, A. (2001). Marketing Images: Construct Definition, Measurement Issues, and Theory Development. *Marketing Theory, 1*(2), 201-224.

Smits, S., McLean, E. R., & Tanner, J. R. (1993). Managing high-achieving information systems professionals. *Journal of Management Information Systems, 9*(4), 103-120.

Taylor, M. S., & Bergmann, T. J. (1987). Organizational Recruitment Activities and Applicants' Reactions at Different Stages of the Recruitment Process. *Personnel Psychology, 40*, 261-285.

Turban, D. B., Forret, M. L., & Hendrickson, C. L. (1998). Applicant Attraction to Firm Influences of Organization Reputation, Job and Organizational Attributes, and Recruiter Behaviours. *Journal of Vocational Behaviour, 52*, 24-44.

KEY TERMS

Candidate Attraction: Candidate attraction is part of the sourcing step of the recruiting process. In contrast to employer branding candidate attraction has a short-term focus on candidates. While the candidate attraction phase the HR-department is publishing job ads or is directly searching for appropriate candidates. Job ads can be published "offline" and "online". Classical offline channels are newspapers or magazines and typical online channels are the company's website or job portal such as monster. Companies can search directly in CV-databases of job portals or online communities (xing, linkedIn) to approach appropriate candidates. The main objective of candidate attraction is to generate applications.

Employer Branding: Employer Branding is a strategic instrument where marketing concepts particularly branding are applied to represent a company as an attractive employer and positions the company on the labor market. The result of employer branding campaigns is the employer brand. That means specific designed perception of the employer by job seekers. The main objective of employer branding are an effective and efficient recruitment and an enduring increase quality of applicants. Employer branding is not only design for external candidates it can be also used to address actual employees to link them with the company (retention). Employer branding has a long-term focus on candidates.

E-Recruiting: E-Recruiting (Electronic Recruiting) means to support the recruitment by the use of electronic media and HR-systems. An effective e-Recruiting system supports employers as well as job seekers. E-Recruiting and its supporting systems represent ideally the entire recruiting workflow. This includes the candidate attraction and all the communications between companies and candidates until the completion of the application. E-Recruiting systems are for example a company's HR-website, an internet job board such as monster and a company's system to manage applications.

HR-Strategy (Hiring Strategy): HR-Strategy is the general strategy of the HR-department. It includes the hiring strategy, talent management strategy and retention strategy. The main objective is to engage employees positively and successfully to achieve the company's corporate purpose and strategic goals. For HR-strategy being successful it is important that the HR-strategy is satisfying the business needs, the needs of customers and the needs of employees. An effective HR Strategy is an integral part of corporate strategy and is deduced from the general business strategy of a company.

IT-Architecture: The term "IT-Architectur" summarizes all static and dynamic aspects of IT (information technology) in organizations. These aspects include the infrastructure like hardware, software and data as well as the management of IT (configuration and capacity planning, load balancing, data backup, availability, reliability, disaster-planning, etc.). Furthermore functional aspects such as the necessary interfaces that provide a frictionless IT support of the business processes of organizations are part of the "IT architecture".

War for Talent: The "War for Talent" was introduced by Elizabeth G. Chambers, Mark Foulon, Helen Handfield-Jones, Steven M. Hankin and Edward G. Michaels III in "The McKinsey Quarterly" (Vol. 1) 1998 discussing an expected talent shortage on the labor market. They pointed out that talent matters and that companies who are successful on the market are those who are the best with locating, assessing, recruiting, and keeping the most talented people. More and more companies start to "fight" for the most talented people and become competitors on the labor market as well.

Chapter XVII
The Enrichment of the HR Intranet Linked to the Regulation's Processes Between HR Actors

Karine Guiderdoni-Jourdain
*The Institute of Labour Economics and Industrial Sociology (LEST),
Université de la Méditerranee, France*

ABSTRACT

The subject of our communication will be a better understanding of how the regulation between the on line HR designers and HR experts is built, and to know about the consequences on the HR intranet's enrichment and the HR reengineering. The author's communication will articulate in two parts. Firstly, she will come back on the e-HR concept in a way to enrich the definition proposed above by a systematic approach. Secondly, individuals will see how this model, mentioned in all the speeches, meets the logic of the different actors and how the differences between them could be managed; which raises an issue to resolve.

INTRODUCTION

In response to a more competitive environment and stronger requirements from the customers and the shareholders in terms of profitability, reduction of the structural costs, the Human Resources Department has to convince the Board of Management of its capacities of innovation, adaptability and flexibility. For this purpose, the

HR Management invests increasingly in a new model of functioning: the e-HR.

According to literature the e-HR, based on a company strategy and linked to the Information and Communication Technology, is a global functioning mode of a company around a significant number of HR processes which leads to the sharing of HR information and its treatment by direct and free access of the employees, the Management and the HR function and to the setting-up of a new HR organisation in order to optimise the customer relationship. This dynamics leads the HR Management to design its own way of changing by optimising its organisation and by trying to convince the HR actors to adopt this role of strategic business partners, in the scope of which they are supposed to reduce the costs of co-ordination and to favour co-operation between the various groups of actors. Achieving a better distribution of messages and optimising the HR service are the first objectives. The middle management is one of the privileged customers to satisfy, because its own role within the company also changes. The improvement of HR communication is generally accompanied by the development and the integration of an HR intranet. There are various steps of development of this tool associated to different functionality. Usually this tool, based on the Information Communication Technology[1], is considered as a technical support with which the required performances can be obtained.

However, as useful as this tool might be, it is first of all a person-related instrument which means that its potential efficiency depends on individual strategies and schemes. A good co-operation between HR actors requires daily efforts. The cost of such efforts is difficult to measure. Our assumption is that the level of internal co-operation influences the elaboration of a stimulating contents, leading to the concrete use of this tool for the HR actors as their customers.

The subject of our communication will be a better understanding of how this regulation between the various HR actors is built, and to know about the consequences on the HR intranet's enrichment. Three parts will be presented. Firstly, we will focus on the e-HR concept in a way to enrich the definition proposed above by a systematic approach. In the second and third parties, we will see how this model, mentioned in all the speeches, meets the logic of the different actors and how the differences between them could be managed. Which raises a issue to resolve.

FOR AN ENRICHMENT OF THE E-HR CONCEPT

The evolution of the HR function has been announced in specialised magazines since the end of the 1990s. Some researchers have made aware HR professionals of their difficult position in the company and of the necessity to transform the function (Ulrich, 1997). Thus, the HR department must show its added business value. To do so, certain guidelines must be followed: become more service-oriented, more focused on its clients, being aware of HR commitment and contribution towards the company performance (Lepark & Snell, 1998 ; Ulrich 1999 ; Wright 1998 ; Rüel, Bondarouk & Looise, 2004). In this context, the support of Information Communication Technology (ICT) is considered to be essential—which leads us to the e-HR concept.

A Brief Story About the E-HR Concept

Different models of this concept exist, but many of them are influenced by a technological determinism. According to us, e-HR is more than a concept. It is a new way of thinking the company and its actors. This is why it seems important to schematise it differently by articulating the evolution of actors of the company in various stages of development of an HR intranet. It is our proposal to exceed the risk of the technological and organisational determinisms and provide us with a more systematic approach.

E-HR as a Basic Element of a New Model of Functioning

Regarding the definition of e-HR, we have been influenced by the thinking of Huub Rüel and his colleagues. According to them, the e-component is not only the symbol of a technical advance, but the imprint of a deeper transformation of the

HR position within the company: a new "*way of thinking about interaction, service-provision, and communication*" in order to "*redefine HR profession*" (Rüel, Bondarouk & Looise, 2004, p 17).

The use of ICT would have an impact on the management of the HR process and would transform the relation between the HR department and its environment. A model of functioning based on e-HR stands for the access to and a treatment of the HR information by all actors of the company, not only the HR staff. Thus, this system would provide employees with the responsibility to manage their own personal data and their own professional development, whereas the manager, without an intermediary, would completely intervene in the HR process. That is the aggregation of new actors in the HR area.

The HR Intranet, an Adequate Support for the Change

In the literature, the HR intranet is presented at the same time as a tool for supporting the middle management (Messeghem & Pierson, 2003) and for improving HR performance (Matmati, 2002). The main question is to know why these two actors would accept to change or not in connection with the development of an HR intranet.

For an HR actor, anxious to show his added value to the business, the intranet tool can become a material support on which a number of new HR applications can be found. These services would provide the HR function with the opportunity to change.

For the middle management, things are different because it is considered a key actor of the company's transformations. Its position is between the Board of Management and the staff, and it is this position, which makes it to manage concretely evolutions of identities, of professions and larger work transformations. It means that the middle management "*becomes the initiator and the founder*" of ICT (Laval, 2000, p85). This is why HR consider him as their first customer to satisfy.

According to this vision, the accessibility of new HR services would give the opportunity to the middle management to explore new forms of organisation and to become more independent (Messeghem & Pierson, 2003; Kalika, 2002).

In their article, Florence Laval, Veronique Guilloux and Michel Kalika explain the Intranet potentialities as the main instrument for the HR department to improve its performance. They present six applications[2] in relation with three stages of HR intranet development.

The first stage corresponds to the "Corporate Intranet", which is mainly focused on internal communications, with a special site for HR information (HR processes, legal elements…). It is dedicated to all employees of the company.

The second stage is called "Non specialised Intranet", of which the originality is e-administration. Using the workflow technology, HR offers to employees some on-line automated administrative services (leaves, bills, certificates …). Others sections are: more information about mobility management; an access to training services; specific applications to support new forms of network organisation. This intranet is currently managed by the HR function. Such on-line administrative services lead the HR intranet manager to create specific interfaces for each actor (employees, managers, HR staff, and the Board of Management). It corresponds to an HR Self-Service approach.

The "Specialised Intranet" is the most accomplished stage. Containing the previous level, it has been further enriched by new applications: e-learning, e-competence and knowledge management. We are in a transversal dynamics, of which one of the main objectives is to capitalise the company's knowledge.

It is evident that the intranet tool has the potential to help the various actors of the company to change. Nevertheless, we think that it is not enough to speak about a concomitant evolution of the role of the manager and of the HR actor, without a strong link to the level of the HR Intranet tool's development.

The essential question is to determine how these transfers of competencies are concretely being made? How the "hierarchical" learns to become this "first HR" according to Ulrich, and then become more and more the "manager-boss". And, on the other hand, how does the HR become a real "business-partner", then a "consultant-expert" while it is currently considered a mere administrator ? How can a compromise between these two actors be found?

Beyond the abstract and normative models, the concrete approach of these crossing points is scarce in the academic literature.

Far from claiming to revolve around these complex questions, we propose an ongoing modelling of these crossings of change's trajectories by adding progressively three hypotheses.

An Ongoing Modeling of the Crossing of Change's Trajectories

We propose three ways to understand the crossing of change's trajectories between the three actors identified in the company (HR actor; Manager actor; Employee) and the technical evolution of the HR intranet. The first hypothesis to take in account is the interdependence of the change's trajectories (1.2.1). The second hypothesis introduces the notion of time in the change's process (1.2.2). The third one concerns the heterogeneity of the company's actors (1.2.3).

Hypothesis 1: The Interdependence of the Change's Trajectories

The first additional hypothesis concerns the interdependent character of these changes which occur in the company. In the figure below, we want to show that these trajectories of change are more than simultaneous, they are interdependent. The level of transformation of an actor has a strong impact on the evolution of other actors on the scene.

Nevertheless, this first figure does not suffice, because the simultaneous character of these changes does not seem real. If it were, this would mean that all actors of the company would change at the same time. However, each actor is different and has his own rhythm of change.

Figure 1. Modeling of the interdependence of the change's trajectories

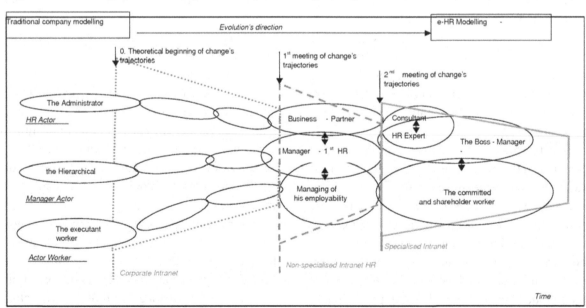

Figure 2. Tendency 1, the HR as main pilot of the change

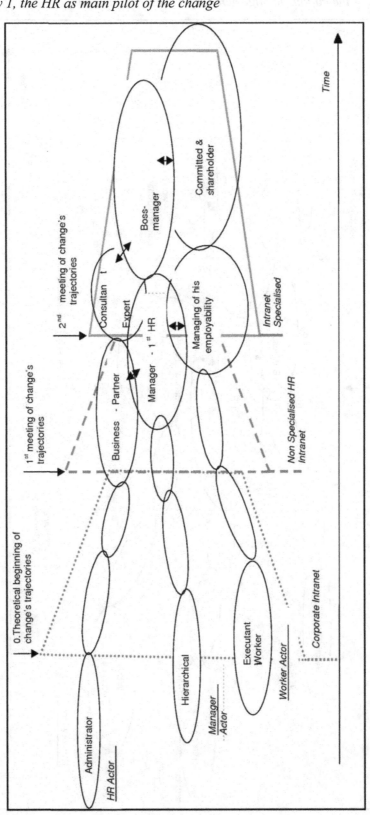

Figure 3. Tendency 2, the middle management as precursor of the change

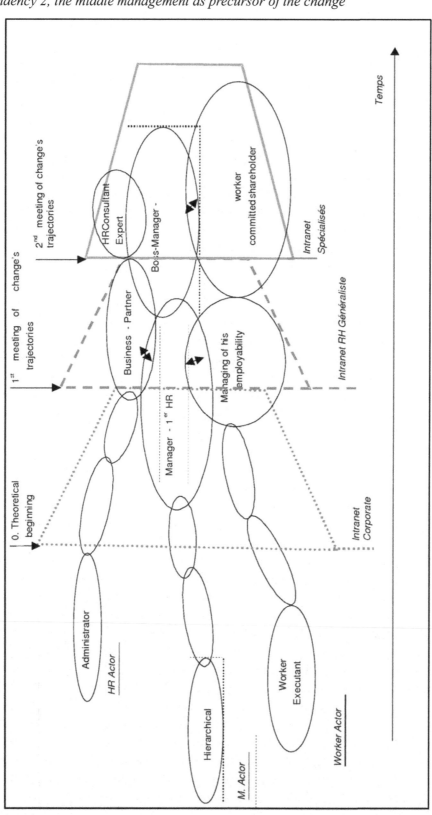

Figure 4. Tendency 3, Employees as pilots of the change

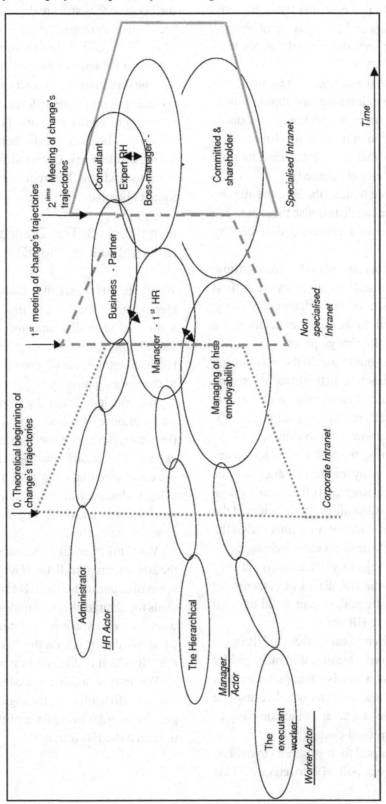

If we follow normative speeches, HR should lead the change. In this case, the HR actor must pull the other actors on his trajectory of change. Hypothesis 2: the consideration of various temporalities of the change

The temporality of the change is the time necessary for negotiations, learning, and appropriation. If we are in a logic of movement of the standards and the construction of new actors (Iribarne, on 2001), this means that change can take its time according to the actor concerned.

Without wanting to describe here the all possible situations, we can distinguish three possible tendencies of evolution according to the motricity of actors.

This first case corresponds to the most optimal situation for the HR staff because they are the first actors who have started their change trajectory. Their evolution will make the other actors of the company enter in the change process.

This situation would remove the outsourcing risk from the HR function. In this case, we assume that the HR intranet would bring to the middle management as to all employees genuine services, which effectively allow them to evolve.

Even if becoming the first HR is not an enthusiastic idea for many middle managers (as this increases their daily workload), their needs oblige them to act and to stimulate the other actors of the company. Here, the middle management takes the lead and concretely implements the change.

However, this trajectory of change is not very advantageous for the HR. Risks of outsourcing or reorganisation are real, except if old internal alliances protect the HR actors.

In this case, we can assume that the HR intranet is not being used. Because it is managed by the HR department which is not in phase with its customers' needs and expectations, because the HR function is the last actor of the company to enter into a dynamics of change.

The employees pull their superiors to evolve, and these managers pull HR to change. This change's trajectory is not favourable for the HR actor, because they still are the last ones to approach the change. Perhaps, the effect of a domestic use of Internet could explain this advanced employee position in change dynamics (Iribarne, 2001).

The interest of all these figures is to show that the change could take different trajectories in the time according to the actors. This last hypothesis makes us conclude on the heterogeneity of the various collectives. Or, we strongly assume that we also find this heterogeneity in one and the same collective.

Hypothesis 3: The Consideration of the Different Actors' Plurality

We made our thesis in a company in management science. During our first year, we realised a survey: 53 middle managers had been interviewed concerning their feeling and use of the HR intranet. This work confirms our hypothesis of the actors' plurality.

We concluded that the middle management was composed by five typical actors[3]. Each of them considered and used the HR intranet and by extension had a different approach on the change. We concluded that the way of understanding and using technology depended on the nature of the user's activity and on the organisational structure in which he evolves.

We think that, like the middle management, the HR actor is pluralistic. If we return to the most optimal situation for the HR function, in which it leads the change, this will imply that the HR must work in a real spirit of co-operation. However, we think that it is exactly this heterogeneity of the HR which is difficult to manage.

We propose to give you concrete examples of the daily difficulties to manage this HR's heterogeneity in order to create useful information and to enrich the HR intranet.

A BRIEF STORY ABOUT THE HR INTRANET OF AN AERONAUTICAL AND SPACE COMPANY

If we admit that the HR intranet is above all a tool built, managed and used by different profiles of individuals, then we can assume that the HR strategy, the level of co-operation within the HR department, the methods and means chosen to stimulate the appropriation and the use of new applications, are essential indicators which lead us to understand the real state of the HR change.

Research Method

As we have already said, we prepare a PhD in management science within the Human Resources direction of a major Aeronautical and Space company, which we shall name *Aero*.

During our first year of study, we realised a survey about the perception and the use of the HR intranet of the middle management. Our method was classic. We collected data through semi-structured interviews (53 middle managers had been interviewed).

Nevertheless, we had to change our method of collecting data for studying the HR actor, because of our real integration in the team in charge of the HR intranet project. What classifies our work in the register of research-action (David, 2002).

The Aero's HR Intranet: Its Implementation and the Consequences of a New High Management for its Evolution

For a better understanding of the difficulties to manage an intranet project, we think it is important to explain you, in few words, the evolution of the Aero's HR intranet.

From 2001 to 2003: The Beginning of the HR Intranet as an Official Vector of Information

At the end of 2001, the director of Human Resource thought it important for his department to have an HR site on the Corporate Intranet, which had recently been created by the department of Communications. For that, an HR intranet manager was appointed to take care of HR information and to work together with the other department in charge of the intranet project: Communications and Information System.

At the same time, the director of HR keeps on investing in the domain of communications. He creates an internal communications service inside his department. Therefore, the simultaneous investment in a HR intranet site and a service dedicated to the communication shows his determination to manage and control better the quality and the distribution of the HR information. His strategy is to transform the HR image. In reality, this directorate is considered being isolated, whose policy and actions are not transparent.

How did the users (the middle management and employees) react to the implementation of this HR tool?

Reactions are mitigated. We note that this tool, as the Aero'Corporate Intranet, had been introduced without any specific communication and training strategies.

Concretely, employees discovered the HR intranet either on-the-job or by friendly relations. Many of them consider the Corporate Intranet, including the HR part, to follow a fashion.

The middle management, who is usually interested in technology, did not massively use the HR intranet. Some of them thought that this type of instrument had to remain in the domain of secretarial work.

Over this period, the HR Intranet was used, but not too frequently. In reality, this tool did not find its place among the other tools of information support which were already used by the Aero's employees and were more settled in their habits of communicating.

Since April 2003: A Dynamics of Communication in Relation with a New Top-Level Management

In spring 2003, a new generation of leaders is arriving at Aero. The new CEO and the new HR director share common interests: their profiles and their methods of management, inspired by American practices, strongly differ from the ones of their predecessors. An important HR re-organisation has begun, which directly impacted on the evolution of the HR intranet. The new HR strategy is closer to the case presented in our first part[4], which considers the HR function as the leader of the change.

According to the new HR director, the HR function must resolve a double difficulty: at the same time, HR must change itself and must help the other departments in their processes of transformation. To succeed these challenges, the internal communications service is considered as an essential support.

The HR re-organisation officially hands over the management of the HR intranet to the internal communications manager. And a new HR intranet manager arrives with more technical skills than his predecessor. This new element provides the internal communications service with a concrete solution to enrich the HR intranet.

The Concrete Evolution of the Aero HR Intranet

Before having the means to develop the HR intranet, an only intranet site exists "Space for Employee" which readily corresponds to the "Corporate Intranet", the first level into the HR intranet typology presented by Michel Kalika and his colleagues (Kalika 2002, p70-74).

The evolution of the Aero's HR intranet drives from a concrete structuration of HR information according to the specificity of the actors. This results in the creation of two additional HR intranet sites: a "Space for Manager" at first and a few months later a "HR Space". There, we can find our three key actors of the company.

In the vision of HR creators, these two virtual spaces have been imagined as a combined answer to resolve the double HR issue: the *Espace RH* must be a tool privileged by HR staff to better work together and to improve the HR service. The interest of the Space for Manager is to bring to the managers a HR and Corporate information that corresponds better to their needs and expectations.

AN EXAMPLE OF AN EXTENSION OF THE HR INTRANET

Though a precise example, we want to describe the difficulties for HR conceptors in charge of the HR intranet to manage the evolution of their on line tool. Firstly, we will present the internal communications service of Aero and his objectives. Secondly, we will focus on the process adopted by designers to involve the HR individuals in the dynamics of a collaborative work, which is an essential element to implement the HR intranet. And at the end, we wonder if this extension of the HR intranet is a success or not.

This Project Derives from the Initiative of the Internal Communications Service

The project concerns the virtual site for the HR staff, "HR Space". It will be an on-line application for a better identification of the HR members.

This project is above all the idea of the internal communications manager. According to her, this tool is indispensable, because the department of Human Resources has known a recent reorganisation. In this context, it is necessary to provide the HR staff, from any hierarchical level, with the possibility to know exactly and find "*who is who*" in its department, and "*who does what*".

This project is a concrete example of an internal solution to the double challenge of HR transformation[5]. In this line, the on-line "*who is who*" could help the HR actor to improve its service. For example, if one of a HR member's customers asks him a specific question, and he cannot answer it because he does not know who in the new HR organisation is now in charge of these questions. With the system proposed, the HR actor can run a specific on-line query (different fields exist as "keyword"). With the tool's answer, he can directly contact the responsible person and provide his customer with a useful answer. Or he can refer to this other HR expert if he judges if it is necessary for revolving customer's issue.

In reality, this on-line tool on the "HR Space" is not so original and innovative, because before its creation the HR department functioned anyway. However, this knowledge of the HR staff depends on the number of years spent in this same department. That is why we think that the tool's originality consists in having created a sort of cultural shortcut, a new solution to reduce functional costs.

An Individual Negotiation Around Contents

After discussion[6], the method, which has been chosen to pilot this project, is composed of four steps. The main objective is to involve the HR individuals in the dynamics of a collaborative work.

Step No. 1: Explanation of the Project and its Learning-By-Doing Methods

From the list of all HR staff and with the first model of this on-line "*who is who*", we contact each HR

member by telephone to present the project of this specific application and globally the philosophy of this HR virtual space. Currently, this exercise goes along with a direct application. We ask the individual to use his keyboard at the same time as we do in order to accompany him in this first discovery of the tool and for many of them the "*HR Space*" too. For testing the application, we ask them to click on the precise name of an HR staff member[7]. Then, they directly obtain a concrete example of which type of information the tool can supply.

Step No. 2: The HR Future-User Becomes a Supplier of Contents: The Beginning of Negotiations

In a second step, the HR individual has to describe his main tasks in some keywords. All the negotiation is focused on the limitation and the choice of the keywords. The user provides us with his proposal of contents either at the phone (we take notes) or by e-mail. It is important to note here the important association of various tools of information support. It refers to the concept of "*wallet of communications*" (Kalika, 2002).

Step No. 3: The First HR Individual Visit for Validation of the Content

After having received the content of his main responsibilities, we enter this information in the tool's system (only the HR intranet team has the access right to do it). Then, we send an e-mail to the HR staff member concerned to ask him/her to verify if our summary is correct, or if she wants us to integrate some modifications. In this e-mail, we purposely refer to the access to the "*HR Space*", without a hypertext link in order to incite her to try to do it alone.

Step No. 4: Last Negotiations for a Final Validation

We think that our first step, reserved to an accompanying discovery of the tool and our direct request around the validation of professional activities, leads us to think that it is a good method to interest and to stimulate a co-operative work inside the HR department.

The HR staff seems enthusiastic to have had the opportunity to describe their jobs without any hierarchical pressure. In 100 % of the cases, we obtained a validation accompanied by only a few modifications (not fundamental).

A Successful Process of Regulation Between HR Actors?

It is difficult today to say if this project is a success. It is obviously too early to interpret the rates of connection. Indeed, these last ones were important, because we asked the HR individuals to verify their on-line contents. That means that these first visits remain on a learning stage and do not translate the real internalisation of this tool.

The interest of this project is to have allowed two HR entities to work collectively: the internal communications service on one side and every HR individual on the other side. Each entity had its own strategy for driving the other in a positive direction: the HR designer with his four step method, trying to push the HR individual to use the on-line tool, and the HR member wanting to impose special keywords to show the value of his/her work to the HR designer.

Regarding this point, we studied some cases where the negotiation around keywords was harder. The phone contact was not enough; a "face-to-face" meeting was useful to find a consensus.

CONCLUSION

We wanted to show throughout this work that the concept of e-HR is much more complex than it appears. This complexity comes from the interdependence between technological evolutions and movements of the standards and the construction of new actors. These transformations have different temporalities.

Our example of an extension of the HR Space demonstrates that thinking concretely the change requires many efforts of negotiations, discussions, in order to find a compromise between the various HR actors (HR designer and HR future-user). The will of being more service-oriented associated to the HR Intranet's development is a new topic for the HR function, which requires a particular learning stage and new competencies (especially in the domain of communications). This concrete example shows that even if the strategy of the HR director strongly incites to adopt a different behaviour by using this tool, it is still difficult to change the current habits.

REFERENCES

Barthe, S., & Castro-Goncalves, L. (2002). Quelles stratégies d'intégration des TIC ? Défis et enjeux des applications Liber-Service RH. In M. Kalika (Ed.), *e-GRH : Révolution ou Evolution? Relever le défi de l'intégration des TIC dans la fonction Ressources Humaines* (pp. 37-61). Paris: Editions Liaisons.

Besseyre-Des-Horts, C. H. (2002). La GRH est-elle créatrice de valeur ? une application au cas du e-RH. *Revue de Gestion des Ressources Humaines, 46*, 8-9.

David, A. (2002). Décision, conception et recherche en sciences de gestion. *Revue Française de Gestion*, juillet –août.

Iribarne, A., & Tchobanian, R. (2001). *Les processus de diffusion et d'appropriation des outils multimédias en réseaux et les transformations des activités professionnelles. Le cas de France Telecom.* Paper presented in Seminaries in The Institute of Labour Economics and Industrial Sociology, France.

Laval, F., Guilloux, V., & Kalika, M. (2002). Les Intranets RH: pratiques des entreprises et problématiques. In M. Kalika (Ed.), *e-GRH : Révolution ou Evolution ? Relever le défi de l'intégration des TIC dans la fonction Ressources Humaines* (pp. 63-90). Paris: Editions Liaisons.

Lepark, D., & Snell, S.A. (1998). Virtual HR : strategic human resource management in the 21st century. *Human Resource Management Review, 8*(3), 215-234.

Matmati, M. (2002). L'Intranet RH, outil de la performance organisationnelle ? In M. Kalika (Ed.), *e-GRH : Révolution ou Evolution ? Relever le défi de l'intégration des TIC dans la fonction Ressources Humaines* (pp. 91-122). Paris: Editions Liaisons.

Merck, B. (2003). *Equipes RH, acteurs de la str@tégie. L'e-rh : mode ou révolution ?* Paris: Editions d'Organisation.

Messeghem, K., & Pierson, F. (2003). *Intranet et rôle de l'encadrement intermédiaire.* Paper presented at the meeting of « la 2ième Journée d'étude " GRH et TIC ", Université Paris-Dauphine, Paris, France.

Ruël, H., Bondarouk, T., & Looise, J. K. (2004). *E-HRM: innovation or irritation ? An exploration of web-based human resource management in large companies.* Utrecht: Lemma Publishers.

Ulrich, D. (1997). *Human Resource Champions.* Boston: Harvard Business School Press.

Wright, P. (1998). Introduction: strategic human resource management research in the 21st century. *Human Resource Management Review, 8*(3), 187-191.

KEY TERMS

Corporate Intranet: It is the first stage of intranet development. It is mainly focused on internal communications, with a special site for HR information (HR processes, legal elements...), dedicated to all employees of the company.

e-HR: Electronic-Human Resource is a group of web-based applications and processes that automate and support HR services and management. The e-HR is a way of working for companies based on a deeper transformation of the HR department.

HR Intranet: Intranet is a network based on TCP/IP protocol, which can be linked to Internet. HR intranet is the part of this tool dedicated to on-line services offered by the Human Resources department.

HR Self-Service: Term employs to characterize the HR on-line administrative services which provide a free access to employees, managers, HR team and the Board of Management for a direct and personal data management.

Intranet Use: The way people daily utilize the on line tools.

Middle Management: The category of population characterizes by its specific position between the Board of Management and the staff. This population is one of the most important HR clients to satisfy, because they are considered as a key factor in the company's transformation through managerial style and discourse.

Non Specialised Intranet: It is the second level of intranet development. It is mainly characterized by the e-administration: leaves, bills, certificates... Other sections are: more information about mobility management; an access to training services; specific applications to support new forms of network organization.

Specialised Intranet: It is the most accomplished level of the HR Intranet tool's development. Containing the "non specialised" stage, some new applications appear like e-learning, e-competence and knowledge management.

ENDNOTES

[1]   We will use the abbreviation «ICT».

[2]   Six applications: HR information, e-administrative; e-mobility; e-recruitment; e-learning; e-competence and applications for knowledge management

[3]   Our five typical actors are «super technicien»; «patron de chaîne»; «artisan industriel»; «électron libre»; «hydride».

[4]   Cf: 5 page.

[5]   As we have already said, the HR department faces a double challenge: changing itself and at the same time helping other departments to change.

[6]   Between the internal communications manager, the HR intranet manager and us, we decide that we will be in charge to contact all HR staff.

[7]   We propose the name of someone who works for a very long time in the HR department. In reality, we assume that this person is known by anyone and especially her tasks too. We have the assumption that if the future HR user of this tool already understands better its utility during the first trial, we can hope of a better internalisation, and finally a better use of it.

Section VI
e–HRM Use and Performance Improvement

Chapter XVIII
Exploring Perceptions about the use of e–HRM Tools in Medium Sized Organizations

Tanya Bondarouk
University of Twente, The Netherlands

Vincent ter Horst
Saxion Knowledge Center Innovation and Entrepreneurship, The Netherlands

Sander Engbers
COGAS BV. Business Unit Infra & Networkmanagement, The Netherlands

ABSTRACT

This research focuses on acceptance of Human Resource Information Systems (HRIS) in medium sized organizations. We look at general SME's in The Netherlands. The goal of this research is to analyse the perceptions about the use of HRIS as there is currently very little knowledge about it in "medium sized organizations". To support the explorative nature of the research question, four case studies were selected in organizations that were using HRIS. Overall we conclude that the use of e-tools in medium sized organizations is perceived as useful, whereas not easy to use. The organizations involved perceive that the use of HRIS helps them to make HRM more effective.

INTRODUCTION

Nowadays IT supports critical HRM functions such as recruitment, selection, benefits management, training, and performance appraisal (Grensing-Pophal, 2001). During last decade large organizations have for several reasons implemented an increasing number of electronic Human Resource Management (e-HRM) solutions (Ruël et al., 2007; Ruta, 2005; Voermans and Veldhoven, 2007). While large organizations are no longer surprised by e-HRM, SME's are at the early stage of its adoption.

Our knowledge about HRM practices in SME's is odd (Huselid, 2003), but even less – about e-enabled HRM in SME's. Only during the last couple of years research into HRM in SME's has taken off. According to Heneman *et al.* (2000), scholars are lamenting the dearth of information about HRM practices in SME's as the existing HRM theories are often developed and tested in large organizations. At the same time, there is a serious need in the development/ application of HRM concepts in the environment of SME's as well-motivated and well-trained workers are probably the most important assets for smaller companies to stay competitive (Huselid, 2003). De Kok (2003) puts forward two main arguments which justify the specific attention for SME's: firstly, SME's form a large and vital part of modern economies; and secondly, despite the heterogeneous character of the SME sector, SME's differentiate from large organisations in many respects.

This bias in HR research is of course understandable. Larger companies have the resources and people available to implement and perform state of the art HR policies and practices and are thus more exciting research playgrounds. They usually have more, and more sophisticated HR in place. But neglecting SME's is inconvenient, given their position in most economies.

In the US for instance, 99,7% of all companies have fewer than 500 employees (the US definition of SME's is all companies with fewer than 500 employees), a startling 78,8% have fewer than 10 employees (Heneman et al. 2000). The European definition of SME's is companies with fewer than 250 employees. If we use that definition, in the Netherlands 714.000 out of a grand total of 717.035 companies are SME's. Only about 1300 companies have more than 500 employees, whereas about 386.890 have no employees at all (Van Riemsdijk and Bondarouk, 2005). According to the Dutch organisation for SME's companies with up to 250 employees (99% of all Dutch companies) provide

2.8 million jobs, more than half of the total of 4.8 million jobs in the Dutch private sector. 48% of the added value and 53% of yearly turnover of this sector is generated by these small and medium sized companies (Meijaard et al., 2002).

Yet good personnel management seems at least as important for small companies as for larger ones, and owners/directors of small companies are well aware of that. Indeed, next to general management issues, personnel policies are seen as the most important aspect of management by owners/directors of smaller companies (Hess, 1987 in Hornsby and Kurato, 1990). At the same time top management in smaller companies find personnel policy issues both difficult and frustrating (Verser, 1987, cited in Hornsby & Kurato, 1990). In other words, many owners/ directors of SME's do find HR important enough to occupy themselves with it directly, but at the same time find it very hard to address the issue in a proper way and could use some help on the topic.

Concluding, what is known is that SME's account for a significant proportion of employment in different countries, and that the owners/ managers of SME's have high interest in personnel issues. However, what is not known is how people are managed in these firms, and to which extent information technologies play a role in people management (if any). The number of articles looking at the HRM issues in small business is increasing (Special Issues in the *Human Resource Management Review* in 1999 and 2006 are good evidence for the growing interest in it). However, as Heneman et al (2000) and Cardon and Stevens (2004) have shown, the progress has been slow.

Research into electronic HRM did not touch SME's yet. There is no clarity whether SME's use e-HRM applications and for what purposes, what the full advantages of e-HRM for SME's are (if any), and to what extent e-HRM improves HR processes. It is hard to accurately capture the extent of e-HRM usage by SME's as the data on e-HRM practices is primarily based on research in large organizations.

Because of the very important position of SME's in our economies, at one hand, but our limited understanding of HRM and specifically e-HRM in SME's, at another hand, we started an explorative research into e-HRM in Dutch SME's. Our goal was to analyse the use of e-HRM tools in SME's, and compare it with what we know about e-HRM large organizations. Research question, therefore was formulated as "How do SME's perceive the use of e-HRM tools?"

This research has been done in cooperation with Unit 4 Agresso. Unit 4 Agresso is a software company that offers to the market IT solutions for the HRM administrative processes.

THEORETICAL FRAMEWORK

In order to build a theoretical guideline for an empirical exploration, we need first to crystallize characteristics of HRM processes in SME's.

Human Resource Management in SME's

It is widely acknowledged that larger organizations benefit from a formalization of the HRM practices as they are more focused on standardizing tasks and formalize HR practices to be more efficient (for example in recruiting). Contrary to that, small organizations are expected to benefit from informal HR practices as they could create jobs around unique experience, skills, knowledge and interests of employees.

From empirical research we learn that especially for the formalisation of HR policies, size is very important. Hornsby and Kurato (1990) in their research on 247 US SME's made a division into three 'size-classes'; 1-50 (53% of their population), 51-100 (22%), 101-150 (25%) employees based on the assumption that with increasing size personnel policies would grow more complex and more formalised. It became clear that the sophistication of the personnel activities was directly

linked with size: the bigger the company, the more sophisticated and extensive were the policies in use. One remarkable result came out with regard to a question on what company owners would consider to be the most important personnel domains for the coming years. All mention the same domains, albeit in a somewhat different order of importance: 1. establishing pay-rates and secondary remuneration 2. availability of good personnel 3. training 4. the effects of government regulations and 5. job security. All of which can be tackled by implementing good personnel policies, they conclude.

This result by Hornsby and Kurato (1990), is mirrored in other research as well. Kotey and Slade (2005) conclude that a blueprint for optimal organisation cannot be given for all companies. They expect that two trends will be discernable whenever companies grow in size: first an increasing division of labour, leading to more horizontal and vertical differentiation and secondly that this differentiation will first increase rapidly and then decline in speed. They therefore also divided their research population of 371 companies into three 'size classes'; micro, 0-5 employees, small: 5-29 and medium sized: 30-100. Again it proved that the formalisation of HR increases with size and that the critical 'turning point' is at about 20 employees. From that moment on informal recruiting, but also direct supervision and other direct management styles become inefficient. The owner starts to get overburdened and has to delegate tasks to other managers.

Yet in another study, Kok et al (2003) looked into the formalisation of HR practices in Dutch SME's. They looked at companies with up to 500 employees and tried to establish which context variables explain HR formalisation. The variables included in the research were size, the existence of a business plan, export orientation, whether the company was a franchise organisation or not, if it was a family owned business and the level of union representation in the company. They further looked at the existence of an HR function, at selection procedures, reward systems, training and development programmes and appraisal systems. Again it proved that with increasing size the formalisation of HR practices increases but as soon as the context variables are taken into account, 50% of the difference in formalisation evaporates.

From the empirical evidence presented so far we conclude that indeed size of the company should be an important predictor of HR sophistication and the formalisation of HR practices. Size not only seems to predict the complexity of the organisation structure, but also seems to provide a justification for applying more standardised jobs, thereby providing an opportunity for standardising important elements of HR policies, such as recruitment and selection, remuneration and appraisal schemes, training and development. Growth in size would lead to more complex structures and might well overstretch the capabilities of the owner/manager, forcing him to delegate responsibilities to subordinates or other managers. Indeed even the existence of a separate HR function or department seems to be dependent on size, and once such a position is created, the formalisation of HR practices might increase because of that.

Strategy and SME's

A literature overview and a research model for "researching personnel management in Dutch Small and Medium Sized Enterprises" were presented by van Riemsdijk *et al.* (2005). They concluded that especially two contingencies were the most important: company size and strategy. According to them the empirical evidence of de Kok *et al.* (2003) showed that size should be an important predictor of HRM sophistication and the formalization of HRM practices. On the other hand they argue that strategy can be relevant for SME's and their HRM. The strategic choices of the so called "dominant coalition", in SME's the owner or director, are very important for the way

an organization is run. In this case the strategy has influence on the way HRM is fulfilled in SME's.

Based on previous research van Riemsdijk *et al.* (2005) conclude that SME's strategic orientation can be based on the Miles & Snow typology (Miles & Snow, 1978; in van Riemsdijk *et al.*, 2005). This typology distinguishes defenders, prospectors, analysers, and reactors. A defender tries to do the best job possible in its area of expertise, it offers a relatively stable set of services to defined markets. A prospector frequently changes its products and services, continually trying to be first in the market. An analyser unites the characteristics of defenders and prospectors, it tries to selectively move into new areas but at the same time tries to maintain a relatively stable base of products. A reactor is in the opinion of Miles & Snow 'the rest', they do not have a consistent strategy. Unfortunately van Riemsdijk *et al.* (2005) were not able to operationalize these typologies of strategy in a proper way into their study at SME's. This was caused by the fact that the used typologies were too difficult for their research population; the operationalization of the business strategy needed more attention.

Next to the typology of Miles & Snow other typologies for the strategic orientation of SME's are used in research. The typology of Porter is also researched at SME's (Gibcus & Kemp, 2003). Porter distinguishes three generic strategies: cost leadership, differentiation, and focus (cost focus & differentiation focus). With a cost leadership an organization tries to become the low-cost producer in its market. They must find and exploit all sources of cost advantage. With differentiation an organization tries to be unique in some dimensions which are highly valued by the customers. When an organization chooses for a focus strategy it focuses on the specific group / segment and creates a strategy which serves the customers optimally to serving them to the exclusion of others. The organizations that do not fit with one of these three generic strategies are called 'stuck in the middle'.

Gibcus & Kemp (2003) conducted research in Dutch SME's, in which SME's are defined as organizations with up to 100 employees. For the data collection they used the so-called 'EIM SME panel'. By computer assisted telephone interviews about 2000 organizations were approached. They concluded that only one out of five SME's have a written strategy and that five distinct strategies came forward: innovation differentiation strategy, marketing differentiation strategy, service differentiation strategy, process differentiation strategy and cost-leadership strategy. These are all based on the typology of Porter but slightly adjusted for SME's. Especially differentiation plays a important role because cost leadership is mainly possible with large-scale production. Next to those conclusions they point to further research in the combination of the typology of Miles & Snow and the typology of Porter.

Based on de Kok (2003) we add growth strategy to the distinguished strategies by Gibcus & Kemp (2003), and van Riemsdijk *et al.* (2005). De Kok (2003) proposed, based on the behavioural and strategic contingency perspectives and other empirical research (Lengnick and Hall & Lengnick and Hall, 1988; in de Kok, 2003), that growth orientation is an important contextual determinant for the existence of HRM practices.

The availability of a business plan or strategic plan can be interpreted as a characteristic of organizations with a relatively long planning horizon. The presence of a business plan can be used to indicate whether the goals and strategies are made explicit. This business plan may be seen as an indicator for enterprises that have a relatively high degree of formalization. Therefore de Kok *et al.* (2003) argue that organizations with a business plan or a strategic plan (or strategy) have more formal HRM practices and are more likely to have an HRM department or HRM manager. We assume that besides the existence of a business / strategic plan, the communication about the strategy is also very important. It is important that employees are aware of the existence of the strategy.

Based on the literature about SME's we expect that the characteristics / content of HRM in medium sized organizations are determined by the size and the strategy of the organization.

HRM Practices in SME's

Cardon and Stevens (2004) sought out scholarly articles concerning human resource practices in entrepreneurial organizations, as defined by the authors of those articles. They found 83 articles in several journals about general management, entrepreneurship and human resource management, as well as several scholarly book chapters in this area. They then coded each article to determine if it was theoretical or empirical and the size and life cycle stage of the organizations it discussed. In the end 37 articles survived their evaluation. Their paper reviews known HRM practices in SME's.

Cardon and Stevens (2004) and others (e.g., Heneman and Tansky, 2002) have stated that the organizations ability to address the challenges faced by small and medium sized organizations depends on organizational approaches to staffing, compensation, training and development, performance management, organizational change, and labour relations. The ability to cope with these challenges influences the organizational effectiveness and survival.

From the literature research about HRM in SME's we can observe some similarities. When looking at these six mentioned practices, we can conclude that these are almost similar to the categorization of de Kok *et al.* (2003); recruitment, selection, compensation, training and development, and appraisal. Others like van Riemsdijk *et al.* (2005) consider 8 traditional HRM fields that are commonly used in a questionnaire research in SME's: HRM planning, Recruitment & Selection, Training & Development, Performance evaluation, Rewarding & Remuneration, Career Development, Employer-Employee relations, and Sickness policies. Van Riemsdijk *et al.* (2005)

choose these HRM fields based on large organizations.

In the following overview we will focus on the six HRM practices in SME's according to Cardon & Stevens (2004).

Staffing

Staffing concerns recruiting, selection and hiring of employees. According to Hornsby & Kuratko (1990) staffing is very important for SME's, and as Heneman & Berkley (1999) argue, may even be the key component of overall effective management of organizational human resources (In: Cardon & Stevens, 2004). But staffing can be problematic due to several reasons. Limited financial and material resources (In Cardon & Stevens, 2004: Hannan & Freeman, 1984), lack of legitimacy as an employer-of-choice (In Cardon & Stevens, 2004: Williamson, 2000), and the high numbers of jobs where employees typically perform multiple roles with unclear boundaries and job responsibilities (In Cardon & Stevens, 2004: May, 1997) are reasons why recruiting is problematic.

The person-organization fit is an important selection criteria (In Cardon & Stevens, 2004: Chatman, 1991). Norms, values and beliefs of the organizations and applicants are considered as important (In Cardon & Stevens, 2004: Williamson 2000, Williamson *et al.*, 2002) Also the focus is more on the match of applicants competences to general organizational needs, than on the match of applicants competencies to specific job requirements (Heneman *et al.*, 2000).

Strategies about staffing are often ad hoc in SME's (In Cardon & Stevens, 2004: Heneman & Berkley, 1999). Often the general manager is responsible for HRM, rather than HR professionals (In Cardon & Stevens, 2004: Longenecker, Moore, and Petty, 1994). A new trend about staffing concerns the outsourcing of HR activities to professional employer organizations (PEO). Organizations also use contingent labour brokers

(e.g. for temporary workers) to recruit employees (In Cardon & Stevens, 2004: Cardon, 2003).

From the literature can be concluded that there are differences between SME's and large organizations in the practice of staffing. SME's seem to be more ad hoc in staffing, the fit between employee and organization (culture) is the most important (more than between the employee and the function). Jobs in SME's also have less typical boundaries, and are more multitasking. Staffing seems to be less formal, but is certainly very important in SME's.

Compensation

Compensation involves all the decisions an organization makes concerning payment of its workers, including pay levels, pay mixes, pay structure and pay raises (In Cardon & Stevens, 2004: Balkin & Logan, 1988). Case study evidence suggests, although more research is necessary (Heneman et al., 2000), that SME's are more likely to view compensation from a total rewards perspective than are large companies (e.g. In Cardon & Stevens, 2004: Nelson, 1994). With a total rewards perspective compensation is seen in addition to monetary rewards in the form of base pay and incentives includes psychological rewards, learning opportunities and recognition (In Cardon & Stevens, 2004: Graham et al., 2002; Heneman et al., 2000))

SME's differ from large organizations in compensation. Especially in pay mix differences occur. In SME's there is more variable at-risk pay in the mix (In Cardon & Stevens, 2004: Balkin & Gomez-Mejia, 1984; Barringer, Jones, & Lewis, 1988; Milkovich, Gerhart, & Hannon, 1991). The pay mix also changes over the life cycle of the organization, when an organization moves from a growth stage to a mature stage of its products (In Cardon & Stevens, 2004: Balkin & Gomez-Mejia, 1984).

Because SME's have usually flat organizational structures with few levels of management and tend to treat employees in an egalitarian way with regard to compensation and rewards, pay structure between large organizations and SME's may differ (In Cardon & Stevens, 2004: Graham *et al.*, 2002). According to Balkin & Logan (1988) small organizations keep traditional hierarchical distinctions to a minimum so that rewards are not indicative of status difference among employees. We assume that through the lack of status difference by rewards within SME's, SME's will not pay much attention to formal compensation (In: Cardon & Stevens, 2004).

Pay raises are also different between SME's and large organizations. Large organizations are common with automatic annual salary increases, whereas SME's usually cannot afford these pay raises because of high uncertainty of sales or profits (In Cardon & Stevens, 2004: Balkin & Logan, 1988).

Because of gaps in education of employees (due to the changing role of employees in the organization and changing organizational and market conditions), SME's often provide educational benefits as a sort of compensation (Balkin and Logan, 1988, In Cardon & Stevens, 2004).

Training & Development

In SME's unstructured training, informal job instruction, and socialization are very important for the training processes (In Cardon & Stevens, 2004: Chao, 1997). These can be seen as a substitute for formal training. Nowadays the process of socialization (through informal and formal training) is seen as very important (In Cardon & Stevens, 2004: Rollag, 2002; Rollag & Cardon, 2003). Due to a faster and more extensive inclusion newcomers might be more productive and satisfied with their job than newcomers in large organizations.

For SME's, the costs of formal training programs and the time spent away from productive work are important considerations for determining what training opportunities to provide to workers, as resources of both money and worker time are constrained (Banks *et al.*, 1987). Next to that sources of formal training are more restricted for SME's than for large organizations. Trade associations, short college seminars, and in-house training are the main sources for employee development within SME's.

An other aspect which increases the importance of training in SME's are the changing roles and expectations of employees within the organization. Due to changing organizational and environmental conditions multitasking is an important aspect of employees (In Cardon & Stevens, 2004: May, 1997).

Performance Management

In the literature topics about performance management (seen as performance evaluation processes, disciplinary procedures, or dismissals of workers (Cardon & Stevens, 2004)) in SME's are very scarce. A reason for this can be the rarity of formalized procedures in SME's for performance management.

Formal appraisals are usually not done in SME's because of a relative lack of concern of venture founders on downstream (post-start-up) management issues, particularly those with negative implications such as workers not performing well or the business needing to lay off workers (Cardon & Stevens, 2004).

Employee issues are often handled arbitrarily rather than consistently (In Cardon & Stevens, 2004: Verser, 1987). But this arbitrary behaviour is not seen as a problem for the productivity or employees morale. Managers of young and small organizations could interpret an informal ongoing communication and feedback related to a highly formalized performance appraisal procedure as preferable, from philosophical point of view (Cardon & Stevens, 2004).

Organizational Change

As stated earlier SME's experience a lot of changes due to changes in the environment. Chu & Sui (2001) found that SME's have a harder time coping with economic downturns than do large organizations.

A research in a large sample of high-technology start ups in Silicon Valley from the Stanford Project on Emerging Companies (SPEC), which tracked the key organizational and HRM challenges of these small companies, shows the implications of changes in particular sets of HRM practice for employees and organizations (Baron & Hannan, 2002). Compared with companies who did not change, the changes in the sets of HRM practices negatively influenced the employee turnover and financial performance of the organizations. Next to that the likelihood of failure of the organizations increased (in relation to organizations who did not change sets of HRM practices). So changes in sets of HRM practices (for technology organizations) can have significant negative implications at an early point in time.

Human Resource Information Systems and SME's

Table 2 does not implicate that the HRM practices in SME's have the same benefits as the e-HRM tools in large organizations. It are only possible benefits. After this table we will discuss the realistic possible benefits for using e-HRM tools in medium sized organizations.

Table 2 shows some contradictory data. For example, generating figures and statistics for Performance management is due to the informal process not preferred in SME's. The process of socialization at Training & Development is seen as important (face to face), but this is not achieved by the use of e-HRM tools.

The contradictory data is caused by the fact that the HRM practices are based on literature about SME's and the e-HRM tools are based on literature about large organizations. This is why there is not much congruence between the specialties of the HRM practices and the expected benefits of the e-HRM tools.

It can be concluded that most of the characteristics of HRM practices in SME's are about cost

Table 1. HRM practices in SME's (Adapted from Cardon and Stevens, 2004)

HRM practice	Specialties
1. Staffing	• Key component of overall HRM management • Person-organization fit is an important selection criteria • Strategies are often ad hoc • Problematic due to lack of legitimacy, multiple roles & unclear boundaries, limited financial and material resources
2. Compensation	• View compensation from a total rewards perspective • Often variable at-risk pay in the mix • Pay mix changes over the life cycle of the organization • Rewards not indicative of status difference • (Annual) pay raises not common • Often educational benefits
3. Training & Development	• Unstructured training, informal job instruction and socialization are very important • Process of socialization important • Costs and time important considerations of training opportunities • Multitasking relevant
4. Performance management	• Formal appraisal usually not done • Employee issues often handled arbitrarily
5. Organizational change	• SME's have a harder time coping with economic downturns than large organizations • Changes in sets of HRM practices can have significant negative implications at an early point in time

Table 2. Linking HRM practices at SME's with e-HRM tools

HRM practices in SME's from literature about SME's	Specialties HRM practices in SME's	e-HRM tools in large organizations	Possible expected benefits from e-HRM from literature about large organizations
Staffing	• Key component of overall effective HRM management • Person-organization fit is an important selection criteria • Strategies are often ad hoc • Problematic due to lack of legitimacy, multiple roles & unclear boundaries, limited financial and material resources	**e-recruitment**	• Creating brand identity • Increasing employee retention levels • Increasing efficiency recruitment process • Decreasing administrative burdens in recruitment process • Increasing organizational attractiveness
		e-selection	• Decreasing administrative paper burden (used for first selection) • Minimizing costs and maximizing utilization of the human capital • Sustainability
Compensation	• View compensation from a total rewards perspective • Often variable at-risk pay in the mix • Pay mix changes over the life cycle of the organization • Rewards not indicative of status difference • (Annual) pay raises not common. • Often educational benefits	**e-compensation**	• Effectively designing, administering and communicating compensation programs • Enabling to look at external payments • Analyzing market salary data • Streamlining bureaucratic tasks • Greater access to knowledge management databases • Internal information process quicker
Performance management	• Formal appraisal usually not done • Employee issues often handled arbitrarily	**e-performance**	• Generating figures and statistics about performance more easily • Enlarging span of control for managers • Facilitating process of writing reviews and generating feedback
Training & Development	• Unstructured training, informal job instruction and socialization are very important • Process of socialization important • Costs and time important considerations of training opportunities • Multitasking relevant	**e-learning**	• Delivering information about learning, knowledge, and skills • Enabling web based training • More flexible & cost efficient than normal training & development • 'Just in time' • Control over learning

reduction and efficiency. This is similar to the goals of SME's for using e-HRM. Implementing e-HRM tools means investing, and this can collide with the goals of SME's for using e-HRM. Investments will not take place if it is not certain that cost reductions or improved efficiencies are reached.

METHODOLOGY

Main condition for the selection of case studies was that the organizations were small and/or medium

sized in the view of Unit 4 Agresso. This resulted in the fact that the size of the organizations was between 50 and 1000 employees. The distinction between the two groups of cases is due to the fact that Unit 4 Agresso offers two different software packages to the market. They have a software package for "general" organizations and a specific software package for the healthcare sector.

Interviews Conducted

Table 4 shows a list of the organizations and the function of the interviewees. In total we did 15

Table 3. Overview of the cases

Organization	Existing HRIS and/or e-HRM tools	Size	Branch
Unidek	Unit 4 Personeel & Salaris	300 employees, 295 FTE	Construction
Van Merksteijn	Unit 4 Personeel & Salaris	500 employees, 500 FTE	Metal
Unit 4 Agresso	Unit 4 Personeel & Salaris e-Recruitment e-Learning e-Performance management	71 employees, 71 FTE	IT
Zodiac Zoos	Unit 4 Personeel & Salaris Unit 4 Personeel & Salaris Webvastlegging	250 employees, 150 FTE	Animal parks

Table 4. Interviews conducted

Organization	Function of the interviewee
Unidek BV	- Personeelsfunctionaris (HRM specialist)
Van Merksteijn	- Personeel / salaris functionaris (HRM specialist)
Unit 4 Agresso	- Managers HRM (HRM specialist) - Hoofd salarisadministratie (Line manager) - Personeelszaken (HRM specialist)
Zodiac Zoos	- Medewerksters P&O (HRM specialist) - Administrateurs (Line manager)

interviews. We did 11 interviews with one person and 4 with two persons. In total we have spoken with 19 persons. Nine of them had a function as an HRM specialist and ten as a line manager. However, most of the time they are also involved with HRM. The interviews took approximately 45 minutes to an hour, so in total we did approximately 15 hours of interviewing. All the interviews were recorded with an voice recorder.

DESCRIPTION OF SOFTWARE UNIT 4 AGRESSO

Unit 4 Personeel & Salaris is a combination of payroll and HRM; two different modules but together one integrated package, using the same basic data. The software keeps all the legislations, CAO's e.g. up to date. Unit 4 Personeel & Salaris is designed on the world standard of Microsoft Windows.

This software has a modular structure. This makes it possible to create a specific software

package the client wishes for. It is also possible for the client to start with a basic structure and extend this in the future. Functional modules are:

- Unit 4 Salaris
- Unit 4 Personeel
- Unit 4 Web (web enabled Payroll and HRM registration)
- Business Intelligence (reporting tool)
- Document Archive (digital personnel dossier)
- VerzuimSignaal (fully web-enabled absence controlling system)
- Import
- External registration (Microsoft Excel)

General Functionalities

Information scout for management information: Filter, sort and group the information. With a link transferable to Microsoft Word or Excel.

Multiple employers: Process multiple administrations (think about a holding). Applicants can be processed in a separate system. When he / she becomes a definitive employee, they are transferable to the other employees.

Design own rubrics and fields: Save extra information.

Signal function: Be sure that the user is noticed on time about for example birthdays, end of contracts and so on.

Information exchange: Exchange information with external parties through digital ways.

Business Intelligence: Direct access to an open database.

Decentralized system / external processing: Get the information from the employees by Excel or by the Internet. Mutations are digitally processed.

- HRM functionalities
- Basic employee data
- From vacancy till resignation
- 'First day of work' (reporting to Tax department)
- Contracts
- Payment agreements
- Extra employee data (partners, children, important addresses)
- Competence management (training, job history, functioning, performance management)
- Sickness information
- Lease data
- Document archive
- Salary mutations
- Automatic signalling if contracts end, birthdays e.g.

FINDINGS

From the interviews and/or document analysis it appeared that all the general SME's do have an HRM department. If we look at the size of the organisations 2 of the 4 organizations fit into our definition of a SME (organizations with 250 em-

ployees). Unidek and Van Merksteijn have more than 250 employees. This non-fit can be caused by the fact that Unit 4 Agresso selected the cases for this research and in their view these 2 organizations can be categorized as a SME.

All the organizations do have an HRM department, so all the organizations have a specialized HRM function. This is in accordance with our expectation that organizations with more than 50 employees do have specialised HRM function. If we look at FTE's at the HRM department we see that all the 4 organizations have an HRM department between 1 and 2,65 FTE's. But if we compare this size of the HRM department with the overall size of the organizations, we see that for example van Merksteijn has an HRM department with 1 FTE for 500 FTE and Unidek has an HRM department with 2,65 FTE for 296 FTE.

All the 4 organizations use Unit 4 Personeel & Salaris as an HRIS. Zodiac Zoos and Unit 4 Agresso have additional e-HRM tools like Unit 4 Personeel & Salaris Webvastlegging, e-recruitment, e-learning, e-compensation and e-performance management.

Strategy, e-HRM Goals

Three of the four organisations do not have a formal business plan and a formal HRM strategy. Only Unit 4 Agresso does have a business plan and a formal HRM strategy. The strategy is only communicated by Unit 4 Agresso. Unidek, van Merksteijn and Zodiac Zoos do not communicate the strategy through the organization with a formal policy. If we look at the types of the strategy of the 4 organizations we see that 3 organizations have (partly) a marketing differentiation strategy. At Zodiac Zoos and Unit 4 Agresso we see a growth strategy, whereas Unidek has also an innovation differentiation strategy (See table 5).

The fact that three of the four organizations have a marketing differentiation strategy can be the signal that this strategy seems to be most important strategy for a SME to survive. At the

Table 5. Overviews of strategies in the empirical sample

Organisation	Business plan	Formal HRM strategy	Clearness of strategy	Characteristics of strategy
Unidek	No	No	Not communicated	marketing differentiation / innovation differentiation strategy
Van Merksteijn	No	No	Not communicated	Marketing differentiation strategy
Zodiac Zoos	No	No	Not communicated	Growth strategy
Unit 4 Agresso Oost-Nederland	Yes	Yes	Clearly communicated	Marketing differentiation / growth strategy

two smallest organizations of our research (Zodiac Zoos & Unit 4 Agresso Oost-Nederland) we see a growth strategy. This in line with de Kok (2003) who said that this is an important strategy for small organizations.

If we look at the mentioned goals for using or starting to use e-HRM we see that most of the goals are related to the quality of the information (making information more visible, all the information located at one central system, clear overview of the available information, clearness of the information, every user has the exact same information). Next to that we see that the goals of e-HRM are related to time reduction / cost reduction (Extra administrative support with Staffing (Recruitment & Selection), saving time, develop a more effective and efficient HRM process).

Use of HRIS

At all the organizations Unit 4 Personeel & Salaris is used as an HRIS at an operational level. The software package is used for administrative tasks. This is mainly caused by the fact that the software package supports functionalities at an operational level. The e-HRM tools at Zodiac Zoos and Unit 4 Agresso Oost-Nederland are also used at an operational level. We can speak of operational e-HRM at these organizations.

The type of operational e-HRM is in line with the expectation that at medium sized organizations e-HRM is only used at an operational (administrative) level.

If we look at the people who are involved with the use of e-HRM we expected that in medium sized organisations the following people are involved: the line management, the employees, and the HRM specialists. We do not expect that suppliers / external users are involved. At unit 4 Agresso we see that this expectation is confirmed, whereas at Zodiac it is partly confirmed. Here the personnel department and line managers are involved with the use of e-HRM.

IT Acceptance

If we look at the answers of the interviewees with regard to the usefulness of the software of Unit 4 we can see that the software is perceived as useful at Unidek, Zodiac Zoos and Unit 4 Agresso Oost-Nederland. The answers of the interviewees with regard to the ease-of-use of the software of unit 4 Agresso show that the software is not perceived as easy to use at Unidek and Unit 4 Agresso. At Zodiac Zoos the software is perceived as easy to use.

In the extra questions about IT acceptance we asked the HRM specialist about his perceptions about the usefulness, ease-of-use and subjective norm for the use of Unit 4 Personeel & Salaris. As stated earlier van Merksteijn does not use the HRM functionalities in Unit 4 Personeel & Salaris intensively. Therefore the questions were / could not be answered in a way that we could say something about the IT acceptance. Because of this we can not say something about the perceived usefulness, perceived ease-of-use and subjective norm with regard to Unit 4 Personeel & Salaris.

The indicators of perceived usefulness show that the software of Unit 4 Agresso is useful for reasons like time reduction, quickly and easily generated information / overviews out of one source and quality of the information.

The indicators of perceived ease of use at Unidek and Unit 4 Agresso show that the software of Unit 4 Agresso is not easy to use because of the experience that is needed to use the software, the software is not flexible and you have to make too many steps to use a functionality. On the other side at Zodiac Zoos they perceive the software as easy to use for reasons like well organized structure of the software, display of different fonts and mutations can be processed in different ways and in the way they want. This can be caused by the fact that at Zodiac they use next to Unit 4 Personeel & Salaris also Unit 4 Personeel & Salaris Webvastlegging.

At all the organizations the use of the software is stimulated. The interviewees indicated that they perceive the influence of other people as stimulating and that the opinion of other people is important for the use of the software of Unit4 Agresso. So at all the organizations subjective norm is important and plays a (positive) role.

DISCUSSION

Based on the interviews we can answer the formulated research questions for the four organisation. If we look at the types of the strategy of the 4 organizations we see that 3 organizations have (partly) a marketing differentiation strategy. At Zodiac Zoos and Unit 4 Agresso we see a growth strategy, whereas Unidek has also an innovation differentiation strategy.

All the organizations do have an HRM department, so all the organizations have a specialized HRM function. If we look at the HRM practices we see that three of the four organisations have

HRM practices. Only at one organization we did not see any HRM practices.

At all the organizations Unit 4 Personeel & Salaris is used as an HRIS at an operational level. The software package is used for administrative tasks. This is mainly caused by the fact that the software package supports only functionalities at an operational level. The e-HRM tools at Zodiac Zoos and Unit 4 Agresso Oost-Nederland are also used at an operational level. We can speak of operational e-HRM at these organizations.

If we look at the people who are involved with the use of e-HRM we expected that in medium sized organisations the following people are involved: the line management, the employees, and the HRM specialists. We do not expect that suppliers / external users are involved. At unit 4 Agresso we see that this expectation is confirmed, whereas at Zodiac it is partly confirmed. Here the personnel department and line managers are involved with the use of e-HRM.

According to the interviewees the 4 organizations have the following goals for using e-HRM:

* Extra administrative support with Staffing (Recruitment & Selection);
* Making the job benefits more visible.
* Saving time
* Making the information more visible.
* Develop a more effective and efficient HRM process
* All the information is located at one central system;
* Clear overview of the available information;
* Clearness of the information;
* Every user has the exact same information.

If we look at the answers with regard to the usefulness of software of Unit 4 Agresso we can see that this software is perceived as useful. The interviewees at the 4 organizations indicated that the software is useful because of:

- reliable information
- reducing administrative tasks
- quickly and easily generated information / overviews out of one source
- time reduction
- all the information can be found at one location.

The answers with regard to the ease-of-use of the software of Unit 4 Agresso show that this software is not perceived as easy to use for 2 organizations. The interviewees at the 2 organizations indicated that the software is not easy to use because of:

- experience needed to use the software easily
- software is not flexible (too much standardized)
- too many steps to use a functionality

At one organization the interviewees indicated that the software is easy to use because of:

- well organized structure of the software
- display of different fonts
- mutations can be processed in different ways and in the way they want

The answers on the questions about subjective norm show that at all the 4 organizations the interviewees perceive the influence of other people as stimulating and that the opinion of other people is important for the use of the software of Unit4 Agresso.

Zodiac Zoos and Unit 4 Agresso Oost-Nederland, who both uses e-HRM tools, perceive that the use of e-HRM helps them to make HRM more effective. In both cases time reduction is seen as the main reason for this.

Overall we can say that from the interviews it appeared that the use of HRIS / e-HRM at an operational level is perceived as useful for three organizations. The software is not perceived

as easy to use at 2 organizations, whereas one organization perceives the software as easy to use. For one organization we were not able to say something about the usefulness and ease-of-use of the software. In relation to the HRM effectiveness we can conclude that HRM is perceived as effective at all the 4 organizations, because goals are perceived as attained and/or the perceptions about HRM are positive. We can not conclude on which factors these (positive) perceptions are based. Two organizations, who both use e-HRM tools, perceive that the use of e-HRM helps them to make HRM more effective. In both cases time reduction is seen as the main reason for this.

There are a couple of limitations for this research at the four organizations. First, there is a non-fit of the size of two of the four organizations with our definition of a SME. Second, we only interviewed a limited number of persons (1-3 persons), so perceptions about IT acceptance and HRM effectiveness are only based on 1-3 persons in the organization.

CONCLUSION

Overall we can say that from the interviews it appeared that the use of HRIS / e-HRM at an operational level is perceived as useful for all organizations. The software is not perceived as easy to use at five organizations, whereas one organization perceives the software as easy to use.

At one organisation the ease-of-use is partly perceived as positive. For one organization we were not able to say something about the usefulness and ease-of-use of the software.

From the organizations who use e-HRM, four organizations perceive that the use of e-HRM helps them to make HRM more effective. At two organizations time reduction is seen as the main reason for this and at two organizations quality of information is seen at the main reasons for this. At the other two organizations is unknown how the use of e-HRM makes HRM more effective.

Overall we can conclude that in this research the use of e-HRM tools is perceived as useful, whereas the use of e-HRM tools is not perceived as easy to use. The organizations perceive that the use of e-HRM helps them to make HRM more effective.

This research has some limitations. The first limitation is the number of cases. We have only done research in 8 organizations. This is just a small fraction of all the organizations in the Netherlands.

The second limitation is the numbers of interviewees. We have only interviewed 19 persons. The perceptions about the use of e-HRM in the organizations are based on 1-3 persons of a organization.

The third limitation is the way of selecting the organization. We have not selected the organizations. The organizations were selected by Unit 4 Agresso, because the organizations are customers of them and use a software package of Unit 4 Agresso.

The fourth limitation is the fact that not all the organizations fit into the definition of a SME. This non-fit can be caused by the fact that Unit 4 Agresso selected the cases for this research and in their view these organizations can be categorized as a SME.

The fifth limitation is the fact that not all the organizations use the software (although the same) as e-HRM. Some organizations use it as an HRIS.

Further Research

Due to these limitations further research is needed. For example research which captures only organizations that fit into the definition of a SME, more in-depth research (larger number of interviewees per organization). Our research was an exploratory research. Further research could use this research for a descriptive or even explanatory research. Next to our qualitative research, in the future more quantitative research would be useful to acquire more knowledge about e-HRM.

ACKNOWLEDGMENT

The authors gratefully acknowledge helpful comments of Maarten van Riemsdijk and Huub Ruël on the early versions of this work.

REFERENCES

Adam, H., & Berg, R. van den (2001). *E-HRM, inspelen op veranderende organisaties en medewerkers.* Schoonhoven: Academic service.

Ball, K. S. (2001). The use of human resource information systems: a survey. *Personnel Review, 30*(6), 677-693.

Balkin, D. B., & Logan, J. W. (1988). Reward policies that support entrepreneurship. *Compensation and Benefits Review,* (pp. 18 -25).

Banks, M. C., Bures, A. L., & Champion, D. L. (1987). Decision making factors in small business: Training and development. *Journal of Small Business Management, 25*(1), 19-25.

Baron, J. N., & Hannan, M. T. (2002). Organizational blueprints for success in high-tech start-ups: Lessons from the Stanford project on emerging companies. *California Management Review, 44*(3), 8-36.

Benbasat, I., Goldstein, D. K., & Mead, M. (1987). The case research strategy in Studies of information systems. *MIS Quarterly September,* (pp. 369 – 386).

Bos, M. van der, & Heijden, H. van der (2004). E-HRM. In F. Kluytmans (Eds.), *Leerboek personeelsmanagement.* Groningen: Wolters-Nordhoff.

Boselie, P., Paauwe, J., & Jansen, P. (2001). Human Resource Management and performance; lessons from the Netherlands. *The International Journal of Human Resource Management, 12*(7), 1107-1125.

Bowen, D. E., & Ostroff, C. (2004). Understanding HRM-Firm Performance linkages: The role of the "strength" of the HRM system. *Academy of Management Review, 29*(2), 203 – 221.

Brown, S. A., Massey, A. P., Montoya-Weiss, M. M., & Burkman, J. R. (2002). Do I really have to? User acceptance of mandated technology. *European Journal of Information Systems, 11*, 283-295.

Cappelli, P. (2001). Making the most of on line recruiting. *Harvard Business Review, 79*(2), 139-146.

Cardon, M. S., & Stevens, C. E. (2004). Managing human resources in small organizations: what do we know? *Human Resource Management Review, 14*, 295 – 323.

Cardy R. L., & Miller, J. S. (2005). eHR and Performance Management. In: H. G. Gueutal & D. L. Stone (Eds.), *The Brave New World of eHR. Human Resources Management in the Digital Age.* San Francisco: Jossey-Bass.

Cascio, W. F. (2000). Managing a virtual workplace. *Academy of Management Executive, 14*(3), 81-90.

Cedar (2001). Cedar 2001 Human resources Self Service / Portal Survey. Fourth Annual Survey. Baltimore: Cedar.

Chu, P., & Sui, W. S. (2001). Coping with the Asian economic crisis: The rightsizing strategies of small- and medium-sized enterprises. *International Journal of Human Resource Management, 12*(5), 845–858.

Cober, R. T., Brown, D. J., Levy, P. E., Keeping, L. M., & Cober, A. L. (2003). Organizational websites: Website content and style as determinants of organizational attraction. *International Journal of Selection and Assessment, 11*, 158 – 169.

Cober, R. T., Douglas, J. B., & Levy, P. E. (2004). Form, Content and Function: An evaluative meth-

odology for corporate employment web sites. *Human Resource Management, Summer / Fall, 43*(2/3), 201-218. Wiley Periodicals, Inc.

Collins, H. (2001). *Corporate portals: Revolutionizing information access to increase productivity and drive the bottom line.* New York: AMA-COM.

Compeer, N., Smolders, M., & de Kok, J. (2005), *Scale effects in HRM research. A discussion of current HRM research from an SME perspective.* EIM, Zoetermeer, the Netherlands.

Davis, F. D. (1989). Perceived Usefulness, Perceived Ease of Use, and User Acceptance of Information Technology. *MIS Ouarterly, 13*(3), 319-339.

Davis, F. D., Bagozzi, R. P., & Warshavi, P. R. (1989). User Acceptance of Computer Technology: A Comparison of Two Theoretical Models, *Management Science, 35*(8), 982-1002.

Duhlebohn, J. H.. & Marler, J. H. (2005). E-compensation: The potential to transform practice? In H. G. Gueutal & D. L. Stone (Eds.), *The Brave New World of eHR. Human Resources Management in the Digital Age.* San Francisco: Jossey-Bass.

European Commission (2000). The European Observatory for SME's. Sixth Report, Office for Official Publications of the European Communities, Luxembourg.

European Commission (2004). Highlights from the 2003 Observatory, *Observatory of European SMEs 2003* no. 8, Office for Official Publications of the European Communities, Luxembourg.

Firestone, J. M. (2003). *Enterprise information portals and knowledge management.* Boston: Butterworth-Heinemann

Flanagan, D. J., & Deshpande, S. P. (1996). Top management's perceptions of changes in HRM practices after union elections in small firms. *Journal of Small Business Management*, 23–34.

Galanaki, E. (2002). The decision to recruit on line: A descriptive study. *Career Development International*, (pp. 243-251).

Gibcus, P., & Kemp, R. G. M. (2003). *Strategy and small firm performance.* EIM, Zoetermeer, the Netherlands.

Grensing-Pophal, L. (2001). HR and the corporate intranet: Beyond "brochureware". SHRM white paper. Retrieved, May 9, 2003, from www. shrm.org/hrresources/whitepapers_publisched/CMS_000212.asp.

Guest, D. E., & Peccei, R. (1994). The nature and causes of effective Human Resource Management. *British Journal of Industrial Relations, 32*(2) June, 219 – 242.

Hageman, J., & van Kleef, J. (2002). e-HRM is de hype voorbij (cited in March 2006). http://www.nvp-plaza.nl/e-hrm/e-HRMvisie&missie_files/frame.htm.

Harrington, A. (2002, May 13). Can anyone build a better monster? *Fortune, 145*, 189-192

Hargie, O., & Tourish, D. (2002). *Handbook of communication audits for organisations.* Hove/New York: Routledge

Heneman, H. G., & Berkley, R. A. (1999). Applicant attraction practices and outcomes among small businesses. Journal *of Small Business Management*, (pp. 53–74).

Heneman, R. L., Tansky, J. W., & Camp, S. M. (2000). Human resource management practices in small and medium-sized enterprises: Unanswered questions and future research perspectives. *Entrepreneurship Theory and Practice*, (pp. 11–26).

Heneman, R. L., Tansky, J.W. (2002). Human Resource Management models for entrepreneurial opportunity: Existing knowledge and new directions. In J. Katz & T. M. Welbourne (Eds.), *Managing people in entrepreneurial organizations,* 5, 55-82, Amsterdam: JAI Press

Hogler, R. L., Henle, C., & Bernus, C. (1998). Internet recruiting and employment discrimination: a legal perspective. *Human Resource Management Review, 8*(2).

Hornsby, J. S., & Kuratko, D. F. (1990). Human resource management in small business: Critical issues for the 1990s. *Journal of Small Business Management*, (pp. 9–18).

Huselid, M. A. (1995). The impact of human resource management practices on turnover, productivity, and corporate financial performance. *Academy of Management Journal, 38*, 635 – 672.

Huselid, M. A. (2003). Editor's note: Special issue on small and medium-sized enterprises: A call for more research. *Human Resource Management, 42*(4), 297.

Hwang, Y. (2004). Investigating enterprise systems adoption: uncertainty avoidance, intrinsic motivation, and the technology acceptance model. *European Journal of Information Systems, 14*, 150–161.

Ilgen D. R., Fischer, C. D., & Taylor, M. S. (1979). Consequences of individual feedback on behaviour in organizations. *Journal of Applied Psychology, 64*, 349-371.

Kane, B., Crawford, J., & Grant, D. (1999). Barriers to effective HRM. *International Journal of Manpower, 20*(8), 494 – 515.

Karahanna, E., & Straub, D. W. (1998). The psychological origins of perceived usefulness and ease of use. *Information & Management, 35*, 237 – 250.

Karrer, T., & Gardner, E. (2003). *E-Performance Essentials.* Retrieved, April 10, 2006,

http://www.learningcircuits.org/2003/dec2003/karrer.htmis.

Keebler, T. J., & Rhodes, D.W. (2002). E-HR: becoming the "Path of least resistance". *Employment Relations Today, summer 2002*, 57-66.

Kehoe, J. F., Dickter, D. N., Russell, D. P., & Sacco, J. M. (2005). E-Selection. In H.G. Gueutal & D. L. Stone (Eds.), *The Brave New World of eHR. Human Resources Management in the Digital Age*. San Francisco: Jossey-Bass.

Klaas, B.S., McCClendon, J. and Gainey, T.W. (2000). Managing HR in the small and medium enterprise: The impact of professional employer organizations. *Entrepreneurship: theorye and Practice, 25*(1), pp. 107-124.

De Kok, J. M. P. (2003). Human Resource Management within Small and Medium-Sized Enterprises, *Tinbergen Institute Research Series, 313*. Amsterdam: Thela Thesis.

Kok, J. M. P. de, Uhlaner, L. M. & Thurik, A. R. (2003). Human Resource Management with small firms; facts and explanations. *Report Series, Research in Management. Erasmus Research Institute of Management.*

Kok, J. M. P. de, Uhlaner, L. M., & Thurik, A. R. (2006). Professional HRM Practices in Family Owned-Managed Enterprises. *Journal of Small Business Management, 44*(3), 441-460.

Kotey, B., & Slade, P. (2005). Formal Human Resource Management in small growing firms. *Journal os Small Business Management, 43*(1), 16-40.

Lai, V. S., & Li, H. (2004). Technology acceptance model for internet banking: an invariance analysis. *Information & Management, 42*(2005), 373-386

Lengnick-Hall, M., & Moritz, S. (2003). The Impact of e-HR on the Human Resource Management Function. *Journal of Labor research, 14*(3), 365-379.

Lepak, D. P., & Snell, S. A. (1998). Virtual HR: strategic human resource management in the 21st century. *Human Resource Management Review, 8*(3), 215-234.

Little, B. L. (1986). The performance of personnel duties in small Louisiana firms: A research note. *Journal of Small Business Management*, October 1986, 66-71.

McConnel, B. (2002, April). Companies lure job seekers in new ways: Corporate web sites snare applicants on line, *HR News*, 1, 12.

Meijaard, J., Mosselman, M., Frederiks, K. F., & Brand, M. J. (2002). *Organisatietypen in het MKB*. Zoetermeer: *EIM.*

Moll, P. (1983). Should the Third World have information technologies? *IFLA Journal, 9*(4), 297.

Morris, M. G., & Venkatesh, V. (2000). Age differences in technology adoption decisions: Implications for a changing workforce. *Personnel Psychology Inc., 53*, 375 – 403.

MKB Nederland (2006). *Het midden- en kleinbedrijf in een oogopslag*. Retrieved, August 22, 2006, from http://www.mkb.nl/Het_midden-_en_kleinbedrijf.

Nickel, J., & Schaumberg, H. (2004). Electronic privacy, Trust and Self-disclosure in e-recruitment. *CHI 2004*, april 24-29, Vienna, Austria

Murray, D. (2001). E-Learning for the Workplace: Creating Canada's Lifelong Learners. The Conference Board of Canada, www.conferenceboard.ca.

Nederlandse Vereniging voor Personeelsmanagement en Organisatieontwikkeling (2006). *On-line resultaten van de NVP e-HRM enquete*. Retrieved, March 2006, from http://www.nvp-plaza.nl/documents/e-hrmresults2005.html

Paré, G. (2004). Investigating informations systems with positivist case study research. *Communications of the Associatoin for informations systems, 13*, 233–264.

Riemsdijk, M. van, Bondarouk, T., & Knol, H. (2005). *Researching Personnel Management in Dutch Small and Medium Sized Enterprises*. A literature overview and a research model. Paper Presented at The International Dutch HRM Network Conference, 4-5 November 2005, Enschede, The Netherlands.

Rousseau, D. M. (1995). *Psychological Contracts in Organizations.* Thousands Oaks, CA: Sage

Ruël, H. J. M., Leede, J. de, & Looise, J. C. (2002). ICT en het management van arbeidsrelaties; hoe zit het met de relatie? In R. Batenburg, J. Benders, N. Van den Heuvel, P. Leisink, & J. Onstenk, (Eds.), *Arbeid en ICT in onderzoek.* Utrecht: Lemma.

Ruël, H. J. M., Bondarouk, T., & Looise, J. C. (2004). E-HRM: innovation or irritation. An explorative empirical study in five large companies on web-based HRM. *Management revue, 15*(3), 364-380.

Ruël, H. J. M., Bondarouk, T., & Velde, M. van der (2007). The contribution of e-HRM to HRM effectiveness. *Employee Relations, 29*(3), 280 - 291.

Ruta, C. D. (2005). The application of change management theory to HR portal implementation in subsidiaries of multinational corporations. *Human Resource Management.* Spring 2005, *44*(1), 35-53.

Saadé, R., & Bahli, B. (2004). The impact of cognitive absorption on perceived usefulness and perceive ease of use in on-line learning: an extension of the technology acceptance model. *Information Management, 42*, 317-327.

Sels, L., Winne, S. de, Delmotte, J., Maes, J., Faems, D., & Forrier, A. (2006). Linking HRM and Small Business Performance: An Examination of the Impact of HRM Intensity on the Productivity and Financial Performance of Small Businesses. *Small Business Economics, 26*, 83-101.

Stone, D. L., Lukaszewski, K. M., & Isenhour, L.C. (2005). E-Recruiting: Online strategies for attracting talent. In: H. G. Gueutal & D. L. Stone (Eds.), *The Brave New World of eHR. Human*

Resources Management in the Digital Age. San Francisco: Jossey-Bass.

Tavangarian, D., Leypold, M. E., Nölting, K., Röser, M., & Voigt, D. (2004) Is e-Learning the Solution for Individual Learning? *Electronic Journal of e-Learning, 2*(2), 273-280.

Taylor, S., & Todd, P. (1995). Assessing IT usage: the role of prior experience. *MIS Quaterly,* December 1995, (pp. 561–570).

Teo, S.T.T., & Crawford, J. (2005). Indicators of Strategic HRM effectiveness: A case study of an Australian public sector agency during commercialization. *Public Personnel Management,* 34(1), 1–16.

Twynstra Gudde (2003). e-HRM onderzoek 2002/2003. Amersfoort: Twynstra Gudde.

UmanID (2006). Wat is e-HRM? Retrieved, March 2006, from http://www.ehrmplein.nl/

Venkatesh, V. (2000). Determinants of perceived ease of use: Integrating control, intrinsic motivation, and emotion into the technology acceptance model. *Information Systems Research, 11*(4), December 2000, 342 – 365.

Venkatesh, V. & Davis, F.D. (2000). A theoretical extension of the technological acceptance model: Four longitudinal field experiments. *Management Science, 46*(2), February 2000, 186–204.

Venkatesh, V., & Morris, M. G. (2000). Why Don't Men Ever Stop to Ask For Directions? Gender, Social Influence, and Their Role in Technology Acceptance and Usage Behavior. *MIS Ouarterly,* 24(1), 115-139.

Venkatesh, V., Morris, M. G., Davis, G. B., & Davis, F.D. (2003). User acceptance of Information technologies: Toward a unified view. *MIS Quarterly, 27*(3), *425-478.*

Voerman, M., & Veldhoven, M. Van (2007). Attitude towards e-HRM: an empirical study at Philips. *Personnel Review, 36*(6), 887 - 902.

Watson, W. (2002). *B2E / eHR. Survey results 2002.* Reigate: Watson Wyatt.

Williamson, I. O., Lepak, D. P., & King, J. (2003). The effect of company recruitment web site orientation on individuals' perceptions of organizational attractiveness. *Journal of Vocational Behaviour, 63,* 242-263.

Wright, P., & Dyer, L. (2000). *People in the e-business: new challenges, new solutions.* Working paper 00-11, Center for Advanced Human Resource Studies, Cornell University.

Wright, P. M., McMaham, G. C., Snell, S. A., & Gerhart, B. (2001). Comparing line and HR executives' perceptions of HR effectiveness: services, roles, and contributions. *Human Resource Management, 40*(2), 111–123.

Yin, R. K. (1993). Applications of case study research. *Applied Social Research Methods Series,* Sage Publications, *34.*

Yu, J., Ha, I., Choi, M., & Rho, J. (2005). Extending the TAM for a t-commerce. *Information Management, 42,* 965-976.

KEY TERMS

e-HRM: The support of HRM processes in organizations with the use of internet technology.

HRIS: Human Resource Information Systems.

Perceived Ease of Use: Degree to which a person believes that using a particular system would be free of effort.

Perceived Usefulness: Degree to which a person believes that using a particular information system would enhance his or her job performance.

SME: Small and medium sized organizations with fewer than 250 full time equivalent employees.

Chapter XIX
Perceived Performance of the Human Resources Information Systems (HRIS) and Perceived Performance of the Management of Human Resources (HRM)

Loubna Tahssain
IAE Graduate School of Management in Aix-en-Provence, France

Mouna Zgheib
IAE Graduate School of Management in Aix-en-Provence, France

ABSTRACT

The changing business environment and increasing technology is redefining the role of the human resources function. Nowadays, corporations have to consistently advance the value of human assets in their own organizations for maintaining their competitiveness. One of the technological changes in this regard is the appearance of Human Resources Information systems (HRIS). How to improve the efficiency of the HR and enhance its status in the organizations has become the top agenda to enterprises. The development of Information Technology (IT) transforms the role of the HR Dept in the organization. It enables HR to be a real strategic partner of corporations through the process of Organization Development. Thus, one of the challenges that face managers nowadays in regard to these emerging technologies, is the need to determine the success factors that play an important role in the implementation of an HRIS and how these factors, that some are Technological, Individual, and Organizational, affect the perceived performance of a HRIS and to measure the impact of this perceived performance on the perceived performance of the HRM.

INTRODUCTION

Regarded as a technical support particularly favorable to obtaining the sought performances, Information and Communication Technologies (ICT) are perceived today as a major tool to ensure the competitiveness of the organizations.

In addition, human resources management is invited to better share its roles, its responsibilities and its functions between the management and the general view of its framing/setting, and to propose relevant creative tools of added value. For this reason, the (HRIS) constitute suitable systems making it possible for the enterprise to manage the flows of information relating to its human resources (HR), as well as improving the quality of decisions related to the HR, which can be either strategic or operational, and this thanks to the automation of the administrative procedures. Many companies maintain the belief that simply by computerizing their HR processes, they will be able to solve all of the noted problems and reach their objectives.

The aim of this research is to identify the determinants of the perceived performance of a HRIS and to measure the impact of this perceived performance on the perceived performance of the HRM. Three types of factors of the perceived performance of HRIS are highlighted right now: technical, organizational and individual. Initially, we will clarify the various solicited concepts. Secondly, we put forward the measure of the perceived performance of the HRM and that of the HRIS. Last but not least, we will draw, based on a literature analysis, the first variables being able to start a modeling, which will be presented in conclusion along with the first methodological tracks.

DEFINITION OF THE CONCEPTS

This first part is devoted to the definition of the concepts related to the ICT then to the clarifica-tion of the concept of perceived performance of the HRM.

ICT, e-HRM and HRIS

Due to their interactive and innovative character, the ICT shake the structures and the "traditional" practices, based in particular on the man-machine correlation. The E-HR, for instance, was defined by Barthe (2001) as "the policies of HRM using the NICT, namely the internal Intranets and the public Internet, to implement dynamic practices". For this purpose, the E-HRM aims at bringing solutions to improve traditional management of HR and to develop the performance.

In addition, the integration of these technological tools passes by a Human Resources Information system (HRIS). This has a main goal to provide the service in the form of information, data, and reports, to the internal as well as to the external customers who use the system. Thanks to the automation of the administrative procedures, the HRIS can improve the quality of the decisions related to the human resources, whether they are strategic or operational, by increasing the available flow of information. In other words, we are talking about a Portal HR where it is possible to acquire, store, handle, analyze, extract and distribute information relevant to the human resources of an organization Tannenbaum (1990).

However, the information related to the human resources changes becomes unforeseeable; from which emanates the need for envisaging a particular management of this information. In response to this need, the HRIS presents certain characteristics which are related to the nature (itself) of this information. Thus, thanks to this system, the organization can manage the important flow of information of which it lays out on its employees. They can modify them and update them without wasting time (See Figure 1).

The Academic work on the HRIS is integrated in a procedural approach of the human resources management (Barthe, 2001, Gilbert, 2001, Lord,

Figure1. The human resources information system (HRIS) (adapted from Reix, 1999)

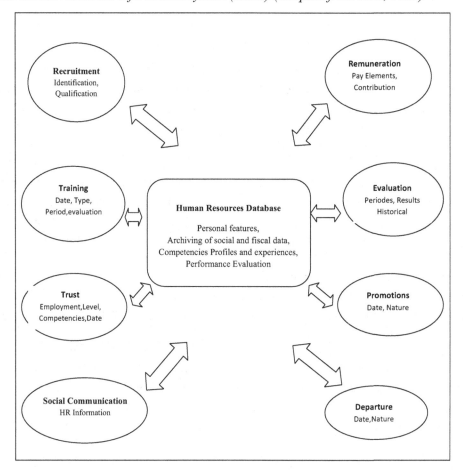

2001; CRIMPED, 2002). Thus, according to Gilbert 2001, "Following the steps of quality, it is usual today to consider the HRM as an assembly of processes in interrelationships. These processes defined as a series of finalized activities leading to a certain service- offer a base of reflection to think of the organization having the information system of HRM (SIRH)". Gilbert underlines the distinction between the information system in human resources and the information processing system of human resource management. Here, the acronym HRIS indicates the information processing systems used for the HRM.

Perceived Performance of the HRM

Behind the concept of performance the question of its measurement arises, as well as the contribution of the various resources to obtaining this objective. Indeed, the performance cannot take effect without its evaluation, and the organizational success cannot be reached without an optimal contribution of the whole committed resources. As underlined by Galambaud (2003), in a company, one cannot speak about only one performance but several ones. The performance is a complex concept which can have several significances which are articulated around three primary meanings: (Burgundian 1996): success, the result of an action and the process of an action (Baird, 1986).

In the literature, the performance is often studied from an angle of the result of the action: the same indicators are used for all the companies. But the relevance of these indicators is not evident for each one of these companies because of their specificities and the strategic objectives which they pursue. In the setting up of a device of evaluation of its HR performance, the company will be shaped by its own problems at a given time. The empirical studies with quantitative dominance make an effort to be released from any conventionality. Finally, if these studies measure the comparative value of a performance on broad samples, they do not sufficiently provide accurate information to allow a given company to take action.

In the sense of a success, the performance can be apprehended like a social construction. If the type of the required performance can differ from a company to another, it can also vary according to the type of actors. It is indeed possible, by prolonging the theory of the *stakeholders* (Freeman, 1984), to interpret the performance according to the stakes of the various actors who compose the organization or those who hold any interest in it. For some, the financial or accounting dimension will be prevalent while for others, the consumer-product dimension, sociopolitical or that of the employment will be more vigorous (Louarn and Wils, 2001). The performance being a socially built category, its level will depend on the "convention": the one which governs its definition. It cannot be single, and while referring to Bourguignon (1996), we will retain, for the continuation of our work, a sufficiently broad definition to adapt to the plurality of the realities lived by the companies: "The performance indicates the realization of the organizational objectives, no matter what the nature and the variety of these objectives are (...) The performance is multidimensional, with the image of the organizational goals, it is subjective and depends on the selected referents".

This prolonged definition of the performance facilitates its operation in a process of evaluation. We will approach it through the perception of the organizational actors.

Concerning the perceived performance of the HRM, it is important to highlight that by bringing together the concept of the performance to that of the human resources is not without significance. The first concept reflects on the ideas of measurement, quantification and evaluation, whereas the second is rather associated with the Human being and his complexity (Louart, 1996). Since the work of the school of the human relations, and more recently the development of a strategic approach of human resources with the RBV[1] (*Resource Based View off the firm*), the contribution of human resources to the performance of the companies is admitted. In addition, the instability of the competitive environment reinforces the requirement of the performance. As indicated by Louart (1996), the positioning of the performance move with the managerial representations in a given context, and the idea of a bond between human resources and performance itself is subjected to these representations. One can think that the good performances of a company make it possible "to invest in the social" and in the installation of practices of the elaborated HRM. But one can also produce the hypothesis of an opposite causality, namely that of a contribution of human resources to the economic and financial performance, and *in fine* to the perpetuity of the company.

Since more than ten years, we have seen appearing an abundant publication on the big role of the human resources management in the organizational performance. The first publications sought to establish bonds between various individual practices, such as the selection, the training or the evaluation of the output and various indicators of organizational performance. Several researchers affirm that the individual practices of the HRM have a limited impact and that in order to have a significant impact on the organizational performance, the practices must be integrated, coherent or complementary (Schuler and Jackson 1988; Snell and Dean 1992; Arthur 1994). Indeed, in certain studies, the combination of some practices involves an improvement of the prediction of the organizational performance (Arthur 1994; Kalleberg and Moody 1994; MacDuffie 1995). On the other hand, other research does not reveal a relation or very marginal relation if any (Delaney and Huselid 1996).

The performance of HR is approached here under its perceptual angle: we measure the performance starting from the diffusion of a judgment concerning the perception of the appraiser on the performance of the provided administrative services. It is a concept which returns to the broader concept of evaluation of the HRM and which is defined as "a systematic and formalized process aiming at giving an opinion on legitimacy, the effectiveness, and the efficiency of the practices, the policies, the programs and the activities of the HRM, conceived and established by the HRM, the direction, the managers; also including a comparison with internal parameters (standards, objectives) or external (benchmarking)" (Saint-Onge and Al, 1998).

MEASURING THE PERCEIVED PERFORMANCE OF THE HRM AND THE HRIS

Within the framework of a customer-supplier aspect applied to the HRM (Zardet, 1995; Peretti, 1993), the employees who are using the services of the HRIS are themselves regarded as internal customers.

Generally, the satisfaction of the users reflects in which measure a product or a service answers their expectations. It is thus essential on the one hand to distinguish the two components of satisfaction – the customers' expectations and the quality effectiveness or perception of the offered service and on the other hand, not to regard the satisfaction as an entity. An adequate measure of the satisfaction thus includes separate appreciations of the customers' expectations and the quality of the offered service.

In addition, certain authors have already underlined the need for focusing on the users of the HRIS, namely the speakers of the HR and the internal clients of the HRM (Boudreau, 1996; Tannenbaum, 1990). The role of the HRM would then consist of evaluating the customers' requirements and answering them (Ulrich, 1989). For this reason, the clients of the HRM can thus constitute evaluators of the effectiveness of the HRM. The criterion of satisfaction of the internal clients as a measure of the efficiency of the HRM tends thus to being more and more used (Lelouarn, Wils, 2001).

Consequently, the service provided by the HRM can be perceived as more powerful for the internal clients through the use of these information systems insofar as the latter allow the speed and the user-friendliness in terms of information access , reliability and the quantity of the provided information. For this reason, it arises that the performance of the HRIS has an impact on the perception of the personnel with respect to the effectiveness of the HRIS provided by the HRM.

The satisfaction of the users of the HRIS thus seems to present one of dimensions of the perceived performance of the HRM. The methods of measurement of this variable will be the subject of an exploratory research making it possible to supplement this indicator.

Concerning the measurement of the perceived performance of an HRIS, Haines and Petit (1997) have developed a first model of evaluation of the information systems of human resources. In this model, the success of an HRIS is defined by two measurements applied in the field of the information systems: the satisfaction of the HRIS' users and the exploitation of the system. These two measurements represent a relatively complete evaluation of the performance of the information system. The first relates to the attitude and the opinion developed by the users with regard to the system, the second is rather related to the conducts adopted vis-a-vis the system, i.e. the effective use of this system.

THE DETERMINANTS OF THE PERCEIVED PERFORMANCE OF HRIS

To approach the determinants of the perceived performance of an HRIS, we will refer to work on the innovation (Romelaer, 2002). We distinguish three categories of determinants: individual factors, organizational factors, and the national culture of the country.

Individual Factors

The success of a new information technology is explained by the characteristics of the user (Zmud, 1979). Many individual variables like age, gender, competencies and experience were studied before by the researches in information systems. Certain researches were interested into studying these variables in an isolated way: the age and the gender constitute variables which operate on the satisfaction with regard to Intranet (Myerscough, 2000).

The acceptance and the appropriation of a new technology by the users constitute essential requirements for the success of its integration in the organization (Hong, Thong & Wong, 2002). Mathieson, Peacock and Chin (2001) showed that the level of acceptance of Technology has an impact on its effective use and the intention to use it. It is also important to note that the simplicity of use of the Information system for an expert is higher than that of a beginner who is not familiarized with the tool. Authors like Bagozzi and Warshaw (1990) put a distinction between the intention to act and the intention to try. From their part, Mathieson, Peacock and Chin (2001) distinguish

between beginners and experts, and underline that the latter will not quickly change their intention to act from their reinforced beliefs, which is not the case for beginners who are more likely to change their initial intention. The researches Hong, Thong & Wong (2001) showed that the perception of the usefulness (defined as being a wide belief of the user that the system will improve his performance at work) has a direct effect on the acceptance of the tool in question. In the same meaning, Davis et al. (1989) underline that the perception of the usefulness constitutes a strong link in the process of the utilization. In conclusion, we estimate that familiarity with the tool and the technical level of the user seems to have a considerable impact on the utilization of the HRIS.

Organizational Factors

The factors that contribute to the success of the information system are also likely to vary according to the organizational characteristics: the size, the internal organizational support, the Information Technology (IT) experience of the organization, in fact that inherent in the technologies of the Web. However, certain constraints coming from the organization and the authority system condition the decision to incorporate or not an innovation, in particular the constraint of the strategic agenda, the acceptability of the risk of failure, the involvement of the authority and the access to the head office, the concern of maintaining a coherent combination of the organization and the strategy, the possibility of collaboration between the various departments, the control of the organization and the position of the innovation in the phases of the development and the constraint of the resources to ensure the continuity of the organization.

The majority of the firms does not have the same capacity for the absorption of the ICT and does not have the same access to these technological opportunities. This idea is illustrated by Cairncross (2001) who underlines that, "the equality of access will be one of the great prizes of the death of distance". However, the inequalities in the adoption of the ICT remain little studied and ignored enough at the micro-economic level. An assumption is generally retained within the vocation framework analyzing the relation between the ICT and the organization. It stipulates that "the utility" withdrawn from their use by the firms strongly depends on their internal organization, in particular on their structures of coordination and communication acting at the same time on the costs and the expected benefit from their use (Brynjolfsson and Mendelson, 1993; Foray, 2000; Creti, 2001). Various organizational features are thus highlighted by these authors. They are primarily relating to the internal organization of the firm (level of centralization/decentralization of the decisions and functional integration of the firm) but also to the organization of the links with its productive environment (customers, suppliers etc).

Generally, the tie between the internal organization and the communication within the firms were underlined in the economic literature of the firm (Chandler, 1962; Williamson, 1975; Aoki, 1986). Chandler (1962) underlined as well that the multi-divisional organization appeared to make it possible to treat increasingly important informational flows. The structure of the firm can thus be seen as an "efficient answer" to its informational costs (Brynjolfsson and Mendelson, 1993), the importance and the nature of the latter can then be more or less favorable to the adoption of the ICT (Hagström and Hedlund, 1999)[2].

In the same way, certain authors have put forward the influence exerted by the delegation of the decision-making power on the individuals and/or the teams of the company (Brynjolfsson and/or Hitt, 2000), and highlighted the existence of a correlation between the use of the ICT and the movement to the decentralization at the individual and structural levels. Moreover, certain empirical studies showed that the decentralized firms adopt these tools in a more intense way (Bresnahan and Al, 2000).

National Culture

The factors of performance of the HRIS raised previously are in most cases, related to the organization, the individual or the characteristics of the HRIS. The cultural diversities remain, nevertheless, insufficiently explored, as for their relationships to the implementation and the orientation of the HRIS. Intercultural researches in HRIS are still recent and largely unexplored. Indeed, the potential influence of the culture on the IS in general is difficult to insulate and measure.

If we refer to the work of Hofstede (1991), in the case of the introduction of new tools such as the ICT, the national culture is important for the formulation and the implementation of the company strategies. Indeed, the ICT imply a democratization of exchange and access of information. In certain countries where the hierarchical spacing is more important, the change induced by the ICT must be incremental which should not generate in the actors the feeling of a loss of legitimacy or authority. In a general way, the ICT allow to reduce the hierarchical distances in the organizations for more reactivity vis-a-vis the constraints of the environment (Kalika et al., 2002).

The degree of individualism, this factor plays a negative part in the case of technologies in the group work (example of the Groupware) which require, as a precondition, a disposition into group work. The ICT are thus supposed to consolidate this logic of collectivism due to the management system which maintains the adequacy of the practices to the group work methods. (Hofstede, 1993) confirms the importance of the degree of individualism in France with an average of 71 (20 for West Africa, 20 for China). The masculinity is a factor which puts forward the performance of the company in relation with the bonds of solidarity between the actors. The masculinity is thus a favorable factor to the creation of value within the framework of the introduction of the ICT into the organization since the vision of the actors is centered on the performance of the company. The study of Hofstede (1993) equates the rate of masculinity in France and West Africa, and confirms that this rate remains very high in countries as Japan where the culture of the performance was the origin of great successes in the industrial field.

Moreover, the control of uncertainty proves to be necessary in the formulation of the strategies in a company as it makes it possible to avoid strategic choices that are not creative of much added value for the company. The ICT, due to the presence of the strategic tools, make it possible to reduce uncertainty relating to the environment of the company. On the other side, the diffusion of the software within the company facilitates the supervision of the processes and the activities, and consequently decreases uncertainty within the organization, which makes of ICT an inevitable way allowing control of uncertainty.

The national culture thus constitutes a big factor which characteristics are modified by the of the introduction of the ICT which induce the reduction of the cultural differences between the countries. This level of culture conditions the strategic options of the company and rather imposes implementation choices in a country than in another or investments in a sector which can be promising in a given country.

CONCLUSION

All the companies are certainly not ready for the installation of such systems. A certain Information Technology (IT) culture proves to be necessary. The risks of the development of a new form of exclusion within the company are real, between those which can use a computer and its resources and those which do not know it. The security of access to information is a vital element, and guarantees the continuity of the system.

This research is of theoretical and practical interest. The theoretical part insists on the importance of the HRIS in the broad sense within the

HRM (management of the flows of information concerning HR, improvement of the quality of the decisions relating to HR, automation of the administrative procedures, etc). Indeed, Information became a very important means on which the competitiveness and the adaptation of the company are carried out. Consequently, it is likely to act on the productivity of the HR, the coordination of the activities and the improvement of decision making, the response times and finally the improvement of the services provided to the customers of the HRM (Snell, Stueber, Lepak, 1998).

From the practical point of view, our research has as an objective to propose important principles to direct the action of the professionals of the HR in the installation, and the usage of the HRIS whose HRM must take into account the importance of the measurement of the performance of these HRIS, as well as the contribution of the various resources to obtaining these objectives.

It is important to note that the performance cannot take effect without its evaluation, and the organizational success cannot be reached without an optimal contribution of the entire committed resources. Thus, the question of the performance evaluation of HR cannot be detached from the more general questions like those aiming at defining the concept of the perceived performance of the HRIS and that of the HRM.

In this article, the perceived performance of the HRIS was approached under its perceptual angle so is the HRM. We measure the performance from the appraiser's perception of the performance of the provided administrative services. This measurement implies the identification of the determinants of the perceived performance of the SIRH, which was gathered in three categories: individual factors, organizational factors, and national culture of the country.

Thus the first modeling comes out from our review of literature that we will be enhanced by implementing a qualitative research undertaken by semi-directing interviews.

This first study will be then supplemented by a quantitative analysis aiming at validating our model of research on a sample of companies integrating HRIS in two distinct countries: France and Lebanon.

REFERENCES

Arthur, J. B. (1994). Effects of Human Resource Systems on Manufacturing Performance and Turnover. *Academy of Management Newspaper*, *37*(3), 670-687.

Aoki, M, (1986). Horizontal versus Vertical information structures of the firm, *American Economic Review, 76*(5), September, 971-983.

Baird, L. (1986). *Managing performance.* New York, John Wiley.

Burgundian, A. (1996). *To define the performance: a simple matter of vocabulary?* In A.–M. Fericelli & B. Sire (Eds.), *Performances and human resources* (pp. 18-31). Paris, Economica.

Barthe, S. (2001). Technologies of the Web: a possible answer to the new challenges of the human resources management. *Revue of Human Resources management, 41,* 5-20.

Boudreau, J. W. (1996). Human resource information system : exploiting the full potential. *Center for Advanced Human resource Studies CAHRS*, (pp. 96-02), Cornell University, USA.

Bresnahan, T., Brynjolfsson, E., & Hitt, L. (2000). IT, Workplace Organization and the Demand for Skilled Labor: A Firm-level Analysis, Mimeo, MIT, Stanford and Wharton

Brynjolfsson, E., & Mendelson, H. (1993). Information systems and the organization of modern enterprise. *Journal of Organizational Computing, 3*(3), 245-255

Cairncross, F. (2001). *The death of distance 2.0; how the communications revolution will change our lives.* Harvard Business School Press, Cambridge

Chandler, A. (1962). *Strategy and Structure.* Boston: MIT Press

Creti, A. (2001). Network technologies, communication externalities and total factor productivity. *Structural Change and Economic Dynamics, 12,* 1-28

Davis, F. D., Bagozzi, R. P., & Warshaw, P. R. (1989). User acceptance of computer technology : a comparison of two theoretical models. *Management Science, 35*(8), 982-1003.

Delaney, J. T., & Huselid, M. A. (1996). The Impact of Human Resource Management Practices on Perceptions of Organizational Performance. *Academy of Management Journal, 39*(4), 949–969.

Foray, D. (2000). *Economy of knowledge,* the Discovery, Reference mark, Paris

Freeman, R. E. (1984). *Strategic management: a stakeholder approach*, Boston, Pitman Press.

Galambaud, B. (2003). HRM and performances. AGEF, Conference of Marrakesh, 23th and 24th January.

Hagström, P., & Hedlund, G. (1999). A three-dimensional model of changing internal structure in the firm. In Jr. Chandler & P. Hagström (Eds.), *The Dynamic Firm* (pp. 166-191). Oxford University Press.

Haines, V., & Petit, A. (1997). Conditions for successful human resource information systems. *Human resource management, 36*(2).

Hofstede, G. (1999). Cultures *and organizations: Software of the mind.* Hill, London.

Hofstede, G. (1993). Cultural constraints in management theories. *Academy of Management Executive, 7*(1), 81-94

Hong, W., Thong, J. Y. L., Wong, W. M., & Tam, K. Y. (2002). Determinants of user acceptance of digital libraries: an empirical examination of individual differences and system characteristics. *Journal of Management Information Systems*, *18*(3), 97-124.

Kalika M., Bellier S., Isaac H., Josserand E. & Leroy I. (2002). E-*management: towards the virtual company? Impact of the ICT on the organization and the management of competences.* Edition Connections

Kalleberg, A. L., & Moody, J. W. (1994). Human Resource Management nd Organizational Performance. *American Behavioral Scientist, 37,* 948–962.

Louarn, J. Y., & Wils, T. (2001). *The evaluation of the human resources management: Control of the costs to the return on the human investment.* Editions Connections, Paris.

Lepak. D., & Snell, S. (1998). Virtual RH : strategic human resource management in the 21th century. *Human resource management review, 8*(3).

Louart. P. (1996). *Stakes and measurements of a powerful HRM.* In A-M. Fericelli & B. Sire (Eds.), *Performances and human resources.* Paris, Economica.

Macduffie, J. P. (1995). Human Resource Bundles and Manufacturing Performance : Organizational Logic and Flexible Production Systems in the World Auto Industry. *Industrial and Labor Relations Review, 48*(2), 197–221.

Mathieston, K., Peacock, E., & Chin, W. (2001). Extending the technology acceptance model: the influence of perceived user resources. *Database for Advances in Information Systems*, New York, Summer.

Myerscough, M. (2000). The relationship of age and gender on user information satisfaction for web-based intranet systems applications. working paper, University of Wisconsin, USA.

Peretti, J. M. (1993). Sharing of the function and sharing of information. *Personnel*, 346, November. - December.

Reix, R. (1999). *Management and Information System.* dictionnaire des systemes d'information. Vuibert.

Romelaer, P. (2002). *Innovations and constraints of management, Book of Crepa*, Paris Dauphine University. *37.*

Schuler, R. S., & Jackson, J. E. (1988). Organizational Strategy and Organizational Levels as Determinants of Human Resource Management Practices. *Human Resource Plannin., 10*(3), 125-141.

Sire, B. (2001). Ten years of HRM which changed France Telecom, Notes of the LIRHE, *350,* November.

Snell, S. A., & Dean, J. W. (1992). Integrated Manufacturing and Human Resource Management : A Human Capital Perspective. *Academy of Management Journal, 35,* 467–504.

Tannenbaum, S. I. (1990). Human resource information system: User group implications. Journal of Systems Management, *41*(1), 27-32.

Ulrich, D. (1998). Delivering results : a new mandate for human resource professionals, Ballantine Bookst, Havard Business School.

Williamson, O. E. (1975). *Markets and Hierarchies: Analysis and Antitrust Implication*s. New York, The Free Press.

Zardet, V. (1995). *The approach of the internal customers-providers: a framework of analysis of the sharing of the HR function.* Acts of the congress of AHRM, Potiers.

Zmud, R. W. (1979). Individual differences and MIS success: A review of the empirical literature. *Management science, 10*(10).

KEY TERMS

HRIS: Abbreviation for Human Resources Information System, is typically a database system that lets you keep track of all types of information related to your company and your human capital.

ICT: Short for Information and Communications Technology, it is the study or business of developing and using technology to process information and aid communications.

Individual Factors: Factors that contribute to the success of the information system according to the organizational characteristics.

National Culture: Refers to the cumulative deposit of knowledge, experience, beliefs, values, attitudes, meanings, hierarchies, religion, notions of time, roles, spatial relations, concepts of the universe, and material objects and possessions acquired by a group of people in the course of generations through individual and group striving that influence the success of the information system.

Organizational Factors: Factors that contribute to the success of the information system according to the users.

Perceived Performance: The degree to which a person believes that using technology will enhance his or her performance.

Technology: Technology is a broad concept that deals with a speicies usage and knowledge of tools, and how it affects a species' ability to control and adapt to its environment.

ENDNOTES

[1] According to this theory, the human resources, apprehended like a reserve of competences, can constitute the source of a durable comparative advantage under certain conditions. Exit of the field of the strategy, this theory differs from the traditional strategic paradigm in the sense that it stresses the bond between the strategy of the company and its internal resources, and not its competing environment.

[2] In this context, the ICT are then considered as tools used by the firms to organize their information system.

Chapter XX
Employee Life-Cycle Process Management Improvement with Web-Enabled Workflow Systems

Leon Welicki
Microsoft, Canada

Javier Piqueres Juan
Systar, Spain

Fernando Llorente Martin
ONO, Spain

Victor de Vega Hernandez
ONO, Spain

ABSTRACT

Employee life-cycle processes management (hiring new employees, changing their conditions, and dismissing them) is a critical task that has a big impact in HR Information Systems. If these processes are not handled correctly the consistency of HR databases is compromised. In many cases (especially in small and mid-size business) these processes are implemented using semi-manual procedures based on unstructured information. In this chapter the authors will present the results of our real-world experience building a Web-enabled workflow system for managing employee life-cycle process instances in the context big Spanish telecommunications company.

INTRODUCTION

Employee life-cycle management is a critical task that affects all companies without regard of their size and business. These processes include hiring new employees, changing working conditions (promotion, demotions, change of cost centre, changes in the compensation package, change of function, change of organizational unit, etc.) and dismissals (end of relationship). In this paper we will present our real-world experience building a web-enabled workflow system for managing employee life-cycle process instances in a big Spanish telecommunications company. In the first section we will present ONO, our company, in order to set the organizational context. In the second section we will present the problem that we faced and set the requirements for building a tool to solve it. In the third section the web-enabled workflow system is presented, making special focus on the agile approach used to build it and how the previously stated requirements are met. Finally we will offer some conclusions and future lines of work

About ONO

ONO is the leading alternative provider of tele-communications, broadband Internet and pay television services in Spain and the only cable operator with national coverage. ONO offers its services to more than 1.8 million residential cable access and 69,000 business customers as of 31 March 2007, through its own state of the art networks which give direct access to nearly six million homes in franchises that cover the majority of Spain, including the nine largest cities. ONO is the principal competitor to the incumbent telecommunications and pay television operators in Spain. For the first Quarter 2007, ONO gener-ated revenues of €1,608 million and EBITDA of €592 million, on an annualized basis. ONO has several offices all around Spain.

Ono is a young company in constant growth in search of excellence. Throughout its history has demonstrated great management skills and solid growth prospects, backed by a strong global investment in an infrastructure that reaches 6.8 million homes. Table 1 shows chronologically the main highlights that significantly transformed our company.

Figure 1. ONO Spanish coverage and operating highlights. ONO offers their services to clients in almost all the national territory, covering more than 17.500 homes in Spain (according the Spanish INE)

Table 1. Company background (chronologically)

Year	Event
1998	The ONO brand was launched in 1998, and was awarded the licenses to provide cable television and telecommunications services in the regions of Valencia, Castellon, Alicante, Murcia, Cadiz, Huelva, Cantabria, Mallorca, and Albacete.
2002	By the end of 2002, ONO was already present in approximately one in every three homes prepared to receive its services.
2003	In 2003, it was awarded the licence to operate in Castilla – La Mancha.
2004	In 2004, it acquired the telecommunications operator Retecal, covering Castilla-Leon.
2005	In November 2005, ONO closed the acquisition of 100% of the telecoms company Auna Tlc, extending its services to the communities of Madrid, Catalonia, Aragon, Andalusia (excluding Cadiz and Huelva, which already belonged to ONO), the Canary Islands, Catalonia, La Rioja, Madrid and Navarra.

BACKGROUND

In this section, we will present our notion of employee life-cycle process and how it is related to e-HRM. Following, we will detail how this processes where run at our company in our initial scenario to show their fragility and resource consumption intrinsic problems.

Employee Life-Cycle Process

We call *"employee life-cycle process"* to any process that modifies the conditions of an employee within our company. These processes include hiring new employees, modifying any of her contractual conditions (changes in the compensation, position, department, location, bonus, etc.), and dismissal. These processes are critical for the reasons detailed in the next paragraphs.

Employee Life-Cycle processes provides the input for HR databases. Therefore, if they are not managed correctly the consistency, organization, and trustworthiness of the information in HR databases are compromised.

They are run collaboratively by groups of persons that may not know each other and may be geographically dispersed (in different cities, states, countries, or continents, depending on the size of the company). Usually each process instance must go through a hierarchical approval workflow (e.g., hiring of a new employee requires an approval of the manager of the requester). When the processes are not formalized enough these workflows mutate on a case-by-case basis, hindering control over the ongoing processes.

Since they deal with information of people and this information is handled by people, there are non-formal issues that may arise (anxiety, envy, information protection, corporate politics, etc.) and may require special attention of the HR team.

The last (but not least) important issue regarding these processes is budget control: each one of these processes affects directly the HR budget for the company. Without budget control departments can hire above the HR budget forecast of the company.

Weak vs. Strong Employee Life-Cycle Process Management

An inefficient (non automated, non formal, non controlled) employee life-cycle process management results in lots of manual, repetitive, boring, low value, and error prone tasks that must be done by the HR team. All companies with a basic implementation of the HR module of SAP (or similar) may be doing a very basic management of employee life-cycle processes (all changes are recorded in a centralized database). However, there is no formal support for the approval workflow, nor management of the people issues at the stages before the data is introduced in the database. In these implementations, the processes may be performed manually (or semi-manually or using unstructured information sources like email). In this case the HR team needs to do an enormous amount of back-office low added-value work: paper chasing, consolidating requests, check for collisions when dealing with a particular request, manually creating reports, deal with each process as a "state-of-the-art" unit, control the HR budget, ensure privacy of information, normalize inconsistent input, etc. (the list could go for several lines more). We call this "weak employee life-cycle process management".

In contrast, when these processes are managed correctly they can change the way HR works within a company since all the manual, boring, error prone, and low added-value work is removed allowing HR people to innovate, drive, envision, and improve the organization. As a plus, upper management has up-to-date just-in-time information on the state of on-going employee life-cycle processes and real time information about the current HR budget. We call this "strong employee life-cycle process management".

Employee Life-Cycle Process and e-HRM

Ruël, Bondarouk and Looise (2004) state that e-HRM is a way of implementing HR strategies, policies, and practices in organizations through a conscious and directed support of and/or with the full use of web-technology. The use of web-technology may render in a set of Intranet based applications distributed within the company. Each one of these applications may focus on a concrete aspect of interest for the employee (Employee's Portal, Vacations Management, Travel Expenses, etc.) or the company (Objectives Management, Work Reports, Planning, etc.).

Each application may have been built to manage its "small universe" of information. However, there is a common denominator for all those applications: all of them deal with information about employees.

When strong employee life-cycle management is implemented within an organization we can expect a trustable source for accessing consolidated up-to-date employee information. In contrast, when weak employee life-cycle management is implemented we cannot guarantee the trustworthiness of our employee information repository (e.g. some processes may have been processed but not introduced in the system; a human error in consolidating thousand-of-excels may result in errors within the hierarchical structure of a department).

eHRM is feasible without a proper employee life-cycle process management, although not

Figure 2. Manual employee life-cycle processes management is error prone and time consuming, resulting in a weak employee's digital corporate identity on the employees. This creates the need for lots of manual or semi formal integration processes as an immediate negative consequence (represented by the arrows from each application to SAP HR)

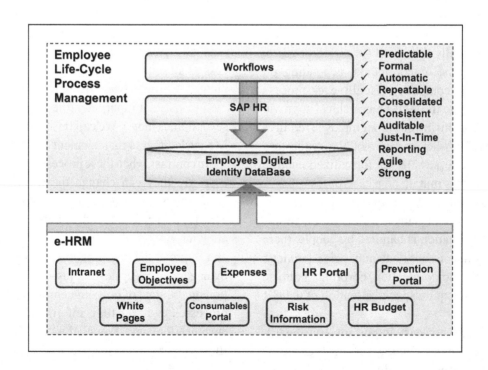

advisable (specially in large companies). Weak employee-life cycle process management has a big impact in all HR applications within a company regarding quality and reliability of its information and workflows. The lack of reliability, auditability, and normalization in employee life-cycle process management leads to a weak employee's digital identity (who is a person within an organization, including position, department, location, duties, professional category, etc.). As a consequence, lots of manual or semi-formal integrations must be done, taking lots of hours of the HR department impeding them to do "interesting things". We could summarize this in the following phrase: *"HR is working for the System, but the System is not working for HR".*

Employee Life-Cycle Processes at ONO

In the last years, ONO experienced a very fast growth in a very short period of time (Table 1). The biggest leap was the merge with Auna (a company that had the same size than ONO at the time of the merge). One of ONO's main characteristics was being very agile, with very simple and human-centred processes. Some of them didn't scale to the new context of the company, since they were designed and implemented having another model of enterprise in mind. The employee life-cycle management support processes (hiring, changing working conditions, and dismissal) fell in this group.

Each of these processes were based on paper-printed documents (that in the best case where based in corporate Excel templates), with all the problems that this implies including inconsistency in the input (files were completed differently by the requestors), traceability (all the Excels were sent internal mail), problems for enabling teamwork (there wasn't any mechanism for dispatching the requests and therefore a single request could

be handled incorrectly by several HR (Human Resources) employees at the same time), lack of a unified way for notifying the participants in the flow, lack of tools for reusing the requests, lack of reporting (there wasn't any automatic way to get a report of what was going on in the company), lot of human effort of very low added-value (HR managers consolidating hundreds of Excel files and e-mails), among other problems. To make things worst, ONO has a region-based organizational model (based on the division of the company in the Spanish geography), increasing the impact of the above mentioned problems.

Description of the Manual Employee Life-Cycle Processes at ONO

ONO is a young company, and therefore some of their processes matured in the last years and some of them are still maturing. The employee life-cycle management processes were manual, based in interactions among people that knew each other (at least by telephone). They were manual-run workflows where all the participants worked collaboratively on the same physical paper document.

Following, we will describe briefly (and in a broad way) how the processes were run:

1. A user creates a request document (for staring a new hire, a change in the conditions of one of his employees, or a dismissal). In the best cases this document was based on a corporate template. While this was the best case, it was far from being ideal: since the requestors weren't HR specialist (a petitioner could be any manager that needs to hire a new employee or to promote one of his employees) usually the document wasn't correctly fulfilled.

2. After the document was created and printed, it was signed by the petitioner and by her manager.

3. The petitioner notifies the HR department (by email or by phone) and then he sends the physical document by internal mail.

4. HR receives the document and validates it. If they need further clarification, they would contact the petitioner or her manager to discuss about the request.

5. In the case that the conditions of the hiring / promotion / change / etc. varied significantly after the discussion, a new physical document needed to be issued and signed again.

6. HR registers the transaction, contacts the employee that would be hired / promoted / fired / etc., does their usual tasks according the type of process, and registers all the information in their HR systems (payroll, SAP HR module, etc.)

7. Periodically (twice a month), the HR staff manually created reports of the ongoing processes to inform the upper management. They also used this information to verify that the HR budget wasn't overrun (this verification was also manual on a process-by-process basis).

The above description is a simplified version of the manual processes, with the goal to illustrate its fragility. It was very error prone, produced lots of unnecessary work, unreliable (in some cases, papers where lost and the process needed to be started over), and unique for each petitioner (according to her personality). It consumed lots of time of the HR team performing tasks of near-to-null value, such as verifying the input data and trying to interpret it, creating reports manually, tracking papers, notifying personally each of the actors in the process, and controlling the budget.

IMPROVING EMPLOYEE LIFE-CYCLE PROCESSES WITH A WEB-ENABLED WORKFLOW SYSTEM: AN AGILE APPROACH

In this section we present the main problem and our solution proposal. We start showing how our weak employee life-cycle processes (detailed briefly in the section "Employee Life-Cycle Processes at ONO") didn't scale when our company increased its size and rapidly became an important issue to be solved. Next is detailed how this problem derives in the need for a tool and establish a set of requirements for that tool. Following we elaborate on our response to the problem: creating a web-enabled workflow system using an agile approach. In order to make our ideas true we benefited from agile concepts for modeling the business processes and building the solution. The use of agile methods allowed us to create a high-functionality and quality application on a low budget with early and frequent deliverables.

ONO-AUNA Merge Related Problems

The process mentioned above worked fairly well in mid-to-low-size environment (less than 2.500 employees), with a relatively small HR department, and a very people oriented culture. Since the process was mainly based in human interactions, it worked better when the participants knew each other. Additionally, each instance of the process was highly dependant in the actors: some requesters (hiring managers in the hundreds of departments of the organization) where good "process players" and sent the information in good shape while others where very chaotic.

When ONO bought Auna and the merge started the company doubled its size. A manual process mainly based in interactions among people that knew each other didn't scale well in the new scenario, in one part because the size of the company increased but mainly because the people running the process didn't knew all their counterparts anymore (and given the new size of the company, it was very improbable that they would do ever).

To worsen things, the amount of HR transactions regarding employee life-cycle increased exponentially: is well known by everyone that in a merge process lots of new people come to the company, lots of people leave the company, and even more people changes position (in the average, there are two employees for each position, since both companies where in the same business).

A final added problem was traceability and auditability: since the process was based in physical paper sheets, it was mandatory to keep the original papers for a time period according with the Spanish law. During the merge, lots of work centre moves were done. Each move affected the paper files and therefore increased the difficulty to locate the papers (they could be lost or at any branch of the company). In these cases, lots of time of the HR was lost just doing "paper chasing".

The Need for a Tool

It was very clear that the company needed a tool to assist the employee life-cycle management, with the goal of making it easier, more reliable, predictable and auditable, to provide all the participants in the process the information they need just in time without any further hassle, and to provide the upper management with reporting tools to know the global picture regarding the overall HR budget of the company.

After jointly studying the problem ONO's HR and IT departments decided to build a set of tools to support the employee life-cycle processes. The main goal of these tools was to enable the collaborative work between all the actors implied in each of the employee life-cycle management processes. Each of these actors should be able to interact with the new tool in a very simple and efficient manner. Additionally, the tool should be

proactive, providing a "push model": each participant in the process should be notified whenever a process instance requires his participation. The tool should support the approval workflow (Workflow Management Coalition, 1995) for each type of process, dynamic headcount validation and automatic reporting.

Requirements for the Tool

The following requirements where established by ONO's HR department:

- **HR budget control:** Provide an automatic control of the HR budget at all the appropriate levels. For example, when a new request is issued it should be checked against the requesting department HR budget to verify if the request is valid. At a higher level the upper management and HR directors need to have reporting facilities to have a general view of evolution the overall HR budget of the company.
- **Support for the approval workflows:** Model the manual processes using a workflow systems. This implies modelling semi-formal processes using formal specifications.
- **Enabling collaborative work:** The tool should allow each employee to participate in the approval workflow at the right moment. It should inform the participant in the flow of the new events that require their attention. It should also give a unique single point for checking the status of the on going processes (eliminating e-mail and phone).
- **Automatic reporting:** Generate all the reports automatically, without manual intervention.
- **Traceability and auditability:** All the process instances should be traceable and auditable, giving a fine grained control over the past events.
- **Reducing manual work:** Reduce all the low value added manual work.

- **Input consistency:** Simplify data input in order to give reduce ambiguity and improve consistency in data that enters to the approval flow.
- **Reduce bottlenecks in the process:** Provide tools to avoid a single person to stop all the ongoing flows when she is not available.
- **Ease of use and far reach:** Create a very easy to use tool in order to make the learning curve as low as possible. It should also accessible by any employee of the organization without the need of any complex setup in his computer.

A Web-Enabled Workflow System as a Response to the Problem: Benefiting from Agile

After the problem was clearly established ONO's IT and HR departments started working on how to deliver a cost and time effective solution following ONO's cultural principles (Davenport & Prusak, 2000). The working group determined that the best approach for solving the problem was building a web-enabled workflow-based system, since it would empower the collaborative work on the employee life-cycle requests without any special requirement in the client computers.

The group also decided to build it with a low budget without sacrificing the quality and functionality, using the technologies and tools available at the company (mainly based in the development framework created by ONO's IT department). An agile approach was the methodological choice since it allowed to build small deliverables in short iterations, delivering value in small (but continuous) slots of time. In the economic side, this approach would allow to build with the resources at disposal: if the team was short on economic resources, it could do less ambitious iterations or even do no iteration without affecting the overall project (whenever any iteration was finished a new fully working module was delivered and deployed in production).

An Agile Approach for Modeling the Business Processes

The processes were modeled after a careful analysis of their manual counterparts. A joint work between One's HR and IT department was performed in order to come out with the most accurate representation of the business processes involved in the employee life-cycle.

The business process modeling was a very important part of the process: lot of tacit organizational knowledge needed to be transformed in explicit knowledge (Nonaka & Takeuchi, 1995) that can be used as a formal specification. It was a big challenge to come out with a model that clearly represents the interactions for each employee life-cycle process: since the process was semi-formal, there where significant ambiguities that needed to be resolved.

The main premise in this specification process was *simplicity*: our goal was to come out with the simplest process definition as possible. All the resulting flows are very similar: this is the result of a commonality analysis (Gamma, Helm, Johnson, & Vlissides, 1995) between all the processes in order to find all the similarities between processes and model them as uniform as possible to make them simpler and easier (Figure 3).

Observing, Learning Building, and Delivering: An Agile Approach for Modelling the Business Processes

We took an agile (Agile Alliance, 1999; Beck, 1999; Martin, 2002; Schwaber & Beedle, 2001) approach built our first model iteratively and incrementally: instead of trying to come out with the final version of the three flows up-front we went through several short iterations on the first one (the hiring process) and improved it using the feedback and experience gained from its real users.

We created a simple implementation of the hiring process according to the more immediate needs of HR. When it was in production we actively

Figure 3. After several iterations and commonality analysis, our "Hiring" and "Change of Conditions" flows are almost identical. In the manual process the flows where significantly different. Currently both flows are formal, determining automatically and in a predictable way their participants. The only difference among both flows is in the control of the HR budget (this is strongly checked on the hiring flow), but does not affect the flow neither the participants (the instance of the flow is marked with special information to indicate if it is or it is not within the forecasted headcount for the ongoing quarter)

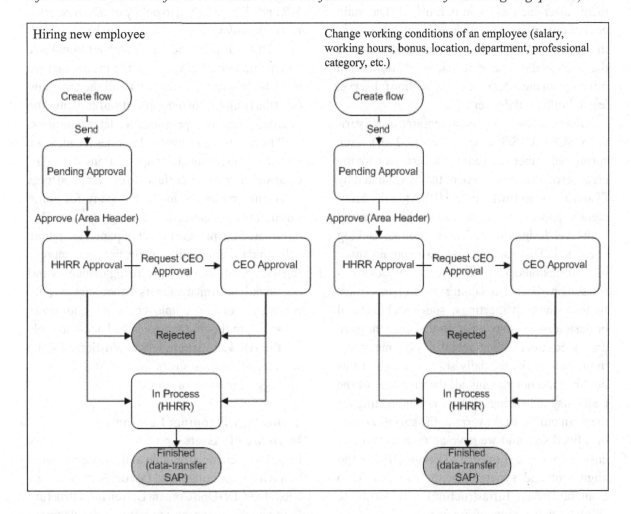

observed the problems and situations that arose to our users when using the tool and the error logs of the system. With all this information we built packages of fixes (in short sprints) and delivered new versions taking the same approach (observing, learning, building, and delivering).

This approach allowed us to constantly deliver value and to supply a working solution to our users without spending unnecessary time in the analysis phase (lot of the changes that we included in the packages where product of our continuous improvement process).

An Agile Approach for Implementing the HR Workflow System

The Software Development area in ONO's IT department works under the principle of dividing big projects in small chunks in order to deliver functionality earlier in shorter intervals of time and with more client checkpoints. This allows building applications with smaller budget, deliver early working products to the clients, and giving them the chance to change or add new requirements after each iteration is finished. The main goal of our approach is to deliver value to clients in the shortest interval as possible and to evolve the functionalities based on real world information mined from the usage of the application (observe, learn, build, and deliver).

ONO's Software Development area uses a variant of SCRUM (Schwaber & Beedle, 2001). Each sprint (Schwaber & Beedle, 2001) starts with the creation of a scope document that is validated by IT and its clients (in this case, HR). After the document is approved, a high level architecture and high level designs are built and a product backlog is created. This backlog may also contain small user stories on each of its items. The backlog is revised on a daily basis doing stand-up meetings. In that stand-up meetings, some architectural or design issues may arise. In that case they are discussed later in other special purpose meetings, in order to make the daily stand ups as short as possible and not keeping all the members of the team busy with things that are not interesting for them. In our SCRUM variant, the sprints are not of a fixed size and we have an architect role to ensure conceptual integrity (Brooks, 1995) and alignment and synergies with Ono.CDI (Ono Content Driven Infrastructure), our corporate software development framework.

We calculate the size of the sprint according to the commitments established with the clients. However, we always work actively with the clients to keep the sprints shorter than six weeks. Ideally, and on the average, the sprints have three weeks duration.

After sprint is finished, a User Acceptance Test (UAT) with the client area is performed. In this test some minor issues may arise, so we always plan some days in our schedule to fix these minor issues. After the UAT is passed and the fixes are approved we deliver the product of the iteration.

Deliverables Planning: Technology for the Masses

HR and IT established to policy of "*Deliver value to 4980 employees first and later to the remaining 20*". This was our guiding metaphor (Nonaka & Takeuchi, 1995; Beck, 1999) and means that we work to deliver functionality to all the company first (the front-end of the application) and leave the detailed back-end operations for later iterations.

The following example illustrates the idea: we focused on creating client applications with very clear and crisp user interfaces to deliver good tools to all the employees in the company for going through the employee life-cycle processes. This eliminated the physical sheet of paper, the phone calls, and the ambiguities in the process, improving the operations of all the hiring managers and organizational unit managers in the company (and potentially of any employee in the company). However, in the first versions the back-end tools for the HR team where less sophisticated since we used all our resources for providing value to the biggest number of users.

Technology Planning: Leveraging In-House IT Assets

In order to create a reliable and fully functional tool with a low budget and fast delivery we leveraged Ono.CDI (Ono Content Driven Infrastructure Framework), our corporate software development framework for intranet based applications. Ono.CDI contains a set of tools and engines that provide core and basic services (Figure 2) that includes a Workflow Engine, Document Management Engine, Business Request Framework, and Caching Engine (Welicki 2006; Welicki & Sanjuan, 2007). It has crosscutting Security and Audit modules that ensure that applications complain with ONO's IT security policies and with legal audit requirements.

Figure 4. ONO's development framework high level architectural view

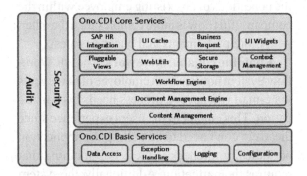

Ono.CDI also includes prescriptive architectural guidelines and blueprints that govern the architecture of ONO's intranet applications. Therefore the application is completely aligned with ONO's development policies lowering its technology transfer and maintenance cost (the maintenance and the development team are formed by different people) and ensuring a quality minimum based proven architectural and design patterns (Fowler, 2002; Gamma, Helm, Johnson & Vlissides, 1995) and development practices.

Financial Planning: More with Less

One of the main goals of the project was delivering within a low budget but still with high level of functionality and quality. On top of our deliverables and technology planning, we created a financial plan to make our developments feasible on time and on schedule.

Our existing software and hardware corporate assets (Ono.CDI development framework and Ono's Intranet deployment infrastructure) set the tooling and deployment costs to the minimum (we where working on proven, reliable, and well-known-to-us components and deploying to a controlled and well known production environment). This also saved us from acquiring new licenses and/or buying new products, since we where building upon (reusing) our in-house IT assets (software and hardware).

The iterative incremental plan allowed us to get a tighter control on budget, having a revision

stage at the end of each iteration. Therefore we didn't pay upfront for something that we couldn't plan in advance and made a more efficient use of money, spending smaller amounts in exactly what we need when we need it.

Unfortunately we cannot disclose economic information (prices of products and services) from our partners and supplier proposals. However, what we can certainly state is that we've built our system within a range of 12.5% and 27% (approximate) of the cost the proposals that we had received.

The HR Workflow System

The result of the process is the HR Workflow System that provides support for the employee life-cycle management processes. In a previous section we established a set of requirements that needed to be fulfilled by the system. Following, we will explain how these requirements have been met by the tool.

HR budget control. The system provides a detailed HR budget control. It has been designed and built to keep track of the budget of each organizational unit on a process instance basis. For example, when a manager requests HR to hire a new employee the system checks if his area is above or below its headcount budget. If the area is above its headcount budget the request is annotated with special information (as shown in Figure 5) in order to make this situation easily noticeable to the rest of the participants in the flow. The application also includes reports to provide the HR experts and the upper management with high level real-time views of the overall HR budget evolution in the organization.

Support for the approval workflow. The system used ONO's Workflow Engine capabilities to model the approval workflows. A workflow definition has been created for each of the flows associated with each type of employee life-cycle process (hiring, change of working conditions, and dismissal). Figure 3 (before in this paper) shows

Figure 5. Fragment of the "hiring request" screen. Notice how the headcount indicators ("HC presupuestado" and "HC real" fields) are highlighted in red. This means that this request is above the headcount of the requesting organizational unit

Figure 6. Change conditions of employee flow (promotions, change of salaries, change of departments, change of location, etc.)

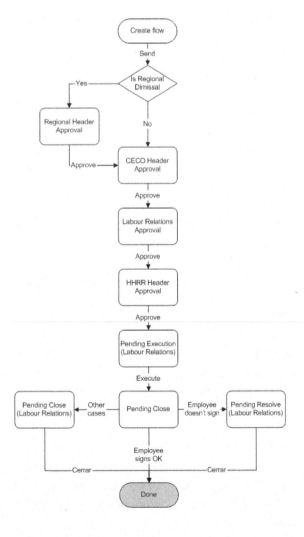

the flows for hiring and dismissing employees are shown. Figure 6 shows the flow for changing the conditions of an existing employee within the company (this flow is more complex than the other, with more participants and business rules).

Enabling collaborative work. The HR Workflow System notifies each employee of new events via e-mail whenever a process needs his participation. This enhances the users experience since the users don't need to be polling the application periodically to check if there is something that requires their attention. Additionally, the system implements an "Inbox" metaphor (similar to the one used in the e-mail systems) that gathers the requests that need participation of the user. When a user enters in the application his inbox is displayed. Additionally a summary of it (Figure 7) is present during all his session within the application.

Automatic reporting. The system generates automatically the necessary reports for HR control and for the upper management control. They are generated dynamically and can be requested at any moment providing an up-to-date picture of the overall active employee life-cycle processes in the organization.

Traceability and auditability. Every action in the approval workflow of the employee life-cycle process instances is recorded in a history log that is displayed within each process instance (Figure 8). Additionally, access information is recorded but not shown (this is used for privacy and access control audits)

Reducing manual work. All the notifications to participants, reporting, and archival of finished processes is done automatically, eliminating the most tedious and error prone manual tasks.

Input consistency. The input screens reduce the work to be done by the users. Each participant only needs to complete a very concrete (and ideally small amount of) information in each step of the flow. The employee and organizational related information is extracted directly from ONO's IT infrastructure, and the rest of the fields

Figure 7. Inbox summary. This widget is displayed in the left menu bar of the screen and is always visible. This widget shows the total number of requests of each type that requires the participation of the logged user. When the user clicks in any of the request types the complete inbox is displayed

Figure 8. History of a process. Each action performed on the request is recorded (including the execution user, date, target state, and observations)

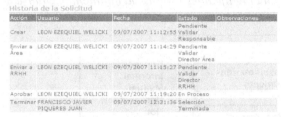

Figure 9. Input screen for working conditions change. After an employee is selected (first field) all his information is retrieved from the corporate SAP HR database and displayed in read only fields. The remaining input fields in the form are parameterized drop down lists

Figure 10. UI consistency and simplicity: the HR Workflow System (right side of the figure) is similar to the corporate intranet (left side of the figure)

are parameterized lists (whenever is possible) simplifying considerably the creation of new requests (Figure 9).

Reduce bottlenecks in the processes. The application provides "delegation" functionality that allows an employee to "delegate" in another employee his functions. There are also "super-users" (HR members) that can act in any request at any time. Therefore, except in the case rare situations that need a careful analysis of a senior

manager, no employee is a bottleneck for a process instance in the system.

Ease of use and far reach. We based our user interface (UI) in our corporate Intranet (OnoNET) that is well known among all ONO employees (Figure 10). We also used all the UI widgets of our development framework having consistency with the existing applications in the intranet. The use of web-based technologies simplifies the deployment and reach of the tool: any user with a browser can access and use the HR Workflow System. Our UI foundation follows the usability guidelines presented in Nielsen (1999) and Krug (2000).

Achieving Strong Employee Life-Cycle Management

ONO HR Workflow System provides support for automated, formally defined, input consistent, predictable, and repeatable employee process life-cycle management. Additionally, all reporting is done automatically at run-time, eliminating manual consolidations.

Another very important outcome is that since we have automated the consolidation of information a single repository for employee corporate information can be easily established and feed with the results of the processes. This repository

(shown in Figure 11 as "Employees Digital Identity Database") is an authoritative up-to-date source of information for all other e-HRM applications, avoiding the need of manual or semi formal small integrations, enhancing the operational quality and information of eHRM within the organization. As soon as a change in an employee's information or hierarchical structure is introduced in the system (through the execution of an instance of an employee life-cycle process) it is available to all applications without the need of performing any manual integration task. Moreover, employee and organizational concepts are normalized within all eHRM applications in the company allowing easier integrations (they all share the same employee and organizational abstractions).

Ono HR Workflow System has all the necessary features to provide strong employee life-cycle process management (Figure 11).

Figure 11. Ono's current "strong employee life-cycle process" model. The process instances go through a formal approval workflow in a web-based application. The results of the processes feed ONO's SAP HR and in return this feeds a centralized corporate information (identity) repository. Applications have a unique source of information for organizational data, reducing the integration and maintenance burden within the whole e-HRM ecosystem

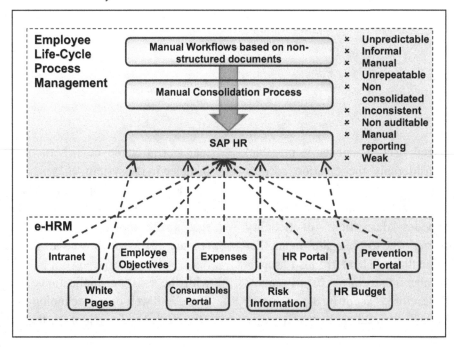

Future Improvements

We improved and normalized the employee life-cycle support significantly, but our work isn't finished yet. Currently, we are working on the following enhancements to the system:

- **Dynamic HR budget with SAP Business Warehouse:** implement SAP Business Information Warehouse (SAP Corporation, 2008) to provide dynamic and up-to-date information on the headcount budget. Currently the budget is loaded in the system upon HR's request. Using SAP's Business Intelligence suite can provide also analytical capabilities when looking at the future (e.g. forecasting budgets) and when looking at the past (e.g. analyzing real versus forecasted)
- **Improving the support for the selection process:** currently some parts of the selection process (for hiring new employees) are done offline. The system doesn't provide support for managing the interviews with candidates and managing offer letters (this two issues need very special attention of ONO's legal department according to Spanish laws on information protection).
- **Automatic creation and archival of formal letters:** Automatically create formal letters within each process and archive them in the process instance. This will eliminate the remaining paperwork associated with the process instances.

CONCLUSION

The workflow system has been in production for more than a year. It has successfully managed a big number of requests (we cannot disclose that information here), bringing reliability, traceability, and audatibility to the employee life-cycle management processes. It has become one of the core systems for supporting HR operations.

The resolution of each employee life-cycle process went down from weeks (in the manual case) to just days or hours (according the complexity of the request). Each participant in the process has to just perform a very concrete action and work with very concrete set of data. Additionally, he is notified via mail every time he needs to perform an action on a request.

Reporting is done automatically. The HR staff doesn't have to spend time on creating reports and the upper management has real-time in information on the on-going employee life-cycle processes.

Everyone in the company knows the processes (they are unambiguous, well documented, and accessible to everyone in the organization) and the processes are always the same for every employee in the organization. They are no longer dependent on the participants. At the same time the processes model the reality of our company and had been tailored to provide as much value as possible to it.

We could summarize the main benefits of the system in these three items:

1. **Reliable information:** The data sources are accurate based on normalized input and each process instance is auditable.
2. **Agile information:** The employees are notified only when they have to participate in a flow eliminating unnecessary and unproductive "polling" in an application.
3. **Improved information management:** The employee process life-cycle processes information is centralized, easy to access, and normalized, making it easy to know about the state of any on going or finished process in a uniform and simple way.

REFERENCES

Agile Alliance (1999) Retrieved September 1, 2008, from, http://www.agilealliance.com/

Beck, K. (1999). *Extreme Programming: Embrace the Change.* USA: Addison-Wesley Professional.

Brooks, F. (1995). *The Mythical Man-Month: Essays on Software Engineering, Anniversary Edition.* Addison-Wesley Professional.

Davenport, T., & Prusak, L. (2000). *Working Knowledge: How Organizations Manage what they Know.* Harvard Business School Press.

Fowler, M. (2002) *Patterns of Enterprise Application Architecture.* Addison-Wesley Professional

Gamma, E., Helm, R., Johnson, R., & Vlissides, J. (1995). *Design Patterns: Elements of Reusable Object-Oriented Software.* Reading, MA: Addison-Wesley Professional.

Krug, S. (2000). *Don't Make Me Think!* USA: New Riders Press.

Martin, R. (2002). *Agile Software Development, Principles, Patterns, and Practices.* USA, Prentice Hall

Nielsen, J. (1999). *Designing Web Usability.* Peachpit Press.

Nonaka, I., & Takeuchi, H. (1995). *The Knowledge-Creating Company: How Japanese Companies Create the Dynamics of Innovation.* USA: Oxford University Press.

Ruël, H. J. M., Bondarouk, T. V., & Looise, J. C. (2004). E-HRM: innovation or irritation? An exploration of web-based human resource management in five large companies. *Management Revue, 15,* 3.

SAP Corporation (2008). Components & Tools of SAP NetWeaver: SAP NetWeaver Business Intellegence. Retrieved September 1, 2008, from http://www.sap.com/platform/netweaver/components/bi/index.epx

Schwaber, K., & Beedle, M. (2000). *Agile Software Development with SCRUM.* USA: Prentice Hall

Seely Brown, J., & Duguid, P. (2002). *The Social Life of Information.* Harvard Business School Press.

Workflow Management Coalition (1995). *The Workflow Reference Model.*

Welicki, L., & Sanjuan Martinez, O. (2007). Improving Performance and Server Resource Usage with Page Fragment Caching in Distributed Web Servers. *Proceedings of International Workshop on Scalable Data Management Applications and Systems.* Las Vegas, Nevada, USA.

Welicki, L. (2006). The Configuration Data Caching Pattern. *Proceedings of the 13th Conference on Pattern Languages of Programs (PLoP 2006).* Portland, Oregon, USA, October 2006.

Yoder, J., & Johnson, R. (2002). The Adaptive Object Model Architectural Style. *Published in The Proceeding of The Working IEEE/IFIP Conference on Software Architecture 2002 (WICSA3 '02) at the World Computer Congress in Montreal 2002, August 2002.*

KEY TERMS

Agile Methodlogies

Corporate Intranet Apps

Employee Process Life Cycle

Hiring Workflow

HR Workflow

Web Based Applications

Web Based HRIS

Workflow

Workflow System

Section VII
Extended e-HRM Topics

Chapter XXI
Information Technologies' Impact on Individual Learning Process:
The Case of a Community of Practice

Manel Guechtouli
ESCEM Business School, France

Widad Guechtouli
CNRS, France

ABSTRACT

Information Technologies (IT) seem to be affecting individuals and organizations' communication and behaviors since many years now. This chapter is about understanding the possible impact of IT on the process of individual learning in a community of practice; in other words the authors wonder if those technologies can possibly help increasing individual competencies in order to improve their learning. They will specifically compare communication in two IT (the email and the web forum) by using agent-based simulation. Results show that each technology has a different impact on individual learning and that communication through emails appear to make individuals learn slower than on a Web forum. Conclusions are widely discussed.

INTRODUCTION

Today, executives have to face a changing and unpredictable environment where the rules of communication are constantly in progress as information technologies (IT) are moving fast. In fact,

with IT development, the access and diffusion of information become easier; technologies like the World Wide Web allow ways of communication that couldn't be imagined some years ago. The profusion of information induced by these technologies makes information abundant and it is no longer considered as a "rare resource" (Feldman and March, 1991). Gathering information is no longer seen as a major problem, but understanding and giving sense to this information seems to be much more problematic. That's the reason why importance is given to improve information management and learning processes, so that companies can develop and be able to face the perceived complexity of their environment.

In this unpredictable and changing context, knowledge is a well kept immaterial capital (Foray, 2000); it can be seen as a potentially provider of competitive advantage to organizations. Knowledge is acquired through a complex learning process which allows individuals to gain new competencies and skills. Improving this learning appears significant to executives as they'll be able to develop their personal abilities, understandings and expertise. Here, information technologies might have a significant impact and support the executive's learning process.

The aim of this paper is to shed light on the impact that IT may have on the process of learning. In a more specific way, we will use agent-based simulation to compare the effects on individual learning process of two types of web-based technologies (the email and the web forum). **The question we ask here is: how can the process of learning be improved according to the technology used?** As a context for this comparison, we choose to focus on communities of practice. Indeed, these communities, seen as informal networks composed of individuals working together in the development of a common practice (Lesser and Storck, 2001), are considered as very efficient tools in the sharing of knowledge within social networks (Lave and Wenger, 1991; Brown and Duguid, 2000). Moreover, according to Cohendet *et al* (2000), an organization can be considered as a set of overlapping communities, which play an important role in the process of organizational learning.

In order to answer the question mentioned above, we will use an agent-based model built upon data collected in an empirical study that we made in a French research centre in June 2005. Our approach of learning here is very simple and specific to the model we build. We won't be talking about the several types of learning that we often come across in the literature; it's not the point here. We are only interested in the way that technologies may affect individual learning and we'll simply consider that an individual "learns" when his competencies rise. Our methodology is based on multi-agent simulation, based on an empirical case study on a specific network (that we'll call the Cormas network). In that network, agents most often interact to solve problems related to the use of the Cormas software, and therefore our approach of learning consists in addressing the learning of agents through the raise of their competencies in a specific practice.

This paper will be structured in three parts: the first part concerns a background literature on communities of practice and learning. In the second one, we will first present the main issues through the description of a case study, and then follows a description of our models and a presentation of the results. The third and last part will contain a discussion of our concluding remarks and some further developments.

LITERATURE BACKGROUND: COMMUNITIES OF PRACTICE (CoP) AND LEARNING

This notion appeared for the first time in the early 1990's, in the work of Lave and Wenger (1991). A CoP is seen as one of the most efficient concepts to study the process of knowledge sharing in groups (Lave and Wenger, 1991; Brown and Duguid, 2000; Lesser and Storck, 2001). A community of practice (CoP) is defined as an informal network composed of agents working together in the development of a common practice (Lesser and Storck, 2001). They interact and exchange knowledge and ideas and build a common repertoire of representations. According to Wenger (1998), a CoP's definition is based on three major points:

- The practice that binds the members of the community together;
- The mutual and voluntary commitment of its members to the community's objectives;
- A repertoire of common representations built through repeated interactions.

According to this author, CoPs' success is essentially due to their informal and independent status, as well as to the voluntary engagement of their members and the knowledge created through their interactions.

First, let us start by giving a brief definition of individual learning. We choose to follow Dibiaggio's definition (Dibiaggio, 1998) who defines this process as a means to reach a goal, solve a problem or answer a question. He considers that it is related to the difference between the knowledge one already has, and the necessary knowledge required to answer a question. In this paper, we will consider that individual learning occurs when an individual increases his/her competency. Salomon and Perkins (1998) state that, in reality, it is not possible to consider individual learning as an isolated process, as it is always related to a social context with social norms and influences. This leads us to a rather social perspective of learning. Zimmermann (2004) gives the following definition: « Social learning corresponds to a situation where agents or individuals are able to modify their behavior, state, opinion or other factor, on the basis of information derived from the observation of their neighbors (Bala and Goyal, 1998) or more generally from the observation of these agents' behavior and performances». Learning is thus a socially constructed phenomenon (Hanneman, 2005).

In the specific context of a CoP, Lave and Wenger (1991) highlight the role of the social participation in the process of learning. Indeed,

according to these authors, new comers play an essential part in the diffusion of knowledge across the community, as stresses by the "Legitimate Peripheral Participation" theory (LPP). We will see to what extent this theory is relevant, according to the technology used.

IT'S IMPACT ON INDIVIDUAL LEARNING PROCESS ON A COP: A CASE STUDY

This section concerns the main thrust of the chapter. It will be divided in two parts: the first one will be dedicated to the development of our major issues through the description of a case study within the Cormas network. The second part will concern the presentation and discussion of our model trying to answer the problems presented in the case study.

Presentation of the Case Study and Main Issues

The study is about understanding the ways of communication and learning in a community of practice. During an investigation made in the CIRAD[1], a research centre in France, we met people belonging to a network that could be identified as a **community of practice**. This network is the Cormas network. It is composed of people interested in natural resources management and multi-agent simulations. Cormas is software that was created by the members of this network; it can be downloaded off the Internet, free of charge and training courses are offered to teach people how to use it. The Cormas community is located all over the world and communicate and interact basically by using the Cormas web forum or via emails.

One of the major goals of the community is the development of this specific tool. It was one of the several criteria that made us point at this network as a community of practice. In fact, the most important feature of a community of practice is the practice that binds the members of this community together. Here, this practice is the software they all use.

In addition to that, we can sum up what made us think of the Cormas network as a CoP in the following points:

- **The status of the network:** the Cormas network is a rather informal community, independent from the CIRAD and autonomous.
- It emerged in 1998 when people working in the same field first felt the need to work together and exchange their knowledge and experiences on the used of multi-agent simulations in natural resources management; this network was not created by a hierarchical authority.
- The voluntary engagement of the network members, on which depends the length of life of this community.
- **The structure of the network:** there are 3 very competent agents (the creators of the software) and 385 less competent, learning agents (the users of the software). This fits perfectly with the structure of a CoP. Indeed, according to Lave and Wenger (1991), the members of a CoP divide into two groups: the most competent ones will represent the core of the community, whereas the rest of the members will step at the periphery of the community.
- **The free access to this community:** people can join and leave the community free of charge. Anyone who shows interest for the use of multi-agent simulations in the natural resources field, and especially for the Cormas software can be a member of this community.

Data were collected in two steps: first we had a of 15 days project research in the Cirad centre, where we met people belonging to several communities of practice, and mostly people belonging to the Cormas community. Each interview lasted from 1 to 2 hours and was immediately transcribed. It was very interesting to approach those individuals and be able to make an *in situ* observation. We contacted the persons we couldn't physically meet in Montpellier by mail and we elaborated a questionnaire to make the gathering of information easier.

We noticed that the Cormas network we were observing was using a forum to communicate most of the time. So we planned to study this particular way of communication in the second part of our research.

We identified 388 individuals using the Cormas forum which was structured as previously seen. We studied the number of question posted on the forum since its creation and the proportion of individuals who eventually posted answers back. We also identified the main aim for insiders to join this community. This aim is to **learn** how to use the Cormas platform. In fact, most posts on the forum are about solving problems that users come across when using the platform.

From these observations, we build a multi-agent model based on the structure of the Cormas network. Multi-agent simulations are considered as appropriate tools to investigate the field of learning in social networks (Phan, 2003). A few empirical studies using multi-agent modelling to explore interactions within communities of practice can be found in the literature (Diani and Muller, 2004; Dupouët et al, 2003; Dupouët and Yildizoglu, 2003). The model we build is different from those found in the literature because it focuses on **learning process** in those communities and it will be described in the next section.

The model built is issued from the confrontation of our case study and literature. Our aim here is to define a structure as close as possible to reality and to use agent-based simulation to test different scenarios in terms of learning and technology use. We'll use this to understand how individuals can learn considering the most often used ways of communication according to them which are **the web forum** and **the email.**

The Model and Main Findings

Agent-based simulation is a bottom-up methodology that is generally used to study complex, self-organising systems, and try to "understand" the mechanisms that take place within these particular structures. It enables the modeller to test different scenarios of simulation, hence, testing the impact of several parameters on the phenomenon studied. As previously mentioned, the model we build aims at comparing two ways of communication through two types of simulations:

- **Simulations with communication though emails:** here, the most competent agents in the community are explicitly identified to answer eventual questions. In this case, agents always ask these particular agents;
- **Simulations with communication through a forum:** where agents simply post a question on a forum, and wait for an answer. Here, agents answer posted questions according to their knowledge and availability.

The Agents

We have a population composed of 110 agents. Each agent is characterized by the following features:

- **Knowledge vector:** This vector is composed of 100 knowledge concerning 100 different subjects. (See Table 1)
- **Competency:** Defined as the number of subjects an agent knows about.
- **Memory:** Where an agent stocks information about past interactions (name of agents previously met and the answer given by each one of them).

Table 1. Example 1: an agent has the knowledge concerning subjects 1, 99 and 100 but knows nothing about subject 2

Subjects	1	2	...	99	100
Knowledge vector	1	0	...	1	1

- **Availability:** Defined by the number of questions that an agent is allowed to answer per time-step.

Tolerance threshold: defined as follows:

- **In simulations with communication through emails:** it is defined as the number of unanswered questions that an agent is willing to accept from another agent, before deciding not to ask it anymore.
- **In simulations with communication through a forum:** it is it is defined as the number of unanswered questions that an agent is willing before deciding to leave the community.

According to these features, every agent is potentially a knowledge-seeker or a knowledge-provider, or both, according to his competency.

In terms of answering questions and providing knowledge, we consider that the population of agents is divided in two parts: priority knowledge-providers (*pkp*) and secondary knowledge-providers (*skp*). The members of the former have knowledge about the 100 subjects of an agent's knowledge vector; they have a competency equal to 100. Whereas the latter members have a competency equal to or higher than a competency threshold (CompMin) defined as the minimal competency required in order to have the ability for answering questions. This threshold is equal to 75^2.

In terms of asking for knowledge, each agent that has a competency smaller than 100 is a knowledge-seeker. This includes *skp* as well.

The initial structure of the population is the following:

- 1 agent with an initial competency equal to 100;
- 9 agents with an initial competency equal to 75;
- 100 agents with an initial competency equal to 0.

Interaction Rules

An interaction is defined according to the type of simulation used:

- **In simulations with communication through emails:** an interaction is defined by a question asked by agent *a* to agent *b*, and an answer given by agent *b* to agent *a*.
- **In simulations with communication through a forum:** an interaction is defined by a question posted by agent *a* on the forum, and an answer posted by agent *b* on the forum.

Each agent can only ask one question per time-step. Moreover, an agent asks a question about a subject it knows nothing about. And an agent answers a question if it has the specific knowledge asked for and if it is available; otherwise, it will ignore the question.

Learning Process

Each time an agent gets an answer to a question; it raises its knowledge of that particular subject to 1, and won't ask questions about this subject

Table 2. An agent learns and acquires knowledge about subject 2

Subjects	1	2	...	99	100
Knowledge vector	1	1	...	1	1

anymore. Following example 1 (cf. Table 1), an agent increases her knowledge of subject 2, as shown in Table 2.

Choosing a Knowledge-Provider

- **In simulations with communication through emails:** agents always choose the most competent agent in the population.
- **In simulation with communication through a forum:** agents don't choose a particular agent, but post a question on a forum.

Parameters of Simulation

- **Availability:** we will make this parameter vary between 1 and 10 questions per time-step.
- **Tolerance threshold:** will also vary between 1 and 10 unanswered questions per agent in simulations with communication through emails, and between 1 and 10 unanswered questions in simulations with communication through a forum.

Indicators

We will observe the following:

- **Number of priority knowledge-providers:** this indicator will show how many agents were able to raise their competencies to the highest level (100).
- **Mean learning of agents who left the community:** measured by the mean competency of these agents at the end of the simulations. This indicator will let us know the level of learning reached by some agents, before leaving the community.

With the several variations of the simulation parameters, we have 100 different scenarios of simulation. We run each scenario 30 times, and the results presented are the mean results of the 30 iterations of each scenario.

The results can be divided in two parts according to the technology used: the email and the web forum.

Results of Simulations with Communication Through E-Mails

Number of Priority Knowledge-Providers

Figure 1 shows the number of *pkp* at the end of the simulations. We can see that this number reaches 110 agents (i.e. all the agents of the network) for all values of tolerance threshold and as soon as agents' availability is equal to or higher than 6.

The same scenario is observed for other values of availability. All agents become *pkp* when certain equilibrium is reaches between values of knowledge-providers' availability and knowledge-seekers' tolerance threshold. These values are:

For all values smaller than the values presented in table 3, the number of *pkp* at the end of the simulations is quite small. Thus, the learning process is poorer.

Mean Learning of Agents who Left the Community

With this indicator, we can have an idea of the number of agents that could increase their competencies to a level equal to or higher than CompMin (75). Thus, we are able to know how much did the knowledge-seekers (i.e. agents that had an initial competency equal to 0) learn before leaving the community. Results are shown in figure 2.

This figure shows the mean competencies of leaving agents for several values of availability. This competency is not observable for some values of availability and tolerance threshold. These values match the values of these two parameters where all the agents were able to become *pkp*. From this figure, we can see that, before leaving the community, knowledge-providers did not

Figure 1. Number of pkp at the end of simulations with communication through e-mails

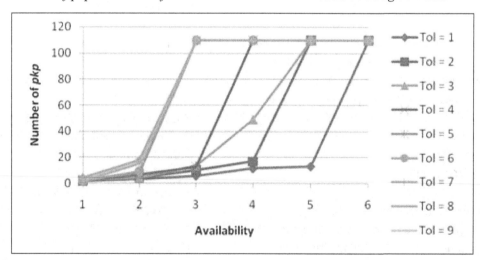

Table 3. Minimal tolerance threshold required for each value of availability in order to have a maximal number of pkp

Availability	1	2	3	4	5	6	7	8	9	10
Tolerance threshold	7	5	4	2	2	2	2	2	2	2

Figure 2. Mean competencies for knowledge-seekers that left the community in simulations with communication through e-mails

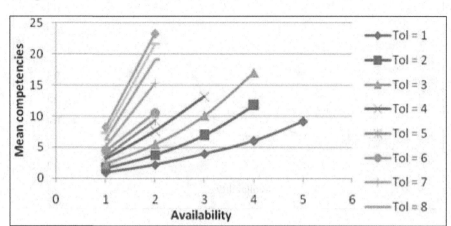

learn that much. The maximal mean competency barely reaches 26.

To sum up the results presented above, it is obvious that the learning process depends on agents' availability and tolerance. But it is likely that it depends more on knowledge-providers' availability than on knowledge-seekers' tolerance. This could be explained by the fact that, as all agents know each-others' competencies and always ask the most competent agents first, there is a **congestion effect**. Thus, access to knowledge is not possible for every agent, and therefore, some of them leave the community with a quite low level of competencies. Agents' tolerance should help for better learning, but this parameter remains at a secondary level, whereas the most important one is knowledge-providers' availability. Let us see now the results obtained by simulations with communication through a forum.

Simulations with Communication Through a Forum

Number of Priority Knowledge-Providers

The figure below shows that the number of *pkp* reaches its highest value as soon as agents' availability is equal to 1. Only tolerance threshold values make a difference, here. All knowledge-seekers become priority knowledge-providers

when tolerance threshold equals 7 and for all values of availability.

Mean Learning of Agents who Left the Community

In general, the mean competencies of leaving agents are quite small. These agents only reach competencies equal to a maximum of 3.2 for values of availability equal to 1 and tolerance threshold equal to 6.

Here, agents left the community with very small competencies. But, according to figure 5, the number of leaving agents is quite small. Hence, the agents that left the community with very small competencies did so before all knowledge was stored on the forum, as we'll explain later.

DISCUSSION AND FURTHER DEVELOPMENTS

Results from simulations above stress that agents increase more their competencies when they use a forum to communicate, than when communication is based on emails. This can be explained by the strong congestion effect observed in the first set of simulations. In fact, because all agents always ask the most competent ones in the community, and because these

Figure 3. Number of pkp at the end of simulations with communication through e-mails

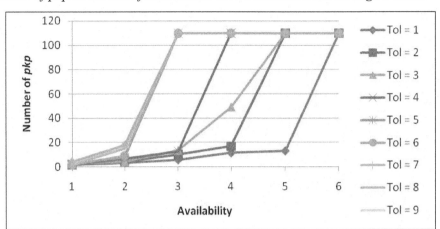

Figure 4. Mean comptences for knowledge-seekers that left the community in simulations with communication through e-mails

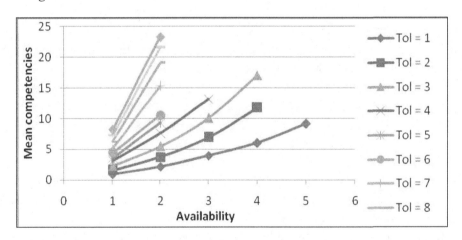

knowledge-providers have limited availability, knowledge-seekers don't always get a chance to access knowledge.

This congestion effect is obvious if we consider the figure below. This figure shows the graph of interactions within the community, based on "who asks who", at the end of a simulation with availability equals 1 and tolerance threshold equals 10. We chose these values because it is likely that the congestion effect is more important when tolerance threshold is larger. In this situation, the community has a star-shaped structure,

with the priority knowledge-providers at the core of the network.

There is a kind of queuing effect observed here, and it really slows down the learning of knowledge-seekers, when using emails. However, we believe that this problem could be overcome if we give enough importance to the legitimate peripheral participation theory, presented by Lave and Wenger (1991). According to this theory, individuals situated at the periphery of a community play an essential part in the process of knowledge diffusion within this community. Indeed, in our case, if new comers

Figure 5. Number of pkp at the end of simulations with communication through a forum

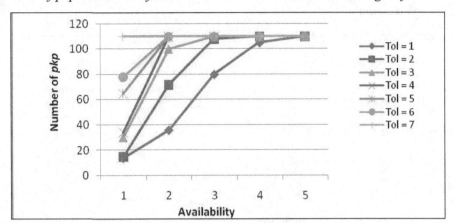

were privileged to have access to knowledge first, it is likely that the knowledge they acquire will soon be transferred to other new comers in the community. Thus, they become priority knowledge-providers over time, and there will be more sources of knowledge within the community.

As a matter of fact, because of the tolerance threshold, it would not be very pertinent that new priority knowledge-providers are initial secondary knowledge-providers. If their availability is not high enough, these agents will soon be ignored by many other agents in the community. Consequently, they won't be asked anymore, and there will not be much new sources of knowledge in the community. Whereas, if new comers are favored in terms of access to knowledge, then the number of sources to knowledge would increase and hence, knowledge would be transferred in an easier way.

Things are different in the second set of simulations. Simulations with communication through a forum show that agents learn better and in an easier way than when they use emails. As we mentioned previously, this is due to the congestion effect that is observed in the first set of simulations. In fact, it makes no sense to talk about a congestion effect when communication happens through a forum. As a matter

of fact, agents don't ask particular agents, but post their questions on the forum, addressing the whole community rather than a particular set of agents.

To make sure of that, we build the graph of interactions based on "who answers who". As we can see from the figure below, the network structure is different from the previous one. We can see little stars emerging around initial knowledge-providers, and a much bigger one around the forum, where most agents find answers to their questions. This entity stores all the answers provided throughout the simulations, and as soon as the 15th time-step on, when availability equals 1, all knowledge is available on the forum. Hence, all the agents that didn't leave the community so far systematically get answers to their questions. This explains the large number of priority knowledge-providers at the end of most simulations.

Moreover, learning is easier in the second set of simulations because knowledge is **stored** on the forum. It becomes available even when knowledge-providers are not. Hence, from a certain time-step on (15 for instance, when availability is 1), all knowledge-seekers can learn and acquire all the knowledge required to become priority knowledge-providers themselves. In this perspective, knowledge can be considered

Figure 6. Mean competences for knowledge-seekers that left the community in simulations with communication through a forum

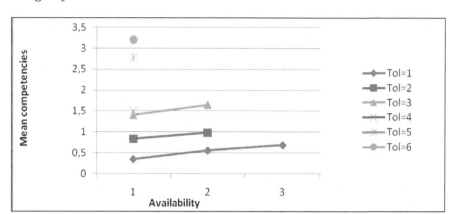

as a public good which no longer depends on the availability of individuals, but on the forum where it can be stored.

Unlike in simulations where communication happens through emails, new comers do not play a central part in knowledge transfer, when a forum is used. Accordingly, the LPP theory is not really relevant in such a context. This theory stresses the importance of a high social participation, in order to enhance individuals' learning. However, this appears not to be essential when using a web-based forum. Though, we are not denying the importance of this theory when using emails as a means to diffuse knowledge.

CONCLUSION

It seems that fast Information Technologies (IT) development had a significant impact on organizational and individual activities since the last decade. Indeed, these technologies changed the rules of communication and made executives reach a wider informational space. Furthermore, adding their constant development to globalization is one of the main factors that give an international aspect to competitiveness.

Today's firms must deal with a complex perceived environment where unpredictability rhymes with uncertainty. In this context, taking advantage of these technologies may help managers and executives to improve individual and organizational learning. Our paper compares two specific IT, the email and the web forum. To do so, we used an agent-based model which characteristics were inspired from a community of practice case we observed: the Cormas network. We run two sets of simulation trying to understand the individual learning process: first where individuals use emails to communicate, and second where they use a web forum.

Results of simulation show that agents learn faster when they use a forum to communicate, than when communication is based on emails. We noticed first that learning depends more on knowledge-providers' availability than on knowledge-seekers' tolerance. This can be explained by the strong **congestion effect** observed when individuals use emails as all agents know each-others' competencies and always ask the most competent agents first. There is a kind of queuing effect which slows down the learning of knowledge-seekers. We suggest that this problem could be overcome by highlighting the legitimate peripheral participation theory, presented by Lave and Wenger (1991).

This congestion effect does not appear when communication happens through a forum as individuals do not address their questions to one or several particular persons but simply post it on the forum. Moreover, knowledge is somehow **stored** on that forum. Hence, it no longer depends on individuals' availability. Thus, learning appears faster and easier in a community of practice when individuals use a web forum than when they use emails.

This result is only relevant to its context. In fact, agent-based simulation is a methodology where results cannot be used as proofs. They can only help us understand what is likely to happen at the macro level if certain parameters were changed at the micro level (Troitzsch, 2004). These results need to be validated, by comparing them to real data. That will be our next step in our research. Another development would be to transpose our model to another real context of learning in order to compare the two situations and stress significant differences. Learning process can be much more relevant in this perspective.

REFERENCES

Bala, V., & Goyal, S. (1998). Learning from Neighbours. *Review of Economic Studies, 65,* 595-621.

Brown, J. S., & Duguid, P. (2000). *The Social Life of Information.* Boston: Harvard Business School Press.

Cohendet, P., Dupouët, O., & Créplet, F. (2000). Communities of Practice and Epistemic Communities : A Renewed Approach of Organisational Learning within the Firm. *Actes du Colloque WEHIA*, 16 juin 2000, Université de Marseille.

Dibiaggio, L. (1998). *Information, connaissance et organisation.* Unpublished doctoral dissertation. University of Nice. France.

Feldman, M. S, & March, J.G. (1991). L'information dans les organisations : un signal et un symbole. In J. G. March (Ed.), *Décisions et organisations* (pp. 255- 284). Paris: Les Editions d'Organisation.

Foray, D. (2000). *L'économie de la connaissance.* Paris. France : Editions La Découverte.

Lave, J., & Wenger, E. (1991). *Situated learning: Legitimate Peripheral Participation.* New York, NY: Cambridge University Press.

Lesser, E., & Storck, J. (2001). Communities of practice and organizational performance. *IBM Systems Journal, 40*(4), 831-841.

Troitzsch, K. G. (2004). Validating computational models. In: *Proceedings of the 18th European Simulation Multiconference.* SCS Europe.

Wenger, E. (1998). Communities of practice: learning as a social system. *The Systems Thinker, 9*(5).

KEY TERMS

Agent-Based Modeling (ABM): Is a bottom approach which enables the researcher to study complex systems and emerging properties.

Community of Practice (CoP): An informal emerging group of people working together toward the development of a common practice.

Individual Learning: A process by which an individual increase its knowledge.

Knowledge Transfer: A process by which knowledge is transmitted from one individual to another.

Knowledge-Providers: Individuals who can be considered as sources of knowledge.

Knowledge-Seekers: Individuals whose aim is to acquire now knowledge.

Network: A collection of individuals (nodes) interacting together, and linked by a set of relations (links).

ENDNOTES

[1] In French "Centre de Coopération Internationale en Recherche Agronomique et Développement»

[2] We led simulations for several values for CompMin and 75 is the value where the highest number of agents are able to increase their individual competencies.

Chapter XXII
What are the Main Impacts of Internet and Information and Communication Technology on Unions and Trade Unionism?
An Exploratory Research in Europe and North America

Valéry Michaux
Reims Management School, France

ABSTRACT

There has been a lot of research on the impact of Internet and information and communication technologies (ICT) on society and on private, public or non-profit organizations. In comparison, there has been far less research specifically dealing with the impact of Internet and ICT on unions and on trade unionism whether in North America or Europe. Moreover trade unionism is a field in which, international comparisons between European countries as well as between Europe and North America are difficult to carry out. The historical background, dialogue and opposition traditions between unions and companies, cultural, institutional and economic contexts, government policies are so many factors that make these comparisons difficult. This research aims to answer two main questions. Is it possible, despite local context differences, to identify main trends and international convergences when analyzing the impact of ICT on unions and trade unionism? And if these major trends do exist, what challenges, opportunities and threats do they pose to trade unions in industrialized countries? This exploratory research, first led to the construction of an analysis grid that presented three main research interests:

- *It made it possible to compare ICT impacts on trade unions and unionism in European countries and North America in spite of their differences of context;*

- *It helped to identify all the different types of ICT impacts whether they were direct (transformation of the unions themselves, transformations in union practices) or indirect (consequences for unions of the transformations of work and in the behavior of employees);*
- *It led to identify main international trends concerning the impacts of ICT on unions and unionism in industrialized countries.*

In a second step, this research shows that ICT poses threats but also offers opportunities for unions and trade unionism. The tensions between opportunities and threats led to the identification of four main types of challenges posed by ICT for unions in the industrialized world today.

INTRODUCTION

There has been a lot of research on the impact of Internet and information and communication technologies (ICT) on society and on private, public or non-profit organizations. In comparison, there has been far less research specifically dealing with the impact of ICT on unions and on trade unionism whether in North America or Europe. International comparisons on the subject are even scarcer. Indeed, trade unionism is a field in which, international comparisons between European countries as well as between Europe and North America are difficult to carry out. The historical background, dialogue and opposition traditions between unions and companies, cultural, institutional and economic contexts, government policies are so many factors that make these comparisons difficult (Hyman, 2001). This research aims to answer two main questions. Is it possible, despite local context differences, to identify main trends and international convergences when analyzing the impact of ICT on unions and trade unionism? And if these major trends do exist, what challenges, opportunities and threats do they pose to trade unions in industrialized countries?

Considering the scarcity and heterogeneity of research on the subject, this research is an exploratory qualitative study. Several stages were necessary to identify international trends. Firstly, an analysis grid was constructed to so that it was possible to make a transnational comparison of the different types of impact ICT has had on unions

whether they were direct (transformation of the unions themselves, transformations in union practices) or indirect (consequences for unions of the transformations of work and in the behavior of employees). This grid reveals four analysis angles which are developed in this paper. This grid also makes it possible to reveal the main challenges that ICT poses for unions and shows that there is indeed a convergence of these challenges in industrialized countries.

In a first part, the methodology and the theoretical framework of this research will be presented. The four analysis angles will be developed in the following four parts. The limitations and lessons to be drawn from this research will be identified in the conclusion.

METHODOLOGY AND THEORETICAL FRAMEWORK: THE CONSTRUCTION OF AN ANALYTICAL GRID ALLOWING INTERNATIONAL AND CROSS CONTINENTAL COMPARISONS ON THE THEME OF UNIONS

A qualitative exploratory approach has been chosen to tackle this problem. Indeed, there are few studies on the impact of ICT on unions and trade unionism. Canadian and American articles are the most numerous on the subject, but their number remains relatively limited. They are still rare in Europe. Moreover these different approaches reveal several analysis angles. Some articles focus more particularly on the difficulties to supervise the use employees and unions make of ICT whereas others focus more on the impact of ICT on the evolution of trade unionism and union practices. In the face of such heterogeneity, several stages of thematic analysis were necessary to identify major international trends. First of all, an analysis of articles devoted to ICT in the trade press and trade union press between 1999 and January 2005 and an analysis of trade union websites helped to highlight a number of observations in the French context. The main themes identified were then compared with the themes and thinking stemming from European research studies (mainly British and Swedish). Thirdly the main trends identified in Europe were compared with the themes and thinking stemming from research work carried out in North America. This threefold exploratory, documentary analysis led to the construction of a reading grid. Indeed, ICT having had many significant impacts on unions and trade unionism, it was necessary, in order to bring out the threats and opportunities it represented, to build a two-dimensional grid that would make international comparisons possible.

An object/subject dimension (c.f. Figure 1). Indeed, some challenges put ICT forward as a vector of union transformation. In this case, the union is an object of transformation. Other challenges put ICT forward as an object of negotiation for

unions. In this second case, the union is no longer an object of transformation but an actor.

A direct/indirect dimension: (c.f. Figure 2). Some challenges lay the stress on the direct impact of ICT on the functioning of unions or on union practices. Other challenges stress the impact of ICT on work and employee behavior and the changes these evolutions result in for unions.

The author has chosen not to come within the theoretical scope of industrial relations. This paper remains within a paradigm that is increasingly common in the field of information systems based on Giddens's structuration theory (1987). In this perspective, technologies are no longer seen as impacting the actors, organizations or society (technical determinism) neither are actors, organizations or society seen as acting on technologies (sociological determinism) in a unidirectional, linear and simple manner. There is increasingly shared consensus on the fact that it is necessary to take into account direct and indirect multidirectional interactions between objects and subjects in order to analyze the impact of ICT[1].

This twofold subject/object and direct/indirect approach led to the construction of an analysis grid to assess the different impacts of ICT on unions and trade unionism (c.f. table 1). This grid presents four angles of analysis.

As shown in the following development, the use of this analysis grid has made it possible to identify four main types of impacts of ICT on unions and

Figure 1. First dimension of analysis

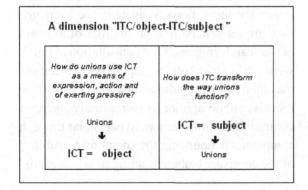

Figure 2. First dimension of analysis

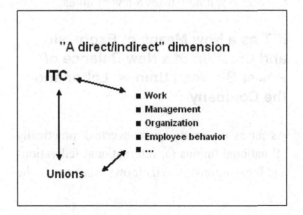

Table 1. An analysis grid based on Giddens's structuration theory (1987)

	ITC/"object How is ICT used?	ICT/ "subject" How does ICT transform?
Direct impacts on unions	Use of ICT by unions	Modification of the internal functioning of trade unions
Indirect impacts on unions	Use of ICT by employees and employers	Evolution in work: evolution in employee behavior

unionism that lead to 4 types of consequences. These impacts and consequences seem to converge in Europe and in North America.

FIRST TYPE OF IMPACT: THE CONSEQUENCES OF ICT AS A NEW MEANS OF EXPRESSION, ACTION AND PRESSURE FOR UNIONS

Around 1850, Karl Marx already underlined that by favoring contacts between workers of different localities, the new means of communication created by modern industry had largely contributed to the development of trade unionism and unions (Merck et al., 2002, p. 171). Indeed, technical breakthroughs in communication have always created new possibilities of action for unions. In their time, the telegraph, the roneo duplicator, the photocopier and then the fax made possible the circulation of information propitious for the creation of a balance of power. Nowadays, the Internet provides the unions with a formidably efficient forum, and a means of spreading information with unequalled speed and reach. Where it once took two months to distribute a union pamphlet to all the workers, it now takes a few minutes.

ICT as a New Means of Expression and Creation of a New Balance of Power Between Unions, Labor and the Company

As far as information is concerned, practically all national unions (or international federations and local unions) have their own websites. In the

French context, studies show that more than the content, it is the tone that varies from one site to another. This particular tone is a reflection of the values of the union organizations. Online information is very diverse, from news bulletins and news flashes to practical files (retirement, pay, leave, employee shareholding, cyber-surveillance...), societal information (unionism abroad, impact of ICT on work...), and historical information (history of the union including social advances obtained...). These websites are also very well documented legal watch tools. The studies carried out by Freeman in the United Kingdom and the United States (2005) show that the quality of these websites keeps improving and they are increasingly interactive (e-mail, forums...).

Trade union websites act increasingly as a counterbalance to institutional websites and companies are very worried by these information practices and are even on the defensive. Indeed they know that the information released can be prejudicial to their competitiveness (internal confidential information released too early on the Net....), to their brand image (trading losses, difficulties recruiting rare competences...). Bietry (2002) observes a referencing race on search engines between official and union websites. Indeed if the union site or sites were launched before the institutional website of the company, they are referenced first on the lists of answers of the search engines. First consultation of union websites by shareholders, suppliers or customers may then prove prejudicial for a company. All the more as public opinion is increasingly aware of contradictory information, in particular through campaigns denouncing the social responsibility of the company (subcontracting in countries using child labor…). As a French unionist pointed out: "*By typing Colgate on a search engine, any internet surfer will fall on our site (…). This does not only give us huge visibility, but also additional nuisance power*" (Dubosc, 2001, p. 37). Bietry notes that the number of connections to alternative sites tends to progressively supplant the unionization rate criteria when assessing the balance of power. Jurisprudence seems to be developing in that direction. In the name of freedom of expression, it has justified the use by dissident sites of the same key words as those used on institutional sites. The web surfer can thus have a global vision of the lines taken at a given moment. However, apart from barely tolerable practices which go as far as to use customer distribution lists to send messages of protest, the trend is to leave aggressive action to other pressure groups (third worldists…) and to remain at the level of contradictory information. But it is still all about the balance of power!

ICT as a New Means of Putting "Pressure" on Companies

Merck and his co-authors (2002) list 3 new union practices: cyber campaigns aimed at recruiting new members, union contact centers, meant to manage all the contacts with members or people susceptible of joining and "cyber strike pickets" used as an information and mobilization vector during industrial conflicts.

Cyber campaigns consist in welcoming on a website forum any person wishing to ask questions on the work environment. Beforehand, an awareness campaign is carried out among members who then act as intermediaries in the field. It is the type of campaign launched by UNI (Union Network International) in the call centre sector. In parallel, a few union contact centers (centers managing telephone or Internet contacts with members or people seeking information) have been started up (for instance: the Digital fagforening. org in Norway…).

The role of cyber strike pickets is to inform all at once the stakeholders, the media, and public opinion. They come in several different forms. Most of the time, specific websites (either autonomous or hosted by federating organizations) are created on a one off basis for the duration of the conflict. It is a matter of transmitting concrete and factual real time information to the strikers, but also to inform other employees, to collect expressions of solidarity, and keep the media informed of the progress of the conflict and more generally alert public opinion. For instance, the use of ICT among all these targets characterized the Boeing conflict in the US and the Calgary Herald Journal conflict in Canada at the beginning of 2000 (see other examples given by Freeman, 2005). The increased mobilization power of union members also comes from their growing ability to manage information. For example the majority union at Delta Airlines created its own databases, which regroup the individual characteristics of each member pilot, his schedule and geographical location. The 10,000 flight crewmembers can thus be mobilized very quickly in real time and at a minimum cost. Staging fast union action and coordinating it on a large scale has thus become possible (Bietry, 2002). These fast and large-scale actions can also help raise funds in the event of strikes. It was the case for AFL-CIO in the United States which in 2004 already regrouped 28 national unions, 88 geographically defined State Federations and City Labor Councils and more than 400 local unions and other union organizations. With its members e-mail addresses, AFL-CIO has an Internet diffusion list of more than 2 million e-activists called « Working Families Network » (Freeman, 2005, p. 11). This enabled them to raise $350, 000 during the Safeway strike in California in 2003 with 2 waves of e-mails sent to 400,000 union members.

Other examples can also be considered as belonging to the cyber-picket category; employees broadcast pictures of union action on the Intranet, or use it to send specific e-mails inviting the employees of a company to lobby the CEO by sending him an e-mail. In this same category, one may also note the use of solidarity messages ready to send with a simple "clic". All one needs to do is "clic on a link and add one's signature". This practice enables unions to trigger fast and almost instantaneous reactions to events.

ICT and more particularly information systems are also resources that can be taken hostage during conflicts. For example, in France, in February 1999, ELF engineers blocked the company's information systems thus completely paralyzing the company's production (Jaubert, 2000). In addition to this action, a special website "ELF putting up resistance" was designed and hosted by employees on strike, both to drain up all the claims of the employees from all the different sites of the group, and to relay the context and history of the movement, the follow up to actions and negotiations, to the outside world.

Generally speaking, the e-conflict is not very costly for well-organized unions whereas it can be very prejudicial for the company (Labbe and Landier, 2001). There are few legal provisions that can be mobilized to counter such actions. The national legal frameworks that regulated conflicts between unions and companies, strikes, tract distribution, blocking production... have become obsolete in the virtual word.

These evolutions lead to a major shift in the balance of power during negotiations.

SECOND TYPE OF IMPACT: THE CONSEQUENCES OF THE USE OF ICT FOR EMPLOYEES, UNIONS, AND EMPLOYERS

The impact of new technologies on work is hardly a recent negotiation theme for unions. However, the massive introduction of ICT in organizations has continued to make it a topical subject. First of all, the impact of ICT on employment (redundancies, worker redeployment...) is far from being

an outmoded problem. For example, in the field of human resources, networking human resource information and making it accessible on the company Intranet enables each employee to manage himself/herself more and more activities online (leave, work time, absences, expense refunding, or enrolling in training...). This revolution has not been without consequences on employment[2]. In the same way, the social consequences of the introduction of *enterprise resource planning* (ERP) and *customer relation management* (CRM) systems are multiple. Indeed, these systems can both cut certain jobs, but also enrich others, the corollary being more responsibilities and claims in terms of employee status, requalifying or salary increases...

In parallel, the use of ICT by unions on one hand, and their use by employees on the other hand, appear as two negotiation themes which have currently tended to boost the role of unions in a context of declining trade unionism everywhere in the world over the past 40 years.

The Use of ICT by Trade Unions to Communicate with their Members: A New Negotiation Theme

Everywhere in the world, unions claim access to company modern means of communication in the same way as they have a telephone and union premises. Nevertheless, in this particular field, existing national legal frameworks are largely obsolete when it comes to the possibilities offered by Intranet and internal electronic bulletin boards. Many conflicts have been recounted worldwide on that subject, and will progressively lead to an evolution of existing rules and the development of new ones. For example, the Canadian civil service union tried to encourage the 3,000 employees of Hydro-Quebec to join through the repeated sending of e-tracts. The management intercepted the messages and ended up forbidding them (Merck *et al.*, 2002). In France, in the early 2000's, a CGT representative (Confédération Générale du

Travail: one of the 5 main French unions) was threatened with being dismissed because he had sent an e-mail to inform the whole workforce of the negotiations over shorter working hours.

As conflicts have developed, current legislation has shown its limitations and new jurisprudence has developed. For example, the use of Intranet by unions conflicts with the French Code du Travail (work code) and the US National Labor Relations Act[3]. In general, unions are in principle limited to informing employees and handing out tracts only at opening and closing hours. What is the meaning of such a rule when facing a tool which can be used 24 hours a day from anywhere? The use of Internet has spread 5 times faster than the telephone (Trogrlic, 2001) and thus requires re-inventing new rules. In France a new legal framework has emerged since 1999, after the unions lobbied both the government and the employers[4]. In France, the new legal framework of labor law provisions foresees that a company agreement can allow union publications and tracts to be made available on a union site set up on the company's Intranet. This text does not recognize the right of unions, or more generally personnel representative institutions to use the Intranet. Currently, the free diffusion of e-tracts without a framework is thus not allowed. However, this text opens the possibility, by means of an agreement between unions and management, to foresee the sending of specific mails or access to a specific Intranet. The purpose of this agreement is to lead to a good balance between the security and responsibility requirements of the employer and union expression within the company. In particular, it should define the conditions of access of unions and the technical rules aimed at preserving the freedom of choice of the employees to accept or refuse the message (a system enabling the employee to unsubscribe on request from the list of employee representatives…). Thus, in France, it is local negotiation on a case by case basis which has currently proved the only possible and relevant solution to manage efficiently this question of the

use of Intranet by the unions. However, whereas works council sites have been developing and have been proving to be more like market places, Merck and his co-authors (2002) notice that companies generally appear to be more reticent to host trade union sites[5].

What can be said about the situation in other European countries and in North America? A study carried out in the United Kingdom, Canada and the United States (Lee, 2004) shows that negotiations of local agreements are not very frequent nowadays. But a finer analysis of the situation shows that in most cases, union members communicate by mail without employers having defined rules either for or against this practice. It all looks as if employers were not aware or did not really anticipate the problems likely to arise from the free use of the Internet by Unions to communicate with employees. It is only when conflicts arise that negotiations are initiated. For example in April 2004 a local union of 400 teachers (Providence, Rhode Island) were obliged to protest against a measure forbidding them to communicate with their members and start ne-gotiating an agreement with the School Council. In Great Britain, the 200 members of the union of the Liverpool Department of Work and Pen-sions office had to go on strike to protest against a management decision forbidding unions to use e-mails (Lee, 2004).

"No legal provision compels Management to grant unions a cyber-forum. However, attempt-ing to deny them any connection to the Web to better limit the means of expression of counter powers is a strategy that is bound to fail" (Bietry, 2002, p. 145). Indeed, if a company introduces too many constraints, even the most recent legal provisions cannot prevent unions from creating their own websites on the Internet[6], outside the company Intranet. They can thus free themselves from the rules governing employee expression in the workplace, and avoid being cut off in the case of tensions with the management. It is then much more difficult for the company to manage

the content and tone of the information released. Here we see the appearance of a new challenge that will be developed further on in this paper. ICT tends to create a new balance of power between unions and companies that still needs to be consolidated.

The ICT use "Charter" or "Code of Practice": A New Field of Negotiations for Unions

Like all technological breakthroughs, ICT is liable to bring the best and the worst according to the use that is made of it. Abuses are possible as well by employees, as by unions or employers. What can be done to avoid an employee spending too much time surfing on the Net? How can one avoid employees "settling scores" directly on the Net[7]? What can be done to avoid management being tempted to spy on unions? How many e-tracts have been open? Who by? With ICT, everything is possible but not everything is allowed[8].

Since the year 2000, cyber-surveillance is a problem that has been raised by all trade unions worldwide. In November 2000, an International conference was organized in Brussels to tackle the problem of the online rights of workers and the surveillance of electronic mail at work. In industrialized countries, employer control of the use made of ICT by the employees is generally authorized. As a counterpart, the employer is obliged to inform the employees of the nature of this surveillance (the way their e-mails, phone calls, their use of internet… are controlled).

French labor law encourages employers and unions to negotiate specific agreements on cyber-surveillance. Moreover, these agreements cover much more ground than just surveillance. Indeed, increasing use of ICT, in particular mobile phones, laptops and other portable means of communication, also has an impact on working hours and the link between private and professional life. It is not so much the fact of having nomadic workers in the company that is new (there have

always been salespeople, sales representatives, maintenance technicians moving around) as the almost permanent link between the employee and his organization. These agreements make it possible to specify "good practice" in the use employees make of the new technologies that are made available to them as well as the rights and duties of each side: respect of the employee's home, the right to a private life (the right to disconnect: phones, computers, e-mails), the different rights linked to employee itinerance.

Concerning this last point, the appearance of new applications like geolocation tends to emphasize this control issue even more[9]. Moreover, the alliance of IT and telephony (in call centers for example) has made it possible to manage and memorize information so as to give a precise account of the activity. All the doings of the employees can thus be controlled through this device (length and number of breaks, hourly performance…).

In principle, these agreements contain several parts (Merck *et al.*, 2002):

- Conditions for employee access to information systems, preservation of IS, abiding by software protection laws;
- Framework for the use of bulletin boards and internal forums (traceability and confidentiality of connections[10];
- Framework for the use of Internet (information downloaded from the net, external forums (traceability and confidentiality of operations carried out…) ;
- Framework for the possible creation of personal employee sites;
- Framework for the use of Intranet by management and unions….

In France, Trade unions have mixed feeling about these charters and existing agreements. Indeed some of these agreements just cumulate all sorts of prohibitions. Nevertheless, as a whole, trade unions encourage dialogue. The CGC (an executives' union) explains that, chart or agreement, what really matters is to create genuine debate around everyone's rights and obligations. That is why it can be considered that in France, technologies have injected dynamism into debate, concertation and negotiation within companies. To a certain extent, this debate has strengthened the role of unions in the co-construction of collective work rules.

In the United States, the National Labor Relations Act offers minimum protection. The law authorizes employers to control phone calls, the use of Internet and the exchange of e-mails between employees. According to the American Management Association, 45% of employers already exerted this type of control in 2000 (75% of large US corporations did so in 2002). The objective was to avoid and protect themselves against excessive, abusive, inappropriate or illegal use of the net by employees. Indeed, as Muhl points out, employers are not protected from the illicit uses their employees can make of the e-mail system of the company and access system to the Internet. That is why lawyers have increasingly been advising companies to formalize the rules concerning the use of ICT by employees and to inform these employees of the company's workplace monitoring policy. These policies must be specifically adapted to the company's type of activity and they must specify (Spognardi et Hill Bro, 1998):

- What is allowed and what is not,
- The scope of monitoring and in particular if the monitoring only applies to calls or to or to all the files recorded,
- The sanctions foreseen...

According to some observers these "codes of practice" must be subject to the agreement of the unions, and the unions must also play a role in the disciplinary procedures that might be conducted against employees (Lee, 2003).

THE THIRD TYPE OF IMPACT: CONSEQUENCES OF ICT AS A FACTOR OF MODIFICATION OF THE INTERNAL FUNCTIONING OF TRADE UNIONS

Will ICT make unions more efficient? An investigation carried out on the basis of 1997 data (Fiorito J. *et al.*, 2002), concluded that ICT mainly changed the organization and the way unions operated[11]. Its impact on a certain number of efficiency criteria remained limited[12].

Towards More Transparency and Democracy

Beyond the possibilities of communication, the new media (and especially Internet) tend to change existing internal balances. For example, Le Coq and Debons (1997) explain how the use of mobile phones between unions and French lorry drivers led to a complete reorganization of union action during conflicts with lorry drivers. Indeed, before mobile phones appeared, the lorry drivers themselves thanks to the use of CB radios coordinated the action, and the unions were often side tracked. The mobile phone enabled them to regain their role in the coordination of actions and the regulation of conflicts. *A contrario,* Green and his co-authors (2003a, 2003b) show how Internet has changed the balance of power between official representatives and field activists by giving power back to the rank and file militants (transparency of information, capacity to act autonomously..)

The biggest French unions have been aware that these changes in internal balances could prove sensitive to manage. That is why it was some time before they encouraged their members to create a Website. In the first place, to a certain extent, the confederations feared the autonomy Internet gave their members and the loss of their centralized regulation power. Moreover, owing to their age and profile, union leaders are not naturally new technology oriented. They have also been marked by the respect for the hierarchy that characterized the industrial "thirty glorious ones"(the thirty years of economic expansion that transformed France between1945-1975); whereas the younger generations have grown up in a network and cooperation-oriented culture largely open onto the Internet. Trade-Union Organizations also wanted to protect themselves from the risks linked to the Internet (everything written leaves traces) and possible "excesses".

However, aware for a few years of the rapid expansion of cyber-unionism, unions encouraged their members to develop and use their own sites to carry out union actions. They offered consultancy and training actions (on line symposiums, specific CD-ROMs) to support their members in this approach. At the European level, as early as March 2002, the European Trade Union Confederation launched a "European plan of action for computer offers at home" which offered equipment, software and internet access….for union members and their families at very attractive prices. In 2004, UNI-Union International Network launched a specific call center to help trade unionists improve their websites.

ICT thus tends to introduce new forms of democracy within union organizations as shown by the example of SIF the largest Swedish union (Hatchuel, 2004). Thanks to participation and consultation provisions put online on the union's website, SIF involved its members in general policy decisions and in the definition of the services to be offered. Thus, in 2004, more than 20,000 members expressed their opinion on the negotiation of branch or national inter-professional agreements in discussion forums on Internet. However, this type of change raised a major internal controversy. Like all organizations that operate on the principle of representative democracy, unions often postulate the uniformity and evidence of their members' needs. *"In contrast, by accepting the variety of individual expectations and by involving their members in the definition of their assignments, some unions like SIF de facto have explored new types of militant collectives"* (Hatchuel, 2004, p. VIII). In the United States, observers (Geere *et al.,* 2003) have also emphasized the introduction of different forms of democracy within trade union organizations (consulting members before a strategic decision, better diffusion and audience for claims by dissident groups which unions are going to have to take into account…).

In conclusion, these impacts lead to more transparency and influence the balance of internal power either to more centralization or decentralization. This impact is not neutral in the context of the 2005 crisis at AFL-CIO especially concerning the problem of lack of link between the activists and the top of the organization (Collombat, 2005).

Towards International Co-Operation and Coordination

Generally, ICT tends to re-enforce international co-operation between union organizations worldwide (relevance of analyzing, discussing and coordinating actions on certain themes at an international level). Thus, new international union structures were created. Union Network International (UNI) was created in January 2000, uniting 900 affiliated unions in one hundred and forty countries. It accounts for 15 million members almost half of whom are in Europe. Its objective is to re-enforce the human dimension in an increasingly globalized economy. The first UNI world congress took place in September 2001 in Berlin and its priority was to discuss new forms of work (teleworking and call centers), and unionization (and in particular the use of Internet as a recruitment tool for unions). In December 2004, a European trade union forum was organized by UNI Europe to tackle the specific problems of the new economy workers.

THE FOURTH TYPE OF IMPACT: CONSEQUENCES OF ICT AS A VECTOR OF THE EVOLUTION OF WORK AND EMPLOYEE BEHAVIOR

All analyses converge to show that ICT has introduced a number of tensions between opportunities and threats which go in the direction of a renewal of traditional unionism (for example, Diamond and Freeman, 2002).

ICT and the Emergence of a New Form of Protest and New Union Actors Providing an Alternative to Traditional Unions

Beyond the opportunities it offers unions, ICT can constitute a threat for traditional union organizations (for example: Chaison 2005). Indeed, they favor the emergence of new hybrid virtual union actors. The example, which got most media coverage, was that of the UBI soft group, one of the world's largest video game publishers. For lack of a union and of an interlocutor in the human resources department, a group of 7 employees on precarious contracts decided to broadcast their discontent on a wide scale. On the 15th December 1998, the 1,000 employees of the group, whatever their location, received a copy of an anonymous open letter to the CEO which denounced working conditions, precarious employment and the absence of any personnel representation, which was made possible by the company's network organization (cluster of companies employing fewer than 49 employees), the hiring policy... Ubi-Free, the first virtual union was thus born. The press picked up the story denouncing the damaging social effects of the race for innovation in the sector as a whole. This experience, illustrates Internet's potential as a means of expression for employees, an alternative to traditional unions. Indeed a few months after the opening of Ubi-Free, other similar sites developed enabling employees to express spontaneously discontent and claims without any union intervention[13]. Internet spaces regrouping a collection of often negative testimonies by former employees or current employees who remain anonymous have emerged (www.tchooze.com...). The Web thus seems in a position to offer a new reactive, interactive, fast, anonymous and difficult to control platform for protest.

This experience needs to be put back into the perspective of the resurgence of autonomous and corporatist trends against the global practices of traditional federations which are no longer able to make specific claims (net economy employees...) ICT favors the emergence of new forms of direct protest by employees in the absence of their traditional unions. It re-enforces forms of individual action, to the detriment of union action, which is based on representativeness (Merck *et al.*, 2002). This context constitutes a threat, or at least is felt as such by traditional union organizations, but also for companies. In contexts of union deficiency, it becomes impossible to foresee and regulate social unrest (Bietry, 2002). The very objective of unionism, which is to offer a credible recognized interlocutor having authority on the employees, thus, tends to be called into question. The possibilities offered by ICT thus emphasize the imbalance in the current system of professional relations (estrangement from unions....).

These new hybrid and virtual species of union actors have become increasingly legitimate. For example, Alliance@IBM[14] was created from 2 groups, which were set up in 1999 in response to the unilateral decision of the IBM management to change the company retirement system (www.ibmemployee.com and www.casepensions.com). Nowadays, this unified group is considered as a full union partner whereas it does not take part in management union negotiations (Diamond and Freeman, 2002). This website which is composed of discussion groups, files offering hypertext links to other more specific sites, and information on the company itself is very active (number of visitors and people having agreed to receive e-mails).

ICT, Opportunities and Threats Introduced by the New Forms of Work

Could the new forms of work, induced by NICT, in particular company break up, have a negative influence on unionization rates? The answers are contradictory.

Work no longer requires sharing the same geographical unit and time. "People increasingly work collectively while increasingly working separately"[15]! Moreover, both mobility of the work place and increased autonomy have led to the development of teleworking and nomadism. These new forms of work do not favor traditional union practices because of the distance between these employees and the company. Moreover, the distance between the employees themselves has detrimental effects on solidarity. Indeed professional communities tend to disintegrate when they are not sustained by human contacts. It is not only the Net-economy sector which is affected, but all companies. Unions speak of "parceling the strength of collective protest"(Merck *et al.*, 2002, p. 174) and have engaged into in-depth thinking about their mission and role in this new work configuration.

However, Greene and his co-authors (2003a, 2003b) show that Internet can have paradoxical effects on solidarity. Indeed, the use of ICT tends to extinguish traditional proximity solidarities, but at the same time it creates the means to develop solidarities of interest which transcend physical presence, hence, the multiplication of virtual communities. That is why, while challenging the foundations of traditional union action, the use of Internet also constitutes an opportunity for union development. Indeed, ICT helps recruit new members and reach out to audiences so far inaccessible: nomad executives, expatriates, employees on temporary posting… who can now keep up with company social news, ask questions or request the help of union representatives with a simple clic, from home, outside working hours. Greene and his co-authors (2003a, 2003b) emphasize that this new context of use introduces greater confidentiality and wider room for maneuver in union practices. Some employees, in particular executives, do not wish to be seen reading union billboards. Nowadays, they can consult union sites whenever they wish. ICT and in particular the use of Internet have contributed to change both unionism as well as the profile of the union activist or militant unionist. New populations (women working flexi-time, itinerant executives, precarious contracts…) can conduct actions and participate in union life from a distance. ICT thus renews the concept of union involvement rooted in the workplace and based on the physical presence of workers during normal working hours (meetings…). This traditional form of activism tended to exclude atypical workers and was perceived as little compatible with the responsibilities of some executives. With ICT, a new type of cyber-unionism and unionists has emerged in addition to traditional forms of activism.

Finally, ICT and in particular the Internet enable unions to target non-unionists. For example, In the UK, the Trades Union Congress developed www.worksmart.org.uk, " to be a one-stop shop for everything to do with your working life", particularly for non-union workers (basic information about workplace problems and worker rights and links to other sources of information and advice). In the USA, the organization Working America provides considerable information to non-union workers on line but under a strong union label (Freeman, 2005).

ICT and the Development of New Services for Members

In the American context, Diamond and Freeman (2002) showed that ICT was going to enable unions to develop policies which provided services to members (on-line connections with national or international experts on different subjects, sending letters of information with legislation updates or current experiments on subjects such as work security, conditions of work in call centers...) these services policies would help introduce and increase union presence in sectors where they were little represented. For example, The National Writers Union helped to create a structured community of 700 independent writers disseminated throughout the country. These services policies are predicted to become as developed as collective bargaining today for unions.

The use of Internet has contributed to develop a new form of service oriented unionism, but without giving up the conflict tool. This dual purpose is illustrated by the example of SIF, the largest Swedish union (related by Hatchel, 2004). This union, which has 300,000 members, caters for white collars (technicians, executives and engineers...) of the manufacturing sector and is largely represented in the new technologies sector. Confronted in the 1990s with stagnating membership, this union went into a process of in-depth analysis of the foundations of union membership. Though current expectations were still oriented towards defending collective rights (salaries, unemployment insurance, working conditions...) they were increasingly oriented towards taking individual needs into account (cyclical crises in certain areas of activity, updating competences, and support when changing jobs...). This new reality and the possibilities offered by ICT helped introduce some innovations. As early as 2000, the website of the union offered personalized on-line tools for career management, in particular a competence balance sheet, that each member could establish himself. In addition, members had the possibility to meet specialized union advisors individually. In 2003, competences and career management were the most consulted services. However this evolution raises questions. One may wonder if, by developing services for members, unionism is not evolving towards a form of managerial unionism that privileges members and experts at the expense of militants. However, the SIF case shows that there was no estrangement from collective

bargaining negotiations with the development of on-line services.

LIMITATIONS, LESSONS AND CONCLUSION

The purpose of this communication has been to answer two main questions. Is it possible, in spite of the differences in local contexts, to identify major international trends and convergences when one analyses the impact of ICT on unions and unionism? And if these major international trends do exist, what stakes, opportunities, and threats do they conjure up for unions in the industrialized world?

This exploratory research, first led to the construction of an analysis grid that presents three main research interests:

- It made it possible to compare ICT impacts on trade unions and unionism in European countries and North America in spite of their differences of context;
- It helped to identify all the different types of ICT impacts whether they were direct (transformation of the unions themselves, transformations in union practices) or indirect (consequences for unions of the transformations of work and in the behavior of employees);
- It led to identify the main international trends concerning the impacts of ICT on unions and unionism in industrialized countries (c. f. figure 3);

In a second step, this analysis grid helps to show that ICT poses threats but also offers opportunities for unions and trade unionism. More precisely, it shows that the same factors, for example: i) the evolution of work, ii) the use of ICT by employees can be both a threat and an opportunity: parceling of the strength of collective protest on one hand, but providing opportunities for recruiting new

Figure 3. Analysis grid of the main international trends of ICT impacts on unions and unionism in industrialized countries

	ITC/"object" *How is ICT used?*	ICT/"subject" *How does ICT transform?*
Direct impacts on unions	*Use of ICT by unions - ICT as a new means of expression, action and pressure for unions* *Use of ICT by unions as an negotiation theme for unions*	*Changes in the internal functioning of union organizations - modifications of internal balances* *Internationalization*
Indirect impacts on unions	*Use of ICT by employees : ICT as a potential vector of gaining news types of union members, ICT as a vector of new services policies* *Regulation of ICT use by employers - participation of unions in implementing policies regulating the use of ICT in companies*	*Evolution of work- Evolution in employee behavior : new opportunities and new threats for traditional unionism* *Emergence of new forms of protest and new alternative union actors*

types of members on the other; leading to the emergence of new forms of protest through an Internet alternative to traditional unions, but also to new opportunities for expression, communication, action and lobbying. Finally, this research has made it possible to show that ICT impacts create tensions today between opportunities and threats. In addition, the impact of Internet in communication, activism or internal democracy depends on the culture and the traditions of each union organization (Lucio, 2003). It can prove to be an opportunity for one organization and a threat for another. More than a threat or an opportunity, ICT poses several challenges for unions. This research has made it possible to identify the 4 main types of challenges ICT represents for unions in the industrialized world.

- Everyday, ICT induces new practices which transform work and render legislation and usage null and void? In parallel these fast

transformations can be very different from one organization to another. This new context could enable unions to regain a place and an active role in the negotiation of agreements, policies or "codes of practices" concerning the "good use of ICT in the company" (c.f. figure 4).

- In parallel, ICT represents an opportunity for the unions to develop new forms of expression, action and pressure which re-enforce their power and change the balance of power within the unions and the companies (c.f. figure 4).

- ICT also tends to change the very functioning of union organizations, by modifying existing balances within these organizations (c.f. figure 5).

- ICT makes unions more likely to be of interest for new employees but also favors the emergence of new forms of alternative employee expression that bypass unions. It is those tensions between opportunities and threats that have made traditional unionism evolve (c.f. figure 5).

This exploratory research presents many limitations. In particular, it is based on putting into perspective threefold documentary research (in France, Europe and North America), but does not include direct interviews with union organization representatives and does not take the union point of view into account. Nevertheless beyond these limitations, this research contributes to provide a comparative analysis grid which could prove useful both for union organizations and employers but also for future research on the subject. (see for example, Michaux, 2009)

REFERENCES

Bietry, F. (2002). *e-GRH, entre promesses et interrogations.* Col. « Management et Société », Colombelles, Paris, EMS.

Bietry, F. (2005). Les syndicats à l'heure des réseaux. *Revue Française de Gestion, 31*(157), 79–102.

Chaison, G. (2005). The Dark Side of Information Technology for Unions. *The Journal of Labour and Society, 8*(4), 395–402.

Chaykowski, R. P. (2002). Re-Inventing Production Systems and Industrial Relations: Technology-Driven Transformation in Canadian Metal-Mining Industry. *Journal of Labor Research, 23*(4), 591–610.

CFE-CGC. (2002). Internet et Intranet dans l'entreprise : un nouvel outil au service de votre action syndicale. *Encadrement Entreprise, 101*(3/4), 2–16.

CNIL. (2001). *Cybersurveillance des salariés dans l'entreprise.* Paris, CNIL Report.

CNIL. (2002). *Cybersurveillance sur les lieux de travail.* Paris, CNIL Report.

Collomba, T. (2005). Crise à l'AFL-CIO, Les leçons du syndicalisme états-uniens. *Le Devoir, 7.*

Coufourier, O. (2001). Quand les nouvelles technologies deviennent mouchards. Retrieved, 26 February, from http:www.cfdt.fr/actualite.

Craipeau, S. (2001). *L'entreprise commutante, travailler ensemble séparément.* Paris: Hermes Science, Lavoisier.

Diamond, W. J., & Freeman, R. B. (2002). Will Unionism Prosper in Cyberspace? The Promise of the Internet for Employee Organization. *British Journal of Industrial Relations, 40*(3), 569–596.

Dommergues, P., Groux, G., & Mason, J. (1984). *Les syndicats français et américains face aux mutations technologiques.* Paris: Edition Anthropos-Encrages.

Dubosc, J. P. (2001). Les syndicats se ruent sur la Toile, au grand dam des enterprises. *Liaisons Sociales ,34,* 34–37.

Duvivier, M. (2002). *Alerter les salariés des risques induits par les TIC.* Retrieved May 14, from www.cfdt.fr/actualite.

Figarol, N. (2005). *Cybersurveillance sur les lieux de travail, Big Brother est-il dans l'entreprise?* Retrived, March 22, from www.cfdt.fr/actualite.

Findlay, P., & McKinlay, A. (2003). Surveillance, Electronic Communications Technologies and Regulation. *Industrial Relations Journal, 34*(4), 305–308.

Fiorito, J., Jarley, P., & Delaney, J. T. (2002). Information Technology, US Union Organizing and Union Effectiveness. *British Journal of Industrial Relations, 40*(4), 627–658.

Freeman, R. B. (2005). The Contribution Of The Internet To Reviving Union Fortunes. In The Webbs To The Web, *National bureau of economic research,* Working Paper, *11298,* 24(December).

Gattiker, U. E., & Paulson, D. (1999).Unions and New Office Technology. *Industrial Relations, 54*(2), 245–276.

Giddens, A.(1988). *La constitution de la société.* Paris: PUF.

Guyodo, A. (2000). NTIC, Des libertés à garantir. *La revue de la CFDT, 35*(11), 24–28 .

Greene, A. M., Hogan, J., & Grieco, M. (2003). E-Collectivism and Distributed Discourses : New Opportunities for Trade Union Democracy. *Industrial Relations Journal, 34*(4), 282–289.

Greene, A. M., & Kirton, G. (2003). Possibilities for Remote Participation in Trade Unions: Mobilising Women Activists. *Industrial Relations Journal, 34*(4), 319–333.

Hatchuel, A. (2004). Le syndicalisme innovateur. *Le Monde, 23 November,* VIII.

Hyman, R. (2002). Trade Union Research and Cross-National Comparison. *European Journal of Industrial Relations, 7*(2), 203–233.

Jaubert, C. (2000). Syndicalisme on-line. *L'hebdo de l'actualité sociale, La vie ouvrière CGT, 2917,* 22–23.

Julliard, C. (2002). Les douze travaux internet de la CFDT Cadres. Retrieved, February 25, from www.cfdt.fr/actualite.

Labbe, D., & Landier, H. (2001). *L'entreprise face au nouveau radicalisme syndical.* Paris: Ed. Liaisons.

Lane, F. S. (2003). *The Naked Employee: How technology is compromising workplace privacy.*

AMACOM, Div American Mgmt.

Le Coq, J., & Debons, C. (1997). *Routiers : les raisons de la colère.* Paris: Les Editions de l'Atelier.

Lee, E. (2004). Trade Unions In The ElectronicWorkplace. In *Proceeding of the Adelaide International Workplace Conflict Conference.* Adelaide, Australia April 21-23.

Lucio, M. M. (2003). New Communication Systems and Trade Union Politics: a Case Study of Spanish Trade Unions and the Role of the Internet. *Industrial Relations Journal, 34*(4), 334–347.

Martinez Lucio, M. (2003). New communication systems and trade union politics : a case study of Spanish trade unions and the role of the internet. *Industrial Relations Journal, 34*(4), 334–347 (September).

Maussion, C. (2002). Il n'est pas temps de légiférer sur l'Intranet. *Libération, November 18,* Paris.

Merck, B., Fabre, M., Proust, M. A., Ridet, F., & Romanet, M. (2002). *Équipes RH, acteurs de la stratégie, l'E-RH : mode ou révolution ?* Paris: Éditions d'Organisation.

Michaux, V. (2009). Comment identifier les nombreux impacts et les enjeux stratégiques diversifiés que représentent les TIC dans le domaine de la GRH?, *Revue Management et Avenir, Special issue: la décentralisation de la fonction RH, 21,* 273-286.

Muhl, C. J. (2003). Workplace E-mail And Internet Use :Employees And Employers Beware. *Monthly Labor Review, February,* 36–45.

Réau, P. (2003). Campagne de syndicalisation au bout du fil, 29 octobre. Retrieved from www.cfdt.fr/actualite.

Spognardi, M. S., & Hill Bro, R. (1998). Organizing Through Cyberspace : Electronic Communications and the National Labor Relations Act. *Employee Relations Law Journal, 23*(4), 141–151.

Trogrlic, J. F. (2001). Impacts de la nouvelle économie et approche syndicale. *La revue de la CFDT, 41*(5), 33–37.

KEY TERMS

Evolution of Industrial Relations: Evolution of the relations between the management of an industrial enterprise and its employee.

Internal Codes of Practices About the Use of Internet in Organizations: The objective of employers is to avoid and protect themselves against excessive, abusive, inappropriate or illegal use of the net by employees.

Means of Expression, Action, and Pressure: The way Internet and ICT becomes means of expression (communication), action (defend of interests) and a new mean to develop and maintain the pressure on employers.

International Coordination Capacity: The capacity of Internet and the ICT to allow large international multi-stakeholders action.

Legal Framework Evolution: The way the legal framework is evaluating to meet the challenges pose by ICT for trade-union.

New Forms of Internal Democracy: Participation and involvement of trade-union's members in general policy decisions of unionists.

New Forms of Protest: Resurgence of autonomous and corporatist trends against the global practices of traditional federations which favours the emergence of new forms of direct protest by employees in the absence of traditional unions.

New Forms of Work: The way ICT and Internet impacts work.

Trade-Unionism Practices Evolution: The way ICT and Internet impacts trade-unionism.

ENDNOTES

[1]   See for example Orlikowsky's work which is based on Giddens's structuration theory.

[2]   For example in the French context, at France Télécom (Merck *et al.*, 2002), a written request for leave generated on average 3 photocopies, several phone calls and at least 2 filings. In a company like France Telecom which has 145,000 employees, this activity required 250 employees working full time. The automation and standardization of documents as well as that of transfer and validation procedures enabled the company to cut within one year 4.8 million written leave requests (73 tons of paper) as well as most of the employees in charge of this administrative task.

[3]   The **National Labor Relations** Board (NLRB) is an independent Federal agency which administers and enforces the **National Labor Relations Act**, a law governing the relationship between unions, employees and employers in the private sector.

[4]   For example in December 2000, then in January 2001 and March 2002, Marc Blondel, general secretary of FO wrote to Mr Sellières, President of the MEDEF (the French employer organisation) to open interprofessional negotiations concerning the use of ICTs in companies.

[5]   In 2001, only 9% of companies had a union site and 15% foresaw to associate personnel delegates to the creation of an Intranet devoted to human resources (Bietry, 2002). At the beginning of 2002, there were only 30 companies to have negotiated a union Intranet agreement.

[6]   Some service providers like GlobeNet have specialised in hosting this type of union Internet site side by side with progressive associations and citizen organizations to avoid dependence on traditional service providers.

[7]   Often, only the central union organization is authorised to use the Intranet.

[8]   Phrase used by the CFDT executives union on February 12, 2002 to introduce its press

[9] conference concerning their 12 proposals on the use of ICT in companies.

[9] For example, geolocation was recently assimilated to electronic shadowing in France.

[10] Some agreements go as far as to specify crossing conditions between the duration of use of resources and working hours

[11] Martinez Lucio (2003) showed that ICT can have a different influence on unions according to their communication strategies (to what purpose does a union mobilize Internet? Is it going to use ICT to a political purpose?) Their identity (how and how often does ICT fit into traditional means of communication?) or even their level of internal democracy (how does ICT put up with or conflict with decision processes?)

[12] The rate of unionization in the union concerned, the rate of member renewal, that is to say the balance between members lost and gained and the perception the leaders of the concerned unions have of their own efficiency

[13] See the examples recounted on the website: http:/freewarriors.org

[14] (www.allianceibm.org)

[15] From an expression introduced by Crepeau (2001)

Chapter XXIII
Coordination of Virtual Teams:
From Trust to Control

Isabelle Parot
Magellan Research Center, France

ABSTRACT

In this communication, the author attempts to answer the question of coordination in virtual teams (or remote teams). Virtual teams can result from economic choices but they can also be a choice in terms of available resources and need of very specific skills. The coordination is thus intra-organizational. How this coordination takes place? Firstly, this chapter will describe conceptually the process of coordination in situations of remote work, and more precisely, in the case of an intra-organizational coordination in virtual teams. The authors will discuss the debate wither it is trust or control that is needed for the co-ordination for virtual teams. Secondly, they are going to present empirical findings about virtual teams' coordination, in high technological firms. Lastly, they are going to illustrate how a number of economic, organizational and cultural factors can impact the coordination process in those virtual teams.

INTRODUCTION

Nowadays, globalization and internationalization are strengthened by the development of the ICT (information and communication technologies). To face the competitions on markets, on suppliers and on customers, more and more companies choose to bet on the cooperation and\or on the network. Organizations thus extend beyond the organizational borders: and the control of those borders becomes crucial. How is made the coordination between partners? How takes place the coordina-

tion outside the organizational borders? And how is made coordination for remote teams?

Since the initial work of Daft and Lewin (1993), evolution of organisation has been taking more and more space in the management literature. Globalisation and internationalisation, together with the development of information and communication technology, are boosting the size of markets, the numbers of customers and suppliers, and meanwhile the number of competitors. This forces companies to become more flexible, reactive and innovative.

To cope with this environment, organisations have developed and implemented many different managerial and organizational approaches. We have chosen to focus on the introduction of virtual teams.

Regarding the lack of precision around the concept of virtual teams, we will begin by giving a clear definition of what is called virtual team in this paper. On one hand, a lot of situation can be hidden behind this term (telecommuting, call centers, e-learning…) ; on the other hand, some comparable situation are described with other terms like remote team, distributed work, global teams….

A virtual team is first defined as a team – that implies a small group of people working together in order to attain the same objectives for which they are collectively accountable (Duarte and Snyder, 1999; Hackman, 1990; Katzenbach and Smith, 1993; Mohrman et al., 1995; Snow et al.,1999; Stewart et al., 1999; Sundstrom, 1990). This team is specific because it uses information and communication technologies to function outside the usual spatial, temporal and organisational boundaries (Duarte and Snyder, 1999; Lipnack and Stamps, 1997, 1999; Snow et al., 1999).

This paper attempts to conceptually describe and theorize the diverse states and evolvements of virtual teams' processes. It includes a discussion of the concepts and provides a definition of virtual teams.

In this paper, based on empirical evidence, we attempt to illustrate some specificity of the coordination process in virtual teams.

The first section based on management literature highlight the interest of new organisational forms and more specifically of virtual teams. The second section will draw the attention on sensitive issues of virtual teams such as the coordination process within those teams. The empirical evidence presented in the third part comes from a field study in international companies. The study has been conducted as a case study about established virtual teams between different countries.

Finally theoretical and managerial implications are discussed, ending with possible future research questions.

EVOLUTION OF ORGANIZATIONS

Since the initial work of Daft and Lewin, the question of "new" organizational forms has became a new trend for management literature (Daft and Lewin, 1993). Daft and Lewin give several types of example of new organizational forms such as virtual corporation, cluster organisation, learning organisation and network organisation.

New Organization Forms

Since ten years some others new forms have appeared and some old forms have changed a lot. Speaking of new organizational forms, we can add communities of practices, remote work, collaborative work, outsourcing and offshoring. It has been a long time since the paradigm of hierarchical organization and bureaucratic structures have begun to fall apart and to be called into question by today's environment. A new paradigm dealing with less central control, more flexibility and adaptability seems to appear (Apgar, 1998).

Those news organizations can be characterised by "flatter hierarchies, decentralized decision-making, greater capacity for tolerance for ambiguity, permeable internal and external boundaries empowerment of employees, capacity for renewal, self-organizing units and self-integrating coordination mechanism"(Daft and Lewin, 1993). All those new forms were made possible by three environmental dimensions: the development and use of technologies, the increased competition and the new strategies of firms such as flexibility, adaptability and efficiency (Cooper, 2000).

The development of technologies of information and their massive entry in the companies are closely linked to the advent of these new forms of work. These technologies made it possible for individuals to work, to communicate and to cooperate, at any time and from any place. The frontiers of organizations are dematerialized by the use of technologies. The localization of individuals in an office is not any more necessary, since they have all the useful information's in their computers. They have an access to the corporate databases; they can communicate with the members of the company, the customers or any other person.

Beside of those contextual dimensions, the creation of new organization forms is also a response to the globalisation of business. To cope with this highly competitive environment, organisations have developed and implemented many different managerial and organizational approaches such as virtual organization, outsourcing or off shoring. New Organizational Forms taken together with the explosion of communication technology in organizations have built new ways of working together, new conceptions of teamwork.

In this paper, we focus on one very special new organizational form: the virtual teams. In the next part, we will first work on defining this new concept; then we will describe those virtual teams using a classical method of comparing advantage and disadvantage.

Virtual Teams: Beyond Spatial, Temporal and Geographical Barriers

The term 'virtual team' combines the notions of team and of virtuality that is to say of remote working. Thus an explanation of these two elements is appropriate.

The team is a group. Analysis of groups and of working groups in particular, has given rise to numerous developments since the 'Hawthorne' studies carried out by Mayo in the 1930s. Based on a review of management, sociological and psychological literature, we define a team according to four criteria.

Firstly, a team is composed of several individuals who represent the group's frontiers; in other words it can be specified who is or is not a member of the group, whatever the criteria of belonging or exclusion.

Secondly, those individuals are together in order to attain an objective for which they are all accountable. And to do so, they need to work together, to communicate and to interact. This notion of a task to be performed could even be said to be the group's raison d'être, the team existing primarily to successfully carry the activity in question (Duarte and Snyder, 1999; Hackman, 1990; Katzenbach and Smith, 1993; Snow and al., 1999; Stewart and al., 1999; Sundstrom, 1999).

Thirdly, these individuals are interdependent, which means that group members depend on each other for achieving common goals, whatever these goals may be.

To this end the members combine tangible and intangible approaches, while developing roles, skills and/or specialist and complementary knowledge within the group (Hackman, 1990; Snow and al., 1999).

Fourthly and lastly, teams are built in a social context. Team are a social construction where there is (or should be) cohesion among the members, creation of norms end trust among the members.

The coming of the new information and communication technologies allows for working relationships at a distance. Thus the team becomes virtual, or remote, when its members can use information and communication technology to function outside the usual spatial, temporal and organisational boundaries (Duarte and Snyder, 1999; Lipnack and Stamps, 1997, 1999; Snow et al., 1999). The members of a virtual team can work together while remaining geographically separated, or even in different countries, in which case they make up a global virtual team.

To summarize the characteristics of virtual teams we can use three dimensions.

The geographic (spatial) dispersion of the members means that people can be located in different site, different countries, and different continent and still work together. Depending on the type of distance, the virtual team will used different type of technologies to communicate.

The organizational dispersion refers to the belonging of the team's member. Do they work in the same company or not. This dimension deals with cultural issues, management practices that can be different between organizations.

Temporal dispersion refers to the possibility of asynchronous work in the team. This can be seen has an advantage, as time difference can enable a worldwide team to work continuously 24 hours a day. It can also be a disadvantage has time difference can implies delay.

Having defined virtual teams, we can now proceed to an examination of their advantages and disadvantages.

The Two Sides of Virtual Teams

The Promises of the Virtual Teams

With the requirements of an increasingly competitive context, companies need to be closer to the resources, the markets and the customers, and to be more reactive. For that, they multiply globalisation and delocalization movements of certain activities.

For some authors, the settled up of Virtual Team should be a new mean to answer these new constraints of speed, flexibility and satisfaction of the customers, imposed by the economic environment (Cascio, 2000; Powell, 2004). The other watchword of the organizations is the importance of flexibility by setting up organizations with decrease hierarchical levels in order to accelerate the decision-makings. In the same spirit, by giving more "flexibility" to the organizations, the virtual teams would offer faster and more effective answers (Dumoulin, 2000).

Current technologies of communication support the exchanges and the cooperation between the various sites of a company. They also facilitate the recourse to foreign consultants or experts in a way much simpler (and less expensive), since that it is not necessary to make the person come (Cascio, 2000). The virtual teams can thus be made up with the best specialists.

Virtual Teams: The Other Side of the Coin

As any change the apparition of Virtual Team disturbs the traditional operation of the companies and can involve certain difficulties.

The principal observations made on this subject concern the managers of these teams. Their dissatisfaction lies in the fact that they have the impression to lose the direct control which they had on their subordinate. It is not obvious to be in an office where there is none of the people you manage (Dumoulin, 2000).

Then, authors agree to say that one of the greatest difficulties of Virtual Teams is the question of the social bond. The members of the team are dispersed in the world, and the majority of their contact is done via means of communication electronic. This mediated communication, often indirect, is proceed mainly in English. Under these conditions, it is difficult to establish relations or more personal bonds within the team.

A last problem posed by the Virtual Teams is the demonstration of some technophobia on behalf of individuals (Townsend and al, 1998). All the communications are done by telephone or Internet. These media of communication remove all the abstract part of the relations. The people can thus feel a fear with respect to these new means of communication. Moreover, all new running of the literature treats harmful consequences of the development of the use of these technologies under name "techno stress" (Lasfargues, 2000).

THE IMPORTANCE OF COORDINATION

The Everlasting Issue of Coordination

At the time of the digital technology, where the ICT penetrated durably and profoundly the management of the company, the traditional relations with time and space are questioned (Kalika, 2002). The relation with time is modified as far as ICT allow new relations, either asynchronous (E-mail, collaborative work) or synchronous (integrated platforms, video conferences). The relation with space is renewed by the speed of data transmission (text, sound, and image) which updates the geographical barriers.

The coordination in and between companies also comes true thus in new conditions. The teams, dispersed in time and space, do not belong any more to the same legal entities. The development of virtual teams asks the question of coordination in a crucial way (Issac, 2002). How from then can one make sure of the realization of the tasks? How to check the progress of a project, a task? How make work a set of the persons who communicate only by e-mail, intranet, groupware and video conference?

At the question of coordination is added the question of control. Actually, in the organizations which use ICT either internally or for remote work and/or collaborative work, the issue of control changes sensibly. Tasks such as the collect and the consolidation of the data are no longer necessary since ICT enables to record, to store and to find very easily informations.

It means that middle management will play more and more administrator's role of the knowledge to the detriment of controller's role (Kalika, 2002).

To look at the mode of coordination of a team thus means identifying what are the mechanisms used. Numerous works bent over the question of the coordination in organizations. The classification establishes by Mintzberg the various modes of coordination is very often resumed in the literature (Mintzberg, 1989).

Mechanisms for coordination are discussed by March and Simon (1958) and Mintzberg (1983, 1998). The first two researchers identify three activities that are necessary in order to perform coordination: coordination through standardisation, coordination through planning, and coordination through feedback. The latter researcher also identifies a set of coordination mechanisms, partly based on March and Simon's (1958) work, mutual adjustment (1), direct supervision (2), standardisation of skills and norms (3), work processes (4), and results (5).(Mintzberg, 1983, 1998).

The six coordination mechanisms are:

- **Mutual adjustment:** Coordination of work is made possible by a process of informal communication between people conducting interdependent work.
- **Direct supervision:** Coordination is achieved by one individual taking responsibility for the work of others.
- **Standardization of work processes:** Coordination is made possible by specifying the work content in rules or routines to be followed. Coordination occurs before the activity is undertaken. Mintzberg adopted Taylorism: procedures are usually specified by work-study analysis.
- **Standardization of output:** Coordination is obtained by the communication and clarification of expected results. The individual actions required to obtain a goal are not prescribed. This goal setting method is closely related to Drucker's Management by Objectives.
- **Standardization of skills and knowledge:** Coordination is reached through specified and standardised training and education. People are trained to know what to expect of each other and coordinate in almost automatic fashion.

- **Standardisation of norms:** Norms are standardized, socialization is used to establish common values and beliefs in order for people work toward common expectations. Mintzberg added this cultural based mechanism at a later stage.

Nizet and Pichault synthesize those coordination mechanisms into three categories. The first mechanism of coordination passes by means of the interpersonal relations, implying an intensification of the side links between the members. The second corresponds to a work of formalization by which the experts are engaged in the planning of the activities and in the controls of the performances. The last one passes by the constitution of appropriate mental representations. (Nizet and Pichault, 2001)

What About Coordination in Virtual Teams?

Virtual Teams: Informal Coordination Based on Trust or...

The institution of the trust is a major element for virtual teams, as for any team. In the constitution of virtual team, (generally), the members do not know each other because they have never had the occasion to work together. The first moments in a virtual team are marked by a feeling of uncertainty towards the other members of the team. It will be necessary to wait for the first actions, or for the first results, to be able to judge the work of a person.

To create a real team, it is necessary that relations are based on trust. Trust can only be established only on the proof of the skill of the others and their integrity. With time this trust will be strengthened by the recognition that the others are right and reliable (Platt, on 1999).

For Handy (2000), the trust is a fragile element, which builds itself in time by means of meeting and of exchanges, which is indispensable for the good functioning of a remote team. «How manage a team that you don't see? By relying on them. "

When we approach the notion of trust in teams, we can be interested in three dimensions of the trust (Lipnack and Stamps, on 1997, p. 226). First of all, we can distinguish the trust in the persons and in their skills. If this trust is not present between the members of the team, we cannot rest on them or on the results of their work. But, so that this trust is established, the persons have to demonstrate their skill in time. It sets more time in the remote teams than in the mode in encounter. The second way of creating some trust), it is by implying the persons in an objective unified with results and shared rewards. It is trust in the objectives. Finally, the trust in the links or the relations is the most difficult to create. The persons have to trust in the information which they receive and in the channels of communication.

The notion of trust and the mechanism of production of this trust in the remote teams aroused the interest of certain number of researcher. The works mentioned above demonstrate the importance of reliable relations in virtual teams, because the "classical" conditions to build and maintain trust such as meetings or verbal exchanges are not meet with those teams. New ways of building trust should be found in virtual teams. Still trust is not the only way to coordinate people; control is also an important issue as we will see.

...Formal Coordination Based on Control?

According to the literature (Galbraith, 1993; Mohrman, 1999; Sundstrom, 1999), team-based organisations are characterised by, among other things, flexibility, reactivity, creativity and efficient decision-making. This means they are especially well suited to the current environment. Thus teams are a source of control: an improved allocation of decision making allows the organisation to achieve its goals in terms of survival, competitiveness, profitability and so on...

However, the literature also indicates that setting up this organisational system involves problems and uncertainty. Even if, as the literature claims, virtual teams represent an organisational means of coping with the new environment, the organisations concerned – like all organisations – are still faced with the problem of control. How can they make sure that their teams and team members are implementing decisions and actions consistent with the organisation's aims?

Merchant (1997) offers three explanations for this problem of individuals control. The first has to do with a lack of direction regarding what is expected of employees: if they are under informed or badly informed of the goals to be achieved and/ or the task in hand, individuals are unlikely to come up with the expected decisions and behaviours. The second explanation relates to motivational problems arising out of divergences of interests between individuals and the organisation. Lastly there is the question of personal limitations, when individuals lack the knowledge, skills, experience and so on needed for correct performance of the task.

These problems of control are common to all organisations and also arise in respect of virtual teams. However, some aspects of them are specific to virtual teams. The question arises, for example, of whether the marked degree of autonomy enjoyed by the teams is not a source of ambiguity in terms of goals and/or of the way they function. Similarly this autonomy can reinforce problems of interest divergence and, by extension, of motivation in Merchant's sense.

This can be true of the team, which may be a homogeneous group whose interests are in conflict with those of the company, and of individual team members: free rider problems are more acute in the case of a group whose members are widely separated. Lastly, personal limitations can be a specific contributing factor within virtual teams, if they touch on the ability to work within a group, the capacity for remote working, knowledge of information and communication technology, etc.

Thus numerous difficulties appear at both the organisational and behavioural levels, and these require the implementation of a control system.

A host of articles and books written by academics and professionals about team and organisation management outline the prerequisites for success. It emerges from this literature that team performance depends on support from the organisation in the form of various appropriate mechanisms. In the view of many authors (Duarte and Snyder, 1999; Lipnack and Stamps, 1997; Mohrman et al., 1995; Sundstrom, 1999) effective teams meet the following conditions: clear, shared objectives complemented by an evaluation and feedback system allowing them to monitor their own performance; group rewards and skill based instead of job-based rewards; appropriate resources in terms of equipment and information and communication systems, as well as of backup from the organisation; and systems of team member selection and training that enhance skills and confidence. Lastly, all these preconditions should fit with each other and with the environment.

If we define control as "the process by which managers influence other members of the organisation to implement the organisation's strategies" (Anthony and Govindarajan, 1998), these prerequisites for success constitute a control system. Here it is the organisation that designs, sets up and applies the systems of control deemed appropriate. This is the approach we shall examine in this paper: control is made up of the set of elements the organisation establishes or on which it acts to ensure success and obtain the desired level of performance.

RESEARCH DESIGN AND METHOD

Method

Desanctis and Monge mentioned in 1999 « given the burgeoning interest in this emerging phenomenon, it is surprising that very little empirical research exists on virtual organization ».

Few years later this statement is still true. Very few empirical studies are done on the question of virtual team and when they are the sample are most of the time students, and even fewer are done in an organizational context.

To try to fulfil the gap between the academic interest and the lack of field knowledge, we decide to build an explanatory research on the processes of virtual teams.

Data Collection

Our data were collected by using a multi-case study. We were involved in three cases in three organizations in the high technology sector. For each case, two teams were studied in the organization. Our first case, Computer, was support service teams characterized by a recent shift to virtual team with Asian area. The second case involved virtual project teams, while the third case considered more functional teams between France and Germany.

For each case study, data were collected through a period of one year primarily through one or two periods of intensive fieldwork lasting one or two weeks. For the case Computer, the fieldwork lasted from March to July 2003; for the case Electronic from March to June 2005; and for the case Aero it was during May and October 2005.

We were using two distinct means of data collection:

1. **Field observations.** Throughout the duration of the study, we spent some time in the office landscape of each unit observing the atmosphere and culture. We also participated to coffee breaks and lunches.
2. **Semi-structured interviews.** Eventually, we performed totally over 50 interviews, lasting from one to two hours. The unit members were selected through a process where we aspired to a diverse sample in terms of hierarchical position type of function and localization of the members. For each virtual team studied, the manager was interviewed as several members of the team located in the French sites. We also did some interviews by phone for the team members located in other countries.

All interviews were recorded and transcribed. In accordance with good research ethic, the data were treated confidentially and made anonymous.

We couldn't use formal documents from the organization, since nothing existed on the subject of virtual teams. Those teams were initiated according to need from the organization (from reorganization globalization strategies) but they were neither communication inside the companies nor any training.

Data Analysis

All of the qualitative data are being analyzed using theme analysis, scanning the material for dominant themes such as communication, coordination and cooperation processes inside the virtual teams. Then, both differences and similarities are identified in the themes between the different cases. In this paper, I will not present all the findings but I want to focus the presentation on certain aspects underlining the changes in the communication process in those teams and their impact on the performance of the virtual teams.

Presentation of the Case Studies

Case A: Computer

In this company, virtual teams are more and more present since ten years. Firstly used for project, virtual teams are now becoming a regular way of working in this organization. They are mainly used to smooth reorganisation and to support new site of the company.

Computer 1 is a computer support team witch members are spread across France, Belgium and United Kingdom. More recently this team has to take in charge clients from the Asia area. This team is characterised by having a lot of "ancient" people used to work in a certain way with some technology. The shift to virtual team and to having all the communication in English with their counterparts in others countries is really hard.

Computer 2 is a virtual team characterized by the fact that all the members are located in France but on different sites of the company, and by the fact that all the members knows each other from a previous team experience.

Case B: Electronic

In this company, virtual teams are very recent, since the first one settled up were the one we have studied. Virtual teams are mainly used to build international projects with the Asian site.

Electronic 1 and Electronic 2 have a lot of similarities in their profile. They are both international project team across Europe and Asia.

FACING THE DIFFICULTIES OF BUILDING A VIRTUAL TEAM

In the various examples met, the mechanism of coordination is mainly done by the manager or the project leader. This coordination is carried out during the weekly meetings or during the phone points that the managers made with their teams. All the follow-up of the team and the coordination thus proceed remotely. This is coordination by direct supervision taking another form that the historical design of Taylor of the foreman, owing to the fact that this function of supervision is carried out remotely. This coordination thus does not go through a visual monitoring and an adjustment of the actions of each one by the manager but more by a prescribed coordination by rules and objectives.

In all the virtual teams studied, the coordination passes by more formalization: often weekly meetings and regular calls of the manager. This coordination is exerted by a line authority - in the teams met, the manager - who "fixes temporal rules and executives". The systems of regular meetings founded in each team are not used for nothing else then to give a progress report on the advance of each one and to lay down new short-term objectives.

Coordination in these teams is thus a mixture between direct supervision and coordination by the results within the meaning of Mintzberg (1989). The mutual adjustment is reduced, insofar as remotely the people cannot follow the advance and the actions of all the other members. The only case of direct coordination between the individuals is that of the data-processing team of maintenance of Computer 1. According to the number of calls

Table 1. Presentation of the case studies

	Computer		Electronic	
Activity	Team Computer 1: Computer support	Team Computer 2: Reporting	Team Electronic 1: International project team	Team Electronic 2: International project team
Number of interviews	8	5	9	10
Origin of the team	Reorganisation	Reorganisation	Project	Project
Countries	France Germany Belgium Asia	Paris Grenoble	France UK Tunisia Asia	France UK Turkey Tunisia Asia

Table 2. Coordination mechanisms in virtual teams

Computer 1	Computer 2	Electronic 1	Electronic 2
Annual objectives	Physical start-up meeting	Physical start-up meeting	Physical start-up meeting
Phone conference	Phone conference	Phone conference	Phone conference
Manager coordinates by telephone at first	Manager coordinates by telephone	Weekly meeting by phone	Weekly meeting by phone
Coordination by the IT tool	Monthly meeting by phone		
(Remote) direct supervision	**(Remote) direct supervision**	**(Remote) direct supervision**	**(Remote) direct supervision**
Coordination by the results	**Coordination by the results**	**Coordination by the results**	**Coordination by the results**
Coordination ex ante			

or specificity of the calls, the people must arrange themselves between them. This coordination "is accompanied" by a data-processing tool which indicates the order of the calls to be taken and their urgency. This coordination is accompanied by an organisational reinforcement of the rules to ensure itself of the correct operation of the team.

As we saw in the presentation of the team Computer 1, this prescribed coordination is quite illustrated for the introduction of the obligation to take international calls in the individual objectives.

CONCLUSION

In the case of the virtual teams, that is in front of an uncertain context, the coordination raises more problems because she cannot use the same mechanisms as in situations of management in encounter. Our results show that in this context of distance, the coordination passes by more formalization, more control. The processes of coordination established in the studied virtual teams are formalized around the weekly meetings and the individual objectives. Furthermore, the role of the project managers is essential in coordination, because it is them who manage it from day to day. In fact, the managers of the teams have essentially coordinator's role. It is no more direct supervision but it is a permanent supervision. The theoretical recommendations on the roles of the managers do not show this coordinator's very time-consuming role. As a result, this result raises questions as for the roles of animation and mediator of the communication of these project managers. It is certainly thanks to this strict and formalized system, and to the past by the managers in their coordinator's role, that through our six examples of virtual teams, the question of the coordination does not seem to rise of particular problems.

Contrary to the vision "libertarian" of the virtual teams, and to the promises of autonomy and management personalized by its working time, the virtual teams require a rigorous coordination. In front of a context made uncertain by the distribution of the members of the team, the coordination can either be made by betting on the interpersonal relations or by betting on a greater formalization.

However, our work presents certain limits as it is here important to remind. On one hand, there is a limit of methodological order because of the restricted size of our sample. On the other hand, it would be interesting to lead a longitudinal study to observe how the mechanism of coordination evolves in the time in both studied contexts Our first results underline that the formalization can understand as a first stage in the construction of these working collectives (inter or intra-organizational). In time, the creation of stronger interpersonal relations the modalities of the coordination can evolve towards more autonomy.

This research is only at his beginning, so is the fields of virtual team research.

We can mention several limits about the methodology used, and especially the limited number of companies met. We will continue this research in a broader sample of companies in order to generalize those first results.

REFERENCES

Anthony, R., & Govindarajan (1998), *Management control*, Tata Mc Graw Hill Publishing.

Apgar, M. (1998). The alternative workplace: changing where and how people work. *Harvard Business Review*, May-June, 121-136.

Cascio, W. F. (2000). Managing a virtual workplace. *The Academy of Management Executive*, *14*(3), 81-90.

Daft, R., & Lengel, R., (1984). Information richness: a new approach to managerial behaviour and organization design. *Research in Organizational Behaviour*, (6), 191-233.

Daft, R. L., & Lengel, R. (1986). Organisational information requirements, media richness and structural design, *Management Science, 35*.

Daft, R. L., & Lewin, A.Y. (1993). Where are the theories for the new organizational forms? An editorial essay. *Organization Science, 4*(4).

Davenport, T.H., & Pearlson, K. (1998). Two cheers for the virtual office, *Sloan Management Review*, Summer, (pp. 51-65).

DeSanctis, G., & Monge, P. (1999) Introduction to the special issue: communication processes for virtual organization. *Organization Science, 10*(6).

Duarte, D. L., & Snyder, N.T. (1999). *Mastering virtual teams - Strategies, Tools and Techniques that succeed*, Jossey-Bass Publishers, San Francisco.

Dumoulin, C. (2000). Le management à distance des équipes virtuelles. *Management et Conjoncture Sociale, 580*(5), 50-60.

Favier, M., & Trahand, J. (1998). La virtualité en pratique : quelques exemples d'Equipes Virtuelles. in M. Favier, F. Coat & J-C. Courbon (Eds.), *Le travail en groupe à l'âge des réseaux*, Economica, Paris.

Fulk, J. (1993). Social construction of communication technology, *Academy of Management Journal*, 36, 921-950.

Galbraith, J. R., & Lawler III, E. E. (1993). *Organizing for the future: the new logic for managing*, San Francisco, Jossey Bass.

Grosjean, M., & Lacoste, M. (1999). Communication et intelligence collective : le travail à l'hôpital. PUF, *Le travail Humain*, Paris.

Hackman, J. R. (1990). *Groups that work (and those that don't)*, Jossey Bass, San Francisco.

Handy, C. (2000). Trust and the virtual organisation, *Harvard Business Review*, 2000, 1-9.

Hertel, G., Geister, S., & Konradt, U. (2005). Managing virtual teams: A review of current empirical research, *Human Resources Management, 15*, 69-95.

Kalika, M. (2002a). *e-GRH : révolution ou évolution*, Editions liaisons, Paris.

Kalika, M. (2002b). Le défi du e-management, in *Les défis du management*, éditions Liaisons, (pp. 221-234).

Katzenbach, J. R., & Smith, D. K. (1993). *The wisdom of teams: Creating high performance organizations*, Cambridge MA, Harvard University School Press.

Lasfargue, Y. (2000). *Technomordus, technoexclus?*, Editions d'Organisation, Paris.

Lipnack, J., & Stamps, J. (1999). Virtual teams, *Executive Excellence, 16*(5), May, 14-15.

Lipnack, J., & Stamps, J. (1997). *Virtual teams: reaching across space, time and organization with technology*. Wiley.

Livian, Y.-F., (2001). *Organisation : Théories et pratiques*, 2ème édition, Dunod, Paris.

Merchant, K. A. (1998). *Modern Management Control Systems: Texts and Cases*. Upper Saddle River. NJ: Prentice Hall.

Mintzberg, H. (1989). *Management, voyage au coeur des organizations*. Editions d'organisation

Mohrman, S.A. 1999. The Contexts for Geographically Dispersed Teams and Networks. In C. Cooper, & D. Rousseau (Eds.), *Trends in Organizational Behavior*, (pp. 63-80). New York: John Wiley & Sons.

Nizet, J., & Pichault, F. (2001), *Introduction à la théorie des configurations*, coll. Management, De Boeck Université, Bruxelles.

Platt, L. (1999). Virtual teaming: where is everyone? *The Journal of Quality and Participation*, Sept.-Oct., (pp. 41-43).

Powell, A., Piccoli, G., & Ives, B. (2004) Virtual teams: A review of current literature and directions for future research. *The Data Base for Advances in Information Systems, 35*(1), 6-36.

Savoyant, A., & Leplat, J. (1983). Statut et fonction des communications dans les activités des équipes de travail. *Psychologie française, 28*(3/4), 247-253.

Simon, H. (1957). *Models of man: social and rational. Mathematical essays on rational human behavior in a social setting.* New York: Wiley.

Snow, C.C., Lipnack, J., & Stamps, J. (1999). The Virtual Organization: promises and payoffs, large and small. In C. Cooper & D. Rousseau (Eds.), *Trends in Organizational Behaviour*, New-York: Wiley.

Stewart, G. L., & Manz, C. C. (1995). Leadership for self-managing work teams: a typology and integrative model. *Human Relation, 48*(7), 747-759.

Sundstrom, E., De Meuse, K. P., & Futrell, D. (1990). Work teams: Applications and effectiveness, *American Psychologists, 45*(2), 120-133.

Townsend, A.M., Demarie, S.M., & Hendrickson, A. R. (1998). Virtual teams: technology and the workplace of the future. *The Academy of Management Executive, 12*(3), 17-29.

Turoff, M., Rao, U., & Hiltz, S. (1991, January). Collaborative Hypertext in Computer Mediated Communications, *Proceedings of the Twenty-Fourth Annual Hawaii International Conference on System Sciences*.

Winkin, Y. (1981). *La nouvelle communication*, éd. du Seuil, coll. "Points", Paris

KEY TERMS

Control: Management process in which the (1) actual performance is compared with planned performance, (2) difference between the two is measured, (3) causes contributing to the difference are identified, and (4) corrective action is taken to eliminate or minimize the difference.

Coordination: Synchronization and integration of activities, responsibilities, and command and control structures to ensure that the resources are used most efficiently in pursuit of the specified objectives.

Trust: Reliance on another's words, integrity or discretion in a relationship.

Virtual Team: A virtual team is a team whose members are interacting primarily through electronic communications. Members of a virtual teal may be within the same building or across continents.

Chapter XXIV
Information Overload in the New World of Work:
Qualitative Study into the Reasons and Countermeasures

Jeroen ter Heerdt
Microsoft B.V., Services, The Netherlands

Tanya Bondarouk
University of Twente, The Netherlands

ABSTRACT

In this chapter the authors present a revision of the information overload concept elaborated by Eppler and Mengis (2004). The main elements of our approach are literature synopsis and analysis, qualitative semi-structured interviews, and discussion. Their review of the information overload concept is multidisciplinary as we identify similarities and differences among the various management perspectives and refine it with the empirical findings. They hope that by doing so, we can identify synergies between the theoretical conceptualization (Epper and Mengis, 2004), and real-life settings. They present results in a highly compressed, visualized format that allows for a more concise representation of the subject domain, easy comparisons, and hopefully – reduction of information overload. The empirical study was done at the Microsoft B.V. (The Netherlands) where Information workers became the most important type of workers within an organization.

INTRODUCTION

In this chapter we present a revision of the information overload concept (Eppler and Mengis, 2004) based on the extensive empirical findings.

The main elements of our approach are literature synopsis and analysis, qualitative semi-structured interviews, and discussion. Our review of the Information Overload concept is multidisciplinary as we identify similarities and differences among the various management perspectives and refine it with the empirical findings. We hope that by doing so, we can identify synergies between the theoretical conceptualization (Epper and Mengis, 2004), and real-life settings. We present results in a highly compressed, visualized format that allows for a more concise representation of the subject domain, easy comparisons, and hopefully – reduction of information overload.

As an empirical setting we take the real-life consultancy world, one of the leaders in knowledge intensive economy. The study was done at the Microsoft B.V. (The Netherlands) that has introduced the New World of Work (NWOW) - a vision of Microsoft Corp. first articulated by Bill Gates in May 2005 (Gates III, 2005) and detailed by Dan Rasmus (2005) in the daily life of employees. NWOW identifies and examines technological trends in the changing world, investigates the challenges they present for workers, organizations and governments in the next ten years and describes how investments in technology and practices to empower Information workers can lead to better outcomes. It thereby argues that Information workers are to become the most important type of workers within an organization. Therefore, the vision mostly focuses on Information workers.

Our study investigated a part of Microsoft B.V., viz. Microsoft Services. Within Microsoft Services we focused on one 'type' of employees, Microsoft Services Consultants, who are in true considered as the main information processors.

The term Information worker is widely used in the New World of Work environment, and we use it in our research, too. In today's knowledge economy, when knowledge-based capabilities are becoming more and more important (Whicker, 2004), information workers are the ones who posses knowledge-based capabilities. The importance of the function of information gathering and processing has already been recognized some time ago, by Tushman and Nadler (1978). Also, several authors stress the need for managing knowledge as a product (Wang, 1998) or even state that knowledge capital is of such importance that it should be listed on the balance of a company (Strassmann, 1999). The knowledge worker sector has become important to overall productivity, because of size and growth (Drury, 1999).

The term knowledge worker has originally been introduced by Peter F. Drucker, in 1959, as a differentiator between employees that do not own the means of production, and those who do own their means of production. This latter group is the people the knowledge workers; they 'produce' with their brain and 'sell' brain-hours to the organization. By contrast, manual workers typically do not own the factory equipment they use to produce their output. This way of identifying knowledge workers is not very clear, and as a result various augmenting descriptions of knowledge workers exist. In particular, Knowledge Work has been defined as a profession, as a characteristic of individuals, as an individual activity and as organizational behavior (see Kelloway, 2000, for a discussion of these four ways of defining Knowledge Work).

INFORMATION OVERLOAD AS THE CHALLENGE OF INFORMATION WORKERS

Organizations and individuals working in those organizations are exposed to ever increasing amounts of data they are required to process (Tushman, 1978) due to increased connectivity and increased use of IT. Individuals and organizations, however have a limited information processing capacity. This gives rise to an important challenge: coping with Information Overload, i.e. the situation that the information processing requirements exceed the information processing capacities. The problem of Information Overload has been noted by Davis (2002) and by Drury (1999) as a challenge posed by unlimited access computing.

Information Overload: Theoretical Concept

As early as 1956, Miller introduced the concept of the 'magical number seven', which describes that people are limited in the capacity of information they can receive, remember and process in a given time (Miller, 1956). According to Eppler and Mengis (2004) later research by Schroder et al. in 1967, has introduced a view on Information Overload that is generally referred to as the inverted U-curve (Eppler and Mengis, 2004), which is reproduced in Figure 1. In this figure it is depicted that when information load increases decision accuracy will presumably increase, up to a certain maximum. From that point on the decision accuracy will decrease. Although decision accuracy is plotted on the vertical axis, it is applicable to other situations. This representation of information load bears close resemblance with the 'channel capacity' as introduced by Miller (see above). In fact, the inverted U-curve of Information Overload is the same as what Miller states, except that it goes one step further, as the inverted U-curve shows that the decision accuracy, or response quality, will decrease after the 'channel capacity' has been reached.

Information Overload can be defined in various ways. One classic definition is based on the information-processing view of organizations as proposed by Galbraith and discussed in (Tushman, 1978). In this definition the information processing capacity of an individual is compared to the requirements set for the information processing. The following formula then describes the situation of Information Overload: $\gamma = \rho > \sigma$ (Eppler and Mengis, 2004), or, $\gamma = \rho - \sigma$, where γ is the Information Overload, ρ represents the information processing requirements, i.e. the amount of information that has to be processed within a certain time period, and σ represents the information processing capacities available in the time period (Eppler and Mengis, 2004). Thus, Information Overload can be viewed as the difference between the requirements set for information processing and the capacities of information processing available. If the requirements posed are higher than the capacities available a situation of Information Overload will occur. In accordance with this definition Schick et al. (Schick, 1990) stress time as a 'critical and scarce resource' (Schick, 1990) regarding the Information Overload problem.

In other studies (for example, Keller, 1987) it is proposed that information has 'at least two dimensions, quantity and quality, and these two dimensions have opposing influences on decision effectiveness' (Keller, 1987). The quantitative dimension of information holds the amount of information that has to be processed in a given time period, and the available information processing capacity in the given time period (Eppler and Mengis, 2004). (Keller, 1987) concludes that decision effectiveness increases and levels off at a certain point as the amount of information available increases, while the average quality level of the information is kept at the same level. The quality dimension of information has been explored by others; according to (Eppler and Mengis, 2004) by Schneider, 1987, who 'distinguishes various information attributes, such as the level of novelty, ambiguity, uncertainty, intensity, or complexity. These information characteristics or quality attributes can either contribute to overload or reduce it' (Eppler and Mengis, 2004). Related to the quality of information is the value of information. An interesting model is the value-added model of information as proposed by (Simpson, 1995). This model proposes five groups of elements of value in information, named Truth (accuracy, validity), Guidance (solution identification, problem awareness), Scarcity (originality, creativity), Accessibility (knowledge of location, ease of access) and Weight (relevance, timeliness, medium). In a context of business, the most important group of elements is Weight, because when an item of information has enough weight, this creates a need for decisions and actions (Simpson, 1995).

Looking at the time span of articles about Information Overload, it seems that Information Overload is not a new phenomenon. Moreover, Noyes and Thomas (Noyes, 1995) point out that as early as in 1880 a desk was promoted as being a solution for storage and filing of books and papers. This seems to indicate that the challenge of Information Overload is not new. But, on the other hand, the amount of information available to a person has significantly increased in more recent years, partly due to advances in telecommunication, such as Internet and email. For example, if one compares the situation that Peter J. Denning describes in his 1982 ACM President's Letter titled 'Electronic Junk' (Denning, 1982) to the situation of a person that is now in the workforce in an knowledge worker job, it seems that the information coming towards a person, either pushed or requested, has increased. Denning describes his situation in 1982 as follows: 'In my own situation, which is not unique, I must deal with a constant barrage of information. In one day I typically receive 5-10 pieces of regular junk mail, 15-25 regular letters, 5 pieces of campus mail, 5 reports or documents, 5-10 incoming phone calls, 10-20 local electronic messages, and 10-20 external electronic messages' (Denning, 1982).

What is important is that Information Overload is a perception, and thus a feeling of receiving too much information.

Causes of Information Overload

Eppler and Mengis (2004) provide an analysis of the causes of Information Overload. The authors relate the reasons for Information Overload to five constructs, as shown in Figure 1. The five constructs are interrelated, and usually Information Overload is caused by a mix of the five causes (Eppler and Mengis, 2004). The constructs influence the information processing requirements and the information processing capacities, as introduced above. Eppler and Mengis (2004) place the organizational design of a company as

Figure 1. Causes of information overload

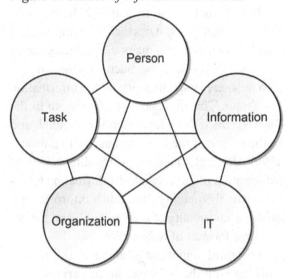

the most important factor influencing Information Overload. Changes in organizational structure, for example decentralization or centralization can lead to greater information processing requirements because of the need for more intensive communication and coordination (Eppler and Mengis, 2004). Various other authors (Schick, 1990; Tushman, 1978), in contrast, show that better coordination through (communication) standards, standard procedures, etc, result in lower information processing requirements ρ and higher information processing capacities.

According to Eppler and Mengis (2004), the next important factor is the information itself. Here, not only the amount of information is important (Jacoby, 1984) argues that when the number of information items rises, information load is increased), but also the characteristics, such as the level of uncertainty, ambiguity, novelty, complexity and intensity (Eppler and Mengis, 2004). Simpson and Prusak (Simpson, 1995) add more elements of value in information to this, such as accuracy, relevance, timeliness, etc. Also, the authors argue that improving the quality, by improving the value, of the information can improve a person's information processing capacity. Sparrow (1999) indicates that information that is of low quality, not relevant, or ambiguous will result in higher load when a person has to deal with the information. (Bawden, 1999) states that it 'is tempting and usual to assume that a major contributing factor (…) is the TMI effect: too much information', but also the increasing 'diversity' of the information is a factor. This diversity can occur both in the form in which the information is presented, and in the nature of the information itself (Bawden, 1999). Ho (2001) identifies three dimensions of information in the context of Information Overload, namely quantity ('too much information'), quality ('low quality of information') and format ('diverse formats of information').

The third important element is the person working with the information. In various older studies it is simply stated that a person's capacity to process information is limited (see for example (Jacoby, 1984; Tushman, 1978)). More recent studies provide a more detailed analysis of the factors limiting a person's information processing capacity. (Swain, 2000) suggests the level of experience of a person is a limiting factor and (Owen, 1992) identifies personal skills as a limiting factor. Hiltz and Turoff (Hiltz, 1985) suggest that the experience a person has with the system that provides the information will increase a person's information processing capacity. Individuals must learn screening skills, and beginners tend to read everything, thus increasing information load (Hiltz, 1985). Maes (1994) suggests that individuals do not change their habit of interaction with computers fast enough to keep up with the technological developments.

Another important factor is the task that is associated with the information, for example the processes that need to be followed while making use of the information (Eppler and Mengis, 2004). If the process is complex and not routine, the information load will be higher, and the time pressure will also increase (Grisé, 2000; Schick, 1990), thus increasing the information processing requirements. Interruptions are also influencing the way information is perceived, used and pro-

cessed (Speier, 1997), as they force the individual to switch attention between various things. Having to do things in parallel can also result in a lower information processing capacity (O'Reilly III, 1980). (Bawden, 1999) indicates that the changing nature of work being carried out by individuals can also be a reason for an increasing information load, as well as the so-called 'disintermediation' of searching for information; people are more and more supposed to find the information they need on their own. This seems to agree with the trend toward knowledge work visible in the modern society (Beardsly, 2006; Johnson, 2005; Rasmus, 2005a).

The last factor Eppler and Mengis (2004) indentify is information technology. Examples of misuse of e-mail are needless 'cc-ing' of messages, huge mailing lists, and spamming (Bawden, 1999). IT has helped to cope with information load, but at the same time created (part of the) problem (Bawden, 1999; Schultze, 1998). For example, e-mail is an asynchronous way of communication, thus the need for direct reaction is suggested to have a smaller interference with normal work (Edmunds, 2000). On the other hand, other authors suggest that the instant notification of an arrival of a new email message, which has been build in into many e-mail systems, results in a high number of interruptions (Speier, 1997) and create the need for immediate answer to the arrived e-mail. Findings from the research of Speier et al. (1997) suggest that these features should be disabled. Also, Edmunds and Morris (Edmunds, 2000) state that a push mechanism for selected information increases the amount of potential irrelevant information a person has to deal with. On the other hand, the same authors indicate that using a push mechanism for information reduces the time needed to retrieve the information. (Schultze, 1998) gives a number of technical reasons for Information Overload, viz.: the increase in storage capacity, the lowering of costs for duplication of information and the increased speed of access to information. Edmunds and Morris add that the usage of various channels for the same content is also increasing information load (Edmunds, 2000).

All in all, the factors playing a role in the occurrence of Information Overload can be divided in five categories, namely: person, information, task, organization and IT. Typically, the cause of Information Overload is a combination of one or more factors from one or more categories. We summarize the causes of information overload in Table 1.

Countermeasures for Information Overload

Solutions to problems should in general not only attack the effects of the problem, but also try to reduce the causes of the problem in order to have not only a softening but a real curing effect.

Schick (1990) uses a tree diagram to investigate (mostly organizational) countermeasures to reduce the likelihood of Information Overload, which is depicted in Figure 2. Although some of

Table 1. Causes of information overload (Adapted from Eppler and Mengis, 2004)

Personal factors	• Limitations in the individual human information-processing capacity
	• Decision scope and resulting documentation needs
	• Motivation, attitude, satisfaction
	• Personal traits (experience, skills, ideology, age)
	• Personal situation (time of the day, noise, temperature, amount of sleep)
	• Senders screen outgoing information insufficiently
	• Users of computer adapt their way of interacting with computers too slowly with respect to the technological development
	• Social communication barriers break down

	• The person:
	  ○ collects the information to show a commitment to rationalism and competence, because they believe that improves decision-making;
	  ○ receives high amounts of unwanted or unrequested information;
	  ○ uses information to check information they already have;
	  ○ feels a need to justify their decision, and use information to do this;
	  ○ collects information, just in case it may prove useful;
	  ○ wants to play safe and use all information possible;
	  ○ uses information as a currency – not to get left behind.

Information characteristics	• Incremental decreases in decision effectiveness due to additional information quantity are greater than the incremental increases in decision effectiveness due to additional
	• Uncertainty of information (info needed vs. info available)
	• Diversity of information and number of alternatives increase
	• Ambiguity of information
	• Novelty of information
	• Complexity of information
	• Intensity of information
	• Dimensions of information increase
	• Information quality, value, half-life
	• Overabundance of irrelevant information
	• Information quality

continued on following page

Table 1. continued

Task and process parameters	• Tasks are less routine
	• Complexity of tasks and task interdependencies
	• Time pressure
	• Task interruptions for complex tasks
	• Too many, too detailed standards (in accounting)
	• Simultaneous input of information into the process
	• Innovations evolve rapidly – shortened life cycle
	• Interdisciplinary work
Environment	• Too many inputs from the environment
	• Inputs follow each other to fast to enable processing
	• The quantity of information produced is too high
	• Failure to create 'high quality' information
Organizational design	• Collaborative work
	• Centralization (bottlenecks) or disintermediation (information searching is done by end users rather than by information professionals)
	• Accumulation of information to demonstrate power
	• Group heterogeneity
	• New Information and communication technologies (e.g. groupware)
	• Pursuing a number of tasks simultaneously, resulting in a tendency to ask for more information than strictly needed
	• Pressure and distraction
Information technology	• Push systems
	• E-mails
	• Intranet, extranet, Internet
	• Rise in number of television channels
	• Various distribution channels for the same content
	• Vast storage capacity of the systems
	• Low duplication costs
	• Speed of access
	• Computers communicate solely by graphical output, straining our visual sense
	• Use and misuse of IT

the countermeasures proposed here are outdated and not all countermeasures proposed in the literature are visible in the tree, the decomposition of the options available in an organization is very clear.

Information

Information should be carrying more value than it is now and should be delivered in the most convenient way and format (Simpson, 1995). Eppler and Mengis (2004) have developed a model of the value of information to make the shift of focus from quantity to quality in information provision clearer. According to Ackoff (1967), the information should be 'visualized, compressed and aggregated', and that, according to Herbig and Kramer (1994), 'signals and testimonials are used to minimize the risk associated with information'. This last addition seems to call for an increase in what (Simpson, 1995) calls the validity of information.

Figure 2. Strategies to reduce the likelihood of Information Overload (Adapted from Schick, 1990)

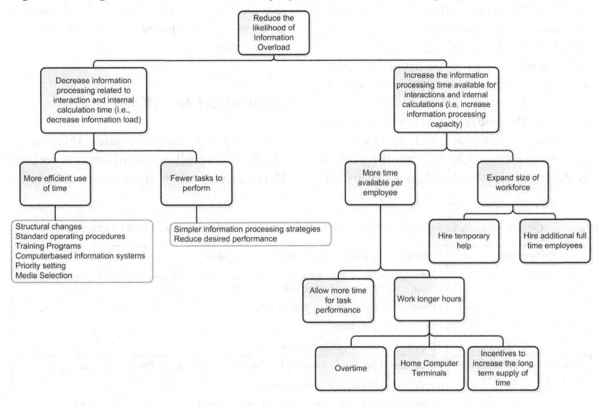

Individual

At the individual level, several authors propose training individuals to ensure a higher information literacy of information consumers (Eppler and Mengis, 2004; Schick, 1990). According to Bawden (2001) companies should give employees the right tools so they can improve their time management skills. Edmunds (2000) advises to supply tooling to employees so they can improve their information management skills.

Organizational Design

Eppler and Mengis (2004) indicate that there are authors, such as Bawden, 2001, who see the focus on collaborative and interdisciplinary work as a cause of Information Overload, instead of as a countermeasure, as Galbraith 1974 does.

Process

Edmunds (2000) suggests a thorough collaboration with information specialists for teams throughout the organization. Schick (1990) points at the need for a standardization of recurring procedures, since that will decrease the information load associated with thinking about how to do a task, because that has already been defined. And Grise (2000) proposes using collaborative tools for cognitive support, thus helping people to cope with the burden of information load.

Information Technology

Information technology should help people with prioritization (Schick, 1990) and quality filtering (Edmunds, 2000; Grisé, 2000; Hiltz, 1985) of information. (Berghel, 1997; Edmunds, 2000;

Maes, 1994). Also, the quality of information could be better evaluated if users could score the information by a simple voting system (Denning, 1982; Hiltz, 1985), something that is already visible at the support part of websites of for example software-companies. Hiltz (1985) considers the use of push technologies instead of pull, in order to decrease the time needed to retrieve information. Other authors have indicated that these push mechanisms could interrupt the work of an individual and therefore have a negative ef-

fect on the information processing capacity of that individual (Speier, 1997). Table 2 lists the countermeasures against Information Overload as described above.

RESEARCH METHODS

The foregoing has investigated Information Overload as a challenge of Information workers. Here we report on a study that was part of a larger

Table 2. Countermeasures against information overload (Adapted from Eppler and Mengis, 2004)

Personal factors	• Improve personal time management skills and techniques
	• Training programs to augment information literacy: information-processing skills such as file handling, using email, classification of document, etc.
	• Improve personal information management
	• Systematic priority setting
	• Improve the screening skills for information
Information characteristics	• Raise general quality of information (i.e. its usefulness, conciseness) by defining quality standards
	• Focus on creating value-added information
	• Promulgation of rules for information and communication design (e.g. e-mail etiquette)
	• Compress, aggregate, categorize, and structure information
	• Visualization, the use of graphs
	• Formalization of language
	• Brand names for information
	• Form must follow function must follow usability
	• Simplify functionalities and design of products
	• Customization of information
	• Intelligent interfaces
	• Determine various versions of information with various levels of detail and elaborate additional information that serves as summaries
	• Organize text with hypertext structures or gophers
	• Interlink various information types (as internal with external information)
Task and process parameters	• Standardize operating procedures
	• Define decision modes developed for specific decision processes (e.g., decision rules)
	• Install an exception-reporting system
	• Allow more time for task performance
	• Schedule uninterrupted blocks of time for completing critical work
	• Adequate selection of media for the task
	• Handle incoming information at once
	• Collaboration with information specialists within the teams

continued on following page

Table 2. continued

Task and process parameters (continued)	• Bring decisions to where information exists when this information is qualitative and ambiguous
	• Install process enablers for cognitive support
	• Use simpler information-processing strategies
	• Regulate the rate of information flow
	• Communicate information needs to providers
	• Provide incentives that are directly related with decisions in order to make decision relevant information be processed more effectively
	• Install a measurement system for information quality
Organizational design	• Coordination through interlinked units
	• Augment into processing capacity through changes in organizational design
	• Creation of lateral relationships (integrate roles, create liaisons between roles, teamwork)
	• Coordination by goal setting, hierarchy, and rules depending on frequency of exceptions (uncertainty)
	• Creation of self-contained tasks (reduced division of labor, authority structures based on output categories)→ autonomous groups
	• Reduce divergence among people (e.g., with regard to expectations) through socialization (e.g., frequent face-to-face interactions)
	• Install appropriate measures of performance
	• Create slack resources
Information technology application	• Use systems that offer various information organization options (e.g. filing systems)
	• Install voting structures to make users evaluate the information
	• Prefer push to pull technologies
	• Facilitator support through (e-)tools
	• Decision support systems should reduce a large set of alternatives to a manageable size
	• Use natural language processing systems (search with artificial intelligence)
	• Information quality filters
	• Intelligent data selectors (intelligent agents)
	• Intelligent information management (prioritization)
	• Multimodal interfaces

study, which aimed at investigating the causes of three key Information Work challenges in the situation of Microsoft Services Consultants and to investigate which solutions for these challenges can be seen in the situation of Microsoft Services Consultants.

Since Consultants are Information workers themselves, it was interesting to investigate the perceptions of individual Consultants on Information Overload. We aimed at giving interviewees the ability to express themselves and therefore use interviewing as a means of gathering data.

The research population for this study consisted of Microsoft Services Consultants, working for Microsoft Services in the Netherlands. The total number of Microsoft Services Consultants was 80, divided over five organizational groups. We took the same size sample out of each of the five organizational groups. With a sample size of three, the total number of interviews conducted was (3x5=) 15. The interviews were performed at a rate of two interviews a day, with transcription of the interviews on the same day. All interviewees were part of Microsoft Services. Interviewees were equally divided between the five organization groups; three interviewees from every group. The working experience ranged from two years to 25 years. Most of the interviewees worked at Microsoft for several years, although there were some interviewees who worked at Microsoft since a couple of months, but had previous experience in other organizations. The average age of the interviewees was 37, which is exactly the average age at Microsoft Netherlands. The youngest of the interviewees was born in 1981 and the oldest in 1961.

All interviews were recorded digitally (after permission of the interviewee) using Microsoft Office OneNote 2007, a tool for making notes. This tool allowed not only to record audio, but also enabled us to keep notes while recording. The notes were linked directly to the moment in the audio stream that the notes were taken, thus making the audio stream easier to process. Interviews have been anonymous, but general questions were asked about the interviewee in order to make the reporting more useful. In order to be able to refer to specific interviews, we chose a nickname together with the interviewee.

The selection of interviewees has been done in collaboration with the manager of each team, by asking him/her to provide a suggestion for three representatives of his/her team.

FINDINGS

New World of Work

General consensus was that the New World of Work is inevitable for branches where the work suits the New World of Work principles, because (future) employees will request this way of working.

The New World of Work is inevitable for branches were it is possible

There is a need for the New World of Work, and organizations will have to adopt the principles in order to be able to retain employees, because sooner or later employees will request these possibilities*

The New World of Work is inevitable for organizations, because employees will want to further control their own life

Also, Consultancy and in general Information Work was considered to be suited for the New World of Work principles.

The New World of Work is not inevitable, because it is dependent on the type of work and employees. It is inevitable for the Information workers

Consultancy is very well suited for the New World of Work principles

The developments on which the New World of Work is based were considered unstoppable, and the New World of Work provides a way to cope with these developments:

The New World of Work is a global development, that is occurring no matter what; it will influence organizations, sooner or later, dependent on their strategy

The New World of Work [provides] a way to cope with the developments in the outside world

Some interviewees indicated that they believe that if many people would work according to the New World of Work principles problems such as traffic jams could be reduced, as people can choose to travel at any time:

If a large portion of the people able to work according to the New World of Work principles would actually do that, the amount of traffic jams would be reduced. An advantage of the New World of

Work is to drive to work after the traffic jams and to go home before the traffic jams.

Also the New World of Work was viewed as beneficial both to employees and customers:

If you can start working according to the New World of Work principles this will result in higher job satisfaction and higher quality of outcomes.

Recognition of Information Overload

Interviewees recognized Information Overload; most of them simply answered 'yes' when asked whether or not they do recognize Information Overload. Some added remarks relating to the amount of information available and the amount of information coming towards an individual:

The amount of information to base a decision on can become too much

The amount of information available is enormous and there are numerous channels

If you want to use all the information available you will get overloaded. You have to find ways to find the truly valuable information and get rid of the rest

The amount of information available is high, and thus, the risk exists that things will not get the attention they need

For most of the interviewees Information Overload was not a problem. Either it has never been a problem for the interviewee or the interviewee has found a way to cope with the problem and get (and keep) it under control. Others indicate that Information Overload is a problem that they are slowly learning to cope with, and few state that they do not know how to cope with Information Overload.

The opinions of interviewees about whether or not Information Overload has increased over time were very different; some of the interviewees perceived no change in the amount of Information Load over time:

The Information Load has increased, but my attitude towards it has also changed; in my situation Information Overload has neither increased nor decreased

No, [Information Load has not increased]; the amount of information has increased, but also the quality of tools to handle the information has increased

Others stated that the amount of Information Load has increased:

Yes, my job has become more demanding over time

The amount of information available over time has increased, partly because of changes in my job. I have to process more information now than before

Yes, the Information Load is still increasing

Yes, there is more information coming towards me and I need to process more information to be able to work well

Causes of Information Overload

Several causes were mentioned by interviewees. Interviewees that did not perceive Information Overload as a problem were asked to try to think of what could cause Information Overload. In Table 3 we present the list of causes mentioned by interviewees, together with relevant quotes from the interviews. Please note that the order in which the causes are presented was randomly chosen.

Table 3. Categorization of causes of information overload illustrated by the quotes from interviews

Amount of information	• The amount of websites [is a cause of Information Overload] • The amount of information available [is a cause of Information Overload] • There is a lot of unstructured information heading our way • The amount of information available is enormous
Easiness of producing, storing, and distributing of information	• The easiness with which information is produced and distributed [is a cause of Information Overload] • A lot more information has been digitalized and can more easily be transported • Information can be more easily transported via electronic means • Producing and transporting information has become much easier • The amount of information produced, stored and made searchable has increased
Internet	• The existence of Internet is the general cause of Information Overload • Internet [is a cause of Information Overload]
Culture within organization	• If the culture within an organization stimulates sharing of information, Information Overload can occur
Email	• Email is the most (mis)used way of communicating [within this organization] • Email is a very confronting way of presenting information • Outlook is the main source of Information Overload
High number of channels for information	• There are many ways of getting information • Having different channels for news [causes Information Overload]
Low quality of data	• Quality of information is low, because the tendency is to complete things quickly
Cell phones	• A mobile phone can also cause Information Overload: a call always comes unexpected
Amount of outdated information	• The amount of outdated information [is a cause of Information Overload]
Broad area of attention	• [My] area of attention is broad, and therefore I need to pay attention to a lot of things
Lack of confidence in the knowledge of others	• Some people lack the confidence in the fact that others will have the information needed
Lack of integrating information systems	• For example, there is no system that integrates and provides all the information about a certain customer
Lack of structure in information	• The lack of structure in the information [is a cause of Information Overload]
Lack of accurate information	• For unstructured data, the lack of to-the-point information [is a cause of Information Overload]
Lack of visualization of data	• For structured data, the lack of visualization of data is the main cause [of Information Overload]
Requesting too much information	• People have the habit to pull too much information towards them, as they are afraid to miss something
Image managing	• People tend to send a lot of information, in order to let others think they actually produce something

Countermeasures Against Information Overload

Several countermeasures were mentioned by interviewees. Interviewees that did not perceive Information Overload as a problem were asked to try to think of what could be countermeasures against Information Overload. In Table 4 we present the list of countermeasures mentioned by interviewees, together with relevant quotes from the interviews. Please note that the order

in which the countermeasures are presented was randomly chosen.

DISCUSSION

The body of knowledge for this study consisted mainly of literature related to the New World of Work and Information Overload. Therefore, some results were not found in the literature studied and are presented as such. This does not mean that

Table 4. Categorization of countermeasures to Information Overload illustrated by the quotes from interviews

(Teach people to) filter incoming information	• Teach[ing] people how to filter [can help solving Information Overload]" • Change your attitude, by starting to filter information • Learn to filter: you are free to choose which information you consume
Use tools to classify and structure information (for example flagging and email rules)	• You can use the tools within Microsoft Office to classify and structure information, [for example you can start] flagging messages for follow-up (for example today, tomorrow, next week) • Structuring your email by using rules [is a countermeasure for Information Overload] • You have to structure information, for example by flagging, or using task-lists
Ask others for information before trying to find it yourself	• Having a network with people can help solve Information Overload, because you can ask others before trying to find information yourself • Use a network for finding information. I myself am a generalist and I know where I should turn to for specific information (colleagues, websites, email aliases)
Disable notifications of new email	• Disable pop-up's of new emails and reminders of things in your calendar • Disables notification of new email
Improve software (intuitive interfaces, natural language)	• Improve software ([for example by providing] intuitive interfaces, [or possibilities to interact using] natural language). Still there are people that are left behind simply because they cannot use the tools properly
Stop searching for information at some point and decide on the information available	• Gathering information to up to some point and then make your decision based on the information then available [can help reduce Information Overload]. Do not be a perfectionist in this, because then you become overloaded. • At a certain moment you just need to stop gathering information and make your decision. If the risk of an erroneous decision is higher the time available for gathering information and thinking about it will be longer
Train people to cope with Information Overload	• People need to be trained to cope with Information Overload • Training. This problem can be solved by changing a personal attitude towards the problem
Communicate clearly and make agreements about communication	• Communicate clearly with others and make clear agreements about communication
Hire an information integrator	• Another solution would be to hire a person to be an Information Integrator: filter and integrate information from different sources and send the result of this process to the rest of the organization
Improve visualization of information	• Provide visualization of data
Improve infrastructure	• We need to improve infrastructure, so more people will get access
Keep professional and private life separated	• Also, keeping your private and work life strictly separated helps to manage Information Overload
Only read communication when needed, not when it arrives	• Only read communication when needed, not at the moment it arrives
Organizations should delete outdated information	• An organization should be deleting outdated information more vigorously
Provide an alternative for email	• Provide an alternative for email
Provide an overview of information from different sources	• Create an overview of information from different sources
Reserve time for email reading	• Reserve time for reading your email and only read your email during the reserved timeslots
Scan your email messages	• Scan your email messages instead of reading them completely
Structure group communication	• [This problem can be solved by] structuring group communication
Structure information hierarchically	• Information should be structured better, to make it easier to search [through] it. We need to structure information hierarchically, from global information down to very specific information
Verify information with colleagues	• Verify information with colleagues
When producing information, provide more quality and less quantity	• When you are producing information you should ensure a high quality and less quantity

the results are completely novel; it means that the results were not discussed in the literature studied for this study.

Novelty of the New World of Work

We can agree with the interviewees who indicated that the New World of Work seems to bring not much new for Consultants. It is important to note here that the implementation of the New World of Work is a company-wide initiative at Microsoft B.V., thus also marketing, sales and finance will go through this change. In our opinion, the New World of Work implementation will indeed bring something new to the Consultants, but in order to ensure a successful company-wide implementation, everyone involved should be brought to the same "level". The Consultants seem to be the group within the company with the highest IT affinity and are indeed working according to the New World of Work principles more than for example someone working in salary administration. Consultants work at the customer's office or at home, at times that fit the tasks at hand and the current situation, whereas someone working in salary administration works at the office of Microsoft all the time, and with less flexible working hours. After everyone has been brought to the same "level" we are confident the New World of Work implementation will start to bring something new to Consultants. What exactly that will be is of course difficult to predict. One of the things that seem to be "New World of Work"-like and is not implemented for Consultants yet is the result-based rewarding.

In addition to that, some interviewees expressed the opinion that the New World of Work vision itself is not new. According to them, Microsoft should consult organizations that have already gone through this change instead of trying to invent "the wheel" again. To some extent we can agree with this, because it seems a good idea to tap into the knowledge others have instead of trying to create that knowledge yourself. On the

other hand, the New World of Work vision was originally written for Microsoft by Dan Rasmus, an internationally recognized expert in knowledge management and collaboration technology, who worked as an analyst with the Giga Information Group and Forrester Research. Thus, in our opinion, the vision of the New World of Work is based on a considerable amount of knowledge and experience in the field.

Concluding, the New World of Work was not perceived as new by the Consultants: it is a natural and logical environment for their tasks; a Consultant is used to working primarily at the office of the customer. So, for Consultants, the New World of Work is a rather natural and logical environment. We are however confident that as soon as the whole company is at the same "level" with the Consultants, the New World of Work will indeed have something new in store for this group.

Information Overload: Causes

Generalized, what the interviewees suggested is that Information Overload is caused by interruptions in an individual's work due to external influences. People tend to store information, even if it has become useless.

In Figure 3 the above findings are depicted. The causes of Information Overload mentioned during the interviews are shown, with their relation to Information Overload. If a cause is, in our opinion, an indirect cause it is connected either via another cause that has been mentioned during the interviews or via a cause that has been found in literature, to which it is related.

Information Overload: Countermeasures

The findings in the literature and in our study were quite consistent, as the top two most mentioned countermeasures against Information Overload found in our study are also present in literature.

Figure 3. Map of causes of information overload

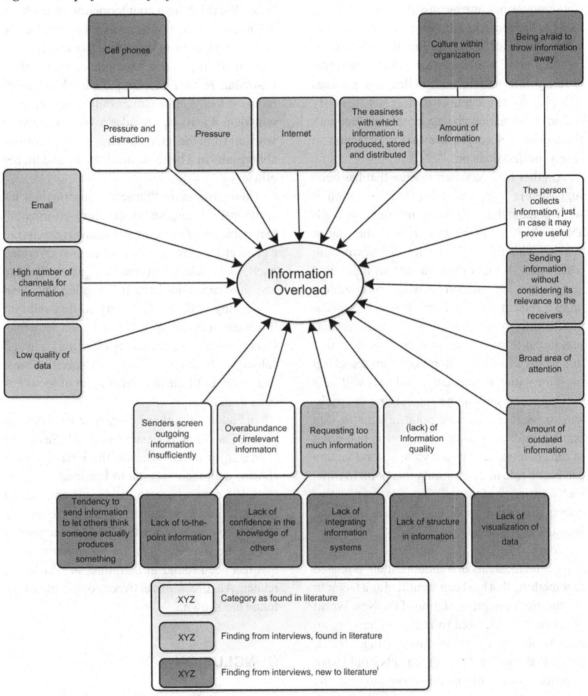

The findings from our study show that a possible countermeasure against Information Overload could be to ask others for help: first ask your colleagues before trying to find the information on your own, while another countermeasures ("Verify information with colleagues") comes into play a little later, as it suggests to verify (found) information about a certain subject with colleagues, before you use that information to base your decisions on.

Another basic countermeasure that has been suggested is "Stop searching for information at some point and decide on the information available", which is indeed, in our view, the way of dealing with the high amount of information, which we call the 'ostrich-tactic': an individual searches for information about a certain subject up to a certain point in time, then stops searching for information and uses only the information found to base a decision on. It is clear that this tactic will indeed stop you from searching for information continuously and thus will help making a decision on the subject, but the problem is: what is a suitable point in time to stop searching for information and how is that point in time determined? In our view, several factors can play a role in determining that point in time, such as priority of the decision, relative negative effects suffered if wrong decisions are made and pressure from others.

Countermeasure "Communicate clearly and make agreements about communication" is related to something that has been identified as a factor in the successful implementation of the New World of Work, viz. the need to make agreements on the way of working and communicating. Thus, it seems that making these agreements would have a twofold effect: Information Overload could be reduced and possibly the New World of Work implementation would have a higher chance of being successful.

Countermeasure "Only read communication when needed, not when it arrives" seems to be contradictory to a countermeasure found in literature, namely 'Handle incoming information at once'. We think both countermeasures can help, because handling information at once will make processing the pile of information easier, because an individual processes the pile of information bit-by-bit, as it arrives. On the other hand, reading/processing information only when needed, not when it arrives, provides a way to shield of yourself from the interruptions and thus presumably results in a better concentration and higher efficiency.

Countermeasure "Structure information hierarchically" suggests to structure information hierarchically. This countermeasure is maybe not a countermeasure against Information Overload itself, but makes information easier findable and thus can reduce the Information Overload originating from the difficulty to find relevant information in the pile of information available. General terms can be used as a starting point and subsequently be refined into more specific terms, and so on, until the desired amount of focus has been found.

In Figure 4 the above discussion has been depicted. The countermeasures against Information Overload mentioned during the interviews are shown, with their relation to Information Overload. If a countermeasure is, in our opinion, an indirect countermeasure it is connected either via another countermeasure that has been mentioned during the interviews or via a countermeasure that has been found in literature, to which it is related. Also, relations between countermeasures found are shown.

CONCLUSION

Concluding, the results from our study suggest that Information Overload is not perceived as a problem, but as a challenge and a possible future problem. Information Overload has to be kept under control as the situation is not likely to improve in the future, although some interviewees

Figure 4. Map of countermeasures against information overload

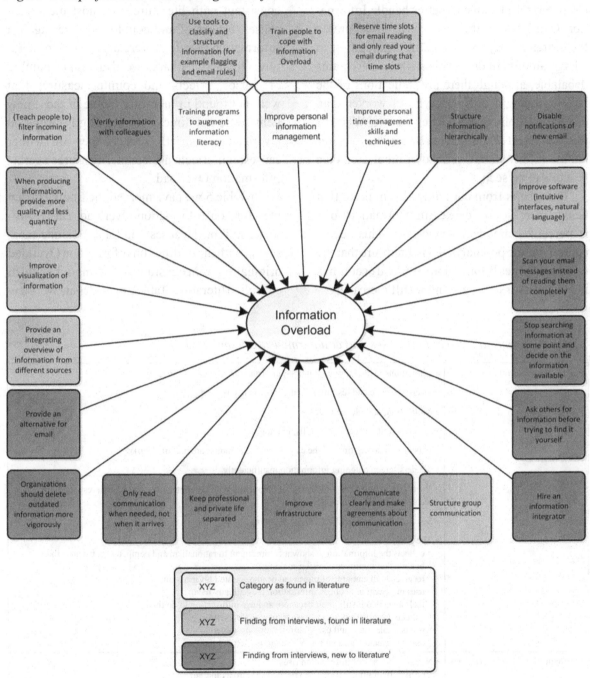

suggested that the next generation of workers (NetGen) will be able to better handle Information Overload, as they may have incorporated the search strategies for finding information in a large amount of data. This suggestion remains debatable, although there are indications of the NetGen being a different type of worker than the Baby Boomers and Generation X. Whether this will result in the NetGen being able to better handle Information Overload or other problems remains to be seen.

The results from our study also indicate that neither increase nor decrease in Information Load is perceived among interviewees. This seems contrary to the popular belief in literature that the number of times Information Overload occurs has increased over the years and it still increasing.

The results from our study are to some extent consistent with literature: the most mentioned causes, effects of and countermeasures against Information Overload were also found in literature. On the other hand, we also found a number of causes, effects and countermeasures that were not found in literature. Some of those new items were not directly influencing Information Overload. So, strictly spoken, they are neither causes, nor effects nor countermeasures against Information Overload.

In Table 5 we have merged the findings from literature on Information Overload, earlier presented in Table 1 (causes) and Table 2 (countermeasures), with the findings on Information Overload originating from our study: the items not found in consulted literature. Table 5 provides an overview

Table 5. Information overload: Causes and countermeasures combined

Personal factors	• Limitations in the individual human information-processing capacity
	• Decision scope and resulting documentation needs
	• Motivation, attitude, satisfaction
	• Personal traits (experience, skills, ideology, age)
	• Personal situation (time of the day, noise, temperature, amount of sleep)
	• Senders screen outgoing information insufficiently
	• Users of computer adapt their way of interacting with computers too slowly with respect to the technological development
	• Social communication barriers break down

	• The person
	  ○ collects the information to show a commitment to rationalism and competence, because they believe that improves decision-making;
	  ○ receives high amounts of unwanted or unrequested information;
	  ○ uses information to check information they already have;
	  ○ feels a need to justify their decision, and use information to do this;
	  ○ collects information, just in case it may prove useful;
	  ○ wants to play safe and use all information possible;
	  ○ uses information as a currency – not to get left behind.

Information characteristics	• Number of items of information rises • Uncertainty of information (info needed vs. info available) • Diversity of information and number of alternatives increase • Ambiguity of information • Novelty of information • Complexity of information • Intensity of information • Dimensions of information increase • Information quality, value, half-life • Overabundance of irrelevant information • Incremental decreases in decision effectiveness due to additional information quantity are greater than the incremental increases in decision effectiveness due to additional information quality

continued on following page

Table 5. continued

Task and process parameters	• Tasks are less routine • Complexity of tasks and task interdependencies • Time pressure • Task interruptions for complex tasks • Too many, too detailed standards (in accounting) • Simultaneous input of information into the process • Innovations evolve rapidly – shortened life cycle • Interdisciplinary work
Environment	• Too many inputs from the environment • Inputs follow each other to fast to enable processing • The quantity of information produced is too high • Failure to create 'high quality' information
Organizational design	• Collaborative work • Centralization (bottlenecks) or disintermediation (information searching is done by end users rather than by information professionals) • Accumulation of information to demonstrate power • New Information and communication technologies (e.g. groupware) • Pursuing a number of tasks simultaneously, resulting in a tendency to ask for more information than strictly needed • Pressure and distraction
Information technology	• Push systems • E-mails • Intranet, extranet, Internet • Rise in number of television channels • Various distribution channels for the same content • Vast storage capacity of the systems • Low duplication costs • Speed of access • Computers communicate solely by graphical output, straining our visual sense • Use and misuse of IT
Personal factors	• Improve personal time management skills and techniques • Training programs to augment information literacy: information-processing skills such as file handling, using email, classification of document, etc. • Improve personal information management • Systematic priority setting • Improve the screening skills for information • Keep professional and private life separated • Reserve time slots for email reading and only read your email during that time slots • Scan your email messages instead of reading them completely • Only read communication when needed, not when it arrives • Verify information with colleagues • Ask others for information before trying to find it yourself • Stop searching information at some point and decide on the information available
Information characteristics	• Raise general quality of information (i.e. its usefulness, conciseness) by defining quality standards • Focus on creating value-added information • Promulgation of rules for information and communication design (e.g. e-mail etiquette) • Compress, aggregate, categorize, and structure information • Formalization of language • Brand names for information • Form must follow function must follow usability • Simplify functionalities and design of products • Customization of information • Intelligent interfaces • Determine various versions of information with various levels of detail and elaborate additional information that serves as summaries • Organize text with hypertext structures or gophers • Interlink various information types (as internal with external information) • Structure information hierarchically • Organizations should delete outdated information more vigorously

continued on following page

Table 5. continued

Task and process parameters	• Standardize operating procedures • Define decision modes developed for specific decision processes (e.g., decision rules) • Install an exception-reporting system • Allow more time for task performance • Schedule uninterrupted blocks of time for completing critical work • Adequate selection of media for the task • Handle incoming information at once • Collaboration with information specialists within the teams • Bring decisions to where information exists when this information is qualitative and ambiguous • Install process enablers for cognitive support • Use simpler information-processing strategies • Regulate the rate of information flow • Search procedures and strategy • Define specific, clear goals for the information in order to contextualize it and turn it meaningful • Communicate information needs to providers • Provide incentives that are directly related with decisions in order to make decision relevant information be processed more effectively • Install a measurement system for information quality • Communicate clearly and make agreements about communication
Organizational design	• Coordination through interlinked units • Augment into processing capacity through changes in organizational design • Creation of lateral relationships (integrate roles, create liaisons between roles, teamwork, etc.) • Coordination by goal setting, hierarchy, and rules depending on frequency of exceptions (uncertainty) • Creation of self-contained tasks (reduced division of labor, authority structures based on output categories)→ autonomous groups • Reduce divergence among people (e.g., with regard to expectations) through socialization (e.g., frequent face-to-face interactions) • Install appropriate measures of performance • Hire additional employees • Create slack resources • Hire an information integrator
Information technology application	• Intelligent information management (prioritization) • Install voting structures to make users evaluate the information • Prefer push to pull technologies • Facilitator support through (e-)tools • Decision support systems should reduce a large set of alternatives to a manageable size • Use natural language processing systems (search with artificial intelligence) • Information quality filters • Intelligent data selectors (intelligent agents) • Use systems that offer various information organization options (e.g. filing systems) • Multimodal interfaces • Improve infrastructure • Disable notifications of new email • Provide an alternative for email

of the causes of and countermeasures against Information Overload originating from literature as well as our study, and thus provides the most complete overview possible in this study.

ACKNOWLEDGMENT

The authors gratefully acknowledge helpful comments of Corrie Huijs and Rene Bouw on the early version of this work; and the Services department of Microsoft B.V. (Netherlands) – for offering access to all relevant documents and cooperation during this study.

REFERENCES

Bawden, D., Holtham, C., & Courtney, N. (1999). Perspectives on information overload. *Aslib Proceedings, 51*(8), 249-255.

Beardsly, S., Johnson, B., & Manyika, J. (2006). Competitive advantage from better interactions. *The McKinsey Quarterly, 2*, 3-9.

Berghel, H. (1997). Cyberspace 2000: Dealing with Information Overload. *Communications of the ACM, 40*(2), 19-24.

Brewster, S. A. (1997). Using non-speech sound to overcome information overload. *Displays, 17*(3), 179-189.

Casonato, R., & Harris, K. (2002). *The Knowledge worker Investment Paradox*. Gartner, Inc.

Davis, G. B. (2002). Anytime / Anyplace Computing and the Future of Knowledge Work. *Communications of the ACM, 45*(12), 67-73.

Denning, P. J. (1982). Electronic Junk. *Communications of the ACM, 25*(3), 163-165.

Drury, D. H., & Farhoomand, A. (1999). Knowledge worker Constraints in the Productive Use of Information Technology. *ACM SIGCPR Computer Personnel, 19/20*(4/1), 21-42.

Edmunds, A., & Morris, A. (2000). The problem of information overload in business organisations: a review of the literature. *International Journal of Information Management, 20*, 17-28.

Eppler, & Mengis, M. J. (2004). The Concept of Information Overload: A Review of Literature from Organization Science, Accounting, Marketing, MIS, and Related Disciplines. *The Information Society, 20*, 325-344.

Gates III, W. H. (2005). The New World of Work [Electronic Version]. Microsoft Executive Mail. Retrieved 01-05-2007 from http://www.microsoft.com/mscorp/execmail/2005/05-19newworldofwork.mspx.

Grisé, M., & Gallupe, R.B. (2000). Information Overload: Addressing the Productivity Paradox in Face-to-Face Electronic Meetings. *Journal of Management Information Systems, 16*(3), 157-185.

Hiltz, S. R., & Turoff, M. (1985). Structuring computer-mediated communication systems to avoid information overload. *Communications of the ACM, 28*(7), 680-689.

Ho, J., & Tang, R. (2001). Towards an Optimal Resolution to Information Overload: An Infomediary Approach. *Paper presented at the GROUP '01.*

Jacoby, J. (1984). Perspectives on Information Overload. *The Journal of Consumer Research, 10*(4), 432-435.

Johnson, B., Manyika, J., & Yee, L. (2005). *The next revolution in interactions*. McKinsey & Company.

Keller, K. L., & Staelin, R. (1987). Effects of Quality and Quantity of Information on Decision Effectiveness. *The Journal of Consumer Research, 14*(2), 200-213.

Kelloway, E. K., & Barling, J. (2000). Knowledge Work as organizational behavior. *International Journal of Management Reviews, 2*(3), 287-304.

Maes, P. (1994). Agents that Reduce Work and Information Overload. *Communications of the ACM, 37*(7), 31-40.

Miller, G. A. (1956). The Magical Number Seven, Plus or Minus Two: Some Limits on Our Capacity for Processing Information. *The Psychological Review, 63*, 81-97.

Noyes, J. M., & Thomas, P.J. (1995). Information overload - an overview. *IEEE Colloquium Digest, 95*(223), 1-3.

O'Reilly III, C. A. (1980). Individuals and Information Overload in Organizations: Is More Necessarily Better? *The Academy of Management Journal, 23*(4), 684-696.

Owen, R. S. (1992). Clarifying the Simple Assumption of the Information Load Paradigm. *Advances in Consumer Research, 19*, 770-776.

Rasmus, D. (2005). Digital Workstyle: The New World of Work [Electronic Version]. Retrieved 01-05-2007 from http://download.microsoft.com/download/B/E/4/BE40F0BC-434B-487C-B788-20052D75A3EC/NewWorldofWorkWP.doc.

Schick, A. G., & Gordon, L.A. (1990). Information overload: a temporal approach. *Accounting, Organizations and Society, 15*(3), 199-220.

Schultze, U., & Vandenbosch, B. (1998). Information Overload in a Groupware Environment: Now You See It, Now You Don't. *Journal of Organizational Computing and Eelectronic Commerce, 8*(2), 127-148.

Simpson, C. W., & Prusak, L. (1995). Troubles with Information Overload - Moving from Quantity to Quality in Information Provision. *International Journal of Information Management, 15*(6), 413-425.

Sparrow, P. R. (1999). Strategy and Cognition: Understanding the Role of Management Knowledge Structures, Organizational Memory and Information Overload. *Creativity and Innovation Management, 8*(2), 140-148.

Speier, C., Valacich, J.S., & Vessey, I. (1997). The effects of task interruption and information presentation on individual decision making. *Paper presented at the International conference on Information systems Atlanta, Georgia, United States.*

Strassmann, P. A. (1999). Measuring and Managing Knowledge Capital [Electronic Version]. Retrieved 28-03-2007 from http://www.strassmann.com/pubs/measuring-kc/.

Swain, M. R., & Haka, S.F. (2000). Effects of Information Load on Capital Budgeting Decisions. *Behavioral Research in Accounting, 12*, 171-198.

Tushman, M. L., & Nadler, D.A. (1978). Information Processing as an Integrating Concept in Organizational Design. *The Academy of Management Review, 3*(3), 613-624.

Wang, R. Y., Lee, Y. W., Pipino, L. L., & Strong, D. M. (1998). Manage Your Information as a Product. *Sloan Management Review, 39*(4), 95-105.

Whicker, L. M., & Andrews, K.M. (2004). HRM in the Knowledge Economy: Realising the Potential. *Asia Pacific Journal of Human Resources, 42*(2), 156-165.

KEY TERMS

Information Workers are employees who posses knowledge-based capabilities.

Information Overload is the situation when the information processing requirements exceed the information processing capacities.

Knowledge Workers are employees that own their means of production (they 'produce' with their brain and 'sell' brain-hours to the organization) in contrast to manual workers.

New World of Work is the vision by Microsoft that investigates technological trends and the challenges they present for workers, organizations and governments in the next ten years.

Chapter XXV
HR Shared Service Centers:
From Brand Management Towards Success

Mitchell van Balen
University of Twente, The Netherlands

Tanya Bondarouk
University of Twente, The Netherlands

ABSTRACT

In this chapter the authors consider articles in professional literature regarding Human Resource Centers, with the goal to explore issues raised by practice: motivation, risk analysis, structure and implementation. Using Grounded Theory approach, they analysed 34 articles, and through open and axial coding, we have modeled the HR SSC's.

INTRODUCTION AND RESEARCH QUESTIONS

A SSC can be viewed as a particular kind of sourcing arrangement having a long-term and strategic impact (Bergeron, 2003). The popularity of SSC's originate in a combination of advantages, including efficiency gains and an increase in service quality without giving up the control of the organizational and technical arrangements and expertise (Janssen and Joha, 2006).

Bergeron (2003) states that SSC's are designed to promote efficiency, value generation, cost savings, and improved service for internal customers of the parent corporation.

Given the hybridisation of centralized and decentralized models in SSC's, their promises reflect that structural dilemma:

- By centralizing HR activities, the basic promise is that HR services are provided by a local unit with relatively low costs (broadening the scope and scale of services, elimination of redundant HR functions, clarification of communication lines, minimizing response time for remote clients);
- By decentralizing HR activities, the basic premise is that HR services become more flexible (alignment with the corporate needs,

synergy of HR services, increase of mutual learning).

Definitions of HR SSC abound, with little consistency or agreement in sight. Why do we need to know those definitions? The answer is rather simple: even minor variants in terminology may result in the study of different phenomenon, or of various subsets of the possible sourcing population (Willcocks et al, 2006).

We follow Janssen and Joha (2006) and define SSC as ... a separate and accountable semi-autonomous unit within an (inter)organizational entity, used to bundle activities and provide specific pre-defined services to the operational units within that (inter)organizational entity, on the basis of agreed conditions (*ibid*, p. 102).

SSCs thus are regarded to enable companies to maintain control of core support functions, avoid duplications, and offer services more efficiently and at lower cost (Cooke, 2000).

Several reasons pushed an HRM field into the Shared Service arrangements. We claim that those reasons are:

- Growth of the HRM function in size and costs that requested new efficient structures;
- Diversity of HR processes and practices that called for unification especially within global and international organizations;
- Emerging of ERP packages that offered enabling technological structures for HR outsourcing;
- Globalization that put a high pressure on organizations when global alliances, acquisitions, joint ventures, and competitors resulted in situations that companies were simultaneously customers, vendors, competitors and distributors. This requested HR to experiment with new organizational forms to increase the speed and accuracy of organizational diagnoses, and to facilitate the allocation of resources to areas where they were most needed (Wright et al., 1999);

- Inflexibility of organizational structure called for SSC's that were viewed to give organizations a greater degree of structural flexibility to respond to business changes (Cooke, 2006).

It is not surprising, therefore, that HR SSC's are popular in organizational life. And it is also true that the first knowledge about HR SSC was accumulated within so-called professional literature since end of 1990's. In our research we were interested in the knowledge developed by practitioners about HR SSC. It is fairly much agreed upon in the HR world that a gap exists between research and practitioner writings (Dipboye, 2005; Deadrick and Gibson, 2007). The practitioner writings on the subject grew significantly, however the academic literature seemed to be lacking behind (Cooke 2006). Therefore, in this chapter we aim to study professional literature in order to gain insights into HR SSCs from practice, and to model the concept of HR SSC's based on the findings from this literature.

CLOSING THE GAP: 'WHAT HRM ACADEMICS CAN LEARN FROM PRACTICE'

SSCs were evermore frequently used for HR purposes during the last two decades. Yet the academic research about this phenomenon contrasted sharply with the attention it had got from HR practitioners and consultancy firms. Issues surrounding this phenomenon were ambiguously spoken of and the urge for academics to pick it up and conduct non ambivalent research was necessary.

Despite of the increase of HR research in general and the growing importance of the HR function, the science and practice of HR remain separated. Dulebohn et al. (1995) argued that this is the result of the different focus of HR researchers. Deadrick and Gibson (2007) showed with an analysis of 4300 professional and academic articles that the interest gap between academics and practitioners is substantial. In that research, HR academics showed a significant interest in Organizational behavior / Motivation related topics, in contrast with HR professionals who wrote four times less about these topics. The magnitude and span of the gap is thus of considerable size. This was confirmed when we looked at the subject of this research, HR SSCs. Searches in several scientific databases gave one single hit on the keywords shared service(s) center. A search with the same keywords within the professional database of Business Source Elite gave us 158 hits. This confirms Cooke's (2006) vision, stated that there is a lack of scientific attention for SSCs.

We agree with Deadrick and Gibson (2007) that probably a real gap in this field can be characterized as *knowing-versus-doing gap*:

We all know the gap between HR research and practice exists, but we have not really done anything to better understand and thus close this gap. (ibid, p.138)

In this study we address this challenge by attempting to better understand the values and knowledge underlying the professional findings in the field of HR SSC's.

Myths, realities and uncertainties can intertwine in the practitioners' writings. But the fact is that in their writings a source of inspirations and facts can be found. From this stance, we will dig up the practitioner's field, explore the experiences, and develop possible new subjects of inquiry about HR SSCs. Hence, we will break a lance for future academic research by developing an insight into the professional findings about HR SSCs.

Selection of Journals

Professional HR journals act as an intermediary that publishes first-hand practitioner experiences while remaining a specialized and traceable source of information. In a mail conversation with Carroll Lachnit, executive editor of *Workforce Management*, we got to know that her professional HR journal was aimed primarily at human resource professionals. Its mission is *to keep them informed of the news and trends that affect workforce management, and that ultimately affect the future of the businesses in which they work*. Five other professional HR journals were contacted to learn their mission statements, but no replies were received.

During selecting HR professional journals, we therefore were looking for those that stated their strict orientation towards human resource professionals. The search for availability of HR professional journals and their accessibility was done by using the Business Source Elite database via EBSCOhost. The following journals were selected: 'Employee Benefit News', 'HR Focus', 'HRMagazine', 'Human Resource Planning', 'People Management', 'Workforce Management', 'Workforce', and 'IntermediairPW'. We do not argue that we selected all HR professional journals, but we took a representative sample of professional journals in the field of HR.

Selection of Articles

The selection process consisted out of two phases. The first was the selection of articles on specific keywords. Keywords chosen were 'shared service' or 'service center'. A total of 78 articles were identified by the initial search.

The second phase enclosed the scanning of articles and judging if they satisfied four parameters. Articles were only included if they matched with the defined parameters: *(1)* Subject area is *specifically* about HR SSCs *(2)* Language is English or Dutch *(3)* Published between 1998 and 2008 *(4)* Information presented is traceable.

From the 78 gathered articles, 34 satisfied the four mentioned parameters. Examples of omitted articles were those focused purely on outsourcing issues or those who contained no relevant information, like business function descriptions. The search was performed in May 2008. A backward reference search was not part of this search, since references were not frequently used and often irrelevant.

Appendix 1 displays articles which were used for further analyses.

GROUNDED THEORY APPROACH

We assumed to start from 'tabula rasa' and take an explorative approach to model HR SSC based on professional writings. For this purpose we have chosen the grounded theory (GT) method (Strauss and Corbin, 1990).

We chose for Grounded Theory for two main reasons. First, it was acclaimed to be suitable whenever the deepening of understanding is required; or, when new ideas, contexts, consequences and recommendations for action for a subject area have to be derived from texts. Secondly, an advantage of GT could be found in its inductive, contextual and processual features which fit well with the research approach of data like we aimed for. Thus with GT we described what was happening in the field and develop a conceptualization from it via an inductive approach (Orlikowski. 1993).

The GT method used exists out of three coding phases. (1) *Open coding* is the process of breaking down, examining, comparing, conceptualizing, and categorizing data. (2) *Axial coding* is a set of procedures whereby data are put back together in new ways after open coding, by making connections between categories. (3) *Selective coding* is the process of selecting the core category, systematically relating it to other categories, validating those relationships, and filling in categories that need further refinement and development (Strauss and Corbin, 1990).

The open coding phase was bounded by a few factors. As Strauss and Corbin (1990) stated, data collection, analysis, and theory stand in reciprocal relationship with each other. One does not

begin with a theory, then prove it. Since the aim of GT is to foster new creative ways to explain phenomena, the development of categories and concepts should be free of previously developed theories. However literature can and was used to help stimulate the theoretical sensitivity, and to foster questions in this phase of the research.

For the development of categories, we used the selected articles. The second author created categories and properties and checked their rigor by constant comparative analysis and discussion with colleagues. The usefulness of the categories and concepts was analyzed with a preliminary scan of all the selected articles. When it was notified that a small sample of articles gave useful data, categories or properties were excluded. An example of this was company size, for which a too small sample of articles gave results. Concepts that remained too poorly developed were rewritten and appropriated for the research.

Category Development

Six categories were identified after the open coding procedure. These were chosen on the bases of presence, pertinence and importance according to the authors' insights. Table 1 has an overview of all five categories. We now define them and explain properties included.

Implementation phase referred to the level of development of the HR SSC(s) mentioned in the text. On the abstract level three phases were identified. *(1) Preparation* was the phase in which the decision is taken to start a HR SSC or a HR SSC will start soon. *(2) Introduction* was selected when it is mentioned that the HR SSC is in the start up phase. An example of this was the reference to the early development processes in Schoeff (2006b). *(3) In Use* was about HR SSCs that are fully functional and operate in the organization. *(4) Unknown* was selected when it is not clear in which level of development the mentioned HR SSC was.

Table 1. Overview of HR SSC's categories and their properties identified in professional literature

Implementation phase	Motivation	Risk	Form	Impact on R	Success
Preparation	Strategic/ organizational	Communication	Administration/Call Center	Consolidated staff	Yes
Introduction	Brand development	Planning	Self service	Improved operations	No
In Use	Service improvement	Power play	Center of expertise	Cost reductions	Unknown
Unknown	Economical	Standardization	Other / Unmentioned	Responsibilities shift	
	Other	De-personalization		Strategic function	
		Other		Other	

Motivation referred to the motives used to choose for adopting the SSC form for HR. Globally they were divided into four groups. *(1) Strategic / organizational* included motives concerning productivity increase, ability to focus more on strategic HR issues (Manocha, 2006b), and standardization and synergy advantages (Martinez, 2002). *(2) Brand development* included credibility (Griffiths, 2007), appearance (Martinez 2002) and compliance (HRfocus, 2007a) motivations. Thus under this property we found motivations that stated that HR could get a higher regard because of a HR SSC. *(3) Service improvement* motivations were those concerned with leveraging technological advantages, higher service levels, and access to more expertise for the HR function. *(4) Economical* motivations were those on lowering costs of services and cost reductions overall. *(5) Other* were motivations which could not be placed in the previous categories. Like 'the sense of urgency' which showed that a real motivation was lacking but the SSC was enforced due to pressure.

Risk referred to the anticipated troubles while or before adopting a SSC in the field of HR. Some risks were more eminent during different phases of implementation. *(1) Communication* included risks concerned with troubles created by improper communication about the HR SSC to those in the organization that were affected by it (HRfocus, 2007c). *(2) Planning* was about troubles concerning the strict or unrealistic planning process and the pressure that was created as a result (Boerman, 2007). *(3) Power play* risks included the frequently mentioned resistance against the HR SSC (Hays, 1999; Boerman, 2007) or the lack of commitment within the organization for a HR SSC (PeopleManagement, 2006c). *(4) Standardization* referred to the risks emerging when the advantage of economies of scale was undermined due to a multitude of exceptions on the standardized services (IntermediairPW, 2005). *(5) De-personalization* risks concerned those troubles with the removal of the 'human side' of the services. Like communication via a telephone while actually there was need for face-to-face contact to discuss a problem (Albertson 1999). *(6) Other* risks were those not described by the previous ones. These were troubles concerned with maintenance (Paradiso, 1999), relocation (FraseBlunt, 2004) or cultural issues (Martinez, 2002; Scott, 2006).

Form referred to the factual or planned setup of a HR SSC within the organization. *(1) Administration / Call Center* was the first form which refered to a unit where transactions were being processed and/or calls were taken. *(2) Self service* includes systems that allowed personnel to perform HR actions themselves, for example via e-HRM. *(3) Center of expertise* was a term invented by Ulrich (1996) and observed in some selected articles. Centers of expertise were centers where HR professionals focused on specialised knowledge (learning, rewarding, recruiting) and implemented those ideas throughout the organization (PeopleManagement, 2007b). *(4) Other / Unmentioned was* selected when there was no clarity about the chosen or desired forms for the HR SSC.

Impact on HR referred to the factual reported consequences/outcomes within the mentioned organization when a HR SSC was deployed. *(1) Consolidated staff* was reported when the amount of HR staff had decreased (Flynn, 2000). *(2) Improved operations* was chosen when the service level increased. *(3) Cost reductions* included the impacts of cheaper processes and operations. *(4) Responsibilities shift* referred to the change of HR responsibilities to different positions. For example from HR professionals to line-managers (Phillips, 2007a). *(5) Strategic function* was included because it was regularly remarked that the introduction of a SSC left more space for HR to act strategic (Hays, 1999). *(6) Other* impacts are selected under option six. Impacts like the increased visibility of HR (IntermediairPW, 2006) or a poor functioning HR staff (Griffiths, 2008).

Success referred to the perceived attitude of the text towards HR SSCs. Since SSCs were commonly perceived as a hyped phenomenon this category was included to see if the practitioners were indeed positive about HR SSCs. This was analyzed with scanning if the HR SSCs in an article (or HR SSCs in general) were indeed perceived as successful. If so *(1) Yes* was chosen. if this was not the case then *(2) Not* was chosen. If the article lacked any (subjective or objective) statements about its success, or there was no clarity *(3) Unknown/Biased* was selected.

Structuring Results

With all the categories and properties operational, the selected articles were rescanned. With a line-by-line analysis the presence of phenomena was analyzed. This form of analysis was chosen on grounds of its generative capacities. This was a labor intensive analysis but generated the most data since all information was taken into account without making samples as other analyses required. It was also useful when the use of metaphors and irony made a deeper analysis necessary to uncover some phenomena. For instance the phrase Where's the money gone?(Griffiths, 2007), which was used as a political motivation to implement a SSC, instead of the more presumable economical one.

The choice had been made that the only dimension of the properties was 'present' or 'not present'. Frequency, intensity, or the extents of properties were thus unmentioned. This choice stemmed from the articles used and their limited information to give real meaning to other dimensions.

While scanning the articles for the presence of phenomena, memos were made. By doing so, combined with careful contemplation about the real meaning of the texts, and the rereading of the articles, information was gathered. A concept matrix was regarded to be the right tool to structure the information, as was supported by Strauss and Corbin (1990). It gave us the ability to put articles alongside the developed categories and conveniently arranged the presence or absence of phenomena. This increased our ability to discover patterns. It was chosen for to order the articles in a chronological order in the matrix. This was done to analyze the developments through time more easily.

FINDINGS

Table 2 shows the general results we observed on the basis of our categorization.

When we looked at the findings we saw an overall increase of articles written about HR SSCs throughout time. Moreover there was also an increase of articles related to HR sourcing, of which a large part was excluded due to the unsatisfactory match with the parameters.

Table2. Concept matrix of the gathered data, bundled per year

	Implementation				Motivation					Risk						Form				Impact						Success		
	Preparation	Introduction	In use	Unknown	Strategic / Org	Brand Development	Service Improvement	Economical	Other	Communication	Planning	Power Play	Standard. excess	De-personalization	Other	Admin / Call	Self service	Center of expertise	Other / Unmentioned	Consolidated staff	Improved operations	Cost reductions	Moved responsibilities	Strategic function	Other	Yes	No	Unknown/Biased
Total 1999	0	1	3	1	4	2	4	3	0	0	0	1	0	2	1	4	3	0	0	1	2	2	3	2	1	4	0	0
Total 2000	1	1	1	0	1	0	1	1	1	0	0	1	0	1	0	1	1	0	0	1	1	1	1	1	0	1	0	0
Total 2002	0	0	1	0	1	1	1	0	0	0	0	0	0	0	0	0	0	1	1	0	1	0	0	0	0	1	0	0
Total 2004	1	0	1	0	1	0	1	1	1	1	0	1	1	1	1	1	0	0	0	0	0	0	0	0	0	1	0	0
Total 2005	2	0	0	1	3	0	1	1	1	0	2	2	1	0	3	2	1	0	0	0	0	0	0	0	0	0	1	2
Total 2006	6	1	2	3	11	1	2	5	1	2	0	3	0	1	4	4	6	4	6	0	1	2	0	0	1	7	1	4
Total 2007	2	1	1	4	7	3	1	6	1	1	2	3	2	0	2	4	2	2	4	0	1	2	1	0	2	6	0	2
Total 2008	1	1	1	1	3	1	2	1	0	1	1	0	0	0	0	1	1	0	3	1	1	0	0	1	1	3	0	1
Absolute totals	13	5	10	10	31	8	13	18	5	6	5	11	4	5	12	17	14	7	15	3	7	7	5	4	5	23	2	9
Percentages	38%	15%	29%	29%	91%	24%	38%	53%	15%	18%	15%	32%	12%	15%	35%	50%	41%	21%	44%	9%	21%	21%	15%	12%	15%	68%	6%	26%

Furthermore we saw a lack of hits in the 'Impact' category due to its causal connection with the 'Implementation' category. Impact phenomena could only be seen if an article wrote about a HR SSC in the 'Introduction' or 'In Use' phase. The 'Impact' category after all only depicted the factual notified implications of HR SSCs. Since only 44% of the articles reported about 'Introduction' or 'In Use' HR SSC, there was a fairly limited amount of hits in the 'Impact' category.

Next to these general observations, there were distinct findings within each category.

Category 1: Implementation Phase

We saw that 'In Use' HR SSCs were relatively more frequently mentioned in the early years. After 2004, there seemed no clear trend present.

Articles reported mostly about HR SSCs in the 'Preparation' phase, followed by 'In Use' and 'Unknown', and closed by HR SSCs in the 'Introduction' phase.

HR SSCs that were in the 'Introduction' phase were more connected with 'Service improvement' and 'Economical' motivations, aware of the risk of 'De-personalization', chose more often for 'Admin/Call' and 'Self service' applications and were much more regarded as successful. Within 'In Use' HR SSCs more attention was given to the different motivations to deploy it. 'Communication' and 'De-personalization' were also more

seriously perceived as risks. When articles did not mention the implementation phase, they tended to mention more that 'Power play' could form a risk for HR SSCs. Also the form of implementation was less frequently mentioned then.

Category 2: Motivation

Chronologically there were two tendencies mentionable. At first we saw the predominance of 'Strategic/Org' motivations throughout the years. Secondly we saw that 'Service improvement' was mostly notified in the early years of the analyzed articles. 'Strategic/Org' motivations were paramount, followed by 'Economical', 'Service improvement', 'Brand development' and finally 'Other'.

Strategic motivation hardly showed anything, because nearly all articles contained 'Strategic/ Org' motivations. Motivations linked with brand development were more conclusive, as it was more mentioned within HR SSCs 'In Use'. They were more tightly connected with 'Economical' motivations, had a negative connection with 'Communication' risks, and 'Improved operations' and success was more often perceived. 'Service improvement' was also more used as a motivation within 'In use' HR SSCs and was also more frequently mentioned in combination with 'Economical' motivations. A wide range of positive impacts were notified when 'Service improvement' was used as a motivation. Success was thus also more frequently perceived. 'Economical' motivations showed as little divergence as articles with 'Strategic/Org' motivations. 'Other' motivations were strongly connected to the mentioning of other risks. Most of the articles with 'Other' motivations described HR SSCs in the 'Preparation' phase.

Category 3: Risk

Figures in this category were affected by a small number of articles reporting about the risks. Interesting findings were nevertheless still distillable from the data. Chronologically, we saw that 'De-personalization' was more reckoned in the early years of the researched data.

'Other' risks were mostly mentioned, followed by 'Power play'. Each of the remaining risks were mentioned in fewer than seven articles. These were, in order from more to less, 'Communication', 'De-personalization', 'Planning', and 'Standard. excess'. It was notified that when risks were spoken of, there was a bigger chance that articles were not merely positive about HR SSCs. The risk of 'De-personalization' was an exception on this. It also showed that risks mentioned differed according to the implementation phase of the HR SSC spoken of.

'Communication' risks were more frequently mentioned in the 'In use' HR SSCs. This while 'Planning' risks were more often mentioned with HR SSCs in the 'Preparation' phase.

Category 4: Form

Within this category we notified that the 'Center of expertise' was more mentioned in later years. The same applied to the 'Other/Unmentioned' property, which showed the tendency of more vague and unclear articles.

'Admin/Call' was mostly mentioned, followed by 'Other/Unmentioned', and 'Self service'. Roughly the same amount of articles reported

about these three phenomena. 'Center of expertise' was seen the least in the articles. We also saw that 'Admin/Call', 'Self service' and 'Center of expertise' were frequently mentioned together.

'Admin/Call' were connected with the 'Service improvement' motivation. No distinct findings were found except that 'Self service' leads to less 'Other' impacts. 'Center of expertise' was more associated with 'Admin/call center' and 'Self service' applications. Also it showed that when a 'Center of expertise' was mentioned, risks or troubles were fewer. A side mark had to be made that it was less frequently mentioned in HR SSCs 'In use'.

Category 5: Impact

The chronological findings in this category were closely attached to the 'Implementation phase' category due to its causal connection. In addition we can say that in the earlier writings impacts were juxtaposed more often. Just like the risk category, this category was susceptible to strong figures due to a small number of articles in which impacts were mentioned.

The order of properties was 'Cost reductions', 'Improved operations', 'Moved responsibilities', 'Other', 'Strategic function', and finally 'Consolidated staff'. Since most of the impact properties had a positive connotation, success was also more frequent perceived. 'Economical' motivation seemed to be mentioned more in articles that contained impacts.

When we looked in detail at the properties some interesting findings were seen, even though they were influenced by the small amount of articles. Staff was more frequently consolidated when HR SSCs were 'In use'. Also, there was more attention for risks concerning 'Communication' and 'Power play'. 'Improved operations' were clearly notified in HR SSCs that were 'In use'. Cost reductions were both realized in 'Introduction' and 'In use' HR SSCs. Still, 'In use' HR SSCs had stronger figures on this property. Moved responsibilities were connected with different motivations like 'Brand development' and 'Service improvement'. Also the risk of 'De-personalization' was more likely to be perceived. We saw that this also led to more clarity on the mentioned implementation form. The same accounted for the 'Strategic function' impact. This impact was also often connected with the 'Service improvement' motivation. The 'De-personalization' risk was also strong for this impact. Finally 'Other' impacts, were more often mentioned when there was no notification of the 'Self service' form of HR SSCs.

Category 6: Success

Commenting on the chronological developments, we could state that in the early years the tendency was to be plainly positive about HR SSCs. After this time, also question marks were introduced into the professional literature.

'Yes' was abundantly perceived the most. 'Yes' was followed on great distance by an 'Unknown/Biased' perceived attitude towards HR SSCs. In only two cases a clear 'No' was perceived.

In this category, we saw that when success was 'Unknown/Biased', more risks were notified. This could support the statement that the reader perceived articles more negatively when more risks were mentioned.

MODELING HR SSC

Further Selective Ccoding consisted out of the following steps:

1. The first step involves explicating the story line;
2. The second consists of relating subsidiary categories around the core category by means of the paradigm as laid out in the story line.
3. The third involves relating categories at the dimensional level.

4. The fourth step entails validating those propositions against the data.
5. The final step consists of filling in categories that may need further refinement and / or development.

Development of the Story line and relating the Categories

The findings gave us a basic insight into the connections between categories. By explicating these connections we created a story which helped us with the further development of our insights. The story describes one salient category which will be the central phenomenon around which all the other categories are integrated. This category is motivation and serves as the core category. Our story therefore, is:

We saw that in the selected articles of the professional HR journals multiple motivations were used for deploying a HR SSC. Still the motivation used to deploy one could differ. We will acclaim that this has a distinct impact on the anticipated risks and eventual perceived success. And thus, motivation will be our core category. In addition to this, anticipated risks influence the desired form of the HR SSC. Eventually the different focus on anticipated risks and the chosen form will result in certain reported impacts. These impacts can be both positive and negative, and are thus describing the consequences of the HR SSC. Also the phase of implementation will affect the vigor of the reported impacts. The eventual impacts will lead to a different assessment of the HR SSC. This perceived success/failure will be expressed in the articles.

It should be notified that the basis of the propositions in the story were the interpretations that were given to the findings. Now each proposition we made in the story will be explained to come to a conceptualization.

Proposition 1: Motivation Influenced the Anticipated Risks

Due to the large quantity of articles mentioning motivations, the figures of this category were less strong in the quantitative analysis. Still we saw some distinct connections between different motivations and the risks that were anticipated. This created the notion that the 'trouble' focus of HR SSCs varied when the 'why' question differed.

Proposition 2: Anticipated Risks Influenced the Chosen Form

We notified in the findings chapter that there were a lot of connections between risks and forms chosen. We will argue that the anticipated risks did have a noticeable impact on the desired form of a HR SSC.

Proposition 3: Anticipated Risks Influenced the Eventual Impacts

Without knowing what different actions were undertaken when certain risks were perceived, we could see a connection between the risks perceived and the eventual impacts. Because the number of articles mentioning risks and impacts were little, some connections between these properties could be disfigured.

Proposition 4: Implementation Phase Influenced the Eventual Impacts

Although there was only a causal connection between HR SSCs in the 'Introduction' / 'In use' phase and the impact category, we saw that figures between these properties differ. We saw that HR SSCs in the 'Introduction' phase had less strong figures on the impacts properties then 'In Use' HR SSCs. Impacts could thus be influenced by chronological developments.

Proposition 5: Impacts Influenced the Perceived Success

The subjective nature of the category 'Success' made that the researcher was, among other factors, influenced by positive statements about HR SSCs. The impact category consisted out of properties with mostly positive connotations. Hence, this proposition will state that the mentioning of impacts had a distinct influence on the perceived success of the HR SSC(s).

Proposition 6: Motivation Influenced the Perceived Success

There are a lot of unknown processes affecting the eventual success or failure of a HR SSC. It is argued that a lot of these factors are not included in this research. Yet, the motivation was used as the core category of our analyses and it was acclaimed that it could be used as a predictor for the success of a HR SSC. This proposition embraces this thought and states that the motivation could be the prime predictor of perceiving HR SSC success.

The propositions laid out the conceptualization. The propositions that we made were validated against the data and one proposition had to be dropped.

Our final conceptualization, which is in line with the data, is put in Figure 1 below.

Figure 1. Model of HR SSC

CONCLUSION

In this research we developed a conceptualization around the articles that were selected out of the professional HR journals with the grounded theory method. This conceptualization gave an insight into a multitude of phenomena that surround HR SSCs with the following main conclusions:

- 'Brand development' or 'Service Improvement' motivations for deploying a HR SSC led to more positive impacts and a higher success rate.
- Solely 'Economical' motivations were not enough to achieve added value
- Risks anticipated were a good predictor for eventual impacts
- HR SSCs had more positive impacts as they grew over time

One recommendation is to examine what will actually change when different risks are anticipated. Do divisions change the service level agreements with the HR SSC, does the culture change, or will the people or the form of the HR SSC be heavily influenced? And does it work as a panacea against certain HR SSC troubles when a certain risk is anticipated?

A second recommendation is to research why HR SSCs, which were deployed for economical motives, did not achieve as many positive aspects as HR SSCs which were deployed for different motivations. Could it be that there simply is no money saved? Or do companies with a 'money saving' motivation hollow the budget of a HR SSC out more, so it can also deliver less qualitative high services?

The third and last recommendation will be to research the development of HR SSCs through time. In our research it was perceived that they seemed to have more positive impacts when time passed by. The question can be raised if this is truly the case. Could it be that it is just perceived because people needed time to adapt to it? Or does the quality really increase over time?

The data in the concept matrix was subject to debate since no inter-rater was used to control if the phenomena witnessed were indeed present in the articles or an error of judgment from the reader. Errors of measurement thus were likely present. Also an impact that was perceived in one article as successful could be perceived as negative in the other due to dependence on the author's wit.

REFERENCES

Albertson, D. D. (1999). Life support. *Employee benefit news, 13*(14), 34.

Bergeron, B. (2003). *Essentials of Shared Services.* Hoboken, NJ: Wiley

Boerman, P. (2007). Dit gaan we aanpakken! *IntermediairPW ,3*(4).

Burke, R. J. (2006). The changing nature of work and organizations: Implications for human resource management. *Human resource management review, 16*(2), 86-94.

Burke, R. J., & Cooper, C. L. (2005). *Reinventing human resources management: Challenges and new directions.* London, Routledge.

Burke, R. J., & Cooper, C. L. (2006). *The Human Resources Revolution: Why putting people first matters.* Amsterdam: Elsevier.

Cooke, F. L. (2006). Modeling an HR Shared Services Center: Experience of an MNC in the United Kingdom. *Human resource management, 45*(2), 211-227.

Deadrick, D. L. D., & Gibson, P. A. P. (2007). An examination of the research–practice gap in HR: Comparing topics of interest to HR academics and HR professionals. *Human resource management review, 17*(2), 131.

Dipboye, R. L. (2005). How I stopped worrying and learned to appreciate the gaps between academic HRM and practice. In R. J. Burke & C. L. Cooper (Eds.), *Reinventing Human Resource Management: Challenges and New Directions.* London: Routledge.

Dulebohn, J. H., Ferris, G. R., et al. (1995). The History and Evolution of Human Resource Management. *Handbook of Human Resource Management.* Cambridge, Blackwell Publishers.

Farndale, E., & Paauwe, J. (2006). HR Shared Service Centres in the Netherlands: Restructuring the HR Function. *First European Academic Workshop on e-HRM*, Enschede.

Flynn, G. G. (2000). Out of the Red, Into the Blue. *Workforce, 79*(3), 50.

FraseBlunt, M. M. (2004). Keeping HR on the Inside. *HR Magazine, 49*(10), 57.

Griffiths, J. J. (2007). Shared services can 'drive NHS reform. *People management, 13*(3), 11.

Griffiths, J. J. (2008). Shared services works for Scottish government. *People management, 14*(4), 13.

Hax, A. C., & Majluf, N. S. (1981). Organizational Design: A Survey and an Approach. *Operations Research, 29*(3), 417-447.

Hays, S. S. (1999). Newcourt's Call Center Streamlines HR Processes. *Workforce, 78*(6), 126.

HR focus (2007a). How Outsourcing & Shared Services Can Help You Now. *HR focus, 84*(7), 1.

HR focus (2007c). How to Maximize Your Return on Outsourcing & Shared Services. *HR focus, 84*(4), S2.

IntermediairPW (2005). Shared services veranderen de grondwet van je bedrijf'. *IntermediairPW,* 1(18).

IntermediairPW (2006). SSC maakt hrm niet per se strategischer. *IntermediairPW, 2*(15).

Janssen, M., & Joha, A. (2006). Motives for establishing Shared Service Centers in Public Administrations. *International Journal of Information Management, 26,* 102-115.

Manocha, R. R. (2006a). Front-line services. *People management, 12*(6), 16.

Manocha, R. R. (2006b). MoD shares HR operations. *People management, 12*(5), 10.

Martinez, M. M. N. (2002). Recruiting Here and There. *HR Magazine, 47*(9), 95.

Orlikowski, W. J. (1993). CASE Tools as Organizational Change: Investigating Incremental and Radical Changes in Systems Development. *Management Information Systems Quarterly, 17*(3), 309-340.

Paradiso, J. J. (1999). Harnessing your benefits knowledge. *Employee benefit news, 13*(2), 21.

PeopleManagement (2006c). NHS shows it shares. *People management , 12*(20), 10.

PeopleManagement (2007b). In the hot seat. *People management, 13*(13), 28.

Phillips, L. L. (2007a). HR centres could help SMEs to recruit long-term jobless people. *People management, 13*(21), 13.

Quinn, B., Cooke, R. et al. (2000). *Shared services: mining for corporate gold.* Harlow, Pearson Education Limited.

Quint (2004). Sharing Shared Services: *Onderzoek naar ontwikkelingen in de Nederlandse markt. Amsterdam,* The Quint Wellington Redwood Group.

Saunders, M., Lewis, P. et al. (2007). *Research Methods for Business Students.* Harlow, Financial Times/Prentice Hall.

Scott, A. A. (2006). Councils unite to cut costs. *People management, 12*(24), 13.

Strauss, A., & Corbin, J. (1990). *Basics of Qualitative Research*. Newbury Park, SAGE Publications.

Strikwerda, J. (2007). *Shared Service Centers; Van kostenbesparing naar waardecreatie*. Assen, Koninklijke Van Gorcum.

Ulrich, D. (1995). Shared Services: From Vogue to Value. *Human resource planning, 18*(3), 12.

Ulrich, D. (1997). *Human Resource Champions*. Boston, Harvard Business School Press.

Van Putten, L. (2008). KPN sluit zich aan. *IntermediairPW , 4*(4).

Ware, J. (2005, 22 August 2005). *The changing nature of work: Basics*. Retrieved 17 June, 2008.

Willcocks, L., Lacity, M., & Cullen, S. (2006). Information Technology Sourcing: fifteen years of learning. In: R. Mansell, et al (Eds.), *Handbook on Information and Communication Technologies*, Oxford Press.

Wright, P., Dyer, L., et al. (1999). What's Next? Key Findings from the 1999 State-of-the-Art & Practice Study. *Human resource planning, 22*(4), 12.

KEY TERMS

Form Chosen: is the factual or planned set-up of an HR SSC within an organization

HR SSC: is a result responsible unit, internally positioned, that works on the basis of agreements for organizational departments on a client-contractor basis (adapted from Jansen and Joha, 2006)

Impact on HR: is the reported consequences/outcomes within an organization when an HR SSC was deployed

Implementation Phase: of HR SSC is the level of development of the HR SSC(s)

Motivation: is the motives used to choose for adopting the SSC form for HR

Risk: is the anticipated troubles while or before adopting an HR SSC

Success of HR SSC: is the perceived attitude towards HR SSCs

APPENDIX A: ARTICLE REFERENCES

Albertson, D. D. (1999). Life support. *Employee benefit news*, 13(14), 34.

Albertson, D. D. (2000). Outsourcing shows limited impact for strategic HR. *Employee benefit news* 14(10), 70.

Arkin, A. A. (2007).Street Smart. *People management*, 13(7), 24.

Bakker, P. (2005). Hoofden P&O in de prijzen. *IntermediairPW*, 1(15).

Bakker, P., & Bosma, M. (2005). Afscheid van de administratie. *IntermediairPW*, 1(15).

Boerman, P. (2007). Dit gaan we aanpakken! *IntermediairPW*, 3(4).

Bosma, M. (2005). We zitten op de goede weg. *IntermediairPW*, 1(8).

Bosma, M. (2006). 10 redenen tegen een shared services center. *IntermediairPW*, 2(18).

Brockett, J. J. (2006a). Outsourcing deal could hit HR. *People management*, 12(23), 10.

Brockett, J. J. (2006b). London bodies plan shared services. *People management*, 12(11), 10.

Chubb, L. L. (2008). Kier division constracts an HR team that's fit for future growth. *People management*, 14(4), 13.

Doke, D. D. (2003). HR Helps Make the Call on Overseas Centers. *HRMagazine*, 48(7), 74.

Flynn, G. G. (2000). Out of the Red, Into the Blue. *Workforce*, 79(3), 50.

FraseBlunt, M. M. (2004). Keeping HR on the Inside. *HRMagazine*, 49(10), 57.

Galante, S. P. S. (1987). Frost Inc. Technological Renewal and Human Resource Management: A Case Study. *Human resource planning*, 10(1), 57.

Geleijnse, A. (2007). Beetje voor beetje is beter. *IntermediairPW*, 3(15).

Geleijnse, A. (2008). Quality time voor p&o. *IntermediairPW*, 4(4).

Grauman, K. K. & Paul, E. E. (2005). Top 10 mistakes when outsourcing benefits. *Employee benefit news*, 19(8), 36.

Griffiths, J. J. (2007). Shared services can 'drive NHS reform. *People management,* 13(*3*), 11.

Griffiths, J. J. (2008). Shared services works for Scottish government. *People management*, 14(*4*), 13.

Hays, S. S. (1999). Newcourt's Call Center Streamlines HR Processes. *Workforce,* 78(*6*), 126.

HRfocus (2000). The Number of Companies That Now Use the Web for HR Surges. *HR focus,* 77(*11*), 8.

HRfocus (2007a). How Outsourcing & Shared Services Can Help You Now. *HR focus,* 84(7), 1.

HRfocus (2007b). Outsourcing and Shared Services Star in Cost Savings, Expertise, and More Time for Strategic HR. *HR focus,* 84(*4*), S1.

HRfocus (2007c). How to Maximize Your Return on Outsourcing & Shared Services. *HR focus* , 84(*4*), S2.

IntermediairPW (2005). Shared services veranderen de grondwet van je bedrijf. *IntermediairPW,* 1(*18*).

IntermediairPW (2006). SSC maakt hrm niet per se strategischer. *IntermediairPW,* 2(15).

Keith, D. D. and R. R. Hirschfield (1996). The benefits of sharing. *HR focus,* 73(*9*), 15.

Killian, M. M. (2001). Shared service approach requires ongoing commitment. *Employee benefit news,* 15(*6*), 64.

Krynski, J. J. (2001). Seven steps to right a capsized outsourcing relationship. *Employee benefit news,* 15(9), 27.

Langendijk, S. (2006). E-hrm systemen zijn nu definitief hot. *IntermediairPW,* 2(*7*).

Leclerc, L. L. (1997). A cost-effective combo: Reengineering plus 'plain vanilla'. *HR Magazine,* 42(*12*), 33.

Lee, K. K. (2004). Call center enrollment can still provide value. *Employee benefit news,* 18(*4*), 14.

Manocha, R. R. (2006a). Front-line services. *People management,* 12(*6*),16.

Manocha, R. R. (2006b). MoD shares HR operations. *People management,* 12(*5*), 10.

Marquez, J. J. (2005). Call centers find savings begin at home. *Workforce Management,* 84(*13*), 6.

Marquez, J. J. (2006). Eastern Europe attracting top HRO providers. *Workforce Management,* 85(*6*), 11.

Marquez, J. J. (2007). Arinso's HRO Ambition. *Workforce Management,* 86(*1*), 1.

Martinez, M. M. N. (2002). Recruiting Here and There. *HR Magazine* , 47(*9*), 95.

Mathys, N. J. N., & Burack, E. H. E. (1993). Strategic Downsizing: Human Resource Planning Approaches. *Human resource planning,* 16(*1*), 71.

Miller, S. S. (2008). Pick and Choose What Is Outsourced. *HR Magazine,* 53(2), 28.

Munniksma, L. L. (2005). Career Matchmakers. *HR Magazine,* 50(2), 93.

Palmieri, F. F. (2007). Assessing the risks and savings of electronic transmissions. *Employee benefit news,* 21(*9*), 56.

Paradiso, J. J. (1999). Harnessing your benefits knowledge. *Employee benefit news,* 13(*2*), 21.

PeopleManagement (2006a). Trust moves to shared services. *People management,* 12(*24*), 12.

PeopleManagement (2006b). People & posts.. *People management.* 12(*22*), 18.

PeopleManagement (2006c). NHS shows it shares. *People management.* 12(*20*), 10.

PeopleManagement (2006d). Councils join forces. *People management,* 12(*17*), 13.

PeopleManagement (2006e). Shared services save RBS £11m. *People management,* 12(*5*), 13.

PeopleManagement (2006f). Unilever grants £1bn contract. *People management,* 12(*12*), 10.

PeopleManagement (2006g). Line manager relationships 'suffering'. *People management,* 12(*11*), 14.

PeopleManagement (2007a). People & posts. *People management*, 13(*14*), 52.

PeopleManagement (2007b). In the hot seat. *People management,* 13(*13*), 28.

PeopleManagement (2008). News in brief. *People management, 14(3), 11.*

Phillips, L. L. (2007a). HR centres could help SMEs to recruit long-term jobless people. *People management, 13(21),* 13.

Phillips, L. L. (2007b). MoD's HR shake-up 'will save £300m.' *People management ,*13(*15*), 14.

Pickard, J. J. (2006). Conflicting schedule. *People management,* 12(*5*), 14.

Quinn, R. D. R. (2000). At the water's edge. *Employee benefit news*, 14(*13*), 35.

Reilly, P. P. (2007). Facing up to the facts. *People management*, 13(*19*), 42.

Rison, R. P. R., & Tower, J. J. (2005). How to Reduce the Cost of HR and Continue to Provide Value. *Human resource planning*, 28(*1*), 14.

Robinson, V. V. (2006). Three legs good? *People management*, 12(*21*), 62.

Schoeff, M. (2006a). Guatemala sees rapid growth in call centers. *Workforce Management*, 85(*23*),10.

Schoeff, M. (2006b). Postal Service streamlining HR operations. *Workforce Management*, 85(*16*), 8.

Schoemakers, I. (2005). ABN Amro ontslaat 200 p&o'ers. *IntermediairPW*, 1(*1*).

Scott, A. A. (2006). Councils unite to cut costs. *People management*, 12(*24*), 13.

Scott, A. A. (2007). Sainsbury's opens £12m shared services centre. *People management*, 13(*16*), 10.

Smith, M. E. M. (1999). Is a benefits call center the right call for your company? *Employee benefit news*, 13(*14*), 23.

Stopper, W. G. W. (1998). Reengineering Levi Strauss & Co.: We Met the Enemy and It Was Us. *Human resource planning*, 21(*3*), 14.

Tyler, K. K. (2000). Recruiting Through Religious Organizations. *HRMagazine*, 45(*9*), 131.

Ulrich, D. D. (1995). Shared Services: From Vogue to Value. *Human resource planning*, 18(*3*), 12.

Van Putten, L. (2008). KPN sluit zich aan. *IntermediairPW*, 4(*4*).

Verheijen, T. (2006). Succesvol generatiemanagement. *IntermediairPW*, 2(*3*).

Walker, J. W. J. (1998). Are We Using the Right Human Resource Measures? *Human resource planning*, 21(*2*), 7.

Weidema, N. (2007). Geen tijd voor Calimero. *IntermediairPW*, 3(*12*).

Weidema, N. (2008a). Een kaasschaaf met een heel dik mes. *IntermediairPW*, 4(*1*).

Weidema, N. (2008b). Vacature wordt merk-event. *IntermediairPW*, 4(8).

WorkforceManagement (2006). New in the c-suite. *Workforce Management, 85(17), 6.*

Compilation of References

Abna, T. (2003). Learning by Telling: Storytelling Workshops in an Organizational Learning Intervention. *Management Learning, 34*(2), 221-240.

Abrahamson, E. (1996). Management Fashion. *Academy of Management Review, 16*, 254-285.

Abrahamson, E. (1997). The Emergence and Prevalence of Employee-Management Rhetoric: The Effect of Long Waves, Labour Unions and Turnover. *Academy of Management Journal, 40*, 491-533.

Abrahamson, E., & Fairchild, G. (1999). Management Fashion. Lifecycles, Triggers, and Collective Learning Processes. *Administrative Science Quarterly, 44*, 708-740.

Adam, H., & Berg, R. van den (2001). *E-HRM, inspelen op veranderende organisaties en medewerkers.* Schoonhoven: Academic service.

Advies Overheid.nl (2005). Webrichtlijnen Overheid.nl 2005, Richtlijnen voor de toegankelijkheid en duurzaamheid van overheidswebsites. Retrieved from http://webrichtlijnen.overheid.nl/webrichtlijnen-1.1.pdf

Advies Overheid.nl (2006). Overheid.nl Monitor, Prestaties van de e-overheid gemeten. Retrieved from http://www.minbzk.nl/contents/pages/54678/overheid.nl_monitor_2005.pdf

Agarwal, R., & Ferratt, T. W. (1998). Recruiting, Retaining, and Developing IT Professionals: An Empirically Derived Taxonomy of Human Resource Practices. In R. Agarwal (Ed.), *Proceedings of the 1998 ACM SIGCPRL-SIGMIS Conference* (pp. 292-302). New York, NY: Association for Computing Machinery.

Agarwal, R., & Ferratt, T. W. (2001). Crafting an HR strategy to meet the need for IT workers. *Communications of the ACM, 44*(7), 58-64.

Agarwal, R., & Ferratt, T.W. (2002). Enduring Practices for Managing Information Technology Professionals. *Communications of the ACM, 5*(9), 73-79.

Agarwal, R., Echambadi, R., Franco, A. M., & Sarkar, M. B. (2004). Knowledge Transfer through Inheritage: Spinout Generation, Development, and Survival. *Academy of Management Journal, 47*, 501-522.

Agile Alliance (1999) Retrieved September 1, 2008, from, http://www.agilealliance.com/

Agre, P. (1998). Building an Internet Culture. *Telematics and Informatics, 15*, 231-234.

Akrich, M. (1998). Users and Players of Innovation. *Education permanente, 134*, 79-89.

Albert, G. (1998). *Betriebliche Personalwirtschaft*. Kiehl: Ludwigshafen.

Albertson, D. D. (1999). Life support. *Employee benefit news, 13*(14), 34.

Alchian, A. A., & Demsetz, H. (1972). Production, Information Costs and Economic Organization. *American Economic Review, 62*(5),777-795.

Allen, C. (1999). Internet Anonymity in Contexts. *Information Society, 15*, 145-147.

Al-Sehali, Saud, H. (2000). *The Factors that Affect the Implementation of Enterprise Resource Planning (ERP) in the International Arab Gulf States and United States Companies with Special Emphasis on SAP Software*. D.I.T. dissertation, University of Northern Iowa, Iowa.

AMACOM, Div American Mgmt.

Ambler, T., & Barrow, S. (1996). The Employer Brand. *The Journal of Brand Management, 4*(3), 85-206.

Amons, P., & Howard, D. (2004). Buy it, Build it, or Have it Built? *Catalog Age, 21*(3), 50.

Anderson, M. C., Banker, R. D., & Ravindran, S. (2003). The new productivity paradox. *Communications of the ACM, 46*(3), 91-94.

Anderson, N. (2003). Applicant and recruiter reactions to new technology in selection: a critical review and agenda for future research. *International Journal of Selection and Assessment, 11*, 121-136.

Anonymous (2001). Headhunters hit by slowdown. *Country Monitor, 9*, (22), 5.

Anonymous (2005). Internet penetration mainly a coastal thing. *Chain Store Age, 79*(10), 80.

Anonymous (2007). The coming crisis in employee turnover. *Growth Strategies, 1004*, 1-3.

Anthony, J. (2003). Adaptive Interfaces and Agents. In J. Jacko & A. Sears (Eds.), *Human-computer Interaction Handbook* (pp. 305-330). Mahwah, NJ: Erlbaum.

Anthony, R., & Govindarajan (1998), *Management control*, Tata Mc Graw Hill Publishing.

Aoki, M, (1986). Horizontal versus Vertical information structures of the firm, *American Economic Review, 76*(5), September, 971-983.

Apgar, M. (1998). The alternative workplace: changing where and how people work. *Harvard Business Review*, May-June, 121-136.

Argiris, C. P. (1960). *Understanding Organisational Behaviour*. Homewood, IL: Dorsey Press.

Arthur, J. B. (1994). Effects of Human Resource Systems on Manufacturing Performance and Turnover. *Academy of Management Newspaper, 37*(3), 670-687.

Ashton, C. (2001). *eHR Transforming the HR function*: Business Intelligence.

Atkinson, J., & Meager, N. (1994). Running to stand still: the small firm in the labour market. In J. Atkinson & D. Storey (Eds.), *Employment, the Small Firm and the Labour Market*. London: Routledge.

Awasty, R., & Gupta, R. (2004). An Indo-Japanese MNC operating in India. *South Asian Journal of Management, 11*(3), 94-113.

Backhaus, K. B. (2004). An exploration of corporate recruitment descriptions on monster.com. *Journal of Business Communication, 41*(2), 115-136.

Bae, J., Chen, S., & Lawler, J. (1998). Variations in human resource management in Asian countries: MNC home-country and host-country effects. *International Journal of Human Resource Management, 9*(4), 653–670.

Bagchi, K., Hart, P., & Peterson, M. (2004). National culture and information technology product adoption. *Journal of Global Information Technology Management, 7*(4), 29-46.

Baird, L. (1986). *Managing performance*. New York, John Wiley.

Bala, V., & Goyal, S. (1998). Learning from Neighbours. *Review of Economic Studies, 65*, 595-621.

Balkin, D. B., & Logan, J. W. (1988). Reward policies that support entrepreneurship. *Compensation and Benefits Review*, (pp. 18 -25).

Ball, K. S. (2001). The use of human resource information systems: a survey. *Personnel Review, 30*(6), 677-693.

Banks, M. C., Bures, A. L., & Champion, D. L. (1987). Decision making factors in small business: Training and development. *Journal of Small Business Management, 25*(1), 19-25.

Barber, A. E. (1998). *Recruiting employees.* Thousand Oaks, CA: Sage Publications.

Bardini, T., & Horvath, A.T. (1995). The social construction of personal computer use. *Journal of communication, 45*(3), summer, 40-65.

Barki, H., & Hartwick, J. (1989). Rethinking the Concept of User Involvement. *Rethinking the Concept of User Involvement , 13*(1), 53-63.

Barley, S., & Kunda, G. (1992). Design and Devotion: Surges of Rational and Normative Ideologies of Control in Managerial Discourse. *Administrative Science Quarterly, 37*, 363-399.

Barney, J. B. (1991). Firm Resources and substantial competitive advantage. *Journal of Management, 17*(1), 99-120.

Barney, J. B., & Wright, P. M. (1998). On becoming a strategic partner: The role of human resources in gaining competitive advantage. *Human Resource Management, 37*(1), 31-46.

Baron, J. N., & Hannan, M. T. (2002). Organizational blueprints for success in high-tech start-ups: Lessons from the Stanford project on emerging companies. *California Management Review, 44*(3), 8-36.

Bartel, A. P., & Lichtenberg, F. R. (1987). The Comparative Advantage of Educated Workers in Implementing New Technology. *Review of Economics and Statistics, 69*, 1-11.

Bartel, A. P., & Lichtenberg, F. R. (1990). The Impact of Age of Technology on Employee Wages. *Economics of Innovation and New Technology, 1,* 1-17.

Barthe, S. (2001). Technologies of the Web: a possible answer to the new challenges of the human resources management. *Revue of Human Resources management, 41*, 5-20.

Bartram, D. (2000). Internet recruitment and selection: Kissing frogs to find princes. *International Journal of Selection and Assessment, 8*(4), 261-274.

Bartunek, J. M., & Moch, M. (1987). First order, second order and third order change and organization development interventions: A cognitive approach. *Journal of Applied Behavioural Science, 23*(4), 483-500.

Bauer, T. N., Truxillo, D. M., Paronto, M. E., Weekley, J. A., & Campion, M. A. (2004). Applicant reactions to different selection technology: Face-to-face, interactive voice response, and computer-assisted telephone screening interviews. *International Journal of Selection and Assessment, 12*, 135-148.

Bawden, D., Holtham, C., & Courtney, N. (1999). Perspectives on information overload. *Aslib Proceedings, 51*(8), 249-255.

Beardsly, S., Johnson, B., & Manyika, J. (2006). Competitive advantage from better interactions. *The McKinsey Quarterly, 2*, 3-9.

Bearman, D., & Trant, J. (2004). *Museums and the Web 2004, Proceedings.* Toronto: Archives & Museum Informatics. Retrieved from http://www.archimuse.com/mw2004/papers/bowen/bowen.html

Beaumont, J. R., Kinnie, N. J., Arthurs, A. J., & Weatherall, C. B. (1992). *Information technology and personnel management: issues and educational implications.* Unpublished paper, School of Management, University of Bath:

Beck, K. (1999). *Extreme Programming: Embrace the Change.* USA: Addison-Wesley Professional.

Becker, B. E., Huselid, M. A., Pinkus, P. S., & Spratt, M. F. (1997). HR as a Source of Shareholder Value: Research and Recommendations. *Human Resource Management, 36(1)*, 39-47.

Becker, G. (1964) *Human Capital: a Theoretical and Empirical Analysis, with Special Reference to Education.* New York: Columbia University Press (for NBER).

Beer, M., Spector, B., Lawrance, P., Mills, Q., & Walton, R. (1984). *Managing Human Assets.* New York: The Free Press.

Bell,B. S., Sae-Won Lee, & Yeung, S. K. (2006). The impact of e-HR on professional competence in HRM: implications for the development of HR professionals. *Human Resource Management,* (Fall), 295-308.

Benbasat, I., Goldstein, D. K., & Mead, M. (1987). The case research strategy in Studies of information systems. *MIS Quarterly September*, (pp. 369 – 386).

Bergeron, B. (2003). *Essentials of Shared Services.* Hoboken, NJ: Wiley

Berghel, H. (1997). Cyberspace 2000: Dealing with Information Overload. *Communications of the ACM, 40*(2), 19-24.

Beyer, H., & Holtzblatt, K. (1999). Contextual design. *Interactions , 6*(1), 32-42.

Beyer, H., & Holzblatt K. (1998). *Contextual Design: Defining Customer-Centred Systems.* New York: Morgan Kaufmann.

Bhagat, R. S., Kedia, B. L., Harveston, P. D., & Triandis, H. C. (2002). Cultural Variations in the Cross-Border Transfer of Organizational Knowledge: An Integrative Framework. *Academy of Management Review, 27*, 204-221.

Bhattacherjee, A. (1998). Management of emerging technologies experiences and lessons learned at US West. *Information and Management, 33*(5), 263-272.

Bietry, F. (2002). *e-GRH, entre promesses et interrogations.* Col. « Management et Société », Colombelles, Paris, EMS.

Bietry, F. (2005). Les syndicats à l'heure des réseaux. *Revue Française de Gestion, 31*(157), 79-102.

Bijker, W. B., & Law, J. (Ed.). (1992). *Shaping Technology/Building Society: studies in socio-technical change.* Cambridge/MA, London: MIT Press.

Bijker, W. E. (1987). The social construction of Bakelite: Toward a Theory of Invention. In W. E. Bijker, T. Hughes, & T. Pinch (Eds.), *The Social Construction of Technological Systems: New Directions in the Sociology and History of Technology.* Cambridge MA/London: MIT Press.

Bingi, P., Sharma, M. K., & Godla, J. (1999). Critical Issues Affecting an ERP Implementation. *Information Systems Management, 16*(3), 7-14.

Bingley, P., & Westergaard-Nielsen, N. (2003). Returns to tenure, firm-specific human capital and worker heterogeneity International. *Journal of Manpower, 24*(7), 774-788.

Biocca, F., Harms, C., & Burgoon, J. K. (2003). Toward a More Robust Theory and Measure of Social Presence: Review and Suggested Criteria. *Presence, 12*(5), 456–480.

Björkman, I., & Lu, Y. (2001). Institutionalization and bargaining power explanations of HRM practices in international joint ventures—the case of Chinese-Western joint ventures. *Organization Studies, 22*(3), 491–512.

Blackburn, J., Scudder, G., & Van Wassenhove, L. N. (2000). Concurrent Software Development. *Communications of the ACM , 43*(11), 200-214.

Blau, P. M. (1964). *Exchange and power in social life.* New York: John Wiley & Sons.

Blomberg, J., Giacomi, J., Mosher, A., & Swenton-Hall, P. (1993). Ethnographic field methods and their relation to design. In D. Schuler, & A. Namioka (Eds.), *Participatory Design: Principles and Practices* (pp. 123-155). Hillsdale: Lawrence Erlbaum.

Blomquist, Å., & Arvola, M. (2002). Personas in action: ethnography in an interaction design team. *Proceedings of the second Nordic conference on Human-computer interaction* (pp. 197 - 200). ACM.

Boerman, P. (2007). Dit gaan we aanpakken! *IntermediairPW ,3*(4).

Bolman, L. G., & Deal, T. E. (1991). *Reframing Organizations: Artistry, Choice and Leadership.* San Francisco, California: Jossey-Bass.

Bondarouk, T. V. (2006). Action-oriented group learning in the implementation of information technologies: results from three case studies. *European Journal of Information Systems, 15,* 42-53.

Bondarouk, T. V., & Ruël, H. J. M. (2006). E-HRM effectiveness at a Dutch Ministry: Results from discursive analysis. In: *Proceedings of the 1st European Academic Workshop on E-HRM,* Enschede (Netherlands).

Bontis, N. (1998). Intellectual Capital: an exploratory study that develops measures and models. *Management Decision, 36(2),* 63-76.

Borland. (2006). Retrieved April 25, 2007, from http://www.borland.com/resources/en/pdf/solutions/rdm_whitepaper.pdf

Boroughs, A., Palmer, L., & Hunter, I. (2008). *HR Transformation Technology: Delivering Systems to Support the New HR Model.* Aldershot: Gower.

Bos, M. van der, & Heijden, H. van der (2004). E-HRM. In F. Kluytmans (Eds.), *Leerboek personeelsmanagement.* Groningen: Wolters-Nordhoff.

Boselie, P., Paauwe, J., & Jansen, P. (2001). Human Resource Management and performance; lessons from the Netherlands. *The International Journal of Human Resource Management, 12*(7), 1107-1125.

Bottazzo, V. (2005). Intranet: A Medium of internal Communication and Training. *Information Services and Use, 25,* 77-85.

Boudreau, J. W. (1996). Human resource information system: exploiting the full potential. *Center for Advanced Human resource Studies CAHRS,* (pp. 96-02), Cornell University, USA.

Bowen, D. E., & Ostroff, C. (2004). Understanding HRM-Firm Performance linkages: The role of the "strength" of the HRM system. *Academy of Management Review, 29*(2), 203 – 221.

Bowers, J. (1995). Making it work. A field study of a CSCW Network. *The Information Society, 11,* 189-207.

Boxall, P., & Purcell, J. (2003). *Strategy and Human Resource Management.* London: Palgrave Macmillan.

Boyd, D., & Ellison, N. B. (2007). Social network sites: Definition, history, and scholarship. *Journal of Computer-Mediated Communication, 13*(1), article 11.

Brancheau, J. C., Janz, B. D., & Wetherbe, J. C. (1996). Key issues in information systems management. 1994-95 SIM Delphi results. *MIS Quarterly, 20*(2), 225-242.

Breaugh, J. A., & Starke, M. (2000). Research on Employee Recruitment: So Many Studies, So Many Remaining Question. *Journal of Management, 26*(3), 405-434.

Bresnahan, T., Brynjolfsson, E., & Hitt, L. (2000). IT, Workplace Organization and the Demand for Skilled Labor: A Firm-level Analysis, Mimeo, MIT, Stanford and Wharton

Brewster, C., Sparrow, P., & Harris, H. (2005). Towards a new model of globalizing HRM. *International Journal of Human Resource Management, 16*(6), 949–970.

Brewster, S. A. (1997). Using non-speech sound to overcome information overload. *Displays, 17*(3), 179-189.

Brèzillon, P., & Pomerol, J.-Ch. (2001). About Some Relationships between Knowledge and Context. In V. Akman, P. Bouquet, R.H. Thomason & R. A.Young (Eds.), *3rd International and Interdisciplinary Conference on Modeling and Using Context* (pp. 461-464). Springer LNCS(LNAI) 2116.

Brice, T. S., & Waung, M. (2002). Web Site Recruitment Characteristics: America's Best Versus America's Biggest. *Advanced Management Journal, 67,* 4-8.

Broderick R. and Boudreau, J. W. (1992). Human Resource Management, Information Technology, and the Competitive Edge. *Academy of Management Executive, 6*(2), 7-17.

Brodt, T. L., & Venburg, M. R. (2007). Managing Mobile Work—Insights from European Practice. *New Technology, Work and Employment, 22*(1), 52-65.

Brooks, F. (1995). *The Mythical Man-Month: Essays on Software Engineering, Anniversary Edition.* Addison-Wesley Professional.

Brown, D. (1996). The challenges of user-based design in a medical equipment market. In D. Wixon, & J. Ramey (Ed.), *Field Methods Casebook for Software Design* (pp. 157-176). New York: Wiley.

Brown, J. S., & Duguid, P. (2000). *The Social Life of Information.* Boston: Harvard Business School Press.

Brown, S. A., Massey, A. P., Montoya-Weiss, M. M., & Burkman, J. R. (2002). Do I really have to? User acceptance of mandated technology. *European Journal of Information Systems, 11*, 283-295.

Brun-Cottan F., & Wall P. (1995). Using Video to Re-Present the User. *Communication of the ACM, 38*(5), 61-71.

Brynjolfsson, E., & Mendelson, H. (1993). Information systems and the organization of modern enterprise. *Journal of Organizational Computing, 3*(3), 245-255

Buchanan, R. (2007). Understanding your users: A practical guide to user requirements: Methods, tools, and techniques. *Design Issues, 23*(1), 92-92.

Buckhout, S., Frey, E., & Nemec, J. Jr (1999). Making ERP Succeed: Turning Fear into Promise. *IEEE Engineering Management* Review, (pp. 116-23).

Budhwar, P., & Baruch, Y. (2003). Career Management practices in India: An empirical study. *International Journal of Manpower, 24*(6), 699-721.

Burgundian, A. (1996). *To define the performance: a simple matter of vocabulary?* In A.–M. Fericelli & B. Sire (Eds.), *Performances and human resources* (pp. 18-31). Paris, Economica.

Burke, R. J. (2006). The changing nature of work and organizations: Implications for human resource management. *Human resource management review, 16*(2), 86-94.

Burke, R. J., & Cooper, C. L. (2005). *Reinventing human resources management: Challenges and new directions.* London, Routledge.

Burke, R. J., & Cooper, C. L. (2006). *The Human Resources Revolution: Why putting people first matters.* Amsterdam: Elsevier.

Burt, R. S. (1992). *Structural holes: The social structure of competition.* Cambridge, MA: Harvard University Press.

Bussler, L., & Davis, E. (2001). Information Systems: The Quiet Revolution. *Human Resource Management Journal of Computer Information Systems, 42,* 17-20.

Butler, M. B. (1996). Getting to know your users: usability roundtables at Lotus Development. *Interaction , 3*(1), 23-30.

Caetano, A., Silva, A., & Tribolet, J. (2004). Separation of concerns in object-oriented business process modeling. *7th International Conference on Information Systems Implementation Modelling,* Rožnov pod Radhoštěm, Czech Republic.

Cairncross, F. (2001). *The death of distance 2.0; how the communications revolution will change our lives.* Harvard Business School Press, Cambridge

Cappelli, P. (2001). Making the most of on line recruiting. *Harvard Business Review, 79*(2), 139-146.

Cardon, D. (1997). Social sciences and machines for cooperation. *Réseaux,* (85), 11-52.

Cardon, M. S., & Stevens, C. E. (2004). Managing human resources in small organizations: what do we know? *Human Resource Management Review, 14*, 295 – 323.

Cardy R. L., & Miller, J. S. (2005). eHR and Performance Management. In: H. G. Gueutal & D. L. Stone (Eds.), *The Brave New World of eHR. Human Resources Management in the Digital Age.* San Francisco: Jossey-Bass.

Carr, N. G. (2003). IT doesn't matter. Harvard Business Review, *81*(5), 41-49.

Carroll, M., Marchington, M., Earnshaw, J., & Taylor, S. (1999). Recruitment in small firms: Processes, methods and problems. *Employee Relations, 21*(3), 236-250.

Cascio, W. F. (2000). Managing a virtual workplace. *The Academy of Management Executive, 14*(3), 81-90.

Cascio, W. F., & Awad, E. M. (1981). *Human resources management: an information systems approach.* Reston (Virg.): Restion publishing company (a Prentice-Hall Company).

Casonato, R., & Harris, K. (2002). *The Knowledge worker Investment Paradox.* Gartner, Inc.

Cassell, C., & Symon, G. (2004). *Essential Guide to Qualitative Methods in Organizational Research.* London: SAGE Publications.

Cedar (2001). Cedar 2001 Human resources Self Service / Portal Survey. Fourth Annual Survey. Baltimore: Cedar.

CedarCrestone. (2006). *CedarCrestone 2006 Human Capital Survey*: Cedar Crestone.

CFE-CGC. (2002). Internet et Intranet dans l'entreprise : un nouvel outil au service de votre action syndicale. *Encadrement Entreprise, 101*(3/4), 2–16.

Chaison, G. (2005). The Dark Side of Information Technology for Unions. *The Journal of Labour and Society,* 8(4), 395–402.

Chan, Y. E. (2002). Why Haven't We Mastered Alignment? The Importance of the Informal Organization Structure. *MIS Quarterly Executive, 1*(2), 97-112.

Chan, Y. E., Huff, S. L., & Copeland, D. G. (1997). Assessing Realized Information Systems Strategy. *The Journal of Strategic Information Systems, 6*(4), 273-298.

Chandler, A. (1962). *Strategy and Structure.* Boston: MIT Press

Charles, J. (2000). Finding a Job on the Web. *Black Enterprise, 30*, 90-95.

Chartered Institute of Personnel Development (2005). People management and technology: progress and potential. London, CIPD.

Chartered Institute of Personnel Development (2006). *Recruitment and Retention 2005*; CIPD, June 2006

Chatman, E. A. (1984). Field research: Methodological themes. *Library and Information Science Research, 6,* 425-38.

Chatzoglou, P. D., & Macaulay, L. A. (1996). Requirements Capture and Analysis: A Survey of Current Practice. *Requirements Engineering, 1*(2), 75-87.

Chaykowski, R. P. (2002). Re-Inventing Production Systems and Industrial Relations: Technology-Driven Transformation in Canadian Metal-Mining Industry. *Journal of Labor Research, 23*(4), 591–610.

Cherry, C., & Macredie, R. D. (1999). The importance of Context in Information System Design: An Assesment of Participatory Design. *Requirements Engineering , 4*(2), 103-114.

Chhokar, J., Brodbeck, F., & House, R. (Eds.). (2007). *Culture and leadership across the world. The GLOBE book of in-depth studies of 25 societies.* Lawrence Erlbaum Associates. Mahwah, New Jersey.

Chin, W., Gopal, A., & Salisbury, W. (1997). Advancing the theory of adaptive structuration: the development of a scale to measure faithfulness of appropriation. *Information Systems Research, 8,* 343-367

Chokkar, J. (2007). India. Diversity and Complexity in Action. In J. Chhokar, F. Brodbeck, & R. House (Eds.), *Culture and Leadership across the World. The GLOBE book of In-depth studies of 25 societies.* Lawrence Erlbaum Associates. Mahwah, New Jersey.

Chu, P., & Sui, W. S. (2001). Coping with the Asian economic crisis: The rightsizing strategies of small- and medium-sized enterprises. *International Journal of Human Resource Management, 12*(5), 845–858.

CIA (2002). *The World Factbook 2001.* Retrieved from http://www.odci.gov/cia/publications/factbook, on 15.07.2002.

Ciborra, C. U. (1997). De Profundis ? Deconstructing the Concept of Strategic Alignment. *Scandinavian Journal of Information Systems, 9*(1), 67-82.

CIPD (2007). *HR and Technology: Impact and Advantages, Research into Practice.* Chartered Institute of Personnel and Development: London

CIPD. (2006). *Technology in HR: How to get the most out of technology in people management.* Wimbledon: CIPD.

Clark, M. S., & Mills, J. (1979). Interpersonal attraction in exchange and communal relationships. *Journal of Personality and Social Psychology, 37,* 12–24.

Clement, A., & Van den Besselaar, P. (1993). A retrospective look at PD projects. *Communications of the ACM, 36*(4), 29-37.

Clemmons, S., & Simon, S. J. (2001). Control and coordination in global ERP configuration, *Business Process Management, 7*(3), 205–215.

CNIL. (2001). *Cybersurveillance des salariés dans l'entreprise.* Paris, CNIL Report.

CNIL. (2002). *Cybersurveillance sur les lieux de travail.* Paris, CNIL Report.

Cober, R. T., Brown, D. J., Levy, P. E., Keeping, L. M., & Cober, A. L. (2003). Organizational websites: Website content and style as determinants of organizational attraction. *International Journal of Selection and Assessment, 11,* 158 – 169.

Cober, R. T., Douglas, J. B., & Levy, P. E. (2004). Form, Content and Function: An evaluative methodology for corporate employment web sites. *Human Resource Management, Summer / Fall, 43*(2/3), 201-218. Wiley Periodicals, Inc.

Cohen, W., & Leventhal, D. A. (1990). Absorptive capacity: A new perspective on learning and innovation. *Administrative Science Quarterly, 35,* 128-152.

Cohendet, P., Dupouët, O., & Créplet, F. (2000). Communities of Practice and Epistemic Communities : A Renewed Approach of Organisational Learning within the Firm. *Actes du Colloque WEHIA,* 16 juin 2000, Université de Marseille.

Collins, H. (2001). *Corporate portals: Revolutionizing information access to increase productivity and drive the bottom line.* New York: AMA-COM.

Collomba, T. (2005). Crise à l'AFL-CIO, Les leçons du syndicalisme états-uniens. *Le Devoir, 7.*

Compeer, N., Smolders, M., & de Kok, J. (2005), *Scale effects in HRM research. A discussion of current HRM research from an SME perspective.* EIM, Zoetermeer, the Netherlands.

Cooke, F. L. (2006). Modeling an HR Shared Services Center: Experience of an MNC in the United Kingdom. *Human resource management, 45*(2), 211-227.

Coufourier, O. (2001). Quand les nouvelles technologies deviennent mouchards. Retrieved, 26 February, from http:www.cfdt.fr/actualite.

Coyle-Shapiro, J. A-M., & Conway, N. (2004). The employment relationship through the lens of social exchange. In J. Coyle-Shapiro, L. Shore, S. Taylor, & L. Tetrick (Eds.), *The employment relationship: Examining psychological and contextual perspectives.* Oxford: Oxford University Press.

Coyle-Shapiro, J. A-M., & Shore, L.M. (2007). The employee–organization relationship: Where do we go from here? *Human Resource Management Review, 17*(2), 166-179.

Cozijnsen, A. J., Vrakking, W. J., & van IJzerloo, M. (2000). Success and failure of 50 innovation projects in Dutch companies. *European Journal of Innovation Management, 3* (3), 150-159.

Craipeau, S. (2001). *L'entreprise commutante, travailler ensemble séparément.* Paris: Hermes Science, Lavoisier.

Cressy, R. (1996). Are Business Start-ups Debt Rationed. *The Economic Journal, 106*(438), 1253-1270.

Creti, A. (2001). Network technologies, communication externalities and total factor productivity. *Structural Change and Economic Dynamics, 12,* 1-28

Cropanzano, R., & Mitchell, M. S. (2005). Social exchange theory: An interdisciplinary review. *Journal of Management, 31,* 874–900.

Curry, J., & Kenney, M. (2006). Digital divide or digital development? The Internet in Mexico. *First Monday, 11*(3), 1-21.

Curry, J., Contreras, O., & Kenney, M. (2001). The Internet and E-Commerce Development in Mexico. Working Paper 144. *The Berkely Roundtable on the International Economy.*

Daft, R. L. (1986). *Organization Theory and Design* (2nd ed.). St. Paul, MN: West.

Daft, R. L., & Lengel, R., (1984). Information richness: a new approach to managerial behaviour and organization design. *Research in Organizational Behaviour,* (6), 191-233.

Daft, R. L., & Lengel, R. (1986). Organisational information requirements, media richness and structural design, *Management Science, 35.*

Daft, R. L., & Lewin, A.Y. (1993). Where are the theories for the new organizational forms? An editorial essay. *Organization Science, 4*(4).

Daft, R. L., & Weick, K. E. (1984). Toward a model of organizations as interpretation systems. *Academy of Management Review, 9*(2), 284-295.

Dahlin, K. B., & Behrens, D. M., (2005).When is an invention really radical? Defining and measuring technological radicalness, *Research Policy, 34,* 717–737.

Dainty, A. R., Raiden, A. B., & Neale, R. H. (2004). Psychological contract expectations of construction project managers. *Engineering, Construction and Architectural Management, 11*(1), 33–44.

Damodaran, L. (1996). User involvement in the systems design process-a practical guide for users. *Behaviour & Information Technology, 15*(6), 363 - 377.

Darses, F. (2004). *Psychological Processes of Collective Problem Resolution Conception: Contribution to Ergonomic Psychology.* Unpublished HDR in Ergonomic Psychology, University of Paris V, France.

Davenport, T. H. (1993). *Process Innovation.* Boston M.A: Harvard Business School Press.

Davenport, T., & Prusak, L. (2000). *Working Knowledge: How Organizations Manage what they Know.* Harvard Business School Press.

Davenport, T.H., & Pearlson, K. (1998). Two cheers for the virtual office, *Sloan Management Review,* Summer, (pp. 51-65).

Davila, A., & Elvira, M. (2005). Culture & Human Resources Management in Latin America in (Ed) *Managing Human Resources in Latin America.* New York: Routledge.

Davis, F. D. (1989). Perceived Usefulness, Perceived Ease of Use, and User Acceptance of Information Technology. *MIS Ouarterly, 13(3),* 319-339.

Davis, F. D., Bagozzi, R. P., & Warshavi, P. R. (1989). User Acceptance of Computer Technology: A Comparison of Two Theoretical Models, *Management Science, 35*(8), 982-1002.

Davis, G. B. (2002). Anytime / Anyplace Computing and the Future of Knowledge Work. *Communications of the ACM, 45*(12), 67-73.

De Chernatony, L., & Dall'Olmo Riley, F. (1998). Defining a 'Brand': Beyond the Literature with experts' Interpretations. *Journal of Marketing Management, 14,* 417-443.

De Jaegher, H., & Di Paolo, E. (2007). Participatory Sensemaking: an enactive approach to social cognition. *Phenomenology and the Cognitive Sciences, 6,* 485-507.

De Kok, J. M. P. (2003). Human Resource Management within Small and Medium-Sized Enterprises, *Tinbergen Institute Research Series, 313.* Amsterdam: Thela Thesis.

Deadrick, D. L. D., & Gibson, P. A. P. (2007). An examination of the research–practice gap in HR: Comparing topics of interest to HR academics and HR professionals. *Human resource management review, 17*(2), 131.

Dean, A., & Kretschmer, M. (2007). Can Ideas Be Capital? Factors of production in the post-industrial economy: a review and critique. *Academy of Management Review, 32*(2), 573-594.

Degani, A., & Wiener, E.L.(1997). Procedures in Complex Systems: The airline cockpit. *IEE Transactions on Systems, Man and Cybernetics-Part A: Systems and Humans, 27*(3), 302-312.

Delaney, J. T., & Huselid, M. A. (1996). The Impact of Human Resource Management Practices on Perceptions of Organizational Performance. *Academy of Management Journal, 39*(4), 949–969.

Delery, J. E., & Doty, D. H. (1996). Modes of theorizing in strategic human resource management: Tests of universalistic, contingency, and configurational performance predictions. *Academy of Management Journal, 39*, 802–835.

DeLone, W. H., & McLean, E. R. (1992). Information system success: The quest for the independent variable. *Information Systems Research , 3*(1), 60-95.

DeLone, W. H., & McLean, E. R. (2003). The DeLone and McLean Model of Information Success: A Ten-Year Update. *Journal of Management Information Systems , 19*(4), 9-30.

Deltour, F. (2004). *Satisfaction, acceptation, impacts: A Multi dimensional and Contextualized Analysis of Individual Intranet Assessment.* Unpublished doctoral dissertation, University of Paris IX, France.

Denning, P. J. (1982). Electronic Junk. *Communications of the ACM, 25*(3), 163-165.

Denzin, N. K. (1978). *The Research Act: Theoretical Introduction to Sociological Methods.* New York: McGraw-Hill.

DeSanctis, G. (1986). Human resource information systems: a current assessment. *MIS Quarterly, 10*, 217-234.

DeSanctis, G., & Monge, P. (1999) Introduction to the special issue: communication processes for virtual organization. *Organization Science, 10*(6).

DeSanctis, G., & Poole, M. S. (1994). Capturing the complexity in advanced technology use: Adaptive structuration theory. *Organization Science, 5*(2), 121-147.

Detchessahar M., & Journé B. (2007). Une approche narrative des outils de gestion. *Revue française de gestion, 174*, 77-92.

Di Paolo, E. (2005). Autopoiesis, Adaptivity, Teleology, Agency. *Phenomenology and the Cognitive Sciences, 4*, 429-452.

Diamond, W. J., & Freeman, R. B. (2002). Will Unionism Prosper in Cyberspace? The Promise of the Internet for Employee Organization. *British Journal of Industrial Relations, 40*(3), 569−596.

Dibiaggio, L. (1998). *Information, connaissance et organisation.* Unpublished doctoral dissertation. University of Nice. France.

DigiD (2008). *Over DigiD.* Retrieved August 2008 from http://www.digid.nl/burger/.

Dignum, V. (2004). *A model for organizational interaction: based on agents, founded in logic.* SIKS Dissertation Series No. 2004-1. Utrecht University, Netherlands.

Dijk, van J. A. G. M. et al. (2005). *Alter Ego: State of the art on user profiling. An overview of the most relevant organisational and behavioural aspects regarding User Profiling,* Telematica Instituut. Retrieved from https://doc.telin.nl/dscgi/ds.py/Get/File-47289/UT_D1.10a.pdf

Dineen B., Ash, S., & Noe, R. (2002). A web of applicant attraction: person organisation fit in the context of web-based recruitment. *Journal of Applied Psychology, 87*(4), 723.

Dineen, B., Ling, J., Ash, S., & Del Vecchio, D. (2007). Aesthetic properties and message customisation: Navigating the dark side of web recruitment. *Journal of Applied Psychology, 92*(2), 356-372.

Dipboye, R. L. (2005). How I stopped worrying and learned to appreciate the gaps between academic HRM and practice. In R. J. Burke & C. L. Cooper (Eds.), *Reinventing Human Resource Management: Challenges and New Directions.* London: Routledge.

Doherty, N. F., King, M., & Al-Mushayt, O. (2003). The Impact of Inadequacies in the Treatment of Organizational Issues on Information Systems Development Projects. *Information & Management, 14*, 49-62.

Dommergues, P., Groux, G., & Mason, J. (1984). *Les syndicats français et américains face aux mutations technologiques*. Paris: Edition Anthropos-Encrages.

Dörrenbächer, C., & Geppert, M. (2006). Micro-politics and conflicts in multinational corporations: Current debates, re-framing, and contributions of this special issue. *Journal of International Management, 12*(3), 251–265.

Dowling, G. R. (1994). *Corporate Reputations: Strategies for Developing the Corporate Brand*. Melbourne: Longman Professional Publishing.

Dowling, G. R. (2001).*Creating Corporate Reputations: Identity, Image and Performance*. Oxford: Oxford University Press.

Doz, Y., & Prahalad, C. K. (1993). Managing DMNCs: A search for a new paradigm. In S. Ghoshal & D. E. Westney (Eds.), *Organization Theory and the Multinational Corporation* (pp. 24–50). MacMillan: Basingstoke.

Drury, D. H., & Farhoomand, A. (1999). Knowledge worker Constraints in the Productive Use of Information Technology. *ACM SIGCPR Computer Personnel, 19/20*(4/1), 21-42.

Duarte, D. L., & Snyder, N.T. (1999). *Mastering virtual teams - Strategies, Tools and Techniques that succeed*, Jossey-Bass Publishers, San Francisco.

Dubosc, J. P. (2001). Les syndicats se ruent sur la Toile, au grand dam des enterprises. *Liaisons Sociales ,34*, 34–37.

Duhlebohn, J. H., Ferris, G. R., et al. (1995). The History and Evolution of Human Resource Management. *Handbook of Human Resource Management*. Cambridge, Blackwell Publishers.

Duhlebohn, J. H., & Marler, J. H. (2005). E-compensation: The potential to transform practice? In H. G. Gueutal & D. L. Stone (Eds.), *The Brave New World of eHR. Human Resources Management in the Digital Age*. San Francisco: Jossey-Bass.

Dukerich, J. M., &Carter, S. M. (2000). Distorted Images and Reputation Repair. In M. Schultz, M. J. Hatch & M. H. Larsen (Eds.), *The Expressive Organization: Linking Identity, Reputation, and the Corporate Brand* (pp. 97-112). Oxford: Oxford University Press.

Dumoulin, C. (2000). Le management à distance des équipes virtuelles. *Management et Conjoncture Sociale, 580*(5), 50-60.

Duncan, T., & Moriarty, S. E. (1998). A Communication Based Marketing Model for Managing Relationships. *Journal of Marketing, 62*(2), 1-13.

Dutch Court of Audit. (2007). Lessons from IT-projects at the government [*Lessen uit ICT-projecten bij de overheid*] Retrieved from http://www.rekenkamer.nl/9282000/d/p425_rapport1.pdf .

Duvivier, M. (2002). *Alerter les salariés des risques induits par les TIC*. Retrieved May 14, from www.cfdt.fr/actualite.

Early, C. P. (1994). Self or Group? Cultural Effects of Training on Self-Efficacy and Performance. *Administrative Science Quarterly, 39*, 89-117.

Eckhardt, A., Weitzel, T., Koenig, W., & Buschbacher, J. (2007). How to Convince People who don't like IT to use IT—A Case Study on E-Recruiting. In: *Proceedings of the Thirteen Americas Conference on Information Systems 2007 (AMCIS)*, Keystone, Colorado, USA.

Eckhardt, A., Laumer, S., & Weitzel, T. (2008). Extending the Architecture for a Next-Generation Holistic E-Recruiting System. In: *Proceedings of the 2008 International Conference on Information Resources Management (Conf-IRM)*, Niagara Falls, Ontario, Canada.

Edmunds, A., & Morris, A. (2000). The problem of information overload in business organisations: a review of the literature. *International Journal of Information Management, 20*, 17-28.

Edvinsson, L., & Malone, M. S. (1997). *Intellectual Capital: Realizing Your Company's True Value by Finding its Hidden Brainpower*. New York: Harper Business.

Edwards, T., & Kuruvilla, S. (2005). International HRM: national business systems, organizational politics and the international division of labour in MNCs. *International Journal of Human Resource Management, 16*(1), 1–21.

Edwards, T., Colling, T., & Ferner, A. (2007). Conceptual approaches to the transfer of employment practices in multinational companies: an integrated approach. *Human Resource Management Journal, 17*(3), 201–217.

Einserhardt, K. M. (1989). Agency Theory: An assessment and review. *Academic of Management Review, 14*(1), 57-74.

Eirinaki, A., & Vazirgiannis, M. (2003). *Web Mining for Web Personalization*. Retrieved from http://www.db-net. aueb.gr/magda/papers/TOIT-webmining_survey.pdf. Athens University of Economics and Business.

Emmond, K. (2005). Investing in IT. *Business Mexico, 15*(5), 22-28.

Empirica (2003). *SIBIS Pocket Book 2002/3*. Bonn, Germany: Empirica GmbH.

Enshur, E., Nielson, T., & Grant-Vallone, E. (2002). Tales from the hiring line: effects of the Internet technology on HR processes. *Organisational Dynamics, 31*(3), 224-244.

Eppler, & Mengis, M. J. (2004). The Concept of Information Overload: A Review of Literature from Organization Science, Accounting, Marketing, MIS, and Related Disciplines. *The Information Society, 20*, 325-344.

Epstein, R., & Singh, G. (2003). Internet Recruiting Effectiveness: Evidence from a biomedical device firm. *International Journal of Human Resources Development and Management, 3*(3), 216-225.

Erez, M., & Early, C. P. (1993). *Culture, Self-Identity and Work*. Oxford University Press, New York et al.

Erickson, T. J., & Gratton, L. (2007). What it means to work here. *Harvard Business Review, 3*, 104-112.

Ettinger, E., Wilderom, C.P.M., & Ruel, H. (Jan 2009). Web recruiters service quality criteria: a content analysis. *Proceedings of the 42nd Hawaii International Conference on System Science*, Hawaii.

European Commission (2000). The European Observatory for SME's. Sixth Report, Office for Official Publications of the European Communities, Luxembourg.

European Commission (2004). Highlights from the 2003 Observatory, *Observatory of European SMEs 2003* no. 8, Office for Official Publications of the European Communities, Luxembourg.

Ewing, M. J., Pitt, L. F., de Bussy, N. M., & Berthon, P. (2002). Employment Branding in the Knowledge Economy. *International Journal of Advertising, 21*, 3-22.

Exclusive IOMA Survey: What do Users Like (and Dislike) About Their HRIS? (2002, December). IOMA's Payroll Manager's Report, *02*(12), 1.

Exxellence Group (2008). *Partner van de elektronische overheid*. Retrieved from http://www.exxellence.nl.

Faerber, F., Keim, T., & Weitzel, T. (2003). An Automated Recommendation Approach to Personnel Selection. In: *Proceedings of the 2003 Americas Conference on Information Systems*, Tampa.

Farndale, E., & Paauwe, J. (2006). HR Shared Service Centres in the Netherlands: Restructuring the HR Function. *First European Academic Workshop on e-HRM*, Enschede.

Favier, M., & Trahand, J. (1998). La virtualité en pratique : quelques exemples d'Equipes Virtuelles. in M. Favier, F. Coat & J-C. Courbon (Eds.), *Le travail en groupe à l'âge des réseaux*, Economica, Paris.

Feldman, D., & Klaas, B. (2002). Internet job hunting: A field study of applicant experiences with online recruitment. *Human Resource Management, 41*(2), 175-201.

Feldman, M. S, & March, J.G. (1991). L'information dans les organisations : un signal et un symbole. In J. G. March (Ed.), *Décisions et organisations* (pp. 255- 284). Paris: Les Editions d'Organisation.

Ferner, A. (2000). The underpinnings of 'bureaucratic' control systems: HRM in European multinationals. *Journal of Management Studies, 37*(4), 521–539.

Ferner, A., & Edwards, P. K. (1995). Power and the diffusion of organizational change within multinationals. *European Journal of Industrial Relations, 1*(2), 229–257.

Ferner, A., & Quintanilla, J. (1998). Multinationals, national business systems and HRM: the enduring influence of national identity or a process of 'Anglo-Saxonization'. *International Journal of Human Resource Management, 9*(4), 710–731.

Ferner, A., Almond, P., & Colling, T. (2005). Institutional theory and the cross-national transfer of employment policy: the case of 'workforce diversity' in US multinationals. *Journal of International Business Studies, 36*(3), 304–321.

Ferner, A., Almond, P., Clark, I., Colling, T., Edwards, T., Holden, L., & Muller-Camen, M. (2004). The dynamics of central control and subsidiary autonomy in the management of human resources: case-study evidence from US MNCs in the UK. *Organization Studies, 25*(3), 363–391.

Ferratt, T. W., Agarwal, R., Moore, J. E., & Brown, C. V. (1999). Observations from 'the front': IT Executives on practices to recruit and retain information technology professionals". In: *Proceedings of the SIGCPR '99*. New Orleans LA, USA.

Figarol, N. (2005). *Cybersurveillance sur les lieux de travail, Big Brother est-il dans l'entreprise?* Retrived, March 22, from www.cfdt.fr/actualite.

Findlay, P., & McKinlay, A. (2003). Surveillance, Electronic Communications Technologies and Regulation. *Industrial Relations Journal, 34*(4), 305–308.

Finn, W. (2000). Screen Test. *People Management, 6,* 38-43.

Fiorito, J., Jarley, P., & Delaney, J. T. (2002). Information Technology, US Union Organizing and Union Effectiveness. *British Journal of Industrial Relations, 40*(4), 627–658.

Firestone, J. M. (2003). *Enterprise information portals and knowledge management*. Boston: Butterworth-Heinemann

Fischer, R. L. (1995). HRIS quality depends on teamwork. *Personnel Journal, 74*(11), 1-3.

Fisher, S., & Howell, A. (2004). Beyond user acceptance: an examination of employee reactions to information technology systems. *Human Resource Management, 43*(2-3), 243–258.

Fister Gale, S. (2003). Three Stories of Self-Service Success. *Workforce , 82*(1), 60-63.

Fitz-Enz, J. (1997). Are Your Human Assets Outperforming the Market? *Management Review, 86*(2), 62-66.

Fitz-enz, J. (2000). *The ROI of Human Capital*. New York: Amacon.

Fitzgerald, M., & Liburt, E. (1999). Spanish-language job site launches. *Editor & Publisher, 132*(48), 3.

Flanagan, D. J., & Deshpande, S. P. (1996). Top management's perceptions of changes in HRM practices after union elections in small firms. *Journal of Small Business Management*, 23–34.

Florkowski, G. W., & Olivas-Luján, M. R. (2006). The Diffusion of Human Resource Information Technology Innovations in US and non-US Firms. *Personnel Review, 35*(6), 684-710.

Flynn, G. G. (2000). Out of the Red, Into the Blue. *Workforce, 79*(3), 50.

Foray, D. (2000). *Economy of knowledge*, the Discovery, Reference mark, Paris

Foray, D. (2000). *L'économie de la connaissance*. Paris. France : Editions La Découverte.

Forsgren, M. (1990). Managing the international multi-centre firm: Case studies from Sweden. *European Management Journal, 8*(2), 261–267.

Foster, S. (2006). A high tech future. *Payroll Manager's Review, November 2006,* (pp. 38-40).

Fowler, M. (2002) *Patterns of Enterprise Application Architecture*. Addison-Wesley Professional

Frank, M. R., & Szekely, P. (1998). Adaptive forms: an interaction technique for entering structured data. *Knowledge-Based Systems, 11,* 37-45. Retrieved from http://citeseer.ifi.unizh.ch/cache/papers/cs/11859/

http:zSzzSzwww.isi.eduzSz~frankzSzPaperszSzkbs98 zSzkbs98.pdf/frank98adaptive.pdf.

Franke, N., von Hippel, E., & Schreier, M. (2006). Finding commercially attractive user innovations: a test of lead-user theory. *Journal of Product Innovation Management, 23*, 301-315.

FraseBlunt, M. M. (2004). Keeping HR on the Inside. *HR Magazine, 49*(10), 57.

Frauenheim, E. (2006). Indian Leaders in demand amid rapid expansion. *Workforce Management, 85*(7), 6-9.

Freeman, R. B. (2005). The Contribution Of The Internet To Reviving Union Fortunes. In The Webbs To The Web, *National bureau of economic research,* Working Paper, *11298,* 24(December).

Freeman, R. E. (1984). *Strategic management: a stakeholder approach*, Boston, Pitman Press.

Friedman, T. (2006). The World is Flat. Updated and Expanded. New York: Farrar, Straus and Giroux.

Fuchs, C. (2003). Structuration Theory and Self-Organization. *Systemic Practice and Action Research, 16*(2), 133-167.

Fulk, J. (1993). Social construction of communication technology, *Academy of Management Journal*, 36, 921-950.

Galambaud, B. (2003). HRM and performances. AGEF, Conference of Marrakesh, 23th and 24th January.

Galanaki, E. (2002). The decision to recruit on line: A descriptive study. *Career Development International*, (pp. 243-251).

Galanaki, E. (2002). The decision to recruit online. *Career Development International, 7*(4). 243-250.

Galbraith, J. R., & Lawler III, E. E. (1993). *Organizing for the future: the new logic for managing*, San Francisco, Jossey Bass.

Gale, S. F. (2001). Internet Recruiting: Better, Cheaper, Faster. *Workforce, 80*, 74-77.

Gamma, E., Helm, R., Johnson, R., & Vlissides, J. (1995). *Design Patterns: Elements of Reusable Object-Oriented Software*. Reading, MA: Addison-Wesley Professional.

Garcia, R., & Calantone, R. (2002). A critical look at technological innovation typology and innovativeness terminology: A literature review. *Journal of Product Innovation Management, 19*, 110–132.

Gardner, S. D., Lepak, D. P., & Bartol, K. M. (2003). Virtual HR: The impact of information technology on the human resource professional. *Journal of Vocational Behavior, 63*(2), 159-179.

Garnier, M., Flos, B., & Romeijn, H. (2007). Overheid. nl Monitor 2007, Overheid heeft Antwoord©. Retrieved from www.advies.overheid.nl/attachment.db?7698.

Gates III, W. H. (2005). The New World of Work [Electronic Version]. Microsoft Executive Mail. Retrieved 01-05-2007 from http://www.microsoft.com/mscorp/execmail/2005/05-19newworldofwork.mspx.

Gatewood, R. D., Gowan, M. A., & Lautenschlager, G. J. (1993). Corporate Image, Recruitment Image and Initial Job Choice. *Academy of Management Journal, 36*, 414-424.

Gattiker, U. E., & Paulson, D. (1999).Unions and New Office Technology. *Industrial Relations, 54*(2), 245–276.

Gayeski, D. M. (2002). *Learning Unplugged; Using mobile Technologies for Organizational Training and Performance Improvement*. American Management Association, New York, :AMACOM.

Gebauer, M. (2003). Information Systems on Human Capital in Service Sector Organizations. *New Library World, 104*(1184/1185), 33-41.

Geppert, M., & Mayer, M. (2006). Introduction. In M. Geppert & M. Mayer (Eds.), *Global, National and Local Practices in Multinational Companies* (pp. 1–14). Basingstoke: Palgrave Macmillan.

Geppert, M., & Williams, K. (2006). Global, national and local practices in multinational corporations: Towards a sociopolitical framework. *International Journal of Human Resource Management, 17*(1), 49–69.

Germanakos, P., et al. (2005). Personalization Systems and Processes Review based on a Predetermined User Interface Categorization, III CONGRÉS INTERNACIONAL COMUNICACIÓ I REALITAT. Retrieved from http://cicr.blanquerna.url.es/2005/Abstracts/PDFsComunicacions/vol1/05/GERMANAKOS_MOURLAS_PANAYIOTOU_SAMARAS.pdf.

Gershon, P. (2004). Releasing Resources to the Frontline: Independent Review of Public Sector Efficiency. In H. Treasury (Ed.).

Ghauri, P. (2004). Designing and conducting case studies in international business research. In R. Marschan-Piekkari & C. Welch (Eds.), *Handbook of Qualitative Research Methods for International Business* (pp. 109–124). Cheltenham: Edward Elgar.

Ghauri, P., & Grønhaug, K. (2002). *Research Methods in Business Studies: A Practical Guide.* Harlow, UK: Financial Times and Prentice Hall.

Ghoshal, S., & Gratton, L. (2002). Integrating the enterprise. *Sloan Management Review, 44*(1), 31–38.

Gibcus, P., & Kemp, R. G. M. (2003). *Strategy and small firm performance.* EIM, Zoetermeer, the Netherlands.

Gibson, H. (1977). Determining User Involvement. *Journal of System Management*, 20-22.

Giddens, A. (1984). *The Constitution of Society: outline of the theory of structuration.* Cambridge, UK: Polity Press.

Gill, R., & Wong, A. (1998). The cross-cultural transfer of management practices: the case of Japanese human resource management practices in Singapore. *International Journal of Human Resource Management, 9*(1), 116–135.

Gillian, P. (1994). Tame the Restless Computer Professional. *HR Magazine, 39*(11), 142-144.

Ginzberg, M. J. (1981). Early diagnosis of MIS implementation failure: Promising results and unanswered questions. *Management Science, 27*(4), 459–478.

Gioia, D. (1986). *The Thinking Organization.* San Francisco, California: Jossey-Bass.

Girgensohn, A. et al. (1995). Dynamic forms: An enhanced interaction abstraction based on forms. In *Proceedings of Interact'95, Fifth IFIP Conference on Human-Computer Interaction,* (pp. 362-367). London: Chapman & Hall.

Glaser, B. G., & Strauss, A. L. (1967). *The discovery of grounded theory: Strategies for qualitative research.* New Tork NY: Aldine.

Globerman, S., & Shapiro, D. M. (1999). The Impact of Government Policies on Foreign Direct Investment: The Canadian Experience. *Journal of International Business Studies, 30*, 513-532.

Gold, J., Watson, S., & Rix, M. (2000). Learning for Change by Telling Stories. In J. McGoldrick, J. Stewart, & S. Watson (Eds.), *Understanding Human Resource Development: A Resource-based Approach.* London: Routledge

Gong, W., Li, Z., & Stump, R. (2007). Global internet use and access: Cultural considerations. *Asia Pacific Journal of Marketing and Logistics, 19*(1), 57-73.

Gooderham, P. N., Nordhaug, O., & Ringdal, K. (1999). Institutional and rational determinants of organizational practices: human resource management in European firms. *Administrative Science Quarterly, 44*(3), 507–531.

Gordon, J. (2002). India or Bust. *Fortune, 169*(8), 65-69.

Gould, J. D., & Lewis, C. (1985). Designing for Usability: Key Principles and What Designers Think. *Communications of the ACM, 28*(3), 300-311.

Gouldner, A.W. (1960). The Norm of Reciprocity: A Preliminary Statement. *American Sociology Review, 25*(2), 161-178.

Gourley, S., & Connolly, P. (1996). HRM and computerised information systems—have we missed a link? *Paper presented at conference—strategic direction of HRM.*

Graham, J. L. (2001). Culture and Human Resource Management. In A. M. Rugman, & T. L. Brewer (Eds.), *The Oxford Handbook of International Business.* Oxford University Press, New York et al., 503-537.

Grant, R. M. (1991). The Resource-based Theory of Competitive Advantage. Implication for Strategy Formulation. *California Management Review, 33*(3), 114-135.

Greene, A. M., & Kirton, G. (2003). Possibilities for Remote Participation in Trade Unions: Mobilising Women Activists. *Industrial Relations Journal, 34*(4), 319–333.

Greene, A. M., Hogan, J., & Grieco, M. (2003). E-Collectivism and Distributed Discourses : New Opportunities for Trade Union Democracy. *Industrial Relations Journal, 34*(4), 282–289.

Greif, I. (Ed.). (1988). *Computer Supported Cooperative Work*. New-York: Morgan Kaufman.

Grensing-Pophal, L. (2001). HR and the corporate intranet: Beyond "brochureware". SHRM white paper. Retrieved, May 9, 2003, from www.shrm.org/hrresources/whitepapers_publisched/CMS_000212.asp.

Griffiths, J. J. (2007). Shared services can 'drive NHS reform. *People management, 13*(3), 11.

Griffiths, J. J. (2008). Shared services works for Scottish government. *People management, 14*(4), 13.

Grisé, M., & Gallupe, R.B. (2000). Information Overload: Addressing the Productivity Paradox in Face-to-Face Electronic Meetings. *Journal of Management Information Systems, 16*(3), 157-185.

Groe, G., Pyle, W., & Jamrog, J. (1996). Information technology and HR. *Human Resource Planning, 19*(1), 56-61.

Grönroos, C. (2000). *Service Management and Marketing: A Customer Relationship Management Approach*. New York, NY: Wiley.

Grosjean, M., & Lacoste, M. (1999). Communication et intelligence collective : le travail à l'hôpital. PUF, *Le travail Humain*, Paris.

Grudin, J. (1988). Why CSCW applications fail. Problems in the design and evaluation of organizational interfaces. *Proceedings of the CSCW'88* (pp. 85-93). New-York: ACM/Sigchi and Sigois.

Grudin, J. (1991). Interactive systems: Bridging the gaps between developers and users. *IEEE Computer, 24*(4), 59-69.

Grudin, J. (1991). Systematic sources of suboptimal interface design in large product development organization. *Human Computer Interaction , 6*(2), 147-196.

Guérin, G., Ouadahi, J., Saba, T., & Wils, T. (2001). La mobilisation des employés lors de l'implantation d'un système d'information: ébauche d'un cadre théorique. *Actes de la 19e université d'été de l'Institut d'audit social*, (pp. 145-159).

Guest, D. E., & Peccei, R. (1994). The nature and causes of effective Human Resource Management. *British Journal of Industrial Relations, 32*(2) June, 219 – 242.

Gueutal, H. G, & Stone, D. L. (2005). *The Brave New World of eHR: Human Resources Management in the Digital Age*. San Francisco: Jossey-Bass.

Guiderdoni, K. (2006). Assessment of an HR Intranet through middle managers' position and users. How to manage the plurality of this group in the beginning of an e-HR conception. In: *Proceedings of the 1st European Academic Workshop on E-HRM*, Enschede (Netherlands).

Guillèn, M. F. (1994). *Models of Management: Work, Authority, and Organization in a Comparative Perspective*. Chicago: University of Chicago Press.

Guthrie, J. P. (2001). High-involvement work practices, turnovers, and productivity: Evidence from New Zealand. *Academy of Management Journal, 44,* 180–190.

Guyodo, A. (2000). NTIC, Des libertés à garantir. *La revue de la CFDT, 35*(11), 24–28 .

Hackman, J. R. (1990). *Groups that work (and those that don't),* Jossey Bass, San Francisco.

Hageman, J., & van Kleef, J. (2002). e-HRM is de hype voorbij (cited in March 2006). http://www.nvp-plaza.nl/e-hrm/e-HRMvisie&missie_files/frame.htm.

Hagström, P., & Hedlund, G. (1999). A three-dimensional model of changing internal structure in the firm. In Jr. Chandler & P. Hagström (Eds.), *The Dynamic Firm* (pp. 166-191). Oxford University Press.

Haines, V.Y., & Petit, A. (1997). Conditions for successful human resource information systems, *Human Resource Management, 36*(2), 261-275.

Hammer, M., & Champy, J. (1995). *Re-engineering the Corporation: A Manifesto for Business Revolution.* London: Nicholas Brealey.

Hammersley, M., & Atkinson, P. (1983). *Ethnography principles in practice.* London: Routledge.

Handy, C. (2000). Trust and the virtual organisation, *Harvard Business Review,* 2000, 1-9.

Hannon, J., Huang, I-C., & Jaw, B-S. (1995). International human resource strategy and its determinants: the case of subsidiaries in Taiwan. *Journal of International Business Studies, 26*(3), 531–554.

Hannon, J., Jelf, G., & Brandes, D. (1996). Human Resource information systems: operational issues and strategic considerations in a global environment. *The International Journal of Human Resource Management, 7*(1), 245-269.

Hargie, O., & Tourish, D. (2002). *Handbook of communication audits for organisations.* Hove/New York: Routledge

Harrington, A. (2002, May 13). Can anyone build a better monster? *Fortune, 145,* 189-192

Harris, L. C. (2002). The future for the HRM function in local government: everything has changed- but has anything changed? *Strategic Change, 11,* 369-378.

Hatch, M. J., & Cunliffe, A. L. (2006). *Organization Theory.* Oxford: Oxford University Press.

Hatchuel, A. (2004). Le syndicalisme innovateur. *Le Monde, 23 November,* VIII.

Hax, A. C., & Majluf, N. S. (1981). Organizational Design: A Survey and an Approach. *Operations Research, 29*(3), 417-447.

Hays, S. (1999). Hiring on the Web. *Workforce, 77,* 76-84.

Hays, S. S. (1999). Newcourt's Call Center Streamlines HR Processes. *Workforce, 78*(6), 126.

Heijke, H., Meng, C., & Ramaekers, G. (2003). An investigation into the role of human capital competences and their pay-off. *International Journal of Manpower, 24 (7),* 750-773.

Henderson, J. C., & Venkatraman, N. (1999). Strategic alignment: leveraging information technology for transforming organizations. *IBM Systems Journal, 38.*

Hendrickson, A. R. (2003). Human Resource Information Systems: Backbone Technology of Contemporary Human Resources. Journal of Labor Research, *24*(3), 381-394.

Heneman, H. G., & Berkley, R. A. (1999). Applicant attraction practices and outcomes among small businesses. Journal *of Small Business Management,* (pp. 53–74).

Heneman, R. L., Tansky, J. W., & Camp, S. M. (2000). Human resource management practices in small and medium-sized enterprises: Unanswered questions and future research perspectives. *Entrepreneurship Theory and Practice,* (pp. 11–26).

Heneman, R. L., Tansky, J.W. (2002). Human Resource Management models for entrepreneurial opportunity: Existing knowledge and new directions. In J. Katz & T. M. Welbourne (Eds.), *Managing people in entrepreneurial organizations,* 5, 55-82, Amsterdam: JAI Press

Herstatt C., & von Hippel E. (1992). From experience: developing new product concepts via the lead user method: a case study in a "Low Tech" Field. *Journal of Product Innovation Management, 9,* 213–221.

Hertel, G., Geister, S., & Konradt, U. (2005). Managing virtual teams: A review of current empirical research, *Human Resources Management, 15,* 69-95.

Hetrick, S. (2002). Transferring HR Ideas and Practices: Globalization and Convergence in Poland. *Human Resource Development International, 5,* 333-351.

Hevner, A. R., March, S.T., Park, J., & Ram, S. (2004). Design Science in Information Systems Research. *MIS Quarterly, 28*(1), 75-105.

Hill, W. F. (1997). *Learning: a survey of psychological interpretations*. New York: Longman.

Hiltz, S. R., & Turoff, M. (1985). Structuring computer-mediated communication systems to avoid information overload. *Communications of the ACM, 28*(7), 680-689.

Hinnings, C. R., & Greenwood, R. (1988). The normative prescription of organizations. In G. Zucker (Ed.), *Institutional Patterns and Organizations: Culture and Environment* (pp. 53-70). Cambridge, MA: Ballinger

Hirschheim, R., & Smithson, S. (1988). A Critical Analysis of Information Systems Evaluation. In N. Bjørn-Andersen & G. B. Davis (Eds.), *Information Systems Assessment: Issues and Challenges* (pp. 17-37). Amsterdam: North Holland.

Ho, J., & Tang, R. (2001). Towards an Optimal Resolution to Information Overload: An Infomediary Approach. *Paper presented at the GROUP '01.*

Hofstede, G. (1983). The Cultural Relativity of Organizational Practices and Theories. *Journal of International Business Studies, 14*, 75-89.

Hofstede, G. (1991). *Cultures and Organizations: Software of the Mind.* McGraw-Hill, London.

Hofstede, G. (1993). Cultural constraints in management theories. *Academy of Management Executive, 7*(1), 81-94

Hofstede, G. (1998). Think Locally, Act Globally: Cultural Constraints in Personnel Management. *Management International Review, 38*(2), 7-26.

Hofstede, G. (1999). Cultures *and organizations: Software of the mind.* Hill, London.

Hofstede, G. (2001). *Culture's Consequences. International Differences in Work Related Values,* second ed. Sage, London/Beverly Hills.

Hofstede, G. (2001). Culture's Recent Consequences: Using Dimension Scores in Theory and Research. *International Journal of Cross Cultural Management, 1*, 11-30.

Hogler, R. L., Henle, C., & Bernus, C. (1998). Internet recruiting and employment discrimination: a legal perspective. *Human Resource Management Review, 8*(2).

Holland, C. P., Light, B., & Kavalek, P. (1996). *A critical success factors model for enterprise resource planning implementation.* Proceedings of the Seventh European Conference on Information Systems, Copenhagen: Copenhagen Business School

Holland, C. P., Light, B., & Kawalek, P. (1999). *Beyond enterprise resource planning projects: innovative strategies for competitive advantage.* Proceedings of the Seventh European Conference on Information Systems, Copenhagen: Copenhagen Business School

Holland, S., Gaston, K., & Gomes, J. (2000). Critical success factors for cross-functional teamwork in new product development. *International Journal of Management Reviews, 2*(3), 231-259.

Holtbrügge, D. (2005). *Personalmanagement,* (2nd Ed.). Springer, Berlin et al.

Hong, W., Thong, J. Y. L., Wong, W. M., & Tam, K. Y. (2002). Determinants of user acceptance of digital libraries: an empirical examination of individual differences and system characteristics. *Journal of Management Information Systems, 18*(3), 97-124.

Hoobler, J. M., & Johnson, N. B. (2004). An analysis of current human resource management publications. *Personnel Review, 33*(6), 665–676.

Hoogwout, M., Vries, de M., et al. (2005). Onderzoek: Digitale indiening omgeving vergunning Mijlpaal op weg naar de Andere Overheid, Zenc. Retrieved from http://www.vrom.nl/pagina.html?id=18487.

Hornsby, J. S., & Kuratko, D. F. (1990). Human resource management in small business: Critical issues for the 1990s. *Journal of Small Business Management,* (pp. 9–18).

House, R. J., Hanges, P. J., Javidan, M., Dorfman, P. W., & Gupta, V. (Eds.) (2004). *Culture, Leadership, and Organizations. The GLOBE Study of 62 Societies.* Sage, Thousand Oaks et al.

HR Technology Trends to Watch in 2007 (2007). *HR Focus, 84*(1), 1.

HRfocus (2007). How Outsourcing & Shared Services Can Help You Now. *HR focus, 84*(7), 1.

HRfocus (2007). How to Maximize Your Return on Outsourcing & Shared Services. *HR focus, 84*(4), S2.

Huang, C. D., & Hu, Q. (2007). Achieving IT-Business strategic alignment via enterprise-wide implementation of balanced scorecards. *Information Systems Management, 24*, 73-84

Huselid, M. A. (1995). The impact of human resource management practices on turnover, productivity and corporate financial performance. *Academy of Management Journal, 38*, 635-672.

Huselid, M. A. (2003). Editor's note: Special issue on small and medium-sized enterprises: A call for more research. *Human Resource Management, 42*(4), 297.

Huselid, M. A., Becker, B. E., & Beatty, R. W. (2005). *The Workforce Scorecard: Managing Human Capital to Execute Strategy.* Boston: Harvard Business School Press

Huselid, M., & Barnes, J. (2002) *Human capital management systems as a source of competitive advantage.* Unpublished manuscript, Rutgers University, New Jersey.

Hwang, Y. (2004). Investigating enterprise systems adoption: uncertainty avoidance, intrinsic motivation, and the technology acceptance model. *European Journal of Information Systems, 14*, 150–161.

Hyman, R. (2002). Trade Union Research and Cross-National Comparison. *European Journal of Industrial Relations, 7*(2), 203–233.

Iansiti, M., & MacCormack, A. (1997). Developing products on the Internet Time. *Harvard Business Review, 75*(5), 108-117.

Ilgen D. R., Fischer, C. D., & Taylor, M. S. (1979). Consequences of individual feedback on behaviour in organizations. *Journal of Applied Psychology, 64*, 349-371.

iLogos Research (2002). *Global 500 Web Site Recruiting: 2002.* Survey, San Francisco.

Imperatori, B., & De Marco, M. (in press). ICT and Changing Working Relationships: Rational or Normative Fashion?" In A. D'Atri, M. De Marco, & N. Casalino (Eds.). *Interdisciplinary Aspects of Information Systems Studies.* London: Springer.

Ind, N. (1990). *The Corporate Image.* London: Kogan Page.

Ind, N. (2001). *Living The Brand: How to Transform Every Member of Your Organization into a Brand Champion.* London: Kogan Page.

IntermediairPW (2005). Shared services veranderen de grondwet van je bedrijf'. *IntermediairPW, 1*(18).

IntermediairPW (2006). SSC maakt hrm niet per se strategischer. *IntermediairPW, 2*(15).

International Organization for Standardization. (ISO) (2001). ISO/IEC: 9126 Software Engineering – Product Quality – Part 1: Quality Model – 2001. Retrieved November 21, 2007 from http://www.iso.org.

Ives, B., & Olson, M. H. (1984). User Involvement and MIS Success: A Review of Research. *Management Science, 30*(5), 586-603.

Ives, B., Olson, M. H., & Baroudi, J. J. (1983). The measurement of user information satisfaction. *Communications of the ACM, 26*(10), 785-793.

Jacoby, J. (1984). Perspectives on Information Overload. *The Journal of Consumer Research, 10*(4), 432-435.

Janssen, M., & Joha, A. (2006). Motives for establishing shared service centers in public administrations. *International Journal of Information Management, 26*(2), 102-115.

Jasrotia, P. (2001). E-recruitment market registers major growth. *Express Computer.* Retrieved from http://www.itpeopleindia.com/20011008/cover1.htm

Jaubert, C. (2000). Syndicalisme on-line. *L'hebdo de l'actualité sociale, La vie ouvrière CGT, 2917*, 22–23.

Jensen, M. C., & Meckling, W. H. (1976). Theory of the firm: Managerial behavior, agency costs and ownership structure. J*ournal of Financial Economics, 3*(4).

Johnson, B., Manyika, J., & Yee, L. (2005). *The next revolution in interactions.* McKinsey & Company.

Julliard, C. (2002). Les douze travaux internet de la CFDT Cadres. Retrieved, February 25, from www.cfdt.fr/actualite.

Kahai, S. S., Sosik, J. J., & Avolio, B. J. (1997). Effects of leadership style and problem structure on work group process and outcomes in an electronic meeting system environment. *Personnel psychology, 50*, 121-146.

Kakihara, M., & Sorensen, C. (2004). Practicing Mobile Professional Work: Tales of Locational, Operational and Interactional Mobility. *INFO: The journal of Policy, Regulation and Strategy for Telecommunications, Information and Media, 6*(3), 180-197.

Kakumanu, P., & Mezzacca, M. (2005). Importance of portal Standardization and Ensuring Adoption in Organizational Environments. *The Journal of American Academy of Business*, Cambridge, *7*(2), 128-132.

Kalika M., Bellier S., Isaac H., Josserand E. & Leroy I. (2002). E-*management: towards the virtual company? Impact of the ICT on the organization and the management of competences.* Edition Connections

Kalika, M. (2002). *e-GRH : révolution ou évolution*, Editions liaisons, Paris.

Kalika, M. (2002). Le défi du e-management, in *Les défis du management*, éditions Liaisons, (pp. 221-234).

Kalleberg, A. L., & Moody, J. W. (1994). Human Resource Management nd Organizational Performance. *American Behavioral Scientist, 37*, 948–962.

Kane, B., Crawford, J., & Grant, D. (1999). Barriers to effective HRM. *International Journal of Manpower, 20*(8), 494 – 515.

Karahanna, E., & Straub, D. W. (1998). The psychological origins of perceived usefulness and ease of use. *Information & Management, 35*, 237 – 250.

Katzenbach, J. R., & Smith, D. K. (1993). *The wisdom of teams: Creating high performance organizations*, Cambridge MA, Harvard University School Press.

Kavanagh, M. J., Gueutal, H. G., & Tannenbaum, S.I. (1990) *Human resource information systems: development and application.* Boston, Mass: PWS-Kent publishing company.

Keebler, T. J., & Rhodes, D. W. (2002). E-HR becoming the 'path of least resistance'. *Employment Relations Today, 29*(2), 57-66.

Keen, P. G. W. (1991). *Shaping the Future: Business Design Through Information Technology.* Cambridge, MA: Harvard Business Press.

Kehoe, J. F., Dickter, D. N., Russell, D. P., & Sacco, J. M. (2005). E-Selection. In H.G. Gueutal & D. L. Stone (Eds.), *The Brave New World of eHR. Human Resources Management in the Digital Age.* San Francisco: Jossey-Bass.

Keim, T., & Weitzel, T. (2006). Strategies for Hiring IT Professionals: An Empirical Analysis of Employer and Job Seeker Behavior on the IT Labor Market. In: *Proceedings of the Twelfth Americas Conference on Information Systems.* Acapulco, Mexico.

Keller, K. L. (2002). *Strategic Brand Management.* Second Edition, New Jersey: Prentice Hall.

Keller, K. L., & Staelin, R. (1987). Effects of Quality and Quantity of Information on Decision Effectiveness. *The Journal of Consumer Research, 14*(2), 200-213.

Keller, R. T. (1986). Predictors of the performance of project groups in R&D organizations. *Academy of Management Journal, 29*(4), 715-726.

Kelloway, E. K., & Barling, J. (2000). Knowledge Work as organizational behavior. *International Journal of Management Reviews, 2*(3), 287-304.

Kelly, & Gennard, J. (1996). The role of Personnel Directors on the board of directors. *Personnel Review, 25*(1), 7-24.

Kelly, G. A. (1955). *The Psychology of Personal Constructs Vol 1 and 2*. New York: Norton.

Kennedy, S. H. (1977). Nurturing Corporate Images. *European Management Journal, 11*(3), 120-164.

Kensing, F., & Blomberg, J. (1998). Participatory Design: Issues and Concerns. *Computer Supported Cooperative Work, 7*(3-4), 167-185.

Kiessling, T., & Harvey, M. (2005). Strategic global human resource management research in the twenty-first century: an endorsement of the mixed-method research methodology. *International Journal of Human Resource Management, 16*(1), 22–45.

King, G., Keohane, R. O., & Verba, S. (1994). *Designing Social Inquiry*. Princeton, Princeton University Press.

King, J. (1997). IT Labor Emergency Promots Feds to Study, Fix Shortage. *Computerworld*, October 6.

Kinnie, N. J., & Arthurs, A. J. (1996). Personnel specialists' advanced use of information technology: evidence and explanations. *Personnel Review, 25*(3), 3-19.

Kirchgeorg, M., & Lorbeer, A. (2002). Anforderungen von High Potentials an Unternehmen. *Arbeitspapier der Handelshochschule Leipzig (HHL), 49*.

Klaas, B.S., McCClendon, J. and Gainey, T.W. (2000). Managing HR in the small and medium enterprise: The impact of professional employer organizations. *Entrepreneurship: theorye and Practice, 25*(1), pp. 107-124.

Klein, H. K., & Kleinman, D. (2002). The Social Construction of Technology: Structural Considerations. *Science, Technology & Human Values, 27*(1), 28-52.

Knox, S., & Freemann, C. (2006). Measuring and Managing Employer Brand Image in the Service Industry. *Journal of Marketing Management, 22*, 695-716.

Kobsa, A., Koeneman, J. J., & Pohl, W. (2001). Personalized hypermedia presentation techniques for improving online customer relationships. *The knowledge Engineering Review, 16*(2), 111-115. Retrieved from http://www.ics.uci.edu/~kobsa/papers/2001-KER-kobsa.pdf

Kohli, R., & Devaraj, S. (2004). Realizing the business value of information technology investment: an organizational process. *MIS Quarterly Executive, 3*(1), 53-68

Kok, J. M. P. de, Uhlaner, L. M. & Thurik, A. R. (2003). Human Resource Management with small firms; facts and explanations. *Report Series, Research in Management. Erasmus Research Institute of Management.*

Kok, J. M. P. de, Uhlaner, L. M., & Thurik, A. R. (2006). Professional HRM Practices in Family Owned-Managed Enterprises. *Journal of Small Business Management, 44*(3), 441-460.

Kolb, D. A. (1984). *Experiential learning. Experience as the source of learning and development*. Englewood Cliffs, New Jersey: Prentice-Hall.

Konradt, U., Christophersen, T., & Schaeffer-Kuelz, U. (2006). Predicting user satisfaction, strain and system usage of employee self-services. *International Journal Human Computer studies, 64*(11), 1141-1153.

Kossek, E. E., Young, W., Gash, D. C., & Nichol, V. (1994). Waiting for innovation in the Human Resources Department: Godot implements a Human Resource Information System. *Human Resource Management, Spring, 33*(1), 135-139.

Kotey, B., & Slade, P. (2005). Formal Human Resource Management in small growing firms. *Journal os Small Business Management, 43*(1), 16-40.

Kotlyar, I., & Ades, K. (2002). Don't Overlook Recruiting Tools. *HR Magazine, 47*, 97-102.

Kovach, K. A., Hughe, A. A., Fagan, P., & Magitti, P. G. (2002). Administrative and Strategic Advantages of HRIS. *Employment Relations Today, 29*(2), 43-48.

Kovach, K., & Cathcart, C. (1999). Human resource information systems (HRIS). Providing business with rapid data access, information exchange and strategic advantage. *Public personnel management, 28*(2), 275-282.

Kovach, K., Hughes, A., Fagan, P., & Maggitti, P. (2002). Administrative and strategic advantages of HRIS. *Employment Relations Today, 29*(2), 43-48.

Kroon, J. P. (1998). *Hoofdstuk 10: Het belang van klantin-formatie voor E-commerce. Ecommerce Handboek.* Retrieved from http://www.netmarketing.nl/downloads/files/Voorbeeldhoofdstuk%20E-commerce%20Handboek.pdf.

Krug, S. (2000). *Don't Make Me Think!* USA: New Riders Press.

Kuiper, P. M. (2006). *Adaptieve Gemeentelijke eFormulieren,* Formulieren die met u meedenken, Universiteit Twente, Exxellence Group, Nederland.

Kujala, S. (2003). User involvement: a review of the benefits and challenges, *Behavior & Information Technology, 22*(1), 1-16.

Labbe, D., & Landier, H. (2001). *L'entreprise face au nouveau radicalisme syndical.* Paris: Ed. Liaisons.

Labovitz, G., & Rosansky, V. (1997). *The Power of Alignment.* New York: Jonh Wiley & Sons.

Lagrosen, S. (2005). Customer involvement in new product development: A relationship marketing perspective. *European Journal of Innovation Management, 8*(4), 424-436.

Lai, V. S., & Li, H. (2004). Technology acceptance model for internet banking: an invariance analysis. *Information & Management, 42*(2005), 373-386

Laing, D., & Weir, C. (1999). Corporate performance and the influence of human capital characteristics on executive compensation in the UK. *Personnel Review, 28*(1/2), 28-40.

Lancaster, J. (2003). Village Kiosks Bridge India's Digital Divide. *Washington Post, Oct 12ᵗʰ*, AOl.

Landis, D., Bennett, J. M., & Bennett, M. J. (Eds.) (2004). *Handbook of Intercultural Training,* (3rd Ed.). Thousand Oaks, CA: Sage.

Lane, F. S. (2003). *The Naked Employee: How technology is compromising workplace privacy.*

Lasfargue, Y. (2000). *Technomordus, technoexclus?,* Editions d'Organisation, Paris.

Lath, S. (2006) The Battle of Two Portals; Yahoo and MSN; are getting ready to fight it out in the Indian market, which may still be small but promises a lot. *Business Today, 128.*

Laval, F., Guilloux, V., & Kalika, M. (2002), HR Intranets: Firms' Practices and Problematics In F. Laval, V. Guilloux, M. Kalika, & M. Matmati (Eds.), *E-GRH: Revolution or Evolution? Manage the Challenge of IT Integration in the HR Function* (pp. 63-90). Paris : Editions Liaisons.

Lave, J., & Wenger, E. (1991). *Situated learning: Legitimate Peripheral Participation.* New York, NY: Cambridge University Press.

Lawler III, E., & Finegold, D. (2000). Individualizing the Organization: past, present and future. *Organizational Dynamics, 29*(1), 1–15.

Lawler, E. E., & Mohrman, S. (2003). HR as a strategic partner—what does it take to make it happen? *Human Resource Planning, 26*(3), 15-29.

Le Coq, J., & Debons, C. (1997). *Routiers : les raisons de la colère.* Paris: Les Editions de l'Atelier.

Lee, C., & Lee, H. 2001. Factors Affecting Enterprise Resource Planning Systems Implementation in a Higher Education Institution. *Issues in Information Systems, 2*(1), 207-212. Retrieved November 24, 2007 from http://www.iacis.org.

Lee, E. (2004). Trade Unions In The Electronic Workplace. In *Proceeding of the Adelaide International Workplace Conflict Conference.* Adelaide, Australia April 21-23.

Lee, I. (2005). An integrated economic decision and simulation methodology for e-recruiting process redesign. *International Journal of Simulation and Process Modelling, 1*(3/4), 179-188.

Lee, I. (2007). The Architecture for a Next-Generation Holistic E-Recruiting System. *Communications of the ACM, 50*(7), 81-85.

Lee, S. H. (1999). *Usability Testing for Developing Effective Interactive Multimedia Software: Concepts, Dimensions, and Procedures,* Hanyang University,

Department of Educational Technology, Seoul, Korea. Retrieved from http://ifets.ieee.org/periodical/vol_2_99/sung_heum_lee.html.

Legge, K. (1978). *Power, Innovation and Problem Solving in Personnel Management.* London: McGraw-Hill

Leidner, D., & Kayworth, T. (2006). A Review of Culture in Information Systems Research: Toward a Theory of Information Technology Culture Conflict. *MIS Quarterly, 30*(2), 357-370.

Lengnick-Hall, C., & Lengnick-Hall, A. (2006). HR, ERP and knowledge for competitive advantage. *Human Resource Management, 45*(1), 79–94.

Lengnick-Hall, M. L., & Mortiz, S. (2003). The Impact of e-HR on the Human Resource Management Function. *Journal of Labor Research, 24*(3), 365-379.

Lepak, D. P., & Snell, S. A. (1998). Virtual HR: strategic human resource management in the 21st century. *Human Resource Management Review, 8*(3), 215-234.

Lepak, D. P., & Snell, S. A. (1999). The human resource architecture: toward a theory of human capital allocation and development. *Academy of Management Review, 24*(1), 31-48.

Lepak, D. P., & Snell, S. A. (2002). Examining the human resource architecture: the relationships among human capital, employment, and human resource configurations. *Journal of Management, 28*(4), 517-543.

Lepak, D. P., Takeuchi, R., & Snell, S. A. (2003). Employment flexibility and firm performance: examining the interaction effect of employment model, environmental dynamism and technological intensity. *Journal of Management, 29*(5), 681-703.

Lesser, E., & Storck, J. (2001). Communities of practice and organizational performance. *IBM Systems Journal, 40*(4), 831-841.

Lettl, C., Hienerth, C. & Gemuenden, H. G. (2008). Exploring How Lead Users Develop Radical Innovation: Opportunity Recognition and Exploitation in the Field of Medical Equipment Technology. *IEEE Transaction of Engineering Management, 55*(2), 219-233.

Levinson, H., Price, C. R, Munden, K. J., Mandl, H. J., & Solley, C. M. (1962). *Men, management and mental health.* Boston: Harvard University Press.

Levitt, T. (1983). The Globalization of Markets. *Harvard Business Review, 61*(3), 92-102.

Liden, R. C., Bauer, T. N., & Erdogan, B. (2004). The role of leader–member exchange in the dynamic relationship between employer and employee: Implications for employee socialization, leaders and organizations. In J. A. -M. Coyle-Shapiro, L. M. Shore, Susan M. Taylor, & L. E. Tetrick (Eds.), *The employment relationship, examining psychological and contextual perspectives.* Oxford: Oxford University Press.

Lievens, F., & Harris, M. (2003). Research on Internet recruiting and testing: Current status and future directions. In C. Cooper & I. Robertson (Eds.), *International Review of Industrial and Organizational Psychology, 18*, (pp. 131-165).

Lievens, F., Hoye, G.V., & Ansell, F. (2007). Organizational Identity and Employer Image: Towards a Unifying Framework. *British Journal of Management, 18*, 45–59.

Lievens, F., van Dam, K., & Anderson, N. (2002). Recent trends and challenges in personnel selection. *Personnel Review, 31*(5), 580-601.

Liff, S. (1997). Constructing HR information systems. *Human Resource Management Journal, 7*(2), 18-30.

Liles, D. H., & Presley, A. (1996). *Enterprise modelling within an enterprise engineering framework.* Winter Simulation Conference, Association for Computing Machinery), San Diego, CA, USA.

Lilien, G., Morrison, P. D., Searls, K., Sonnack, M., & von Hippel, E. (2002). Performance Assessment of the Lead User Generation Process for New Product Development. *Management Science, 48*, 1042-1059.

Lim, K., Leung, K., Sia, C., & Lee, M. (2002). Is e-commerce boundaryless. Effects of individualism-collectivism and uncertainty avoidance on Internet shopping. *Journal of International Business Studies, 35*(1), 545-559.

Limburg, D., Looise, J. C., & Ruël, H. (1998). HRM and ICT in the Knowledge Company. An explorative study to the integration of strategic HRM, production organization and ICT. In *Conference Proceedings of the Sixth conference on International HRM*. Paderborn (BRD).

Lin, B., & Stasinskaya V. S. (2002). Data warehousing management issues in online recruiting. *Human Systems Management, 21*(1), 1-8.

Lin, W. T., & Shao, B. B. (2000). The relationship between user participation and system success: a simultaneous contingency approach. *Information & Management, 37*(6), 283-295.

Link, A. N., & Siegel, D. S. (2007) *Innovation, Entrepreneurship and Technological Change*. Oxford: Oxford University Press.

Lipnack, J., & Stamps, J. (1997). *Virtual teams: reaching across space, time and organization with technology*. Wiley.

Lipnack, J., & Stamps, J. (1999). Virtual teams, *Executive Excellence, 16*(5), May, 14-15.

Little, B. L. (1986). The performance of personnel duties in small Louisiana firms: A research note. *Journal of Small Business Management*, October 1986, 66-71.

Littlejohn, S. W. (2002). *Theories of Human Communication*. Belmont: Wadsworth/Thomson Learning.

Livian, Y.-F., (2001). *Organisation : Théories et pratiques*, 2ème édition, Dunod, Paris.

Louarn, J. Y., & Wils, T. (2001). *The evaluation of the human resources management: Control of the costs to the return on the human investment*. Editions Connections, Paris.

Louart. P. (1996). *Stakes and measurements of a powerful HRM*. In A-M. Fericelli & B. Sire (Eds.), *Performances and human resources*. Paris, Economica.

Lucas, H. J. (1974). Systems Quality, User Reactions, and the Use of Information Systems. *Management Informatics, 3*(4), 207-212.

Lucio, M. M. (2003). New Communication Systems and Trade Union Politics: a Case Study of Spanish Trade Unions and the Role of the Internet. *Industrial Relations Journal, 34*(4), 334–347.

Luftman, J. (2000). Assessing Business-IT Alignment Maturity. *Communications of the Association for Information Systems, 14*, 1-51.

Luftman, J., Kempaiah, R., & Nash, E. (2006). Key Issues for IT Executives 2005. *MIS Quarterly Executive, 5*(2), 81-99.

Lupton, B., & Shaw, S. (2001). Are public sector personnel managers the profession's poor relations? *Human Resource Management Journal, 11*(3), 23-38.

Lüthje, C., & Herstatt, C. (2004). The Lead User method: An outline of empirical findings and issues for future research. *R&D Management, 34*(5), 553-568.

Lykkegaard, B. (2007). *Western European Human Capital Management and Payroll Applications Forecast, 2007-2011*: IDC.

Macduffie, J. P. (1995). Human Resource Bundles and Manufacturing Performance : Organizational Logic and Flexible Production Systems in the World Auto Industry. *Industrial and Labor Relations Review, 48*(2), 197–221.

MacKenzie, D., & Wajcman, J. (Eds.). (1985). *The Social Shaping of Technology: How the Refrigerator Got Its Hum*. Milton Keynes: Open University Press.

Madill, A., Jordan, & A., Shirley, C. (2000). Objectivity and Reliability in Qualitative Analysis: Realist, Contextualist and Radical Constructionist Epistemologies. *British Journal of Psychology, 91*(1), 1-20.

Maes, P. (1994). Agents that Reduce Work and Information Overload. *Communications of the ACM, 37*(7), 31-40.

Magnusson, P. R., Matthing, J., & Kristensson, P. (2003). Managing user involvement in service innovation. *Journal of Service Research, 6*(2), 111-124.

Majchrzak, A., Rice, R. E., Malhotra, A., King, N., & Ba, S. (2000). Technology adaptation: the case of a computer-supported inter-organizational virtual team. *MIS Quarterly, 24*, 569-600.

Malladi, R., & Agrawal, D. P. (2002). Current and Future Applications of Mobile and Wireless Networks. *Communications of the ACM, 45*(10), 144–146.

Manocha, R. R. (2006). Front-line services. *People management, 12*(6), 16.

Manocha, R. R. (2006). MoD shares HR operations. *People management, 12*(5), 10.

Mantei, M. M., & Teorey, T. J. (1988). Cost/Benefit Analysis for Incorporating Human Factors in the Software Lifecycle. *Communications of the ACM , 31*(4), 428-439.

Marakas, G. M., & Hornik, S. (1996). Passive resistance misuse: Overt support and covert recalcitrance in IS implementation. *European Journal of Information Systems, 5*(3), 208-219.

March, J. G., & Simon, H. A. (1958). *Organizations*. New York: Wiley.

Markus, M. L. (1983). Power, Politics and MIS Implementation. *Communications of the ACM, 26*(6), 430-444.

Markus, M. L., & Benjamin, R. I. (1997). The magic bullet theory in IT enabled transformation. *Sloan Management Review, Winter*, (pp. 55-58).

Markus, M. L., & Connoly, T. (1990). Why CSCW applications fail. Problems in the adoption of interdependent work tools. *Proceedings of the CSCW'90* (pp. 7-10). Los Angeles.

Marschan, R., Welch, D., & Welch, L. (1997). Language: The forgotten factor in multinational management. *European Management Journal, 15*(5), 591–598.

Marsden, R. (1993). The politics of organizational analysis. *Organization Studies, 14*(1), 93-124.

Martin, G., & Beaumont, P. (1998). Diffusing 'best practice' in multinational firms: prospects, practice and contestation. *International Journal of Human Resource Management, 9*(4), 671–695.

Martin, G., & Beaumont, P. (1999). Co-ordination and control of human resource management in multinational firms: the case of CASHCO. *International Journal of Human Resource Management, 10*(1), 21–42.

Martin, G., Reddington, M., & Alexander, H. (2008). *Technology, Outsourcing and Transforming HR*. Oxford: Butterworth Heinemann.

Martin, G., Wood, G., & Collings, D. (2006). Institutions, HR strategies and the Adoption and exploitation of e-HR. In: *Proceedings of the 1st European Workshop on e-HRM*. Enschede , Netherlands.

Martin, R. (2002). *Agile Software Development, Principles, Patterns, and Practices*. USA, Prentice Hall

Martinez Lucio, M. (2003). New communication systems and trade union politics : a case study of Spanish trade unions and the role of the internet. *Industrial Relations Journal, 34*(4), 334–347 (September).

Martinez, M. M. N. (2002). Recruiting Here and There. *HR Magazine, 47*(9), 95.

Martinez, M. N. (2000). Get Job Seekers to Come to You. *HR Magazine, 45*, 44-52.

Martinsons, M. G., & Chong, P. K. C. (1999). The influence of human factors and specialist involvement on information systems success. *Human Relations, 52*(1), 123-152.

Mason, R. O. (1978). Measuring information output: A communication systems approach. *Information & Management , 1*(4), 219-234.

Mathieston, K., Peacock, E., & Chin, W. (2001). Extending the technology acceptance model: the influence of perceived user resources. *Database for Advances in Information Systems*, New York, Summer.

Matta, N. F., & Ashkenas, R. N. (2003). Why Good Projects Fail Anyway. *Harvard Business Review, 81(9)*, 109-114

Matthing, J., Kristensson, P., Gustafsson, A., & Parasuraman, A. (2006). Developing Successful Technology-Based Services: The Issue of Identifying and Involving

Innovative Users. *Journal of Service Marketing, 20*(5), 288-297.

Maussion, C. (2002). Il n'est pas temps de légiférer sur l'Intranet. *Libération, November 18,* Paris.

McConnel, B. (2002, April). Companies lure job seekers in new ways: Corporate web sites snare applicants on line, *HR News,* 1, 12.

McGaughey, S., & De Cieri, H. (1999). Reassessment of Convergence and Divergence Dynamics: Implications for International HRM. *International Journal of Human Resource Management, 10,* 235-250.

McGregor, D. (1960). *The Human Side of Enterprise.* New York: McGraw-Hill.

McKeen, J. D., & Guimaraes, T. (1997). Successful strategies for user participation in systems development. *Journal of Management Information Systems , 14*(2), 133-150.

McKeen, J. D., Guimaraes, T., & Wetherbe, J. C. (1994). The Relationship between User Participation and User Satisfaction: An Investigation of Four Contingency Factors. *MIS Quarterly , 18*(4), 427-451.

McKinlay, A. (2002). The Limits of Knowledge Management. *New Technology, Work & Employment, 17*(2), 76-88.

McLean Parks, J., & Kidder, D. L. (1994). «Till Death Us Do Part...» Changing Work Relationships in the 1990s. In C. L. Cooper, & D. M. Rousseau (Eds.), *Trends in Organisational Behaviour,* 1 (pp. 111-136). Chichester, England: John Wiley & Sons.

Meijaard, J., Mosselman, M., Frederiks, K. F., & Brand, M. J. (2002). *Organisatietypen in het MKB.* Zoetermeer: *EIM.*

Mejias, C. (2000). *Latin American Trends in Human Resources. Society for Human Resource Management.* V.A.: Alexandria

Mense-Petermann, U. (2006). Micro-political or intercultural conflicts?—An integrating approach. *Journal of International Management, 12*(3), 302–317.

Mercer. (2007). *HR Transformation 2.0: It's all about the business.*

Merchant, K. A. (1998). *Modern Management Control Systems: Texts and Cases.* Upper Saddle River. NJ: Prentice Hall.

Merck, B., Fabre, M., Proust, M. A., Ridet, F., & Romanet, M. (2002). *Équipes RH, acteurs de la stratégie, l'E-RH : mode ou révolution ?* Paris: Éditions d'Organisation.

Messenger, R. (2004). Style Matters. *Business Mexico, 14*(7), 30-32.

Miles, M. B., & Huberman, A. M. (1984). *Qualitative Data Analysis, 16.* Newbury Park, CA: Sage.

Miles, M. B., & Huberman, A. M. (1994). *Analysis for qualitative data: collection of new methods.* Bruxelles : De Boeck University.

Miles, M. B., & Huberman, A. M. (1994). *Qualitative data analysis: An expanded sourcebook.* (2nd Ed.). Thousand Oaks, CA: Sage.

Miller, G. A. (1956). The Magical Number Seven, Plus or Minus Two: Some Limits on Our Capacity for Processing Information. *The Psychological Review, 63,* 81-97.

Mingers, J. (2001). Information, Meaning and Communication: an autopoietic approach. In F. Geyer & J. van der Zouwen (Eds.), *Sociocybernetics: complexity, autopoiesis and observation of social systems.*Westport, CT: Greenwood Press.

Ministerie van Binnenlandse Zaken en Koninkrijksrelaties. (2007). *Nota Vernieuwing Rijksdienst.* Retrieved Februari 08, 2008, from http://www.minbzk.nl/aspx/download.aspx?file=/contents/pages/89897/notavernieuwingrijksdienst.pdf

Ministry of Internal Affairs (2006). Press statement Retrieved July 21, 2007, from P-Direkt: http://www.p-direkt.nl/index.cfm?action=dsp_actueelitem&itemid=QKNGJL8E.

Minneman, W. A. (1996). Strategic justification for an HRIS that adds value. (Human resource information systems). *HR Magazine, 41*(12), 35-38.

Mintzberg, H. (1989). *Management, voyage au coeur des organizations*. Editions d'organisation

Mitchell, C. (2002). Selling the Brand Inside. *Harvard Business Review, 1-2,* 73-80.

Mitra, K. (2006). The New Dotcom Millionaire. *Business Today* (p. 124).

MKB Nederland (2006). *Het midden- en kleinbedrijf in een oogopslag*. Retrieved, August 22, 2006, from http://www.mkb.nl/Het_midden-_en_kleinbedrijf.

Mohrman, S.A. 1999. The Contexts for Geographically Dispersed Teams and Networks. In C. Cooper, & D. Rousseau (Eds.), *Trends in Organizational Behavior*, (pp. 63-80). New York: John Wiley & Sons.

Moll, P. (1983). Should the Third World have information technologies? *IFLA Journal, 9*(4), 297.

Mollison, C. (2001). The Internet World Interview. *Internet World Magazine*. Retrieved from http://www.iw.com/magazine.php?inc=050101/05.01.01interview.html.

Mooney, J. (2002). Pre-Employment Testing on the Internet: Put Candidates a Click Away and Hire at Modem Speed. *Public Personnel Management, 31,* 41-52.

Morris, M. G., & Venkatesh, V. (2000). Age differences in technology adoption decisions: Implications for a changing workforce. *Personnel Psychology Inc., 53,* 375 – 403.

Morrison P. D, Roberts J. H., & von Hippel E. (2000). Determinants of user innovation and innovation sharing in a local market. Management Science, *46*(12), 1513–1527.

Muhl, C. J. (2003). Workplace E-mail And Internet Use :Employees And Employers Beware. *Monthly Labor Review, February*, 36–45.

Muller, M. (2001). A participatory poster of participatory methods. *Conference on Human Factors in Computing Systems, CHI '01 extended abstracts on Human factors in computing systems*, (pp. 99 - 100).

Murphy, H. L. (1999). Top Job Sites. *Marketing News, 33,* 13-17.

Murphy, T. E., & Zandvakili, S. (2000). Data and metrics driven approach to human resource practices using customer, employees and financial metrics. *Human Resource Management, 39*(1), 93-105.

Murray, D. (2001). E-Learning for the Workplace: Creating Canada's Lifelong Learners. The Conference Board of Canada, www.conferenceboard.ca.

Murray, S. (2001). From tiny job boards into mighty career networks. A brief history of online recruitment. *Financial Times*, 04.

Myerscough, M. (2000). The relationship of age and gender on user information satisfaction for web-based intranet systems applications. working paper, University of Wisconsin, USA.

Nah, F. F., Lau, J. L., & Kuang, J. (2001). Critical Factors for Successful Implementation of Enterprise Systems. *Business Process Management Journal, 7*(3), 285-296.

Nahapiet, J., & Ghoshal, S. (1998). Social capital, intellectual capital, and the organizational advantage. *Academy of Management Review, 23,* 242–66.

Navarrete, C., & Pick, J. (2002). Information technology expenditure and industry performance: The case of the Mexican Banking Industry. *Journal of Global Information Technology Management, 5*(2), 7-29.

Nederlandse Vereniging voor Personeelsmanagement en Organisatieontwikkeling (2006). *On-line resultaten van de NVP e-HRM enquete*. Retrieved, March 2006, from http://www.nvp-plaza.nl/documents/e-hrmresults2005.html

Newman, K. L., & Nollen, S. D. (1996). Culture and Congruence: The Fit between Management Practices and National Culture. *Journal of International Business Studies, 27,* 753-778.

Ngai, E.W.T., & Wat, F.K.T. (2006). Human Resource information systems: a review and empirical analysis. *Personnel Review, 35*(3), 297-314.

Nickel, J., & Schaumberg, H. (2004). Electronic privacy, Trust and Self-disclosure in e-recruitment. *CHI 2004*, april 24-29, Vienna, Austria

Nielsen, J. (1993). *Usability Engineering.* San Diego: Academic Press.

Nielsen, J. (1999). *Designing Web Usability.* Peachpit Press.

Nielsen, J. (2000). *Designing Web Usability.* New Riders Publishing, Indianapolis.

Nizet, J., & Pichault, F. (2001), *Introduction à la théorie des configurations,* coll. Management, De Boeck Université, Bruxelles.

Nonaka, I., & Takeuchi, H. (1995). *The Knowledge-Creating Company: How Japanese Companies Create the Dynamics of Innovation.* USA: Oxford University Press.

Nonaka, I., von Krogh, G., & Voelpel, S. (2006). Organizational knowledge creation theory: Evolutionary paths and future advances. *Organization Studies, 27*(8), 1179–1208.

Norman, D. (1988). *The Psychology of Everyday Things.* New-York: Basic Books.

Noyes, J. M., & Thomas, P. J. (1995). Information overload - an overview. *IEEE Colloquium Digest, 95*(223), 1-3.

Noyes, J., & Baber, C. (1999). *User-Centered Design of Systems.* Heidelberg, Germany: Springer Verlag.

Noyes, P. M., Starr, A. F., & Frankish, C. R. (1996). User involvement in the early stages of an aircraft warning system. *Behaviour & Information Technology , 15*(2), 67-75.

O'Connell, M., Hattrup, K., Doverspike, D., & Cober, A. (2002). The Validity of "Mini" Simulations for Mexican Retail Salespeople. *Journal of Business and Psychology, 16*(4), 593-599.

O'Donohue, W., Sheehan, C., Hecker, R., & Holland, P. (2007). The psychological contract of knowledge workers. *Journal of Knowledge Management, 11*(2), 73-82.

O'Leary, B., Lindholm, M., Whitford, R., & Freeman, S. (2002). Selecting the best and brightest: leveraging human capital. *Human Resource Management, 41*(2), 325-340.

O'Reilly III, C. A. (1980). Individuals and Information Overload in Organizations: Is More Necessarily Better? *The Academy of Management Journal, 23*(4), 684-696.

OECD (2002). *Standardised Unemployment Rates.* Retrieved from http://www.oecd.org/pdf/M00030000/M00030784.pdf, on 15.07.2002.

Oh, W., & Pinsonneault, A. (2007). On the assessment of the strategic value of information technologies: conceptual and analytical approaches. *MIS Quarterly, 31*(2), 239-265.

Olivas-Lujan, M., Ramirez, J., & Zapata-Cantu, L (2007). E-HRM in Mexico: Adapting innovativeness for global competitiveness. *International Journal of Manpower, 28*(5), 418-434.

Oliver, C. (1991). Strategic responses to institutional processes. *Academy of Management Review, 16*(1), 145–179.

Olson, E. L., & Bakke, G. (2001). Implementing the Lead User Method in a High Technology Firm: A Longitudinal Study of Intentions versus Actions. *Journal of Product Innovation Management, 18*, 388-395.

Olson, T. K., & Teasley, S. (1996). Groupware in the wild. Lessons learned from a year of virtual collocation. *Proceedings of the CSCW'96* (pp. 362-369). Boston: ACM Press.

Organ, D. W. (1997). Organisational Citizenship Behaviour: Its Construct Clean-Up Time. *Human Performance, 10*, 85-97.

Orlikowski, W. & Robey, D. (1991). Information technology and the structuring of organizations. Working paper No. 220, CISR. Sloan School of Management, Massachusetts Institute of technology.

Orlikowski, W. (2000). Using technology and constituting structures: a practice lens for studying technology in organizations. *Organization Science, 11*(4), 404-428.

Orlikowski, W. J. (1993). CASE Tools as Organizational Change: Investigating Incremental and Radical Changes in Systems Development. *Management Information Systems Quarterly, 17*(3), 309-340.

Orlikowski, W., & Gash D.C. (1994). Technological frames: Making sense of information technology in organizations. *ACM Transactions on information systems, 2*(2), 143-169.

Orlikowski, W., & Gash, C. (1994). Technological frames: making sense of information technology in organisations. *ACM transactions on Information Systems, 12*(2), 174-207.

Orlikowski, W., & Robey D. (1991). Information Technology and the Structuring of organisations. *Information Systems Research, 2,* 143-169.

Osterman, P. (1994). How common is workplace transformation and who adopts it? *Industrial and Labor Relations Review, 47*(2), 173-188.

Othman, R. (2003). On developing the informated work place: HRM issues in Malaysia. *Human Resource Management Review, 13,* 393-406.

Othman, R., & Musa, N. (2007). E-reccruitment. Pros Vs Cons. *Public Sector ICT Management Review, 1(*1), 35-39.

Overheid heeft Antwoord (2008). *Actueel.* Retrieved August 2008 from http://www.advies.overheid.nl.

Owen, R. S. (1992). Clarifying the Simple Assumption of the Information Load Paradigm. *Advances in Consumer Research, 19,* 770-776.

Paauwe, J. (2004). *HRM and Performance: Achieving long-term viability.* Oxford University Press.

Paradiso, J. J. (1999). Harnessing your benefits knowledge. *Employee benefit news, 13*(2), 21.

Paré, G. (2004). Investigating informations systems with positivist case study research. *Communications of the Associatoin for informations systems, 13,* 233–264.

Paré, G., & Elam, J. J. (1995). Discretionary Use of Personal Computers by Knowledge Workers: Testing of a Social Psychology Theoretical Model. *Behavior and Information Technology, 14 (4),* 215-228.

Parry, E. (2008), Drivers of the adoption of online recruitment: An analysis using diffusion of innovation theory.

In. T.V. Bondarouk & H.J.M. Ruël (Eds), *E-HRM in theory and practice.* Amsterdam: Elsevier.

Pascal, A. (2006). *Conception of an IT Solution to Favorize Innovative Project Emergence: Approach by Use. The KMP Experience.* Unpublished doctoral dissertation, University of Nice-Sophia Antipolis, France.

Pascal, A., & Thomas, C. (2007). Role of boundary objects in the coevolution of design and use: the KMP experimentation. *Proceedings of 23rd EGOS Colloquium.* Vienna July 5—7.

Pearce, C. G. & Tuten, T. L. (2001). Internet Recruiting in the Banking Industry. *Business Communication Quarterly, 64,* 9-18.

Pearce, J. (2005). In-House or Out-Source? Three Key Elements for IT Development. *Franchising World, 37*(4), 93-95.

Pekkola, S., Niina, K., & Pasi, P. (2006). Towards Formalised End-User Participation in Information Systems Development Process: Bridging the Gap between Participatory Design and ISD Methodologies. *Proceedings of the ninth Participatory Design Conference 2006 ,* 21-30.

PeopleManagement (2006). NHS shows it shares. *People management , 12*(20), 10.

PeopleManagement (2007). In the hot seat. *People management, 13*(13), 28.

Peretti, J. M. (1993). Sharing of the function and sharing of information. *Personnel, 346,* November. - December.

Perrow, C. (1967). A Framework for the Comparative Analysis of Organizations. *American Sociological Review, 32*(2), 194-208.

Peterson, A. (2000). Opening a Portal: E-Commerce apostle target Latin America. *Wall Street Journal (Eastern Edition), A1.*

Phillips, L. L. (2007). HR centres could help SMEs to recruit long-term jobless people. *People management, 13*(21), 13.

Piturro, M. (2000). The Power of E-Cruiting. *Management Review, 89,* 33-37.

Platt, L. (1999). Virtual teaming: where is everyone? *The Journal of Quality and Participation*, Sept.-Oct., (pp. 41-43).

Polachek, S., & Siebert, W. (1993) *The economics of earnings.* Cambridge, England: Cambridge University Press.

Polanyi, M. (1958, 1998) *Personal Knowledge. Towards a Post Critical Philosophy.* London: Routledge.

Polanyi, M. (1967) *The Tacit Dimension.* New York: Doubleday & Co.

Pollitt, D. (2005). E-recruitment gets the Nike tick of approval. *Human Resource Management International Digest, 13*(2) 33-36.

Pomerol, J.-Ch., Brèzillon, P., & Pasquier, L. (2002). Operational Knowledge Representation for Practical Decision Making. *Journal of Management Information Systems, 18*(4), 101-116.

Poole, M. S., & DeSanctis, G. (1989).Use of group decision support systems as an appropriation process. In: *Proceedings of the 22nd Annual Hawaii International Conference on System Sciences* (pp. 149-157). New York: ACM

Poole, M. S., & DeSanctis, G. (1990). Understanding the use of group decision support systems: the theory of Adaptive Structuration. In J. Fulk, & C. Steinfield (Eds.), *Organizations and communication technology* (pp. 173-193). Newbury Park/London/New Delhi: Sage Publications

Poole, M. S., & DeSanctis, G. (1992). Micro-level structuration in computer-supported group decision-making. *Human communication research, 19*, 5-49.

Powell, A., Piccoli, G., & Ives, B. (2004) Virtual teams: A review of current literature and directions for future research. *The Data Base for Advances in Information Systems, 35*(1), 6-36.

Powell, W., & DiMaggio, P. J. (Eds.). (1991). *The New Institutionalism in Organizational Analysis.* Chicago-London: University of Chicago Press.

Prahalad, C. K., & Hamel, G. (1990). The Core Competence of the Corporation. *Harvard Business Review, 68*, 79-91.

Preece, J., Nonnecke, B., & Andrews, D. (2004). The top five reasons for lurking: Improving community experiences for everyone. *Computers in Human Behavior, 20*(2), 201-223.

Pressman, J. L. & Wildavsky, A. B. (1973). *Implementation. How Great Expectations in Washington are dashed in Oakland.* Berkeley, L.A.: University of California Press.

Puck, J. F. (2002). *Personalrekrutierung über die Personalhomepage.* Ibidem, Stuttgart.

Puck, J. F., Mohr, A. T., & Holtbrügge, D. (2006). Cultural Convergence through Web-Based Management Techniques? The Case of Corporate Web Site Recruiting. *Journal of International Management, 12*, 181-195.

Purcell, J. (1999). Best practice and best fit: Chimera or cul-de-sac? *Human Resource Management Journal, 9*(3), 26-34.

Quinn, B., Cooke, R. et al. (2000). *Shared services: mining for corporate gold.* Harlow, Pearson Education Limited.

Quint (2004). Sharing Shared Services: *Onderzoek naar ontwikkelingen in de Nederlandse markt. Amsterdam,* The Quint Wellington Redwood Group.

Ramamurthi, R. (2001). Wipro's Chairman Azim Premji on building a world class Indian company. *Academy of Management Executive, 18*(12), 13-19.

Rasmus, D. (2005). Digital Workstyle: The New World of Work [Electronic Version]. Retrieved 01-05-2007 from http://download.microsoft.com/download/B/E/4/BE40F0BC-434B-487C-B788-20052D75A3EC/NewWorldofWorkWP.doc.

Rastogi, P. N. (2000). Sustaining enterprise competitiveness - is human capital the answer? *Human Systems Management, 19*(3), 193-203.

Rastogi, P. N. (2003). The Nature and Role of IC - Rethinking the Process of Value Creation and Sustained

Enterprise Growth. *Journal of Intellectual Capital, 4(2)*, 227-248.

Réau, P. (2003). Campagne de syndicalisation au bout du fil, 29 octobre. Retrieved from www.cfdt.fr/actualite.

Reddington, M., & Martin, G. (2007). Theorizing the links between e-HR and strategic HRM: A framework, case illustration and some reflections. *Proceedings of the First European Academic Workshop on Electronic Human Resource Management.*

Reddington, M., Williamson, M., & Withers, M. (2005). *Transforming HR: Creating Value Through People.* Oxford: Butterworth Heinemann.

Reich, B. H., & Benbasat, I. (2000). Factors that Influence the Social Dimension of Linkage Between Business and Information Technology Objectives. *Management Information Systems Quarterly, March,* 81-113.

Reix, R. (1999). *Management and Information System.* dictionnaire des systemes d'information. Vuibert.

Remus, U. (2007). Critical Success Factors for Implementing Enterprise Portals: A Comparison with ERP Implementations. *Business Process Management Journal, 13*(4), 538-552.

Riemenschneider, C., Moore, J. E., & Armstrong, D. (2008). Call for papers - Special Issue on Meeting the Renewed Demand for IT Workers. *European Journal of Information Systems (EJIS).* Retrieved from http://www.palgrave-journals.com/ejis/CFP-EJIS-ITWorkers.pdf.

Riemsdijk, M. van, Bondarouk, T., & Knol, H. (2005). *Researching Personnel Management in Dutch Small and Medium Sized Enterprises.* A literature overview and a research model. Paper Presented at The International Dutch HRM Network Conference, 4-5 November 2005, Enschede, The Netherlands.

Rifkin, G. (1989). Recruiting in MIS: Facing Up to Hire Stakes. *Computerworld, 23*(6), February 13.

Robey D., Ross, J. W., & Boudreau, M.-C. (2002). Learning to Implement Enterprise Systems: An Exploratory Study of the Dialectics of Change. *Journal of Management Information Systems, 19*(1), 17-46.

Robey, D., & Farrow, D. (1982). User Involvement in Information System Development: A Conflict Model and Empirical Test. *Management Science, , 28*(1), 73-85.

Robinson, S. L., Kraatz, M. S., & Rousseau, D. M. (1994). Changing Obligations and the Psychological Contract: A Longitudinal Study. *Academy of Management Journal, 37*(1), 137-152.

Romelaer, P. (2002). *Innovations and constraints of management, Book of Crepa*, Paris Dauphine University. *37.*

Rondeau, P. J., Ragu-Nathan, T. S., & Vonderembse, M. A. (2006). How involvement, IS management effectiveness, and end user computing impact IS performance in manufacturing firms. *Information and Management, 43*(1), 93-107.

Rose, J. G. (2003). The Joys of Enterprise portals. *The Information Management Journal, Sept/Oct,* (pp. 64-70).

Rosen, D. E., Purinton, E., & Lloyd, S. J. (2004). Web Site Design: Building a Cognitive Framework. *Journal of Electronic Commerce in Organizations, 2,* 15-29.

Rosenzweig, P., & Nohria, N. (1994). Influences on human resource management practices in multinational corporations. *Journal of International Business Studies, 25*(2), 229–251.

Rousseau, D. M. (1989). Psychological and Implied Contracts in Organisations. *Employee Responsibilities and Rights Journal, 2,* 121-139.

Rousseau, D. M. (1995). *Psychological Contracts in Organizations.* Thousands Oaks, CA: Sage

Rousseau, D. M., & Mclean Parks, J. (1993). The Contract of Individuals and Organisations. In B. M. Staw & L. L. Cummings (Eds.), *Research in Organisational Behaviour, 15,* 1-43. Greenwich, CT: JAI Press.

Rowley, D. E. (1996). Organizational considerations in field-oriented product development: Experiences of a cross-functional team. In D. Wixon, & J. Ramey (Eds.), *Methods Casebook for Software Design* (pp. 125 - 144). New York: Wiley.

Rucci, A., Kirn, S., & Quinn, R. (1998). The employee-customer-profit chain at Sears. *Harvard Business Review, 70*(1), 82-87.

Rudich, J. (2000). Job hunting on the web. *Link up, 17*(2), 21-25.

Ruël, H. J. M., Bondarouk, T. V., Velde, & M. van der (2007). Does e-HRM influence HRM effectiveness? *Employee Relations, 24*, 16-25.

Ruël, H. J. M., Bondarouk, T., & Looise, J. C. (2004). E-HRM: innovation or irritation. An explorative empirical study in five large companies on web-based HRM. *Management revue, 15*(3), 364-380.

Ruël, H. J. M., Bondarouk, T., & Velde, M. van der (2007). The contribution of e-HRM to HRM effectiveness. *Employee Relations, 29*(3), 280 - 291.

Ruël, H. J. M., Leede, J. de, & Looise, J. C. (2002). ICT en het management van arbeidsrelaties; hoe zit het met de relatie? In R. Batenburg, J. Benders, N. Van den Heuvel, P. Leisink, & J. Onstenk, (Eds.), *Arbeid en ICT in onderzoek.* Utrecht: Lemma.

Ruel, H., & Magalhaes, R. (2008). *Human Resource Information Systems: an Integrated Research Agenda.* Forthcoming book chapter, Elsevier Science.

Ruta, C. D. (2005). The application of change management theory to HR portal implementation in subsidiaries of multinational corporations. *Human Resource Management.* Spring 2005, *44*(1), 35-53.

Ruta, C. D. (in press). HR Portal Alignment for the Creation and Development of Intellectual Capital. *International Journal of Human Resource Management.*

Ryan, A.M., McFarland, L., Baron, H., & Page, R. (1999). An International Look at Selection Practices: Nation and Culture as Explanations for Variability in Practice. *Personnel Psychology, 52*, 359-391.

Saadé, R., & Bahli, B. (2004). The impact of cognitive absorption on perceived usefulness and perceive ease of use in on-line learning: an extension of the technology acceptance model. *Information Management, 42*, 317-327.

Saarinen, T. (1996). SOS An expanded instrument for evaluating information system success. *Information & Management, 31*(2), 103-118.

Sambamurthy, V., Bharadwaj, A., & Grover, A. (2003). Shaping Agility though Digital Option. *MIS Quarterly, 27*(2), 237-263.

SAP Corporation (2008). Components & Tools of SAP NetWeaver: SAP NetWeaver Business Intellegence. Retrieved September 1, 2008, from http://www.sap.com/platform/netweaver/components/bi/index.epx

Saunders, M., Lewis, P. et al. (2007). *Research Methods for Business Students.* Harlow, Financial Times/Prentice Hall.

Saunders, M., Lewis, P., & Thornhill, A. (2003). *Research Methods for Business Students*, 3rd edition. Essex: Pearson Education Ltd.

Savoyant, A., & Leplat, J. (1983). Statut et fonction des communications dans les activités des équipes de travail. *Psychologie française, 28*(3/4), 247-253.

Sawyer, R. K. (2005). *Social Emergence: societies as complex systems.* Cambridge, UK: Cambridge University Press.

Scarbourgh, H., & Elias, J. (2002) *Evaluating Human Capital Chartered Institute of Personnel and Development.* London

Schein, E., (1980). *Organisational Psychology.* Englewood Cliffs, NJ: Prentice-Hall.

Schick, A. G., & Gordon, L.A. (1990). Information overload: a temporal approach. *Accounting, Organizations and Society, 15*(3), 199-220.

Schmitt, M., & Sadowski, D. (2003). A cost-minimization approach to the international transfer of HRM/IR practices: Anglo-Saxon multinationals in the Federal Republic of Germany. *International Journal of Human Resource Management, 14*(3), 409–430.

Schneider, B. (1995). *Personalbeschaffung.* Frankfurt: Peter Lang Europaeischer Verlag der Wissenschaften.

Schramm, J. (2006). HR technology Competencies: New Roles for HR Professionals. *HR Magazine, 51*(4), special section, 1-10.

Schreier, M., Oberhauser, S., & Pruegl, R. (2007). Lead users and the adoption and diffusion of new products: Insights from two extreme sports communities. *Marketing Letters, 18*(1–2), 15–30.

Schryer, C. F. (1993). Records as Genre. *Written Communication, 10,* 200-234.

Schuler, R. S. (1992). Strategic human resources management: linking the people with the strategic needs of the business. *Organizational Dynamics, 21*(1), 18–32.

Schuler, R. S., & Jackson, J. E. (1988). Organizational Strategy and Organizational Levels as Determinants of Human Resource Management Practices. *Human Resource Plannin., 10*(3), 125-141.

Schuler, R. S., & Rogovsky, N. (1998). Understanding Compensation Practice Variations across Firms: The Impact of National Culture. *Journal of International Business Studie, 29*(1), 159-168.

Schuler, R. S., Dowling, P. J., & Cieri, H. D. (1993). An Integrative Framework of Strategic International Human Resource Management. *Journal of Management, 19,* 419-459.

Schultz, T. W. (1961). Investment in human capital. *American Economic Review, 51(1),* 1-17.

Schultze, U., & Vandenbosch, B. (1998). Information Overload in a Groupware Environment: Now You See It, Now You Don't. *Journal of Organizational Computing and Eelectronic Commerce, 8*(2), 127-148.

Schwaber, K., & Beedle, M. (2000). *Agile Software Development with SCRUM.* USA: Prentice Hall

Schwarzkopf, A. B., Mejias, R. , Jasperson, J., Saunders, C., & Gruenwald, H. (2001). *Effective practices for IT skills staffing",* Communications of the ACM, 47(1), 83-88.

Scott ,W. R., & Meyer, J. W. (1994). *Institutional Environments and Organizations: Structural Complexity and Individualism.* London: Sage.

Scott, A. A. (2006). Councils unite to cut costs. *People management, 12*(24), 13.

Seely Brown, J., & Duguid, P. (2002). *The Social Life of Information.* Harvard Business School Press.

Sels, L., Winne, S. de, Delmotte, J., Maes, J., Faems, D., & Forrier, A. (2006). Linking HRM and Small Business Performance: An Examination of the Impact of HRM Intensity on the Productivity and Financial Performance of Small Businesses. *Small Business Economics, 26,* 83-101.

Senge, P. M. (1990). *The fifth discipline.* Century Business.

Serengul Guven Smith, A. (2000). *Application of Machine Learning Algorithms in Adaptive Web-based Information Systems,* School of Computing Science Technical Report Series. Retrieved from http://www.cs.mdx.ac.uk/staffpages/serengul/Pdf/chapter%204.PDF.

Sessa, V., & Taylor, J. (2000). *Executive Selection: Strategies for Success.* San Francisco: Jossey-Bass and The Center for Creative Leadership.

SFIA (2008) *The Skills Framework for the Information Age (SFIA)* Retrieved 23 May 2008, 2008 from http://www.sfia.org.uk/

Shanks, G., & Seddon, P. (2000). Editorial Enterprise resource planning (ERP) systems. *Journal of Information Technology, 15*(4), 243-244.

Shannon, C. E., & Weaver, W. (1949). *The mathematical theory of communication .* Urbana: University of Illinois Press.

Shapiro, D. (2005). Participatory design: the will to succeed. *Proceedings of the 4th decennial conference on Critical computing: between sense and sensibility,* (pp. 29-38). Aarhus, Denmark.

Sheng, H., Siau, K., & Nah, F. (2005) Strategic Implications of Mobile Technology: A Case Study Using Value-Focused Thinking. *Journal of Strategic Information Systems, 14*(3), 23-55.

Shilakes, C. C., & Tylman, J. (1998). *Enterprise Information portals.* New York: Merrill Lynch, Inc.

Shore, L. M., & Tetrick, L. E. (1994). The psychological contract as an explanatory framework in the employment relationship. In C. Cooper & D. Rousseau (Eds.), *Trends in organizational behavior, 1* (pp. 91–109). New York: Wiley.

Shrivastava, S., & Shaw, J. B. (2003). Liberating HR through technology. *Human Resource Management, 42*(3), 201–222.

Siegel, D. S. (1999). *Skill-biased Technological Change: Evidence from a firm-level Survey.* Kalamazoo, MI: W E Upjohn Institute Press.

Siegel, D. S., Waldman, D. A., & Youngdahl, W. E. (1997). The Adoption of Advanced Manufacturing Technologies: Human Resource Management Implications. *IEEE Transactions on Engineering Management, 44,* 288-298.

Sierhuis, M., & Clancey, W. J. (1997). Knowledge, Practice, Activities and People, AAAI Spring Symposium on Artificial Intelligence in Knowledge Management, 142-148. AAAI Press.

Sierhuis, M., & Clancey, W.J., (2002). Modeling and Simulating Practices, a Work Method for Work Systems Design. *Intelligent Systems, 17*(5), 32-41.

Sierhuis, M., Clancey, W. J., Hoof, R., & Hoog, R. (2000). *Modeling and simulating work practices from Apollo12 .* 6th International Workshop on Simulation for European Space Programmes, ESTEC.

Silverman, D. (2001). *Interpreting Qualitative Data: Methods for Analysing Talk, Text and Interaction.* London: Sage.

Silverman, R. (2006). Buying Better to Buy Better. Contract Management, 46(11), 8-12.

Simon, H. (1957). *Models of man: social and rational. Mathematical essays on rational human behavior in a social setting.* New York: Wiley.

Simonsen, J., & Kensing, F. (1997). Using ethnography in contextural design. *Communications of the ACM , 40*(7), 82-88.

Simpson, C. W., & Prusak, L. (1995). Troubles with Information Overload - Moving from Quantity to Quality in Information Provision. *International Journal of Information Management, 15*(6), 413-425.

Sippola, A., & Smale, A. (2007). The global integration of diversity management: A longitudinal case study. *International Journal of Human Resource Management, 18*(11), 1895–1916.

Sire, B. (2001). Ten years of HRM which changed France Telecom, Notes of the LIRHE, *350,* November.

Smale, A. (2007). *Mechanisms of Global HRM Integration in Multinational Corporations.* Unpublished dissertation, No.181, University of Vaasa, Finland.

Smale, A. (2008). Foreign subsidiary perspectives on the mechanisms of global HRM integration. *Human Resource Management Journal, 18*(2), 135–153.

Smith, A. D., & Rupp, W. T. (2004). Managerial challenges of e-recruiting. *Online Information Review, 28*(1), 61-74.

Smits, S., McLean, E. R., & Tanner, J. R. (1993). Managing high-achieving information systems professionals. *Journal of Management Information Systems, 9*(4), 103-120.

Snape, E., Thompson, D., Yan, F. K., & Redman, T. (1998). Performace Appraisal and Culture: Practice and Attitudes in Hong Kong and Great Britain. *International Journal of Human Resource Management, 9,* 841-861.

Snell S. A., Youndt, M., & Wright, P. (1996). Establishing a Framework for Research in Strategic Human Resource Management: Merging Resource Theory and Organizational Learning. In G. Ferris (Ed.), *Research in Personnel and Human Resource Management.* Greenwich, CT: JAI Press, *114,* 61-90.

Snell, S. A., & Dean, J. W. (1992). Integrated Manufacturing and Human Resource Management : A Human Capital Perspective. *Academy of Management Journal, 35,* 467–504.

Snell, S. A., Stuebner, D., & Lepak, D. P. (2002). Virtual HR departments: Getting out of the middle. In D. B. G.

R. L. Henneman (Ed.), *Human Resource Management in virtual organisations* (pp. 81-101). Greenwich: Information Age Publishing.

Snell, S., Stueber, D., & Lepak, D. (1992). Virtual HR departments: Getting out of the middle. In R. L. Heneman & D. B. Greenberger (Eds.), *Human resource management in virtual organizations* (pp. 81-101). Greenwich, CT: Information Age Publishing

Snow, C.C., Lipnack, J., & Stamps, J. (1999). The Virtual Organization: promises and payoffs, large and small. In C. Cooper & D. Rousseau (Eds.), *Trends in Organizational Behaviour*, New-York: Wiley.

Soderberg, A.-M. & Holden, N. (2002). Rethinking Cross Cultural Management in a Globalizing Business World. *International Journal of Cross Cultural Management*, 2, 103-121.

Solomon, J. (2005). India poaches U.S executives for tech jobs. *Wall Street Journal*. (Eastern Edition), B1.

Som, A. (2006). Bracing for MNC competition through innovative HRM practices: The way ahead for Indian firms. *Thunderbird International Review, 48(2)*, 207-237.

Sparrow, P. (2006). Global knowledge management and HRM. In G. K. Stahl & I. Björkman (Eds.), *Handbook of Research in International Human Resource Management* (pp. 113–138). Edward Elgar, Cheltenham.

Sparrow, P. R. (1999). Strategy and Cognition: Understanding the Role of Management Knowledge Structures, Organizational Memory and Information Overload. *Creativity and Innovation Management, 8*(2), 140-148.

Sparrow, P., Brewster, C., & Harris, H. (2004). *Globalizing Human Resource Management*. London: Routledge.

Speier, C., Valacich, J.S., & Vessey, I. (1997). The effects of task interruption and information presentation on individual decision making. *Paper presented at the International conference on Information systems Atlanta, Georgia, United States.*

Spognardi, M. S., & Hill Bro, R. (1998). Organizing Through Cyberspace : Electronic Communications and the National Labor Relations Act. *Employee Relations Law Journal, 23*(4), 141–151.

Sridhar, B. (2005). E-Recruitment, the right way. *The Hindu*. Retrieved from http://www.hinduonnet.com/jobs/0503/2005030900350600.htm

Srinivasan, P., Babu, V., & Sahad, P. (2005). Durable Dotcoms. *Business Today*, 60.

Starng, D., & Meyer, J. W. (1994). Institutional Conditions for Diffusions. In R. Scott & J. W. Meyer (Eds), *Institutional Environments and Organizations: Structural Complexity and Individualism* (pp. 100-112). Newbury Park, CA: Sage.

Stern, B., Zinkhan, G. M., & Jaju, A. (2001). Marketing Images: Construct Definition, Measurement Issues, and Theory Development. *Marketing Theory, 1*(2), 201-224.

Stewart, G. L., & Manz, C. C. (1995). Leadership for self-managing work teams: a typology and integrative model. *Human Relation, 48*(7), 747-759.

Stewart, T. A. (1997). *Intellectual Capital*. New York: Doubleday-Currency

Stone, D. L., Lukaszewski, K. M., & Isenhour, L.C. (2005). E-Recruiting: Online strategies for attracting talent. In: H. G. Gueutal & D. L. Stone (Eds.), *The Brave New World of eHR. Human Resources Management in the Digital Age*. San Francisco: Jossey-Bass.

Stone, D. L., Stone-Romero, E. F., & Lukaszewski, K. (2006). Factors affecting the acceptance and effectiveness of electronic human resource systems. *Human Resource Management Review, 16*(2), 229-244.

Stone, D., & Gueutal, H. (2005). *The brave new world of e-HR: human resources management in the digital age*. San Francisco: Jossey-Bass.

Stone, D., Stone-Romero, E., & Lukaszewski, K. (2006). Factors affecting the acceptance and effectiveness of electronic human resource systems. *Human Resource Management Review, 16*, 229-244.

Stover, M. (1999). *Leading the Wired Organization*. New York: Neal Schuman Publishers

Strassmann, P. A. (1999). Measuring and Managing Knowledge Capital [Electronic Version]. Retrieved 28-03-2007 from http://www.strassmann.com/pubs/measuring-kc/.

Strauss, A., & Corbin, J. (1998). *Basics of qualitative research: Techniques and procedures for developing grounded theory*. (2nd Ed.), Thousand Oaks, CA: Sage.

Strikwerda, J. (2007). *Shared Service Centers; Van kostenbesparing naar waardecreatie*. Assen, Koninklijke Van Gorcum.

Strohmeier S. (2007). Research in e-HRM: Review and implications. *Human Resource Management Review*, *17*(1), 19-37.

Strohmeier, S. (2006). Coping with contradictory consequences of e-HRM. In: *Proceedings of the 1st European Workshop on e-HRM*, Enschede (Netherlands).

Strohmeier, S. (2006). Coping with contradictory consequences of e-HRM, *Proceedings of the 1ˢᵗ academic workshop on e-HRM research*, University of Twente, The Netherlands .

Strohmeier, S. (2007). Research in e-HRM: Review and implications. *Human Resource Management Review* , *17*(1), 19-37.

Subramanian, M., & Youndt, M.A. (2005). The influence of intellectual capital on the types of Innovative Capabilities. *Academy of Management Journal, 18*(3), 450-463.

Sundstrom, E., De Meuse, K. P., & Futrell, D. (1990). Work teams: Applications and effectiveness, *American Psychologists, 45*(2), 120-133.

Suryanarayanan, M. (2001). A Guide to Better Positions and Better Performance. *The Hindu*. Retrieved from http://www.hinduonnet.com/jobs/0105/05230014.htm.

Swain, M. R., & Haka, S.F. (2000). Effects of Information Load on Capital Budgeting Decisions. *Behavioral Research in Accounting, 12*, 171-198.

Szmigin, I., Canning, L., & Reppel, A. E. (2005). Online community: Enhancing the relationship marketing concept through customer bonding. *International Journal of Service Industry Management, 16*(5), 480-496.

Tannenbaum, S. I. (1990). Human resource information system: User group implications. Journal of Systems Management, *41*(1), 27-32.

Tansley, C., Newell, S., & Williams, H. (2001). Effecting HRM-style practices through an integrated human resource information system: An e-greenfield site? *Personnel Review, 30*(3), 351-370.

Tavangarian, D., Leypold, M. E., Nölting, K., Röser, M., & Voigt, D. (2004) Is e-Learning the Solution for Individual Learning? *Electronic Journal of e-Learning, 2*(2), 273-280.

Tayeb, M. H. (1998). Transfer of HRM practices across cultures: An American company in Scotland. *International Journal of Human Resource Management, 9*(2), 332–58.

Taylor, J. (2003). Decisions. Jeff Taylor founder and chairman, Monster. *Management Today*, 26.

Taylor, M. S., & Bergmann, T. J. (1987). Organizational Recruitment Activities and Applicants' Reactions at Different Stages of the Recruitment Process. *Personnel Psychology, 40*, 261-285.

Taylor, S. (2006). Emerging motivations for global HRM integration. In A. Ferner, J. Quintanilla & C. Sánchez-Runde (Eds.), *Multinationals, Institutions and the Construction of Transnational Practices* (pp. 109–130). Basingstoke: Palgrave Macmillan.

Taylor, S., & Todd, P. (1995). Assessing IT usage: the role of prior experience. *MIS Quaterly*, December 1995, (pp. 561–570).

Taylor, S., Beechler, S., & Napier, N. (1996). Toward an integrative model of strategic international human resource management. *Academy of Management Review, 21*(4), 959–985.

Taylor, S., Fisher, D., & Dufresne, R. (2004). The Aesthetics of Management Storytelling: A Key to Organizational Learning'. In C. Grey & E. Antonacopoulou (Eds.), *Essential Readings in Management Learning.* London: SAGE

Taylor, W. C., & LaBarre, P. (2006). *Mavericks at work: why the most original minds in business win.* New York: William Morrow.

Teece, D. J. (2000). *Managing Intellectual Capital.* Oxford University Press, Oxford.

Teo, S.T.T., & Crawford, J. (2005). Indicators of Strategic HRM effectiveness: A case study of an Australian public sector agency during commercialization. *Public Personnel Management*, 34(1), 1–16.

Terri, A. C., Goes, P. B. & Gupta, A. (2004). GIST: A Model for Design and Management of Content and Interactivity of Customer-Centric Web Sites. *MIS Quarterly*, 28, 161-182.

Thaler-Carter, R. E. (1998). Do-It-Yourself Software. *HR Magazine, May 1998*, 22.

Thomke, S., & von Hippel, E. (2002). Customers as innovators: A New Way to Create Value, *Harvard Business Review*, 4(80), 74-81.

Thompson, L. (2003). Improving the creativity of organizational work groups. *Academy of Management Executive*, 17(1), 96-109.

Thompson, M. (2005). Structural and epistemic parameters in communities of practice. *Organization Science*, 16(2), 151-164.

Timm, N.H. (2002). *Applied Multivariate Analysis.* New York et al., Springer.

Tomer, J. F. (1987). *Organizational Capital: The Path to Higher Productivity and Well-Being.* Praeger Publishers.

Tong, D., & Sivanand, C, (2005). E-recruitment Service Providers Review. International and Malaysian. *Employee Relations, 27*(1/2), 103-118.

Townsend, A.M., Demarie, S.M., & Hendrickson, A. R. (1998). Virtual teams: technology and the workplace of the future. *The Academy of Management Executive*, 12(3), 17-29.

Traylor, P. (2006). To Buy or To Build? That is the Question. *Info World, 28*(7), 18-23.

Triandis, H.C. (1995). *Individualism and Collectivism.* Boulder, Westview.

Trogrlic, J. F. (2001). Impacts de la nouvelle économie et approche syndicale. *La revue de la CFDT, 41*(5), 33–37.

Troitzsch, K. G. (2004). Validating computational models. In: *Proceedings of the 18th European Simulation Multiconference.* SCS Europe.

Turban, D. B., Forret, M. L., & Hendrickson, C. L. (1998). Applicant Attraction to Firm Influences of Organization Reputation, Job and Organizational Attributes, and Recruiter Behaviours. *Journal of Vocational Behaviour, 52*, 24-44.

Turoff, M., Rao, U., & Hiltz, S. (1991, January). Collaborative Hypertext in Computer Mediated Communications, *Proceedings of the Twenty-Fourth Annual Hawaii International Conference on System Sciences.*

Tushman, M. L., & Nadler, D.A. (1978). Information Processing as an Integrating Concept in Organizational Design. *The Academy of Management Review, 3*(3), 613-624.

Twynstra Gudde (2003). e-HRM onderzoek 2002/2003. Amersfoort: Twynstra Gudde.

Tyson, S. (1995). *Human resource strategy.* Pitman.

Tyson, S., & Selbie, D. (2004). People processing systems and human resource strategy. *International Journal of HR Development and Management, 4*(2), 117-127.

Ulrich, D. (1995). Shared Services: From Vogue to Value. *Human resource planning, 18*(3), 12.

Ulrich, D. (1997). *Human Resource Champions: The Next Agenda for Adding Value and Delivering Results.* Boston MA: Harvard Business School Press.

Ulrich, D. (1998). Delivering results: a new mandate for human resource professionals, Ballantine Bookst, Havard Business School.

Ulrich, D., & Brockbank, W. (2005). *The HR Value Proposition.* Harvard Business School Press.

Ulrich, D., & Lake, D. (1991). Organizational capability: Creating competitive advantage. *Academy of Management Executive, 5*(1), 77-92.

UmanID (2006). Wat is e-HRM? Retrieved, March 2006, from http://www.ehrmplein.nl/

Urban, G., & von Hippel, E. (1988). Lead user analyses for the development of new industrial products, *Management Science, 34*(5), 569-582.

Valenduc, G., & Vendramin, P. (2001). Telework : from distance working to new forms of flexible work organization. *Transfer - European Review of Labour and Research, 7*(2), 244-257.

Valverde, M., Ryan, G., & Soler, C. (2006). Distributing HRM responsibilities: a classification of organisations. Personnel Review, *35*(6), 618-636.

Van Dyne, L., Cummings, L. L., & Mclean Parks, J. (1995). Extra-Role Behaviours: In Pursuit of Construct and Definitional Clarity. In B. M. Staw & L. L. Cummings (Eds.), *Research in Organisational Behaviour, 17*, 215-285. Greenwich, CT: JAI Press.

Van Putten, L. (2008). KPN sluit zich aan. *Intermediair PW , 4*(4).

Varela, F. J. (1984). Two Principles of Self-Organization. In H. Ulrich and G.J.B. Probst (Eds.), *Self Organization and Management of Social Systems.* New York: Springer Verlag.

Varela, F. J., Thompson, E., & Rosch, E. (1991). *The Embodied Mind.* Cambridge, MA: MIT Press.

Varshney, U., & Vetter, R. (2000). Emerging mobile and wireless networks. *Communications of the ACM, 43*(6), 73-81.

Vendramin P., & Valenduc, G. (2000). *L'avenir du travail dans la société de l'information, enjeux individuels et collectifs.* Paris: L'Harmattan.

Venkatesh, V. & Davis, F.D. (2000). A theoretical extension of the technological acceptance model: Four longitudinal field experiments. *Management Science, 46*(2), February 2000, 186–204.

Venkatesh, V. (2000). Determinants of perceived ease of use: Integrating control, intrinsic motivation, and emotion into the technology acceptance model. *Information Systems Research, 11*(4), December 2000, 342 – 365.

Venkatesh, V., & Morris, M. G. (2000). Why Don't Men Ever Stop to Ask For Directions? Gender, Social Influence, and Their Role in Technology Acceptance and Usage Behavior. *MIS Ouarterly, 24*(1), 115-139.

Venkatesh, V., Morris, M. G., Davis, G. B., & Davis, F.D. (2003). User acceptance of Information technologies: Toward a unified view. *MIS Quarterly, 27*(3), *425-478.*

Verheijen, T. (2007). Gestrikt: E-HRM komt er uiteindelijk toch. *Personeelsbeleid , 43*(11), 20-23.

Vinuta, V. (2005). E-Recruitment is here to Stay. *Express online Computer.* Retrieved from http://www.express-computeronline.com/20050418/technologylife01.shtml

Voerman, M., & Veldhoven, M. Van (2007). Attitude towards e-HRM: an empirical study at Philips. *Personnel Review, 36*(6), 887 - 902.

von Hippel, E. (1986). Lead users: A source of novel product concepts. *Management Science, 32*(7), 791-805.

von Hippel, E. (1988). *The Sources of Innovation.* New York: Oxford University Press.

von Hippel, E. (2005). *Democratizing Innovation.* Cambridge: MIT Press.

von Hippel, E. (2007). Horizontal innovation networks: By and for users. *Industrial and Corporate Change, 16*(2), 293-315.

Voth, D. (2002). Why Enterprise portal are the Next Big Thing. *E-learning,* (pp. 25-29).

Wagner, E. L., & Piccoli, G. (2007). Moving beyond user participation to achieve successful IS design. *Communications of the ACM, 50*(12), 51-55.

Walker, A. (2001). *The Technologies and Trends that are Transforming HR: Web-Based Human Resources.* NewYork: McGraw Hill/Towers Perrin.

Walsh, J. P., & Ungson, G. R. (1991). Organizational memory. *Academy of Management Review, 16,* 57–91.

Wang, R. Y., Lee, Y. W., Pipino, L. L., & Strong, D. M. (1998). Manage Your Information as a Product. *Sloan Management Review, 39*(4), 95-105.

Ware, J. (2005, 22 August 2005). *The changing nature of work: Basics.* Retrieved 17 June, 2008.

Watson, W. (2002). *B2E / eHR. Survey results 2002.* Reigate: Watson Wyatt.

Weick K. E. (1969). *The social Psychology of Organizing.* Reading, MA: Addison Wesly.

Weick, K., Sutcliffe, K. M., & Obstfeld, D. (2005). Organising and the process of sensemaking. *Organization Science, 16*(4), 409-421.

Welicki, L. (2006). The Configuration Data Caching Pattern. *Proceedings of the 13th Conference on Pattern Languages of Programs (PLoP 2006).* Portland, Oregon, USA, October 2006.

Welicki, L., & Sanjuan Martinez, O. (2007). Improving Performance and Server Resource Usage with Page Fragment Caching in Distributed Web Servers. *Proceedings of International Workshop on Scalable Data Management Applications and Systems.* Las Vegas, Nevada, USA.

Weller, S. C., & Romney, A. K. (1988). *Systematic Data Collection.* London: Sage Publications Ltd.

Wellman, B., Boase, J., & Chen, W. (2002). The networked nature of community on and off the Internet. *IT and Society, 1*(1), 151-165.

Wenger, E. (1998). Communities of practice: learning as a social system. *The Systems Thinker, 9*(5).

Wheeler, B., Mennecke, B. E., & Scudder, J. N. (1993). Restrictive group support systems as a source of process structure for high and low procedural order groups. *Small group research, 24,* 504-522.

Whicker, L. M., & Andrews, K.M. (2004). HRM in the Knowledge Economy: Realising the Potential. *Asia Pacific Journal of Human Resources, 42*(2), 156-165.

Whisler, T. L. (1970). *The impact of computers on organisations.* New York: Praeger.

Wilcox, J. (1997). The evolution of human resources technology. *Management Accounting, June 1997,* 3-5.

Willcocks, L., Lacity, M., & Cullen, S. (2006). Information Technology Sourcing: fifteen years of learning. In: R. Mansell, et al (Eds.), *Handbook on Information and Communication Technologies,* Oxford Press.

Williams H. (2008). *How do organisations make sense of their talent as valued assets?* The Literature Human Resource Management Nottingham Business School, Nottingham Trent University: Nottingham

Williams, H. (2000). *How Can Human Resource Information Systems Inform and Enable Strategy Making?* Human Resource Management Nottingham Business School, Nottingham Trent University: Nottingham

Williamson, I. O., Lepak, D. P., & King, J. (2003). The effect of company recruitment web site orientation on individuals' perceptions of organizational attractiveness. *Journal of Vocational Behaviour, 63,* 242-263.

Williamson, O. E. (1975). *Markets and Hierarchies: Analysis and Antitrust Implications.* New York, The Free Press.

Winkel, N. (2005). *Publieke dienstverlening 65% elektronisch, Viermeting van de elektronische dienstverlening van de overheid in 2005,* Advies Overheid.nl en Ministerie van Binnenlandse Zaken en Koninkrijksrelaties. Retrieved from http://advies.overheid.nl/3137/.

Winkin, Y. (1981). *La nouvelle communication,* éd. du Seuil, coll. "Points", Paris

Wood, L. E. (1997). Semi-structured interviewing for user-centered design. *Interactions , 4*(2), 48-61.

Woolgar, S. (1991). Configuring the user The case of usability trials. In J. Law, (Ed.), *A sociology of monsters. Essays on power, technology and domination* (pp. 58-99). London: Routledge.

Workflow Management Coalition (1995). *The Workflow Reference Model.*

Wright, P. M., & Dyer, L. (2000). People in the E-business: New Challenges, New Solutions. Working paper 00-11. Center for Advanced Human Resource Studies, Cornell University.

Wright, P. M., McMaham, G. C., Snell, S. A., & Gerhart, B. (2001). Comparing line and HR executives' perceptions of HR effectiveness: services, roles, and contributions. *Human Resource Management, 40*(2), 111–123.

Wright, P., & Dyer, L. (2000). *People in the e-business: new challenges, new solutions.* Working paper 00-11, Center for Advanced Human Resource Studies, Cornell University.

Wright, P., & McMahan, G. C. (1992). Theoretical perspectives for strategic human resource management. *Journal of Management, 18*, 295-320.

Wright, P., Dyer, L., et al. (1999). What's Next? Key Findings from the 1999 State-of-the-Art & Practice Study. *Human resource planning, 22*(4), 12.

Wright, P., McMahn, G., & McWilliams, A. (1994). Human Resources and Sustained Competitive Advantage: A Resource-based Perspective. *International Journal of Human Resources Management, 5*, 301-326.

Yeow, A., & Sia, S.K. (2007). Negotiating "Best Practices" in Package Software Implementation. *Information and Organization.* Retrieved from doi:10.1016/j.infoandorg.2007.07.001.

Yin, R. K. (1993). Applications of case study research. *Applied Social Research Methods Series*, Sage Publications, *34.*

Yin, R. K. (2003). *Case Study Research: Design and Methods.* 3rd edition, Thousand Oaks, CA: Sage.

Yoder, J., & Johnson, R. (2002). The Adaptive Object Model Architectural Style. *Published in The Proceeding of The Working IEEE/IFIP Conference on Software Architecture* 2002 (WICSA3 '02) at the World Computer Congress in Montreal 2002, August 2002.

Youndt, M. A., & Snell, S. A. (2004). Human Resource Configurations, Intellectual Capital and Organizational Performance. *Journal of Managerial Issues, 16*(3), 337-360.

Youndt, M. A., Snell, S. A., Dean, J.W., & Lepak, D. P. (1996). Human resource management, manufacturing strategy and firm performance. *Academy of Management Journal, 39*(4), 836-866.

Youndt, M. A., Subramaniam, M., & Snell, S. A. (2004). Intellectual Capital Profiles: An Examination of Investments and Returns. *Journal of Management Studies, 41*(2), 335-361.

Yu, B.-M., & Roh, S.-Z. (2002). The Effects of Menu Design on Information-Seeking Performance and User's Attitude on the World Wide Web. *Journal of the American Society for Information Science, 53*, 923-933.

Yu, J., Ha, I., Choi, M., & Rho, J. (2005). Extending the TAM for a t-commerce. *Information Management, 42*, 965-976.

Yumiko, I. (2005). Selecting a Software Package: From Procurement System to E-Marketplace. The Business Review, Cambridge, *3*(2), 341-347.

Zacarias, M. S. (2008). *A Conceptual Framework for the Alignment of Individuals and Organizations.* PhD Dissertation. Lisbon, Portugal: Instituto Superior Tecnico.

Zahra, S. A., & George, G. (2002). Absorptive capacity: A review, reconceptualisation and extension. *Academy of Management Review, 27*(2), 185-203.

Zakaria, F. (2006). India Rising, *Newsweek, CXLVII* (10), 34-43.

Zall, M. (2000). Using the Internet to find your next job. *Strategic Finance, 81*, 74-78.

Zardet, V. (1995). *The approach of the internal customers-providers: a framework of analysis of the sharing of the HR function.* Acts of the congress of AHRM, Potiers.

Zeithaml, V. A. (2000). Service quality, profitability, and the economic worth of customers: What we know and what we need to learn. *Journal of the Academy of Marketing Science, 28*(1), 67-85.

Zellner, A. (1962). An Efficient Method of Estimating Seemingly Unrelated Regressions and Tests of Aggregation Bias. *Journal of the American Statistic Association, 57,* 348-368

Zhao, H. (2006). Expectations of recruiters and applicants in large cities of China. *Journal of Managerial Psychology, 21*(5), 459-475.

Zizakovic, L. (2004). *Buy or Build: Corporate Software Dilemma.* Retrieved November 11, 2007, from http://www.insidus.com

Zmud, R. W. (1979). Individual differences and MIS success: A review of the empirical literature. *Management science, 10*(10).

Zuboff, S. (1988). *In the age of the smart machine.* New York: Basic Books.

Zusman, R., & Landis, R. (2004). Applicant preferences for web-based versus traditional job posting. *Computers in Human Behaviour, 18,* 285-296.

About the Contributors

Tanya Bondarouk is an assistant professor of human resource management at the University of Twente, the Netherlands. She holds two PhDs: in didactics (1997) and business administration/HRM (2004). Since 2002 she has been busy with the emerging research area of electronic HRM. Her main publications concern an integration of human resource management and social aspects of information technology implementations. Her research covers both private and public sectors and deals with a variety of areas such as the implementation of e-HRM, management of HR-IT change, HRM contribution to IT projects, roles of line managers in e-HRM, implementation of HR shared service centers. She has conducted research projects with the Dutch Ministry of Interior and Kingdom Relations, Dow Chemical, Ford, IBM, ABN AMRO bank, Shell, Unit4Agresso. Among her current research projects are implementation of HR shared service centers at the Dutch Ministry of Defense, Essent (Dutch Energy Supplier), large non-academic hospitals, and the Belgian Federal Public Health Service. Since 2006 she is involved in organizing European academic workshops on e-HRM,and international workshops on HRIS.

Huub Ruël works as an assistant professor of HRM and international management at the University of Twente, before that at the Kuwait-Maastricht Business School (Kuwait), and the University of Utrecht (The Netherlands). He holds a PhD in business administration/human resource management. His thesis focused on implementation of IT's in office-environments. After that his main research focus became e-HRM, combining his IT and HRM knowledge. In 2004 he published a book *e-HRM: Innovation or Irration?* together with Dr. Tanya Bondarouk, in which the results of e-HRM implementation in five large international companies were described. Articles derived from this e-HRM study have been published in academic and professional journals.

Karine Guiderdoni-Jourdain is in PhD position, in management science in the Institute of Labour Economics and Industrial Sociology (LEST—Unité mixte de recherche CNRS 6123), under the direction of Ariel Mendez, professor of management science in the University of Mediterranean (Aix-Marseille 2). (LEST—Unité mixte de recherche CNRS 6123). Her doctoral research is focused on the appropriation of an specific ICT, an HR intranet by the middle management. She is the author of several communications in scientific conferences and chapters in books on the topics of e-HRM. She is also member organizing committee of the first and second *European Academic Workshop on e-HRM*.

Ewan Oiry is assistant professor in human resources management in the University of Mediterranée and in the Institute of Labour Economics and Industrial Sociology (LEST—UMR CNRS 6123). He is actually responsible of an MBA and a national thematic think tank on the subject of «competencies management». He published several books and articles on HRM, appraisal systems. He works on the theme of construction and uses of management tools (especially electronic management tools). He is also member of the organizing committee of the first and second *European Academic Workshop on e-HRM*.

* * *

Nawaf H. Al-Ibraheem, MBA (Kuwait, 1975) earned his Bachelors of Science degree in computer engineering from the University of Arizona, Tucson, AZ. After graduation, he started his career working for more than five years as a software engineer at StorageTek in Louisville, Colorado, currently a subsidiary of Sun Microsystems Inc. In 2004 he continued his professional career working for Shared Electronic Banking Services Company, or KNET. He is in charge of ATM's, Online payment gateway, and the E-Government project. In 2008 he earned his MBA from the Maastricht School of Management (MSM).

Mitchell van Balen is enrolled as a master student in public administration with the 'Management, Economy and Law' curriculum. At the moment he is working on his thesis project at Capgemini Nederland B.V. about the impact of sourcing arrangements on HR

Ronald Batenburg (1964) obtained his masters at Utrecht University and his PhD in 1991 at Groningen University based on the dissertation, "*Automation at Work. The Influence of Automation on the Job Structure of Organizations*". Since then, he worked at the universities of Utrecht, Tilburg and Nijmegen as assistant professor in organizational sociology, strategic policy making and HRM. Since 2000 he is associate professor at Utrecht University, Department of Information and Computing Sciences. His research interest and publications are in field of business-IT alignment, implementation of ERP-systems, teleworking and CRM, as well as inter-organizational issues as the extended enterprise and e-procurement. As of 2006, he combines his academic activities with a part-time senior research and consultancy position at Dialogic Innovation and Interaction, Utrecht, The Netherlands.

Rolf van Dick earned his PhD from Philipps University in Marburg (Germany). He is professor of social psychology at Goethe University in Frankfurt (Germany). He was visiting professor at the University of Alabama (2001) and the University of the Aegean, Rhodes, Greece (2002). Prior to his current appointment, Rolf was Chair of Social Psychology and Organizational Behavior at Aston Business School in Birmingham (United Kingdom). His primary research interests are in the application of social identity theory in organizational settings such as diversity, leadership, mergers. Rolf served as associate editor of the *European Journal of Work & Organizational Psychology* and is editor-in-chief of the *British Journal of Management*. He has published more than 60 papers in academic journals including the *Academy of Management Journal, Journal of Organizational Behavior, Journal of Applied Psychology, Journal of Marketing, Journal of Vocational Behavior,* and *Journal of Personality and Social Psychology.*

Betsy van Dijk is an assistant professor at the Human Media Interaction group of the Faculty of Electrical Engineering, Mathematics and Computer Science of the University of Twente in The Netherlands. She studied mathematics (MSc) at the University of Nijmegen and obtained a PhD on teaching methodology in computer science from the University of Twente. Since 1996 her research interests are in the field of human-computer interaction where her focus is on multi-modal and multi-party interaction and ambient intelligence environments. The main research topics are interface and interaction design, user evaluation, user modeling and personalization. She is involved in several national and international research projects.

Andreas Eckhardt graduated in business administration from Nuremberg University. In 2006 he joined the Centre of Human Resources Information Systems where he serves as a PhD candidate. His research interests include the adoption and value of human resources information systems (HRIS) for personnel recruitment, business process standardization and information system architectures. Andreas published several papers in scientific journals like *Information Systems Frontiers* (ISF) and in the proceedings of conferences like HICSS, ECIS, PACIS, AMCIS and Conf IRM.

Sander Engbers currently works as a financial staff member at Cogas Infra & Netbeheer BV in the Netherlands. Cogas Infra & Netbeheer BV is an organisation responsible for the quality and safety of the net which provides energy (gas and electricity) to regional customers. His current job contains among others writing new procedures/processes, solving problems in existing procedures/processes, taking care of customer complaints, analysing government policy and analysing financial data. He studied business economics at Saxion and finished his master business administration, track human resource management at the University of Twente. For his master thesis he conducted, together with Vincent ter Horst, an exploring research about the perceptions of the use of e-HRM tools in SME's.

Elfi Furtmueller is an assistant professor at the University of Twente, the Netherlands. She obtained a DBA (Doctor of Business Administration) in organizational behavior from the University of Linz, Austria and is currently working on a PhD in information systems. Before joining the University of Twente, she researched at the Institute of Management, Innovation and Organization at the Haas School of Business, University of California. She also spent a year at the University of Charleston, USA. She has experience in corporate recruiting and consulting and has been working in communications at this paper's e-recruiting firm during the past 3 years.

Carley Foster is currently a senior lecturer in marketing & retail management at Nottingham Business School. Carley's research interests include diversity management, fairness/justice in the workplace, employer branding and retailing. More recently she has embarked on research which explores how the diversity of customer facing retail staff might influence the shopping experiences of customers, women's career progression in retailing and flexible working in the retail/service sector.

Steve Foster is manager, business consultancy at UK based HR/payroll systems and services provider NorthgateArinso. Steve has an extensive human resources management background, gained in a variety of line practitioner roles including compensation & benefits, industrial relations and generalist HR management. As a managing consultant, he has worked with a wide range of major clients, helping them transform their HR operations. He brings specialist knowledge of HR business process improvement, e-HRM planning and implementation, outsourcing and change management. Steve regularly presents at HR/technology conferences, has published several articles on technology strategy and human capital management and is regularly quoted in professional magazines and journals.

Manelle Guechtouli holds her PhD in management, with the interests in business intelligence information systems' engineering. She worked as the consultant in business intelligence information system of a big technological firm.

Widad Guechtouli is a PhD student in economics at GREQAM–CNRS (Groupement de Recherche en Economie Quantitative d'Aix Marseille), Paul Cezanne University. She is working also as a teaching assistant in microeconomics at Paul Cezanne University. Her research topics include the dynamics of knowledge transfer and learning within knowledge-intensive communities.

Jeroen ter Heerdt is currently working as next generation consultant at the services department of Microsoft, the Netherlands. He holds a masters degree in business informatics from the University of Twente. As next generation consultant he is investigating and experiencing the New World of Work firsthand. In addition, he is working on various projects, both inside and outside Microsoft; Current projects include data analysis for project management data, a marketing related project around UMPCs and an internal project involving hospitality management for meetings at the office of Microsoft. His areas of interest are business intelligence, unified communications and the New World of Work.

Jukka-Pekka Heikkilä works as a project researcher in the Department of Management at the University of Vaasa. He is currently writing his PhD thesis about the standardization–localization dilemma in the field of e-HRM. His other reserach interests lie in the outcomes of e-HRM and cultural issues within e-HRM, especially China. He also has an MA in Asian Studies and has published in Finnish journals.

Victor de Vega Hernandez Víctor de Vega worked for Siemens from Sept 99 til June 2005 as the C&B responsible for the Telco areas within the C&B+Development area. After that, he joined the Mobile phones Merger of BenQ Mobile and Siemens, acting as the HR Manager. Nowadays he is responsible for the C&B area within the Spanish Cable operator ONO.

Dirk Holtbrügge (PhD and habilitation, University of Dortmund) is professor of international management at the University of Erlangen-Nuremberg, Germany. His research interests include international management, human resource management, and management in Asia and Eastern Europe. He has published eight books and more than 70 articles in journals such as *European Management Journal*, *Journal of International Business Studies*, *International Business Review*, *Journal of Business Ethics*, *Journal of International Management* and *Management International Review*, among others. He serves as a member of the editorial board of *Management International Review*.

Vincent ter Horst currently works at Saxion Kenniscentrum Innovatie en Ondernemerschap in the Netherlands. Saxion Kenniscentrum Innovatie en Ondernemerschap is part of Saxion, an organisation for higher education. The goal of Saxion Kenniscentrum Innovatie en Ondernemerschap is to stimulate entrepreneurship and innovation within Saxion. He currently works on projects about entrepreneurship and innovation. For example a project "learning innovation", where a cooperation of entrepreneurs in East-Netherlands and students of Saxion work together on innovative projects. He studied business economics at Saxion and finished his master business administration, track human resource management at the University of Twente. For his master thesis he conducted, together with Sander Engbers, an exploring research about the perceptions of the use of e-HRM tools in SME's.

Barbara Imperatori is assistant professor of organization design and organizational behavior for the Economics and Business Administration Sciences Department of the Catholic University. She received her PhD degree in management and business administration at Bocconi University. She is currently coordinator of the international HR management master programme at Catholic University and senior professor in the Organization and Human Resources Management Department for the SDA Bocconi School of Management, where she teaches and manages various executive training programs and courses, such as organization and HR management master, MBA, people management and project management. Her research interests are HR systems and strategic HR, extra-role behaviors, work motivation and organizational solidarity, employment relationships and social enterprises. Before embarking upon her academic career she worked as HR Manager for Commercial Union Group, an organization of international reach.

Francisco Javier Piqueres Juan is a software architect at ONO. He holds a telecomunication engineering degree from Universidad Politecnica de Valencia and is a PhD student at Universidad Pontificia de Salamanca.

Gerwin Koopman (1982) obtained his business informatics master's degree at Utrecht University. He has done research on information technology and users both at governmental organisations as well as at IT service organizations. Currently he is employed as a product manager at Syntess Software in The Netherlands. His main research interests are in the field of user involvement & participation, user satisfaction, usability and the implementation of ERP-systems.

Pieternel Kuiper is a project manager at the Exxellence Group in Enschede, the Netherlands.
Pieternel Kuiper, a project manager, has done research on adaptive municipal e-forms since 2005. She was born in Amsterdam, the Netherlands, on February 10, 1981. She grew up in Amsterdam and now lives in Enschede, the Netherlands, with her boyfriend. She graduated in 2006 in business information technology and with honours in human media interaction at the University of Twente, the Netherlands. She participated in the 2006 International Conference on Adaptive Hypermedia and Adaptive Web-Based Systems in Dublin, Ireland. Since January 2007 she works as a project manager at the Exxellence Group in Hengelo, the Netherlands. This is her first book publication.

Sven Laumer graduated in information systems at Bamberg University (Germany). He currently works as a PhD candidate for information systems at the Centre of Human Resources Information Systems, a research centre founded by southern German universities (Otto-Friedrich University of Bamberg, Goethe University Frankfurt a. Main) to investigate information systems and human resources. His research interests are business process standardization, information system architectures, e-recruiting and the adoption and diffusion of human resources information systems (HRIS). Sven has published papers in scientific journals like information systems frontiers (ISF) and in the proceedings of various conferences, including AMCIS, Conf IRM, PACIS, HICSS and ECIS.

Rodrigo Magalhães is the academic director of Kuwait Maastricht Business School and invited associate professor at Instituto Superior Técnico of Lisbon. He holds a PhD in information systems from the London School of Economics, a MBA from Sheffield University, and a MA from Leeds Metropolitan University, UK. He is also lecturer in postgraduate programmes at the Portuguese Catholic University

(UCP) and at the Instituto Superior de Ciências do Trabalho e da Empresa (ISCTE) in Lisbon. He has been involved in consultancy projects in Information Systems and Organization areas for over 20 years and has several books and publications on organizational change, knowledge management, organization learning, information systems management, business process management and e-learning.

Marco De Marco is full professor of organization and information systems at the Catholic University in Milan. Before embarking upon his academic career he worked in the aerospace and computer industries as a research engineer. He is author of 4 books and numerous essays and articles, he has written mainly on the development of information systems and the impacts of technology on organizations. Marco De Marco has worked as a consultant for a wide range of important public institutions. He is also a member of the editorial board of the *Journal of Information Systems* and the *Journal of Digital Accounting Research*. Marco De Marco is President-elect of the Italian Association for Information Systems (ITAIS), and he served as conference officer for ECIS and ICIS. Since July 2008 Marco sits as an elected member in Council of the Association for Information Systems representing Region 2 (Europe, Middle East, Africa).

Fernando Llorente Martin is a Sr HR Director in ONO. He has extensive experience working with HRIS.

Valéry Michaux is professor at Reims Management School (France) in the department management, organisation and strategy and is a member of the team of professor in research methodology. She holds a PHD in sciences of management (Prize of the FNEGE thesis, in 2004). At the operational level, she worked 8 years in the private sector and 8 years in the public area. She is a member of several academic associations and is a member of the Research Centre in Management and Organisation of the University of Nantes. Her research topics are: the collective performance in different types of situation (teams, networks, lateral coordination and cooperation, communities of practice...) when people work face-to-face and when they work through information and communication technology. Especially, she analyses the impacts of ICT on organizations, workplace, practices, team behaviour and management. She had already written several academic publications on these topics.

Alexander T. Mohr (PhD, University of Erlangen-Nuremberg) is Reader of International Business and Management at the Bradford Centre in International Business. His research focuses on the management of international joint ventures and issues related to international human resource management. His research has been published in journals, such as the *International Journal of Human Resource Management*, *Journal of International Business Studies*, *Management International Review*, *Long Range Planning* and the *Journal of World Business*.

Isabelle Parot is connected with the research group Magellan of the University of Lyon 3. She realized her PhD on the subject of virtual teams in order to underline their specificities. Her researches concern the question of the virtual teams and their functioning. She is interested in various processes of those virtual teams, such as communication, coordination or cooperation. The author writes several communications in scientific congress, and she published articles in *Gérer et Comprendre* and in joint publications.

Emma Parry is a senior research fellow in the Human Resource Research Centre (HRRC) at Cranfield School of Management. Her research interests include recruitment and selection, particularly the use of the internet for recruitment and selection, the use of technology in HR, age discrimination at work, and HRM in the voluntary sector. Emma earned her BSc (Hons) in psychology from London Guildhall University in 1993 and her MSc and PhD in applied (Occupational) psychology from Cranfield University in 1996 and 2001 respectively. Emma worked as a consultant to the human resources department of a large retail chain before joining the HRRC in April 2002. Emma also manages Cranet, an international network of business schools that conducts a comparative survey of HRM policies and practices in around 40 countries worldwide. Emma is the author of numerous publications and conference papers in the field of HRM.

Jonas F Puck (PhD, University of Erlangen-Nuremberg) is senior lecturer of international management at the University of Erlangen-Nuremberg, Germany. His research focuses on management and business in emerging markets, international human resource management and cross-cultural management. His research has published four books and articles in journals such as the *Journal of International Business Studies*, *Journal of International Management*, *Long Range Planning*, *European Journal of International Management*, *International Business Review* or the *International Journal of Human Resource Management*.

Pramila Rao is employed as an assistant professor in human resource management in Marymount University, Arlington since fall of 2005. She got her doctorate from George Washington University (2005) and her dissertation focused on pioneering research, namely, executive staffing practices in US-Mexican Joint Ventures (JVs) located in Mexico. Her current research interests include executive staffing practices, cross-cultural management (Mexico, India and Spain) and case study research.

Cataldo Dino Ruta is assistant professor of organization and human resource management at Bocconi University and SDA Bocconi School of Management. He is director of the master in organization and human resource management at Bocconi University and Director of the FIFA International Master in Humanities, Management and Law of Sports at SDA Bocconi School of Management. After receiving a MSc in management from Bocconi University, he obtained a PhD in business administration at University of Bologna. He was visiting at University of Illinois at Urbana Champaign (USA) and he is currently visiting the School of Management and Labor Relations at Rutgers University, USA. His research activities are focused on human resource management. Main topics: the intersection of human resource management and information technologies: how firms can leverage technology to increase workforce management efficacy. The HR function's role in creating competitive advantage: the role of social value for competitive advantage. sport management and human resources management.

Adam Smale works as an assistant professor in the Department of Management at the University of Vaasa. His main research interests lie in HRM and knowledge transfer in multinational corporations, but more specifically in the mechanisms through which multinational corporations globally integrate HRM practices throughout their foreign subsidiaries. He has published articles on these topics in international academic journals, including *International Business Review*, *International Journal of HRM*, *HRM Journal*, and *Personnel Review*.

Loubna Tahssain holds her PhD in sciences of management within the IAE Graduate School of Management in Aix-en-Provence–France. She's a temporary instructor and researcher within the IAE Graduate School of Management in Lyon–France. Her research interests include ICT and employees' behavior, ICT use processes, change management and HR politics, Extranet's implementation.

Carole Tansley is director of the International Centre for Talent Management and Development, leading a team of applied researchers, PhD and knowledge transfer partnership students engaged in exploring dimensions of talent management for research councils such as the ESRC and for corporate clients. Carole led the Chartered Institute of Personnel Development's research on talent management between 2007-2008 and has published widely in journals such as *British Journal of Management, Journal of Managerial Psychology* and *Personnel Review* in the areas of talent management, e-HR, knowledge management, organisational behaviour and human resourcing. She has spoken at many international conferences and gives masterclasses at events in the UK, Sweden, United Arab Emirates and Greece. She speaks on topics such as the nature of talent; undertaking talent management in turbulent times; the key facets of employer branding; developing leaders and a balanced scorecard approach to human capital management.

José Tribolet is a full professor of computer engineering and information technology at Instituto Superior Técnico, Technical University of Lisbon, Portugal. He holds a PhD degree in electrical and computer engineering from the Massachusetts Institute of Technology, USA. He was a visiting fellow at the center for coordination sciences in MIT's Sloan School of Management (1998). He leads of the Organizational Engineering Center (CEO) at the Institute for Systems and Computer Engineering (INESC), a private sector, contract-based research organization, which he founded in 1980. He has been involved in several research and consultancy projects concerning organizational engineering, including organizing the ACM SAC Organizational Engineering special track.

Shaun Tyson is emeritus professor of human resource management at Cranfield School of Management. He has experience of human resource management in the public sector and private sectors. He holds a PhD from London School of Economics and is a Fellow of the Chartered Institute of Personnel and Development, a Fellow of The Royal Society of Arts and a Member of the British Psychological Society. He is also a member of the Association Française de Gestion des Ressources Humaines and was awarded a doctorate (honoris causa) from the University of Lyon. He was a visiting professor at the University of Paris for 5 years, and is currently a visiting professor at the University of Westminster. He has written 19 books on human resource management and has published extensively on human resource strategy and policies. He currently Chairs the Remuneration Committee of the Law Society and broadcasts regularly on industrial relations and people management issues.

Leon Welicki is the head of the intranet development department and lead software architect at Ono. He holds PhD and MSc in software engineering from Universidad Pontificia de Salamanca.

Celeste P.M. Wilderom is a full professor in 'Management & Organizational Behavior in the Private and the Public Sector' (University of Twente, the Netherlands). She obtained a PhD from the State University of New York at Buffalo (USA) in 1987. Her main research pertains to organizational leadership, change and culture. She is one of the three editors of the award-winning *Handbook of Organizational Culture*

& Climate (2000, Sage). Currently she serves as a senior editor of the *British Journal of Management*, previously also of the *Academy of Management Executive* and the *International Journal of Service Industry Management*. She is the initiator and trackchair of the European Group for Organization Studies standing workgroup "Professional Service Organizations and Knowledge-intensive Work".

Hazel Williams is senior lecturer in human resource management at Nottingham Business School, The Nottingham Trent University, UK. She has 15 years experience as a human resourcing professional in a range of industry sectors. Hazel has been teaching and researching human resourcing information systems since 1997. She leads on this subject for post-graduate and corporate programmes based in the UK, Russia and Azerbaijan. Her research interests also include strategic human resourcing, talent management, e-HR and human capital, with a particular interest in the hospitality and leisure, and engineering and construction sectors. With colleagues, she published research in 2007 commissioned by the CIPD on Talent Management, titled *Talent: Strategy, Management, Measurement*. Hazel has presented conference papers and contributed to international journals and book chapters. Hazel is currently studying for her DBA, with a working title of *"How Do Organisations Make Sense of Their Talent as Valued Assets?"*

Marielba Zacarias is an assistant professor of information systems, software engineering and data base systems at the Algarve University, Faro, Portugal. She holds a PhD in informatics and computers engineering from the Instituto Superior Técnico of Lisbon, a MSc in information systems from Simón Bolívar University of Venezuela and has background education on computer engineering. She has a professional experience of over 20 year in the information systems field, both as a developer and project manager. Currently, she is a PhD candidate at the Instituto Superior Técnico, Technical University of Lisbon, Portugal. Her research work focuses the development of a conceptual framework to enable the dynamic alignment between individuals and organizations, and has written 18 scientific papers on this topic.

Mouna Zgheib is Lebanese / Colombian residing in Beirut where she was born on 37 years ago. She is in her third year PHD at IAE Aix-Marseille III. She has graduated from the Lebanese American University in spring 1993 in computer science. She did her Master MBA in the same University and graduated in spring 2005. She continued her doctoral studies in 2005. She has more than 14 years of working experience in the banking sector, where she is currently a head of the Unit of IT Project Management and Quality assurance Unit at FRANSABANK–Lebanon.

Index